THE ANOINTMENT OF DIONISIO

· THE ·
ANOINTMENT
OF DIONISIO

Prophecy *and* Politics
in Renaissance Italy

•

Marion Leathers Kuntz

THE PENNSYLVANIA STATE UNIVERSITY PRESS
UNIVERSITY PARK, PENNSYLVANIA

Library of Congress Cataloging-in-Publication Data

Kuntz, Marion Leathers.
The anointment of Dionisio: prophecy and politics in Renaissance Italy / Marion Leathers Kuntz.
p.   cm.
Includes bibliographical references and index.
ISBN 0-271-02134-9
1. Gallo, Dionisio, 16th cent.   2. Reformation—Italy—Venice—Biography.   3. Humanists—Italy—Venice—Biography.   I. Title.

BR350.G28 K86 2001
945´.07´092—DC21
[B]
2001021964

Copyright © 2001 The Pennsylvania State University
All rights reserved
Printed in the United States of America
Published by The Pennsylvania State University Press,
University Park, PA 16802-1003

It is the policy of *The Pennsylvania State University Press* to use acid-free paper. Publications on uncoated stock satisfy the minimum requirements of American National Standard for Information Sciences—Permanence of Paper for Printed Library Materials, ANSI Z39.48–1992.

Contents

	Preface	VII
	Introduction	XI
I	Gallus Cantans: *The Singing Gaul*	1
II	Religio and Politia: *Emanuele Filiberto of Savoy, Pope Pius V, and Dionisio Gallo*	31
III	Religio and Politia: *Cosimo I, Alfonso II, and Dionisio Gallo*	67
IV	Venice, Prophetic Reform, and Dionisio Gallo	99
V	Among Friends and Foes in Venice: *The Trial and Imprisonment of Dionisio Gallo*	139
VI	Conversations and Letters from the Prisons of the Palazzo Ducale	177
VII	The Horseman of the Apocalypse and the Course of the Church Militant	209
	Conclusion	245
	Notes	259
	Bibliography	403
	Index	427

For
Maria Francesca Tiepolo

&

In memory of
Paul Oskar Kristeller
Paul Grimley Kuntz

PREFACE

THIS BOOK HAS been long in coming to fruition. Originally conceived as a study of Venetian chronicles that would develop the theme of Venice as a prophetic city, its course changed when I discovered the documents pertaining to the proceedings against Dionisio Gallo before the Venetian Inquisition and his numerous writings, which the Inquisition had preserved along with the records of his trial. Happily for me, the years of reading chronicles provided a good background for studying the fascinating, if complicated, documents that concerned the man known as Dionisio Gallo, who had captured my interest from the beginning.

In the long pursuit of Dionisio, many people have provided indispensable help. My many conversations with Professor John Martin over the years enabled me to focus upon significant questions about the trial and Dionisio's writings. In this regard I must also mention Professors Edward Muir, Guido Ruggiero, and Jonathan Glixon. Anne Jacobson Schutte read a preliminary sketch of three chapters about Dionisio and made interesting suggestions. Each has provided valuable insights as well as factual information. The late Professor Paul Oskar Kristeller read early versions of the manuscript, made precious suggestions, and gave constant encouragement, as did my late husband, Professor Paul Grimley Kuntz.

From almost the moment in which I found the records of Dionisio, Dr. Maria Francesca Tiepolo, former director of the Archivio di Stato, encouraged me to pursue this difficult study and provided invaluable help with interpretation and textual problems. She always listened patiently to my questions, especially about Dionisio and Postel, and provided brilliant insights on this vexing problem.

The Archivio di Stato in Venice became my second home, as it were, and the archivists and personnel have been exceptionally helpful. I am indebted to the former director, Dr. Maria Francesca Tiepolo, and to the present director, Dr. Paolo Selmi, for the use of rare materials, for the interest they have demonstrated in my research, and for countless courtesies through the years. The archivists have aided me in numerous ways: by helping me to understand the organization of the *archivio*, by assisting me in reading difficult words and thereby avoiding pitfalls, by showing interest in my work. For these and for many other things, I am deeply indebted to Drs. Michela Dal Borgo, Edoardo Giuffrida, Elisabetta Barile, Maria Pia Pedani, Alexandra Sambo, Pietro Scarpa, and Alessandra Schiavon. Dr. Viola Visentini, *ricercatrice* at the Archivio di Stato, provided information from testaments that were not available for my consultation, and I am deeply grateful for her assistance. Dr. Elisabetta Barile also provided me with precious information about the University of Padua that was essential for my argument. The *personale professionale* graciously accepted my constant requests for *buste*, and I am very grateful for this and the numerous kindnesses they have extended to me.

Dr. Marino Zorzi, director of the Biblioteca nazionale di San Marco, made available to me all the magnificent materials necessary for my research and extended me every courtesy, for which I am deeply grateful. I am also deeply indebted to Dr. Daniela Ambrosini for invaluable suggestions about representations from art, to Giancarlo Verdica for his extraordinary kindness to me in providing photographs for illustrations, to Drs. Margherita Carbone and Anna Maria Zanotto for their excellent bibliographical advice, to Dr. Suzy Marcon for her extraordinary knowledge of watermarks and paper and for her advice in regard to these and other problems. I am also very grateful to all the personnel of the Biblioteca nazionale di San Marco, who have extended to me every kindness and made me feel very much at home.

I am indebted to Dom Bruno Bertoli, director of the Archivio Patriarcale for the use of valuable materials and for his help with various problems. In addition, the directors of the Biblioteca del Museo Correr and of the Biblioteca Querini Stampalla have allowed me the use of rare sources, and to them I am very grateful. I am also grateful for the courtesies of the personnel of the *biblioteca* of the Istituto Veneto.

For many years I have been privileged to use the collections of the Biblioteca Apostolica del Vaticano and the Archivio Segreto, and to the late Monsignor José Ruysschaert I am deeply indebted for his unusual kindness to me and for his vast knowledge of the Vatican collection. I am also very grateful to Herr Doktor Paul Rabbe, former director of the Herzog August Bibliothek, Wolfenbüttel, and to Herr Doktor Milde, director of research, for the use of rare materials.

The librarians in the reference section of Georgia State University have been very helpful, especially Dr. Stanley Voorhaven; Mrs. Marjorie Patterson of Interlibrary Loan has assisted me in every way, and I am very grateful to her. Dr. William Sessions, my colleague for many years, has encouraged me in my work and has engaged me in conversations that clarify my understanding. The editors of The Pennsylvania State University Press have been very helpful, especially Peter Potter and Keith Monley.

I am indebted to the Fuller E. Callaway Foundation and to Georgia State University, especially to Dr. Carl Patton, president, and to Dr. Ahmed

Abdelal, dean of the College of Arts and Sciences, for support of my research. To all who for many years have shown interest in my work, I am deeply appreciative, especially to my late husband, Professor Paul Grimley Kuntz, to the late Professor Paul Oskar Kristeller, and to Dr. Maria Francesca Tiepolo.

My practice in transcribing manuscripts is to follow the orthography of the documents. Therefore, I have not regularized *u* and *v*, *i* and *j*, or any variant spellings of names.

Introduction

THE STORY OF Dionisio Gallo, an almost unknown French humanist of the sixteenth century, provides the modern reader with a fascinating view of prophecy and reform in France and Italy after the conclusion of the Council of Trent. Dionisio's story especially reaffirms the significance of prophecy in regard to religious reform, although scholars of the modern era have often considered prophecy an almost insignificant factor after 1530. This is only one of the paradoxes that arise from a study of Dionisio Gallo.

Who was this man who called himself Dionisio Gallo? From the documents which are today found in the Archivio di Stato of Venice and which record his trial before the Venetian Inquisition in 1566–67,[1] we learn that he had been rector of the Collège de Lisieux; letters to Italian princes, preserved along with the records of the trial, demonstrate not only his familiarity with court circles but also his erudition and his utopian vision of a reformed Church and a reformed world.

The story of Dionisio Gallo illustrates once again the close, if enigmatic, relationship between humanism and reform. Like his fellow countryman Guillaume Postel (1510?–81), Dionisio Gallo was a learned humanist-teacher who had a profoundly moving spiritual experience, which he called his "anointment on the inside and on the outside" by the Virgin Mary. A virgin whom Postel called the "Venetian Virgin," in whom Christ dwelled most fully, participated in Postel's mystical-spiritual reawakening by appearing to him at night and engrafting herself into his body, burning out the "old man," in whose place a new spiritual man was born. Both Gallo and Postel, one of the most learned humanists of the sixteenth century, used humanism and the rhetoric of humanism to bring about a reform of the Church and society at large. As we pursue Dionisio Gallo in France and in Italy, we are drawn into princely and aristocratic circles and find that Dionisio's humanism is not atypical, especially in Venice, after the midpoint of the sixteenth century and after the conclusion of the Council of Trent. Granted that his use of Latin was flawless in syntax and elegant in style, his main purpose was to accomplish by his writing and discourse a reform of the Church—a truly catholic reform. Dionisio did not hesitate to criticize the pope, the Curia, and many cardinals as harshly as did the Protestant reformers against whom he railed for severing the unity of the Church.

Dionisio Gallo speaks to us through the records of his trial by the Holy Office of the Inquisition in Venice in 1566–67 and through the many letters to Italian princes that were preserved by the Inquisition along with his trial. His explicit descriptions of the horrors of prison life in Venice, his ability to represent conversations apparently verbatim, his revelations about his princely friends, his almost hallowing references to two Venetian benefactors, and his own additions to the myth of Venice draw us intimately into his company, but at the same time confound and frustrate.

Our knowledge of Dionisio is confined to about the first seven years of the 1560s. In Paris, as rector of the Collège de Lisieux, Dionisio was knowledgeable of events in the king's circle. His conviction that the Virgin had anointed him on the inside and outside as God's messenger and servant for the restoration of the Church caused him to lose favor with the royal court. Before he departed France for Italy, this conviction had earned for him the mockery of his fellows, who called him derisively "king of the Gauls." In Italy he signed his name Dionisio Gallo or, when writing in French, Denys des Gaulois. Was this a pseudonym rich in associations for his prophetic persona? One cannot be certain, but on several occasions he referred to himself as the one whose name no one knew except him who bore it. The unanswered questions about Dionisio are frustrating, and one could well ask, Why spend so many years of research on a figure as elusive as Dionisio Gallo, whom some could consider a minor figure? I, however, must point out that a so-called minor figure can become a major figure when he or she represents a number of converging elements.

The example of Domenico Scandella detto Menocchio comes immediately to mind. This sixteenth-century miller from Friuli, almost unknown until recreated by Carlo Ginzburg in *The Cheese and the Worms*, has become a topos for *studiosi* of the sixteenth century.[2] By focusing attention on Menocchio, Ginzburg has unequivocally demonstrated the significance of so-called minor figures for historical understanding. When many historical threads converge in such minor figures, weaving a multilayered tapestry for our historical vision, the minor figures may become major.

Such a figure is the man who referred to himself as Dionisio Gallo, a so-called minor figure who brings into our vision the converging elements of King Charles IX of France, beset by civil and religious strife, and "most serene" Venice, determined to deflect her enemies within and without; the converging elements of Duke Emanuele Filiberto of Savoy, Duke Cosimo I of Florence, Duke Alfonso II of Ferrara, Papal Rome, Venice, France, and our prophet, Dionisio; the converging elements of heresy and heterodoxy and prophetic vision as responses to the troubled Cinquecento; the converging elements of high and low culture in regard to prophecy and the reform of the Church. The number of converging elements into which a study of Dionisio draws us is vast, and from these converging elements the historian receives another vision of what prophecy meant in the sixteenth century and how prophecy was related to reform of the Church.

Dionisio's narrative has numerous surprises and turns. His trial before the Venetian Inquisition was atypical because the accused often played the role of inquisitor by posing questions of his own to the inquisitor. His trial seems less an inquisition than perhaps a dialogue between the inquisitor and the defendant, who almost always dominated the discourse. Among the *processi* of the Holy Office of the Inquisition in Venice, Dionisio's case is surely one of the most interesting, not only because of Dionisio and his lengthy discourses and outbursts but also because of the tension between Dionisio and the inquisitor, Giovanni Trevisan, and the patience of the latter. Additionally, the Holy Office preserved Dionisio's numerous letters to Italian princes, and these provide us with a fascinating study of his mindset, his circles, and his convictions about the restoration of the Church and his role in making this a reality in his own day.

Our humanist self-styled prophet caused quite a stir when he arrived in Venice in 1566, since he was a flamboyant personality whose stunning clothing and elegant speech, usually Latin, lent him a strange charisma and "star quality." He knew exactly how to choose the proper political and religious space in which to speak in order to enhance his claims about his prophetic persona. According to J. G. A. Pocock, Machiavelli emphasized that "the prophet's inspiration and mission do not deliver him from the political context created by innovation and that he must continue to use the secular arm for reasons inherent in that context." The prophet, whether true or false, is an innovator and consequently requires the sword. Moses and Savonarola are significant in this context because the "legislator is part of the definition of the ideal type of innovator and the prophet part of the definition of the ideal type of legislator."[3] Dionisio saw himself in both roles, and hence his choice of space—a princely court of the cortile of the Ducal Palace in Venice—in which to present his innovation for the Church and the world. Dionisio's sword was the "sword of truth," revealed to him by the Virgin and honed by the rhetoric of his metaphorical language. His elegant use of Latin was an essential part of his "star quality" as innovator, but certainly not the only part. His exotic dress, his boldness, and his certainty about his role as prophet all blended together to give him an aura which was fascinating for princes and the princely courts and for the patricians and *cittadini* of aristocratic Venice.

Dionisio captured the imagination of large numbers in Venice as he proclaimed his innovations for a reformed Church, a reformed society, and a reform of the universities. His prophetic voice was directed not to the future but to the ills of his own day, as were the voices of Savonarola and Postel. For Dionisio, a prophet was a "servant and messenger of God" who had received his message directly from divine sources, with no outside intervention. In this sense a prophet was the essential ingredient in the program of reform. As an innovator-prophet Dionisio was also an innovator-legislator who drafted a charter, or platform, of seventy-two articles for the reform of the Church and the world. He made several copies of these articles, which differed not at all in substance or wording but only in the numbering. As an innovative legislator, to use Pocock's phrase, he called these principles for a new world order his *Legatio*. Always linking religious reform to the political state and its well-being, Dionisio sought the aid of certain Italian princes, hoping to join their political expertise and power with his prophetic authority, which he believed had been granted directly by God through the intervention of the Virgin Mary.

In 1566 Dionisio arrived in Venice, the culmination of his prophetic journey, since he believed that Venice held a unique role as defender of justice and consequently should play a major part in his program of reform. Since Dionisio's eye was always fixed on the political aspects of religious reform, Venice, with its political-religious balance, safeguarded by the political sphere, was the ideal state from which his grand vision for reform should originate. In addition, Venice had for many centuries claimed a prophetic origin, with Saint Mark as patron and protector. The four splendid ancient bronze horses that grace the western façade of the Basilica di San Marco as the Quadriga Domini surely would have underscored for Dionisio the significant role of Venice not only in her prophetic past but in her prophetic present.[4] There was an urgency in all of Dionisio's exhortations to princes and to people, but especially to the Venetians—the Venetian Senate, Venetian senators, and the Venetian Inquisition. He insisted that enactment of the reforms adopted by the Council of Trent was going too slowly. He was convinced that drastic and immediate steps were necessary, to be set in motion by himself, with the aid of chosen princes and even the pope, should he be willing. In fact Dionisio called himself the *auriga* (charioteer) of the Church Militant, and the horses of San Marco were perhaps his inspiration. In Dionisio's *Legatio*, completed in Venice in 1566 in the home of a Venetian citizen, Rocho de Mazzochis, our humanist-prophet signed his proemium "totius ecclesiae militantis auriga Dionisius Gallus." As charioteer of the Church Militant, exemplified by the prancing horses that awe any spectator viewing the façade of the Basilica de San Marco, Dionisio Gallo hoped, with the aid of Venetian friends and chosen Italian princes, to lead the Church into a renewed and pristine state that would reflect its ancient origin. Although he listed more than seventy points in his various *Legationes,* he consistently reiterated the general foundation of his program of action, namely: (1) the clergy must be reformed; (2) heresy must be extirpated; (3) the poor must be consoled; (4) all the infidels, Turks and Jews, must be led to Christ; (5) a third part of the goods of the Church must be returned to the poor. He also urged the clergy to choose truth and follow charity. He was insistent that these general principles plus more than seventy specific points be acted upon immediately. The urgency in his proposals revealed his impatience with what he considered the slow pace of reform. One could describe Dionisio as a political activist, a religious revolutionary, and a humanist-prophet who wore all of his mantles at the same time.

The story of Dionisio begins for us in Venice, where the records of his trial and his numerous letters are found. We are ultimately confronted with King Charles IX's court and the Wars of Religion in France; we also get an intimate view of the princely courts of Savoy, Florence, and Ferrara from Dionisio's letters written from these courts and preserved by the Venetian Inquisition. In order to hear Dionisio's words, we need only to study his letters, which accompany the documents of his trial. In order to comprehend Dionisio in his milieu in Italy and in France, however, much more is required. Since Dionisio's story reflects numerous converging elements, it is necessary to acquire an independent account of the persons, places, and events mentioned by Dionisio in his own writings and his trial as recorded by the scribe of the Venetian Inquisition. In pursuit of such an account I have studied the dispatches of the Venetian ambassadors to Savoy, Florence, Ferrara, Rome, and France from 1560 to 1567; the letters to the Capi del Consiglio dei Dieci (Council of Ten); the records of the Collegio and Senato; numerous trials found in the records of Santo Uffizio; wills and tax records. To follow the trail of Dionisio in the archives was at times baffling but always exciting. To pursue Dionisio one needs to be a detective who leaves no stone unturned. Common sense and intuition, as well as critical methodology, are also required. Especially perplexing was the identification of Dionisio's friend and benefactor whom he identified only as Rocho Veneto. His identification was essential to a comprehension of Dionisio's milieu in Venice and to the veracity of his story. Dionisio never mentioned the cognomen of Rocho, referring to him only as Rochus Venetus. To locate this particular Rocho seemed an impossible task, since the name was common in Venice both as given name and family name. After exploring many dead ends, I hit upon a commonsense approach: if Rocho was a friend of

Dionisio, perhaps he was also a friend of others who had had problems with the Holy Office of the Inquisition, and perhaps had been summoned as a witness. This commonsense hypothesis led to a perusal of all the *processi* of the Holy Office from 1560 to 1566. In one, that of Zuane de Vancimugio of Vicenza, in July 1566, Rocho de Mazzochis, *senser di biave*, was called as a witness. It seemed reasonable to assume that Rocho Veneto and Rocho de Mazzochis were one and the same.

A commonsense hunch had helped identify a person whose identity had hitherto seemed unascertainable. With the discovery of Rocho's cognomen, the story of Dionisio in Venice and of his friends in the Serenissima began to unfold. When a name took on flesh and bones, the history began to come into focus. Prophetic voices belonged not only to self-styled prophets like Dionisio Gallo but also to businessmen like Rocho de Mazzochis and patricians like Giusto Morosini, who also apparently agreed with Dionisio's plan for reform. This plan was not derived from a particular set of social or political circumstances; rather, it developed from Dionisio's conviction that the Church must be reformed and that God had chosen him, "a weak little man," to lead this grand enterprise.

Dionisio's crusade for reform was a personal one that he intended to make universal. Dionisio's program focused on the reform of the pope, the papal Curia, and every person who had clerical responsibilities, from the "lowest to the highest." Society at large also came under his scrutiny, and though he believed he spoke with authority from on high about religious reform, he was not averse to calling upon the aid of secular princes in his quest for a reformed society and a reformed Church. This is not surprising, because to Dionisio the Church was the *Ecclesia militans*, that is, the social, political, and religious world of mankind.

I spoke earlier of the prophet as innovator, yet Dionisio's ideas in many ways reflect the medieval worldview of Joachim and later of Savonarola. He was an innovator, however, in his blending of medieval and Renaissance worldviews, in his insistent conflation of the political and religious, and in his theatricality and his piety. He was also an innovator in his demands for an immediate response to the religious crisis, boldly ignoring the work of the Council of Trent and indicating in his numerous *Legationes* his own plan for a reformed Church. In keeping his own agenda for reform, Dionisio resembled the Jesuits, who had ministries the Council of Trent underplayed or ignored, even though Lainez, Salmerón, and Jay attended the council. The Jesuits' program for adult education grounded in Scripture, their emphasis upon moral issues through "sacred lectures," and their preaching in the streets, hospitals, or wherever they found an audience were not dissimilar from the goals and methods of Dionisio.5 We should also note that Guillaume Postel, whom Dionisio resembled in many respects, was a Jesuit in the early days of the society and was considered a radical reformer by both Protestants and Catholics. Dionisio, like Postel, demanded immediate action in regard to the reform of the Church and was considered either a fool or a radical or often both. The Venetian Inquisition tried both men; Postel was sent to Rome at the insistence of Pope Paul IV; Dionisio was sent back to Ferrara, presumably to his friend, Duke Alfonso II. Dionisio's life has not been documented as completely as Postel's, yet their ideas, which often seem part of one fabric, and also their ambience are examples of the "converging elements" alluded to earlier.

Although many questions about the life of Dionisio Gallo remain unanswered, the evidence we have and the more than three hundred pages of his writings present a vivid picture of the civil and religious strife in France and of three princely courts in Italy, especially in the city of Venice, where Dionisio preached, received hospitality, suffered in the prisons of the Ducal Palace, and made his most ardent challenge to the Serenissima and especially the Venetian nobility to render justice, since this responsibility had been granted to the city by God. All of these converging elements make the history of Dionisio Gallo a subject worthy of scholarly inquiry. From the study of Dionisio Gallo there is much to learn, not only from his trial and his remarks to the inquisitor during the process but also and especially from his own writings, preserved along with his trial, which clarify the milieu in which he moved, especially in Venice.

Dionisio reconfirms for us the Old Testament meaning of a prophet as one who speaks for God. Dionisio's certainty about his role as God's prophet calls to mind the transforming experience of Saint Paul on the road to Damascus, where he heard God's voice speak to him and thereafter became God's prophet. Dionisio also encourages us to rethink prophecy, in the sense in which he meant it, as direct response to the religious and social ills of the sixteenth century. Dionisio's prophetic voice reveals his fervid insistence on man's response to God's voice. Through the appearance of the Virgin, God had instructed him in His program for reform of the Church and had given him a double anointment to confirm him, Dionisio Gallo, as *servus* and *nuntius Dei*, God's prophet for the sixteenth century. He sees himself as the culmination of medieval expectations of the angelic pope; in addition, as the "man from Bosra," Dionisio intensifies his identification with Christ in the temporal work of restoration. Although he did not claim to be Christ, Dionisio believed himself, as God's prophet, to be His, and therefore Christ's, messenger and servant.

His story is fascinating, but more important, his story demonstrates the numerous paradoxes of the sixteenth century. Ambiguous himself, his story is also; from the ambiguities, however, we arrive at a clearer picture of the prophet and his audience in the Cinquecento. The story of Dionisio Gallo is open-ended and invites us to participate in it and perhaps to conclude it.

· I ·
GALLUS CANTANS
The Singing Gaul

Iterum noui apostoli qui predicabunt iterum euangelium dei ut omnes conuertantur ad deum. Deinde cantabit gallus optimaque fiet restauratio. . . . Cantet gallus optimus et uerus papa fietque restitutio scilicet erroribus extirpatis.

—Venice, Biblioteca nazionale di San Marco, MSS latini, Cl. III, Cod. CLXXVII (= 2176), c. 27

he exotic prophet who arrived in Venice in the late spring of 1566 called himself Dionisio Gallo. He became well known in a few days because of his unusual dress.[1] His colorful attire would have distinguished him immediately as a stranger, since Venetian patricians and citizens wore sober black.[2] His habit was wine red, long, and ample, and over it he wore many crosses of various sizes. His long vest with long sleeves had a high collar extending from shoulder to shoulder in the back and was bound with cords of gold.[3] Around his neck he wore a scarf of red silk. The stranger's appearance was sparkling, and some who saw him thought that he was a French bishop.[4] All commented on the beauty and elegance of his attire. He was often seen in the *calle* and *campielli* of Venice. He could be found most often, however, around the Piazza San Marco, in the basilica, in the curia of the palazzo, or in the cortile of the Palazzo Ducale, where for many days he was seen preaching. In the vast space of the courtyard Dionisio chose the most dramatic spot from which to address the numerous persons who passed through daily to attend to their sundry duties or to transact business at the palace. For his discourses, or sermons, he stepped upon the *banca*, or ledge, that ran along the sides of the white marble grand stairway leading to the loggia of the Ducal Palace.[5] This magnificent *scala* was designed by Antonio Rizzo; its construction began shortly after the fire that destroyed parts of the palace in 1483.[6] Completed in 1497, it would soon be called the Scala dei Giganti, from the huge sculptures of Mars and Neptune, representing Venice's prowess on land and sea; these figures were designed by Jacopo Sansovino and placed at the top of the stairway in 1566.[7]

The Scala dei Giganti intersects the cortile of the Palazzo Ducale and provides the most advantageous position for addressing those gathered in the courtyard. The *banca* upon which Dionisio stood was on the side of the stairway that faces the large court. From this vantage point he could be seen by all in the large cortile and even by those passing along the *piazzetta* of San Marco, since the Scala dei Giganti was in full view even to the campanile.[8]

Dionisio chose to speak not outside, in the Piazza San Marco, but inside the cortile of the Palazzo Ducale because of its political and religious connotations.[9] The Ducal Palace was the seat from which the doge, in conjunction with the elected nobles, administered justice and directed the governance of the Serenissima; it was also the doge's dwelling place. Adjacent to the Palazzo Ducale the private chapel of the doge was erected, the Basilica di San Marco, to replace the ancient Church of Saint Theodore and to serve as a fitting home for the body of the saint, which had been spirited away from Alexandria by two Venetian merchants.[10] Indeed, the relics of Saint Mark became the palladium of the doge and of Venice. From the time Saint Mark became the protector of Venice, the position of the doge was enhanced, as it were, by a heavenly light.[11] The doge upheld the republic's laws and God's Laws to assure the continued protection of "Messer San Marco" and was the "grand officiant" in the devotion to the saint: Venetians often remarked that they were *prima veneziani, poi cristiani*; they also considered Saint Mark, first, the patron of the state and, second, one of the evangelists.[12] From the palace the doge could enter directly into the Basilica di San Marco through the door that opens into the Capella di San Clemente. In this chapel, under the mosaic that depicts Saint Mark's translation to Venice and under a beautiful mosaic of Saint Clement, is a border with an inscription sculpted in stone, still visible today.[13] This inscription served as a reminder to the doges of Venice to cherish justice both political and religious. The inscription, beginning on the side of the chapel under the mosaics and continuing around the vault and over the door through which the doge entered, advises the doge as follows:

> *Love justice, Oh Doge; render its rights to all; the poor, the widow, the child, and the orphan look to you as their patron. Oh Doge, be pious to all people. Do not let fear or hatred or love draw you away, nor gold. As the flower will fade, so will you, Doge, become ashes. And just as you will do, so will you be after death.*[14]

fig. 1
The courtyard of the Ducal Palace. Dionisio addressed the crowds from the banca (ledge) of the grand stairway, to the right. On this stairway the doge received the symbols of his authority. Biblioteca nazionale di San Marco, Venice

This ancient inscription was a constant witness to the dual nature of the doge as guardian of political and religious justice. The question of justice was to underpin a key challenge our prophet would direct to the Venetians. A significant part of Dionisio's message for Venice concerned Venice as the upholder of justice and as the new Jerusalem.

One of the most beautiful depictions of the doge's role as upholder of God's Law and the laws of the Serenissima, the symbol of justice for the Venetian republic, is an exquisite miniature at the beginning of the ducal proemium of the *Libro d'oro vecchio* of the Maggior Consiglio, which shows Saint Mark, seated, handing the Law to Doge Andrea Gritti, on his knees before the saint.[15] In the proemium the doge promised "to preserve and safeguard the laws without corruption and with holiness and to entrust them to be preserved to our other magistrates, judges, and citizens."[16] Other visible examples reminded all Venetians and visitors of Venice's dedication to justice. On the capital of the first column of the colonnade of the Palazzo Ducale, adjacent to the Porta della Carta, Moses is sculpted on his knees before God, who is handing him the Decalogue; God's Law provided the direction for the laws of the Serenissima. It appears likely that in the miniature of the *Libro d'oro* Saint Mark is presenting God's Law to Doge Gritti as a paradigm for the laws of the Venetian republic.

The careful blending of sacred and secular in the person of the doge was not lost upon Dionisio. His choice of dramatic space in the cortile of the Palazzo Ducale demonstrated his understanding of the nature of the doge and of the Venetian republic. This stunning setting, with all its implications, was the appropriate space from which Dionisio Gallo announced to the prophetic city of Saint Mark that he had come to the Serenissima as God's messenger with the resolution to all the conflicts of the Cinquecento. If his dazzling garments bordered with gold and his many crosses had not sufficiently aroused the curiosity of those who were passing through the courtyard, his words about his own mission and about the pope would have quickly captured their attention. From the *banca* of the grand *scala* in the courtyard of the Palazzo Ducale, Dionisio announced in excellent Latin to those gathered around: "Venetian lords, I have been sent by the Holy Spirit; you have seen the dove, and it is a sign of my truth. I say that the pope and his cardinals do not understand well the true and Catholic teaching, because they do and say things that are contrary to the evangelical doctrine, as I shall show you in my discourse."[17] To support the truth of his prophetic mission, he stated that he was prepared to suffer fire, water, and every kind of torment.[18] In effect Dionisio believed himself to be one of the "new apostles chosen to preach the gospel of the Lord and to convert all to Him," as proclaimed in medieval prophecy. Dionisio Gallo saw himself as the "singing Gaul" who had been chosen to proclaim "the restitution after sins have been removed."[19] And he believed Venice had been elected to fulfill the divine mission of salvation. As we shall see, Dionisio's life became intertwined with that of Venice. The story of Dionisio Gallo, an "angelic pope" for the sixteenth century, begins and ends in Venice.[20] Many things emerge, however, between the beginning and the end.

In Venice the vividness of Dionisio's words and his dress did indeed attract large crowds of patricians and churchmen, who listened intently to his statements, always spoken in elegant Latin. He managed to preach, without permission, from his chosen location for eight days or more before he was imprisoned, though imprisonment did not silence him. He had also spoken in other strategic places around the city. On one occasion he spoke from the

fig. 2
Girolamo Priuli, Doge of Venice from 1559 to 1567. Biblioteca nazionale di San Marco, Venice

choir of the Basilica di San Marco in the presence of the doge, the patriarch, and Venetian noblemen. He had even been successful in entering the hallowed space of the Senate of Venice, where he identified himself to the august body as God's messenger, with a special message for the doge and the senators about imminent dangers to Venice. He admitted that he spoke "as long as he was allowed," and then was escorted toward an exit. Before he reached the exit, however, a white dove flew across the huge room and perched above his head; it then followed him to the front of the Senate, where he addressed the august body. This white dove represented for him a sure sign of his divine calling. He reminded the senators that the dove indicated the Holy Spirit, which directed him. He was to repeat the same interpretation of the dove on many occasions, pointing out that the dove that hovered over his head certified his claim that he was God's messenger. Dionisio considered it very significant that this had taken place on the Feast of Pentecost.

His appearance and his erudition soon made him a well-known figure. He preached in the public places of Venice as well as in the privacy of Venetian homes. His activities in Venice, however, did not escape the notice of the Holy Office of the Inquisition, which had been advised by many "worthy of faith" about the strange claims of the mysterious stranger.[21] Among those who denounced Dionisio Gallo was the Venetian patrician

Daniel Reiniero, who was shocked by Dionisio's claims.²² A religious, Stephanus de Franciscis, subdeacon of the Church of San Giovanni Eleemosinarii di Rialto, had engaged Dionisio in friendly conversation one day outside of the Basilica di San Marco. Stephanus asked him who he was and by what spirit he was led. After Dionisio repeated his usual declarations about being God's messenger, Stephanus retorted that messengers carried testimonial letters, and asked to see his.²³ Not at all hesitant, Dionisio responded that the dove was one testimony and the letter of Christ that he carried in his hands was the other. Because of remarks like this, the authorities noted Dionisio's presence in Venice. Consequently, the Holy Office of the Inquisition, to which Reiniero had directed his *denuntia,* sent its messenger Nicolas Lapicida to tell the stranger to stop his preaching, since he had no license; otherwise he would suffer banishment *sub poena triremis.*²⁴ Dionisio did not cease his preaching and his commerce with his Venetian friends. On Saturday, June 8, 1566, four days after the first warning, the mysterious stranger was again found preaching, to a large audience in the curia of San Marco.²⁵ On this occasion the papal nuncio, Giannantonio Facchinetti, seized the documents from which he was reading, and warned him again that if he did not cease preaching publicly, he would be detained and thrown into prison. Dionisio ignored this second warning as well. The following day, Sunday, June 9, 1566, he was again observed preaching in the cortile of the Ducal Palace,²⁶ and a third time was warned to stop. That evening, the papal nuncio sent his agent to apprehend Dionisio while he was in bed. Dionisio complained that he had been seized by the nuncio's agent like a dove in its nest.²⁷ The stealth of the agent was graphically contrasted with the helplessness of Dionisio, "the dove in the nest." The Inquisition had apparently been aware of Dionisio's activities, but Reiniero's denouncement spurred them into action. Dionisio was subsequently incarcerated in the prisons of the Consiglio dei Dieci in the Palazzo Ducale. The number of nobles and "persone di qualità" who had listened intently to Dionisio preach caused grave concern to the Venetian Inquisition and especially to the papal nuncio, Facchinetti. There had been much speculation about who he was, what he was doing in Venice, and if he was one of those who believed that "all must be in common."²⁸

Information about Dionisio Gallo is scarce. Except for the records of the Venetian Inquisition and his numerous writings, preserved along with his trial in the Archivio di Stato of Venice, we would know little about this mysterious Frenchman. Most of our information about him is derived from his own writings, though witnesses at his trial, Parisian monks visiting Venice, provide us with some additional facts. Secondary literature has yielded only two references to our prophet, mocked as "king of the Gauls" in Paris. The name he used in Venice and in other Italian cities cannot be found in the testimony of French witnesses or in the secondary literature. The man who called himself Dionisio Gallo in Italy was referred to in Paris and by Parisian witnesses in Venice only as "the one who was called king of the Gauls." The name Dionisio Gallo may have been a pseudonym chosen to reveal what he believed was his prophetic calling. Who was this man?

Dionisio said he was born in Gisors, France, and on one occasion gave a fanciful derivation for the place of his birth. He wrote that he came *de urbe gi sorte, id est, terra sortis*.[29] No mention is made of his father or mother or any relatives. On one occasion, however, he claimed that he was descended from an ancient lineage of Norman princes.[30] No records of Dionisio Gallo exist today in the Archives de l'Eure.[31] Dionisio tells us nothing of his early life in Gisors or of his mature years there, for that matter. He often wrote of being the rector of the *collège* of the "citè et ville" of Lisieux. From his words one could assume that he meant that he was rector of the Collège de Lisieux in Lisieux, but this presents a problem, since the Collège de Lisieux was established in the city of Lisieux only in 1571 and began its active works only in the beginning of the year 1572.[32] The Collège de Lisieux in Paris, on the mountain of Sainte Geneviève, was established in 1336, but records concerning the rector of the *collège* for the period under consideration do not exist.[33] Therefore, the records from the Venetian archives are all the more precious, since they supply quintessential information about at least one of the rectors during the turbulent years before and during the Wars of Religion in France.

Dionisio was in all likelihood a member of a religious order who also served as the rector of the Collège de Lisieux. He was a frequent visitor to the Carthusian monastery in Paris and engaged in long conversations with the monks.[34] He appeared to have an intimate knowledge of events taking place in Paris, especially regarding the king, the queen mother, and the King's Council. Although he often related events connected with the king's activities, his most frequent statements about France concerned a mystical anointment that he experienced in Lisieux in February 1563. He was to describe again and again, to King Charles IX and to Italian princes, this spiritual anointment, which forever changed his life as a rector. His insistence on the truth of this anointment caused him to be mocked in Paris and eventually was one of the causes of his departure from France. He never changed his story, however, in countless retellings:

The queen of heaven, the most sacred mother of Christ and virgin . . . she herself sent by the eternal Trinity, descended from the sky. She appeared to me and surely told me supreme news. What was the news? . . . I announce a new heaven, a new earth, a solution of the century: the Antichrist has been born; the clergy must be reformed and their errors abolished; the poor must be consoled; all the unfaithful must be converted to Christ. These are my duties, once and for all, according to the divine will of the eternal Trinity. Three years have elapsed, toward the end of February recently past. She appeared about the middle of the night, the night of the Sabbath, if I remember well, when I was alone in my little room, lying on my bed. I am not ashamed to say that at that time I was rector of the collège of the city of Lisieux. . . . She stood and addressed me with a most serene face. When so many messages were understood, I asked her: "Since I am alone, so inexperienced in human affairs, a man of almost no strengths, should I dare, or could I dare, to accomplish so difficult and so dangerous deeds . . . ?" With signs and arguments she explained all things to me, having promised the favor of God and Heaven and His aid. At length I agreed, although my weakness and fragility were declared. I vow my whole body and my whole soul to God Omnipotent, and I dedicate myself to him, saying, "Let there be the will of the most blessed Trinity in heaven and on earth."[35]

Dionisio's mystical experience had two phases. The first, described above in his own words, was the Virgin's calling of Dionisio to the great task of reforming the clergy, consoling the poor, and converting all the unfaithful to Christ. Essential to this calling was Dionisio's acceptance of his role. Only after the covenant was accepted could his divine anointment take place. Dionisio described it thus: "Then that Virgin, clothed in white and girdled as if she were a certain bishop about to consecrate presbyters and ordain them, began with all reverence to anoint me with heavenly oil on the outside of my body from the top of my head to the tip of my toes. And I was thinking that there had been sufficient unction; and then she begins to anoint all the interior parts of my body from the top of my head to the tip of my toes." After the anointment, the Virgin gave Dionisio specific instructions, according to the mandate of the Holy Trinity: "Announce to kings, princes, peoples, and nations of the earth and likewise to all the shepherds of the Church."[36] The Virgin then touched him on the right side of his head, made some slight sound, and disappeared.

In the three years following his anointment Dionisio often repeated the story to indicate God's choice of him as reformer of the Church with specific duties, expecting this fantastic experience to be believed. He began his mission, the very day after this nocturnal anointment, by attacking what appeared to him to be the errors of the heretics and the universal iniquities of the clergy. The day was Sunday, but even on the Sabbath he was thrown into prison for his harsh criticism of the clergy, the bishop, and canons of the city of Lisieux. After three days, the Virgin, clad in a triumphant habit, appeared to him again, while he was imprisoned. She appeared in the middle of the night and consoled him against Satan, who was tempting him with an old desire for luxury. Dionisio, however, says he conquered Satan, "who was bound by the soldiers of Christ." He does not say who freed him from prison, indicating only that God freed him.[37]

As he departed from the prison, he saw his adversaries, the bishop and canons, captives in the middle of the city. They had been stopped in flight by the king's soldiers, who were ready to defend the city against the army of heretics who were surrounding it. After his release from prison, he renewed his challenges to all men to reform themselves.[38] His new role was that of God's messenger and servant, confirmed by the mystical anointment by the Virgin in late February 1563. The simple but learned rector of the Collège de Lisieux no longer existed. Whatever tranquillity he may previously have enjoyed in his scholarly life was now concluded. An active and often tormented life lay ahead.

Dionisio, in writing about his life after his anointment, noted that "good men" supported and protected him but wicked men constantly abused him in countless ways.[39] He apparently suffered the greatest ills at the hands of the "heretics." Dionisio had access to young King Charles IX, perhaps as a tutor.[40] On a daily basis he admonished the king, in the name and in the virtue of Christ, to unite his kingdom in the holy religion of God or else lose his crown.[41] He also addressed the queen mother, the royal Senate, the cardinals, and princes, both Catholic and Huguenot, who at first received him cordially, when the court was in residence in Gaîllon, but became silent and confused when they heard Dionisio condemn them.[42]

Among the courtiers at Gaîllon was Constable Anne Montmorency, whom Dionisio quoted as saying: "If wise men of all the world were gathered together to resolve the problems of Christianity, they could not do this in a more true or holy way."[43] It was Dionisio's usual practice to read his writings to his various audiences, but on this occasion Dionisio spoke without notes, which feat seemed to impress his noble listeners. Although he spoke from memory, he had already written his program for reform of the Church, according to his divine mandate. He called his platform for the reform of the Church his *Legatio,* which he was to transcribe many times but with very few changes. He admitted that in his remarks to the assembly of nobles he was not as forthright "about the kingdom of France divided in religion" as he would be in his later *Legatio.*

The young king asked for a copy of the *Legatio* and evidently read it. He heard Dionisio speak for several days and apparently approved his words. According to Dionisio, however, when the king realized from the passionate pleas of Dionisio that this strange prophet expected him to execute the *Legatio,* punish the heretics, and send the cardinals and "other shepherds" away from his court to watch over their own flocks, he was not able to do it.44 One of the principles in the *Legatio* that the young king read concerned Clement Marot. Dionisio had written: "Clement Marot receu par les Docteurs correct." Marot, the French humanist and poet, had inherited from his father the responsibility of *valet de chambre* of King Francis I. He had enjoyed great popularity at court until he was accused of heresy and compromised in the famous *affaire des placards,* after which he sought help from Marguerite of Navarre and later from René of France, duchess of Ferrara.45 Marot's translation of the Psalms had long been censured by the Sorbonne, and Francis I had suspended the printing.46 One might wonder why Dionisio mentioned Marot in his *Legatio* if one did not recall that young Charles IX in 1560 had given "par grâce spéciale, pleine puissance et autorité royale, un privilège pour réimprimer les Psaumes de Marot." In granting the privilege, the king declared: "[L]es dit Psaumes traduicts selon 'la vérité hébraique,' et mis en rime françoise et bonne musique, comme a este bien veu et congneu par gens doctes en la Saincte Escriture, et aussi en l'art de musique."47 At the time Charles gave permission for the printing, he was about ten years old and was a great lover of poetry and a disciple of Ronsard. It seems likely, however, that he received advice from someone regarding the reprinting of Marot's versification of the Psalms in French. It could have been his tutor, Jacques Amyot, or even Dionisio himself. Dionisio's brief statement in his *Legatio* about Clement Marot is an example of a little piece of information that leads to fascinating "convergences." It shows the young king's appreciation of Marot's poetry; it may also indicate Dionisio's role in the king's decision, since the mention of Marot seems strange in the context of other points in the *Legatio.* The statement also allows us to speculate that Dionisio had been preparing an agenda for the reform of the Church for some years before his "divine anointment." It would be difficult to imagine that a person with literary talents such as Dionisio's would not be in touch with humanistic ideas connected to reform. Many humanists, like Marot, were sympathetic to reform regardless of the persuasion, and their ideas of a reformed Christianity were nondogmatic, centering upon praise and worship of God and simple acts of piety and charity.[48] Like many humanists, Dionisio may have arrived at some of his ideas about reform from his linguistic and literary studies. He knew well prophetic texts from the Latin Middle Ages, and he recommended the teaching of Hebrew, Latin, and Greek in all the schools. He was obviously sympathetic to certain ideas of the reformers, but he was so single-minded about the need for reform that he never seemed to realize the difficulties, political and religious, that a general reform of the Church would entail. Without guise he spoke his mind, and expected all reasonable men to come to his aid in reforming the Church.

In spite of the king's hesitation about the execution of Dionisio's *Legatio*, Dionisio was allowed to preach, especially in Paris: in the churches, in the palace, and in all the public places. He evidently read his *Legatio* or excerpts from it in as many parts of Paris as possible. In spite of the provocative nature of Dionisio's program for reform, and although our prophet had no skills for diplomatic discourse at this point, he obviously found audiences who listened to his sermons, and he still had access to the king. Charles IX perhaps knew Dionisio because of his duties as rector of the Collège de Lisieux, and the erudition of the rector would certainly have impressed the boy king. Dionisio was fluent in Latin, and his skill in oratory, *de memoria*, was considerable. He often wrote of Charles IX with affection and excused his shortcomings, attributing them to youth. Yet he was constantly warning that the clergy in Gaul had to be reformed and that heresies had to be extirpated.[49] Dionisio had often complained of the many heretical French bishops and the ineffectiveness of the French Crown in implementing reform of the clergy and bishops and in restraining heresy.[50] As a Frenchman, Dionisio was keenly aware of the growing power of the Protestants and the threat of imminent civil war. He was especially harsh in his opinion of Catherine de' Medici, who, he complained, was too tolerant of heretics. Dionisio seemed unable or unwilling to comprehend the difficult situation in which Catherine found herself after the death of her husband, Henry II (in 1559), whose heir was Francis II, the fifteen-year-old husband of Mary Stuart. The boy king delegated the administration of his realm to the Catholic Guises, thereby arousing the ire of the princes of the blood, the Protestant Bourbons. The Huguenots by sheer numbers had become a power to be reckoned with, and the overthrow of Guise rule was their common cause.[51] After the Bourbon-inspired coup, known as the Conspiracy of

Amboise, in March 1560, Catherine de' Medici took a more active role in the political arena. She developed a working relationship with the Huguenots, among whom was Gaspard de Coligny, admiral of France in 1552, who became a supporter of the royal cause. Catherine, in return, upheld the side of toleration.[52] On December 5, 1560, the young king Francis II died, and the power of the Guises fell with him. Charles IX, second son of Catherine and Henry II, was ten when he ascended to the throne, and his mother assumed the regency, without commitment to either Bourbon or Guise. Huguenots were advanced at court, and Anthony, king of Navarre, was appointed lieutenant-general of the kingdom. George Cassander wrote in 1561: "All Gaul is divided into three factions."[53] One was the "papists," headed by Tournon; another was the Huguenots. The third was called the "third party," which was moderate and pacific. This group included Catherine, Michel de L'Hôpital, the chancellor of France, Jean de Montluc, bishop of Valence, the cardinal of Lorraine, and the king of Navarre.

Dionisio did not seem to comprehend that Catherine's tolerant policies toward the Huguenots were based more upon circumstance and desire to keep the throne independent than upon conviction.[54] He perhaps also had in mind the politics of the cardinal of Lorraine who in 1560–61 urgently had called for a national council of the Gallican Church. Lorraine's tolerant stance encouraged the Huguenots, and violence again broke out. Because of the belief that the court was on their side, Calvinist pastors preached without restraint. Catherine even took the king and her other children to hear a sermon preached by a Calvinist pastor. This certainly scandalized the Catholics and was perhaps one of the reasons that Dionisio had abandoned hopes that the Crown of France could settle its religious problems and usher in a true reform of the Church. One must say, in fairness, that Catherine de' Medici's attempts to lessen the tensions on both sides of the religious spectrum, especially in light of her intense fear of Spain, and to pursue a more moderate policy were doomed to failure in view of the hostile climate preceding the outbreak of civil war in France.[55] As the Wars of Religion increased in violence, however, and as the efforts of the king and his mother proved ineffective in spite of the Edict of Pacification, Dionisio became more frustrated and openly critical of the king and especially of Catherine de' Medici. What Dionisio most abhorred was the fragmentation of Christianity that neither Catherine nor anyone else seemed able to stop. In spite of his constant challenges to the king, he reserved his harshest criticism of Charles IX until after his departure from France.[56]

When the king left Paris to survey his realm in 1563, Dionisio was still a conspicuous figure in the city. In the king's absence, however, Dionisio's movements were restricted, and he was "forced to suffer whatever was pleasing to those enemies," to the point of being "closed in the darkest prisons." Dionisio wrote that "it is sweeter to be crucified once and for all than to suffer for almost three years the things that I have suffered in Gaul because of the truth." Yet he was mysteriously freed from prison; Dionisio's dry comment was: "God finally freed me."57

As soon as he was released from prison, he determined to remind the sovereign "of the things that God had commanded him," and toward that end made his way to Mont Marsan to join the king and his party on a tour of the realm. He warned the king that if he did not unite his kingdom in a short time, he would be "sitting on two seats, as in a divided kingdom, and would fare ill, being deprived of each."58 It is not surprising that the "king, the queen mother, the royal Senate bore the truth badly," according to Dionisio's words. The heretics, however, bore it "very badly." Dionisio's plainly spoken warning from an ancient proverb led to his dismissal from the king's presence; the king uttered words to the effect that Dionisio could go wherever he wished with that truth.59

After Dionisio's dismissal from the king's court in Mont Marsan and the severance of what had previously been cordial relations with the king and some of the king's ministers, like Constable Anne Montmorency, Dionisio began to be mocked. Dionisio claimed that it would be impossible to tell how much effort he had given to the king on behalf of the unity of religion. He had urged the king to act against the heretics and against the abuses of the clergy. He had advised Charles IX that if he would punish a few of the heresiarchs who were with him in his palace in Paris, the other heretics would be silenced. It is no wonder that our prophet wore out his welcome with the king and the courtiers. Dionisio wrote that one day, in the king's palace in Paris, he cried out: "O Charles, king of the Franks, let those mad and raging dogs be captured (if you please), those who have laid waste your whole kingdom. If you allow them to escape, if you do not do justice, your crown perishes." He argued that the Edict of Pacification had no validity and should be revoked. The king's action in regard to the edict was against God and against the faith and belied the king's stature as most Christian king. He partially excused the king because of his youth and the pressures to which he had been subjected when he had agreed to the Edict of Pacification. Dionisio argued, however, that the kingdom had become ungovernable because of the edict. "Now God has restored this kingdom to you. You love peace; do justice," Dionisio warned.60 Our prophet interpreted the problems in France as both religious and political because the king had in his household enemies of both the Church and the Crown.

In spite of Dionisio's agitated state and rash words, his appraisal of the crisis in France in 1563 was similar to that of many modern critics.⁶¹ His attitude toward Catherine de' Medici was less than balanced, however.⁶² He blamed her, as did many others, for yielding to the heretics in granting the Edict of Pacification and therefore dividing the kingdom. The idea of a divided kingdom of France was inconceivable to Dionisio and a situation contrary to God's plan for the Gauls. In spite of Dionisio's harsh criticism of Catherine after he left France, the queen mother had, according to his own words, shown him some favor after his "mystical anointment" in Lisieux. One knows that Catherine was not averse to prophets and on occasion had consulted Nostradamus. Dionisio, for his part, never mentioned Nostradamus in his writings, even though he could have used a prediction of the famous prophet to his own advantage. In foreseeing events of 1566 Nostradamus wrote: "Sun and Mercury in the beginning of the cycle of the year indicate many legations [*legationes*] for the sake of faith and religion."⁶³ As we know, Dionisio called his plan for the reformation of the Church his *Legatio*.

As the civil wars increased in violence, Dionisio's rhetoric increased in intensity. Believing that the Edict of Pacification had increased the religious and civil problems, Dionisio harangued the young king: "You [Charles IX] can have no reason for the accursed and Satanic peace that you have made with those [heretics]; otherwise, in the strength and virtue of eternal God who sent me, I declare to you the rights of your kingdom have been broken and shaken."⁶⁴ While the king and his mother were trying to calm the situation in France, Dionisio's inflammatory words were surely having the opposite effect. Given the situation, it is amazing that the king allowed him to preach for almost a year after his "mystical anointment" in Lisieux.

Dionisio had harangued the king in Paris as well as in the palace in Gaîllon. During his stay in the palace in Paris, there came a great storm "contrary to every disposition of time and contrary to nature." Unheard-of thunder, horrible winds, and constant rain lashed Paris for eight days; during these stormy days Dionisio had a captive audience of cardinals, bishops, and clergy, to whom he preached with passion, calling them thieves and robbers because they had usurped the rights of the poor.⁶⁵ It may have been during this great *mal tempo* that Dionisio indicated to the king's religious guests that he had been sent as "king of the Gauls" by God. He obviously did not bother to explain that in his florid vocabulary a "king" was one who served God; his usual designation for himself after his anointment was "the servant and messenger of God." After his challenges to the king at Gaîllon, Paris, and Mont Marsan, Dionisio lost the *escu* that he had received each day for sustenance according to the ordinance of the king.⁶⁶ But though he had lost his financial support from the king, he was still allowed to preach in Paris.⁶⁷

After this encounter in Paris and especially in Mont Marsan, the king, exasperated with Dionisio's challenges and his unsettling words, probably recalled Dionisio's boast in Paris during the storm and hurled back the epithet "king of the Gauls" in derision. This epithet stuck, and Dionisio became known in Paris and in the king's circle as "king of the Gauls." This epithet and the activities described by Dionisio Gallo can be confirmed by two secondary sources, one from the sixteenth century. Jehan Baptiste de La Fosse, the *curé* of the parish of Saints Leu and Gilles during the years 1557–90, noted in his *Journal* for November 1563: "En ce temps il avoit ung jeune homme bon latin et aussi de grand esprit, lequel estant déguisé simuloit le fol et faisoit de grandes exclamations contre les huguenots et n'épargnoit personne à son parler. Il se faisoit appeler le roy des Gaulois."⁶⁸

There is no question but that this "young man, good in Latin," is our prophet, Dionisio Gallo, who appeared in Venice in late May 1566. De La Fosse, in his entry for January 1564 (1563 *more antiquo*), also confirms Dionisio's description of the consequences of his encounter with the king in Mont Marsan and his subsequent dismissal from the king's presence:

> *En ce moys fut défendu à Postel de ne plus prescher.*
> *Ledict mois, le roy des Gauloys fut mené prisonnier, puis il fut baillé en garde en une religion au païs de Normandie, et ce par délibération du privé conseil.*⁶⁹

These precious notices confirm for us Dionisio's account of his relationship with King Charles IX. They also arouse curiosity about the *déguisé* noted by de La Fosse. As I have already suggested, Dionisio used his attire to enhance his persona. We have examples of this from his appearance in Venice and in Rome. When he appeared in Paris and even in the king's presence, Dionisio chose external garments to reflect his message and his internal persona.

In addition to de La Fosse's *Journal*, the *Memoires de Condé* also confirm Dionisio's account. The *Memoires* explain that the one "who called himself king of the Gauls" was sent back to Gisors to be guarded unless the king himself ordered otherwise. The king also wrote a letter "to those of the *ville*" (Gisors), probably to explain the circumstances of Dionisio's banishment to Gisors, the place of his birth, according to Dionisio's account and apparently confirmed by the *Memoires de Condé*.⁷⁰ The king's edict of January

29, 1564, sent to the president of the Parlement de Paris, was issued "pour la conservation du repos de cette Ville." It is interesting to note that on the same day that King Charles IX ordered Dionisio to be sent to Gisors, he also directed the Parlement to put Guillaume Postel in the Priory of Saint Martin, "to be nourished and detained until the king should advise otherwise."[71]

It is obvious from the royal edict of January 1564 that Dionisio (and Postel, for that matter) had become more than the subject of children's laughter, as they followed him through the streets of Paris, calling him a fool. He had become a potential source of tension, even violence, as he openly insulted the Catholic clergy and demanded punishment of the heretics. With Dionisio in Paris it would have been even more difficult for Catherine de' Medici to steer a middle course between the extremes.[72]

After January 29, 1564, the citizens of Paris could have "some repose," since Dionisio was returned to Gisors, probably under some type of "house arrest." We have no indication of Dionisio's activity, if any, from January 1564 until October 1565, when he appeared in the Midi. Since he traveled extensively in the south, he may have remained under guard in Gisors for only a year. It is unclear whether the king had relaxed his previous edict.

Inquisition records also confirm Dionisio's account of events in France and Venice. This confirmation, together with those of the *Journal* and the *Memoires de Condé*, tends to bolster confidence in his statements about his activities in Savoy, Florence, and Ferrara. In addition, Dionisio was so convinced of his mystical experience that he would seem to have had no need to falsify. His forthrightness was part of his folly. His claims of having received the approval of two important Venetians, one a patrician, the other a Venetian officeholder, can be confirmed by their signatures. Given Dionisio's prophetic fervor and his firm belief that he had been sent to reform the Church and society, one could assume that he left Gisors without permission of the king, in the hope of finding support for his message at a distance from Paris, where he had lost favor.[73]

Therefore, he traveled south to Languedoc, visiting the cities of Bordeaux, Toulouse, and Carcassonne, where he preached his "legation of reform." He also preached in Tours before his arrival in the Midi.[74] While in the Midi, Dionisio wrote a letter to the king's governor of Languedoc, Henri de Montmorency, duke of Damville, who has been called the "uncrowned king of the South" because of his influence not only in Languedoc but also in Paris and Rome.[75] In addition to the letter to Damville, Dionisio also directed a letter to the "messieres, tenans les estatz du pais de Languedoc."[76] Since the Estates of Languedoc were among the most important provincial assemblies in France, Dionisio obviously hoped that the representatives to the Estates could use their considerable power to bring religious peace to Languedoc, where the influence of the Huguenots was strong.[77] In a letter written on October 22, 1565, to the representatives of the Estates of Languedoc, Dionisio revealed that he had been interrogated by the magistrates in their council and placed under arrest. He continued, however, to proclaim the truth of his "legation" and chided "you bishops, grand prelates and vicars, who ought to be the lights of people, you, governor, knights, and lords, who ought to fight for the faith. You, chosen for the cause of people. . . . Do you not wish to hear the truth?"[78]

Dionisio's stinging criticism of the existing state of affairs in Languedoc was directed at those in the political as well as the religious realm.[79] Without attention to diplomacy and without tempering his words, he beseeched the Estates of Languedoc to hear from him the truth that had been given to him by Jesus Christ. He asked for an audience to explain his legation, and concluded the letter with these words: "Jesus Christ made the kings, and virtue made the nobles. Jesus Christ and virtue, with truth, are one and the same thing."[80] In the letter, Dionisio also indicated that he had preached his message as "ambassadeur et seruiteur de Dieu" to the court of the Parlement and throughout the city of Paris. Two days after Dionisio wrote to the Estates, he composed a long letter to the governor, Damville, reiterating his desire to proclaim the truth in the land of Languedoc. He admitted that the wise of the world called him a fool;[81] however, he appealed to Damville to intercede with the bishops, who had not allowed him to present his legation. Many years earlier Savonarola had expressed the same idea about one's being so filled with the love of God that the men of the world consider one a fool. Fra Hieronimo wrote, for example, that "those who are filled with the love of Christ do and say certain divine things that sometimes seem to men to be folly."[82]

Savonarola said that when the love of Christ makes a man a fool to the world, he has reached the grade of *Ebrietà* (drunkenness) because "just men speak or do, not more human things, but divine things, and these exceed the capacity of reason."[83] Guillaume Postel, Dionisio's contemporary, was also to speak of being drunk for Christ and of being considered a fool by men in France and also by the Venetian Inquisition.[84] Anton Francesco Doni presented the problem of men's opinion of each other in comic dialogues that made the same profound impression as had Erasmus's *Praise of Folly* several decades earlier. In a dialogue between Giove and Momo, Doni makes the point very clear by having Giove ask Momo: "Who will be the one to judge whether that one is crazy and the other wise? To judge a crazy man [*pazzo*], we need a wise man, but where is this wise man [*savio*]? And to judge a wise man [*savio*], who else but the 'crazies' are there to judge?"⁸⁵ This little dialogue expresses the opinion that Dionisio conveyed, since he took pride in being considered a fool by the so-called wise. After he was derided as "king of the Gauls" by Charles IX, he enhanced the epithet by walking through the streets of Paris with a homemade tin crown on his head and a staff in his hands. According to Dionisio's use of the word, he was truly the "king of the Gauls" because a "king" must serve God, not man. Therefore, by his shabby attire as "king of the Gauls," he was making a statement about the service of kingship. To those who saw him, however, he was *pazzo*.

Dionisio did not hesitate to admit, even to the duke, the contempt in which he was often held. He noted that the bishops were very skeptical that he had been sent by God and asked for his proxy. Dionisio pointed out that neither Saint Peter nor Saint Paul, neither the Apostles nor the prophets, had carried proxies. He sharply criticized the bishops and prelates for their lack of charity to the poor and indicated that they were unwilling to suffer for Christ. He then warned Henri de Montmorency, duke of Damville, that it was his responsibility, given by Christ, to seize the revenue of all the bishops and the benefices of the land of Languedoc in order to subvent the poor.⁸⁶ Damville obviously was no more prepared for such a move than the king had been. Dionisio's proposals in France were revolutionary, confirming that he did not believe that the Church, even after the conclusion of the Council of Trent, could reform itself. Stronger medicine was needed, and only the king and secular officials in France had the power to administer the medicine that Dionisio believed was necessary for a reformed Church and state.⁸⁷

Our prophet never seemed to realize that the medicine he prescribed might be lethal for the institutions of both Church and state.⁸⁸ It is certain, however, that Montmorency understood the ramifications of Dionisio's statements. Therefore, it is doubtful that he interceded with the bishops and equally doubtful that Dionisio was allowed to read his *Legatio* in the governor's presence.⁸⁹ This *Legatio*, according to Dionisio, contained the resolution to all the problems that were dividing Christianity. Although young King Charles IX had read the *Legatio* and apparently approved of it, Dionisio's demand that the *Legatio* be enacted immediately was one of the chief reasons for his loss of favor in the royal circle. We are not told whether Dionisio had known Damville in Paris. However, he may have assumed that Constable Montmorency's favorable response to his *Legatio* implied the likelihood of a similar response from Constable's son, Henri.⁹⁰ At any rate, Dionisio's movements in the Midi obviously did not remain secret, since, according to his own words, he had traveled rather widely in the South. The king no doubt heard from his governor about the "king of the Gauls" preaching in Languedoc and about the letters he had written to Damville and to the Estates. Since Languedoc was already in a volatile situation, the royal governor probably made Dionisio unwelcome for the same reasons that had led to his banishment from Paris. For these reasons or others, Dionisio left Languedoc sometime after October 23, 1565, and two months later, two days before Christmas, he was in Turin.

In writing of his departure from France, he only noted that the Italian princes were more pious that the French, obviously assuming that they would be more amenable to his reform initiatives. Whatever the case was, he had become a *cause celebre* in France and could certainly have been imprisoned again if he had remained. In France few doors would have been open to him, and Italy seemed a logical choice for his mission. He may have reasoned that the Italian princes, joined by many ties to the Italian pope Pius V, would be more successful in correcting the abuses in the Curia and in the papal hierarchy. It is obvious that Dionisio believed that curial reform was still possible in the 1560s; other Catholic reformers in the Tridentine period and later also continued to denounce abusive practices and to demand reforms.[91] Although Dionisio was never specific about how to change the Church bureaucracy, he believed that the Italian princes and some Italian cardinals could persuade the pope to effect change, especially in regard to the wealth of the Church and its officials.[92] Reformers of both Catholic and Protestant persuasions often discussed the question of the Church and its wealth. Barbara Hallman cites Cardinal Marcello Cervini's remarks to one of his agents on the subject of the Church and wealth: "Watch more, if you can, the hands of men than their mouth."[93] As Professor Hallman has demonstrated, much of the Church's wealth was dispersed from the pope's private treasury, called the dataria. "The dataria thus provided a less visible means of providing for functionless relatives, and, paralleling the use of ever larger ecclesiastical pensions as incomes for churchmen, the increasing use of datarial moneys for relatives helped to conceal the practice somewhat from the public eye."[94] Dionisio evidently felt that secular authorities could administer the wealth of the Church better than the pope was doing through the dataria.

The abuses Dionisio cited are similar to those enumerated by Martin Luther in his *Address to the Nobility of the German Nation* in 1520 and those noted by the reform commission established by Pope Paul III in the *Consilium de emendanda ecclesia* of 1537.[95] These problems were also a cause of concern to the churchmen at the Council of Trent in 1546. In the *Consilium* Gasparo Contarini and the other authors saw the pope's power as the leading cause of the Church's corruption. Guillaume Postel, writing in 1564, noted: "Car le pape estant reforme, tout le monde le sera, et en parfaicte vnion."[96] As noted earlier, Dionisio argued that the pope should be worthy of the chair of Saint Peter. The abuses listed by the commission Contarini headed were reiterated by Dionisio almost thirty years later. The commission of 1537 noted as abuses "the appointment of unfit clergy, the reservation of incomes from church benefices, even by the sons of priests, the use of 'expectative graces' or the reservation of benefices not yet vacant, pluralism in sacred office, non-residence of clergy, simony, and other scandals."[97] Dionisio's program of reform differed, however, from the previous reform councils' basic premise, which held that churchmen could and should reform the Church. Dionisio argued that a council of princes should be called together to reform the Church, since he believed that lay reformers could breathe new life into the Church. The new life would come, however, only when the abuses were removed. The *Consilium de emendanda ecclesia* of 1537 was very precise in reproving certain practices against which Juan Luis Vives had spoken in 1525 and against which Dionisio would speak in 1565–66. The following statement from the *Consilium* is reminiscent of both Vives and Gallo, and many others, for that matter: "The license for bequeathing the goods of the church ought not to be given to clerics except for an urgent reason, lest the goods of the poor be converted into private delights and the amplification of houses."[98]

Dionisio's decision to go to Italy was influenced not only by his opinions about the piety of the Italian princes but also by the relative tranquillity in Italy in 1566, as compared with the situation in France, engulfed in religious and civil strife. Other factors were also at work in this regard. The medieval prophetic tradition was well established in Italy, as many scholars, such as Marjorie Reeves, Delio Cantimori, Cesare Vasoli, Donald Weinstein, and Ottavia Niccoli, have shown.[99] Countless prophecies had predicted dire happenings under a series of antipopes, often portrayed as ugly beasts. After the reign of the final antipope an angelic pope would appear, and he would preside over a reformed Church in a world of harmony and peace.[100] Some prophecies announced a series of angelic popes, just as there had been a series of antipopes. Joachim of Fiore, for example, saw the Third State, or the Age of the Holy Spirit, the age in which the Church would be reformed, as representative of a prophet, not a demiurge. When heaven and earth were harmoniously reconciled, the new order would clearly accompany that accord: it would not bring it into being.[101] Our prophet, Dionisio, believed that his role was to bring about the accord between heaven and earth by demanding that the Church be reformed. The reformation of the Church would then signal a reformation of society, a universal brotherhood, as it were, in which all men should care for and help each other as they praised and served God. Service to God, according to Dionisio, was demonstrated by charitable acts toward one's fellowmen. Dionisio considered his anointment as God's servant and messenger, therefore God's prophet, as a calling higher than that of pope and cardinals. The exaltation of the prophet was not without precedent in Italy in the years before Dionisio's arrival. Lodovico Lazzarelli had adopted as his spiritual father Giovanni da Corregio, the prophet who called himself Enoch and appeared in Rome in 1484 calling for repentance in preparation of the coming *renovatio*.[102] He glorified Giovanni as prophet and also the role of prophet:

> *Happy beyond measure is*
> *he who knows*
> *The fruits of his fate and who*
> *will have brought them*
> *freely to pass.*
> *For he ought to be counted*
> *among the gods*
> *And not lower than the*
> *highest of them.*[103]

In addition, large numbers of devotional works concerning various aspects of reform were circulating in Italy before and after the Council of Trent.[104] One of the most significant was the *Trattato utilissimo del Beneficio di Gesu Christo Crocifisso*, published in Italy about 1542.[105] In spite of its placement on the *Index* of prohibited books in 1549, it was extremely influential as a devotional book among Catholics and Protestants. The authorship was contested from the beginning.[106] Guillaume Postel attributed the work to Cardinal Reginald Pole.[107]

In 1545 Gioan Domenico Tharisia translated the *De subventione pauperum* (1525) of Juan Luis Vives into Italian, giving it the title *Il modo del sovvenire a poveri* and dedicating the translation to Monsignor Pietro Carnesecchi.[108] The translator noted the great value of this work and indicated he felt obligated to translate it into Italian so that many could have it in their hands, "percioche non molti sono che si dilettino delle lettere latine." Tharisia equated the significance of the book with that of the subject matter, namely, the poor: "percioche nessuna sorte di persone è che più habbia di noi bisogno ne che più ci sia stata ricommandata da Christo di quelli che sono i poveri, dobbiano a questi del continuo in ogni modo a noi possibile sforzara di far bene."[109] The ideas expressed in Vives's work reflect some of Dionisio's most cogent ideas for reform.

Peter Galatinus, best known for his *De arte kabbalistica*, in 1515 wrote a devotional work entitled *Oratio de circumcisione dominica*, dedicating it to Pope Leo X. The writing in the work, reminiscent of Dionisio Gallo's, is filled with powerful images about the need for reform of the Church. Galatinus noted: "Christ, by his own example, taught us to be circumcised [in the heart]. . . . But who today has been thus circumcised? Who does not abound in faults? Who serves the contract of peace? Who guards the sacraments of faith?"[110] The language of Dionisio Gallo reflects the rhetorical language of religious devotion such as that expressed by Vives and Galatinus.

Many preachers in Italy during the first part of the Cinquecento, following in the steps of Savonarola, proclaimed the need for reform of the Church. Cardinal Egidio da Viterbo, in his inaugural address to the Fifth Lateran Council of 1512–17, declared that he had preached for twenty years about the times prophesied in the Apocalypse.[111] The cardinal's statement is all the more significant in light of the fact that the council in 1517 prohibited "free and inspired preaching" and prophesying about the last days.[112] The *Mirabilis Liber* of 1524, a rare but very influential book in the sixteenth century, prophesied the reform of the Church and the conversion of the enemies of Christianity. Revelations, according to the *Mirabilis Liber*, would be sent by God: "[T]hen He deemed it worthy to reveal these things to several either in spirit or in vision as if in an enigma or through angels openly sent and to certain others in secret ways; He shows the future to certain men so that they will pronounce truly the things of the future."[113] The *Mirabilis Liber* also speaks of the role of the French king in bringing about the reformation of the Church. Also included is a prophecy of Saint Bridget's in which the saint was said to exclaim in reference to France: "Correct your conscience. May you consider whether you are from a good *gallo* or a bad. For an ancient prophecy is found to be thus about the good *gallo*: 'The lily will be allied to the grand eagle and will be moved from west to east against the lion.'"[114] Some mosaics in the floor of the Basilica di San Marco show two *galli* (cocks) carrying a wolf; these mosaics were said to be designed by Joachim of Fiore to indicate future events. The cocks were supposed to represent Charles VIII and Lodovico XII, "who are carrying outside the Signoria of Milan the Duke Lodovico Sforza, a prince compared to the wolf because of his own astuteness."[115]

The prophecies in the *Mirabilis Liber* allowed for much creative interpretation, as did other prophecies circulating at the time, especially those concerning the Apocalypse. Devotional and prophetic literature abounded in Italy in the sixteenth century, and many works by Joachim and Savonarola were published in the first half of this era. One rare work, *Flagellum et Renouatio mundi et Ecclesiae Dei*, portrayed Savonarola as the new prophet who had been sent by God for a renovation of the Church. This treatise, composed of prophecies of Saint Bridget, Joachim, and Bernardino, to name only a few, proclaimed the need for renovation: "This renovation Christ grants in order that his precept be observed. . . . Love is no longer found. . . . Belief is missing. Each great sin reigns in the world, homicide, luxuries, and sodomy."[116] God has seen the need of His Church, and "a new prophet thus has announced death and grief." He has the mark of a true prophet of God, "I mean Savonarola the Ferrarese, whose holy works make his own defense."[117]

In the second decade of the sixteenth century Father Zacharias Ferrer wrote a devotional tract about the reformation of the Church, *De reformatione ecclesiae*, which he sent to Pope Hadrian VI. On the title page one reads the prophetic question *Tu es qui venturus, an alium expectamus?* In this work a connection is made between prophetic ideas and the need to reform the Church Militant. Ferrer made the following challenge:

> *We are awaiting, surely for a long time, on behalf of renewing this mystical Jerusalem, which threatens ruin because it is worn out and corroded by age, the coming of the angelic pope. Are you the one who is to come, or are we awaiting another? . . . If, entering Jerusalem with a whip and that triple rope made from faith, hope, and charity that is difficult to break, you do not throw out from the temple of God the buyers and sellers of birds, who else will cast them out?*[118]

The author, like Dionisio, was passionately devoted to the unity of Christianity, "one sheepfold and one shepherd."[119] Consequently, he challenged the pope, just as Dionisio was to do in 1566 in Rome, to correct the faults and abuses in the Church, for "who will build the new state of Jerusalem and will plant in this state the beauty of virtues, piety, religion, and a new man who had been created according to God?" Dionisio, as we have seen, believed that he was the "new man" created to lead the reformation of the Church to its completion. Father Ferrer made the same point Dionisio was constantly to make about priests sent by God instead of by man. Ferrer asks: "Who will eliminate these pseudopriests coming from

Illuftra faciem tuam fuper feruum tuum domine, &
doce me iuftificationes tuas.

fig. 3
Father Zacharias Ferrer receiving the inspiration for his devotional tract, De reformatione ecclesiae. Such devotional and prophetic literature abounded in Italy in the sixteenth century. Biblioteca nazionale di San Marco, Venice

themselves and not sent by God from the house of the Lord?" "Who was to be the new Moses if not the pope?"[120] Sins had become so intolerable that the author predicted that the Church would become Sodom and Gomorrah unless the Lord had left in the pope the seed of heavenly grace and spiritual renovation as an example for mankind. Ferrer, like Dionisio, was shocked to hear of and to see the vices of priests. He drew the same conclusions as Dionisio about the results of this decay in the lives of the clergy, who had become just like the people: "Hence arise schisms, hence heresies, hence scandals in the Church of God. The flock does not obey the shepherd; the princes do not obey the bishops; and the people do not esteem the priests."[121] Ferrer was especially harsh in his condemnation of poor choices of men (often ignorant boys) for the priesthood and especially for the chair of Saint Peter. The degeneration of the priesthood and the papacy had given rise to Martin Luther. He believed that the key to the reformation of the world was Rome. He urged the pope: "Purge Rome; the world is purged. Renew, reform Rome; the whole world is renewed and reformed."[122] There is no mention of doctrinal issues in the *De reformatione ecclesiae*, only the great need for a reform of the practices of the Church. This is typical of prophetic and devotional literature before the Council of Trent. The documents written by Dionisio Gallo in 1565–67 make clear, however, that in numerous circles, especially in Italy, and in Venice in particular, many believed that a true reform of the clergy and the Curia would signal a reform of society in general. Piety, acts of charity, and praise and love of God would transform the world into a new Jerusalem. This medieval conception was kept alive in the later decades of the sixteenth century by men like Dionisio Gallo.

The devotion of Dionisio to Saint Bridget demonstrates the continuity of medieval spirituality in the Cinquecento. His devotion was a renewal of the bond that had existed between Saint Denis and the Blessed Bridget in the fourteenth century.[123] Many prophecies of Saint Bridget became central to the prophecies of Dionisio. For example, Bridget had predicted that "magnificent brothers will come to a council and will preach union."[124] Dionisio insisted on a council of princes to bring about reform of the Church. Under the signature to one of the letters in which Dionisio described his mystical anointment by the Virgin, he wrote: "The sacred words of the prophets vouch for me and represent me with the divine Bridget."[125] Dionisio made explicit his belief that Bridget had prophesied his coming and that therefore he was associated with her. The Holy Virgin, in anointing him, confirmed the prophecy made by the Blessed Bridget. In arguing for the truth of his role as God's servant and messenger, Dionisio wrote: "Comprehend my legation. Be aware of the prophets. Read the scriptures, and [if it serves the cause,] understand what Saint Bridget says."[126] The saint's voice was a constant source of encouragement to our prophet, and a constant guide were her numerous acts of charity. Saint Bridget's *Revelationes* had great influence in the sixteenth century, and especially for Dionisio Gallo, whose devotion to her was steadfast. A libretto entitled *Onus mundi*, in which *leggenda* and prophecies of Saint Bridget and others are found, recounts the story of Saint Denis's (Dionisius's) appearance to Saint Bridget and her subsequent calling by the saint. Denis says: "I . . . am Dionisius, who has come from Rome to these parts of France to preach the word of God in my lifetime. Because you cherish me with special devotion, I prophesy to you that God wishes to speak to the world through you; and you have been handed over to my care and to my protection, and I shall help you always. And this will be a sign to you that your husband will not die in that infirmity of his."[127]

Dionisio Gallo knew the *Revelationes* of Saint Bridget and also the *Onus mundi*. If his name was a pseudonym, one can infer that it was chosen, not only because of the rich associations that can be made with the several persons called Dionisio, but also because of the special relationship Dionisio claimed to enjoy with Bridget. Perhaps he believed himself to be a new Saint Denis who had preached his legation first in France and, having been rejected, would now proclaim his message in Italy, a reversal of the *iter* of Saint Denis. Whereas Bridget had been called by Saint Denis, the new Saint Denis, our Dionisio, in a change of sexual roles, had been proclaimed by Saint Bridget. In the *leggenda* that reveal Bridget's calling by Saint Denis, we are told that God had chosen Bridget "to enjoy the duty and office of the legation of the Most High God." In like manner Dionisio called his program for the restoration of the Church his *Legatio*.

In European literature of the Cinquecento, visions of the Antichrist and the universal judgment were commonplace. Between the nights of Wednesday and Thursday before Pentecost of 1525, Albrecht Dürer dreamed that the end of the world had arrived with a dire flood that covered the world; even the sky was obscured by a tremendous column of water. The dream made such an impression on the painter that the morning after the dream he painted his vision in watercolors and annotated in the margins various aspects of the dream.[128] Dürer also represented the Antichrist. Luther became convinced between 1521 and 1525 that the pope and the institution of the papacy were the Antichrist.[129] During the same period, the vision of the Antichrist from the Apocalypse became entrenched in the religious conceptions of the age. The Antichrist, in addition to opposing Christ, was viewed as a false prophet who was trying to turn mankind away from the Truth.[130] In 1562 Anton Francesco Doni wrote *Dichiaratione del Doni supra il XIII capitolo dell'Apocalisse*, where he used numbers to interpret the chapter from the Apocalypse in which is described the beast with seven heads and ten horns, above which are ten diadem, and above whose heads is the name "blasphemy." Doni calculated the letters in Martin Luther's name and arrived at the number 666, the sign of the beast.[131]

Thomas Müntzer and the Anabaptists gave a social reading to the statement in the Apocalypse about the "new heaven and new earth." Müntzer believed himself to be "the messenger of Christ," and he and the Anabaptists identified themselves with the "saints" from the twelve tribes of Israel who were to establish a "new Jerusalem" on earth, which they tried first in Strasbourg and later in Münster, with tragic results.[132] At Münster, Jan Bockelson called himself "king of Sion."[133] Thomas Müntzer had denounced the vast holdings of the nobles and had urged the peasants to struggle to retain their own parcels of land. Although Müntzer did not speak against private property in and of itself, but rather against the abuses of those who had great wealth, he was often accused of "wanting to hold all things in common."[134] Müntzer believed that a universal upheaval of the established order was part of God's design and that peasant demands heralded the beginning of God's kingdom on earth.[135] A Lutheran who was later condemned by Luther for his views of illumination and radical reformation, Müntzer was associated with the Anabaptists, although he never established any formal ties with the group. Professor Aldo Stella has noted that the followers of Jakob Hutter in 1533–35 had organized an Anabaptist community at Staupitz in Moravia, a community more radical and rigorous than the typical Anabaptists, who had made inroads into northern Italy.[136] The Hutterite Anabaptists listened for the prophetic voice that would proclaim the next installation of God's kingdom on earth.[137] Even Erasmus, in one of his *Colloquia*, in 1526 wrote that "the Antichrist is awaited."[138] Pope Clement VII believed that the end of the world was at hand and consequently asked Michelangelo to paint the universal judgment on a wall of the Sistine Chapel. Ottavia Niccoli notes the significance of the brief citation from Erasmus, since it points to the fears behind the facts of the sixteenth century: the continuing wars among the princes of Europe, uprisings of the people, the break in Christian unity, and the threat of the Turks. The discovery of America was also seen as a fulfillment of prophecy.[139]

Into this milieu of religious, apocalyptic, and political elements Dionisio Gallo thrust himself, "according to God's command." Cesare Vasoli, in his *Profezia e ragione*, has emphasized the importance in France of the mystical ideas of the Venetian Fra Francesco Zorzi.[140] It would be strange indeed if Dionisio had not been acquainted with Zorzi's *De harmonia mundi* or *Problemata*, in which, Vasoli notes, one can easily recognize "the sincere aspiration to a free and interior faith, founded on the supreme basis of the 'word of God' and on the primitive virtue of the Church of Christ, the hope of a final liberation from the slavery of the 'world,' the certainty of the 'rebirth' for all who have believed and are reborn in the 'supercelestial water' of the Son."[141]

Dionisio is an interesting example of the religious cross-fertilization between France and Italy. France was not without other prophetic voices in the Cinquecento. In 1543 the learned Guillaume Postel had prophesied the need for reform of King Francis I, his court, and his realm; he soon became an unwelcome figure in the king's circle;[142] Postel, like Dionisio twenty years later, left France and went to Italy, where he joined the small group around Ignatius Loyola in Rome. The newly formed Society of Jesus accepted Postel as a member in 1544, and he pledged his loyalty to Ignatius in seven of the major churches in Rome. It is significant that the men around Loyola joined together in a body at the College of the Lombards in Paris, and they, like Postel, who knew these men in Paris in the 1530s, conceived of the restitution of the whole world under God.[143] The early ideas of the men who became the first Jesuits, of men like Postel and Dionisio Gallo, were revolutionary and caused them to be feared in France.[144] A prophet like Nostradamus (Michel de Nostredame, 1503–66) may have had more success in prophesying future events than a prophet like Dionisio Gallo (and certainly Guillaume Postel), who prophesied the need for reform in his own age. Catherine de' Medici consulted Nostradamus on occasion, but in all likelihood found Dionisio's persistent challenges to her son, King Charles IX, and to herself too controversial to accept. Louise of Savoy, the mother of Francis I, often listened to the prophecies of San Francesco di Paolo (b. 1416), who lived in a cave, apart from men, and was often consulted because of his sanctity. In 1436 he built a monastery and called the new order the Eremiti of San Francesco. The marvels told of him, his miracles, and his prophecies caught the attention of Pope Paul II, who sent a legate to ascertain the facts about Francesco. The legate went to the archbishop of Cosenza, who confirmed "that Francesco seemed inspired by God to make known his power through His hand."[145] San Francesco di Paolo was also revered by the French kings Louis XI, Charles VIII, and Louis XII, husband of Louise of Savoy, for his sanctity and for his prophetic powers.[146] Francesco di Paolo told Louise of Savoy, when she was expecting a child, that she would bear a son destined for great things if he would reform the kingdom of France and lead the world in a universal reformation of the Church. If he did not reform his kingdom and the Church, dire calamities would ensue for him. Louise named her son Francesco as an eternal reminder of the prophecy.[147] When Guillaume Postel recounted this story to King Francis I, the king was moved to tears; however, Diane de Poitiers consoled him and told him that he should not listen to the voice of a fool.[148] In 1543 Postel warned the king of his proper course of action, necessary to fulfill the prophecy. Shortly thereafter he lost favor with the king (Postel claimed it was because of Dame de Poitiers) and left France for Italy. Postel's prophecies announced to King Francis I in 1543 are similar to those Dionisio Gallo announced to King Charles IX, and the results that followed them were much the same. A beautiful broadsheet entitled *Miracolo fatto dal glorioso San Francesco de Paula nella città di Venetia*, published in Venice in the sixteenth century, pictures a woman being robbed in her home by vandals. While she was restrained by ropes on her neck, "within her heart, with vows and humble prayers, she beseeched him who is called Minimo . . . and this one suddenly appeared, the grand

fig. 4
Sixteenth-century broadsheet from Venice depicting San Francesco di Paolo aiding a woman who has been robbed in her home. Archivio di Stato, Venice

Francesco, who, to give her aid, extended his hands in order to free her from the great peril."[149] This charming representation provides graphic confirmation of the cross-fertilization of prophetic ideas between France and Italy in the Cinquecento.

Dionisio was not deterred by his fall from favor in France. His prophetic soul, guided by the certainty of his divine calling, seemed to be inspired by suffering even as he complained against it. Following in the steps of Christ seemed to entail suffering. In his choice of clothing and public space, Dionisio also emphasized his public persona as prophet to heighten the effect of his mission as "servant and messenger of Christ." Therefore, like a sixteenth-century apostle, Dionisio turned his face toward Italy, where in the Cinquecento numerous groups of artisans, professionals, priests, and friars labored for the reform of the Church and of society and longed "for a world in which churches would be transformed into inns for preaching, and shops and *piazze* would become churches."[150] There is no reason to suppose that Dionisio Gallo was unaware of the prophetic ideas that had circulated in Italy in the early decades of the Cinquecento. Convinced of his own divinely appointed role, the new angelic pope, as it were, Dionisio Gallo departed for Italy not only because of his lack of success in France and the threat of new imprisonment but also and especially because prophetic ideas had not been completely smothered in Italy. Dionisio intended to fan them back into a burning flame that would purge the corruption in the Church and bring forth a pristine and renewed *Ecclesia militans*.

The following chapters explore Dionisio's connections in Italy, focusing especially on Venice and Dionisio's prophetic warning to the Serenissima. The particular climate that fostered prophetic ideas, especially in Venice, made Venice seem to Dionisio the ideal receptacle for his prophetic call for the reform of the Church and society. In Venice, Dionisio Gallo was to meet his greatest success and his greatest failure. Before these events, however, he was to meet the most important princes of Italy, to whom he proclaimed with fervor his program for reform of the Church.

· II ·
RELIGIO AND POLITIA
Emanuele Filiberto of Savoy, Pope Pius V, and Dionisio Gallo

ionisio remained in France a year or less after his departure from Gisors, where he had been sent for the repose of the city of Paris on the king's order.¹ Since his departure from the place of his birth was without royal permission, his travels in the Midi, especially his visits to Toulouse, were necessarily abbreviated and potentially dangerous. Therefore, he turned his path toward Italy, because, as he was often to repeat, the Italian princes were more pious than the French.² In spite of Dionisio's laudatory remarks about the princes, his decision to go to Italy was a result of the personal danger to himself in France and perhaps associations he had previously made in Italy. The princes whom he chose to visit were not selected for their piety alone. In the case of each—the duke of Savoy, the duke of Florence and soon-to-be grand duke of Tuscany, and the duke of Ferrara—there was a French connection that Dionisio obviously considered advantageous, and there were other reasons as well. In addition, there were compelling reasons for his arrival in Venice, where his persona as prophet was accentuated.

From the Midi, Dionisio headed east to Savoy. We do not know by which route he traveled, but considering that he was in flight from the authorities in Gisors and Paris, a direct route into Savoyard territory would have been circumspect. He arrived in Turin some time in December 1565, as evidenced by a letter he wrote to Emanuele Filiberto, duke of Savoy, on December 23 of that year. Dionisio made clear in the opening sentence that he had come expressly to tell the duke the good news that God had recently sent to the whole human race. Written in elegant French, the letter reveals at the outset Dionisio's purpose in Savoy: "It is to make known the news of truth, good judgment, the resolution of all the differences that are presently in Christianity."[3]

Dionisio's letter to Emanuele Filiberto would certainly have captured the duke's attention and especially that of his wife, Margaret Valois, duchess of Berry, who was the daughter of King Francis I, sister of Henry II, and sister-in-law of Catherine de' Medici. The political and religious concerns in Savoy and the close but delicate relations with France through marriage ties at the time of Dionisio's arrival in Turin are significant for our story and for an understanding of the interrelationships between religion and politics, between prince and prophet. Since Dionisio had been rector of the Collège de Lisieux and since Margaret was interested in humanists and their ideas of reform, the two could have known each other in Paris.[4] Margaret inherited from her father a lively desire for culture. She could read Latin and Greek correctly, could speak Italian and Spanish without any show of pedantry. Her goodness of soul made her "la protettrice de quanti protezione le richiesero, la soccorritrice di tutti le miserie che conobbe."[5] In the royal family she became the representative of arts and letters and their natural protector. Her duchy of Berry, which she governed from Bourges, rapidly became one of the liveliest centers of culture.[6] Duke Emanuele Filiberto found in his wife a "donna che più si conosce, più si ammira per l'altezza della mente, la bontà e la nobiltà dell'animo, la saggezza politica; e che, finche visse, fu sola a conoscere a fondo le mire ed il gioco politico del marito, la sola che su di esso esercitasse influsso serio e duraturo."[7]

Margaret Valois was a disciple of Michel de L'Hôpital, whom she had made president of her council in 1560, before he became chancellor of France. He owed much of his power to Catherine de' Medici, who at this time was opposed to the unyielding policies of the dukes of Guise. She supported instead the tolerant and conciliatory political policy of L'Hôpital, who had refused, for example, to sign the order that would condemn to death the prince of Condé because of his complicity in the conspiracy of Amboise. Margaret's choice of L'Hôpital as president of her council and chancellor of her duchy of Berry indicated her receptiveness to creative thinking and new ideas, philosophic, literary, and religious.

Margaret was deeply concerned with the religious strife in France and perhaps welcomed any new approach to resolving the dissensions among Christians. She wrote a letter to the French ambassador in Venice on October 12, 1567, expressing her concern about the religious ruptures. She was particularly sensitive to the various rumors circulating in Italy about the troubles of the boy king Charles IX. She reiterated her earnest prayer that God give the king the strength to bring peace and order to France. In addition, she instructed the ambassador to advise the Venetians of the true state of affairs in France, with its inherent dangers, and to beg the doge to give the young king his sage advice.[8] The French ambassador carried out Margaret's wish on October 17, 1567, sharing with the Collegio a letter describing in great detail the tumults in France occasioned by the religious quarrels. He referred to the conflicts as *seditioni*, in which the Huguenots had taken the lands near Mâcon and Valenza. He also revealed that the king, his mother, and brothers had had to flee Meos, a town ten kilometers from Paris where they had gone to celebrate the Feast of San Michele, since Admiral Coligny was marching toward Meos with three thousand horsemen. Luckily for the royal family, six thousand Swiss soldiers had rebuffed the cavalry of Coligny, thus allowing the king and his party to return safely to Paris. The ambassador warned the Venetians of the perils of civil strife and indicated that the present problems in France were also problems for Venice, since both shared mutual concerns and interests. The Venetians would surely have been aroused by the words of the ambassador as he pointed out the dangers of civil strife and upheavals, "because nothing can disturb and offend a kingdom and state more than seditions and wars."[9]

Although the queen mother, Catherine de' Medici, had pledged to do everything possible to lessen the tensions and to make the state secure, the Venetians were advised by Margaret Valois "a consigliar il Re, come hora debba proceder et gouernarsi."[10] The doge's response was surely less than Margaret would have wished; he said that since God had preserved the French king through such great danger, he prayed that He would always favor him and would be his secure guide and protector. As for Venice's help, the doge's words suggested that God was a refuge stronger than Venice. Not satisfied with the doge's response, the ambassador again advised that Madama di Savoia believed that the king "ha bisogno del conseglio prudente di vostra serenità la qual potrà consolar la Maestà sua."[11] The seasoned diplomacy of the doge was in sharp contrast to the youth and inexperience of the French king.

As the situation in France continued to deteriorate, in spite of the Edict of Pacification, Venice was evidently becoming ever more wary of any action that could upset the tenuous harmony of la Serenissima.[12] In 1562 Venice had given 25,000 scudi to the French king to be used "nelli bisogni della religione et della fede."[13] When the ambassador, however, requested speedy payment and increased support, the doge noted that the things of France concerned the world and that he desired the prosperity of France as he did of his own state. All things in his state, however, were subject to discussion, the doge noted further. His tone implied the superiority of the Serenissima, where decisions were made after debate in council. The doge pointed out the great expenses his republic incurred in fortification of the city: fortresses on land and on sea, the maintenance of a large armada, and many other things "che sonno necessarie ad un stato che uogli conseruarsi et continuare con l'aiuto di Dio in reputatione et sicurta."[14] By 1567 the doge appeared reluctant to give even advice to the king. He was perhaps reflecting the criticisms that were circulating in Venice because of the king's action in signing a second Edict of Pacification. Some were saying that the king had made war on his own subjects, while others said that in making peace with the Huguenots he had betrayed his own beliefs.[15] The French ambassador, conscious of the criticisms that were circulating, explained that the king did not agree to anything that had not been agreed upon in 1562. He also noted that the king had shown the greatest clemency in the war with the Huguenots and again warned of the horrors of civil war, in which no one was the winner.[16]

The letter of Margaret Valois to the French ambassador in Venice reveals the sensitive perception of the duchess of Berry and puts the civil tumults in France on a personal as well as a political level. The youth of the king was repeatedly stressed, and his inability at the tender age of ten years to cope with such complex issues aroused sympathy as well as frustration. The letter of the duchess was more than a plea for financial aid; it was a cry for maturity, which should signify wisdom, to come to the aid of unseasoned youth. The personal tragedy of a family became abundantly clear in Margaret's letter. Yet affairs of state demanded more than sympathy and understanding. They also demanded action. The cogent statements of Margaret to the French ambassador did not fall on deaf ears, although the Venetians obviously shared some of Dionisio Gallo's criticisms about the inability of the French Crown to handle its own religious quarrel. If Dionisio ever had any understanding of the sincere attempts of Catherine de' Medici to solve the religious dissensions, he never expressed them in his writings, although he expressed great sympathy, even affection, for the young Charles IX. He blamed the king's councillors as well as his mother for the escalating tensions in France and for his own problems. Dionisio's hostility toward Catherine and the Royal Council stemmed both from their rejection and mockery of him and from his own exasperation with a divided Church and kingdom.[17]

Like Dionisio, Margaret was absorbed with the perilous situation in France. Like Dionisio also, she comprehended the enormity of the French problem and therefore turned to sources outside of France for help. Through the French ambassador in Venice she had sought intelligent understanding and advice from the Venetians, who in 1566–67 were hesitant to say or do anything except to call upon God's support for the kingdom of France.

From the point of view of the Venetian ambassador Andrea Boldù, writing in 1561 to the Signoria, Margaret Valois was a paragon of virtue. Boldù described her as "virtuosa, savia, prudente et dotta quanto sia religiosa, pia, humana, et liberalissima del che ne rendono testimonio li numerosissimi doni et elemosine che ha fatto in ogni tempo."[18] She lived in splendor in Savoy as she had in France; her servants in Savoy were French except for one young girl from Piedmont, and she was surrounded by French advisers in her own quarters. In order to allay excessive French influence, none of Margaret's French ministers was allowed in the duke's quarters or in the court when the duke was absent. The Venetian ambassador noted, however, the affection that many Savoyards had for France. In spite of the duke's distancing himself from too much French influence at his court, he remained very fond of his wife and was always concerned for her welfare. She often participated in the duke's discussions with his ministers, although her counsel was not always heeded.[19] Boldù also reported that the duchess of Savoy was very kindly disposed to the Serenissima, "tanto affettionata, quanto è, et in tal modo osseruatrice del prudentissimo gouerno di questo serenissimo dominio."[20] On one occasion, when she had no money to spend, the ambassador arranged for her, in the duke's absence, some financial help through diplomatic channels. Consequently, the duchess was very grateful to Venice, "onde quanto si tiene, obligatissima alla Serenità vostra tanto ne resta grandemente affettionata a questa carissima Republica et desideriossissima d'ogni suo bene."[21] Margaret astutely observed that her state was a bastion for Italy, and if Savoy should be weakened, so much weaker would be Venice.

Dionisio, whether he knew Margaret in Paris or not, probably reasoned that she might be amenable to his pleas for reform and perhaps could help him receive an audience with the duke. Since Margaret surrounded herself with Frenchmen, a learned Frenchman like Dionisio might have found favor in the circle of the duchess, who seemed drawn to brilliant, if eccentric, humanists. In addition, Margaret was a strong advocate for peace, although she was well aware of the difficulties of attaining it, as she had made clear to the French ambassador in Venice, beseeching him to secure the sage counsel of the Venetians for the young king Charles IX. The Venetian ambassadors were generally impressed with Margaret's virtues and intelligence and continued to praise her for her virtues, which the world esteemed; they also pointed out the respect for the Crown of France that this most serene republic had always held.[22]

Margaret's influence was felt in many circles. In August 1560, a year after her marriage to the duke, she expressed to the Venetian ambassador Andrea Boldù how great was the duke's desire to have returned to him the five *piazze* of Piedmont.[23] She also requested that Paulo Stoppa *padouana* be freed from a Venetian prison.[24] The dispatches from the Venetian ambassadors in Savoy often related Margaret's opinions and always pointed out her love and admiration for Venice. Dionisio certainly would not have been unaware of her influence.

From 1560 to 1579 news from France dominated the numerous letters sent from Turin and Nice by the Venetian ambassadors. Based on the eyewitness accounts of the religious civil wars in France from the point of view of the Venetian ambassador in Savoy, it is clear that the duke was also completely preoccupied with the French wars and how they might affect his efforts to recover lands from France.

Since affairs in France had been steadily deteriorating during the year of Dionisio's arrival in Turin, the duke of Savoy was especially sensitive to any disturbance that might ensue from the Huguenots. On January 6, 1565, only a few weeks after Dionisio's arrival in Savoy, the Venetian ambassador Zuan Corner wrote that the duke had notified him of a certain Provençal named Schigniragni, a man very important to the Huguenots, who had come into that city from the valley of Angrogna.[25] The duke wanted the doge to know about this Schigniragni in case he should come to Venice. Corner wanted more details about this person as well as a good description, which the duke promised to give. The duke, in conversation with the Venetian ambassador, indicated his grave concern about the instability of his state that could develop as a result of the Huguenots' presence. He noted that "nothing could more easily disturb the quiet life of the Italian princes than this animosity of a new religion, because the people who are contaminated by a similar pest call us idolators and under such cover say that they are not bound to obey."[26] The duke's concern found a ready response from Ambassador Corner, who agreed that "nothing is more dangerous to a prince than the diversity of religions."[27]

Dionisio's arrival in Savoy coincided with the duke's anxiety about religious disturbances. The challenges Dionisio made in his letter to Emanuele Filiberto evoked a positive response from the duke of Savoy.[28] It also would not have been out of character for Margaret Valois to take note of a prophet-humanist like Dionisio, who called for reform of the Church as a means of obtaining religious peace. The duke and his duchess could have considered the catholicity of Dionisio's prophecies an antidote to the poison the Provençal Schigniragni might spread.

Certain aspects of Duke Emanuele Filiberto's character would also suggest a possible rapport with Dionisio Gallo. Emanuele Filiberto was interested in reform of education at all levels, a subject dear to Dionisio.[29] The duke instituted primary schools for commoners. Secondary schools and colleges for the upper classes were directed by the Jesuits, who taught in Piedmont in 1561, in Mondovì.[30] The most distinguished Jesuit teacher in Mondovì was Roberto Bellarmino, who taught Latin eloquence from 1564 to 1566 and later became a cardinal. A second college (after the Collegio Romano) was established in Chambéry, and in 1567 a third was founded in Turin. All the lower schools carefully observed orthodoxy in teaching. Those in the universities, however, practiced freedom of investigation. The duke was interested in all branches of knowledge and knew five languages in addition to Latin. He was especially devoted to the mathematical arts and the sciences. His interest in botany was demonstrated by the establishment of the *studio della botanica*, since he believed that knowledge in this area could be put to practical use in the development of agriculture. His scientific interests were also directed with passion to chemical and alchemical studies. Furthermore, he neglected neither literary arts and culture nor architecture. Many buildings, some under Palladian inspiration, and a famous park were erected during his reign.[31]

The duke chose not only well-known and erudite Italian scholars to enhance his court and dukedom but also notable foreigners; Dionisio's erudition and mysticism would have been appealing to the duke. Emanuele Filiberto was convinced that an educated populace with a religious conscience sensitive to the dangers of heresy was necessary for the stability and progress of his realm. Education was the energizer that would quicken all aspects of the life of his state. He also held the opinion, shared by the Venetians, that disobedience in religious matters could be easily transferred to the political realm.[32] In addition to his desire to restore the intellectual, social, and political life of his duchy, he had great enthusiasm for religion and for religious reform. Emanuele Filiberto was originally destined for the priesthood, for which he seemed well suited because of his deeply spiritual nature. Upon the death of his brother Luigi in 1535, however, the course of his education changed, since he was now heir to the throne. But he never gave up his interest in religion or his desire for religious harmony in his realm. The Venetian ambassador described Emanuele Filiberto's character favorably: "As to his gifts of soul, he is religious and very devout, a virtue derived from his ancestors, most of whom have founded many abbeys and built different monasteries in their state, and many times have gone to fight for the faith of Christ against the Turks and infidels."[33]

His deeply religious nature developed from his education and from the deeply religious nature of the house of Savoy. His father, Carlo II, was most pious, and perhaps this instinct was passed on to his son. His religiosity did not spring only from political considerations, as one scholar has stated, noting that he was not a Henry IV. "Certo l'atteggiamento religioso e lo zelo per la causa cattolica servì anche alla politica e vi arrecò non pochi vantaggi: ma ciò non vuol dire che il Principe sia stato e si sia mostrato religioso per quella."[34] From his religious feeling he drew inspiration not only for reforming religion but also for renewing his state. He went to Mass every day and spent Holy Week in pious contemplation. He had great faith in prayer, and he favored pious orders such as the Carthusians in Mondovì and the Capuchins at the Madonna di Campagna. The religion of Emanuele Filiberto was derived from Christian practice, which had the spirit as its foundation, not external manifestations.[35] To renew the spiritual life in his realm and to reform religious observances, the duke passed a series of ordinances that applied to teaching in the schools. He decreed, for example, that the catechism must be taught and that the text of Canisius must be learned by heart. Regarding those who were illiterate or too young to read, heads of the households were enjoined to instruct their children and servants in the meaning of holy days. Legislation was passed that forbade the duke's subjects to go outside the realm to study.

The penetration of foreigners into his state, many with heretical beliefs, caused the duke anxiety. As a Catholic prince surrounded by Protestants, he was obliged to defend the faith. On January 25, 1563, the Compagnia di San Paolo was formed with the purpose of counteracting the invasion of Protestant preachers, who, during the French occupation of Turin, were encouraged by the success of the Huguenots in France.[36] In addition, the Jesuits were welcomed in Turin in December 1566, and they worked closely with the Compagnia di San Paolo. A year after their arrival they opened their first college and received an annual bequest from the duke. Emanuele Filiberto also aided the Compagnia di San Paolo in its work with the *poveri vergognosi*. Help for the poor was a special concern of the duke's, and his contributions to the *compagnia* for this work were largely responsible for its success. This devotion to the poor was another aspect of his character that was reflected in Dionisio.

Emanuele Filiberto founded the Religion of San Lazzaro and San Maurizio, which was approved in 1572 by the pope, who named him *gran maestro* and *patrone* of the order. The duke was overjoyed with the honor and vowed to make the order greater than that of San Stefano in Florence and even, in time, equal to the Knights of Malta. The Venetian ambassador

Girolamo Lippomano indicated that the duke was more delighted with the establishment of this order than with any other thing that could be bestowed upon him.37 The duke chose the ambassador as a *cavaliere* of the "Religion" and sent Count Cesare Cambiano, a senator, to Venice to explain the honor bestowed by the pope and to ask the Venetians' help in strengthening this order.38 The ambassador said that "it is clear to see that every honor and favor that will please the most excellent Signoria to give me will return to the appropriate glory of that republic."39

Relations between Savoy and Venice had not always been cordial. They made conflicting claims about Cyprus; in addition, Savoy had joined the League of Cambrai against Venice. However, when Emanuele Filiberto became duke, relations began to improve and soon became cordial, although there were still quarrels in diplomatic channels about the primacy of Venice or Savoy. By 1573, however, Lippomano had been named a *cavaliere* of the Religion of San Lazzaro and San Maurizio, and in 1574 Emanuele Filiberto had been named a Venetian patrician.40

Because of the duke's religious inclinations Dionisio Gallo obviously felt that he would have a sympathetic ally for the reform of the Church and society. In addition, the duke's mystical nature would have made him amenable to Dionisio's program. Livio Sanuto dedicated his *Astrologia divinativa* to the duke and duchess; however, since the work was proscribed by the theologians, Andrea Boldù and Girolamo Lippomano advised the author to send the document in manuscript to the duke.41

Dionisio Gallo spoke constantly of the need to reform the Church by putting Christ's life into practice with help to the poor. The duke's generous charities to the poor through the work of the Compagnia di San Paolo exemplified the true calling of a prince in Dionisio's mind.42 Emanuele Filiberto's example of daily Christian piety and his desire to strengthen the Catholic faith and combat heresy by persuasion, if possible, reflected the same understanding of religion that Dionisio expressed. Like Dionisio, Emanuele Filiberto was mystical as well as pious. He had deep faith that the holy shroud, the most precious reliquary of the ducal chapel of Chambéry and of the house of Savoy, was the authentic shroud, that in which the Divine Redeemer had been wrapped by Joseph of Arimathea. After the duke had secured Turin from the French, his great desire was to return the shroud there. He was finally successful on the fifth of September in having the holy relic again in Turin. On September 14, 1578, in a solemn procession of the court, the papal nuncio, five bishops, and the magistrates, the holy shroud was carried and was placed in the Chapel of Saint Lorenzo. On September 28 the shroud was exhibited publicly in the cathedral.43

During his youth Emanuele Filiberto participated in the Council of Trent and was the guest of Cristoforo Madruzzo, who became cardinal, bishop of Trento, in 1539, upon the death of Cardinal Clesio.[44] The associations Emanuele Filiberto made as a guest of Madruzzo were important for the young duke's development, since among the friends of Madruzzo were Cardinals Gonzaga, Sadoleto, Morone, and Pole. Madruzzo's insight and intellectual boldness surely impressed the duke, who enjoyed intellectual challenges and was not averse to visionary ideas. Madruzzo had spoken in favor of having the Bible translated into the vulgar languages. For his attitude during the debate on justification, he was suspected of being the head of the German party and therefore favorable to the Lutherans.

Emanuele Filiberto was deeply concerned about the religious strife that was enveloping Christendom. In his own realm he was especially concerned about the threat of the Calvinists, who were very aggressive in religious matters and also antimonarchical.[45] This latter aspect of Calvinism was particularly disturbing to Emanuele Filiberto, who believed in unified, absolute control of his state.[46] He had visions of the Catholic powers and the pope designating him the leader of a kind of Crusade against the Protestants of Switzerland in 1560, but his enterprise was considered a utopian dream and was never formalized. His attitude toward the Waldenses was more restrained, and in many instances they enjoyed the duke's favor. His tolerance of the Waldenses and other groups of dissidents drew remonstrances from Pope Pius IV and his successor, Pope Pius V, who exercised greater rigor against heresy.[47] Some suspected that his duchess, Margaret Valois, was responsible for the duke's tolerance of the Waldenses. He had used moderation in his approach to them in 1560, but their open rebellion in 1561 forced him into war. The duchess advised again that he should find a peaceful solution to the religious dispute, and accordingly, he signed an agreement that gave the Waldenses freedom of worship within their territory, le Valli. He wanted to check heresy not only with the power of arms but also with persuasion.[48]

Emanuele Filiberto sent Bishop Allardet to Geneva in 1559 after the Treaty of Cateau-Cambrésis was concluded with France. The bishop made a speech before the Great Council, in the presence of Calvin and "two wicked Frenchmen," in which he urged the Genevans to return to the realm of the duke, as had been the ancient custom.[49] Calvin called for the immediate arrest of the bishop, but the Great Council observed that Allardet had acted legally and with sincerity, that he had been granted safe conduct, and that he was dear to the duke. However, the council made clear that Geneva had no intention of returning to the hegemony of Savoy. Bishop Allardet was told "che Ginevra aveva scelto a sovrano Dio e che, pur riconoscendo i meriti indiscussi di Emanuele Filiberto, riteneva più potente e migliore la Maestà Divina e che non volevano altra autorità."[50] When the duke's representative failed to persuade the Genevans to rejoin the ancient patrimony of Emanuele Filiberto, the duke tried to persuade the pope and the kings of France and Spain to engage in military action against the feared city. In 1560 the duke, through his ambassador, had also sought the help of Venice in this regard. On February 8, 1560, in the Collegio, the ambassador was told that, although the doge would like to help with arms, the Collegio and the doge had decided, after discussion, that "peace was the greatest good that Christianity could have and that everyone must see to it that Christianity remains for many years in this quiet, so that it can breathe free from its past troubles."[51] The ambassador was also assured that Venice had always loved and desired peace, which carries every good and happiness to states; that God had now introduced peace among the Christian princes, which the Venetians were most desirous of maintaining, so that they could remedy with discussion so many disparate ideas in Christianity. The Venetians also indicated that if any military operations were attempted, the Protestants would not come to the council.[52] From this response it appears that the Venetians were hoping that a unified Christianity was still possible and might result from the discussions at the Council of Trent. They certainly did not want to upset the delicate balance of the moment or to see a war develop in Italy. The Venetians were especially distressed when in 1561 they sent their ambassador Boldù to find out if Emanuele Filiberto was meeting in secret with Alfonso II, duke of Ferrara, and the marchese of Pescara, governor of Milan, and were told that indeed Alfonso II had gone incognito to Piedmont and that it was likely "che tale viaggio si ricollegasse al progetto di lega tra i principi cristiani ideato da Emanuele Filiberto, coll'intenzione apparente di combattere il Turco, ed invece nel fatto di assalire Ginevra."[53] The Serenissima consequently advised its ambassador Tiepolo in Spain to indicate to King Philip II the incipient danger. The ambassador to France was also advised to tell the king and queen mother about the meeting, "esprimendo il desiderio che tutti si adoperassero a mantenere la pace in Italia."[54] Venice took the same noninterventionist stance in regard to the civil wars in France. The French ambassador, in a letter to the Collegio dated August 12, 1562, beseeched Venice to help with the war, "which has been decided and begun with the advice and direction of His Holiness and of the Catholic majesty for the defense of the true Christian faith and the holy Church and for the removal of errors."[55] The ambassador warned the Venetians that "since France, which is placed in the center of Christianity, is infected" with the plague of the new religion, "the surrounding provinces of Italy and

Spain could be infected from hand to hand."[56] He urged Venice not "to remain only a spectator of the miseries and ruin of that kingdom, with universal damage for Christianity and particularly for your republic."[57]

The duke of Savoy was also beset with the same problems, since he struggled with the numbers of Huguenots who came into Savoy from France and Switzerland.[58] Emanuele Filiberto also pointed out to the Venetian ambassador the danger to the Italian princes that would follow the introduction of a new religion into the various states of Italy. The duke noted that the quiet life of Italian princes could be suddenly changed by those, "contaminated with this pest," who refuse to obey the princes.[59] He urged that "i nostri Signori" use every diligence to protect their state from such a deadly plague.

In dispatches sent from Turin to the Capi of the Council of Ten in 1568, Vincenzo Tron said the political ills of France resulted from the introduction of a new religion. Reporting on what he had heard in Turin about the strife in France, he noted that the leaders of the civil strife "could not be called gentlemen or vassals of His Majesty but rather rebels who had taken up arms against their own Signor and the Catholic and Christian religion. Whence it seemed necessary to purge this infected body with those appropriate medicines that were necessary for the sickness; otherwise, in a short time the other uncontaminated members would be corrupted, with the greatest danger to the religion of the kingdom and to the life of his Christian Majesty."[60]

In addition to the geography of the duke's realm, which gave easy access to those fleeing the religious and civil strife in France, internal problems caused grave concern. The daughter of the count of Antremon, a very rich nobleman, decided to marry Admiral Coligny of France. Dismayed by her choice, the duke nevertheless had to decide whether to give or refuse permission for the marriage. If he gave permission, this "most wicked man" would probably come to live in Savoy and would encourage Huguenots to do likewise. The duke understood the difficulties involved in whatever decision he might make. He finally gave permission, since he feared that his denial might cause the admiral to bring his troops into Savoy to effect the marriage. His troubles did not end there, however. A minister from France brought invitations to the wedding in the name of the king and the queen mother. Although the duke was disinclined to attend the wedding, the French minister put pressure upon him in this regard as well as in regard to a league against the Turks and the heretics in France. The French hoped to persuade the duke to head such a league, using as an incitement the return of two of the duke's *piazze*.[61] The duke denied that he knew anything about this league, noting that "he could only attend to the government of his own states." If His Majesty wanted to restore the fortresses, however, the duke would be "much obliged, because if he had these, he would strongly hope that he would have the other two from Spain."[62]

As the civil wars increased in intensity after the death of Coligny and the massacre of Saint Bartholomew's Day, many Huguenots fled France. The duke issued an edict that forbade anyone, under severest punishment, to lodge or help in any way the Huguenots who had come into Savoy from France.[63] Huguenot refugees were ordered to leave Savoy within three days. The daughter of the count of Antremon, after the death of her husband, Admiral Coligny, returned to her *castelli* in Savoy, where she, along with her two young sons and her daughter, born after her return to Savoy, became a prisoner in her own castle. Duke Emanuele Filiberto took possession of her *castelli* after the admiral's death, so anxious was he, according to the ambassador's report, that all live as Catholics in Savoy.[64] Emanuele Filiberto's dream of a unified state coincided with his belief in a unitary religion. However, from time to time he would yield on the second point in hope of attaining the first.[65]

The crusade of Dionisio Gallo to reform the Church and society presented a platform not alien to the goals of the duke of Savoy. In spite of the duke's pragmatism, Dionisio hoped to arouse him to overt acts of reform. In the letter that Dionisio wrote to the duke on Sunday, December 23, 1565, a few days after his arrival on Thursday, December 20, he made clear his own role in the reform of the Church as well as the basic points in his platform.[66] In the heading of the letter Dionisio called himself "maistre . . . par la grace celeste ambassadeur, et seruiteur de Dieu: Roy incogneu et plusque Roy, pasteur oinct vniuersellement . . . par la benoiste ancelle de la trinité." He defined his role as that "pour appaizer, composer, iuger, et reigler, attraire a la foy de nostre Redempteur, et saulueur Jesuschrist, toutes les partz du monde."[67]

In addressing the duke, Dionisio made clear his heavenly calling, referring to himself as "ambassador and servant of God, King unknown, and more than King, Shepherd universally anointed without and within by the blessed handmaiden of the Trinity." Dionisio used the word "King" to indicate one who serves God, who through His handmaiden had chosen him as His ambassador to unite all parts of the world under Christ. Dionisio's purpose in coming to Turin, according to his story, was to inform the duke of the good news of truth, good judgment, and the resolution of all differences that were dividing Christianity. The reform that Dionisio envisioned was to include the reform of both Church and state. The Church must be reformed from the top to the bottom of the episcopal hierarchy. The abuses of the pope as well as those of the simple presbyter must be removed. In the temporal realm, kings must be regulated as much as the beggar. False belief must be eradicated, beginning with the leaders who teach erroneous belief and following all the way down to the poor man who has fallen into error through ignorance. As one can see from Dionisio's statements at the outset of his letter to the duke, he envisioned a complete renewal, a renovation and restoration of both Church and state.

Although only one letter from Dionisio to the duke of Savoy remains, it is one of Dionisio's most interesting letters, since in the first part of the letter he reveals his prophetic persona and establishes his identification with the apocalyptic vision of John the Evangelist. Since Dionisio obviously knew the mystical and religious nature of Emanuele Filiberto, he wrote about the Apocalypse and his relationship to John's vision on the island of Patmos. All aspects of reform, according to Dionisio, are found in "the seventy-two laws that are the open book, sealed with seven seals, of which Saint John speaks in the fifth chapter of his Apocalypse." According to the Apocalypse (5:5), the book was opened by the Lamb, a reference to Christ. Dionisio, in the letter to Emanuele, wrote that Christ, sitting on His throne, had allowed him to open the book. Dionisio equated his mystical anointment by the Virgin "on the inside and on the outside" with the opening of the book sealed with seven seals, written on the inside and on the outside, and described in Apocalypse 5.

Prophetic and apocalyptic literature and especially interpretations of the Apocalypse abounded in the early part of the sixteenth century. Dionisio's frequent use of the Apocalypse in citations and in appropriation of meaning makes clear the significance of this book and of prophetic literature well after the middle of the century. Dionisio was obviously acquainted with the prophetic tradition and especially with the Psalms and the Apocalypse. Joachim's commentary on the Apocalypse, which was published in Venice in 1527, provided inspiration for Dionisio, since he followed Joachimite interpretations very closely, applying the meaning to himself.[68]

The Apocalypse mosaics in the Basilica di San Marco also provided inspiration for prophetic groups in Venice, whose teachings resembled those of Dionisio.[69] Although Dionisio did not specifically mention the mosaics, as his countryman Guillaume Postel had done, he often went to the basilica before his incarceration, and his references to Apocalypse 12, where the "woman clothed in the sun" is described, would certainly lead one to believe that he was aware of the mosaics.[70] His preoccupation with the Apocalypse, as revealed in this letter to the duke of Savoy before his arrival in Venice, would substantiate the supposition that he had previously seen or heard of the fascinating mosaics, which depict the substance of the twelfth chapter of the Apocalypse and which Joachim, according to tradition, was said to have designed.[71]

Medieval prophecy frequently predicted the arrival of an angelic shepherd or shepherds.[72] Dionisio saw himself in the role of this angelic shepherd, as certified by his own mystical experience. His quasi-religious-political role as adviser to kings and princes and reformers of the Church resembled that of the angelic popes described in the *Mirabilis Liber* of 1524.[73] This was also the role of Old Testament prophets like Jeremiah.[74]

Dionisio did not hesitate to make his divine calling clear to the duke of Savoy, who he obviously believed would find his apocalyptic references pleasing. He was also very precise about when the "mystically sealed book" was opened; the opening of the book was synonymous with Dionisio's divine anointment, which took place "depuis deux ans, dix mois ou ennyron ce temps par mystere celeste."[75] According to Dionisio's statement to the duke of Savoy, his mystical anointment, or "the opening of the book," took place around October 1562. Dionisio was to refer many times to his mystical anointment and the opening of the book sealed with seven seals. The profundity of this religious experience never left him. He described in great detail his divine anointment by the Virgin. Dionisio's description of the Virgin, "dressed in white, with a girdle like a bishop who was about to consecrate and ordain presbyters," evokes the beautiful watercolor of the angel holding the "open book" in the manuscript of Teolosphoro.[76] The Virgin anointed him first on the outside "from the top of his head to the bottom of his feet," and he believed his anointment was complete. This was not the case, however. It was complete only after the Virgin anointed him on the inside of his body. Dionisio's twofold anointment was more thorough than any described in the Old Testament. Taking in all parts of the body, instead of only the head, the exterior-interior comprehensiveness of Dionisio's anointment indicated its universality.

The mystical nature of Dionisio's anointment was not the only quality in his experience that was of importance to him. In the letter to Emanuele Filiberto our prophet also emphasized good judgment, which could be equated with reason. Good judgment, or reason, was necessary for a universal restoration. All men must use their reason and practice good judgment to accomplish a restoration of the Church and society. Dionisio referred to Apocalypse 5 and his own double anointment to support his claim of spiritual and rational authority as God's servant and messenger. Although his letter to the duke was filled with apocalyptic associations, there was no hint of theological debate. He evidently accepted Catholic doctrine, since he had often noted that heresies must be removed. He obviously believed that the practices of the Church, not the teachings of the Church, should be corrected by men who used their reason, that is, "good judgment." Also inherent in Dionisio's claim of opening the seals is his conception of himself as the one who would preside over the judging and condemning, since he referred to the Apocalypse as the book that contains the decrees of God's justice against His enemies. This book was never opened except in extreme cases, that is, for judging and condemning.[77]

It is interesting to note here that in the third stage of messianism the foundation of the future king's throne is to be justice. He will be distinguished by his zeal for justice and will be endowed with the sense of right and wrong and with the ability to judge.[78] Dionisio's comments in the letter to Emanuele Filiberto link him to the apocalyptic tradition with inherent messianic claims.

His enthusiasm for his heavenly selection was expressed in his preaching, in discussions, and in his own apocalyptic book, whose title, *Liber, quem Nullus aut in coelo aut in terra aut subtus terram, antea poterat aperire ne quidem respicere,* is reminiscent of the Apocalypse.[79] He completed this work in Florence, as indicated by the long dedication to Cosimo I, dated March 7, 1566, from Florence. In his letter to the duke of Savoy he asked for an audience with the duke and his council. Dionisio was given an audience with the duke sometime after the twenty-third of December, the date of Dionisio's letter to Emanuele Filiberto. The archbishop was also in attendance.[80]

Dionisio's meeting with the duke can be confirmed by an important statement from his long work entitled *Haec est causa,* which was completed in Ferrara during his visit with Duke Alfonso II and his uncle Francesco d'Este, marquis de Masse. Dionisio wrote that the pope ought to reform the Church, but since he had not done so, the princes must assume this authority. Then he noted: "The first of the dukes of Italy, the duke of Savoy, also approved this [legation], and after I had urged him to put it into execution, he declared that he, with all his effort, was as prepared as possible to do this. It is uncertain? It is certain to him and to me."[81]

Emanuele Filiberto's encouragement of Dionisio should be seen in light of the duke's long-cherished desire to head a league of Italian princes to rout the heretics from the lands he claimed. One also knows that the prince had worked actively between 1559 and 1562 to organize a general Catholic league whose purpose would be to rout the Protestants. The French and Spanish were unwilling to cooperate in any action that could bring more prestige to the duke. The Italian princes such as the Gonzaga of Mantua and the Medici of Florence were motivated by jealousy, and the Farnese of Parma and the d'Este of Ferrara did not hold any effective power.[82] Venice was at this time preoccupied with the defense of the Levant against the Turks and limited its help to demonstrations of sympathy and friendship for the duke of Savoy.

The duke's personal efforts in regard to a league of Catholic princes were unsuccessful. However, they found an echo in the program of Dionisio, who called again and again for a league of Italian princes to settle the religious problems of the day and to reform the Church. Dionisio admitted that he had had little success in France when he had presented his program for reform to the king, his mother, the Royal Council, and the cardinals. He had no more success in Paris than in Rouen, Bordeaux, Toulouse, or Carcassonne.[83] He frankly acknowledged that no one in France accepted his program. The duke well understood rejection, and for this reason Dionisio may have captured his attention. After noting that Emanuele Filiberto and other Christian princes must put into execution his legation, which he hoped to present to the duke, he promised that upon execution of the legation all the duke's lands now occupied by others would be returned to him. The recovery of the duke's lands prophesied by Dionisio had been uppermost in the duke's mind since the treaty of Cercam on October 18, 1558, which gave to Emanuele Filiberto the state as it was in 1536; however, Turin, Chieri, Pinerolo, Chivasso, and Villanova d'Asti still remained with France.

The duke directed his attention, however, to reclaiming Turin and other lands occupied by the French. A conference was held in 1561 with ministers from France, but nothing was decided. Upon the outbreak of civil war in France in 1562, an offer was made for partial restoration, which the duke was advised to refuse.[84] Later, not wanting "to help throw France into the arms of the heretics," the duke proposed that he cede Pinerolo, Savigliano, and Perosa in exchange for Turin, Chieri, Chivasso, and Villanova d'Asti.[85] On December 12, 1562, the French withdrew from Turin, and on February 6, 1563, the duke and duchess made their solemn entrance amid much exultation. Emanuele Filiberto next turned his attention to the lands to which Dionisio referred when he spoke of the lands that would soon be restored to the duke. Diplomatic pressures were applied to Bern, Fribourg, and the Valais, since the duke could use the restoration of Turin as a precedent. The five Catholic cantons of Switzerland eventually yielded to the pecuniary incentives of the duke, and they in turn exerted pressure on Solothurn and Bern.

Emanuele Filiberto's willingness to receive Dionisio was evidently based on their mutual desire for a league of Italian princes. A second confirmation by Dionisio that the duke granted him an audience supports this conclusion. Dionisio described the duke's reaction and his advice: "Monseigneur the Duke of Savoy heard and understood and greatly approved the [legation]. The Duke, whom I urged to give his support for the legation's execution, said that for his part it would be very soon and that I should go to the other Dukes and Princes of Italy."[86] The duke's response makes clear that he continued to nourish his desire to unite the Italian princes in a league against the heretics. Dionisio's conception of the league's mission was first to reform the Church and society, then to remove heresy. Dionisio's priorities were different from the duke's, since he was convinced that if the Church were reformed, most heretics would return to the fold. His reception in Savoy evidently encouraged him to follow the duke's advice and his own inclination to visit other Italian princes. Dionisio's letter was addressed to the duke alone; the name of the duchess did not appear in its heading. In all likelihood, however, the duchess was present when Dionisio read his legation, given Margaret's interest in humanists, especially learned Frenchmen.

The legation Dionisio read in the presence of the duke of Savoy was probably the same as the one he read in Languedoc but apparently with more success. Dionisio followed the advice of Emanuele Filiberto about soliciting the aid of other princes, but not before he went to Rome to see the prince of the Church, Pope Pius V. In the conclusion of his letter to the duke of Savoy, Dionisio wrote of the problems of his own day: "There are two most harsh enemies of Truth itself: one, the avarice and ambition of the prelates of the Church; the other, the error of the heretics. Truth, however, will confound each."[87] The conclusion of Dionisio's letter to the Estates of Languedoc serves as a fitting gloss on the conclusion of the letter to the duke and clarifies Dionisio's concept of Truth: "Jesus Christ made the kings, and Virtue made the nobles. Jesus Christ and Virtue with Truth are one and the same thing."[88] In these two statements Dionisio declared that the clergy and the heretics were fighting against Christ. Because of Dionisio's conviction that the clergy must be reformed, he left Savoy sometime in January and made his way to Rome in order to challenge the vicar of Christ and his clergy to reform Christ's Church so that all could be united in one sheepfold. A purified Church was the essential element for a universal brotherhood of mankind under Christ. Dionisio departed from the duke on friendly terms. On June 5, 1566, the duke arrived in Venice, where Dionisio had been for some days. Whether the prince and the prophet met in Venice is a matter of conjecture.[89]

Dionisio apparently left Savoy by mid-January of 1566, since he was in Rome toward the end of the month to address the pope, the cardinals, and the Roman people. Dionisio's arrival in Rome was nothing less than spectacular. He walked through the public squares, carrying a wooden cross seven feet long on his shoulders. He must have made a startling appearance, since he walked through Rome with his clothes on backward, with his hat turned askew, and with an old breastplate slung over his shoulders.[90] Dionisio's outrageous attire was carefully chosen to demonstrate his role as prophet. As is evident from his choice of space for preaching in Venice, the cortile of the Ducal Palace and the Basilica di San Marco, Dionisio was very astute in appropriating symbols to illustrate his message. He used the streets and squares of Rome, even the Basilica of Saint Peter, as the stage on which he performed his greatest role, that of God's servant and messenger. Indeed, Dionisio saw the world as the stage to which he had been sent to pronounce the cosmic vision of John the Evangelist and Old Testament prophets, the vision he had received directly from the Virgin. He also used his carefully chosen clothing to indicate his prophetic persona, as he did in Venice.

In his symbolic attire he went through the streets, carrying his huge wooden cross and presumably stopping at certain strategic points to read his long letter addressed to the pope but presented publicly in Rome, according to Dionisio's statement. In the letter, written in the form of a broadsheet, he first stated his divine credentials (*suscitauit me dominus, Christo mecum cooperante*) and then detailed his suffering in France on account of the Truth. "It is sweeter to die more often (if it were possible) than to suffer what I have suffered among those Gauls." He did not hesitate to blame the bishops of France as well as the heretics for his suffering, since the Truth was hateful to both groups. So dire were the conditions in France, according to Dionisio, that if Christ had come into France and had preached His message "as freely, as openly, as intensely," as had Dionisio, the French would have wanted to crucify Him. The strife in France was the result of Satan's invasion. Dionisio noted that Satan had been conquered and bound "by holy men" up to the coming of the Antichrist, which was imminent. Now he had been unleashed in France. Dionisio urged the pope to rejoice, since he had been sent by God to the pope, to the Roman people, and to the whole world, with the message of peace and mercy. The message of peace and mercy was fourfold: "(1) the reformation of the clergy, (2) the consolation of the poor, (3) the conversion of the Turks and Jews, (4) the resolution of all the controversies that are and were in Christianity."[91] Dionisio never strayed from these four points in all his writings. Two of his premises were very similar to the two objectives that the Council of Trent hoped to achieve when it was convoked on March 15, 1545, by Pope Paul III. The council had as its aims (1) to attempt a reconciliation with the Protestants and (2) to reform the life of the clergy. The council was in session first in Trent, then briefly in Bologna; then, after a hiatus because of the death of Paul III in November 1549, it resumed its work in Trent in 1551. That work was suspended in 1552 and remained that way through the rest of Pope Julius III's reign, as well as those of Marcellus II and Paul IV, the latter having had no enthusiasm for the council. Its duties resumed only in 1562, through the efforts of Pope Pius IV. The last session of the council was held on December 3–4, 1563.[92]

The problems connected with the resumption of the Council of Trent were astutely analyzed by Alvise Mocenigo in 1560 on his return to Venice after having served the court of Rome as ambassador.[93] He noted that the princes were not encouraging the return of the prelates to Trent and that the French spoke of a national council, as opposed to the general council, "which will place confusion and schism in Christianity."[94] Although the popes spoke of their desire for a general council, their deeds revealed the contrary. The cardinals and prelates abhorred the idea of the council, and therefore "they go, always saying there is no need for such a thing, because all the difficulties were removed by the other councils."[95] Pope Paul IV, on the other hand, according to Mocenigo, was determined to accomplish reform and was trying as hard as he could to correct the abuses.[96] Pius IV, in the beginning of his reign, spoke of reform that he would attempt through the College of Cardinals and the council when all the Christian princes were in agreement.[97] Dionisio, like Mocenigo, criticized the pope for attempting to reform the Church through the College of Cardinals. Dionisio rebuked the pope for his timidity, for not taking action without consultation and approval of the cardinals. Dionisio saw this dependence upon the cardinals, who did not want, for the most part, to change their luxurious lifestyles, as a sign of papal weakness. Mocenigo, in his report to the Collegio, also mused over the pope's loss of authority, which in the past had been greater than "any other power on earth that God had given to men."[98] Previously, Mocenigo wrote, "the people willingly agreed to do what was ordained by the popes as a thing that seemed to them commanded by God Himself."[99] In his age, because of schisms and heresies in the Church of Christ, Mocenigo believed that things had come to such a bad pass "that if the Lord God does not place His hand on us, the things of religion soon, soon will be found in the worst, and, as if, desperate, straits."[100] This negative appraisal of papal authority and the health of the Church was repeated in the letters written by Dionisio to the pope and the Roman people.

We find the same concerns expressed by Mocenigo and Dionisio also articulated by Girolamo Soranzo, Venetian ambassador to Rome, upon his return to the Serenissima in 1563.[101] To describe the Church's sickness he used a medical metaphor similar to that used by Dionisio in his papal letter of 1566.[102] Soranzo warned that the medicine needed might kill the patient: "The council at these times cannot have an effect other than that which wishes to work as a strong and powerful medicine in a weak and worn-out body that does not revitalize but is killing itself. Thus, when the world is in such great disorder and travail, [the council,] wanting to work a remedy so powerful, runs the risk of not setting in order the apostolic see but of making it collapse." Soranzo placed the blame for the sickness of the Church upon the court of Rome; the sickness of the Church, "with the example of that court, is then passed to the temporal princes." Under the pretext of religion, Soranzo wrote, the pope began to make laws, break the peace, and lead arms into one state or another, "to introduce so many abuses into the Church . . . that it will be no less long than scandalous to recite them."[103] Like the Venetian ambassador, Dionisio placed the blame for the Church's sickness upon the pope and the papal court. Everyone, however, was in need of reform. All needed a common medicine, according to Dionisio.[104]

Opinions about the ill health of the Church and the papal see similar to those expressed by Dionisio Gallo were voiced many times during the spasmodic sessions of the Council of Trent. Questions were also raised about the outcome of the council. Soranzo saw no other solution than that which the Collegio had wisely observed and considered, namely, that the pope should give orders of such import to his legates to the council that decisions on matters already begun would be made and that an effective and true reform would be implemented. Soranzo warned that if nothing should be accomplished by the council, greater mockery of the Church would ensue.[105] Soranzo advised that diplomatic pressure from the Serenissima be applied to bring about changes in the Church. Dionisio, with the same goals in mind as Soranzo and the Venetians about the reform of the Church and the role of the council, went to Rome in person, without diplomatic protocol, to reveal his prophetic persona to the pope and the Roman people and urge that reform be instituted immediately. Dionisio's criticisms and fears about the spiritual state of Christendom were very similar to the Venetian ambassadors' opinions expressed in various *relazioni* of the 1560s. Dionisio, however, differed from all others in his "method and art" of accomplishing a universal healing. Since his art had been taught him by God, he appealed to the pope and the Roman people to aid him in this great enterprise.

Although in its early sessions the council resolved specific reform issues such as the obligation of the pastor to his flock, the use of the Holy

Scripture in preaching, and the residence of the bishop in his diocese, dogma and theology dominated the later sessions of the council.[106] Dionisio's criticisms of the life of the clergy indicated his conviction that the council had not accomplished either of its major goals;[107] and two years after its conclusion, his proclamation of his own legation as the resolution of all difficulties in Christianity indicated that he did not acknowledge any accomplishment of the Council of Trent. In the letter written to the pope on January 27, 1566, and read throughout Rome, Dionisio implied that the revelations he had received from God took precedence over the council, since he had received them before and also after the council had been convened. He noted: "All these things have been revealed to me from Heaven before the Council of Trent was held, and after."[108] Had Dionisio warned King Francis I and his court of the need for reform before the Council of Trent began in 1545? Since a divine revelation had taken place before the Council of Trent, according to Dionisio's words, it is unlikely that he would have been silent for twenty years, given his personality and his passionate desire for the reform of the Church. It appears from his words that he experienced some kind of revelation in France before the council opened, March 15, 1545. The reference to a revelation after the end of the council indicated without doubt his divine anointment that took place in February 1562 (1563), of which he was to speak again and again to kings, princes, and prelates. With his statement about the revelations before and after the Council of Trent, Dionisio was defining a two-part stage of his prophetic development. Divine revelations before the council explained what must be done. The divine anointment following the council made clear God's choice of Dionisio as servant and messenger. The tacit assumption of Dionisio's statements to the pope was that his own solutions were conceived by God, while the council's resolutions were the conclusions of men. Dionisio was not reluctant to indicate to the pope himself the priority of his prophetic voice because it had been given to him by God. It is interesting to note that Cardinal Morone, on his way to the council, was quoted as saying that only "God, with His own hand, could provide a remedy for the divided Church and its ills."[109]

In Dionisio's mind the council solved neither the problems of reform of the clergy and charity for the poor nor the problems dividing Christianity. Some were saying that the pope had called the council not so much to reform the clergy and to unite the Church as to keep the French from calling a national council, which they had desired since the time of King Francis I.[110] Whatever results the Council of Trent produced, there were those, like Dionisio, who grieved over the problems still remaining in the Church after the council's conclusion. Pietro Bembo, bishop of Veglia, in a letter dated July 11, 1566, to the doge of Venice and to the members of the Collegio, decried the abuses in the Church and even in his own diocese of Veglia.[111] He admitted that his bishopric was not the house of God but the house of Satan.[112] The aberrations of bishops described by Bembo still existed after the Council of Trent, and it was to those prelates of the Church that Dionisio directed his remarks. Ignatius Loyola also wrote that the sins of a priest were more offensive to God than all the sins of the people.[113]

Throughout Rome, Dionisio read other letters he had written to the pope. In a high voice he challenged the Roman people as well as the pope to accept God's servant and reform the Church, "since Rome formerly was and now is, with a double name, the head of the whole world." Dionisio wrote mysteriously of the dual role of Rome. He noted that "at Rome the Royal Dignity has been joined with the priestly dignity in a certain man still unknown."[114] Dionisio was perhaps referring to himself as angelic pope with temporal and spiritual duties. As he described the ills of the Church especially in France, he urged the pope and the Roman people to realize that "there will be the greatest remedy for the greatest evil; there will be a common medicine for a common sickness." Dionisio was presenting himself in Rome metaphorically as a physician who had the proper medicine, prescribed by God, for a sick world. His credentials were derived from God and predicted by the Blessed Bridget.[115] He named two illnesses that were attacking France: (1) "the greedy ambition of many prelates of the Church," (2) "the error of the heretics."[116] He quickly pointed out, however, that although the sickness of France was greater than that in other nations, the illnesses he named were also common to the other nations.

Dionisio appealed to the pope and to the Romans to accept God's servant and to allow the healing to begin in Rome, since Rome was the head of the nations and the apostolic seat, which is Christ's abode. Christ was working with Dionisio, and it was His medicine Dionisio recommended. Dionisio's prescription for the sickness of the Church was the same as he had proclaimed in France and in Savoy.[117] His vision of the Church healed and restored is reminiscent of Joachim's prophecies about the restoration of the Church under one "holy man" who would lead all to the state of the primitive Church, under "one shepherd, one law, one lord true and humble, fearing God."[118] Joachim proclaimed the results of Christ's medicine: "He will set all things in order beyond that which the human mind can believe, because He is the highest lord and true physician, who, after the wounds, will grant the honeylike medicine."[119] This was the same promise that Dionisio made to the pope and the Romans if they would heed him and put his *Legatio* into practice.

Dionisio's desire to heal took a concrete form. As a challenge to the papal hierarchy Dionisio walked through Rome in his prophetic attire, distributing alms to the poor: "I had called the poor to me; with my purse hanging from my neck, I was distributing money to the poor. Moreover, I did this as an example to arouse the cardinals and shepherds of the Church to pursue charity."[120] From Dionisio's statement it is clear that he deliberately chose this public mode of charity to set an example for the cardinals and bishops and implicitly to criticize their own opulent lifestyles. Active works of charity were second only to the reform of the clergy in Dionisio's prescription for reform. He believed that the Church should return to the practices of the primitive Church, which emphasized the love of God through Christ and exemplified this love through works of charity.[121] In the Church of the tenth and the eleventh centuries, money was brought to the altar for the poor. When the priests began to receive money for themselves for private masses, the number of masses rose while charity for the poor fell.[122] Dionisio harshly criticized the bishops and canons "who follow[ed] avarice and vanity and not charity."[123] If the shepherds of the Church followed charity, the Church and society would be greatly improved. The evils of the Church and the lack of brotherhood in society were the causes of God's chastisement of Christianity at the hands of the Turks, according to the *Prophetia de maometani et altre cose Turchesche*, which was translated by Lodovico Domenichi. If charity and brotherhood were practiced at all levels of society, if the ecclesiastics would leave their pomp, and if the princes "in common, leaving their errors, would conspire to the unity of faith and to the harmony of the Church, God would soon send a remedy."[124]

A variety of thinking men in the sixteenth century, from reforming cardinals to those considered heretics, repeated in one form or another Dionisio's advice to the pope and his challenge to the hierarchy of the Church and to the Roman people. Hieronimo Donzellino, a learned physician from Brescia who had practiced his medical art in Venice for fourteen years, was interrogated by the Holy Office of the Inquisition in 1559 and again in 1560–61. Whereas he admitted he had read prohibited books and had engaged in discussions about faith, he denied that he had ever strayed from the teachings of the Catholic Church in his practice. In a long letter written to the men sitting on the tribunal, Donzellino acknowledged that he had thought about the abuses in the Church, which were "outside the intention of the holy Roman Church and occurred partly through the evil of men, partly through negligence."[125] In addition to the scandalous lives of ecclesiastics, he defined for the Inquisition what he meant by abuses. He identified an abuse as "the evil use of a thing that according to its own nature was good." The abuses Donzellino described were the same as those pronounced by Dionisio a few years later. The Inquisition in Venice and the pope and his Curia in Rome could hardly deny that those things mentioned by Donzellino (and later by Dionisio) were abuses. Donzellino enumerated abuses as (1) the naming of a bishop who was incapable because of age or ignorance or vice, (2) the residence of a bishop outside his diocese,[126] (3) the holding of more than one bishopric, (4) the giving of benefices to persons incapable and unworthy and the giving of multiple benefices, (5) the bestowal of benefices before the bishoprics were vacant, (6) the holding of benefices when the position was changed, (7) the acceptance of money for performing burials and, especially odious, the acceptance of money from the poor, (8) the dispensing of the monies of the Church contrary to the sacred canons, (9) questioning in a confessional simple persons, especially women, about wicked things unknown to the confessants, (10) saying the Paternoster to the Madonna and the Ave Maria to the crucifix or to one of the saints, (11) praying without devotion and intent. With the exception of the last three abuses, the same criticisms of the practices of the clergy are found in Dionisio Gallo's *Legatio* that he read in Rome.[127]

The discussions that engaged Donzellino were often held in the *corte* of the Palazzo Ducale, where he heard a Venetian, Signor Spatafora, dispute with the patriarch of Venice, Pierofrancesco Contarini, about a passage in Saint Augustine.[128] Dionisio chose the same space, the court of the Doge's Palace, with its proximity to the seat of religious and political authority, from which to proclaim his message of reform. In Rome Dionisio was also very conscious of choosing the appropriate space. The streets of Rome offered opportunities to make his message popular. The Church of Saint Peter, the hallowed center of Christianity, provided sacred space in which he could urge the pope and clergy to reform Christ's Church.

In a long letter to the pope Dionisio asked permission to read the *Legatio* to him in the presence of the clergy and the Roman Senate.[129] In his letter he wrote: "You will hear [this *Legatio*] in French when you wish. No woman pregnant and ready to give birth desired parturition more than I want Truth—that Reformatrix, Extirpatrix, Consolatrix, Reconciliatrix, Victrix, and Imperatrix—to be carried out."[130]

It is significant that Dionisio compared his desire that Truth become a reality to that of a pregnant woman waiting to give birth; he was obviously thinking of 4 Esdras 16, where the evils of the world are compared to a woman's labor pains that continue even after she has given birth. The passage from Esdras was well known and loved because of its prophetic character, and it appeared in almost all editions of the Bible and especially in that of Brucioli.[131] Dionisio, with his excellent knowledge of scripture, would have been familiar with the passage from Esdras, using it as a prophetic reminder in his exhortation to the pope.

Dionisio informed the pope that his *Legatio* contained the "art and method," a phrase he was often to repeat, for accomplishing the reforms of the Church, which he referred to as the Truth.[132] On one occasion Dionisio begged the pope, sitting on his papal throne in Saint Peter's and "by the apostolic authority the Pontiff received willingly when he was chosen pope," to call together the Christian princes. Dionisio noted that the opportunity for speaking to the pope was offered by God. He also told the pope that if he could not call together the princes, he must say so. Dionisio advised that it was not necessary to call together all the Christian princes, only Philip II, the Holy Roman Emperor, the Italian princes, and especially himself. Dionisio claimed that if the pope tried and he was received, the Turks and the Jews would convert, and there would be peace in the whole world.[133]

Dionisio emphasized that on his tenth day in Rome, which was the Feast of the Purification of the Virgin, February 2, 1566, he called out to the pope, who was genuflecting toward the altar "of the body of Christ": "Christ greets you through me, O Pontifex. Recognize the cause of Christ and the Church. I shall also reveal that cause to you."[134]

As he spoke to the pope, he held out a letter. One of the pope's attendants received the letter and gave it to the pope. The pope read the letter, and according to the story of the papal attendant and others, the pope afterward kept the letter on a table near his bed. After the Mass on that same day Dionisio again addressed the pope, sitting on his papal throne. Dionisio was close enough to the pope to see that he was nodding his head, as if in agreement, when Dionisio spoke about consoling the poor. Four days later, however, Dionisio was thrown into prison. In these four days his activities were frenetic. He assailed cardinals in the choir of Saint Peter's, demanding that they take him to the pope in order to discuss with him his *Legatio*, which he had already presented in Saint Peter's in French.[135] He admitted that he had beaten on the pope's doors in an effort to present what Dionisio called "his laws." He noted that his lack of success in obtaining an audience was a result of the novelty of his proposal, of his not being known, or of his harsh statements about reforming the clergy. He had more success in the piazze of Rome, where great crowds of the poor pressed so closely to him, while he was distributing money, that he had to throw the money a good distance to free himself. Of this event, Dionisio remarked dryly: "The cardinals and the Romans were watching me. The cardinals were silent; the Romans praised the deed."[136]

On February 6, 1566, Dionisio was thrown into prison, still carrying his cross on his shoulders. He was seized near the doors of Saint Peter's, crying out: "The Cross of Christ is a fortress strong and unassailable. Crucify your hearts, O Romans and all peoples, so that the clergy be reformed, heresies be extirpated, the Turks and Jews be baptized."[137] Dionisio indicated that for those words and for carrying the cross the judges put him in prison, along with the cross. There were other reasons, however, of which Dionisio seemed unaware. Dionisio had challenged the pope's authority in numerous statements. He had explained his divine calling and his anointment by the Virgin in every letter written to the pope and the Romans. His appeal to the Romans and especially his distribution of alms in his spectacular attire could easily be viewed not only as a challenge but also as a conspiracy against the pope and the ecclesiastical hierarchy. On the day before his arrest he had written to the pope a letter that he read publicly and that began with the following plea: "Pray the same thing for me, O Pope, that I pray for you, namely, blessing and pardon. I have been conceived in sin, and in sin my mother conceived me. But not only I, but also you and the whole world. Pray for mercy and salvation." The vicar of Christ on earth was probably not pleased to be reminded of his sinful nature by this strange Frenchman. He was obviously not amused when Dionisio reminded him that they both were servants of Christ, though Dionisio's position had greater authority. Dionisio wrote to Pius V: "On account of your virtue and merits you have been elected by men, that is, by the clergy representing Christ, legitimately congregated; you, as a man, sit in the apostolic chair. But I, not by merits but by the grace of God, I, a worm, not even a man, have been made a servant and messenger of Christ."[138] The legitimacy of Dionisio as servant of God surpassed that of the pope because the former received his position directly from God, not from men. Since Dionisio believed himself, as God's servant, to be the angelic pope who would lead all back into one sheepfold, the position of the pope in Rome was left in the balance. In addition, Dionisio concluded his first letter to the pope with a citation from Saint Paul—"God chose the fools of the world to reprove the wisdom of the wise"—which could be construed negatively by Pius V, especially in light of Dionisio's criticisms of the clergy.[139] The question of folly and wisdom had come to the forefront in the Cinquecento as a means of criticizing the Church and society. In addition to the famous work of Erasmus, the *I Mondi* of Antonio Francesco Doni, in a dialogue, pointed out the difficulty of judging *un pazzo* from *un savio*.[140] In Rome Dionisio had certainly played the *pazzo* with his "backward" clothes and his foolish actions. In effect he was presenting the same problem to the pope, the cardinals, and the Romans as had the interlocutors in Doni's dialogue. The appearance of Dionisio seemed foolish, but in reality he was God's servant and messenger. This was certainly the message he wanted to convey in Rome both by his public persona and by his statements in his letters; the citation from Saint Paul cited above is an excellent example.

In spite of Dionisio's conviction about himself, his words and actions, especially his biting criticism of the ecclesiastical hierarchy,[141] were enough to cause concern about his intentions. It is not surprising that he was placed in prison by the mandate of the pope.[142] He wrote of his imprisonment in several letters. According to his own testimony he spent eleven anxious days in prison and was often questioned by the judges, who blushed at Dionisio's responses. He also remarked that they were "less than truthful," noting also that they had not crucified their hearts, but his.[143] When Dionisio was arrested, he was carrying two letters addressed to the pope and his *Legatio*, which contained seventy-seven principles for accomplishing the reform of the Church and society. The judges of the pope took these documents from him and questioned him at length about their meaning. They finally returned the documents to him upon his request; Dionisio declared that "all things were pleasing to them, approving and praising me in all things and through all things."[144] However, one thing was intolerable to them and to the pope: that he went about Rome preaching about reforming the clergy. He also was advised not to speak about calling together the princes. If he would be silent on these points, he could live in Rome and find favor with all, he was told.[145]

The question of a league of princes had been discussed in various circles and often in Rome by the pope, who had hoped for such a league "to return Christianity to a good union and conformity of religion." The topic was fraught with problems, however. There was no unanimity about which prince would serve as the head of such a league. The duke of Florence was not acceptable to some. While the duke of Savoy seemed a good choice, some opposed because "sia Francese per rispetto dello stato et della moglie o forse inclinasse ad accrescer lo stato et che sia nimico de Suizzeri et non piaceria a Vostra Santità."[146] The Venetians, as noted previously, never favored a league; on November 3, 1563, the Consiglio dei Dieci sent a sharp response to the Venetian representatives at the Council of Trent about a Venetian prelate who had favored statements, approved by the council, about the reform of the princes. The Consiglio dei Dieci advised: "We have taken no small displeasure because of this, being amazed that such as these have so little consideration and so little charity for their country that they, spent, as one must reasonably believe, by ambition and desire to increase their jurisdiction, wish to advance themselves and give favor to something so prejudicial to our dominion and of so great dissatisfaction to the other Christian princes."[147] The need for harmony among kings and princes was also discussed in literary circles; for example, Francesco Sansovino wrote a poem, *A Principi Christiani*, about conflicts and desire for power. Sansovino noted that these conflicts would finally be resolved, and then prophetically stated: "poi, sia vn solo Ouil, sola vna Verga."[148] The pope, however, did not want such a volatile person as Dionisio speaking about a league of princes, which had already shown itself to be a divisive political issue.

The Roman judges had changed their original sentence of banishment to a demand for silence on Dionisio's part, according to the points named by them. Dionisio indicated that he had the remission of his banishment that they had signed; he claimed, however, that he probably would have remained in prison had not God sent to him a certain French hermit. This unnamed hermit pled Dionisio's cause, "like a wife for her dearest husband," before the Roman judges until they freed him. The hermit gave many testimonies about Dionisio's work in France for the king and for the princes and against the heretics. He also enumerated the imprisonments and punishments that Dionisio had received at the hands of the heretics.[149] The unnamed hermit's strong defense was obviously responsible for Dionisio's release from prison and for the remission of his banishment from Rome. Dionisio remarked that he had been freed by truth, truth being the testimony of the French hermit. The Roman judges made certain stipulations that Dionisio must follow if he remained in Rome. To these Dionisio replied: "O Judges, do you want heresies removed and the clergy not reformed? Indeed, whence are heresies born? . . . There is one single remedy for reforming [the clergy] and for removing [heresies]: to gather together Christians and to unite the princes."[150] Dionisio noted that the judges were confused and had no response. After his release from prison he remained in Rome for twelve days, hoping the pope would still give him an audience. When this was not forthcoming, he made his way to Florence in great need. He expressed spiritual anguish that the guards had forced him to give them his money and his horse, which Cosimo I had given him when he was previously in Florence.[151] The wretched state of a mendicant was very depressing to Dionisio, who had enjoyed the hospitality of the duke of Savoy and of Cosimo I, duke of Florence, to whom in his miserable state he was now returning.

As one reflects on Dionisio's dramatic public appearances in Rome, his prophetic sermons in Saint Peter's, and his encounter with Pius V in the basilica, one realizes, surprisingly, the similarity between some of Dionisio's proposals for reform and those of the pope. In his *Legatio* Dionisio had outlined many corrections that must be made in the lives of the clergy. Of these points, only a few concern us here. Dionisio wrote that each bishop was to hold only one bishopric, and no benefice would be given if the bishop was absent. The same applied to every prelate. All religious who were devoid of virtue and intelligence were to be dismissed. The rich would not receive pensions. Prelates created by simony would be dismissed. The luxurious lives of the cardinals and bishops must be replaced by the "beautiful poverty of Christ." Only a month after Dionisio had preached throughout Rome and in Saint Peter's, Pope Pius V, on April 6, 1566, in an extended consistory, urged the cardinals to attend to spiritual matters and to live in such a way that their lives would be an example to others. He urged the cardinals to live modestly and to dress without pomp. He was very distressed over the lavish households that the cardinals maintained for themselves and for their families.[152] This lavish way of life exposed them to the mockery of the heretics, according to the pope, and was reprehensible when seen in others. The pope's nephew, Cardinal Paul Ghisliere, was one of the worst offenders, along with Cardinal Alessandrino. Neither heeded the directions of the pope, who in desperation had ordered that the fine silks and brocades used in the cardinal's bedroom and throughout his quarters be replaced with simple cloth.[153]

Shortly after the pope's coronation he addressed the various ambassadors and the cardinals in a general audience in which he described the difficulties of the times, the afflictions of Christianity, and the loss of so many souls and so many provinces because of the divisions of religion. He sadly noted that the principal duty now was to preserve whatever remained, to help the weak, to seek the lost, and to placate God with prayers and with good life and good example. The pope evidently believed at this time that the rupture in Christian unity was irreparable, but the reforms must be made to deter further loss. In this regard Dionisio was more optimistic than the pope, since he believed that true reform would signal a return to the unity of the Church as well as of society. The pope recognized that princes and people had made their cities beautiful and the Church ornate, but they had given more care to temporal affairs than to spiritual affairs. The lack of attention was evident in the loss of devotion and reputation. Because of the loss of spiritual vigor resulting from the sumptuous lives of cardinals and bishops, the heretics had a pretext for seducing the people.[154] The pope especially emphasized that the bad lives of the clergy more than anything else had fueled the heretics' arguments against the Church.[155] He urged the cardinals to make certain that the clergy reformed itself, "so that they not only would not offend God but would be an example for consoling the good and for confounding the heretics." He urged the cardinals to make their works shine, continually reminding them of the "office they were holding and whom they were representing."[156]

To the average person, the lavish life of the cardinals and of many clergy more than any question of dogma was responsible for the divisions in the Church. The deplorable condition of the poor, when contrasted with the luxury of the cardinals, had caused countless men and women to ally themselves with the Protestants. One Francesco Milanese, when summoned before the Inquisition of Venice, admitted that he had observed that the cardinals feed their dogs but allowed the poor to die of hunger.[157]

The Venetian ambassador Paolo Tiepolo reported that Pius V was moved to tears when he thought of the places in Asia, Africa, and in the greater part of Europe that were lost to the Christian religion.[158] The pope was convinced that the Huguenots had been successful because of the sin of the ecclesiastics whose lives had given the opportunity to the heretics to mock the Roman clergy. The only remedy seemed to be to placate the divine majesty with prayers and alms; in addition, the principal members of the ecclesiastical hierarchy were to provide an example for all others and especially to exhort their families, that is, the members of their ecclesiastical households, to "live well" (*ben vivere*) and to refrain from every kind of vice so that others would want to imitate them. For this purpose the pope had ordained a solemn jubilee.[159] To placate the wrath of God the pope also made solemn processions with the cardinals, bishops, and ambassadors from the Church of Saint Peter to Saint John Lateran, a distance of more than a mile. The churchmen protested bitterly against their discomforts as they marched in the hot Roman sun.[160]

As Dionisio Gallo walked through the streets of Rome, he made the same criticisms of the ecclesiastical hierarchy as Pope Pius V would make several months later. The prophet and the pope each made public displays of piety in order to challenge the clergy and the people to reform themselves in the pious mode of Christ. Pius V made pilgrimages to various Roman churches and often dispensed alms along the way. On other occasions he would distribute dowries for young women of poor families. By precept and example, the pope hoped to persuade the Romans and the Christian world to perform acts of charity. He also exerted his influence against practices in society that he considered sinful. He abhorred the act of sodomy and, in his eagerness to punish all who were guilty of this sin, exacted harsh punishments. One man was burned alive on a bridge; a rich

Roman citizen along with many others was put into prison. The pope indicated that anyone, even a cardinal, who was guilty of this mortal sin would be punished.[161] In his desire to reform the morals of the Romans, the pope also had a plan to move the prostitutes outside Rome. As the women were leaving the city, however, they were robbed, some even killed. Moved by compassion as well as by public outcry, the pope decided to place them in certain houses separated from the rest of the populace. This episode concerning the Roman prostitutes, reflecting as it does the pope's good intentions but his inability to carry them to fruition, seems typical of Pius's desire to reform the Church but his impotence in effecting such reform. His inability to bring about reform seemed to drive him toward severity in punishing heresy and moral offense and toward rigidity in interpreting the faith. The Venetian ambassador in Rome, Paul Tiepolo, noted that the pope thought only of the Inquisition and the new prisons that he was to build.[162] Force and harsh punishments were the pope's major responses to heresy. In spite of his rigidity, the Romans considered him a holy person. His pious acts throughout Rome had obviously impressed the Roman people more than the cardinals, whom he had urged to make their works shine before men. The pope had refused the Venetian ambassador's request for renewal of indulgences for churches, monasteries, and hospitals, replying that he had annulled many indulgences and rescinded many concessions, since he was not granting any plenary indulgence unless the cause pertained to the whole of Christianity. The pope's response indicated his sensitivity to the Protestant attack against indulgences.[163]

The remonstrances that Pope Pius V articulated to the cardinals and bishops in 1566–67 had also been pronounced by Dionisio Gallo in Rome in 1566 and had been responsible for his imprisonment there. Dionisio's actions and words could easily have been interpreted by the pope as usurpations of papal dignity and power, since Dionisio had indicated that the source of his authority was God and that the authority itself was therefore higher than that of the pope. The persona Dionisio assumed following his anointment by the Virgin was replete with religious and political implications. His actions in Rome were especially suggestive of his prophetic persona. In his role as God's prophet and messenger he assumed the authority to warn and advise princes, kings, churchmen, even the pope himself.

Dionisio, in voicing his dismay and disgust over the evils of the Church, seemed to be following in the steps of his prophetic predecessors. Savonarola before him had preached and written about the reformation of the Church and of society. In a passionate plea for reform that reminds one of Dionisio, Savonarola wrote:

> O Italy, do penance. O tepid, O religious, on account of you this tempest has arisen; because of you and your actions these storms arise; . . . O citizen, do penance; render justice, leave your iniquities; leave your oppressions. O merchant, restore the ill-gotten gains, and soon. Give to the poor what you do not need . . . O wicked Sodomites, leave that indescribable and wicked vice. . . . You usurer, leave your usuries, and you poor, leave your evil words and leave your blasphemy. . . . You women, leave your vanities . . . , and you husbands and fathers, constrain them to leave them, because all are cursed things. . . . O Italy, O Florence, do penance, because on account of your sins evils will come to you.[164]

The *Mirabilis Liber*, which was widely circulated in the Cinquecento, also contained many prophecies about the reform of the Church, including the prophecies of the Blessed Bridget, who, according to Dionisio, had predicted his own divinely given role. Bridget had warned each one "to trust in God and do good so that the evils that God had revealed to His own, he may mercifully avert."[165]

Five years after Dionisio had carried his cross through the streets of Rome and had read his *Legatio* in the Basilica of Saint Peter, the pope was still being urged by average citizens to reform the Church. A letter addressed to the pope in May 1571 by Paul Pasqualitius, a notary of Tragurien, is a case in point. The notary's letter had been circulated among a wide audience, since the Venetian Inquisition was eager to find the author "lest some tumult result."[166] Pasqualitius contrasted the life of the early popes and leaders of the Church with the stupor of the Church grown sluggish in its desire for honors in the sixteenth century. "The light of the early Church, seen in all parts of the world, in its innocence had poverty as a companion and a true simplicity of divine worship, which made it flourish; the same church now is almost overturned by the acquisition of riches. For in place of holiness and virtue, honor is believed to reside in riches."[167]

The author of the letter contrasted the lives of the shepherds of the Church, who constantly sought wealth and honor, with the lives of the Apostles, "poor, unlearned, most despised men who were not instructed in clever syllogisms or in the wisdom of the world but were clothed only with the breastplate of faith and guided by the sword, that is, by the word of God."[168] The writer, like Dionisio, was appalled that uneducated bishops created by Christian kings lived like satraps in the king's court.[169] Dionisio had treated this problem in his *Legatio*, saying that all bishops, cardinals, and other churchmen in the court of King Charles IX must be sent immediately to their dioceses.[170] Dionisio, like Pasqualitius, emphasized the need for educated priests and bishops who should be chosen for their virtue.[171] Dionisio also shared with Pasqualitius a conviction that the advance of the Turks in Europe was linked to the ineffectiveness of the Christian Church, divided by religious strife and burdened with a clergy more desirous of riches than of spreading the message of Christ. Dionisio believed that Turks and Jews would be converted and heretics would return to the Church when it was reformed. Since Dionisio believed in the theological dogma of the Church, he did not hold that the teachings of the Church were responsible for its problems. He upheld the seven sacraments and verified that all must confess "the actual presence of the true body of Jesus Christ in the material bread." The real problem was that the Church was no longer filled with the Holy Spirit and the pope no longer demonstrated this heightened spirituality.

Dionisio also proposed that the name of the pope be changed in the reformed Church. Instead of being called the pope, the head of the Church, restored to its ancient purity, would be known by a name more excellent, that is, "king and more than king."[172] Dionisio explained that "Christ makes good princes and magistrates [to be] kings and priests" when they give aid to the poor.[173] Likewise, if the pope fulfilled his duties by subventing the poor and reforming the Church, he would indeed be "king and more than king," that is, king and priest. In Dionisio's understanding of Christianity overt acts of charity were the foundation and the cornerstones of the Church. If the Church were truly inspired by the Holy Spirit, which Dionisio claimed directed him and even his quill as he wrote, it would be aflame with burning charity. The power of the Holy Spirit to transform was a frequent topic for sermons in the sixteenth century. A book of sermons by an unknown preacher in Venice in the Cinquecento explained the relationship of the Holy Spirit to sanctification. The ideas and the language recall Dionisio: "This is of so great excellence and perfection, brothers, that without it you could never be able to know God.... Through this, by the goodness of God and the merit of His Son, we acquired the living faith through which we are sanctified and full of goodness, of peace, hope, burning charity, continence, chastity, and even more, this most Holy Spirit renders us full of incalculable joy."[174] Dionisio believed that he had been anointed with the oil of the spirit; hence the spirit of God could speak through him.

Although the words of Dionisio about the reform of the Church were not unlike the many admonitions of the pope about reform or the ideas of many reforming cardinals and preachers in the Roman Church, his claims about himself and his mission were enough to render him a suspect person. The pope may have kept Dionisio's letter by his bed, but he did not choose to hear more from him. The words and prophetic persona of Dionisio Gallo may have recalled the fiery prophet from Florence, Savonarola. Many themes expressed in Savonarola's *Trattato della reuelatione della reformatione della Chiesa diuinitus fatte*, published in Venice in 1536, found an echo in Dionisio's numerous writings about the reform of the Church.[175] Especially significant are Savonarola's ten petitions, which were required of him and of the city of Florence; these petitions were like gems culled from the Decalogue, according to Savonarola.[176] The Law of God was also central to Dionisio's program for reform of the Church, and the emphasis upon God's Law and upon "flaming charity" was common to both Savonarola and Dionisio.

It is also interesting to note another theme Dionisio shared with Savonarola and the Blessed Bridget, an interpretation of the role of the prophet in fostering the renewal of the *Ecclesia militans*. On the cover of the parchment in which Dionisio enclosed his writings read in Rome and elsewhere, he wrote: "Nos insensati vitam illorum putabamus insaniam. Ecce quomodo computati sunt inter filios Dei."[177] This statement was also used by the Blessed Bridget when she admonished those Christians who scorned prophetic revelations. The words of Bridget vary only slightly: "Nos insensati uitam et reuelationes predicte domine insaniam estimabimus. Ecce nunc intelligimus quia computata est inter iustos et inter sanctos sors illius."[178] Savonarola also used the same theme in writing about the impossibility of pleasing men and God. He, like Dionisio, agreed that we must be "fools for Christ" and must be held in derision by the wise of the world. Then he expressed the hope of hearing those who mocked God's servants, that is, His prophets, or fools, say: "Nos insensati vitam illorum estimabamus insaniam et finem illorum sine honore. Ecce quomodo computati sunt inter filios dei et inter sanctos sors illorum est."[179]

The original text that Bridget, Savonarola, and Dionisio used is found in the Book of Wisdom, 5:4. Savonarola cited the text exactly as it appeared in Scripture. Dionisio's use of the theme from the Book of Wisdom as a heading for all of his writings is important especially for his prophetic persona in Rome. Like Jesus entering Jerusalem on the back of an ass, Dionisio entered Rome on foot, proclaiming the message taught him by God and by Christ and hoping that Rome would become the new Jerusalem. What more fitting place could Dionisio have chosen to present himself as God's servant and make known his *Legatio* inspired by the Holy Spirit? It was essential that he attack the problems of the Church in the heart of Christianity.

Consequently, his certainty of his divine calling, his discourses before the pope in Saint Peter's, and his attempts, though futile, to explain his program for reform of the Church to the pope in private were essential elements in establishing his prophetic persona in Rome and in revealing his prophetic voice. Dionisio's extravagant claims about himself, however, and his revolutionary challenge to the pope for immediate reform of the Church won him no favor with Pope Pius V, although the pope's ideas about reform and Dionisio's were similar. The pope and many others accepted the need for reform. How to accomplish it without destroying the Church and its ecclesiastical hierarchy was the point of contention. Dionisio's *Legatio*, which he claimed would solve the problems of the Church if enacted, was a radical and revolutionary solution that the Pope and princes admired but none dared to implement.

After remaining in Rome for twelve days following his release from prison in expectation of a meeting with the pope, Dionisio decided to return to Florence, where he had previously received the hospitality of Duke Cosimo I. In spite of Dionisio's limited success in Rome, he wrote with enthusiasm to Cosimo I about what they could accomplish together. "We shall renew the earth in this year," he wrote; "that is, we shall reform the clergy; we shall remove heresy; we shall endow the poor; in a short time we shall baptize the Turks and Jews."[180] These four points Dionisio often reiterated to the pope, to princes, and to any who would listen. Undaunted by rejection, he lived on the hope that the Truth he believed he had received would conquer. On the parchment cover that enclosed his writings was also written a second theme, which was a corollary to the words about God's prophets, namely, the theme of truth. As Dionisio departed from Rome, these words, written with care on the parchment cover as a subtitle for all his writings, must surely have been uppermost in his mind, especially in regard to his encounter with the pope: "Now Truth, the 'Victrix,' spares no one but judges all in truth from the highest to the lowest so that she may reconcile all to God in these most recent days."[181]

· III ·
RELIGIO AND POLITIA
Cosimo I, Alfonso II, and Dionisio Gallo

ionisio's bizarre behavior, such as carrying a cross throughout Rome and wearing his clothing backward, reveals that he was appropriating for himself the symbols of a prophet. His fiery call for reform is reminiscent of the prophets of the Old Testament, while the passionate language he used to describe his divine anointment by the Virgin recalls the mysticism of Catherine of Siena and Saint Bridget of Sweden, to whom Dionisio attributed prophecies about his own calling. His insistence that the pope, the Curia, the clergy, and the Romans "crucify their hearts" was consciously chosen to recall the Old Testament prophet Joel,[1] since Dionisio was as certain of his prophetic role as the prophet of old. Strange as his behavior appears to us today, he consciously and knowingly acted and spoke in ways to emphasize his divinely appointed role of prophet. Dionisio's public *persona* was also replete with political overtones. Before his incarceration in Venice he had chosen the cortile of the Palazzo Ducale as an appropriate setting for his sermons. This courtyard was circumscribed by the seat of justice, the Palazzo Ducale, and the seat of worship, the Church of Saint Mark. Dionisio's vision of his role as God's messenger incorporated the aspects of *politia* and *religio*, both of which are identified and defined in the cortile of the Palazzo Ducale and the adjacent Church of Saint Mark,[2] the private chapel of the doge. The cortile, as the site of Dionisio's preaching, provided the obvious associations he intended to make. Medieval prophecies that identified the dual nature of the angelic pope (most angelic pope and most pious king) were also apparent in Dionisio's psyche and in his public presentation of himself.

One recalls that witnesses who testified at his trial indicated that he had preached throughout Paris with a crown of tin on his head and a staff in his hand to indicate royal and priestly authority. He consciously intended to project the image of the humble servant chosen for a divine undertaking. His letters to Italian princes and to the pope also demonstrate a conscious linking of political and religious authority. In the manner of Old Testament prophets, he solicited leadership for his grand enterprise of reform of the Church and the world from the most important dukes in Italy. Dionisio's choice of princes to entreat for help also reveals his understanding of the use to be made of political symbols in religious causes. Emanuele Filiberto of Savoy had hoped to be the leader among Italian princes in a union against the heretics. Cosimo I, also wanting to be first among Italian princes and grand duke of Tuscany, was aware of the value of religious symbolism in enhancing the authority of the prince. As history has shown, Cosimo I was masterful in appropriating religious symbols to enhance his political ambitions.[3]

After Dionisio was released from the Roman prison on February 15, 1566, he remained in Rome several days, awaiting the pope's summons. When it became clear that was not forthcoming, Dionisio made his way to Florence to rejoin Cosimo I. Writing to Cosimo I somewhere between Rome and Florence, Dionisio indicated that, burdened down with his writings, he was returning to the duke.[4] It is not clear when Dionisio had previously been in Florence, but he had enjoyed the duke's patronage before his visit to Rome. Recounting in his letter many of the events that had happened in Rome, he added an interesting account of the French hermit whom he claimed God had sent to him. This was the hermit who, according to Dionisio, had shown much concern for him. In addition to showing the judges many testimonies concerning Dionisio's efforts in France for the king and for the princes against the heretics, he had revealed the countless punishments and imprisonments Dionisio had suffered in France. Cosimo may have been instrumental in securing Dionisio's release from the Roman prison.

In order not to shock Cosimo because of his dress, Dionisio reminded his patron that his clothes were worn and ragged; he begged not to be scorned because of his appearance. As indicated earlier, the prophetic call did not keep Dionisio from affecting a striking appearance. In a letter to Cosimo's son Francesco, Dionisio asked for new clothing, even describing the cut and color he preferred. He wanted his cloak and pants to be red or violet and worthy of a patriarch or servant of God. For the rest of his clothing he chose the colors cerulean or violet, "the kind noble youths wear."[5] He requested a military girdle, a sword, and a *pugio* (short-sword), noting that "my soul desires to wage some kind of best war; give me that which befits a soldier of Christ."[6] He also asked Cardinal Ferdinando for new shoes or the money to buy them. Dionisio's desire for colorful clothing worthy of a soldier and servant of Christ, often noted in his writings, illustrates his use of clothing as a religious symbol.[7] Contrary to many prophets whose dress has been described by Niccoli,[8] Dionisio did not intend to wear rags. His dress should be appropriate for one chosen as "king and more than king," that is, one who served God and was chosen by God to reform His Church on earth. Dionisio's language, his dress, and his actions constituted political and religious symbolism that he used to demonstrate what he considered his prophetic calling.

Cosimo I apparently understood and appreciated Dionisio's appropriation of political and religious imagery, since Dionisio did not hesitate to recount to Cosimo his strange behavior in Rome, recalling his experiences to clarify his conscious use of prophetic symbols.

Cosimo would also have been interested in Dionisio's boast that his origin was "the ancient line of Gallic princes." The Etruscan-Aramaic origins of Florence and its language, as proclaimed by the humanists Gelli and Giambullari, had provided Cosimo I with ideological support for his political expansion. Since Dionisio claimed as ancestors the ancient princes of Gaul, who, in the forgeries of Annius of Viterbo, had been descendants of Noe, Cosimo may have believed that Dionisio could be used as a propagandist for Medicean politics. As it happened, Dionisio tried to enlist the Medici in his own grand crusade of reform.[9]

Dionisio's description of his actions also indicates the security he felt in Cosimo's household. Expecting to be received again by Cosimo I, he beseeched the duke to join with him and other Christian princes in order to renew the land, reform the clergy, stamp out heresy, endow the poor, and convert the Turks and Jews.[10] His expectation of welcome was fulfilled, since Dionisio enjoyed Medici hospitality for an extended period in 1566, as several letters written from within the palace to members of the princely family reveal. His writings had found favor with Prince Francesco, whose virtues Dionisio praised. In a letter to Cardinal Ferdinando, Cosimo's son who had been named cardinal after the untimely death of Cardinal Giovanni, Cosimo's natural son, Dionisio advised the young cardinal: "Since the world is governed by ineffable divine providence and since, on account of the splendor of your dear parents, God has honored you with the highest dignity of cardinal, I urge you to rejoice that in your youth you have been established as a column of the Church, that you have assumed the yoke of Christ. Therefore, do work worthy of your office. Trust in Christ, hope in the Lord, and follow charity."[11]

Dionisio did not hesitate to remind his patron's son of the sacredness of his role as cardinal. In all of his letters to the duke and his sons, he wrote in a familiar yet elegant idiom. In one long letter Dionisio explained that he was writing a large work containing the resolution of all controversies that were dividing Christianity and that he hoped to finish the book in eight days. The work, written in both Latin and French, is his *Liber, quem Nullus aut in coelo aut in terra aut subtus terram, antea poterat aperire ne quidem respicere* and is preserved, along with other documents written by Dionisio, among the records of his trial.[12] He beseeched the young cardinal: "Do I not seem 'captured' in my mind as I write these things? It is necessary that I write this book, not 'captured' but 'raptured.' For whoever has been 'captured' is able neither to propose nor to continue nor to conclude and correct the things proposed. But when a person is in rapture, because there is a certain special grace of God present to him, it is possible to accomplish correctly all these things."[13]

Dionisio made a clear distinction between God-given rapture, a spiritual state, and the physical state of "possession," which he called *captus in mente*. He claimed for himself a state of rapture reminiscent of medieval prophetic writings. Saint Bridget, whose influence on Dionisio, according to his own statements, was significant, wrote often of being in rapture.[14] The headings in the *Apocalypsis nova*, attributed to the Beatus Amadeus and widely circulated in Italy during the Cinquecento, are designated not as chapters but as "raptures."[15]

In a letter to Cosimo and his sons, Dionisio wrote that his book had been completed but that revisions were needed because "of countless interruptions from the duke's sons."[16] Dionisio seemed secure enough with Cosimo's favor to complain about his room. Since he had to share a room with the children, he blamed the crowded conditions for the necessary revisions. From Dionisio's words about his living arrangements at the palace, it appears that he had been engaged as a tutor for Cosimo's children and possibly as a scholar in residence. Dionisio received Cosimo's hospitality as soon as he arrived in Florence, as the date of a letter written soon after his arrival in that "most illustrious and excellent Florentine home" indicates. This visit was obviously not Dionisio's first within the princely household, since Cosimo had already given him a horse and some money, which had been stolen in prison.[17] Dionisio's associations with Cosimo I and his family could have begun before his arrival in Italy in 1565, since Dionisio knew the young French king and Catherine de' Medici, who seemed to favor Dionisio, according to his account.[18] If Dionisio had been employed as a tutor for the duke's sons, this would explain his apology for leaving Florence and his responsibility to the young princes.

Dionisio's arrival in Florence around the first of March 1566, after his Roman imprisonment, followed a period of great sadness in the life of Cosimo I. In November–December 1562, Cosimo I suffered the deaths of his two young sons Giovanni and Garzia and also his beloved wife, Eleonora.[19] In May 1564, Cosimo I ceded to his son Francesco the reins of government, while still appropriating for himself the ducal title and the responsibility of naming those who would serve in the most important offices of government. In December 1565, Cosimo inaugurated the festivities for the marriage of Francesco with Johanna of Austria, sister of the emperor Maximilian II. A little more than a year after the marriage, Dionisio wrote to the young bridegroom from Florence. The letter is filled with compliments for the young prince and especially for his bride, Johanna. "What can I say," Dionisio wrote, "about the most generous and sweetest, about the exceptionally outstanding and wisest Johanna, dear imperial daughter?"[20] He continued his extravagant praise by noting "that heaven gave her to you as your wife; that you love her alone as you love yourself; you love her deeply; you will treat her most pleasingly and most lovingly." Although Dionisio wrote that he did not have the strength to extol the family sufficiently, his fulsome praise belied his claim. In this letter to the young Francesco, whom Dionisio addressed as his patron most esteemed, Dionisio asked, in addition to new clothes, for amenities such as a servant, some wine, a little heat, and supplies for writing, in order to complete his legation. He concluded his letter with the request that the prince "include him in the happy number of those whom you love on account of truth."

Dionisio's hyperbole did not faithfully represent the prince's rather weak character. However, at the conclusion of the letter, he added a postscript that could have served as a maxim for the prince. Dionisio advised: "Everything that is an excellent work and will be outstanding in the future has difficult beginnings and slow increments. As gold in a furnace, God tests those whom He has chosen. His own rewards will never fail outstanding virtue."[21]

Although Dionisio gave counsel to Francesco only in a veiled manner, Duke Cosimo I pointed out that his son and heir needed moral improvement.[22] Francesco had demonstrated unruly behavior at an early age, and Cosimo, the most loving father, endeavored to lead him to better conduct. In a letter to his son before Francesco's marriage, the father sagely noted that the actions of men are observed, not their words. In this regard, he

fig. 5
Dionisio enjoyed the patronage of Cosimo de' Medici, pictured on the title page of this funeral oration in his honor. Biblioteca nazionale di San Marco, Venice

pointed out that his son's habit of roaming through the streets alone at all hours of the night was not behavior behooving a young prince. Cosimo reminded his son that the Florentines considered the youth one who was easily led by others rather than one who led others.[23] Obviously this behavior was not befitting one who would inherit his father's titles. Cosimo perhaps thought that Dionisio's encouragement would influence his son for the better. Dionisio could surely serve as a model for a man of action.

Cosimo would also have found Dionisio an appropriate addition to his household because of his academic and religious inclinations. Cosimo himself was very interested in all the religious and political developments stemming from the Council of Trent, as his correspondence with his petitioners to the council made clear.[24] While he was apparently dedicated to reform, his religious zeal was ever weighed against the political consequences. For example, Giovanni Battista Strozzi advised the duke in 1562 that although the prelates beyond the Alps professed the desire to reform the pope and the Curia, in reality their intention was to "abbassare quelle grandezza e quella autorità e diminuire lo splendore di quel collegio."[25] Strozzi warned that the weakening of papal authority was not in the best interest of Italy. Cosimo obviously knew that it would also not be in his own best interest. The tension between Cosimo's religious and political considerations is especially obvious in the case of Pietro Carnesecchi, whom he handed over to the Roman Inquisition in June 1566. Carnesecchi had enjoyed a close friendship with the duke, whom he served as chancellor. But Cosimo, in spite of his favor and support of Carnesecchi, finally yielded to papal pressure.

Since Cosimo had great hope that the pope would name him grand duke of Tuscany, the extradition of Carnesecchi to Rome appeared to be expedient in regard to Cosimo's expectations.[26] Pope Pius V used Cosimo's extradition of Carnesecchi to Rome as an example of the loyalty and religious fidelity he expected from the Venetians in regard to Guido di Fano, a heretic imprisoned in Venice whom the pope greatly desired to be sent to Rome. The pope pointed out to the Venetian ambassador, Paolo Tiepolo, that even though Carnesecchi had been the duke's *amico intrinsico*, the duke had complied with the pope's wishes.[27] Cosimo I was to receive more than praise, however. In 1569 he was named grand duke of Tuscany by Pius V and was solemnly crowned in Rome on March 5, 1570. Cosimo's increasingly strong religious sentiments in his mature years appear to be genuine. In 1561 Duke Cosimo had received the license from Pope Pius IV to establish the Cavalieri di Santo Stefano under the rule of Saint Benedict, and he was especially devoted to this enterprise as a Medicean response to the Turkish aggression along the Tyrrhenian Sea.[28] He was apparently attracted to Dionisio because of our prophet's passionate religiosity.

Dionisio's return to Cosimo in the early spring of 1566 preceded by only a few months Carnesecchi's consignment to Rome. One can only guess whether Dionisio's presence in Cosimo's household brought any consolation to the duke, given the contradictory arguments concerning Cosimo's decision to extradite Carnesecchi. The death of Cosimo's wife, Eleonora, caused an apparent change in the duke's character. During his marriage he had been a most loving husband and devoted father. After the death of his wife, however, he tossed decorum to the winds by engaging in countless amorous affairs well known to all Florence.[29] None of Dionisio's letters to Cosimo made even a veiled reference to these amorous adventures.

At the end of March 1566 Dionisio completed the book he had promised to Cosimo.[30] In a long letter appended to the book Dionisio justified his claims about himself by using the example of Saint Paul, who did not err "when he call[ed] himself the apostle of Christ or when he name[d] the multitude of kindnesses, with the action of grace, that he received from God." Saint Paul did not make these claims for his own glory but for the glory of Christ, Dionisio noted, nor did he have letters from God about his own apostolate. Saint Paul's authenticity was revealed through his faith and virtue, which he preached to Jews and Gentiles in spite of countless torments and dangers to his life. In like manner Dionisio clearly associated his calling with the prophetic calling of Saint Paul as well as John the Evangelist and David.[31] His challenge to the princes and to the pope himself was based on the belief that God still spoke to His prophets in the Cinquecento. He repeated to Cosimo that his appointment had been made three years before and that he had proclaimed the truth for two years in France and for one year in Italy. After his mystical anointment, his experiences in France, "divided in religion," had left him depressed about any chance for religious peace in that divided land and fearful for his life. He wrote: "Indeed, I would prefer to be crucified once and for all rather than suffer the things that I suffered in Gaul on account of truth."[32] Dionisio noted that the Italians were more patient than the French in searching out the truth. They were also less harsh with Dionisio. In Italy, he had only been incarcerated, not tormented and punished as in France. He pointed out that as soon as the judges in Rome learned the truth, he was freed.[33] His numerous imprisonments seemed to him necessary for a servant of Christ.

Dionisio's admiration for Italy and the Italian princes was based upon the generosity and interest he had found there; he also maintained that Italian princes were more pious than their French counterparts. He praised Cosimo and his sons for their humanity and magnificence, which put to flight past evils. The "past evils" could be a reference to the death of Cosimo's beloved wife, Eleonora, and his sons Giovanni and Garzia. Dionisio's remarks could also have been a reference to the unstable conditions in Florence concerning the succession after the assassination of Alessandro de' Medici.[34]

Dionisio indicated to Cosimo that the clarity of the duke's mind and also his virtue prepared him to receive "the most excellent, truly heroic and divine understanding" that the Paraclete would give to him.[35] In spite of the certainty about his appointment as God's messenger, Dionisio was equally certain that he could not accomplish God's great task without the help of others. For this reason, he indicated, "I cry out, I urge; I warn, I write. I challenge princes and people." He obviously expected Cosimo to provide help, and perhaps not without reason, since Dionisio was not alone in calling for a league of Italian princes to help with the ills of the Church. The pope had often called for such a league against the heretics.[36]

The French king, aided by the pope, had often urged the Italian princes to bolster, especially with their finances, the fight against heresy that was dividing the kingdom of France. The Venetian ambassador to Rome, Michiel Surian, advised the Capi del Consiglio dei Dieci of the discussions and of the pressure from the pope. The ambassador wrote that instead of calling for a league against the heretics, Rome now called for a league "against anyone who disturbed the peace of Italy and the states of the confederated princes."[37] Surian noted that Cardinal Farnese had indicated that all were in favor except the Venetians and that the duke of Florence, backed by the Spaniards, was a supporter of the plan.[38] Dionisio's call for a league differed in substance from the other proposals, however. The main point of Dionisio's plan was the formation of a league to help reform the Church, which appeared unable to reform itself. The main objective of the pope was to remove heresy. The princes obviously wanted to suppress heresy, but they were also eager to obtain political advantage from their cooperation. Dionisio, never failing to attach divine authority to his mission, made clear to Cosimo the universality of his work, as foreseen by prophets and predicted by Saint Bridget.[39] In his own eyes, his enterprise seemed a blending of heavenly calling with human perseverance. Cosimo was urged to "put on his armor" as an example of a Christian Italian prince, along with Dionisio, to do battle against the evils in the Church and in the world. Dionisio was also quick to point out that he always had Christ as his coworker *(Christo cooperante)*.

Dionisio referred to his utopian program for the reform of the Church as a "true and absolute art and method."[40] The fundamental principle of his art was truth, which must be executed quickly. Dionisio often personified truth as the Victress, the Reconciler, and the Empress. A great part of Dionisio's passion for and absorption with the need for reform was linked to his conception of truth. Truth to him was "divine, universal, and complete." Truth was essential in the world if God's *Ecclesia* was to succeed. He was equally convinced that he spoke the truth that would solve the problems of the Church and society. In his long letter to Cosimo I and his sons, Dionisio confounded his emphasis on truth and reason with the medieval notion of the Antichrist, who had to be bound. In Dionisio's idiom, to bind the Antichrist meant to reform the Church. Metaphors pervade the prophetic language of Dionisio, whose skilled use of words would certainly have aroused interest.[41] Dionisio used his rhetorical skills to combine fact with his prophetic visions, repeatedly appropriating the words of Old

Testament prophets to describe himself and his mission. The "book of nature" that he had opened was like honey in the mouth, he wrote, and must be devoured. He claimed that his *Liber, quem Nullus . . . antea poterat aperire,* which he called the book of truth, revealed the solution for purging and restoring the Ecclesia militans. The metaphor of devouring the book was drawn from the prophet Ezekiel, whom God instructed to eat the book, that is, His words, written within and without.[42]

In his letter to Cosimo that accompanied his *Liber, quem Nullus,* Dionisio demonstrated in the spring of 1566 an awareness of the fear that the Turkish menace inspired among the princes of Italy. The deliberations of the Venetian Senate confirm the Serenissima's preoccupation with the advance of the Turkish fleet in the Venetian dominion. So concerned were the Venetians with the Turkish threat that the Senate advised the *proveditor* of the armada to dispatch the Venetian fleet to the port of Malamocco if the Turks continued to advance.[43] Dionisio used the very real fear of the Turkish threat to encourage Cosimo to adhere to his reform program. He argued that there would no longer be any need to fear the Turks if the Church were reformed, since both Turks and Jews would be quickly baptized into a reformed Church.

Dionisio's rhetorical and literary ability and his excellent use of language enhanced his passionate program for reform. In spite of his extravagant claims he obviously found favor with Cosimo I, since Dionisio again and again repeated that he had spent all of the Lenten season of 1566 in the ducal palace of Florence. He often commented upon the duke's generosity in his regard. More significantly, Dionisio claimed that when he returned to Florence from Rome and informed Cosimo of all that had transpired in Rome, "the duke strongly approved and rejoiced because of Dionisio's actions before the pope and the cardinals." Dionisio often beseeched the duke for his help in initiating his program for reform, and, according to Dionisio's story, Cosimo promised that he and his sons would join with other princes to help Dionisio in his enterprise.[44] Dionisio declared to the princes of Florence "that Christ was crying out through him and the Church in vehement complaint about the pope's not reforming the clergy, not removing heresy, not consoling the poor, and not convoking the princes, although he had been urged to do so."[45] Dionisio was especially harsh in his criticism of the clergy, whom he accused of holding the goods that were owed to the poor. Some of the clergy had driven the poor away from their doors and had even beaten them. According to Dionisio, the right of the poor had been established by Christ, but no one was willing to come to their defense.[46] Dionisio believed that one of his major responsibilities was to feed the poor. He also urged Cosimo and the other Italian princes to assume their appropriate roles as defenders of the poor, since "Christ himself through me tells you: This is indeed the time in which Christ makes you kings and priests. Therefore, render to the poor their right to a third part of the goods of the Church."[47]

If the clergy should be unwilling to do this, Dionisio suggested the use of force.[48] In fact, he appropriated the rights of the state as well as the rights of the Church for the princes of Italy, since he said that God had given them the rights of judges, kings, and priests in order to render justice to the poor. Dionisio pointed out that God created all men equal, whether they were kings, princes, popes, cardinals, potentates—rich or poor—who were Christ's members.[49] Our prophet obviously believed that the pope and the clergy were in need of secular help if the Church were to be reformed. Dionisio seemed unaware of the problems that the precedence of princes over the pope would spawn. He sincerely believed that the implementation of the teachings of Jesus expressed in the beatitudes would solve this thorny religious and political problem.

Dionisio contrasted the misery of the poor with the luxury of cardinals. The poor had been scorned and abused in many countries, but he singled out France for its excessive neglect, claiming that he had seen the poor dying of hunger in the public squares under the eyes of cardinals who did nothing to help.[50] The pope also did not escape Dionisio's harsh censure: "I have seen the Curia of the pope. I have seen his servants, royally clothed."[51] In spite of his harsh criticism of the clerics, he did not deny the power and authority of the pope or the dignity of the cardinals. In fact, he demanded that the pope and cardinals live according to their power and dignity, which should be directed toward making Christ's kingdom on earth a reality. His constant complaint against the Church hierarchy was its lack of concern with its own proper objectives, chief among which was the care of the poor. In a long document that Dionisio began in the palace of Duke Cosimo I and that was addressed to Cosimo, to the duke of Ferrara, and to his uncle, the marquis de Masse, Dionisio asked questions he considered pertinent to Christianity:

> *What do you say, O dear princes, chosen peoples and nations? The pope should without delay reform the clergy, blot out heresy, console the poor. If he cannot do it, he ought to call us together and beg our aid. What should I do? . . . If the pope does not wish it, if the cardinals are a hindrance, if the king of France, the royal Senate, and the heretics urge all that we not be convened . . . this is the knotty problem. . . . This is the difficulty with all the present task.*[52]

Some of Dionisio's questions had already been posed by the Protestants. In regard to heresy, the Protestants would also have agreed that it needed to be eliminated; however, from their point of view heresy stemmed from the Roman Church itself because of the failures Dionisio had pointed out. To Dionisio, on the other hand, the abuses of the clergy and the destruction of Christian unity were equally culpable as heresies. He sincerely believed that the correction of clerical abuses would eliminate the disunity of Christianity. The growth of heresy had been abetted by Satan because of the avarice, ambition, negligence, iniquity, and ignorance of the clergy.[53] He never took into account the theological arguments of the Protestant reformers, evidently believing that they did not constitute the main points of disagreement among Catholics and Protestants.

In urging the reformation of the clergy, Dionisio, quoting the prophet Isaiah—"Moab will wail"—compared the shepherds of the Church to Moab.[54] Unless the shepherds walked in simplicity, in sincerity, and in newness of life and fed and clothed the poor, they would understand how true were the words of the prophet David: "He cast the powerful from their abodes and exalted the humble. He filled the needy with goods, and He divided needless riches."[55] The situation was urgent, Dionisio proclaimed, and the sooner the Church was reformed, the better. Everyone who was truly Christian must desire, pray for, and try to effect the changes necessary. Yet Dionisio was quick to point out that the pope was the major obstacle to change. He wrote, as if he were in a dialogue with the pope, what the pontiff would say when urged to call together a council of princes. He would say that he was the head of the Church Militant and that he recognized no one since the time of Peter above himself as judge and reformer. In addition, he would say that he could not call together the Christian princes to reform the clergy, to extirpate heresies, and to console the poor without the advice and consent of cardinals and the clergy. He would perhaps say that the consistory of cardinals had not approved a convocation of princes.[56] Dionisio compared the pope and the cardinals to a wayward student who never wanted to be corrected.[57]

The frustration of the teacher turned prophet was very apparent, since he noted in desperation that neither the pope nor the cardinals wanted a convocation of princes to discuss the reformation of the Church's abuses.[58] "The abuses of the clergy," Dionisio wrote, "are the root and origin, the cause and beginning, of errors and civil wars." In his statement about the wayward student who never chooses to be corrected, Dionisio implied that the princes were to be the *maestri* of the pope and the cardinals, who resembled wayward students. Dionisio's statement about the abuses of the clergy repeated the reasons Francesco Spinola had given for his apostasy. Our prophet seemed unaware that his complaints about the clergy and the pope had much in common with the charges made by the Protestants. He also chose to ignore the Council of Trent and its efforts to bring about reform. However, when the inquisitors pointed out to Dionisio that many of his articles had already been approved by the Church and by "the sacred, Holy, ecumenical, universal Council of Trent," he responded that the articles must be carried out immediately, before Christ should come and the Antichrist rage among the elected. Those principles, and others that were absent from the council's documents, must be put into effect with all haste, according to a revelation made to him from on high. It is significant that the council that Dionisio was trying to call together was a secular council. Though our prophet did not say so, it is clear that he believed the reforms proposed by the Council of Trent and by his *Legatio* must be put into effect by the political sphere. He obviously believed that the clergy would never bring about change in the Church or in themselves. In addition to the pope and cardinals, Dionisio also accused the king of France and the royal Senate of fearing a convocation of princes who would send into France true reformers and Catholic rectors to unite the divided kingdom. Although Dionisio admitted that pope, cardinals, king of France, and royal Senate were unwilling to bring about reform, he believed that "truth nevertheless will conquer." Dionisio, like many of Catherine de' Medici's critics, believed that she was ineffective in bringing peace to the divided realm of France and was perhaps even under the influence of Protestant advisers. He was horrified that heretic and Catholic could live with equal liberty in France and that truth had been confounded with error. One could even think that God had made a pact with Satan to throw France into confusion and impiety.[59] However, Dionisio assured the princes that God had made no pact with Satan, but had permitted Satan to seem victorious so that his fall would be all the greater. Dionisio blamed Satan for the divisions in the French realm, since he had seduced princes and people away from the truth.

Dionisio gave a fascinating account of a mock dialogue with Satan. In this feigned exchange our prophet pointed out that Satan knew the clergy could never be reformed without a convocation and union of the princes.[60] Dionisio used a mock heroic style to personify Satan, who had been set loose in Gaul. His realistic dialogue with Satan demonstrated the medieval perception of the Devil as a person against whom a soldier of Christ and the Church Militant must fight.[61] Dionisio used military terms reminiscent of Saint Paul to describe the battle against Satan.[62] In this imaginary dialogue, Satan pointed out that the pope and cardinals had been anointed by

God, before all kings and princes, with spiritual power. He concluded, however, that all Christian princes gathered together could not reform the pope from any sin if there were pleasure in sinning and if the cardinals and the clergy did not want to be reformed.[63] Therefore, Satan asserted that he would be victorious and God would fall, that the rights of Christ would be abolished and heresies would increase more and more. As a result the poor would suffer graver discomforts, since charity would be obliterated, and life would be worse for all.[64] In his response to Satan, Dionisio did not directly refute the particular charge about the pope. He said instead that God was not without a plan and wisdom to satisfy the charges of Satan. God had foreseen both the order and the confusion that would come to His Church, whose head was His son, Jesus Christ. For this crisis a new order and a new messenger had been directed by God. Dionisio noted that he had been anointed and consecrated without the pope and without the cardinals. His task was to announce a new heaven and a new earth. His apocalyptic fervor is apparent throughout his writings but especially in his *Haec est causa*, where he linked himself not only to the prophets of the Old Testament but also to John the Evangelist. For example, he used the word *annuntio*, which appears many times in the first chapter of the first letter of John the Apostle. Dionisio's announcement of a new heaven and a new earth projected John's vision of the new Jerusalem descending from heaven as a tabernacle of God, who dwelled with mankind.[65] Dionisio's allusions to his role as a second John are surely intentional. In this context he regularly demanded help from all, especially the princes, in reforming the Church so that the new Jerusalem could descend.

Dionisio's long fictitious dialogue with Satan revealed his belief that the pope could not or would not effect reform of the Church and that Dionisio's divine anointment in effect superseded the qualifications of the pope to bring about the reform requisite to the new Jerusalem.[66] Dionisio's feigned dialogue was also an implicit rebuke to the Council of Trent, which had not been able to reunite Christendom or reform the clergy, according to Dionisio. At the same time, Dionisio's criticism never precluded the power, dignity, and authority of a reformed papacy or clergy. However, since it appeared that the pope and cardinals were not prone to reform, and since Dionisio was certain of his calling as the second John, his pressure upon the princes became more frantic and more insistent with every passing day. In a letter to Cosimo I, Prince Francesco, and Cardinal Ferdinando, "on behalf of the other princes and all nations," Dionisio made explicit his claim to be the shepherd promised by Christ and described by John the Evangelist. The shepherd is called in the Apocalypse the Lamb. This Lamb, or shepherd, has been struck with swords and has almost died from various torments he has suffered at the hands of heretics and wicked men on account of the truth. Dionisio related in a passionate flow of words John's description of the Lamb whose role as the promised shepherd he believed he had been called to assume. In this long and fascinating letter, which served, in Dionisio's mind, as the confirmation of his prophetic *persona* for the duke of Florence, he interpreted passages in the Apocalypse that seemed to him to refer to his role as shepherd. For example, when the Evangelist wrote of the Lamb with seven horns and seven eyes, Dionisio interpreted the seven horns to be the divine authority and strength of soul that had been granted by heaven to that shepherd "to announce to kings, princes, peoples, and nations that very truth which is truly that open book." The seven eyes represented various gifts of the Holy Spirit that had been bestowed upon the shepherd. Dionisio cited the passage from Apocalypse 5: about the four animals and the twenty-four elders who fell before the Lamb and said that the Lamb was worthy to open the book. It is useful to consider this passage, with Dionisio's interpretation, in full, since in this context he makes the most forceful claims about his own role of shepherd under Christ:

> But how will you interpret for us these words of the divine John that follow in the same fifth chapter of the Apocalypse? "And when he had opened the book, four animals and twenty-four elders fell before the Lamb, each having lyres and golden vials full of perfumes, which are the prayers of saints; and they were singing a new song, saying: 'You are worthy (O Lord) to receive the book and to open its seals, since you have been slain and you have redeemed us for God in your blood. From every tribe and language and people and nation, you have made us for our God a kingdom and priests, and we shall reign above the earth.'" All these words in the first place must be understood about Christ. Then they must be understood about the shepherd who has been incorporated and comingled with Christ in a certain heavenly mystery, almost ineffable. To open that very book pertains to Christ and to the shepherd. Christ, revealing, opens the book; the Redeemer, already triumphant, opens the book. The shepherd, announcing, proclaiming, writing, suffering, and challenging, will do greater things when the Christian princes are joined and united. Christ and the shepherd, moreover, each is called the Lamb. Christ is the Lamb crucified and sacrificed for the redemption of the whole world. The shepherd is the Lamb under Christ, almost killed, beaten, struck with swords, whipped, and now for almost three years overcome with various torments for the reconciliation of the whole human race.[67]

From this long exegesis of the Apocalypse it is clear that Dionisio considered himself the divinely appointed angelic shepherd who would lead the Church to a true reformation. Dionisio's open confession of his role as angelic shepherd (or angelic pope) reveals that medieval concepts about the angelic pope who would reform the Church were still alive after the middle of the Cinquecento and could command an audience in Florence, even in the palace of the duke. Dionisio's experiences in Turin, Florence, Ferrara, and Venice demonstrate the vitality of prophetic ideas in Italy in the middle of the sixteenth century. His prophetic challenge to the prophetic city of Venice would reveal the paradoxical nature of prophetic understanding as well as of the desire for a reformed Church. In Venice all of Dionisio's prophetic claims would reach their culmination.

But while in Florence with Duke Cosimo I, Dionisio wasted no time in trying to win the duke's aid in forming a league of princes to initiate the reform of the Church. Dionisio's spiritual challenges were seldom free of political implications. His quotation from Psalm 32 made clear his warning that unless the princes fulfilled their obligation to feed the poor, reform the shepherds of the Church, and walk in simplicity and sincerity of life, they could be overthrown. He was also not reluctant to reveal the support he had received from the duke of Savoy, whom he pointedly called "the first of the dukes of Italy." He quoted Emanuele Filiberto as saying that he was as prepared as possible with all his strength to accomplish the goal outlined by Dionisio.[68] As noted earlier, Emanuele Filiberto had dreams of heading a league of Italian princes whose purpose was to rout the heretics. Although the duke's hopes had not come to fruition, he perhaps saw Dionisio as a catalyst for his own political as well as religious program. For his part, Dionisio used the rivalry between the dukes of Savoy and Florence to spur them into action.

Our prophet's enthusiasm for reform, abetted by his apparent success in winning Cosimo's favor, led him into further excessive rhetoric about the pope, which resulted in an open conflict with the papal nuncio, Bernardino Brisegno.[69] In the duomo of Florence, in the presence of the clergy, Duke Cosimo, the papal nuncio, and others gathered for the Feast of the Annunciation of the Virgin, Dionisio boldly declared that the "pope was culpable for occupying the apostolic chair, until he should call together those Christian princes."[70] Not surprisingly, the papal nuncio became enraged, but he could do nothing against Dionisio, because of the duke's protection. When Cosimo left town, however, the nuncio ordered Dionisio to leave Florence. Dionisio recounted the circumstances: "I, the messenger of God, went to the messenger of the pope so that he could tell me why he wished me to depart and if he had the power [to order this] in the duke's absence."⁷¹ The nuncio, not amused, ordered Dionisio to leave Florence, but Dionisio responded that he was unwilling to go in the duke's absence and without taking leave of him "who had received and nourished me."

A long exchange between Dionisio and the nuncio followed, during which Dionisio challenged the nuncio's authority, claiming it was less than his own; he pointed out that the nuncio's authority came only from the pope, while the prophet's authority was derived from God.⁷² In his *Haec est causa* Dionisio repeated the discourse between himself and the nuncio apparently verbatim.⁷³ The nuncio denied that Dionisio spoke with authority from Christ and said that the self-proclaimed prophet had to leave Florence, since he had publicly declared that the pope was an "invader of the apostolic chair."⁷⁴ The long exchange between the papal legate and the prophet-preacher reveals that Dionisio's certainty about his divine anointment produced the same rhetorical boldness whether in the presence of the pope's representative or princes of state. Dionisio's lack of caution caused the nuncio to call him insane, noting that Dionisio's madness, not Christ, was responsible for his outrageous remarks.

When Dionisio refused to leave Florence in the duke's absence, the nuncio had him thrown into prison, where he remained for three "most wretched nights." With Cosimo's return to Florence, Dionisio's enemies freed him, out of fear of the duke. However, they led him outside the city and forced him to leave the area. Cosimo I perhaps remained unaware of the reasons for his eccentric prophet's sudden departure. However, in light of the difficulties surrounding the duke's friend Pietro Carnesecchi and his subsequent extradition to the Roman Inquisition in 1566, Cosimo I probably breathed a sigh of relief when he learned that Dionisio had departed. Dionisio's encounters with the pope's nuncio would undoubtedly have caused trouble for Cosimo had Dionisio remained under the duke's protection in the ducal palace. Dionisio's words about the pope were certainly interpreted by the nuncio as a challenge to papal authority and the Church's magisterium. There had been previous Florentine examples. Massimo Firpo and Paolo Simoncelli have noted the continuity of problems, from the Church's point of view, in the inquisitorial proceedings against Savonarola and Carnesecchi. The Holy Office was shown to be knowledgeable of the ruptures that the ecclesiastical institutions had suffered in the last ten years. Here the necessity of going back over that past and understanding the teaching of "heresy" as doctrinal deviation or as disobedience to papal authority could unite Girolamo Savonarola to Giovanni Morone, to Pietro Carnesecchi, and to many other protagonists of the "internal dissent," against which the inquisitors were now taking count. They considered them much more dangerous than every type of "external contagion" that had come from outside the Church.[75]

A similar connection could be made among Savonarola, Carnesecchi, and Dionisio. Like Savonarola, Dionisio proclaimed the truth of his prophecies, since they came from God. Like Carnesecchi, who had called the believers of the Waldensian dogma the "elect of God," Dionisio considered himself God's elect, since he had been chosen by God and anointed by the Virgin, whom he called the "handmaiden of the trinity."[76]

No doubt Dionisio's forced departure saved Cosimo I from further embarrassment, since Dionisio's criticism of the pope could have suggested the opinions of disciples of Valdes, such as Pole, Flaminio, Morone, Priuli, and others of the "same school."[77] Although Dionisio cannot directly be linked with any of the aforementioned reformers, he surely ranks among the *spirituali* and *profeti* who desired reform of the Church from within and reformed leadership from the papal throne.

It is surprising that the nuncio released Dionisio from prison and banished him from Florence. Because of Dionisio's direct challenge to the nuncio and especially because of his direct assault upon papal authority, one would expect Dionisio to have suffered a harsher fate. In spite of the fact that the pope in 1551 had urged "tutti i principi e rettori delle provincie, città e terre ed a qualunque altra persona secolare di non porre ostacolo ai vescovi e agli inquisitori nell'esercizio della loro autorità contro gli eretici,"[78] the nuncio was disinclined to take stronger action against Dionisio, evidently because of the duke's patronage. Although the nuncio had told Dionisio that madness propelled him, not Christ, the prophetic certainty with which Dionisio spoke and his overt criticism of the pope were obviously challenges to the nuncio and to the pope.[79] Cosimo's jealous guarding of his own power relative to Rome had been the subject of numerous letters and negotiations between Rome and Florence regarding the implementation of the Index of Paul IV in Florence in 1559.[80] The nuncio was certainly aware of the delicate balance that had been established between the pope and the duke and consequently took the least controversial approach to the problem posed by the preacher-prophet Dionisio Gallo. It was easier, from the nuncio's point of view, to call Dionisio insane than to deal directly with the charges made by Dionisio about the pope and the clergy. The nuncio in all likelihood did not relate to Cosimo the reasons for Dionisio's departure. To the duke the prophet's absence perhaps did not appear unusual, since he had earlier left abruptly for Rome, as he himself had indicated. The paradox is that Cosimo had received in his palace one who had so harshly criticized the pope and the cardinals.

Cosimo I was in partial retirement in 1566, when Dionisio was his guest, but Dionisio's learning and his passion for reform obviously struck a responsive chord. However, our preacher-prophet's unrestrained criticisms of the pope while under Cosimo's protection, especially his strident suggestion that the pope was a "usurper of the Holy See," presented a bold contradiction, since Cosimo I, who had been awaiting the title of grand duke of Tuscany from Pope Pius IV, continued to hope for this honor, which was indeed awarded in 1569 by Pius V, the object of Dionisio's harsh criticisms.[81] In spite of the implications inherent in Dionisio's belief in the ineffectiveness of the pope in bringing about reform, Cosimo I continued to favor him until the papal nuncio forced him to leave Florence.[82] Before Brisegno's expression of rage at Dionisio's words in the duomo of Florence, Cosimo I had enthusiastically approved Dionisio's call for reformation. Even more surprising was Cosimo's apparent willingness to engage in some kind of military enterprise that Dionisio was urging upon the princes. Dionisio wrote on several occasions of the approval of several Italian princes and of Cosimo I himself.[83] He indicated that even in France the good princes and Parlements, when they had understood his program, agreed "that it would be good according to God and reason, very universal and Catholic but very difficult to put into practice."[84] As I have indicated, the duke of Savoy had given his approval and was ready to provide his part, but he had advised Dionisio to seek the help of the other princes as well.[85] Cosimo listened to Dionisio's plan and indicated that he was ready to march with the other dukes and lords of Italy.[86] Dionisio admitted, however, that all the princes of Europe joined together would not be sufficient to reform the clergy, to extirpate heresies, to render the right of the poor to a third part of the goods of the Church, without the help of the Holy Spirit, which would make the Turks, along with the Jews, lay down their arms and receive baptism into the Christian faith.[87] Dionisio frankly admonished that resisting the Turks, which was perhaps uppermost in Cosimo's mind and in the mind of the pope, was secondary to reforming the clergy, removing heresies, and helping the poor.[88] Dionisio never wavered in his priorities, believing that true reformation would solve the Turkish problem.[89] The dukes of Savoy and Florence, each with his own particular agenda, apparently gave tacit assent to Dionisio's scheme, some aspects of which had been bandied about by one prince or another for several years. A league of princes had also been uppermost in the mind of the pope, who in December 1567 had instructed his nuncio Giannantonio Facchinetti to urge the Venetians to help him in acting against the heretics in France. The papal nuncio pointed out that when there was a fire, it was better to help put out the blaze in a neighbor's house than have the blaze spread to one's own house. The pope had asked all the princes of Christianity to help in this enterprise. The nuncio noted that Venice was subject to great danger from the Calvinists in the Serenissima and surely would not want to be the only state unwilling to help. The papal nuncio also warned that the heretics wanted to overturn obedience to the princes and to the Church. In addition, they wanted to refute all superiority of the nobles, a point extremely cogent for the Venetians.[90]

The pope's concept of a league of princes under his leadership was not what Dionisio had in mind. Dionisio's insistence upon a league of Italian princes that would immediately confront the problem of Church reform and reform of the clergy was one motive for his travels in Italy. As noted previously, he had challenged Pope Pius V to call together the princes to help him reform the Church from within and without. The pope was himself frantically trying to call together the princes, but his aims were quite different from those of Dionisio. The pope wanted a league to fight the heretics, especially in France, and to stop the advance of the Turks. According to Dionisio's plan a league of princes would help the pope implement reform on all levels of the Church hierarchy.

Religious reform was not devoid of social implications in Dionisio's program. All levels of society were equal in Dionisio's plan, and hierarchy was based only on a measure of virtue. The poor were to be fed from a third part of the Church's wealth. The care of the poor, coupled with the reform of the clergy, would bring immediate improvements in society. Dionisio believed that the heretics would return to a reformed Church and that his reforms would lead not only to religious peace but also to social justice. He was convinced that a league of Italian princes could accomplish these goals. The Pope, too, had religious peace in mind when calling for a league of Italian princes, but his concept of society was different. He certainly wanted religious reform and had taken measures to effect this;[91] the Church hierarchy was unwilling, however, to give up its privileges, and the pope was unwilling to force change upon them. Although the Council of Trent had spoken to many of the ills of the Church and had codified Catholic dogma, the Church remained divided. Dionisio believed that the council had not solved the problem of Church reform. Hence he supported a program of action that would radically alter the face of Christianity.

In addition to Dionisio's statement that Cosimo I was ready to send troops, a dispatch sent by Michiel Surian, Venetian ambassador to Rome, to the Capi del Consiglio dei Dieci verified Cosimo's support for an Italian league.[92] Cosimo I wanted to win favor with the pope in order to foster his pursuit of the title of grand duke as well as to receive all the help available for any disturbances the heretics might produce. Dionisio's forced departure from Florence, seen in the light of the discussions that were under way concerning a league of princes, relieved Cosimo I of the embarrassment that Dionisio's undiplomatic proposals would surely have produced, especially in regard to the pope, as his fiery discourse with Bernardino Brisegno, the papal nuncio in Florence, illustrated.

Whereas caution and diplomacy were not facets of Dionisio's character, perseverance was. Consequently, not dismayed by his expulsion from Florence, he made his way to Ferrara to espouse his cause before the duke of Ferrara, Alfonso II. Dionisio arrived in Ferrara sometime in April 1566. We cannot be certain if this was his first contact with Duke Alfonso II or if he had previously known the duke in France. Alfonso II, son of Hercole II d'Este and Renée of France, was born in 1533 and was well educated in letters and in the duties of a cavalier.[93] Without his father's permission he went to France in 1552 to join King Henry II, who gave him a company of one hundred men, whom he led in the war in Flanders. Alfonso returned to Ferrara in 1554 after a reconciliation with his father. He returned to France two years later, this time with his father's permission. Alfonso married Lucrezia Medici, the fourteen-year-old daughter of Cosimo I, in Florence on June 18, 1558, but continued his service to Henry II until the king's untimely death in a joust. Alfonso remained in France until his father's death on October 3, 1559.

In November 1559 the Dodici Savi of Ferrara chose Alfonso to succeed his father. In celebration of the entrance of Lucrezia Medici into Ferrara on February 27, 1560, the dukedom enjoyed a series of grand festivals, which increased the renown of the Estense court. The brother of the duke, Prince Luigi, was named cardinal in 1561, and this elevation also presented an occasion for spectacular tournaments.

The young Duchess Lucrezia died in 1561 without issue. Her brief residence at the court of Ferrara had been eclipsed by the intelligence and spiritual endeavors of her mother-in-law, Renée of France, and by the beauty of her sisters-in-law, Lucrezia and Leonora. On December 5, 1565, Alfonso II celebrated his marriage to Barbara of Austria, the sister of the emperor Maximilian II, and again Ferrara enjoyed fantastic festivals. In 1566 Alfonso II led a small army of men to Vienna to help his brother-in-law in his invasion of Hungary and in his preparations against the threat of the Turks.[94] When Soliman II died in 1566, the emperor negotiated an armistice and withdrew his troops. Alfonso II returned to Ferrara on December 18, 1566, with the goodwill of the emperor but with no concrete advantage.

The duke had been back in residence in Ferrara only four months before Dionisio's arrival. Dionisio had again chosen to come to a princely court where there were close ties with France. There had also been ties between Alfonso II and Dionisio's patron, Cosimo I, who had been the father-in-law of the duke.[95] Dionisio's contacts in Italy reveal a network of associations that he obviously used to the fullest extent. Since Alfonso II had gathered around him a splendid group of *letterati* and artists, he would have been inclined to receive at his court a Latin-speaking French humanist who claimed to have the solution to the religious problems of the day. Religious persuasion, however, was an especially sensitive issue in Ferrara in 1566, since Alfonso II had already faced the thorny question of his mother's religious loyalties because of her friendship with John Calvin.[96] On September 2, 1560, Renée had departed from Ferrara and had taken up residence in the castle of Montargis.[97] She traveled to Poissy for the colloquium and allowed Reformed sermons to be preached in her lodgings.[98] The cardinal of Châtillon had loaned her his mansion during the Colloquy of Poissy.[99] Renée returned to Montargis after the colloquy, determined to make Montargis a Protestant city. In addition to François Morel, the *sieur* of Colonges, whom Calvin had sent as preacher and adviser to Renée, the duchess also requested that Peter Martyr, Peter Viret, and Theodore Beza visit her on their return from Poissy.[100]

Renée's influence on her son is difficult to assess, but his early devotion to France and to King Henry II reflected his preference for his mother's lineage.[101] For a brief period Francis II, the young king who succeeded his famous father, Francis I, was especially devoted to Alfonso and treated him as a brother. Renée's interest in theology may have sparked Alfonso's devotion to religious causes. She, however, was truly dedicated to the teachings of Calvin, whereas he was a staunch supporter of the Roman Catholic Church. On the other hand, her tolerance, which enabled her to maintain friendships at both ends of the religious spectrum, may have had its counterpart in the duke's resistance to ecclesiastical pressure in regard to the heretics.

Nevertheless, when Alfonso II in 1564 journeyed to the Château Rousillon near Lyon to visit his mother, his motive was to urge the queen mother in residence in Lyon to take harsh measures against the Huguenots more than to show filial duty.[102] He was acting in consort with the duke of Savoy. His visit to his mother in Lyon and his pressure on Queen Catherine of France to take new measures against the Huguenots help to clarify his reception of Dionisio Gallo in the late spring of 1566.[103] In addition, the family d'Este had not been reluctant to seek the help of a prophet in generations past, as witnessed by the correspondence and friendship between Savonarola and Hercole d'Este, great-grandfather of Alfonso II.[104] The duke of Ferrara received his prophet sometime in April, as Dionisio's letters to the duke and his uncle, Francesco d'Este, marquis de Masse, indicate.[105] As had been Dionisio's practice with the other princes, he wrote to his hosts long letters in which he outlined his mission and the princes' roles in helping him to accomplish it. He often read the letters in the presence of the dukes; the letter to Alfonso II and his uncle indicates that it was written and read in Ferrara the next to the last day of April 1566. Dionisio wrote in rhetorical style to describe his divine calling, envisioning himself a knight errant protected by his sword, the spiritual sword of truth. Dionisio claimed that his sword had been fashioned from truth and knowledge divinely infused by the Virgin. This sword of truth and knowledge allowed Dionisio to know with certainty what had to be done to reform the Church and society. He told the duke and his uncle that with the "sword of truth" their battles could accomplish great victories for Christ and His Church. Dionisio certainly was not the first to use military metaphor to describe his struggle to reform the Church. Saint Paul, writing to the members of the Christian community in Ephesus, admonished them: "Stand, therefore, having girded your loins with truth, and having put on the breastplate of justice, and having your feet shod with the readiness of the gospel of peace, in all things taking up the shield of faith, with which you may be able to quench all the fiery darts of the most wicked one. And take unto you the helmet of salvation and the sword of the spirit, that is, the word of God."[106] The sword of the spirit of which Saint Paul spoke became for Dionisio the platform for the reformation of the Church and society that he articulates in his so-called legation. This legation, inspired by God through the Virgin, was the word of God, described metaphorically as the sword of truth. Dionisio's language is also reminiscent of Ignatius Loyola, who in his *Spiritual Exercises* had used military language in order to instruct his followers in becoming soldiers of Christ.[107]

Dionisio described his *glayve* (sword) as faithful because "God, Who gave it to me, is the true Worker Who made it." He also declared that God has sent the "sword" to Duke Alfonso II and Francesco d'Este to be unsheathed against the abuses of the clergy and the heresies of the world. "Take up the sword," Dionisio challenged. "It is of divine efficacy." His "sword" of truth had seen battle in France with the king, his mother, and "his council with all the princes."[108] Dionisio's hope was that Alfonso II would see combat with this "sword of truth," which the king of France had refused to do. Dionisio noted that though he was weak, he had been fighting for the truth for three years. Since the princes were very powerful, their battle, with the "sword of truth," could accomplish great victories for Christ and his Church.

Dionisio read his letters and also his platform for the reform of the Church in the presence of the duke and his uncle in the ducal palace of Ferrara. After hearing Dionisio's program for reform of the Church, Francesco d'Este advised Dionisio to go to the Catholic king for help. D'Este's advice perhaps stemmed from his knowledge of Philip's interest in a league to fight the heretics. Philip II had been outraged, on religious grounds, by the toleration of Calvinism, which the Edict of Amboise had allowed; he was also fearful, for political reasons, that England might recover Calais, thereby increasing the power of the heretics and threatening Spain's hegemony.[109] At the conclusion of the Council of Trent on December 4, 1563, Philip's representatives had intimated to King Charles IX that he would assist the young sovereign in stamping out heresy in his kingdom. When the cardinal of Lorraine had proposed on the floor of the council the formation of a league to be known as "The Brotherhood of Catholics in France," he had already made overtures to Philip II, who responded cordially but with no definite commitments.[110] However, after the English seized Le Havre-de-Grâce, Philip II was more resolute and placed money and troops at the disposal of the dukes of Guise.

As early as 1562 provincial leagues began to form in France to combat the rise of heresy. Blaise de Montluc was instrumental in forming provincial leagues in Agen and later in Toulouse. The Guises had more far-reaching designs; they informed Montluc that a league was in process of formation "wherein were several great persons, princes and others."[111] Although Montluc had been asked to join the group, he was cautious on several counts. Catherine de' Medici, fearing the consequences of a league that perpetuated, at least in part, the feud between the houses of Guise and Montmorency, asked Montluc for advice. Montluc responded that the league, though intended to ensure the peace and security of the kingdom, could, since formed in private, have the opposite effect. However, princes and others should become part of a league of the king and "take a great and solemn oath not to decline or swerve from it upon penalty of being declared such as the oath should import."[112] Montluc's advice prevailed, and all agreed that "all the Princes, great Lords, Governors of Provinces, and Captains of Gens d'armes should renounce all Leagues and Confederacies whatsoever, without as within the Kingdom, excepting that of the King, and should take the oath upon pain of being declared rebels to the crown." In spite of this proclamation and Montluc's support of it, Montluc, angered over what he considered personal affronts by the queen mother, urged Philip II to intervene in France. He proposed the formation of a league "between the Pope, the Emperor, the Spanish King, and the leading Catholic princes of Germany and Italy to avert a union of Huguenots with outside Protestant princes for the overthrow of the Catholic religion in France." The plan was to kidnap Jeanne d'Albret, who was to be handed over to the Inquisition, and to seize possession of Béarn. Philip's participation would accomplish for him the destruction of the "hearth of Calvinism" in France and the advancement of Spanish power north of the Pyrenees. The plan was thwarted when the French ambassador in Madrid learned of the plot and informed Catherine de' Medici, who took quick action. Upon discovery of the plan, Philip II dissimulated his role and grew reluctant to push the league, at least until a more favorable time.[113] Perhaps Francesco d'Este, the duke's uncle, in advising Dionisio to go to Spain to seek Philip's help, was "testing the waters." At any rate, the talk of a league of Christian princes to remove heresy had been discussed in one form or another since 1560–61 and was a volatile topic.

The league of Italian princes for which Dionisio relentlessly pressed was not unlike many of the associations being formed in France to combat the menace of heresy. Nor was it dissimilar from the league that Philip II had previously joined upon the urging of Montluc. In *Haec est causa*, Dionisio addressed the Italian princes and, for the first time, the Catholic king Philip II and also the emperor. These additions represent the composition of the league Philip II had joined, with the exception of the Catholic princes of Germany, whom Dionisio did not include. The inclusion of the Catholic king and the emperor resulted from the counsel of Francesco d'Este, in all likelihood, since Dionisio clearly stated that his *Haec est causa* was written in Ferrara, where subsequently he read the document in "ipsa noua dicendi forma more velut oratorio."[114] Dionisio also indicated that the cause of Christ was "most worthy of examination by the emperor and the Catholic king, two of the bravest and most excellent defenders of the Church Militant." Since Dionisio had not included the Catholic king or the emperor in any of his writings before coming to Ferrara, this acknowledgment reveals perhaps more about the loyalties of the family d'Este than about those of Dionisio. The brother of Francesco d'Este was Cardinal Ippolito II d'Este, who was sent as papal nuncio in 1561 to urge the French crown to revoke the actions that had alienated the revenues of Church property and to refuse any change in religion or religious observance.[115] The brother of Alfonso II was Cardinal Luigi d'Este. Although the family d'Este had a long history of loyalty to the papacy and numerous connections to France, they were obviously willing to listen to Dionisio, who was convinced that he, as God's messenger, had the solution to the religious crisis of the Church. Dionisio's proposal for a Catholic league that would reform the church as its chief goal was not a new idea, as I have shown; the originality of Dionisio's call for a league of princes resided in the leadership of a prophet instead of a prince or the pope and in the platform of reform that Dionisio called his legation.

To the advice of Francesco d'Este that he visit the Catholic king, Dionisio replied that he had never withdrawn from fighting the enemies of the faith, nor did he refuse to go to the king of Spain. However, he wanted time to consider the plan and also to make a trip to Rome. The marquis de Masse had given not only advice but also letters and reasonable aid. Dionisio felt the need to take up arms if the "sword of truth" did not prevail, and the duke and his uncle evidently agreed with him. Alfonso II and Emanuele Filiberto had already pressured Catherine to take action against the Huguenots, and Emanuele Filiberto had long dreamed of leading a league of princes to route the Huguenots. Each prince, however, seemed reluctant to take the initiative and continued to wait until someone else made the first move toward a functioning league.[116] The pope's nuncio, on various occasions in 1566–68, and the pope himself had encouraged organization of a league of Italian princes to fight heresy. Cosimo I appeared to favor such a league, perhaps to please the pope and help his pursuit of the title of grand duke of Tuscany. The Venetians, less willing to be involved in such a league, believed the wiser course to be for each prince to resist the enemies of the Church. The Venetians sagely counseled the papal nuncio that if such a league were declared in writing and if the heretics should discover its existence, which they probably would, they would arouse their own kind and disturb those who wanted peace and quiet. In addition, the need for a league of princes would cause "a great fear that would serve no other purpose than to make the faithful fearful and to increase the boldness of the unfaithful, who would be encouraged in that which now they judge to be impossible."[117]

Dionisio's mission in Ferrara was to enlist support for a league to reform the Church. In the *Haec est causa*, which was read in Ferrara to Alfonso and the marquis de Masse, Dionisio again recounted his divine anointment by the Virgin and her charges to him. The duke of Ferrara, like Cosimo I, obviously accepted Dionisio's prophetic persona, since our prophet did not hesitate to describe the mockery hurled against him in France, nor did he soften his warning of disaster to the French throne in spite of Alfonso's close ties with France.[118] In his *Legatio* dedicated to the dukes of Florence, Ferrara, Venice, Savoy, and Mantua and written in French, Dionisio also made abundantly clear his prophetic voice, which he believed to be sanctioned by God: "I am the Lamb under Christ, as if slain; I am the voice of many waters to teach the wicked so that the impious be converted; I, conceived in sin, made like to those descending into the lake, born in the city of Gisors, touched by heaven, called, anointed, and sent, in the state of Lisieux, promised by the prophets in these last days and prophesied by the divine Bridget."[119]

These same claims were made in another *Legatio*, directed especially to Cosimo I de' Medici.[120] The *Legatio* read to Duke Alfonso and the marquis de Masse has two additional documents appended: one entitled *Proces clos de la cause de Dieu pour les droictz de Jesuschrist en son egglise militante* . . . , the other entitled *Premyer auditeur des hommes de ceste cause en ce stille ainsy que premyerement l'auyons escripte a este, monseigneur le Marquis de Masse oncle de monseigneur le Duc de Ferrare du quel l'aduis et iugement ensuyt.*[121] On the first of these appendixes Dionisio also included the names of the emperor and the Catholic king. In the general introduction to this *Legatio* Dionisio also praised the duke of Mantua, although there is no indication that he had visited the duke or had any communication with him.

Although in the *Legatio* Dionisio had intensified his prophetic persona by applying countless epithets to himself, in the *Proces* he described himself as "l'ung petit corps de trespetites forces, presqu'ainsi comme vng fol, entre les aultres hommes." The *Proces* was directed especially to the duke of Ferrara and his uncle. Throughout Dionisio contrasted the wealth of the cardinals with their true responsibility to serve the poor; he also noted that the pomp of the pope and the papal court contrasted with the humility necessary for a vicar of Christ.[122] The cries of the poor in their grief should challenge the pope and his court to serve Christ as His true servants. Dionisio was dismayed at the disorder within the papal court, within the papal palace, and even up to the doors of Saint Peter's Basilica. Dionisio admitted that he had irritated and angered some members of the ecclesiastical hierarchy with his constant challenge that they practice the charity of Christ. Although he defended the right of the pope to be head of the Church, the pope must be a true representative of Christ. Dionisio explained that his criticisms stemmed from his eyewitness view of the travails of Christianity. The plight of the poor, whom he called "the members of Christ," was uppermost in Dionisio's mind, and his own suffering had made him especially compassionate for those in need. He repeated his encounter with Pius V in Saint Peter's, where Dionisio said that he looked into the pope's face as he warned him to convoke the princes in order to reform the clergy, remove heresies, and console the poor, as was his obligation. Dionisio spoke to the pope in Latin, and the pontiff nodded in agreement when Dionisio said that the poor must be comforted. No papal reaction was indicated regarding the other points.

In the documents Dionisio directed to the duke of Ferrara and the marquis de Masse, our prophet used his success with Cosimo I to encourage the Estensi to become partners with the duke and the prince of Florence in the enterprise of renewing Christianity. Dionisio argued that he had performed his obligation as God's messenger, and he in turn challenged Alfonso II and the marquis de Masse to give more than tacit approval. With all his rhetorical skills, Dionisio chided and cajoled his hosts in Ferrara. In spite of his single-minded zeal, he nevertheless realized that to effect a plan of action, he needed support from more Italian princes than those five whose support he claimed—that is, the duke of Florence, his son the prince of Florence, the duke of Savoy, the duke of Ferrara, and the marquis de Masse. Dionisio's objective was to force the duke of Ferrara to become the catalyst for action among the princes who seemed to approve his program but were unwilling to take the initiative. The Italians should join with the emperor and with the Catholic king in a league capable of accomplishing its purpose. Was the purpose to resist the Turkish advance? Only in part, according to Dionisio. The principal goal was to reform the clergy. One can easily ascertain the difference between the priorities of the pope and those of Dionisio.[123]

Our prophet did not hesitate to describe the king of France and his Royal Council as enemies of the truth. He also recounted his challenge to the king and his council at Gaîllon and later at Mont Marsan. After his strong words to King Charles IX about the absolute necessity of uniting his realm before his kingdom and his throne were destroyed, Dionisio had lost favor at court. He apparently had no fear of losing the patronage of the marquis de Masse and the duke of Ferrara, since to them he made his most forceful claims about his own divinely given role. He stated emphatically that he was, "under Christ, the king of the clergy, the supreme pontiff, and sovereign shepherd of all the Church Militant."[124] Because of his double anointment and his titles, Dionisio told the princes of Ferrara that they owed him aid.

Dionisio seemed to be following the example of Jeremiah, who had made a habit of prophesying before kings, priests, prophets, and elders. In fact, in the prophetic literature of the Old Testament the prophet, receiving God's commands, went to the rulers and urged them to repent. He predicted destruction of cities and countries if the rulers did not heed him. In like manner Dionisio had gone to the king of France to prophesy. Rejected especially by the King's Council, Dionisio came as prophet to the princes of Italy. He reiterated certain aspects of his anointment by the Virgin, who had announced great marvels to him, a new heaven and a new earth. The certainty Dionisio had about this heavenly apparition made him less than circumspect in his relationships in Ferrara and elsewhere. He seemed amazed, as others surely were, that Christ had chosen him, a simple man in great poverty, a little man, as if a fool among other men.[125] These characteristics described by Dionisio did not diminish his certainty about his role, however.

As if to illuminate his specific tasks, Dionisio, in a long discourse, claimed that he carried the scepter of Christ in the world and upheld the rights of Christ because "He is with me, and I am with Him, incorporated together, united by will."[126] Because of his role as God's servant and messenger and because of his oneness with Christ, Dionisio saw himself as ancillary to the Trinity.[127] Was Dionisio expanding the Trinity into a quaternity? Someone who read the *Proces* obviously thought so, since an annotation at the bottom of the page on which Dionisio had described his relationship with the Trinity reads as follows: "Dice di sopra che lui è incorporato e unito per uolonta co'il Padre, figliolo e spirito santo e che lui è la quarta persona in diuinis."[128] The author of this interpretation was suggesting that Dionisio claimed to be a fourth person alongside the three divine essences, thereby claiming divinity of a sort. Dionisio's words, taken out of the Pauline context in which he was writing, could be viewed as heretical or insane. Our prophet had said in other documents that he was not of the same substance as Christ but that he shared in the graces of Christ because Christ lived in him, and that he followed the precepts of Christ. Dionisio's words about being united with Christ through the will closely resemble the language of Saint Paul. Dionisio took seriously the Pauline precept that "Christ is all things and in all things."[129] The unknown writer of the brief commentary did not see Dionisio's remarks in this light. We cannot ascertain who wrote this comment or others that appear throughout the *Proces*, although it is certain that all comments were written by one hand. One could suggest that a member of the Inquisition, perhaps the papal nuncio or his secretary, had written the comments after Dionisio's writings had been seized from his person while he was speaking in San Marco or from the house of his host, Rocho de Mazzochis. In whatever way Dionisio's words were interpreted by others, it is clear that he believed himself to be God's servant and messenger, an angelic pope for the sixteenth century, as it were, with both religious and political prerogatives.

Comments and interpretations of a different sort were recorded by Dionisio in a second appendix to the letters and articles read in Ferrara.

He recounted the responses of the marquis de Masse to some of his principal points. The marquis agreed that it was necessary to defend the cause of God and the rights of Christ, and he believed without doubt that God would gain His cause. In regard to the rights Dionisio had asked of the princes, the marquis said that it was difficult to believe all the claims could be true. He seemed to believe them, however, and agreed that Dionisio should receive help from the princes. He sagely concluded that the holy doctors "and the Holy Spirit must be entreated for assistance." In regard to the most significant point, about the validity of Dionisio's title as ambassador of God, the marquis de Masse said that "he believed all that was a work of God and that God had chosen us to accomplish this task."[130]

The statements of Francesco d'Este, uncle of the duke of Ferrara, provided the most overt acceptance Dionisio had received for his utopian dream of the Church Militant, truly reflective of the teachings of Christ. Dionisio acknowledged that these conclusions of the marquis de Masse had been read on Monday, May 20, 1566, in the palace of the marquis in Ferrara, in the presence of many noblemen. He did not specifically indicate that Duke Alfonso II had been present when the marquis's comments were read, although the duke had been in attendance when Dionisio read his *Legatio*. Dionisio made abundantly clear that his support was derived from the marquis de Masse. The public reading of the comments of the duke's uncle was perhaps Dionisio's attempt to encourage the duke to give him open approval.

In the letters directed to the duke of Ferrara and Francesco d'Este, Dionisio wrote in the ornate style of a rhetorician.[131] In fact, all of Dionisio's writings to princes were composed in the same elegant style. In the *Proces*, however, Dionisio acknowledged that he had modified his style, in the form of a trial, in order to avoid difficulties. His new style was only slightly more abbreviated than his customary, ornate style. Dionisio's use of language would certainly have been admired by the princes he addressed, especially Cosimo I and Alfonso II.[132] His gifts of style were considerable, and he made the most of his linguistic abilities in order to persuade the princes to his cause.

The depth of Alfonso's commitment to Dionisio's proposals about Church reform remains in the shadows. His marriage to Barbara of Austria in 1565 had been the occasion for many literary and artistic fests. In 1566–67 Alfonso II was very concerned over the problem of succession, since he remained childless, and Pope Pius V on May 23, 1567, published the bull *Prohibitio alienandi et infeudandi civitates et loca Sanctae Romanae Ecclesiae*, which forbade the investiture of illegitimate sons to the fiefs of the Church. Although Dionisio indicated that Alfonso II had approved his remarks, the duke in

1566 was involved in matters that seemed far more pressing to him and his political ambitions. Dionisio remained in Ferrara for six weeks and then made his way to Venice. The fact that the Venetian Inquisition sent him on a boat in the direction of Ferrara at the conclusion of his imprisonment in Venice would lead one to believe that Dionisio had found enough favor in Ferrara to support his return there sometime after August 12, 1567.

· IV ·
VENICE, PROPHETIC REFORM, AND DIONISIO GALLO

n a day in late spring or early summer of 1566 Dionisio Gallo arrived in Venice. Having had modest success in Florence and Ferrara, he made his way to Venice, the culmination of his long prophetic journey. Venice seemed the logical place for Dionisio to go, given his belief in his own prophetic persona. In fact, all of his previous visits with Italian princes were preparatory to his Venetian experience. The so-called myth of Venice, or rather the *leggenda* connected with Venice's prophetic origin, was widely circulated in the Cinquecento and was obviously well known to our learned Frenchman.[1] What is not so obvious is why Dionisio believed that Venice would be the appropriate place to culminate his prophetic preaching and why he believed that the city would be receptive to his summons for reform of the Church and society.

Prophecy had been associated with Venice from its early history, as the ancient chronicles demonstrate.[2] The cult of saints and prophets of the Old Testament flourished in Venice, as in Greece, quite unlike other parts of Italy, or Europe, for that matter, with the exception of Ireland.[3] Churches in Venice were dedicated to Old Testament saints—namely, Moses, Samuel, David, Job, and Simeon—as well as Old Testament prophets—for example, Habakkuk, Daniel, Elisha, Ezekiel, Jeremiah, Jonah, Isaiah, Samuel, Simeon, and Zechariah.[4] All these prophets were called saints, and most saints of the Old Testament were prophets. They were represented in the mosaics of the Basilica di San Marco and also in the ceilings of the Churches of Santa Maria della Visitazione and of Santa Maria dei Miracoli.

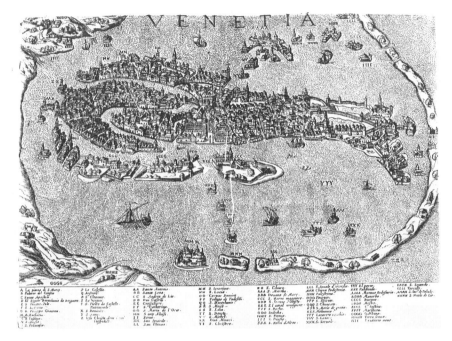

fig. 6
Venice in the sixteenth century. Biblioteca nazionale di San Marco, Venice

There were also many prophetic preachers in Venice in the early days of the sixteenth century, especially at the Churches of the Carmini, Santi Apostoli, and San Mattio di Rialto, where they often delivered sermons about "the last days." Fra Bonaventura dedicated his book of prophecies to the Senate of Venice, although he believed that the king of France would lead the Church in a grand reformation. Delio Cantimori argues that the book was dedicated to the Senate of Venice because Venice had accepted the friendship of France after the treachery of the League of Cambrai. Bonaventura was imprisoned in Rome in 1516 because he was preaching the advent of the angelic pope "announced by the prophets and elected by God" to be the savior of the world and of the *universae humanitatis*. Bonaventura believed that the reform of the Church would come not from the pope but from the political realm, since "rex Franciae sit a Deo minister electus pro translatione ecclesiae Dei in Syon."[5]

Silvana Seidel-Menchi has amply demonstrated that numerous preachers in Italy were conveying Erasmian ideals in their sermons. Of particular interest is a Franciscan conventual, Sebastian Castello, who had preached in Venice at Santi Apostoli, during Lent in 1551, on the beginnings of the universal apostolate. Noble Venetians heard the preaching of Fra Sebastian, and some gave testimony to the inquisitor concerning his sermons.[6] Other preachers were accused of saying that God spoke through them to confound the Serenissima, the ecclesiastical laws, and the apostolic faith. These same preachers had also been accused of receiving pay "from one who is in the government of the most Christian king of France."[7] Francesco Scudieri Cremonese, a brother of the Canonici Regolari who had taken holy orders and had begun preaching in Venice, said that the true Church was the union of the faithful and that the pope was the Antichrist predicted in medieval and early Renaissance prophecies.[8] When Scudieri was called before the Inquisition of Venice, he was accused of having in his house the *Doctrina* of David Joris, a leader of the Dutch Anabaptists, a friend of Hendrik Niclaes (head of the Family of Love), and a proponent of the teachings of Guillaume Postel.[9] He was also accused of believing the Talmud, the Koran, and the rabbis.[10] According to Scudieri's own statements in 1569 about his former opinions, which he now recanted, his belief that the pope and the bishops were never superior to the civil magistrates but were subject to them would surely have caught the attention of the Venetian Inquisition.

Ottavia Niccoli has demonstrated that prophetic preachers were common in all parts of Italy in the fourteenth century and in the first part of the fifteenth, and Venice was certainly no exception. She has also noted that many tractates predicted disasters resulting from the sins of the clergy.[11] The prophetic preaching of the Franciscans and the Dominicans in Venice was significant for the religious life of the city, since the Venetian inquisitor was a Franciscan until 1560, and thereafter was chosen from the Dominicans. Prophetic preachers could also be found in the gardens of Giudecca, where young Venetians often congregated. The number of preachers in Venice in the Cinquecento was vast, so I shall mention only a few points about them that seem especially pertinent to this study.

The preaching of the Jesuits in Venice and their active works of charity at the Incurabili added to the spiritual climate of the city.[12] Ignatius Loyola and Francis Xavier had worked with the infirm at the Hospital of the Incurabili in 1537, before Ignatius received the charter for the Society of Jesus from Pope Paul III in 1540, and the Jesuits had attended the sick there ever since. Ignatius and Xavier wanted to be occupied in the service to the sick, whose care would test their natural repugnance for "quelle schifose e sciagurate creature."[13] The work of the Jesuits at the Incurabili revealed what they believed was the evangelical message of Christ.[14] In their sermons and in their daily lives the Jesuits made clear that right living and loving "were central to the life of every Christian."[15] Guillaume Postel was one of the early Jesuits whose ideas about the restitution of all things apparently were shared by the small group around Loyola in Paris and later in Rome.[16] Although Postel was given license to depart from the Jesuits in Rome in 1545, he always considered himself a Jesuit and a priest. In 1546 he came to Venice and worked at the Ospedaletto of Saints John and Paul, hearing confessions and ministering to the sick; he also said the Mass at the Churches of Santa Maria Formosa and Santa Maria dei Miracoli.[17] The hearing of confessions was a vibrant part of the spiritual work of the Jesuits in Venice.[18] Large numbers of penitents, even Lutherans and Anabaptists, came to confess their sins. Through the confessional the Jesuit confessor was able not only to absolve the sinner but also to guide the penitent into active works of charity and profound reform, as the penitent began his own spiritual exercise guided by a Jesuit confessor.[19]

The Jesuit Postel, a contemporary of Dionisio Gallo, had made Venice the focus of his concepts about the restitution or reformation of the world, calling Venice "la magistratura più perfetta," "Gerusalemme nuova," and "Roma nuova."[20] In spite of his great admiration for Venice, Postel, like Dionisio later, had warned the Venetians that they must reform themselves immediately if Venice was to assume its providential role in divine and human history. Postel wrote a letter to the doge of Venice warning him that Venice was in great danger, since the Devil envied God's love for Venice, which was greater than His love for all other cities except Jerusalem.[21] Postel noted that he had delivered "to the Venetian Senate, through the hands of the doge," a work in which he explained how Venice could convert the Turks and bring about peace in the world.[22] During Postel's trial by the Holy Office in 1555, he wrote to Maffeo Venier, *procuratore sopra la heresia*, explaining his concern for Venice's safety.[23] Postel's warnings about Venice had their origin in the prophecies of a Venetian mystic, a pious woman known as Madre Giovanna, or the Venetian Virgin.

Bernardino Ochino, Pietro Paolo Vergerio, and Guillaume Postel, among many others, expected Venice to lead in the reform of the Church. Dionisio seemed to follow in their direction, especially that of Postel, since Dionisio also expressed lavish praise of Venice and its institutions yet issued warnings similar to Postel's. Dionisio, like others before him, had specific reasons for expecting Venice to live up to its prophetic origin.

In the Quattrocento and in the early part of the Cinquecento, long before Dionisio's arrival in Venice, the reform impulse was not confined to ecclesiastics.[24] In the middle of the Quattrocento, Francesco Barbaro compared the decline of the Church in his day with the holiness of the primitive Church. He also exalted Franciscan poverty.[25] Reform had already made

inroads into Venice, and many, like Bernardino Ochino, hoped
would be the door "through which reformation ideas would en
Others at the end of the Quattrocento looked to Venice for lea
reforming the Church, as Dionisio would do in the Cinquecento.[27]
esting unpublished text written in 1480 contains the prophecy th
is the state that will effect a reform of the Church. Accompanying the text
is a drawing showing a rose in the middle of a quadrangle; the name *Venecia*
pierces the center of the rose, and from the rose hangs a key. The key indicates that Venice, where reform is flowering, holds the key to a renewed and
reformed Church. Fra Laurentius da Monte, the author of the text and the
drawing, gave the following explanation: "The description of the rose in
the middle of the second quadrangle shows through its letters that [the
rose] is Venecia. There is a key in the middle, hanging perpendicular [to the
rose]. The key shows that the ecclesiastical power of the new, or restored,
Church will come into this holy state with many signs and miracles."[28]

Savonarola's preaching in Florence had also quickened the zeal for reform
among many patricians and *popolani* in Venice, but the desire for reform had
to be weighed against political considerations.[29] In Florence, Savonarola's
preaching had obvious political results. The expulsion of the Medici brought
about the restoration of the Florentine republic, yet the Florentines faced
a threatening future. Piero de' Medici had ceded to King Charles VIII of
France strategic towns on the northern border of Tuscany and also the
citadels of Livorno and Pisa, which were Florence's access to the sea. As
Donald Weinstein has noted: "The Tuscan state which had taken the
Florentines over a century of labor to put together had come undone in a
matter of days, and this just when Florence found herself dangerously iso-
lated from powerful neighbors on the north, east, and south who were furi-
ous with her for allying with the French invader."[30]

The Florentine example surely provided occasion for reflection for the
Venetian republic, making its leaders all the more anxious to extend their
control outside its *terraferma* possessions.[31] The Florentines, fearful of the
Venetians' dominance in Italy, continued the anti-Venetian propaganda that
had been formulated by Duke Francesco Sforza of Milan from 1447 onward.
When peace finally came between Milan and Venice in September 1449,
Sforza, through his ambassador to Florence, urged Cosimo de' Medici to
give him financial and diplomatic support "in order to prevent the Venetians
from becoming lords of Milan and of Lombardy." He insisted that it was
"the intention of the Venetians to take possession of Milan . . . and that
once they were lords of Milan, one could say that they were lords of the
whole of Italy."[32]

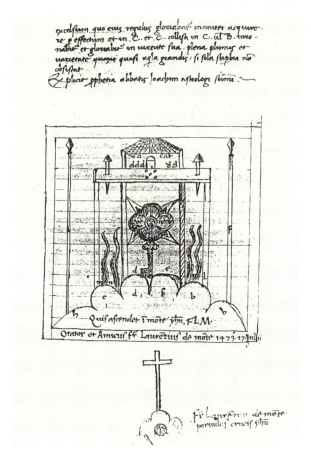

fig. 7
This 1480 drawing depicts Venice as a rose above a key. For many, Venice was the key to church reform. Biblioteca nazionale di San Marco, Venice

The anti-Venetian propaganda of the Quattrocento was again to erupt with the formation of the League of Cambrai; consequences for Venice soon followed. The war also evoked self-criticism. Moral corruption, according to the opinion of many *popolani* and *patrizi* alike, was the chief reason for the decline of Venice's power. The humiliations Venice suffered as a result of the League of Cambrai resulted from God's will to chasten His people.33 Doge Loredan (1501–21) regularly criticized the immorality of the Venetians and their desire for luxuries and urged greater piety among all the citizens. In the summer of 1509, after all the Venetian possessions on the *terraferma* except Treviso had been lost, Girolamo Priuli reflected about the causes for Venice's sudden fall. Priuli, as well as Marino Sanudo and others, were confident that the change in Venice's fortune resulted from the will of God.34 Instead of fulfilling the responsibilities toward their most

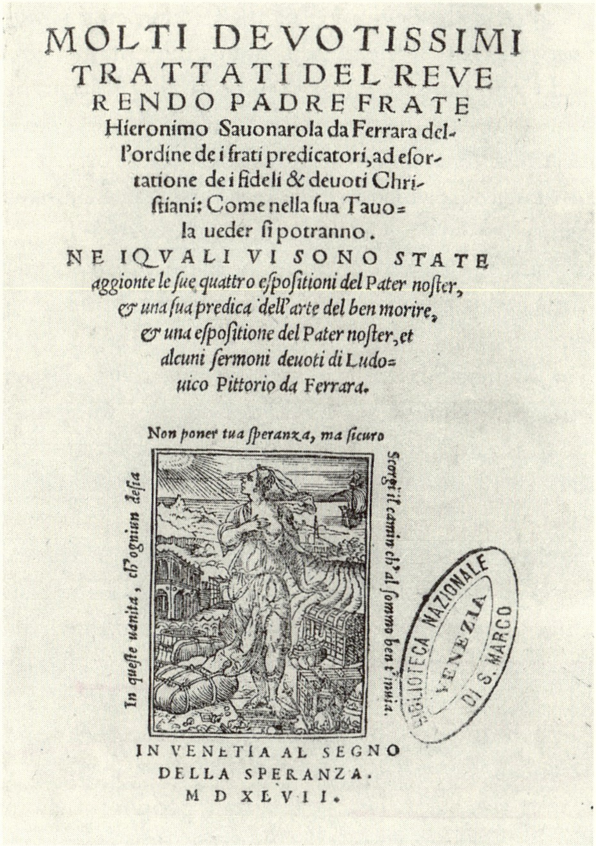
MOLTI DEVOTISSIMI TRATTATI DEL REVE RENDO PADRE FRATE Hieronimo Sauonarola da Ferrara del-l'ordine de i frati predicatori, ad esor-tatione de i fideli & deuoti Chri-stiani: Come nella sua Tauo-la ueder si potranno.

NE IQVALI VI SONO STATE *aggionte le sue quattro espositioni del Pater noster, & una sua predica dell'arte del ben morire, & una espositione del Pater noster, et alcuni sermoni deuoti di Ludo-uico Pittorio da Ferrara.*

Non poner tua speranza, ma sicuro
Scorgi il camin ch'al sommo ben t'inuia.
In queste uanita, ch'ogniun desia

BIBLIOTECA NAZIONALE VENEZIA DI S. MARCO

IN VENETIA AL SEGNO DELLA SPERANZA. M D XLVII.

fig. 8
Savonarola's influence was felt in Venice as well as Tuscany. This title page is from a compilation of works by Savonarola published in Venice in 1547. Biblioteca nazionale di San Marco, Venice

serene republic, founded under the divine protection of God, Saint Mark, and Saint Peter, the Venetians had forsaken their God-given duties of governing well and justly. Poor governance was symptomatic of moral corruption, according to Priuli. Homosexuality was openly practiced; many nuns broke their vows; many noblewomen were eager for luxuries and frivolities.[35] Some of Priuli's criticisms can also be found in the diaries of Marino Sanudo. Priuli, however, had a political ax to grind, since he regarded Venice's expansion on the *terraferma* a mistake. He believed that Venice's greatness had developed from its possessions overseas and from its trade routes. In effect, Venice had risen from the sea and had become powerful and great because of the sea. The life of Venice as a maritime republic was difficult and demanding.[36] Priuli argued that the expansion on the *terraferma* provided a "softer," easier life for the Venetians.[37]

Priuli's assessment of Venice at the beginning of the Cinquecento is significant, but one cannot assume that all the nobility were guilty of the vices Priuli described.[38] Nor did Priuli himself mean to indicate this. Rather, he intended his remarks to be a warning to the guilty. Priuli wanted to challenge Venice to reassume the role of maintaining God's *ecclesia* on earth. Because of the dire circumstances in which Venice found itself and perhaps because of Priuli's criticisms, legislation against luxury was effected. In 1512 the Senate decreed that it was necessary to "placate the anger of our Lord" and to establish a magistracy whose duty would be to prevent "immoderate and excessive expenditure."[39] The three *provveditori sopra le pompe* issued a decree against all types of luxury. Sumptuary laws were passed to lessen expenditure and to discourage lasciviousness. In addition to the laws against luxury, efforts were made to regain God's favor. The doge asked the patriarch to arrange for prayers in all churches "so that God would assist this republic against its enemies."[40]

As Felix Gilbert has pointed out, the patricians often demonstrated contradictory feelings, love of Venice and loyalty to it as well as self-interest. Gilbert writes that we cannot doubt, however, Priuli's contention that "the great mass of the people 'loved the republic and [were] devoted to it' and [were] convinced that 'the freedom of Italy depended on the defense of Venice.'"[41] They felt they had upheld Christianity against the Turks and that, even if their present enemies were Christians, they were again fighting to defend civilization against the barbarians.[42] The only people to whom the Venetians could compare themselves were the Romans, as is evident in the words of Hieronimo Borgia, who noted that "the true Romans did not demonstrate greater bravery against Hannibal than the Venetians did against their enemies."[43]

Among the ruling class it was often difficult to distinguish moral obligation from personal interests, as Gaetano Cozzi has noted.[44] During the crisis of the League of Cambrai and the years immediately following, however, the Senate, with the recovery of Verona, repealed the laws that had allowed irregularities in election to the magistracies upon payment of loans to the republic.[45] The new decree, ratified on January 16, 1517, proclaimed that no more money would be received for the purpose of election. Marino Sanudo commented upon this happy circumstance: "Verona being recovered by divine favour, and the fortunes of our state being in the condition well known to this council, it is proper to give notice to all, that if certain offerings of money in the form of gifts or loans have been accepted for offices and posts, it was done out of necessity and contrary to our ancient customs and out of the most ardent desire for the restoration of our state."[46]

The peace that finally came in 1517 brought a renewal of intellectual life, to which the reopening of the *studio* of Padua in October 1517 bore witness.[47] In 1521 a chair of philosophy was established in Venice, and humanistic studies and the arts flourished.[48] Gino Benzoni states that in Venice the Renaissance had its own prolonged gilded autumn.[49] In addition, the revival of religious fervor was encouraged in an effort to return Venice to the favor of God and to its divinely appointed role.[50] Patricians such as Gasparo Contarini saw the need for reform before the shadow of heresy should weaken both Church and state.[51] Felix Gilbert has pointed out that Contarini "had become deeply convinced that all secular activities had to be placed in a Christian framework and that social life had to be ordered in such a way that man would be ready to receive what only God could give—the salvation of man's soul."[52]

Gasparo Contarini, in his *De officio episcopi*, warned the princes of the Church against luxury, against absence from their bishoprics, and against superstitions.[53] He urged a concern for the moral and spiritual well-being of the bishop's flock. Contarini's call for Church reform is similar to that of his Venetian friends Tomaso Giustiniani and Vincenzo Querini, the Camaldolese monks who wrote the *Libellus ad Leonem x*, which has been called "the most comprehensive and most radical of all reform programs since the conciliar period."[54] As already noted, Contarini, after he was appointed cardinal by Pope Paul III in 1553, was named to the commission that would produce a project for reform of the Church, the *Consilium de emendanda ecclesia*, in 1537. Elisabeth Gleason has pointed out that Contarini, one year after his appointment, was definitely perceived as a champion of reform among the cardinals.[55]

In the *De magistratibus et republica venetorum* Contarini wanted to demonstrate how the proper social order could help man in his spiritual ascent. "No state has existed which possesses institutions and laws equally apt to lead to a good and blissful life," wrote Contarini.[56] In this work Contarini, nevertheless, relates Venice's need for a return to its ancient piety to the Church's need for a return to its spiritual origin. Contarini's emphasis upon Venice's ancient piety reminds one of the work of Contarini's friend Giambattista Egnazio, specifically his *Nove libri de gli essempi de gli illvstri Vinitiani e altri stranieri* . . . , a chronicle of Venetian history organized around the theme of virtues and vices.[57] Egnazio, a humanist and friend not only of Contarini but also of Marino Sanudo, states in the preface of his work that all who have followed the rule of the elders to *ben vivere* through the practice of simple purity have understood that a life of wisdom depends upon poverty, scorn of human things, and religion.[58] He then discusses the religion of the Venetians and their origins. In the margin of the manuscript I consulted, which is an Italian translation of the printed Latin text, rendered by Dom Leonardo Cemoti, Venetian, canon of S. Salvador, the author or the translator notes: "the reason why God prefers Venice to all other cities," "how Venice is different from other cities," "the origin of Venice."[59] There is also an interesting citation from Plato, which states that "no city can be established with prosperity or governed with happiness without the help of God."[60] Egnazio then illustrates the ancient piety and religiosity of the Venetians and God's continual care for His Own. Divine providence has bestowed upon Venice many miracles but also natural disasters. Even the disasters, however, which could have destroyed Venice, indicated God's love of Venice.[61] For example, fires that destroyed countless houses and churches caused the Venetians to rebuild in stone; thereafter, the city became the wonder of the world.[62] A terrible earthquake and pestilence had warned the Venetians that Doge Marino Falier was trying to suppress liberty and establish a tyranny.[63]

Egnazio also stresses the natural order of the universe, exemplified by the Law of Moses and the coming of Christ, which he claims the Venetians have respected and followed since their origin.[64] In the first two books he uses many examples to illustrate the stability of Venetian institutions; in book three, however, he discusses the beginnings of virtues and of vices. Among the virtues, he names fortitude (*fortezza*), patience (*patienza*), moderation of soul (*moderatezza all'animo*), poverty (*povertà*), shame (*vergogna*), scorn of human things (*disprezzo*), which he describes as a most happy passage from poverty, generosity (*liberalità*), humanity (*humanità*), piety (*pietà*), modesty (*pudicitia*), justice (*giustitia*), and happiness (*felicità*). Egnazio identifies these as the virtues that have made Venice great in the past and that are essential for its present and future success. The virtues he chooses to illustrate combine Graeco-Roman and Christian virtues, many of which are especially representative of Franciscan Christianity, with its the emphasis upon evangelical poverty.[65]

Egnazio's book, a humanist work illustrating pagan as well as Christian virtues, can also be recognized as a prophetic *cronaca*. The author noted Venice's prophetic origin but also issued a prophetic warning to the Venetians to refrain from the vices that were the opposite of their ancient virtues. Stability of Venetian institutions and religion must be maintained because the continuity of Venice reflected Venice's continuous covenant with God.[66] Lest any Venetian nobleman think of upsetting this stability, he reminded his readers, while discussing the virtue of patience, that the impatient Baiamonte Tiepolo was called a second Catiline.[67] By using many examples of noble poverty, Egnazio was implicitly warning the Venetians about the consequences of the love of money. He made this warning explicit in the ninth book, where he wrote of the vice of *lussuria,* which easily followed love of money.[68] He chided the Venetians for their new desire of pleasure and praised their ancient temperance.[69] Egnazio's work, published in Venice in 1554, served not only as a glorification of Venice but also as a warning that the Venetians of the Cinquecento must purify all aspects of society, secular and religious.

The influence of Joachim of Fiore and his prophetic admonitions for reform of the Church was especially strong in Venice in the Quattrocento and also in the Cinquecento.[70] As I have already indicated, the tradition according to which Joachim designed the mosaics of the Basilica di San Marco was part of the mentality of Venetians and non-Venetians alike. The learned Guillaume Postel wrote about Joachim's role in the design of the mosaics.[71] The tradition maintained that Joachim had had a small room in the upper section of the basilica while he worked on his designs. His prophecies were known not only from his designs in the basilica but also from beautiful editions of his works that were published in Venice in 1516–17, and especially from his commentary on the Apocalypse, published in 1527. Both works seemed to have a special meaning for Venice in the early days of the sixteenth century. In Joachim's *De magnis tribulationibus et statu Sancte matris Ecclesie* one finds great expectations of an angelic pope, chosen by God for his sanctity.[72] Some of the prophecies for the Venetians would have made a great impression in Venice in 1517, after the cessation of hostilities resulting from the League of Cambrai. Joachim wrote that the patriarch of the Venetians would warn his flock and that the Venetians would be reformed from their iniquities.[73] In fact, Joachim noted that the reform would continue until the day of judgment, so much so that "not such good men among all nations of Christians will be found, as Merlin says in his own revelations."[74] The race of "good sailors" who inhabit the "great island of the sea will distinguish themselves by the purity of their lives more than all men of the world, and their 'prince' will be holy. This holy 'prince,' or doge, because of his merits, will receive great gifts from God for his people."[75]

Joachim's favorable prophecies about the Venetians were surely welcomed in the Serenissima, since they predicted that a Venetian commander would be chosen to lead the ships in victory against the infidel. Venice's future successes would be the result of her great reformation, according to Joachim.[76] The concept of the Antichrist was also dominant in Joachim's prophecies; he foretold that before the son of perdition should arrive, a certain man, chosen by God, would come forth in Italy, although he would not be an

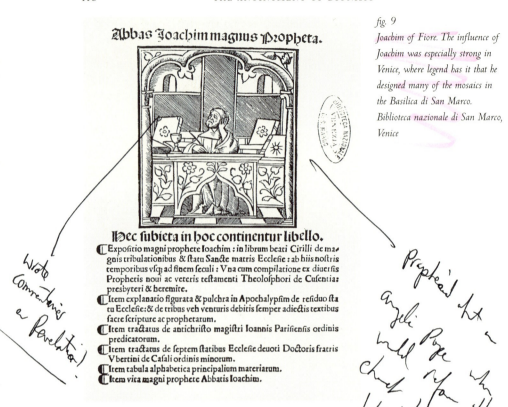

fig. 9
Joachim of Fiore. The influence of Joachim was especially strong in Venice, where legend has it that he designed many of the mosaics in the Basilica di San Marco. Biblioteca nazionale di San Marco, Venice

Italian, and would help to free Italy from her servitude to Lombardy.77 These fascinating prophecies were widely read, especially in Venice. Their recurring theme was the reform and restoration of the Church to the pristine state of its origin through the effort of an angelic pope. The idea of a reformed Church was a pressing one in the sixteenth century, and the need for pure leadership by an angelic pope was greatly desired and expected. The long-awaited shepherd would preside over the Eastern and Western churches, and the faith of each would flourish. Joachim thus described the angelic pope: "The virtue of this kind shepherd will be so great that he will bend down the ridges of the mountains as if having nothing and possessing all things. This holy man will lay low the haughty horns of the religious, and all will return to the state of the primitive Church; thus there is one shepherd, one law, one lord true and humble, fearing God."78 Numerous woodcuts illustrate this work, and the millenarian expectations of the age are everywhere apparent, since the Apocalypse was the basis of many prophecies throughout the text.

fig. 10
In Joachim's prophecies, an angelic pope will restore the Church to its pristine state, and the doge will lead in the reformation. From a printed edition of De magnis tribulationibus et statu ecclesie. *Biblioteca nazionale di San Marco, Venice*

The *Tractactus de antichristo* of John of Paris, in which the so-called Mestre prophecy appears, follows the prophecies of Joachim in the *De magnis tribulationibus;* also included are various prophecies of Ubertino da Casale.[79] The Mestre prophecy is filled with political overtones about France and Germany and also the need to reform the Church. The fact that this often-repeated prophecy was found in Venetian Mestre enhanced the prophetic aura of Venice. Venice, as a pious, free, and prophetic city, was a symbol for those searching for a guide to the complexities of life in the sixteenth century. In addition, Joachim's commentary on the Apocalypse, published in 1527, provided prophetic inspiration for interpreting the mosaics of the Basilica di San Marco and for comprehending pure Christianity in its simplest forms, expressed in the most suggestive metaphoric language. For example, in Joachim's commentary on the first books of the Apocalypse, he wrote about names and the name by which man is known in the book of life. Then he noted: "No one ought to be believed to have a name with God because he is called Christian but because he is innocent, fearful, and just."[80]

The concept of a moralizing religion is clearly expressed in the explanation of the word's being written in the heart rather than on tablets of stone, since the word written in the heart is written "by the spirit of the living God." Words of God that are written in the heart are not formed with letters but with the knowledge of the spirit of the living God that has been granted to us. God gives to each just man, according to Joachim's exegesis, a gift of his own name "so that he is known from the name, as was Moses, to whom God said: 'I have known you from your name.'"[81] The gift that defines the just man is the gift of charity. Joachim wrote: "The common gift that is the charity of God develops a common name in the universe of the just so that they are called citizens of Jerusalem."[82] Venice was well known for its charity and charitable institutions, which were abundant in the city.[83] The prophetic city of Saint Mark defined itself by works of charity, which showed the city's love of God. Perhaps for this reason in the Cinquecento Venice became known as the *Jerusalemme nuova*.[84]

The concept of Venice as the new Jerusalem would have had great appeal for our prophet, Dionisio Gallo, since Venice as the new Jerusalem would confirm his own belief, and it would seem to have been confirmed by others. The numerous editions of Joachim published in Venice in the Cinquecento would seem to indicate that the Serenissima was prepared for Dionisio's prophetic platform. More than twenty years after the publication of Joachim's commentary on the Apocalypse, Anton Francesco Doni published in Venice a commentary on the Apocalypse in which he demonstrated that the book had secrets and that one should read the mysteries in chapter thirteen according to number.[85] He revealed a complicated scheme in which he calculated the name of Martin Luther to be equal to the number of the beast, that is, 666.[86]

The prophetic voice was heard in Venice from many quarters. In 1516 Laçarus de Soardis published the *Cronica breuis ab initio ordinis vsque ad presens tempus . . .* , which details the founding of the Dominican Order and describes the mysterious anointment of the teacher Reginald by the blessed Virgin Mary. Appearing to him at night while he was very ill, shortly after his entry into the order, the Virgin anointed him, restored his health, and showed him the new habit of his order, which had not changed since the time of Saint Dominic. Abbot Joachim, according to the *Cronica*, greatly impressed with his divine anointment and manifestation, told the story in paint in a monastery in Calabria and in the mosaics in the Church of San Marco in Venice.[87] He also said to his brothers: "Quickly there will rise up a new order of teachers; one greater will be in charge of this order, and with him and under him there will be twelve who will direct the order. And just as Jacob the patriarch with his twelve sons entered Egypt, so he with those twelve in that order will go forward after him and will illuminate the world."[88] So great was the prophetic impulse in sixteenth-century Venice that Marino Sanudo the younger, in his diary entry for May 30, 1509, noted that

> at San Clemente there was a certain brother of the Order of Charity who had been there with a converso for a long time; his name was Piero Nani, our gentleman, ninety years old; and he says many things that treat of prophecies. And I was with him today, and he said many things to me. To a large group of patricians he says: "This land will lose all its dominion because of sins; . . . and the Turk will become Christian, and the Signoria will take back its own state; the king of France will live a few months; and this flagellation will last twelve and a half years, and then in this year there will be hunger and the greatest plague; nevertheless, Venice will remain untouched." And this, he says, is written through the prophecies of which he has grand supply. And he notes the conversation of the pope at present turns often to prophecies, and they go into the Church of San Marco, seeing prophecies in mosaic that Abbot Joachim made.[89]

Two figures in the basilica were especially fascinating because one of them was believed to be the angelic pope. Located opposite the altar of San Giacomo in two arches, the figures, unnamed but designated *sancti*, were avidly studied for their presumed messianic connotations. Under one figure was inscribed the motto *Fiet unum ouile, et unus Pastor*, although the words are no longer visible today.[90] The figure in simple blue garments but with an exceptionally beautiful mystical face would appear to be, in my opinion, the one believed to be the angelic pope. However, the other figure, "clothed *pontificalmente*" and carrying a bishop's staff, was held to be the angelic pope, according to Francesco Sansovino, who was himself influenced by the expectation of the angelic pope and "one sheepfold."[91]

The influence of Joachim and the acceptance in Venice of his authorship of the designs for San Marco can best be substantiated in an action taken by the Procuratoria di San Marco on December 22, 1566, which indicated that no writing or figure in the mosaics could be changed without first taking note "acciò che si possi lavorar e formar quelle istesse opere e profetie le quali si dicono esser state ordinate da San Joachino."[92] The two unnamed saints, therefore, in place in the second quarter of the thirteenth century, were generally considered to be, one or the other, the angelic pope.[93] From the association of the unnamed saints with the angelic pope described by Joachim, "the entire mosaic decoration or at least its plan became the work of the prophet."[94] A *chronica* of the Cinquecento mentioned Joachim specifically as having a role in the plan of the mosaics: "The church was all in mosaic and decorated with many prophecies . . . by the Abbot Joachim, a spiritual man and close to God; this abbot made many designs."[95] The author of the chronicle also spoke of many mysteries and of prophetic signs. The prophetic mosaics with scenes from the Apocalypse in the west vault of the dome were executed around 1570, according to Otto Demus, but they must have been planned in conjunction with the mosaics of the *pozzo* in the fourth decade of the sixteenth century.[96]

The prophetic voices in Venice in the sixteenth century were sounding "the trumpet" for the reform of the Church. The many contributions of Francesco Zorzi to the spiritual and intellectual life of Venice have been carefully documented. Cesare Vasoli, in his *Profezia e ragione*, discusses in detail the contributions of the Venetian Fra Francesco Zorzi to the "reform movements" in Venice and in other parts of Italy as well as, especially, his influence in France.[97] Vasoli notes that the modern reader of Zorzi's *De harmonia mundi* or the *Problemata* can recognize "la sincera aspirazione ad una fede libera e interiore, fondata sulla suprema norma dei 'verba Dei' e sulla virtù primitiva della chiesa di Cristo, la speranza di una finale liberazione della schiavitù del 'mondo,' la certezza della 'renascentia' per tutti coloro che hanno creduto e si sono rigenerati nell'acqua sovraceleste del Figlio."[98] Zorzi was an influence in intellectual as well as evangelical circles in Venice.

Before Dionisio Gallo arrived in Venice in 1566 and began his prophetic preaching, a feminine mystic who had organized a hospice to care for the sick and the poor after the terrible plague of 1528 had proclaimed with prophetic zeal the need for reform of the Church, for active works of charity, and for the union of all peoples under God, a message quite similar to that of Dionisio Gallo. Francesco Zorzi had been, in all likelihood, her confessor.[99] This woman has only recently been mentioned in connection with Venetian evangelism, yet through her works at the little hospice, which became known as the Ospedaletto of Saints John and Paul, since it was adjacent to the great Dominican church of the same name, and in the *calle* and *campi* of Venice, she preached the need for reform of every individual.[100] She demonstrated by her work with the poor what she believed to be essential for all who claimed to love and serve God. She was successful in "begging from the rich to feed the poor," and her makeshift hospice was rebuilt into permanent quarters to feed the poor and minister to the sick. Many influential Venetian patricians contributed to the work of the Ospedaletto and served on its board of governors.

This feminine evangelist-prophetess was known simply as Mother Johanna (Giovanna) or the Venetian Virgin. In the records of the Ospedaletto she is called Zuana. There is no evidence to connect her with any religious group outside the Church, but she clearly hoped for a reformation of the Church and a return to its pristine unity.[101] Mother Johanna was heralded by the French humanist Guillaume Postel (1510–81) as the one in whom Christ dwelled most fully, indeed as the feminine Christ and as the angelic pope.[102] In the year 1540, according to Postel, the spiritual, or heavenly, body of Christ descended into the "most holy virgin, Johanna by name," and she became truly one with the living Christ and carried His substance in her body.[103] The Divine Presence acting within her person revealed to her the mystery of the restitution of all things. These mysteries became the foundation for Postel's millenarian ideas. They are also important for an understanding of the millenarian and prophetic ideas that were circulated in Venice in the Cinquecento as well as for what they reveal about the mysterious Giovanna. She prophesied to Postel, when he was in Venice in 1546–49, as follows:

(1) *The beginning of the reformation of the world will take place in Venice.*

(2) *The minister prince of this papacy will be the most Christian prince who is most Christian in deeds and not in words alone.*

(3) *All the Turks will soon be converted, and they will be the best Christians in the world; but if the Christians do not turn to the good life, the Turks will castigate them before they become Christians.*

(4) *All those who have faith in God, love for all, and the Good Life will be secretly blessed by the Venetian Virgin's Spouse [Christ] and will be given two bodies, one white in the bread, one red in the wine, which are changed.*

(5) *The time will come when all who have been lost through Satan will be restored, as if the first parents had never sinned. There will be one Pasqua, or universal raccolta (gathering).*

(6) *Human nature will be led to such perfection that all men will be as Christ, except for His Divinity; in men will be seen the living Christ, as root, fount, and trunk.*

(7) *The Lord of Lords has so ordered His world that it is all made, as the nature of the Palm (Thamar), of a perfect substance, immortal and incorruptible like the body of gold or gems. . . . The Lord wants to be known through the substance of the Palm, not only because of its sweetness, nourishment, concord, and duration but because of its perfect love.*[104]

These prophecies reveal Giovanna's conceptions of herself as prophetess and vessel of Christ, and the providential role of Venice in bringing about the "new age," or the restitution of all things. The Venetian Virgin's prophecies influenced Postel to the extent that they became for him a platform of restitution and the basis of a universal monarchy under the rule of God in which Venice would be the center of the temporal monarchy. Giovanna believed herself to be the angelic pope who had so often been proclaimed by Joachim of Fiore. The Venetian Virgin, in defining her providential role, stated: "I am the Signor [the Lord] because He lives in me, and because of this I am in Him the pope, the holy reformer of the world."[105] The prophecies of the Venetian Virgin reveal the influence of Joachim as well as the Jewish mystical tradition, and they also show an originality in making Venice the catalyst for the reformation of the Church and society. Some of these ideas had been expressed by Fra Laurentius da Monte, as we have noted. Many chronicles, medieval and sixteenth-century, also contained statements about Venice's providential origin and the piety of its citizens. Because of Giovanna's work with the poor at the Ospedaletto and her ability to obtain funding from wealthy Venetians to enlarge her hospice, she certainly had an audience for her prophecies in addition to Postel. Lorenzo Lotto was on the board of governors of the Ospedaletto, and he may have included the figure of the Venetian Virgin in the painting of 1542 entitled *L'elemosina di sant'Antonio*, which is in the Church of Saints John and Paul in Venice. Lodovico Domenichi wrote a biography of Giovanna Veronese in *Historia di Messer Lodovico Domenichi, di detti, e fatti Degni di Memoria di Diversi Principi e Huomini privati antichi et moderni*, which was published by Gabriel Giolito de' Ferrari in 1558; a second edition, issued in 1564, also included the biography of Giovanna Veronese.[106] There is no doubt that Giovanna Veronese, whom Domenichi called *donna santissima*, is the Giovanna called the Mother of the World and the Venetian Virgin by Guillaume Postel. In fact, it has been demonstrated that Domenichi drew heavily from Postel's life of the Venetian Virgin, which appeared in the appendix of the *Chronica* of Carion, published in Paris in 1557.[107] Domenichi's biography is an Italian translation of Postel's original Latin. Postel had indicated that the prophetess Giovanna, or the Venetian Virgin, had in Venice a following who considered her almost a saint. Lodovico Domenichi also believed that the mysterious woman and her prophecies were very significant. He prefaced his biography of Giovanna with the following remarks: "Because this did not happen recently but many years ago, and not least because it happened in Venice and seemed to me a thing not only most worthy but also necessary to be known, I have wished to record it in this place."[108] Domenichi noted that "she acquired in Venice so much light about the things of God that in all the sacred scripture and especially in the most secret sentences of the ancient Hebrew interpreters there was not anything so abstract, secret, and hidden that she could not clearly explain it."[109]

Postel met Mother Johanna (Giovanna) at the Ospedaletto in 1546, where he had come to work as a confessor after his separation from the Jesuits in Rome. He became the "reed," to use his own words, by which the prophecies of the Venetian Virgin about Venice and the reformation of the Church would be proclaimed.[110] His writing and pronouncements bear witness to his stated intention. Until his death in 1581 he never ceased to proclaim the mysteries of the Virgin of Venice and the divine infusion of Christ in her person. Although he was forced to recant his beliefs and his writings about the Venetian Virgin—whom he had equated with Sara, wife of Abraham, with Rebekah, wife of Isaac and mother of Jacob, and even with the Virgin Mary—he never gave up his belief in her prophecies or in her divine efficacy. In 1555 the Venetian Inquisition tried Postel for his heretical writings.[111] Among the books cited were *Il libro della divina ordinatione* and *Le prime nove del altro mondo*, printed in 1555 in Padua; both books detailed the miracles and prophecies of the Venetian Virgin and Postel's unusual relationship to her. He defined her as his spiritual mother and himself as her confessor and divinely ordained son.

The inquisitors confiscated as many of the books as they could find and burned them. No copy of either work printed in Padua in 1555 remains in the libraries of Venice today; it seems almost certain, however, that copies of the prophetic books remained in Venice in private hands.[112] In the Cinquecento, manuscript copies were made from the printed texts and found their way to France, England, and Germany.[113] That those works were influential in prophetic circles and in reform and millenarian conventicles is altogether likely. Joanna Southcott, an English mystic of the eighteenth century, named Postel, along with his Mother Johanna, as a spiritual guide whose writings she had studied. In addition, in the early part of the twentieth century *Il libro della divina ordinatione* was translated into English.[114]

The prophecies of the Venetian Virgin are important for understanding the prophetic currents in Venice in the Cinquecento as well as for the development of Postel's thought. In 1549 he wrote to his friend and fellow Hebraist André Maes that he was as certain of his "divine ordination" and the truth of the Mother of the World, his Venetian Virgin, as he was that "two plus two equals four." He also noted: "And that I may speak very clearly to you, that person is a Virgin, born fifty years before, in whom the plenitude of the substance of Christ dwells just as in Him lives corporally the plenitude of Divinity. Without enigma I speak. I am ridiculed and mocked universally. But I know whom I have believed, what I have seen and heard. But the Lord orders silence be maintained."[115]

Postel, of course, did not maintain silence about the prophecies of the Venetian Virgin, which he had adopted for his own, as his trial in 1555 demonstrated.[116] As early as 1548 he was summoned to appear before the Capi del Consiglio dei Dieci because of words he had spoken during the Mass at Santa Maria dei Miracoli. On March 19, 1548, the Capi summoned Marino Pisani, a Venetian nobleman, to give his account of what the officiant had said at the Mass.[117] Pisani responded that a foreigner, unknown to him, who worked at the Ospedaletto of S. Zanipolo, had said the Mass, and that when the foreigner was consecrating the host, he turned to the people and exhorted them to live well. Then he said to the people that they should say a Paternoster and ask the help of God for their city, which had more need of help than at the time of Tiepolo.[118]

The foreigner was quickly identified, for on the same day Guillaume Postel was brought before the Capi.[119] When asked where he lived, he said he lived in the house of Messer Zan della Speranza, *libraro*. He also indicated that he said Mass at Santa Maria Formosa, when he preached there, as well as at Santa Maria dei Miracoli. When Postel was questioned about what he had said during the Mass, he confirmed Signor Pisani's testimony. He also noted that Venice was in more danger now than at the time of the conspiracy of Baiamonte Tiepolo because Venice had a great abundance of Lutherans and wicked men, who would influence the youth.[120] He indicated that he had also spoken about the ineffectiveness of the princes, both secular and ecclesiastical, in bringing about a solution to the religious and moral crisis. He noted especially the weakness of France in this regard.

When the Capi asked him if he had any further information to give, he said: "I have no other information, Signori, except that the spirit told me that Venice was in great danger and needs to pray to God continually for her own conversion."[121] The Capi praised him for his good works but warned him that he must not mention Tiepolo or any other person again.[122] As Postel departed from his meeting with the Capi, he urged them *da parte di Dio* to order that every parish say a Paternoster and an Ave Maria at Mass. He also expressed his hope of seeing a grand conversion in the city of Venice, since the Devil had more hatred of Venice than any other city under heaven because of divine protection and divine favor bestowed upon her. Postel apparently left the interview on good terms with the Capi del Consiglio dei Dieci; during this period of 1548 he wrote that he had given to the Senate of the Venetians, through the hands of the doge, a book of sacred commentaries about what Venice should do for its own protection or its ruin, if neglected.¹²³

The hope of universal concord, that is, "one sheepfold and one shepherd," can also be found in the writings of Francesco Sansovino, who wrote a prophetic poem entitled "A Principi Christiani," in which the evils of his day are described. After many travails are suffered, however, there will be a renovation of the Church. The conclusion of the poem is significant: "Et poi, sia vn solo Ouil, sola una Verga."¹²⁴ The idea of a return to Christian unity and a purified Church under the direction of an angelic pope was more widespread in Venice after the middle of the sixteenth century than has previously been believed. Only a few years before Dionisio Gallo arrived in Venice in 1566, other prophetic voices had been raised to proclaim the reception of a special illumination directly from God. These men were from different stations in life and followed different occupations. Giacomo Brocardo was a grammarian, scholar, and teacher; Giorgio Siculo was a *frater*; Benedetto il Corazzaro was an artisan who made armor; the Venetian Virgin, already discussed, worked for the poor and the sick as the founder of a hospice that later became known as the Ospedaletto; Guillaume Postel, learned humanist polyglot, was known in various circles in Venice. All had gained a certain notoriety in Venice, and they also had followers. These prophets had prepared the way, so to speak, for the prophecies of Dionisio Gallo. It is not surprising that Dionisio found audiences willing to listen to him all over Venice.

Having looked at the prophecies and warnings made by the Venetian Virgin, which resembled in many ways the platform of Dionisio, we shall now look briefly at the prophetic voices of some men who were witnessing in the Venetian dominion a few years before or during Dionisio's sojourn in Venice. Giacomo Brocardo is a fascinating figure to consider in relation to Dionisio Gallo and prophecy, since Brocardo also was greatly influenced by prophecies and used them to try to implement reform in Church and state. Brocardo, born about 1518 in Pinerolo in Piedmont, had lived about thirty-five years in the Venetian dominion, according to his own statement.¹²⁵ His father had died when Brocardo was a young child; and when Brocardo was about fifteen, he left Piedmont. He had some schooling in France but returned to Italy and the Venetian dominion, where he studied in 1543–44. He was extremely precocious and mastered subject matter easily. He was vivacious and had a wide circle of friends, among whom were Pietro Carnesecchi, Giulio Camillo, and Alessandro Cittolini. He knew Carnesecchi intimately. Brocardo called himself a Platonist, but he also translated Aristotle. In 1548–49 he was in Paris, where in 1549 he published a translation of

Aristotle's *De arte rhetorica*, probably with the help of his friend Carnesecchi, with whom he associated in Paris and in Venice.[126] In Paris he also met Giulio Camillo, who did many kindnesses for Brocardo and later came to Venice to continue his association with him.[127] It was Camillo who placed Brocardo in the home of the bishop of Lodi, since Camillo was also friends with some leading families of Portogruaro and Venice.[128] In his *Grammatica* Camillo included a letter of dedication to Antonio Altano, conte di Salvarolo, to whom he wrote with great affection, asking that Altano greet the "Magnifici Signori Fratini."[129] It was probably Giulio Camillo who introduced Brocardo to the family of Marco Frattina of Portogruaro.

In Venice, Brocardo had studied Aristotle with Giorgio Cornaro, bishop designate of Treviso. Brocardo's *In tres libros Aristotelis de arte rhetorica Paraphrasis* (1549) was dedicated to his former teacher, who had inspired him to study letters so that he might bring some advantage to others.[130] It is clear from Brocardo's *praefatio* that he felt great affection and admiration for the bishop.[131] Always interested in rhetoric, he published the *Partitiones oratoriae* ten years after his first book. Returning again to Venice after a stay in France, he became a *maestro di schola* at San Lorenzo. His distinction in humane letters made him a sought-after teacher, and consequently he instructed the sons of many prominent Venetian patricians, among whom were Andrea Pasqualigo and Zuan Cornaro, in whose home he remained about eleven years.[132] He was also employed by Vincenzo Pellegrini, a lawyer, and by Marco Frattina of Portogruaro. He taught the children of Marco Frattina and his wife, Isabella, for about two and a half years. Both Brocardo and Isabella were denounced to the Holy Office of the Inquisition in 1568. Isabella was denounced because of the enmity of several women and also because of her friendship with Giacomo Brocardo, who had openly expressed opinions that caused him to be suspect.[133] He was not reticent in his criticism of the pope. His reading of prophecies had led him to predict the end of the papacy and the renovation of the Church and had political implications, as well. His friendship with Pietro Carnesecchi was also a factor in his problems in Venice, since Carnesecchi had been identified in 1565 as one of the heads of a conventicle in the Campo of San Fantin, where many young noblemen often gathered.[134] In addition, Carnesecchi, familiar with other notorious heretics such as Andrea da Ponte before he fled to Geneva, also read and taught in the *ridotto* and collected *limosine* for Bartolomeo Fonzio, imprisoned and later put to death as a heretic.[135] Francesco Spinola had been a part of this conventicle before his incarceration in 1563–64 and his death by drowning in 1567.[136] Brocardo was very likely known to the friends of Carnesecchi. At any rate, he had aroused the suspicions of the Venetian authorities because of his associations and his teachings.

The Tre Savi sopra Eresia, Federico Valaresso, Lorenzo da Mula, and Francesco Bernardo, Venetian patricians who served on the tribunal, made a request to the Capi del Consiglio dei Dieci sometime before May 11, 1568, that they notify the podesta of Portogruaro to detain Brocardo, since the Holy Office of the Inquisition wished him in their hands.[137] They also wanted to see Brocardo's writings and his books. Salvador Surian, podesta of Portogruaro, reacted immediately upon receipt of the letter from the Capi.[138] He summoned Brocardo to the palace, and the captain of the guards, Probo Gianà, restrained him there.[139] He was then placed under guard on a boat while Gianà went to the home of Marco and Isabella Frattina to confiscate Brocardo's writings and his books. When this was accomplished, Gianà rejoined Brocardo on the boat and set sail for Venice, arriving there on May 11, 1568, the very day the podesta had received the Capi's letter in the early hours of the morning.[140] Brocardo was quickly placed in the prisons of the Consiglio dei Dieci. He had indicated to the guards that he had important things to tell the Capi, so he was led into their presence.[141] The Capi asked him to say whatever he wished; he began by saying that he assumed that he had been summoned and that his books and writings had been confiscated because he was suspected of heresy, or *luterannità*. He claimed, however, that he did not dissent from the Holy Roman Church, although he admitted that he had actively studied prophecy.[142] He asked the Capi to take care of his books of prophecy and added: "I believe that I have been sent here by God, because I wish to say to your most excellent *signori* how much in those prophecies pertains in an important way to your state."[143]

Brocardo's warning to the Capi del Consiglio dei Dieci was similar to the admonitions Guillaume Postel sent to the doge in 1548; in a letter as yet missing but described by Postel in an unpublished text, Postel warned the doge that Venice was in grave danger.[144] In 1555 he reiterated his message of imminent catastrophe in two books published in Padua in Venetian dialect, *Il libro della divina ordinatione* and *Le prime nove del altro mondo*. Because God loved Venice more than all other cities save Jerusalem, the Devil, Postel wrote, was very envious of Venice and had unleashed many travails against the city. The number of heretics in Venice, the Turkish advance, and Venice's own sins were the Devil's work. During Postel's trial by the Venetian Inquisition, while he was imprisoned in San Giovanni in Bragora, he again repeated the ominous warning in a letter to Maffio Venier, one of the Tre Savi sopra Eresia. "I know of the greatest dangers in which your republic is," Postel wrote, "and there are things that I cannot put in writing here because they in neighboring princes."¹⁴⁵ Postel had often written that Venice must [lead] the world in a general reformation by assuming her rightful role as the [n]ew Jerusalem." Dionisio Gallo was to issue the same warning to the tri[b]unal and to the Venetian Senate, as Postel had and as Brocardo was also to do. Venice must be reformed in order to lead the world in a *restitutio omnium*.

Brocardo told the Capi that he did not want to say any more about the prophecies that concerned Venice until they had time to think about his statements. Brocardo's mysterious words about Venice and prophecies make clear that he, like others, including Dionisio Gallo, did not hesitate to blend religion and politics, since the prophetic voice of the sixteenth century seemed to demand this union.

Many years before Brocardo had published his interpretation and translation of the Apocalypse, he had had a mystical conversion from an unexpected divine illumination. Returning home on a Sunday afternoon after spending time with friends, he was reading the prophet Haggai when a voice from heaven reprimanded him for his desire for riches. At that moment he committed himself to a life of active religion, and he never ceased reading prophecies to understand the present. Brocardo, like Joachim, believed that a new age in human history had begun. He, however, believed that Luther would usher in a *restitutio* of evangelical doctrine and religious unity. He saw Venice as the setting for the renewed kingdom of Christ after the defeat of the papists. Two general councils would be held in Venice, and they would reunite all Christian people, inaugurating the general reformation and the beginning of the heavenly Jerusalem.¹⁴⁶ Brocardo's mystical and millenarian ideas were published late in his career, but while in Venice he was also formulating and discussing his theories about the *restitutio*. Brocardo's ideas about Venice and the reformation of the Church seem to reflect Postel's ideas and those of the Venetian Virgin. Dionisio Gallo also believed that Venice had a prophetic role to fulfill. Even while imprisoned in Venice, he wrote to the Venetian Senate, the Venetian Inquisition, and especially to the Tre Savi sopra Eresia, urging Venice to administer justice, as God had intended. Postel also believed that Venice was to be the new Jerusalem and that these ideas derived from the Venetian mystic whom he called the Venetian Virgin.

When Brocardo appeared before the Venetian Inquisition, he was questioned about the prohibited books in his possession, especially about his annotations of the Targum. The inquisitor wanted an explanation about his notes concerning images, or idols. Brocardo had a ready response: "About the images, I have written that the prophets rebuke the exterior cult without the interior, and temporal honors without divine worship. And as to the things I have written in all those annotations, I have written them because I was thinking that prophecy rejects them inasmuch as they are like the things of the Gentiles."[147] Brocardo also admitted having and having read the *Chronica* of Carion, the *De arte cabalistica libri tres* of Ioannes Reuchlin, the *De celesti agricultura* of Paul Riccius, and some works by Cornelius Agrippa.[148] Brocardo's reading is important for understanding his particular type of prophetic vision.

The Cabala was another source from which Brocardo drew inspiration for his prophetic vision. In his testimony before the Venetian Inquisition he specifically mentioned that he had "il libro della Cabala," in which he had found nothing contrary to the Church.[149] Brocardo may have been referring to the *Zohar*, which Postel in 1546–48 was translating in Venice from the original Aramaic into Latin. The Cabala was an appropriate source for prophetic thinkers, since they considered the books of the Cabala and other cabalistic literature an aspect of ancient wisdom that must always be expressed in symbolic or poetic language in order to veil its truths from the "common crowd."[150] The books of the Cabala, especially the *Zohar*, were a significant influence on the Venetian Fra Francesco Zorzi, especially in his *De harmonia mundi* and *In Sacrum Scripturum Prolemata*, on Guillaume Postel, the translator of the *Zohar*, and on Giulio Camillo, whose *La Idea del Theatro*, *Sermoni*, and *De l'humana deificatione* reflect the influence of the *Zohar*. Vasoli has underlined the connections in Camillo's writings with the Venetian *spirituali* who were hoping for a profound reform of the Church.[151] Camillo was in rapport with the Venetian Alvise Priuli and also with Cardinal Reginald Pole.[152] His friendship with Brocardo would only have strengthened Brocardo's mystical tendencies.

A recent biographer has noted that cabalistic, hermetic, and magical-astrological opinions made Giulio Camillo attentive and sympathetic to radical renewal of spiritual and ecclesiastical life.[153] In Paris and in Venice, Camillo and Brocardo had ample opportunity for mutual influence. In Camillo's *De l'humana deificatione* one finds a deeply spiritual work similar to his other writings and also those of other humanist-prophets and *spirituali*, in which the love of God, who is man's health, and the separation from the pleasures of the world are paramount.[154] One finds here the blending of the spiritual with the prophetic. Camillo notes that in the *Timaeus* Plato wrote about the need to believe the testimony of the "little sons of the gods who are the prophets."[155] The "most profound" books of the *Zohar*, which have been received from the mouth of the spirit of Elias by their author, also have great influence in the *De l'humana deificatione*. Camillo clarifies the relationship of God and man, made in the likeness and in the image of God, making use of the *Zohar*, which says that likeness, image, and the rational soul are different. The likeness of God (*similitudine*) is the most excellent and is called *Nessamah;* the image is excellent and is called *Rauch;* the rational soul, along with man himself, is the lowest and is called *Nephes.* The image is to the angels as the similitude is to God.[156] These mystical ideas expressed in the *Zohar* are significant for the thought of many *spirituali*, who concentrate on man's inner relation to God more than on the outward practices of their cult.

Giulio Camillo was an important influence on Brocardo's thought, especially in the mystical works published late in his career, namely, the *Interpretatio et paraphrasis libri Apocalipseos* (1580) and the *Mystica et prophetica libri Geneseos interpretatio*.[157] Other prophetic works remain in manuscript.[158] Long before these works were published, however, Brocardo, as I have observed, was engaged in reading the prophets and prophecies to interpret events in the present.

According to the testimony of a religious, Brocardo was also among those who gave special credence to the passage from the Apocalypse about the "woman clothed in the sun and ready to give birth." This theme had been very important in prophetic literature, especially since the time of Joachim, whose commentary on Apocalypse 12 had become a leitmotif, as it were, for *spirituali* like Brocardo, Doni, Postel, and Dionisio Gallo. Joachim glosses the passage as follows: "O truly great and remarkable sign. The Church in the uterus of the heart: the word of God is crucified, afflicted, oppressed. Therefore, she does not cease crying. And what does she cry out? My little sons, whom again I suffer for in parturition, until Christ be formed in you. . . . That woman generally signifies the mother church, who in the word of prophecy, by crying and giving birth, was laboring."[159] Brocardo had used the same passage about the woman giving birth to indicate the suffering of the Church in his day, which resulted from the lack of reform. According to Dom Vincentius Julianius Romanus, when news had reached Venice that the pope was ill, Brocardo leaped up with joy and exclaimed that the time had come of which the prophet spoke, namely, "the pangs of the woman giving birth."[160] Brocardo had also predicted the demise of the papacy, either in the present or in the future.[161]

The inquisitor's questions reveal that he had carefully read the testimonies about Brocardo and the accused's statements. Brocardo's responses demonstrate his keen intelligence and his use of rhetorical language in his own defense. The inquisitor wanted an explanation concerning the "shadows" of which Brocardo had written and also concerning the errors of the Church. He especially wanted to know how Brocardo interpreted the reformation of the Church. This question was full of pitfalls; skillful use of language was essential here. Brocardo's response met the challenge:

> *As to the shadows, I understand the practices, the discord, the disobedience that are now among Christians, all of whom ought to obey the Holy Mother Church. For the errors, I mean the particular ones that are in Christianity, that follow the heresies of the ancients or introduce new ones. I mean then that the Church must be renewed, that good practices must be in all people; there should be no error, no lack of harmony, no discord in the Church, and all must be obedient to the Holy Mother Church.*[162]

Joachim also had written of the *tenebre*, which in the Cinquecento became a code word used by *spirituali*, who believed that true religion was the illumination of man's mind by the Divine Light, which cast away the shadows.[163] In "Mondo massimo," the concluding chapter of *I mondi*, published in Venice in 1552 by Francesco Marconlini, Anton Francesco Doni wrote of the shadows (*tenebre*) that could be dispersed only by Divine Light: "O Light that gleams in the shadows; light that the shadows of my intellect do not comprehend unless such light is infused in me by you, so that I can penetrate the loftiness of your splendor."[164] Doni, like the *spirituali*, emphasized Love as the spark that kindles the illumination of the mind. In trying to comprehend divine secrets, this can only happen "if you love the Divine Goodness with your whole heart, with your whole soul, and with your whole mind; therefore, as wood cannot receive light, but by being set on fire becomes smoke, so you will become divine not by searching out only the Divine Light but by being inflamed with Divine Love."[165] One of the *medaglie* that precedes the chapter "Mondo massimo" bears a striking resemblance to Guillaume Postel. The inscription over the engraving reads: "Dovea aprir gli occhi et non tardar al fine." These words are especially appropriate for Postel, who never tired of proclaiming his own divine illumination, which restored his reason, according to his frequent accounts. Postel called his divine illumination his "immutation," which represents the spiritual engrafting of the body of the Venetian Virgin onto the "dead" body of Postel. This "immutation" restored Postel's reason, since Christ lived fully in the person of the Venetian Virgin and now lived fully in him.[166] In the left hand of the person represented in Doni's engraving is a compass, the instrument that often appears in representations of Postel.[167] If I am correct in my assumptions about Postel's representation in the *medaglia*, it is another example that links our *spirituali* together in their work for an inner religion, a prophetic religion, expressed by love of God and love of mankind.

Giacomo Brocardo had been an insistent prophetic voice in Venice in the years before and during Dionisio's arrival. Brocardo's intelligent, if tempered, response to the inquisitor, however, could not alleviate the fears his prophecies seemed to inspire. The damning words of his friend Pietro Carnesecchi could only aggravate Brocardo's situation. Carnesecchi had been sent by Cosimo I to the Roman Inquisition at the insistent request of Pope Pius V. After a lengthy imprisonment in the Torre di Nona and after an exhausting trial, Carnesecchi was handed over to the secular arm for sentencing in 1567. At this point, perhaps in an effort to escape death, he implicated his friend Brocardo, whom he described as "infected with heretical opinions," demonstrated "not only in his conversation but also in his writings."[168] Carnesecchi also noted that Brocardo was "one worth noticing" because of his influence among Venetian patricians whose children he had taught. He also named a member of the patrician family of Pasqualigo as one who shared Brocardo's ideas. As we know, Andrea Pasqualigo had been an intimate of Brocardo for many years. The evidence about Brocardo that Carnesecchi gave in a confession shortly before he was put to death was presented to the Holy Office of the Inquisition in Venice on August 12, 1568.[169]

The final resolution of Brocardo's case would be important for our consideration, had the process gone to judgment. But Brocardo's escape thwarted the decision of the Holy Office. As he was being brought from the prison of San Giovanni in Bragora to the office of the Inquisition in the Chapel of Saint Theodore in San Marco, four men attacked the two guards escorting Brocardo, throwing one of them in a canal.[170] There were suspicions that the four men had been in the service of Marco Frattina, although Marco and his wife denied it.[171] Brocardo's two guards were also suspect, since they seemed to have allowed the escape, according to the papal nuncio, Facchinetti.[172]

Brocardo's escape marked the end of his activity in Venice. He lived out his days in Germany, Switzerland, and Holland and continued to interpret prophecies, as his publications attest. His prophetic interpretations also caused him some problems outside Italy. His influence in Venice, however, and his prophetic vision were not quickly extinguished.

In addition to humanists like Postel and Brocardo a group of artisans was reading the signs, "being especially attentive to the prophetic mosaics in San Marco."[173] Although several of these artisans were investigated by the Venetian Inquisition in 1573, they had been instructed in their prophetic outlook by one Benedetto Corazzaro, a maker of shields, who many years before had interpreted the mosaics in San Marco for his followers.[174] Benedetto Corazzaro is important for our consideration of prophetic ideas in Venice before Dionisio's arrival, since he awaited "the one proclaimed in prophecies" and used the Apocalypse, especially the passage about the "woman clothed in the sun," to interpret the present. Benedetto probably drew some of his ideas from Guillaume Postel, who had been proclaiming the restitution of all things and translating the *Zohar* when he acted as confessor for the infirm at the Ospedaletto of Saints John and Paul in Venice. As I have indicated earlier, Postel's prophetic vision was influenced greatly by the Venetian Virgin, who in turn may have had Francesco Zorzi as her confessor and may have been a *conversa*.

Benedetto had been dead ten years when his followers were brought before the Venetian Inquisition; this indicates that his prophecies were still very much alive when Dionisio arrived. We learn a great deal about the prophetic ambience of Venice from testimony of these artisans. Domenego Callegher, Benedetto Florian, Lunardo Cimador, along with others, were charged with interpreting the scripture in a bad sense and writing and arguing scandalously about the Bible, which they read in the vernacular.[175] Alessandro Callegher, called as a witness, reported that Domenego Callegher had said that the Hebrews were saved without baptism, that the Council of Trent had erred in some things, that Saint Augustine had not understood some of things he had said. More significantly, Domenego had indicated that one would come who would rule with an iron rod and that the Messiah the Hebrews expected had not come.[176] He also accused the theologians of not understanding the Scripture. Ideas such as these were being discussed in shops, with the fathers at the Carmini, and even at vespers in San Marco.[177] Alessandro testified that he thought, but without certainty, that some of those followers of prophecy were in a *scuola grande*.[178] The meetings often took place in the homes of Domenego and Benedetto. Sometimes they went to talk with Jews in the *gheto de Zudei*.[179] The practice of going to the ghetto reveals an emphasis upon Old Testament prophecy and also the *Zohar*.[180]

The harpsichord maker Benedetto Florian also was accustomed to going with his friends who were interested in prophecies to the Churches of Santa Maria Maggiore, Anzolo Raphael, and then to the Carmini, where there were often discussions about the *sol pastore* and the *sol ovile*, which were taken from the tenth chapter of John.[181] Florian admitted he did not know who the *sol pastore* was, but he believed that he would be "that faithful servant whom the Lord has established above His family in order to give food in His own time and ... that he will be like the son of man, of whom Saint John writes, who was walking in the midst of the seven candlesticks of gold."[182]

Florian and his group had been instructed in prophecy by Benedetto Corazzaro before his death ten years before. Although the group did not have a name, the members met frequently to discuss the meaning of the passage from John's Gospel and to express their opinions concerning the shepherd. Florian told the inquisitor, Fra Aurelio Schellino, that he believed that the faithful servant would be he who did the will of God; he also noted that God had chosen many servants, for example, Moses.[183]

Although Benedetto Florian refused to name the *sol pastore*, he and his friends clearly had been taught by Benedetto Corazzaro to await "this faithful servant."[184] Domenego Callegher, in his testimony before the Inquisition, made the expectations of the followers of Corazzaro very clear.[185] In response to a question about the son of God about whom David spoke, Domenego explained:

> *This is a man whom God generates not as He has generated Christ, but He generates [him], that is, He chose him, to destroy the infidels and the heretics and to put the world under this faith and to do that which Christ has said: "There will be one sheepfold and one shepherd." And this man is not Christ but is that sun of which Malachi speaks when he speaks of the sun, because Christ is the light that gives light to the sun, that is, to this man. And this man is the son of God and of the Church and that one of whom the Psalms say: Demand from me, and I shall give to you the nations as your inheritance. It was not said of Christ, but of that captain general who is to come and give execution to the laws of God, for the redemption of the human generation and to make all come to the laws of God.*[186]

Domenego's explanation of the "man who will come" introduced an additional element to the concept of the *sol pastore*, since he referred to him as the *capitano generale*. This designation was probably derived from Joachim, who had used the term to describe the captain general of the naval fleet of the Venetians and of the union of the Holy Church, who, after returning from duties in England, would be chosen *generalis capitaneus* of a great armada.[187] In the context of the "captain general," Joachim also wrote of a holy patriarch of the Venetians who would lead his people back to a purified religion and purified customs.[188] The *generalis capitaneus*, after serving as head of the armada, was to be chosen by the Senate of Venice "to serve the Holy Mother Church according to the precepts of the angelic shepherd," and then he would have a victory over the infidels.[189]

The prophecies of Joachim that placed Venice in such a favorable light would have been especially useful for the prophecies of this group of Venetian artisans. Merlin had also prophesied about the great reform of the "good sailors," that is, the Venetians: "these good sailors will have a holy prince who, while still living, will be famous for his miracles."[190] Because of the reform of the Venetians, God "will reward them with many favors, especially the favor of *perennitas*. The Venetians will also have good doges and holy patriarchs." So great was their piety that "after the death of the Antichrist they will be reformed above all men of the world, and they will be better and more holy. Likewise their dominion will not cease until the end of the world."[191]

This prophecy about the divine protection of Venice was often repeated in the sixteenth century and was part of the prophetic ambience in which many lived. Domenego was not at all reluctant to explain the teachings of Benedetto Corazzaro, whom he had known for twenty years. Corazzaro had interpreted the Psalms, John's Gospel, and the Apocalypse for his followers, and his interpretations reflected to a large degree the influence of Joachim and also Old Testament prophecy. The followers of Corazzaro were especially concerned with the idea of prophetic parturition. Callegher had said that the man whom they awaited as the angelic pope would be "the son of God and of the Church, which gives him birth with great pain."[192] To explain the mystery of the Church's birth pangs, Callegher resorted to metaphor: when the pope dies, the cardinals are pregnant and give birth to another pope. In like manner the doge of Venice: when the doge dies, the Signoria gives birth to another doge. "And it did not give birth to a baby but to a grown man."[193]

By the use of metaphoric language Domenego provided an original explanation of the New Testament concept of being born again. In addition, he explained that whatever was good in him came from God and from the Holy Spirit.[194] Domenego Callegher, although an artisan, had an excellent grasp of the metaphysical ideas expressed in the New Testament. He had obviously studied the teachings of Benedetto Corazzaro from the book that explained Corazzaro's interpretation of prophecies.[195]

Other followers of Corazzaro, like Lunardo Cimador, when questioned by the inquisitor, testified that they had spoken of the "seven seals" and of the one shepherd over one sheepfold. The "seven seals" were to be interpreted spiritually, since they were the work of the Holy Spirit. The first seal was of Adam, the second of Noah, the third of Shem, the fourth of Abraham, the fifth of Moses, the sixth of David, and the seventh of

Salomon.¹⁹⁶ When asked why the Gospel had been omitted, Lunardo said he understood the seven seals to be the seven ages. Another artisan, Biasio, interpreted the seven seals to mean the woman who will give birth to one who will be the shepherd of one sheepfold. In his interpretation of the twelfth chapter of the Apocalypse, he noted that the twelve stars over the woman's head represented the twelve apostles; the sun indicated the Holy Spirit; and the moon under her feet revealed the victory of the woman, that is, the Church, over the Turks.¹⁹⁷ In fact, these artisans, taught by Benedetto Corazzaro, were awaiting a universal restitution that included Turks, Hebrews, and other infidels; in this restitution each would be saved in his own law.¹⁹⁸ Although the artisans recanted this opinion when questioned by the inquisitor, they obviously had adhered to this teaching of Corazzaro's.

The twelfth chapter in the Apocalypse provided ample opportunity for prophetic interpretation and was the common link between humanists who also looked to prophecies and artisans who had been instructed by Benedetto Corazzaro. Both groups were awaiting the reunification and reform of the Church under the *sol pastore*.¹⁹⁹ The book that Corazzaro had written was also mentioned by the son-in-law of Lunardo Cimador, Ioannes Baptista de Ravaiolis, as being a book of prophecies that Benedetto Florian and Domenego Callegher read to the disciples of Corazzaro. The prophecies included the conquest of the Turks and the taking of Constantinople, the conversion of the Turks, the demise of the "empire in the house of Austria," and the belief that for all people there would be *uno solo Ouile et un sol Pastore*.²⁰⁰ The artisans apparently believed that the shepherd had already come and was in France at the time of their inquisition. They strangely described him as born "from the royal line in *Domo Priullia Venetiis*."²⁰¹ This "cavalier had been sent by God as His servant and chosen one, who must lead all the world to one faith, under one shepherd and one sheepfold."²⁰² Ioannes Baptista confirmed that he had copied a letter about this servant of God from a letter written by Domenego Callegher, who also had in his possession an exegesis of the first part of Genesis.²⁰³

Benedetto Florian, as a disciple of Corazzaro, often read from his books of prophecies and then explained the passages to his followers. He often gave an exposition of the twelfth chapter of the Apocalypse, interpreting "the woman clothed in the sun" as the Holy Mother Church, the twelve stars as the Twelve Apostles, and the dragon as Martin Luther and the Turks.²⁰⁴ The torments of the woman represent the Turks, Martin Luther, and the heretics. This interpretation is typical of many of the prophets of the sixteenth century. The interpretation of the child born from the woman and taken by an angel to the Holy Spirit is different, however. The child represented the one "who had been born" and was now in France. This *putto* was, in fact, a man who had a sword (*spada*) and the keys. With the sword he would defend the Holy Mother Church, and with the keys he would establish one shepherd and one sheepfold. The seven-branched candelabra represented the seven bishops who were to go throughout the world preaching the Gospel. The seven churches were those that had been established in Venice by Saint Magno, bishop of Altin.[205] Ioannes Baptista testified that he did not believe all of the teachings of Corazzaro, but he did believe that there had to be one shepherd and one sheepfold.

To illustrate to his disciples his written prophecies, Corazzaro gave lectures about certain mosaics in San Marco that confirmed for him the truth of his prophecies. The mosaics were probably those two figures without names, identified only as *sancti* but assumed by Corazzaro to represent the angelic pope and perhaps his disciple.[206] In Ioannes Baptista's testimony he made clear that Benedetto Florian, his father-in-law, Lunardo, and other artisans in this prophetic conventicle "mi mostrauano depinte in la chiesa di San Marco in Venetia." He probably described the "apocalyptic mosaics" in the western vault of the basilica as well as those two known only as *sancti*. If one follows Demus's dating, the apocalyptic mosaics would not have been completed during the life of Corazzaro (d. 1561) but would have been in place for his followers to describe and discuss. The testimony of Ioannes Baptista, however, makes this dating less certain, since Corazzaro's interpretations seem to have been fueled by the apocalyptic mosaics in San Marco. As we know, Postel had been greatly influenced by the mosaics, which he attributed to Joachim and which he believed prefigured the holy virgin whom he called the Venetian Virgin. At any rate, to Corazzaro and his followers the mosaics represented the "one shepherd" and the holy bishops prophesied by Joachim. To Postel the mosaics represented his "holy ordination" by the Venetian Virgin as the new angelic pope who would lead in the reform of the church.[207] Postel may have been the *cavaliere* described by Corazzaro and awaited by his followers. Postel had been in Venice in 1530, 1540, 1550, and had returned in 1560, using the pseudonym Petrus Anusius, which clearly announced his "divine ordination" and grand plan for a universal monarchy.[208] Postel's sojourn in 1560 may have been the final spark that convinced Corazzaro of his "divine ordination" and ignited the apocalyptic expectations of his followers. We cannot be certain, however, that Corazzaro had met Postel, but it would be probable, since their prophetic expectations were very similar and the prophetic ambience of Venice was closely knit.

The prophecies of the artisan Corazzaro were also similar to those of the learned humanist-grammarian Giacomo Brocardo and our prophet,

fig. 11
Angelic pope and disciple, the two unnamed sancti mentioned by Joachim, Corazzaro, and Dionisio. Biblioteca nazionale di San Marco, Venice

Dionisio Gallo, who claimed to be descended from a line of ancient Norman kings. The many prophetic statements of Postel about the beginning of the "restitution of all things" in Venice in 1566 and Dionisio's arrival in Venice in 1566, where he proclaimed the same program for reform as had Postel, seem to be more than coincidental. It is clear that similar prophetic expectations were circulating in Venice among various groups awaiting the inauguration of the *respublica mundana* under the leadership of a divinely appointed angelic pope.

The arrival of Dionisio in Venice in 1566, following Postel's appearance in the Serenissima in 1560, and his high-profile sermons in the *campi* and the *campielli* of Venice, especially in the cortile of the Palazzo Ducale and in the Basilica di San Marco, would surely have been noticed by Benedetto's followers in Venice and would have fueled their messianic expectations.[209] Dionisio's language resonated with phrases often repeated by the prophetic-minded adepts of Corazzaro, who had warned that the one who would come would rule with a "rod of iron," a phrase Dionisio had often repeated in his discourses. Although it would seem likely that the various prophetic groups in Venice would have known each other, this cannot be demonstrated in every case. One can be certain, however, that all of them were drawing directly or indirectly from the same medieval and Biblical sources. Also significant is the cross-fertilization of prophetic ideas between France and Italy, which can be demonstrated in regard to Francesco Brocardo, Pietro Carnesecchi, Guillaume Postel, and Dionisio Gallo.[210] This had also been true in the case of Francesco Zorzi, as Vasoli has pointed out.[211]

This cross-fertilization of ideas was related to both prophecy and reform, insofar as these humanist-prophets were also reformers who dreamed of a general reformation of the Church that would in turn bring about a reformation in society. The responsibility for reform of the Church lay with the pope and the ecclesiastical hierarchy, yet the princes had an important part to play in administering justice and making society in general more Christian.[212] Brocardo, Carnesecchi, and Postel had emphasized the role of the prince in relation to the reform of the Church, and Dionisio followed their lead. He probably came to Venice in 1566 as a result of prophetic currents that had been circulating in the Serenissima even after the Council of Trent. Since he had tried to bring other Italian princes into his movement of reform, it would appear natural that the political-religious structures of the Venetian republic would seem to him the ideal space for the reform to begin, since prophetic voices had long been heard there.

In addition to the learned Brocardo, Postel, and the artisan followers of Corazzaro, still others had dreamed of a reformed Church and society before Dionisio's arrival in Venice. At least twenty years before, Giorgio Siculo of Ferrara was spreading his prophetic doctrines, which he claimed were divinely inspired by Jesus Christ.[213] Siculo, who had been a Benedictine monk of the Cassinensis Congregation, had claimed that the justification he had received from Christ was that justification granted to the Apostles and other holy men of the primitive Church.[214] Such justification was that true justice and redemption which Christ had given with His passion and which had remained in the early Church for about two hundred years but could no longer be found. Siculo claimed that Christ had appeared to him in order to bring this justice again to the world and had taught him how to follow it.[215] Siculo's teachings were recorded in a book called *libro grande*, which was read especially by a large group of his disciples in Ferrara and in Venice.[216] Francesco Severo, a physician of Argenta during his investigation by the Inquisition of Ferrara, admitted in his testimony that he had been a disciple of Siculo and had read his book, entitled *Della ueritate Christiana et doctrina apostolica riuellata da nostro signor Iddio a Giorgio Siculo suo seruo della terra di Santo Pietro, seu De iustificatione.*[217]

Severo carefully outlined Siculo's teachings, and these provide us with the reasons for the Inquisition's fear of him. His heresies appeared to be a direct assault upon the Church's teachings. He denied baptism by water, for example, since he claimed that the only true baptism was by the Holy Spirit; he also denied the true body of Christ in the altar. He did not believe that power had been granted by Christ to men for loosing sins; therefore priests who claimed this power were false prophets.[218] He also argued that doctors of the Church had turned heavenly matters into carnal ceremonies and rites from which human perdition has flowed, and "for this reason it is shown to the whole world that the Christian faith is a diabolical and cursed sect, full of deception above all the sects of the unfaithful. Severo also indicated that Siculo urged all not to believe the doctors of the Church but the revelation made by Christ to him in the *libro grande*.[219] Indeed, Siculo had attacked and consequently denied almost every teaching of the Roman Church. From the Church's point of view, most damning were Siculo's teachings about justification and the Law. According to the testimony of Severo, Siculo had taught that "those who received the grace of God once and for all could no longer sin from inclination; that the remnants of sins do not remain in the person justified through grace and that the flesh does not fight against the spirit; that if one falls into mortal sin after justification or after grace has been received, he cannot be forgiven of his sin, which is against the Holy Spirit."[220]

Giorgio Siculo also claimed that for a thousand or more years before his vision there had been neither truth in the land nor mercy nor knowledge of God: "However, now Christ in His own person revealed the truth of sacred scripture to Giorgio Siculo, His own servant, and made this Giorgio his own legate to show to the world the teaching and truth of Christ, which had been hidden even till the present day because of the work of the Devil and the presumption and rashness of the doctors of the Church."[221] Siculo's teachings, contained in his *libro grande*, completely bypassed the magisterium of the Church, the pope, and the hierarchy. Siculo believed that as Christ's messenger he was about to address the Council of Trent in his own first legation.

The similarity of language used by Siculo and Dionisio to describe their missions is striking. Each called himself the *servus* and *nuntius* of God, and Siculo, like Dionisio, called his writings a *legatio* that had been revealed by Christ. Each prophet also became involved in temporal affairs. As noted previously, Dionisio had urged the king of France and the princes of Italy to help him in the reform of the Church, which seemed ineffective in reforming itself. Siculo had advised the temporal lords that they should not allow justice to be rendered according to canonical or civil laws but according to the precepts of the Mosaic Law.[222] Both Siculo and Dionisio strongly criticized the luxurious lives of the bishops of the Church; Siculo called for a removal of such bishops from their bishoprics if they did not lay aside their pleasurable lives.[223] Ten years afterward Dionisio was making the same point in France and later in Italy. It is not surprising that clerical officials were distressed over the revolutionary messages of Giorgio Siculo and Dionisio Gallo, whose claims for himself about the proper interpretation of the Holy Scriptures completely eliminated the need for interpretation by the clergy. Since Siculo claimed to have had all the interpretation of Scripture revealed to him by Christ Himself, his comprehension of scripture would far surpass that of any human agent. Siculo's emphasis on human reason obviously had its basis in his claims about being taught directly by Christ.

There is an important relationship in the sixteenth century between the prophetic voice and the emphasis upon human reason. Christ's restoration of his servant's reason was considered by certain prophets a sign of redemption through the justification of Christ. Prophet-reformers like Siculo, Brocardo, Postel, and Dionisio Gallo all shared this concept of the prophet as one whose reason had been restored by Christ. Each had had a mystical experience in which Christ had either directly or indirectly appeared to His servant and restored His reason: in person, in the case of Siculo; in a vision, in the experience of Brocardo; through the agency of the Venetian Virgin, in the case of Postel; and through the charity of the Virgin Mary, in the case of Dionisio Gallo. When one was taught directly by Christ, his understanding was restored to its state before the Fall; therefore, he was justified by Christ and would sin no more. The teachings of Siculo and Postel were considered heretical not only by the Roman Church but also by Calvin, who polemicized against Siculo because the prophet who had written against predestination had disciples not only in the Grison but also among the Italians in Geneva.[224] A year after Siculo's death, Calvin wrote in regard to Siculo that "eius libri per Italiam volitantes, multos passim dementant" and therefore "cum tanta ecclesiae iactura insania eius grassetur."[225] It is interesting to note that those who were immersed in prophetic and millenarian thought in Venice often relied on the prophets of the Old Testament for their inspiration and could often be found in the ghetto. Savonarola's commentaries on the Old Testament prophets, especially Jeremiah, Amos, Zechariah, and Malachi, were regularly found among the books of those charged with heresy. Venetian visionaries were awaiting "that servant who will do the will of God in that fact because God elected many as He did Moses."[226] Moses as servant and prophet of God was a fitting paradigm for Venetian expectations about the "one shepherd who will preside over one sheepfold."[227] I have already pointed out the number of churches in Venice dedicated to Old Testament prophets. Moses, to whom the Church of San Moisé was dedicated, was considered in some circles a paradigm for Saint Mark, who had given the Law and the Gospels to the Venetians.[228] Jewish prophetic thought was easily molded into Christian apocalyptic hopes. The Psalms of David translated into the vernacular by Antonio Brucioli were also studied for their prophetic utterances. Dionisio himself frequently cited David the prophet.

Although Giorgio Siculo was condemned to death for his heresies in 1551, his prophecies and teachings continued to be influential among many in Venice and the surrounding regions. In addition to Francesco Severo, another disciple was Nascimbene Nascimbeni, a well-known and esteemed teacher in whose Ferrara house Siculo had lived.[229] Nascimbene had been questioned in Ferrara by the Inquisition in 1551 and again in 1560 and had sworn that he no longer followed the teachings of Siculo.[230]

When Nascimbene was questioned on October 31, 1560, by the inquisitor of Ferrara, Camillo de Campegio de Papia, he admitted that he had met a monk at the Benedictine monastery of San Faustino in Brescia who said that he had had visions and that he was interpreting some passages from the Apocalypse.[231] Nascimbene acknowledged that he had told the monk, Dom Thomas, that he considered it unworthy to speak of so great a prophecy, although Nascimbene's friend, Pietro Todesco, placed great store in the things said by the monk. Nascimbene denied at this time that he continued to believe the teachings of Siculo, adding that he considered Dom Thomas crazy, rather than heretical, because of his prophecies. As it turns out, Nascimbene was disingenuous in his confession to the Inquisition in Ferrara in 1560, in regard to Siculo and to his statements about the prophecies of Dom Thomas.[232]

About twenty years after his first abjuration in Ferrara, Nascimbene was questioned in Venice by the Holy Office of the Inquisition for following the teachings of Giorgio Siculo. He admitted that he had been a disciple of Siculo from 1550, and although an ordained priest, he had continued to say Mass and administer the sacraments while he was member of the "Giorgian sect."[233] He admitted that in 1551 he had made a feigned abjuration in the room of the bishop of Ferrara because Giorgio Siculo was still alive, although in prison, and he, Nascimbene, was still following the prophet's teachings.

In his final abjuration he even admitted that he had had doubts that the Church understood the true meaning of Scripture.²³⁴ Our prophet, Dionisio, had also accused the priests of not understanding Scripture.

Nascimbene's trial reveals the power of Siculo and his message before and after the prophet's death. Nascimbene recorded the names of many of Siculo's *complici*, among whom were an abbot, monks, priests, physicians (like Francesco Severo), organists, a bookseller, and a philosopher. A monk, Don Antonio Montavano da Bozzolo of the Benedictine Congregation Cassinensis, admitted before the Inquisition of Brescia that he had held all the beliefs of the notorious Giorgio, confessing that he had believed that Jesus Christ had appeared to Giorgio "and in his own breast showed him in mystery and in writing all our redemption with the true intelligence of the Sacred Scriptures, conforming them to the doctrine and to the infernal errors and heresies."²³⁵ Like Nascimbene, Don Antonio acknowledged that he did not believe that priests had the power to absolve sin; that only Christ could pardon sins; "that the priests for this false power of absolution from sins are false prophets and false Christs, of whom Christ prophesied in Saint Matthew, saying: 'If anyone shall have said, "Look, here or there is Christ," do not believe, for pseudo-Christs and pseudoprophets will rise up and will give great signs and prodigies.'"²³⁶ Siculo's success with priests and monks was especially hateful to the Church, since he had been able to undermine the authority and the magisterium from within. A priest named Giovanni Battista Clario frequented a conventicle in Udine, and among his books, which were confiscated by the Inquisition, were the *Prediche del Reverendo p. fra Giorgio da Ferrara*.²³⁷ The influence of Siculo was not easily removed from religious or lay communities.

Nascimbene's flourishing career in humane letters had been ruined because he could not put aside the prophetic vision of Giorgio Siculo. Finally, in 1571, he was condemned by the Venetian Inquisition to perpetual confinement in the prison of San Giovanni in Bragora.²³⁸ The physician Francesco Severo, because of his adherence to Siculo's teachings, paid with his life in 1567.

The power of the prophetic voice was evident in Venice before and after the Council of Trent, a fact that is obvious from a careful scrutiny of the documents of the Holy Office of the Inquisition and made abundantly clear by the trial of Dionisio Gallo. But though Dionisio had the same certainty in his prophetic persona as had Siculo, he escaped the fate of Siculo and Severo.

In addition to prophets and preachers who appeared in Venice in the middle of the sixteenth century, there were also those, like Floriano Turchi, who had made a study of astronomy and had read the stars in order to warn Venice of the threats of a grave fire and of the days that were to be propitious or contrary.[239] All these ideas were a part of the complex of currents, often in conflict, that were flowing here and there in Venice at midcentury.

We shall turn our attention in the next chapter to Dionisio's successes and failures in Venice, looking first at his audience and especially at two Venetians, one a Venetian citizen, the other a Venetian patrician, who subscribed to Dionisio's prophetic program for reform and gave him shelter and moral support before his incarceration. We shall also see Dionisio before the Venetian Inquisition. His trial was atypical of cases heard by the Inquisition, since it appears to have been a conversation between Dionisio and the inquisitor rather than an inquisition. We shall consider what life in a Venetian prison in the Cinquecento was like. We shall also focus upon the conversations between Dionisio Gallo and Francesco Spinola, a famous humanist heretic enclosed in the same cell in the prisons of the Consiglio dei Dieci in the Palazzo Ducale.

· V ·
AMONG FRIENDS AND FOES IN VENICE
The Trial and Imprisonment of Dionisio Gallo

enice was still pregnant with ideas for reform at the time of Dionisio's arrival sometime before June 1566. Although the Council of Trent had been concluded, the question of reform was not settled for men like Dionisio Gallo, who believed in divine guidance for setting the agenda for reform of the Church and society. Dionisio believed his divine anointment and the Virgin's words to him about his mission as servant and messenger of God gave him precedence over the Council of Trent, since his charge had come from God through the Virgin, while the council had received its mandate only from men. There was still much work to be done, and Venice seemed to be the logical place from which Dionisio's program for reform could be set in motion. The general ambience of Venice seemed propitious for Dionisio's plans, but specific factors also worked to his advantage. In the other Italian cities where he had made clear his program for reform, he had exploited French connections, as previously indicated. In Venice, however, the connections were with Venetian citizens, even Venetian patricians. His decision to come to Venice was obviously intentional, and he may have come at the invitation of his Venetian friends. If this is the case, it indicates some prior relationship with Venice and Venetians.

After Dionisio arrived in Venice in the early summer of 1566, he lived in the house of a Venetian friend until his imprisonment. He also enjoyed the friendship of at least one Venetian patrician, possibly more. In addition to his personal friends in Venice, many other Venetians came to know him because of his preaching and his assertions that he was a messenger of God. In several of Dionisio's writings he mentioned the names of his friend and host Rochus Venetus, *senser di biave,* and his patrician friend, Giusto Morosini. We need not trust only Dionisio's words about his Venetian benefactors, however, since external evidence confirms his words. On June 7, 1566, in the home of Rochus Venetus, both Rochus and Giusto Morosini signed their names to a lengthy document written by Dionisio Gallo and directed to the patriarch of Venice, the clergy, the nobles, and the whole dominion of "most Christian Venetians." Their signatures, confirmed by numerous other documents as authentic, attested to their agreement with the proposals of Dionisio's *Articuli pacis Redemptoris atque salvatoris nostri Jesu Christi reuelatae coelitus a spiritusancto archipraeceptori . . .* , which was the subtitle to his *Legatio electi serui Dei,* prepared for the Venetians. Dionisio mentioned Rochus Venetus and Giusto Morosini in several documents that were preserved along with his trial, and his references to them were always laudatory. He suppressed the real cognomen of his friend Rochus, however, using only the designation Venetus. At the conclusion of the document subtitled *Articuli pacis Redemptoris,* dated June 7, 1566, Dionisio wrote: "The most famous Venetian men, the lords Justus Maurocenus, in vulgar language, Mauresini, and Rochus Venetus, *sensarius bladorum,* in vulgar language, *senser de biave,* heard [this work] partly in the hospice of an outstanding foreign man, partly in the home of that most humane and Christian lord Rochus Venetus."[1] In Rocho's home Dionisio read not only this work but also another large work, entitled *Haec est causa.*

On the final page of this latter work Dionisio noted that Rochus Venetus and Giusto Morosini had also heard the reading of this text, evidently in great sympathy, since he wrote that their attention was a consolation and help to him.[2] He read his *Haec est causa* also in the home of Rocho and that of "the outstanding foreigner," whose identity remains a mystery.[3] Under this attestation the two Venetians signed their names. Morosini wrote: "Justus Maurocanus subscripsi."[4] Rocho wrote: "Io Rocho da Venezia sanser da biave io sotto scritto." After Dionisio read his program aloud to his friends in Rocho's home, discussion evidently followed. Reading followed by discussion seemed to be Dionisio's regular practice, as evidenced by his discourse and subsequent discussion and criticism in Ferrara.[5] He was obviously an effective orator and chose to read his text. The signatures of Rochus Venetus and Giusto Morosini confirmed their approval and commitment to Dionisio's program for reform.

In order precisely to define Dionisio's milieu in Venice it is essential to determine the cognomen of the man whom Dionisio called Rochus Venetus, who also referred to himself in the same way.

A lengthy search among the *processi* of Santo Uffizio revealed the cognomen of Rochus. He was evidently in the habit of choosing friends who often found themselves in trouble with the authorities. He was summoned on July 18, 1566, to the Holy Office of the Inquisition to give testimony in the proceedings against Zuane de Vancimugio Vicentino, who had been accused of holding opinions derived from either Lutherans, Calvinists, or Anabaptists.[6] Responding to the inquisitor's question about his identity, he indicated that he was Rocho de Mazzochis, *senser di biave*, son of Messer Andrea, and he lived in the *parrochia* of San Moisé in the home of Bartholomeo Nani, a Venetian patrician.[7] Since Rocho was *senser di biave* in 1566, as he had indicated, and since Dionisio always noted Rochus's occupation as *senser di biave*, Rochus Venetus was obviously Rocho de Mazzochis.

From Rocho's testimony at the trial of Zuane de Vancimugio we learn that Zuane and Rocho had been friends for six years and that Zuane was an associate of Rocho's patron Messer Baldassare Moro.[8] Rocho testified that Zuane was a good Catholic who had previously worked with the Jesuit fathers. Another witness, Alvise Moro, indicated that Zuane could often be found in the Hospital of the Incurabili, where the artisans and merchants had an oratorio and held devotions and where certain teachers expounded Christian doctrines to young boys.[9] Zuane had fallen into trouble under the bad influence of a lawyer named Santohim, who claimed that the Jesuits were betrayers of the faith and that the true faith resided in Geneva.[10] The influence of Santohim on Zuane was probably the cause of Zuane's reversal of fortune. Zuane had visited in Rocho's home about a year and a half before the investigation. Clearly Rocho de Mazzochis, Zuane de Vancimugio, and Baldassare Moro had common interests, since they were all close friends. Some of their common concerns were religious, and these interests would have drawn Rocho to the preacher-prophet Dionisio. Rocho obviously found friends among patricians of important families. Baldassare Moro, son of Agustin, was a patrician with ancient lineage; his ancestor Niccolò was elected to the Maggior Consiglio in 1304. He himself was received into the Maggior Consiglio on July 4, 1531, when he was nineteen years old.[11] Rocho de Mazzochis (1511–92), Baldassare Moro (1510–76), and Giusto Morosini (1514–73) were about the same age, and at the time of their association with Dionisio Gallo they were mature gentlemen whose interests often centered upon religious questions. Moro's name, for example, appeared in the inquisition of Fra' Cherubino on October 24, 1565, where he testified that he had been scandalized when he heard the friar in his sermon at Santi Apostoli say that "le nostre opere sono come il pano menstruato" and "senza la gratia sono pecchi."[12] Giusto Morosini's concern with the wicked lives of some

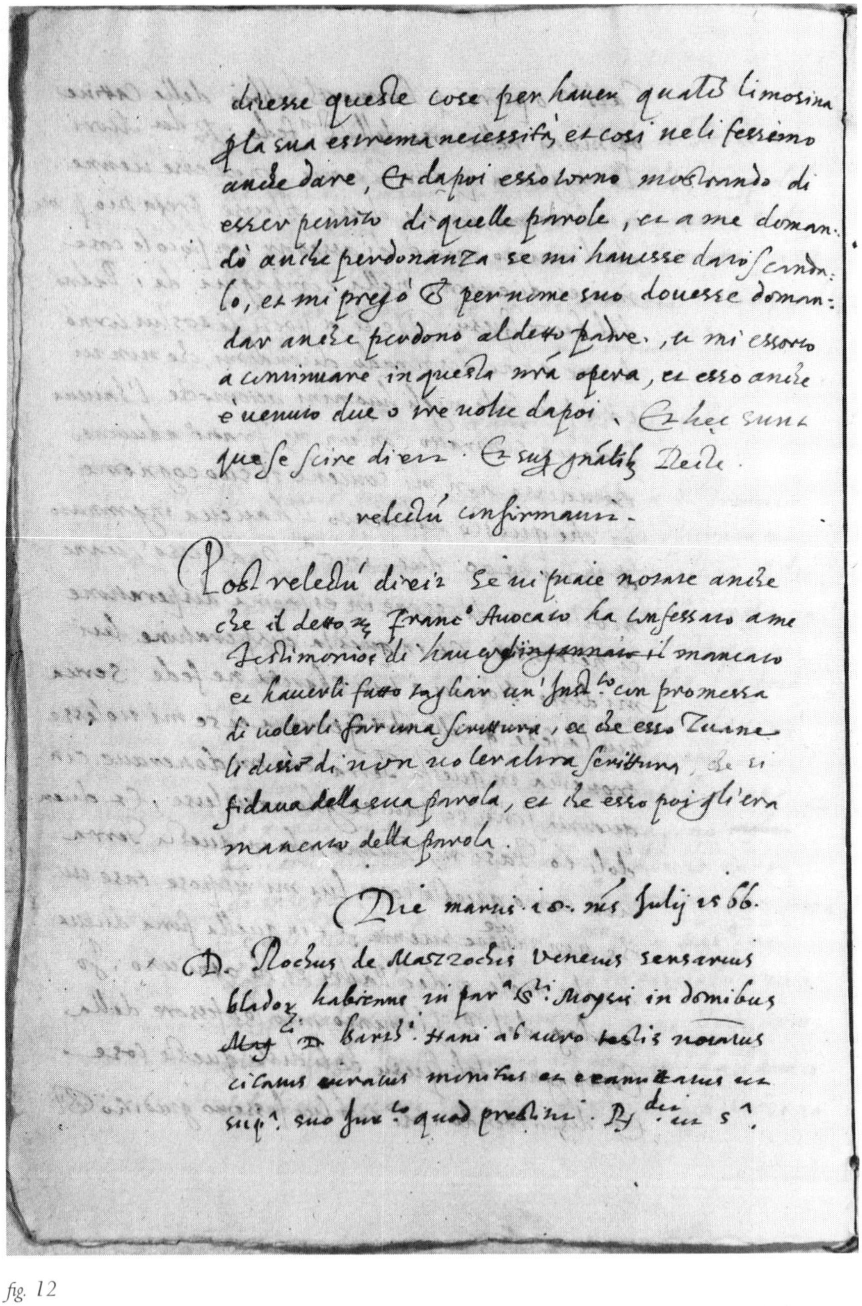

fig. 12
Page from the 1566 Inquisition proceeding against Zuane de Vancimugio recording the testimony of Rocho de Mazzochis. Archivio di Stato, Venice

clergy and their associates was articulated in a complaint to a priest named Gidonus about the wickedness of the lawyer Paulo Magno, who was a friend of the notorious Fra' Aurelio.[13] Morosini was dismayed that the patriarch had not taken action in regard to this wicked man.[14] Morosini, Moro, and de Mazzochis exemplified patricians and upper-class citizens who continued to work for reform from within the Church.[15] Yet each of these Venetians did not hesitate to criticize the Church or churchmen, though not always publicly; but if not openly critical, as in the case of Moro and de Mazzochis, their friends often were. Consequently, they sometimes found themselves in difficulty with the Venetian authorities. Dionisio's harsh criticisms of the pope and the Curia, in addition to his radical proposals for reform of the Church, did not deter Rocho de Mazzochis from extending his hospitality to him, or Giusto Morosini and Rocho from approving his proposals. Since Baldassare Moro was the patron of Rocho, one might assume that he also shared the opinions of Dionisio Gallo.

Dionisio's particular circle in Venice consisted of patricians and upper-level Venetian citizens, as in the case of Rocho de Mazzochis. Information about him is not plentiful, but one can reconstruct some of his lifestyle in which Dionisio played a part. Rocho, like his father, was born in Venice and held the office of *senser di biave* at the time of his association with Dionisio in 1566.[16] His duties as *senser di biave* were to act as a buyer and seller of grains. His work would have required that he often be at the Rialto; he also had an office at the Dogana di Mar.[17] His business associations also put him in touch with commercial interests in Venice. He married Andriana Centani, whose family was well known. Some Centani were *cittadini originarii,* and some were noble.[18] Rocho and Andriana had three children, Giacomo, Zuanmaria, and Anzola. The testament of Anzola shows that Rocho had provided his daughter a sizable dowry, between five hundred and one thousand ducats.[19] Anzola was married to Bartholomeo de Bressan; they had one child, Camilla, at the time Anzola's will was written.[20] One can assume that Rocho would have provided for his sons properties and/or goods equal in value to his daughter's dowry.

Rocho always dressed in the elegant and sober style of a Venetian gentleman, in black. Many items of clothing were among his personal effects at the time of his death—silk shirts and handkerchiefs, silk hose, satin vests, numerous wool pants and coats, and an ermine cassock. Rocho was probably a member of a *scuola,* since a cape from an unnamed *scuola* was listed among the effects. His furniture was antique, and in his home there had been an antique *spaliere* of thirty *bracchia;* this wall hanging, or elaborate drapery for a bed, was embroidered with the coat of arms of Zantani-

Mazzochis.[21] He obviously enjoyed a comfortable lifestyle and had some wealth. His marriage to Andriana Centani (Zantani) would have improved his social status and increased his upper-class connections, which were considerable.[22] His association with Bartholomeo Nani, in whose house he was living when he offered hospitality to Dionisio, continued for many years.

Obviously blessed with good health, since he lived to be eighty-six years old, Rocho de Mazzochis married for a second time, Giulia di Franceschi, when he was seventy-six years old.[23] Giulia's family, though not noble, was well established as *cittadini originarii*.[24] Throughout his life Rocho was active in commercial affairs in Venice. Even in his advanced years he was involved in the life of Venice, often acting as a witness to numerous legal contracts for the clients of his son-in-law Bartholomeo Bressan, a Venetian notary whose office was in the Piazza San Marco. He also conducted business affairs in his home in the Ca'Corner at San Samuele, where he witnessed land exchanges or the sale of properties.[25] Rocho never moved far from San Marco, the center of Venetian life and culture, although he had several residences during his lifetime. He rented a *mezado* in San Moisé from the patrician Nani until 1582.[26] Rocho's association with Nani lasted many years. Several years before his marriage to Giulia di Franceschi he lived in the Ca'Corner at San Samuele in the Corte della Vida, where he continued to live until his death.[27] He perhaps maintained two residences, for on March 14, 1587, the day the contract was signed for his marriage to Giulia, he was living "de confinio Santi Paterniani," which is near the Piazza San Marco.[28] Rocho de Mazzochis was obviously comfortable in the business and social life of aristocratic circles in Venice. He also maintained his position as *senser di biave* until about 1582. Since Rocho was very active and sought after as an old man, there is no reason to assume that he was not equally active and well known in the prime of his life, when he knew Dionisio Gallo.

Rocho's circle of friends was not limited to his business contacts, since Giusto Morosini was among his acquaintances. It seems likely that de Mazzochis introduced Dionisio to Morosini, but Dionisio could have known each independently. Whatever the precise circumstances may have been, all three were together in Rocho's home in San Moisé, the Palazzo Nani, when Dionisio read his program for reform of the Church and society. Dionisio did not mention whether others were present; he mentioned only Rocho de Mazzochis and Giusto Morosini, and only they affixed their signatures to the document. This fact, however, does not preclude the presence of others, since Dionisio also mentioned being in the home of a distinguished foreigner. One would assume that the unnamed friend was also present at Rocho's house and vice versa. Since Rocho de Mazzochis had been a friend of Zuane de Vancimugio before his problems with the Inquisition and since Zuane had formerly worked with the Jesuit fathers, one could speculate whether some Jesuits in Venice had been invited to hear Dionisio's concept of reform. However that may be, we can be certain that two Venetians heard Dionisio speaking in the privacy of Rocho's home.

The association of Giusto Morosini with Dionisio Gallo is an interesting and important link between the Venetian nobility and prophetic preacher-reformers such as Dionisio Gallo. Giusto Morosini, from the lineage of Benetto Morosini of Santa Maria Formosa, was the son of Pietro Antonio Morosini and Laura Venier, a Venetian noblewoman.[29] Giusto was received into the Maggior Consiglio on Saint Barbara's Day, December 4, 1537, assuming his civic duties at the age of twenty-three.[30] He evidently was not destined for an important political career, since his name is not found among those who served in important magistracies or as ambassadors.[31] His interests lay in religious matters, as his association with Dionisio would indicate. He often went to hear sermons in the various churches and, as I have indicated previously, expressed dismay that action had not already been taken by the patriarch against the scandalous priest Fra Aurelio.[32] Giusto apparently never married, although his inheritance was sufficient to support a family. He received from his father the Villa of Lovedo near Mirano, with its nine fields, which he rented to his cousin Vittorio Morosini. He also had other fields to rent near those of his Villa of Lovedo.[33] In addition, he had the usufruct of properties in Venice, which provided him the means for "living, clothing himself, and paying the rent on his house."[34] At the time he knew Dionisio Gallo, he was living in the *contrada* of San Pietro in Castello, in the home of the archbishop of Spalato, Alvise Michiel.[35] Although information about Giusto Morosini is not plentiful, it is clear he and Dionisio shared many interests in the reform of the Church. His concern for purified religion was obviously more important to him than political and social advancement.

On June 7, 1566, Giusto Morosini and Rocho de Mazzochis affixed their names to the lengthy document written by Dionisio Gallo, in which he set forth his program for reform of the Church, indicating that Venice, like Dionisio himself, had been chosen by God to accomplish the great goal of reform.[36] This *Legatio . . . Articuli pacis* was directed to the patriarch of Venice, the clergy, the nobles, and the whole dominion of "most Christian Venetians." But Giusto Morosini and Rocho de Mazzochis, as noted earlier, continued to work for the reform of the Church from inside.

A core of patricians some years younger than Morosini and de Mazzochis gives evidence of the relationship of the patriciate to the reform movement within and without the Roman Catholic Church. The records of the Holy Office of the Inquisition reveal the names of scions of noble Venetian families, such as Carlo Corner, Andrea Dandolo, Marc'Antonio da Canale, Alvise Mocenigo, Giacomo Malipiero, Francesco Emo, Antonio Loredan, and Alvise and Polo Malipiero. The young patricians, even the illegitimate sons of noble fathers, shared numerous interests, such as music, chess, literature, and philosophy, in addition to their religious concerns. As a group they were rather closely allied and spent a good deal of time together, often at the Fontego dei Tedeschi, where they enjoyed the music and also absorbed heterodox ideas. They enjoyed hearing the Psalms read in the vernacular at the Fontego and also in the garden of San Giorgio Maggiore on the Giudecca, where they often debated religious topics and the Huguenots in France.[37] They also read prohibited books like the *Institutes* of Calvin, the sermons of Fra Bernardino Ochino, and especially the works of Savonarola, among which were cited *Oracolo della renovatione della Chiesa* and *Trattato della revelatione della reformatione della Chiesa*. The youths in this group had eagerly studied these latter works, especially the *Oracolo*.[38]

When these Venetian patricians were summoned to appear before the Venetian Inquisition, they denied that they were part of a formal organization or conventicle. In spite of their denials, they clearly met in groups at the homes of various members, and they shared many ideas about the reform of the Church. From their testimony before the Inquisition one recognizes that they were not adept at theological argumentation. However, they voiced a variety of concerns: some were preoccupied with the sale of indulgences and the wicked lives of some priests; others questioned the doctrine of the pope, the veneration of images, auricular confession, purgatory, and the celibacy of the clergy, which Antonio Loredan claimed was impossible to maintain. Loredan said that he based his opinions upon natural law and natural reason, and summarized his beliefs by stating that only the Old Testament, the Gospels, the Acts of the Apostles, and the Epistles should be believed.[39] The inquisitor asked Loredan if he followed the good custom of the nobility and put the stole on his neck and knelt on both knees when taking communion. The inquisitor's question served as a reminder to Loredan of the nobility's responsibility in regard to religious practice. Antonio Loredan and Giacomo Malipiero seemed to be leaders in this group. Malipiero even admitted that he had learned his bad opinions from the humanist heretic Francesco Spinola, who had taken him to hear a preacher at San Mattio di Rialto.[40] Spinola had been a teacher of Venetian patricians' children and had also been a leader in a conventicle that met in San Fantin.[41] He had success in spreading his heterodox ideas among the

Venetians and was eventually incarcerated. Most interesting for our concerns is the fact that Spinola and Dionisio Gallo shared the same cell in a Venetian prison, about which I shall speak later. When Malipiero recanted his heretical views before the Venetian Inquisition, he indicated that he had learned all of his heresies from Francesco Spinola. These young Venetian patricians, though not adept in theology, were concerned with moral regeneration within the Church, and in this regard they would have had ideas in common with Dionisio Gallo, although there is no hard evidence to indicate that they had heard his discourses. One could argue, however, that any one of the young Venetian patricians mentioned might have been among the large crowds of noblemen who heard Dionisio speak in the cortile of the Palazzo Ducale. Giacomo Malipiero and Antonio Loredan, among others, had looked to prophetic works such as Savonarola's *Oracolo* as an aid in solving the religious problems of the day; Dionisio's claim to be God's servant and messenger would not have fallen on deaf ears if indeed any young members of Loredan's circle had heard his prophetic utterances. The young nobles had studied and admired Savonarola's prophetic utterances and his urgent call for a renovation of the Church, and these could have provided a common ground for interest in the words and warnings of Dionisio Gallo.[42] It is not known whether any of Dionisio's writings had circulated among his friends or among the closely knit group of young patricians or whether they had been copied.[43] It is quite clear, however, that the prophetic call for reform made by Savonarola and the reforming ideals expressed by Erasmus were still influential among patricians, *popolani,* and preachers in Venice in 1566.[44]

In addition to Dionisio's actual association with Rocho de Mazzochis and Giusto Morosini in Venice and a possible audience among young Venetian nobles, he had at least one connection in Padua. He received the hospitality of one of the rectors of the Studio of Padua, in whose home he put the finishing touches on the *Haec est causa totius ecclesiae militantis,* before he arrived in Venice.[45] Dionisio had himself been rector of the Collège de Lisieux in France, and the hospitality extended to him by the rector of the Studio of Padua could have been a courtesy of one rector to another. Dionisio did not indicate which of the two rectors had been his host. Joannes a Boteren (also written as Joannes ab Hoboken Antwerpiens) was rector of the *iuristarum* in 1566, and he would certainly have been interested in Dionisio's concern about the reform of the Church hierarchy.[46] Pope Pius V had accused Joannes of being a Lutheran and of holding Lutheran sympathies, expressing his concern to the Venetian ambassador Giacomo Soranzo that a heretic should not be tolerated as rector of the scholars. The pope had even ordered Cardinal Alvise Pisani to initiate proceedings against the rector because he was a heretic. Ambassador Soranzo, in his response, was grieved to point out "that this was not a good way to make a case, especially since the rector was living as a Christian inside and outside his house." The ambassador also noted that without any other indictment of the rector, a case could not be made; however, should other evidence be found, His Holiness must so indicate this specifically to Cardinal Pisani.[47]

The other rector, Andreas Gostiath Polonus (also written as Andreas Ctostinto Polonus), rector of the *artistarum,* also would have made the pope uneasy, since he also was known to hold heterodox opinions.[48] Dionisio did not indicate which rector was his host, but he remained long enough to complete *Haec est causa* and to make some contacts. While in Padua, Dionisio also read his legation to the podestà of Padua, Gerolamo Cicogna,[49] who listened patiently, according to our prophet. When the dinner hour approached, however, Cicogna advised Dionisio to speak to Cardinal Alvise Pisani, bishop of Padua, so that the bishop could approve the cause of Christ.[50] The bishop was not in Padua, however, when Dionisio went to call.

Dionisio's visit to the podesta reflected his emphasis on justice and the role of the Venetians in executing justice.[51] The podesta was the Venetian official chosen to administer justice in Padua, which was part of the Venetian dominion, a fact not lost on Dionisio. While he was completing the *Haec est causa* in the home of the rector of the Studio of Padua, he wrote at length about who should be chosen as judges. In a rhetorical discourse he claimed there were four persons who spoke with authority in the cause of the Catholic faith: the three persons of the Trinity as well as the "small and humble man whom you see." Dionisio indicated that he was *sub, pro,* and *cum* the three persons of the Trinity.[52] In an interesting passage, he rhetorically questioned the nature of man and the nature of justice:

> *What is man? What indeed are men whom you and eternal God established as judges in your cause with them? O highest and eternal Trinity, are you not able to do all things in heaven and on earth? Have you not created angels and men? Have you not judged and condemned by eternal decree the haughtiness of Lucifer and of all the angels who were his cohorts? . . . Wherefore do you not judge and condemn men who sin daily—from kings even to the lowest persons, from the chief authority of the Church even to the lowest ministers?*[53]

As a warning to all secular persons chosen to judge (including the podesta of Padua) Dionisio reminded lay officials and princes of their responsibility in regard to divine justice: "O divine justice, greatly to be heard, resisting most fairly the haughty and the rebellious! Consider these things, O dear prince, elected people, and nations. Recognize the divine honor that Christ himself shows to you. You establish judges in His cause and in your cause and in the cause of the whole Church; moreover, you are executors of His judgments in the land."[54] Dionisio's reminder about justice would hold great significance for Venice, which represented itself in its iconography as the upholder of justice. An example is found in the little book *Sitto e forma della chiesa di Santo Marcho posta in Venetia*, which describes the beauty and the splendor of the basilica.[55] On the frontispiece a woodblock depicts Venice as a beautiful woman, enthroned and crowned, surrounded by six maidens with crowns, representing the virtues. The two maidens in the foreground represent justice and temperance, while Venezia, the beautiful woman, holds the scepter of authority in her left hand and the gonfalon in her right. Two lions sit on either side. Venezia is obviously the summation of all the virtues, especially justice. Venice as justice is a central part of the program of sculptures on the facade of the Palazzo Ducale that faces the Bacino and also on the facade that overlooks the *piazzetta*.

Given Dionisio's prophetic certainty about his mission as God's servant and messenger, his visit to the podesta had a certain logic. Moreover, the potential for a sympathetic audience in Padua was large, since many students from Germany, France, and Italy would have been in accord with Dionisio's call for a reformed Church. Whether Dionisio ever addressed a public audience in Padua, however, cannot be determined at present. At any rate, he left Padua probably on the last day of May, leaving his horse with his friend, the rector of the Studio of Padua.

Dionisio timed his arrival in Venice to coincide with the Feast of Pentecost. He made use of many associations and symbolic meanings to emphasize his divinely given role. His strange clothing in Rome, with crown askew while carrying a massive cross, his request for appropriate clothing from Cosimo I, his reading and explanation of his prophetic text, his choice of space in which to unfold his message, no less than the time of his arrival in Venice on the eve of Pentecost—all point to Dionisio's purposeful presentation of himself and his message. And never was this more so than in Venice. Upon his arrival he evidently went directly to the home of Rocho de Mazzochis, for on the day of the Feast of Pentecost, June 2, 1566, he appeared in the Basilica di San Marco after a morning Mass and read his *Legatio*, his long proposal for the reform of the Church.

Since the day of Pentecost represented the return of Christ in the form of the Holy Spirit, Dionisio chose this day to reveal himself in Venice as God's chosen messenger. God had filled his person with the Holy Spirit, and he had become a "sacred agent," as it were, revealing on this sacred day of the Holy Spirit God's message in "sacred space."[56] The "sacred agent" in the physical presence of his own "sacred space" became part of the "sacred space" of San Marco, with its religious and political associations. Dionisio's presentation of himself as individual "sacred space" and "sacred agent" is significant for the interaction between the individual and the community, religious and political, in the grand scheme of *renovatio*.[57] Dionisio indicated that he had spoken "in the middle of the choir of San Marco in the presence of Christ, in the sight of the most illustrious Venetian prince and senators, in the presence of the legate and many other very famous men and people."

Dionisio was very much in evidence in the public spaces of Venice on the day of Pentecost. After vespers on the feast day he went to the Zattere, to the Church of the Holy Spirit, and again read his program for the reform of the Church, "with the clergy and people listening intently."[58] Again it is clear that Dionisio carefully chose the space in which he would present his message as God's servant for the second time in one day. The Church of the Holy Spirit was obviously a significant space for one chosen, according to Dionisio's belief, as God's messenger and servant. The Basilica di San Marco, where he had spoken earlier, not only had religious implications as the center of the Venetian religious cult but was also important as a political space, since it was the private chapel of the doge. This point has been made previously, but it bears repeating, since Dionisio's program for reform had both political and religious implications. The very nature of the Venetian republic, in which the political was ever entwined with the religious in a peculiarly Venetian fashion, was intimately related to Dionisio's choice of Venice as the culmination of his religious pilgrimage.

An example of the blending of political and religious ideas can be found in the records of the Consiglio dei Dieci; in this succinct statement the *consiglio* reminded the Venetians that God had given them the responsibility of governing and that they must assume this responsibility by turning from vices to virtues: "Our most prudent elders, who with authority and blood have acquired and left to us their posterity, this dominion, to safeguard its preservation, ordained many laws and ordinances to call the inhabitants in this city from vices and to lead [them] to virtue, and particularly the nobles, to whom the majesty of God has given the responsibility of ruling and governing the others in order to restrain immoderate ambition by the path of virtue."[59] Dionisio hoped that the Venetians would be the catalysts for the summoning of a league of princes to bring about a true reform of the Church, which he clearly believed the Council of Trent had not accomplished.[60] In addition, his appearance in Padua, in the home of the rector, and his discourse before the podesta before his arrival in Venice indicate Dionisio's understanding of the political-religious nature of Venetian politics. In fact, Dionisio seemed to have carefully orchestrated the revelation of his prophetic persona with multiple symbols, and in this sense he was very different from many of the itinerant preacher-prophets described by Niccoli.[61] He may have had expectations that his proposals for reform and the recounting of his "divine anointment" would allow him to become a "prophet in residence" in Venice, as he seems to have been in Florence and Ferrara. Gabriella Zarri has demonstrated that princes in the Quattrocento and the Cinquecento were not averse to having mystical women in their courts as a sign of divine protection for the city.[62] Because of his mystical anointment by the Virgin Mary and the commands from the Holy Spirit, Dionisio hoped for similar acceptance.[63] He understood the complex relationship between politics and religion, but he misread the practice of the Venetians, who had labored so diligently to maintain a delicate balance and to keep the pope's interference in Venetian affairs to a minimum.

After a busy feast day of preaching in two important locations, the Basilica di San Marco and the Church of the Holy Spirit, Dionisio lost no time in asking for an audience with the doge, Girolamo Priuli. He acted to enlist the political realm in his religio-political plan for reform. It is unknown whether Dionisio was given a formal audience with the doge, but his elegant purple robes and his cultivated demeanor would have made this a possibility. According to his own story, he was encouraged by the dignity of the Venetian doge and the senators and therefore presented himself as the "servant and messenger of God" who had an important message for Venice. He apparently read a formal statement written in elegant Latin and addressed "to the most serious, first, and most powerful dominion in the world and to the most famous Venetian Senate." In this document Dionisio claimed to have been shown by divine revelation what must be done in Christianity and in the whole world. He saw the problems of the Cinquecento in simple terms: the reformation of the clergy, the extirpation of heresy, the consolation of the poor, and the conversion of all the unfaithful to Christ. Noting his credentials as "the elected servant and messenger of omnipotent God," he acknowledged that his message had been heard and approved in many parts of France and Italy, naming specifically the dukes of Savoy, Florence, and Ferrara. He referred to his speech of the previous day in the

Basilica di San Marco, reminding the senators that his revelation had come from God, with grace infused. At the conclusion of his statement he offered "peace, happiness, and an eternal kingdom" to the doge and the Venetian senators. Dionisio signed his greeting "the elected servant and messenger of God, your friend and friend of the whole world, charioteer of the whole Church Militant, Dionysius Gallus."[64] He read from his prepared text "for as long as was possible." In addition to the unaccustomed appearance of one who claimed to be God's servant and messenger, a white dove, which Dionisio said had followed him into the Senate and had hovered over his right shoulder while he was speaking, added to the drama of the day.[65] From Dionisio's prophetic perspective the appearance of the dove provided absolute confirmation, at least to him, of his divine calling. He had claimed that his credentials were from the Holy Spirit, and the dove that followed him proved the point.

After this eventful day following the Feast of Pentecost, Dionisio was more determined than ever, because of the miraculous "sign," to reveal in full his plan of action to the Venetians. Consequently, he could often be found preaching in the cortile of the Ducal Palace and in the vicinity of the Basilica di San Marco. He chose these spaces because of the large number of people who passed through the piazza daily.[66] The cortile of the Palazzo Ducale would also have provided contact with patricians, who would more likely have understood his discourse in Latin. Dionisio's exotic dress, his cultivated speech, and his passionate sermons about reform never failed to draw a large audience, and he soon became a familiar figure in Venice. His notoriety also sparked the attention of the Venetian Inquisition. Consequently, the Inquisition sent its messenger Nicola Lapicida to the colorful preacher on June 4, 1566, and told him to stop his preaching, since preaching without a license was strictly forbidden. If he did not comply with the Inquisition's order, he would suffer banishment *sub poena triremis*.

Dionisio did not heed the warning and continued his practice of speaking in private space in the evening and in public space during the day. He could most often be found in the cortile of the Palazzo Ducale, preaching from the *banca*, or ledge, that is attached to each side of the Scala dei Giganti. Dionisio spoke from an advantageous point of the *banca* that looked toward the large court, so that he could be seen and heard by the greatest number of people. Dressed in magenta and gold and speaking in eloquently rhetorical Latin, Dionisio could always depend on a large audience of those who were passing through on business in the palazzo. When Dionisio was found preaching to a large group in the curia of San Marco on Saturday, June 7, and when news of his disregard for the orders of the Inquisition reached the members of the Holy Office and the Consiglio dei Dieci, Dionisio was admonished for the second time to desist from preaching, or else he would be apprehended and placed in prison. Our passionate, if rash, prophet ignored this warning as well. The record of the Holy Office at this point is terse: "And thus, when on Sunday, which was the ninth of the present month, he had been seen preaching, he was detained by the ministers of the Holy office and thrust into the prisons of the most illustrious Capi."[67] Dionisio, however, amplified the circumstances of his arrest and wrote metaphorically about his incarceration. The nuncio of the papal legate took him from his bed, presumably in the home of Rocho de Mazzochis in San Moisé. Dionisio vividly described the event: the nuncio surrounded "me, alone and simple and quiet in my bed, and he captured me like a dove in its nest; he bound me, covered my eyes, and led me into the dark prisons with evildoers, who oppressed me."[68] Dionisio's use of Latin was especially effective in contrasting the gentleness of the dove, representing the Holy Spirit, which had hovered over him as he spoke in the Senate, with the cruelty of the "hunter," the nuncio of the papal legate.

We recall that Dionisio had challenged the papal legate Brisegno in Florence and never missed an opportunity to place the papal legates in a bad light. He had also been critical of the pope and the cardinals, who did not understand Catholic doctrine.[69] Criticism of the papal legates, however, was not unfamiliar to the Venetians. On one occasion, in 1544, Francesco Venier, Venetian orator at the papal court, wrote to the pope, urging him to leave the responsibility of judicial matters and of heresy to the patriarch. He noted that the nuncios had previously been like other ambassadors, but now the papal legates were "like medicine that sometimes and for some reasons may be useful but must not be used as a daily diet."[70]

Dionisio's arrest followed the third warning by the messenger of the Inquisition that he stop preaching and a denunciation by the magistrate, Daniel Reiniero, who had heard his sermon in the cortile of the Palazzo Ducale. Reiniero surmised from hearing the stranger that he was "one of those who held the opinion that all things must be in common." He also noted in his denunciation that Dionisio had much to say about the education of children and the choice of their teachers. The Venetian patrician evidently believed that Dionisio was an Anabaptist who believed that God still revealed himself to those "prepared through suffering to receive His illumination." The Anabaptists were considered especially dangerous in Venice, since they did not accept any authority except the rule of God.[71] It is not surprising that Dionisio appeared to be a cause for alarm, especially if he had been sent by agents in France.

The operation of the Venetian Inquisition has been amply clarified by Andrea Del Col and will not be redescribed here.[72] However, the men who constituted this body in June 1566, when Dionisio appeared before them, were the father inquisitor, Monsignor Valerius Faventius; the patriarch of Venice, Ioannes Trevisan; the papal legate, Giovanni Antonio Facchinetti; the auditor; the vicar; and the three secular representatives, the Venetian patricians Paolo Corner, Marco Morosini, and Giulio Contarini, procurator of San Marco. The Inquisition met on Tuesday, Thursday, and Saturday in the Chapel of San Teodoro, adjacent to the sacristy of the Basilica di San Marco. On some occasions, however, the Inquisition met in the loggia; during the trial of Dionisio all investigations were held in the regular meeting place.[73] The day after Dionisio's incarceration in the prisons of the Consiglio dei Dieci in the Palazzo Ducale, the Holy Office ordered that information be gathered about what the Frenchman had preached in his public discourses. Several witnesses provided information about the stranger. Jacobus Gambacurta, an important citizen of Verona, was summoned to testify about a certain Frenchman whom he had heard preaching "sopra quella banca alla scala di palazzo uerso la Corte." Gambacurta painted a vivid picture of the stranger who had been going through Venice teaching and arguing "evil doctrine," which often meant Lutheran or Anabaptist beliefs. Gambacurta was fascinated by Dionisio's clothing and described in detail his long purple-red cloak with long sleeves, his long vest, and his red shawl with a high collar, bound in gold braid. In addition to his colorful attire, the witness noted that Dionisio was adorned with many crosses of different sizes. All the witnesses who were summoned by the Inquisition commented in detail about Dionisio's clothing, and all presented a consistent portrait of our prophet. Dionisio's exotic appearance obviously represented his own concept of how God's chosen prophet should present himself.[74] As I have noted previously, Dionisio often spoke of clothing and asked for new clothing appropriate to his calling. He was attentive to "sacred space" for preaching and to himself as a "sacred vessel" properly attired as God's anointed.

Dionisio's appearance as described by various witnesses recalls the late-Quattrocento painting by the anonymous painter of Aix-en-Provence that depicts the prophet Jeremiah clothed in crimson robes and looking like a beautifully attired cardinal.[75] Vestments associated with divine service and other occasions are well attested in Judaism and Christianity. Dionisio's conscious choice of prophetic symbolism reflects the cultural model of the "humanist-prophet" of the Cinquecento rather than that of the itinerant *romito* described by Ottavia Niccoli, who went through the streets, dirty and

fig. 13

Diagram showing the seating plan of the Holy Office of the Inquisition in the Chapel of San Teodoro, adjacent to the sacristy of the Basilica di San Marco. Biblioteca nazionale di San Marco, Venice

in rags, crying "Do penance!" as bystanders mocked.[76] Dionisio also used additional outward symbols in Paris and Rome to convey his own concept of renovation of the Church and society. He moved through Paris, wearing a tin crown and carrying a wooden scepter as he preached the need for reform from the "highest to the lowest." Similarly, in Rome he dressed the part of a "fool for Christ" as he carried a huge cross through the streets, warning the Romans "to crucify their hearts." The role of "sacred actor" was ever present as Dionisio consciously and carefully chose his garments and his "sacred space," that is, his "sacred theater," for presentation of his divinely inspired drama of restoration and regeneration. The clothing he chose for himself as "sacred actor" was successful in capturing the attention of the Venetians and drawing it to his words. Gambacurta noted that the Frenchman repeated many times the following words: "Venetian Lords, I have been sent by the Holy Spirit. You have seen the dove, and it is a sign of my truth. Indeed I say that the pope and his cardinals do not understand well the true Catholic doctrine, since they do and say many things contrary to the evangelical doctrine, as I shall show you in my discourse."[77]

Almost as an incantation Dionisio repeated his credentials and their verification. The witness from Verona indicated that the stranger read from a handwritten book that contained many propositions, some of which seemed to have been taken from Saint Paul, others from different Gospels. All passages had been abridged, and the preacher was interpreting them in his own manner, always speaking in cultivated Latin. Gambacurta mentioned that a large crowd had listened intently to the Frenchman, among whom were the magistrate Zuan Francesco Pisani, son of Marc'Antonio Pisani, and a priest from the Church of San Zuane di Rialto.

The Inquisition made note that noblemen and clergy had come under the spell of this flamboyant preacher, and immediately called Fra Augustinus de Martinis of San Zuane di Rialto to testify. Like Gambacurta, Fra Augustinus described in detail the clothing of Dionisio and confirmed the previous testimony. He defined more specifically, however, Dionisio's remarks that (1) the elections of the pope and the cardinals were not made according to the ancient tradition but rather through simony and indirect paths; (2) the pope was a simple bishop of the Lateran; (3) he, Dionisio, had been sent by God and the Holy Spirit; (4) God had sent the Holy Spirit in the form of a white dove to indicate his divine appointment; (5) to prove the truth of his assertions, he was prepared to suffer fire and water and every kind of torment.[78] Fra Augustinus had obviously listened attentively, since he reported accurately what Dionisio had written in his *Legatio*, which he had read to those in the cortile of the Palazzo Ducale. Fra Augustinus noted that many nobles, as well as a subdeacon of San Zuane di Rialto, were in attendance as Dionisio spoke.

Patrician support for evangelism, in addition to the support from other social classes, kept reform ideals in Venice alive even after the midpoint of the sixteenth century, as the case of Dionisio and those of nobles, prelates, and artisans make clear. While support for reform along traditional Catholic and Venetian lines was welcomed by Venetian authorities and the Holy Office, the preaching of Dionisio presented a paradox. On the one hand, his call for reform of the clergy and the Church struck a chord with Venetian religious ideals;[79] on the other, his unorthodox dress, his prophetic claims, and the excitement his preaching aroused made him suspect. Religion was viewed not only as a spiritual concern but also as a means of securing social and political stability. The effect of the Dionisio's preaching on the customary Venetian piety, religion, and politics was cause for concern.

The Inquisition was anxious for names of those who had listened to the preaching of the Frenchman, but Fra Augustinus named only the subdeacon. On June 20, 1566, five days after the testimony of Augustinus, the

Inquisition summoned the subdeacon, named Stephanus, for testimony. Stephanus admitted that he had spoken with the stranger in a friendly manner outside the Basilica di San Marco and had asked him several questions about who he was and by whose spirit he was led. Dionisio had responded that he was a *gallus* and a messenger of God sent by the Holy Spirit. Stephanus had asked where his testimonial letters were, since messengers carried such letters. Dionisio had replied, according to the witness, that the dove that followed him into the Senate was his witness.[80]

The Inquisition probably searched for additional witnesses, since the investigation did not resume until July 2, when the magistrate Zuan Francesco Pisani testified that some people thought that the stranger was a French bishop because of his attire. Pisani apparently was fascinated by Dionisio's dress, which he, like others, described in detail. He noted that Dionisio had asked for lighter-weight clothing, since it was becoming warm in Venice, but he could not remember the names of the many nobles in attendance. He did indicate, however, that the papal nuncio had taken some papers from which Dionisio had been reading, and then led him outside the courtyard of the palazzo.

A week after Pisani's testimony the subject of the investigation was brought before the Holy Office. Investigations customarily began with questions about the accused's name, place of birth, and occupation. These questions were not asked of Dionisio, however. Instead, the inquisitor first asked what usually came second in an inquisition: namely, did the defendant understand why he was being detained? Dionisio responded that he had no idea except that he had not left Venice as he had been enjoined by the messenger of the Holy Office. When asked whether he had stopped preaching as he had been ordered, Dionisio engaged in a bit of verbal subtlety, as was his custom, noting that he had not been preaching but rather had been showing his writings, reading them and interpreting the passages he read. He admitted, however, that he had said a few words in addition to reading the documents.

The inquisitor wanted to know where his writings were, and Dionisio acknowledged that they had been taken from him by the papal legate's representative while he was speaking in the curia of San Marco. When asked if there were other documents, Dionisio said that there were three others, two written in Ferrara and one in Florence; among these were letters to princes, about thirteen in number, according to Dionisio's recollection, and also letters to the pope and to the Romans. He also reported that he had entrusted these letters to a Venetian citizen, Rocho by name, who held the office of *sensarius bladorum* (*senser di biave*). Dionisio did not give the cognomen of Signor Rocho, who evidently made a practice of opening his home to free thinkers or at least to those whose reforming ideas appeared suspect to the Inquisition. Dionisio indicated that Giusto Morosini and Signor Rochus Venetus had heard and had approved his articles for reform of the Church, and that they had signed their names at the conclusion of the *Legatio* he had completed in Rocho's home. Since thirty-six documents written by Dionisio are found among the records of his trial by the Venetian Inquisition, it is probable that the members of the tribunal knew of Dionisio's friendship with Rocho de Mazzochis and Giusto Morosini, both of whom had affixed their signatures to the *Legatio* that Dionisio had completed in the home of Rocho on the Feast of Pentecost. With such knowledge they would have had at their disposal not only the documents seized directly from Dionisio in the curia of San Marco but also any he may have left in the home of Rocho. The names of Rocho and Giusto appeared often in Dionisio's various writings in the hands of the tribunal. The Venetian Inquisition was zealous in gathering all information pertinent to a proceeding and in calling all witnesses who could supply accurate information. In Dionisio's trial what is surprising is that the inquisitor did not summon either Rocho or Giusto, although they could have supplied pertinent information about the defendant.

The precise reason for the inquisitor's unusual oversight cannot be stated with absolute certainty. It seems highly possible, however, that Giusto Morosini was not summoned to give testimony, in order not to embarrass his family or Marco Morosini, one of the Tre Savi sopra Eresia. Marco and Giusto were cousins from the Morosini dalla Sbarra. Marco's grandfather, Lorenzo, was the brother of Giusto's great-grandfather Benetto. The cousins were only one year apart in age and probably had many things in common.[81] Familial ties may have been at work in the reluctance shown by the Inquisition to summon Giusto Morosini for testimony. The Inquisition's circumspection in regard to Giusto may also have been the reason that Rocho de Mazzochis was not summoned; if one were called upon to testify, the other must also logically be summoned, since both Giusto Morosini and Rocho de Mazzochis had signed Dionisio's *Legatio*, which was already in the hands of the Inquisition.

Other aspects of Dionisio's inquisition were atypical of cases held during the same period. For example, the inquisitor did not ask him to state his name or where he was staying in Venice. In light of his harsh criticism of the pope, it is unusual that he was not asked his beliefs regarding Catholic dogma. Of the approximately fifty-nine heretics who were summoned for investigation by the Holy Office of the Inquisition in 1566 and 1567, almost all were asked similar questions: their beliefs concerning the Eucharist, the role of the pope, the validity of images and purgatory, and other aspects of Catholic practice, such as dietary habits. Not only was Dionisio not asked these types of questions, he was allowed greater freedom in his responses than was customary. He gave indirect answers to the questions of the inquisitor, and on one occasion he began to question the inquisitor, who often demanded that he respond with simple and precise answers. Dionisio seldom followed the inquisitor's instructions, however. For example, when he was shown a list of documents with their *incipits* and was asked if he recognized them, he responded that they were his writings. When asked, however, if he approved all the articles and propositions contained in these writings, he did not give a simple yes or no answer. Instead, he responded that his writings should be judged by a council of princes who were most virtuous and without any suspicion of heresy. He had also indicated that the nobleman Paolo Corner, one of the Tre Savi sopra Eresia, should evaluate his works. Dionisio's reference to Paolo Corner was less than tactful, since he was implying that a lay member of the tribunal was better qualified to judge his writings than were the ecclesiastics and that a lay council of princes could better assess the truth of his words than could the tribunal.

The inquisitor Faventius lost patience with Dionisio's responses about being judged by laymen and sharply demanded that he should answer with a simple yes or no. In his typical manner Dionisio responded: "All these works have been written about just causes and are true; they are partly prophetic, which an event will prove, partly real, that is, true and approved in themselves, and they ought to be approved by all sane judgment. For their approbation the grace of the Holy Spirit, which oversees all, has been implored. Unless these things are approved with the predicted solemnities preserved, I wish to be burned alive or crucified."[82] Dionisio had the last word, since the inquisition was abruptly halted, and he was returned to his cell.

Three days elapsed before Dionisio was again called to testify, on July 12, 1566. He insisted that after his name, the words "called in Gaul king of the Gauls, elected servant of omnipotent God and messenger to whom the most blessed Virgin appeared and spoke" should be appended. Surprisingly, these words appear in the transcription of the trial, indicating that the scribe of the Holy Office had followed Dionisio's request. Dionisio obviously wanted the words added because to him they represented his appropriate credentials and his mission. The fact that he was mocked in France did not seem to disturb him. Although his revilers had called him king of the Gauls in jest, their disbelief in his mission only strengthened his own certainty. As his testimony indicates, he recounted to the Inquisition his divine anointment by the Virgin "first on his skin, from the top of his head to the bottom of his feet over his whole body." Before the inquisitor could pose the first question, he denied that he was stubborn (*pertinax*), because this term applied "to the infidels, to heretics, and to those who hold foolish and evil opinions." Dionisio's passionate claims were in contrast to the calm, measured questions of the inquisitor, yet his unusual boldness seemed to divert the usual line of questioning. The inquisition became a reaction to Dionisio rather than reactions by Dionisio to questions asked. The inquisitor finally asked Dionisio whether all the propositions contained in his writings were true or false. Never answering yes or no as instructed, Dionisio responded that all of his writings were "true, according to the irrevocable affirmation of God, and just, according to God's wisdom in contrast to the earthly, animal, and diabolical wisdom of men." When Dionisio was asked if a good and true Catholic would write and declare publicly that the pope was unfit for the papacy, he again did not answer the question directly. Instead, he said that he would present his argument before the Venetian Senate and the congregated princes, with the pope present, if it was agreeable. In effect Dionisio declared that the authority of the Venetian Senate was superior to the authority of the Venetian Inquisition. This delicate point was not lost on the inquisitor, who immediately asked if the defendant thought that he could be judged by the holy tribunal and held responsible for answering the questions put to him by that body. Dionisio responded that in spite of the honor of the sacred tribunal, it could not appropriately judge him, because of the universality and generality of the case. The inquisitor impatiently asked how he, as a Catholic, could hold, in his writings, that "the pope was a defendant of the apostolic see that he occupied." Our prophet again responded that he could not answer unless all his writings had been seen by the congregated princes. Dionisio was again making clear that he believed that secular princes were better prepared intellectually and spiritually to understand his writings than were the ecclesiastics on the tribunal.

The inquisitor's exasperation was clear when he asked Dionisio what reason he could possibly give for his opinions; he obviously was not assuaged when the defendant noted that the problem was most universal, since the controversies in Christianity were not limited to only one part of the universe; rather, all must confess one God and one Son, true God and true man. The inquisitor, again in amazement, wanted to know how Dionisio could think that articles universally held by the Catholic Church and reaffirmed by the "Sacred Holy Ecumenical Universal Council of Trent" were points of controversy.

Dionisio's response at this point made clear that he did not believe that the Council of Trent had solved all the controversies in Christianity, since its acts still had to be put into execution. More important, however, was his statement that "the things that were lacking" should be completed "in the highest and final council before Christ should come and the Antichrist should rage against the elect."[83] Dionisio clearly believed that "his legation," inspired by the Holy Spirit and put into practice by a council of princes, would supplement the Council of Trent.

The inquisitor, strangely, did not pursue Dionisio's denial of the Inquisition's right to judge him. He did, however, question Dionisio about his claim that the pope should defend his right to occupy the apostolic chair. Dionisio again refused to answer this question until a full council of princes should review his writings. He insisted that the council be convoked immediately, so that it could render its truth before Christ's imminent coming, which, Dionisio claimed, had been revealed to him from on high. He emphasized that he had been chosen to reveal the divine will not because of his own merits but because of the decree from God revealed to him by the most sacred Virgin, who appeared to him, spoke to him, and hallowed his appointment as God's servant and messenger. Because of this heavenly decree, he professed "to reveal what he reveals, to do what he does, and to proclaim what he proclaims."[84] In Dionisio's mind the role of prophet was higher than that of pope or cardinal, since a prophet was chosen by God, the pope and cardinals by men. He had made this point to the papal nuncio in Florence when he had challenged the nuncio's authority to judge him whose authority came from God. Dionisio's concept of the prophet and his conviction that he was God's messenger led him into bold, sometimes audacious discourse with the Venetian Inquisition.

The exaltation of prophets was not without precedent in Italy in the years before Dionisio's arrival. Lodovico Lazzarelli had adopted as his spiritual father Giovanni da Corregio, the prophet who, appearing in Rome in 1484, called for repentance in preparation for the coming *renovatio*. Lodovico glorified Giovanni as prophet and also the role of the prophet: "Happy beyond measure is he who knows the fruits of his fate and who will have brought them freely to pass. For he ought to be counted among the good and not lower than the highest of them."[85] One of the disciples of Marsilio Ficino, Giovanni Nesi, who followed Savonarola's call for a *renovatio mundi*, endorsed Savonarola as a prophet in the tradition of Hermes Trismegistus.

Savonarola, however, denied any relation between the prophet and his prophetic powers, since prophecy was a gift from God and man had no power of prophecy without divine infusion.[86] Dionisio was similar to Savonarola in this respect. His boldness before the Venetian Inquisition was based upon his certainty of his divine illumination. He had been mocked and considered foolish in Paris and Italy, but this did not deter him before the Inquisition, so certain was he of his mission.

The Franciscan Chronicle of 1572 speaks of Fra Giovanni, a Spanish Franciscan, as one whom God had inspired, a claim Dionisio made for himself, and notes that "questo huomo de Dio fosse de nobile generatione quanto al seculo, nondimeno molto se humiliò et anichilò per amore de Dio."[87] The Franciscan Bartolomeo Cordoni, sometime before his death in 1535, wrote the *Dialogo dell'unione spirituale di Dio con l'anima*. Paolo Simoncelli has demonstrated that the *Dialogo* should be considered a link between the ideas generated from the medieval Free Spirit and the quietism of the Seicento.[88] The work is important in the context of Dionisio Gallo, since it shows that the man who is illumined by divine wisdom can become like God. This belief may explain Dionisio's claim that he was higher than the pope and the cardinals. Simoncelli cites a passage in which the *Anima*, in dialogue with *Amore* and *Ragione*, states that "[t]he universal desire of all mortals is to wish to come to one final end, to a state perfect and completely quiet." In this state of quiet, "if a man wished, he could surpass the seraphim and be made God."[89] The *Dialogo* appears to have its source in Jacopone da Todi and Ubertino da Casale. Simoncelli also points out that during the years when the *Dialogo* was being printed and reprinted, Giorgio Siculo and a group of Benedictines of the Congregation Cassinese were preaching the fullness of the mercy of God and a general pardon for all, two themes dear to Dionisio.[90] Fra Bartolomeo, in order to humble himself, feigned madness so that he would be humiliated the more. During the same period of the 1530s the mystical Benedictines "Cassinesi" theorized that madness (*pazzia*) was a most important avenue for inhuman humiliations as a preparation for uniting man's soul with God.[91] Savonarola was of the same mind in regard to illumination. Writing to the brothers of San Marco about how to resist temptation and arrive at perfection, he noted that "many are wiser and more illuminated by God than you, and you need especially . . . to become fools [*pazzi*] to be saved in the sight of God. As the Apostle says, 'If anyone among you seems to be wise in this generation, let him become foolish in order to be wise.'"[92] Dionisio followed Saint Paul's words about being God's fool and refused to be "wise" in the eyes of the world.[93] His certainty or his stubbornness in this regard was the cause of many of his troubles. As Savonarola often retold the story of Balaam and his ass, Dionisio often wrote of himself as a humble little man in a weak body whom God had chosen to glorify as his prophet. Dionisio Gallo was indeed an unusual presence in the Chapel of Saint Theodore, where the Inquisition met.

When the inquisitor questioned Dionisio about some of his writings that stated that the reasons for the pope's dominion over men were diabolical arguments introduced by the Devil and Satan against Christianity and the truth, he smiled and began to walk back and forth before finally answering. "Whatever he wrote as the orator and messenger of God, let the congregated princes judge if he had written correctly," Dionisio replied.[94] He then became angry and said that he would answer no more questions, because the members of the Inquisition were the defendants who needed to be reformed. He also accused them of being his enemies and most cruel judges, who daily killed him. Because of the injuries he had suffered at their hands, he was forced to speak out. At this remembrance of his suffering in the prison of the Capi del Consiglio dei Dieci and perhaps frustrated because of the inquisitor's questions, he threw himself on the floor, out of sight of the inquisitor, uttering insults against anyone who tried to intervene. He was led back to his cell by the guards, whom he attempted to kick. After this outburst during his inquisition of July 12, 1566, he was placed in the prisons of the Signori di Notte instead of the prisons of the Consiglio dei Dieci, where he had been incarcerated since his arrest on June 8, 1566.[95]

The prisons of the Consiglio dei Dieci were in the Palazzo Ducale, and they were acknowledged by the Venetians to be places of horror. The stench from feces and the subsequent pollution caused misery and often death for the prisoners. There was little space in which to move about, and sickness was common.[96] The prisons in the Palazzo Ducale were often cause for concern to the Consiglio dei Dieci, and many records indicate the council's preoccupation about the small spaces in which the incarcerated had to live and about the obvious health problems.[97] Houses adjacent to the Palazzo Ducale were purchased to provide more space, and some prisons were enlarged.[98] The wretched conditions continued, however. Various other locations were used for prisons, such as San Giovanni in Bragora or Sant'Apostoli, but these were equally unsatisfactory, usually occupying the first level of their respective buildings and therefore very damp and difficult to secure. Dionisio had always been incarcerated in the prisons in the Palazzo Ducale. When he was moved from one prison to another, his conditions did not improve— quite the contrary. Dionisio's account of the suffering he endured and about which he complained to the Inquisition in words and in writing was no exaggeration, since records of the Consiglio dei Dieci confirm his description.[99] The prisons of the Signori di Notte, also in the Palazzo Ducale, were equally terrible, and Dionisio described in detail many of his torments instead of answering the questions put to him by the inquisitor.[100] He complained that the other prisoners had beaten him, kicked him, and stolen his money and that a guard named Cesare had beaten him with keys, causing him to bleed profusely. He scolded the inquisitor and the judges on the tribunal about his vile treatment and about life in the Venetian prisons. After his transfer to the prisons of the Signori di Notte, he complained that he was dying of hunger, yet remained in his right mind in spite of his extreme deprivation. At night he had to endure the cold and damp with no blankets or bedding, sleeping on the bare earth. The greatest horror he suffered was at the hands of a Turk, a prisoner in the same cell, who beat him first with his fists and then with a board. Afterward the Turk pulled Dionisio by his beard and threw him on the ground; next he seized him by his genitals and lifted him above his head. Dionisio said that the Turk tried to strangle him and boasted that he had been a torturer among the Turks. Because of this violence he demanded that the Venetian Senate take note of his travail. He also stated that even the guards and the other prisoners were disturbed over the tumult but obviously were ineffective in quelling the attack.[101]

We are not told why the Turk chose Dionisio to abuse; from subsequent testimony, however, we learn that he probably was offended by Dionisio's constant preaching, which apparently continued within the prison. Life in a Venetian prison in the Cinquecento was harrowing, to say the least, and Dionisio's description of his torments was especially vivid. If the inquisitor was moved by the account of his suffering, he did not reveal his sentiment. Instead, he began to read word for word the document that Dionisio had written to the Venetian Senate. Dionisio interrupted the reading, however, saying that he should be allowed to interpret the document. He also attacked the sacred tribunal with harsh words, calling them "lords who were becoming tyrants," and accusing them of resisting the reformation he had proposed. After this final outburst the inquisitor sent him back to the prison of the "Lords of the Night."

Three weeks passed before the Frenchman was again summoned from the prison to appear before the Inquisition, on July 30, 1566. The respite from questioning did not improve Dionisio's prudence. When he was asked about his purpose, he in turn asked the members of the Inquisition to declare themselves either friends or foes of Christ and His Gospel.[102] The inquisitor was obviously startled by the accused who was becoming the accuser, and the other members of the tribunal responded that they were friends of Christ and the evangelical truth and avengers and defenders of the Catholic faith. Shortly after responding, they regained their composure, and the inquisitor warned Dionisio that he was the defendant and must answer their questions in a direct manner. He resumed his investigation by asking Dionisio's opinion about the wealth of the Church.[103] Dionisio said that although it was not evil for the Church to have riches, the clergy should use the riches of the Church for the consolation of the poor and for the removal of heresy. The question of the Church's riches evidently interested the Venetian Inquisition because Dionisio was asked if he wrote or taught that the riches of the Church should be acquired by the secular authorities.[104] Again the defendant evaded the questions, suggesting that he should be asked about his writings, which were now in the hands of the tribunal. He was then asked if he approved all that he had written about the removal of the Church's wealth by the secular authorities. He replied that he approved all that he had written and then added that the judges would also approve the accord of the Holy Spirit. Dionisio's suggestion that he and the Venetian authorities would be in agreement over the disposition of the wealth of the Church is significant, since it perhaps contained more than a grain of truth, a fact that surely would cause embarrassment to the lay members of the Inquisition.[105]

Venetian legislation in the fifteenth century reflected the Serenissima's distrust of clerical influence. For example, nobles who had received income from ecclesiastical benefices were in 1498 excluded from membership in the Great Council and from all public office. The *papalisti*, the families of Venetians who held ecclesiastical positions, were excluded from all deliberations that concerned ecclesiastical matters. In addition, no clergyman could serve the Venetian state in any capacity or have access to the archives.[106]

Especially after the League of Cambrai and the concessions Venice had to make, the Serenissima was determined to maintain its traditional authority over the Church. As Paolo Sarpi wrote, "Chiesa e Stato vengono ambedue da Dio, e la prima obbedisce al secondo nel temporale, questo a quella nello spirituale ma conservando ciascuno i propri diritti." In its relations with Rome, Venice treated the papacy as an equal among other lay states and allowed the spiritual character of the papacy minimal influence over the city's political relations with Rome. Venice also followed this policy "nelle relazioni politiche dovute a cause diverse dalle questioni di possessi o di confini."[107] The city occasionally taxed the clergy without the pope's consent and sought to bring them to trial in the secular courts despite the protests of the papal nuncio.

In 1535 the Venetian Senate passed one of the most significant laws about the Church and property in order to validate Venice's authority with respect to the Church. The law stated that real property of the city that had been given to ecclesiastics through legacies or donations for pious causes must be sold after two years to a layman, "the proceeds to go to the procurators of Saint Mark, the normal administrators of charitable bequests."[108] The Venetian patricians were also solidly opposed to the Tridentine decree that forbade the laity from possessing ecclesiastical property.[109]

Dionisio's responses to the inquisitor's questions about Church ownership of property were ironic, since the statements of the man suspected of strange or heretical teachings were not antithetical to the laws passed by the Senate of Venice to maintain Venice's authority over the Church. Dionisio enlarged his original statements about the wealth of the Church by noting that the right of Christ and the right of Saint Peter did not establish any riches or temporal dominions of the Church, since Christ was poor and had no temporal dominion and Saint Peter did not leave any temporal dominion to his successors but gave them equal authority to rule the Church. He noted that temporal dominions often produced wicked quarrels instigated by the Devil, who was called "Prince of the world."

When the inquisitor asked Dionisio if he was prepared to "sustain the flames of fire" for his belief, he noted that he had already professed that point. Reluctant to abandon the question of Church property, the inquisitor asked whether the Church could justly possess a temporal kingdom and whether or not this would be good. The defendant responded that, since they had put him in chains and threatened prison even till Judgment Day, this question was unnecessary. His impertinence again produced a reprimand; the inquisitor told him to answer the question seriously and briefly. Dionisio said that the Church was justly entitled to possess both dominion and kingdom. After this response, the questioning resumed about the Church's possession of a temporal kingdom and temporal dominion. Dionisio responded that all the possessions of the Church could be held justly if they were used well.

Up to this point in Dionisio's interrogation the inquisitor seemed to engage in discussion with the accused rather than in an investigation, in spite of his attempts to control the questioning on his terms. After the lengthy remarks about the Church and property, the inquisitor turned to the usual questions that were asked of suspected heretics. He wanted to know what Dionisio meant when he spoke of the Church. This question was critical for determining heretical ideas, since many heretics said that the Church was the body of Christ and those who believed in Him and that the Roman Catholic Church was not the Church of Christ. Dionisio's answer was equivocal, since he said that the Church was the Church of the Just and the Church of Christ, whose members were the faithful, not heretics or the unfaithful. When asked whether the Church contained the unjust and sinners, the defendant responded that the Church Militant contained them. It is interesting to note that throughout the interrogation about the nature of the Church the inquisitor always used the term *Ecclesia* (Church), and Dionisio also spoke of the *Ecclesia* until pushed to explain what the Church was. Then, instead of *Ecclesia*, he used the word *congretatio*. The inquisitor obviously understood the implications of the turn of the phrase, for he then asked if the Roman Church was the Church (*Ecclesia*) of Christ. Dionisio, contrary to his previous imprecise responses, stated that the Roman Church was the true and only Church, which could be called Catholic and which was approved by Christ, that there was no other Catholic Church that could be called the Church of God, and that the others were churches of evil.

Apparently satisfied with this Catholic response the inquisitor returned to the question of the Church's right to possess dominion or a temporal kingdom. Dionisio answered in his typically indirect manner by noting that the Church justly holds dominion when it uses its authority for the consolation of the poor and the guidance of the Church. The inquisitor reminded Dionisio that he had taught or written that the riches of the Church should be taken away and dispensed by lay authorities. The question of the Church's right to hold riches and property was apparently the most vexing concern of the inquisitor up to this point in the investigation and one that the defendant, by his responses, had not clarified to his satisfaction. He was again vague, stating that he had written that the Church should have its wealth taken away if it did not use it well. The inquisitor became repetitious in his questions, and the responses followed the same pattern. Finally, he asked who should determine how the Church used its wealth. Dionisio's answer was surprisingly forthright. He said: "The princes by whom, in large part, those dominions have been piously given and by the chosen shepherds [bishops] along with them."[110] Dionisio's response, which indicated the Church must share with lay princes the responsibility of distributing its wealth was surely displeasing to the papal nuncio, Facchinetti; however, to the three lay members of the Inquisition the defendant's answer probably seemed to represent a commonsense approach. For the rest of the day the inquisitor continued to pursue Dionisio's teachings about the relations of the clergy and laypersons. He wanted to know who was to select the "chosen shepherds" and if the defendant had written that the selection of bishops pertained to princes and secular authorities. Dionisio responded that the clergy, together with the princes, should select the bishops. Although he had written that the selection of bishops pertained to princes or to secular authority, he had not indicated that the clergy should be excluded; however, in order to remove many abuses, virtuous men and those princes and magistrates who performed their duties well should be chosen to select the bishops. He pointed out that if a good magistrate, free from all heresy, should choose the bishops, they would not by right be accused after their selection.

The questions posed by the inquisitor about the Church and property were the most substantial issues raised in Dionisio's inquisition. They were also central to reform proposals of both Catholics and Protestants. In addition, the abuses that resulted from the Church's possession of property and the clergy's holding of plural bishoprics were also major themes in Dionisio's plan for reform.[111]

Many of the ideas articulated by Dionisio were already practiced in Venice as part of the religious and civic interaction. For example, the patriarch of Venice and other members of the higher clergy were chosen by the Venetian Senate, which sent names to the pope for confirmation. Parish priests were chosen by the property holders in the parish and confirmed by the patriarch. Church property in Venice was taxed. Clerics accused of crimes were tried in state courts. The letters of the Venetian ambassadors in Rome reflect the pope's disapproval of Venice's Church-state relations. As Frederic Lane has pointed out, in other Italian cities "papal power was not limited as much as it was in Venice, nor was the Church as firmly policed by the state."[112] Yet in spite of reform-minded cardinals like Gasparo Contarini and other Venetian patricians, some Venetian politicians used their influence to gain bishoprics for siblings or other family members, thereby adding to the wealth and prestige of their families, although no one could hold office in both the Church and the republic. Although alien to the ideals of Cardinal Contarini, "wealth cast a dark shadow over the competition for honors within the Venetian nobility."[113] It should also be noted that the Senate had to approve the assignment of a bishopric in Venetian territory, and if a Venetian accepted a bishopric contrary to the will of the Senate, he and his family would be punished. Another abuse related to benefices was the inheritance of Church money. Contarini and the authors of the *Consilium* of 1537 viewed will-making an abusive practice, as they noted.[114]

The remarks of Dionisio about the role of princes in effecting reform led to questions concerning who was to judge whether the Church had used well or badly its wealth and temporal property. Again Dionisio emphasized the importance of the princes. He noted that the chosen bishops should oversee the Church's stewardship in conjunction with the princes. He also urged that princes who were upright men without any taint of heresy should, in conjunction with priests, choose the bishops. The situation in France, where there were heretical bishops, according to Dionisio, had obviously impressed him with the urgency of reforming the episcopacy. His belief that the princes, especially Italian princes, should choose the bishops reflected his desire that virtuous men, whether lay or clerical, participate in the reformation of the Church. The significant role Dionisio assigned to the princes was also a compliment to the princes of Ferrara, Florence, and Savoy who had befriended him and extended him hospitality, and especially to the doge of Venice, who, along with the Venetian Senate, according to Dionisio, had a special role in bringing about the reform of the Church. Dionisio's repeated call for a council of princes to effect reform in the episcopacy seemed to reiterate Venice's vain appeal for a council in the early years of the Cinquecento, contrary to the desires of the pope.[115] Yet the Venetians were aware of the dangers inherent in some reform ideas as proclaimed by the Protestants and their princes. Recognizing the political as a potential sphere of danger, Girolamo Soranzo, Venetian ambassador to Rome in 1563, wrote: "According to my opinion, in the estrangement of Germany and England the self-interest of the princes has played a much greater part than the opinion of Martin Luther or of Melanchthon; and concerning the present disturbances of France, Your Serenity knows very well that the principal motive has been neither Calvin nor Beza, but the particular hatreds and the desire to govern."[116]

The general temporal and spiritual reform of the Church that Dionisio proposed bore a resemblance to the reforms suggested by Giustiniani and Querini in the *Libellus ad Leonem x* of 1513. The emphasis of the *Libellus* was on the spiritual renewal of mankind.[117] Gasparo Contarini also shared these concerns for the individual renewal of man; in addition, he stressed the role of the episcopacy in the reform of the Church. Contarini's emphasis upon the role of the bishops was not unlike Dionisio's call for true reform of the "shepherds of the flock." Contarini and his group, who presented a proposal for reform of the Church under orders of Pope Paul III, noted in 1537 that one of the first abuses that must be corrected concerned the bishops who held multiple bishoprics and were often absent from their churches. They wrote: "By our immortal God, what more miserable sight could present itself to a Christian traveling though Christendom than the deserted state of the churches? Almost all shepherds have abandoned their flocks, nearly all of which are entrusted to hirelings. Therefore a severe penalty and no mere censure should be imposed especially on bishops, but also on parish priests who are absent from their flocks."[118]

Dionisio's remarks about the princes' role in reform aroused the inquisitor's interest; he asked Dionisio if he had taught or written that princes and secular authorities could remove bishops and place others in their office. Dionisio's response was again indirect. He said: "When the pope is in accord and when bishops are uncorrupted, it is good." He then added that Christ had established kings and priests. He also noted that what he had written was for the help of the clergy, not in contempt of them. The final question of the day's lengthy interrogation was whether the Frenchman had ever written that secular persons and princes were priests. Dionisio's answer confirmed his prophetic persona: "He had never written or talked plainly, but according to the intelligence of the Holy Spirit, just as the first chapter of the Apocalypse says. He made us a kingdom and priests for God."[119] Dionisio boldly identified himself with John, author of the Apocalypse, who wrote in the prologue to the first chapter: "This is the revelation given by God to Jesus Christ so that He could tell His servants about the things that are now to take place very soon; He sent His angel to make it known to His servant John . . . to Him who has loved us, and washed us from our sins in His own blood and made us to be a kingdom and priests for God His Father—to Him belong glory and dominion forever and ever."[120]

The prophecies of Dionisio that were discussed by the Inquisition in the first month of questioning did not concern the doctrinal issues that occupied reformers of both persuasions in the first two decades after Luther. The principles advanced by Dionisio were spiritual and moral and contained a social and political message, reflecting, as I have noted, the concerns of reforming cardinals such as Contarini, Pole, and Morone and the spiritualist zeal of the Theatini and their Oratorio of Divine Love.[121] Dionisio's prophetic dreams were not unique, as previously demonstrated. After the Council of Trent the visionary hopes that had first been placed in the council now found credence among noblewomen such as Giulia Gonzaga and Vittoria Colonna, by prelates like Pietro Carnesecchi, and by the circles of Waldensians and Erasmians. Giorgio Siculo's claim that he had received knowledge of God directly from Him was not dissimilar to the claims of Dionisio Gallo.[122]

The inquisitor asked Dionisio who had sent him and who had appointed him a minister to preach and spread abroad the doctrine found in his writings. Although warned to speak the truth and reply simply, Dionisio launched into a long discourse about his divine anointment, noting that the Virgin had reported the mysteries of these "most miserable, most new times"; that he, in spite of all dangers, must speak and preach the truth to kings, to people, to nations, and to all men without exception; that the truth of his prophetic message was that the clergy must be reformed, heresy must be removed, the poor must be consoled from a third part of the goods of the Church, and all infidels must be converted to Christ.[123] By emphasizing his outer and inner anointment by the Virgin, Dionisio was indicating the transfer of divine gifts to himself through the virginal female presence that represented the Divine Trinity.[124] At least in his own eyes, his anointment confirmed the truth of his prophecies and increased his boldness before the inquisition, which continued spasmodically throughout the summer of 1566.

In spite of the customary efficiency of the Venetian Inquisition, Dionisio's trial did not move smoothly, at least from the Inquisition's point of view, because Dionisio usurped the inquisitor's questions with long discourses of his own, which often led the inquisitor to remind him that "it was not his right to question but to be questioned, also to respond, because he is the defendant and faces the judges of the holy tribunal convoked as representatives of Christ."[125] The inquisitor seemed unable to keep the questioning under control, however. Even when dismissed from the presence of the Inquisition, Dionisio continued to speak, begging to be sent to the "most illustrious Venetian Senate" so that the Senate could take account of his innocence and afflictions.[126] However, before he was sent back to prison, he ominously warned that he had "certain things that must be said [to the assembled Senators] for the conservation of this Venetian dominion and republic."[127]

Three weeks later, on August 20, 1566, the Inquisition, in response to Dionisio's request to be heard and to confess the truth, gave him an audience but warned him to tell the truth, since the truth would cause them to be sympathetic to him.[128] When received into the presence of the Venetian Inquisition, Dionisio began a long soliloquy:

> *I, Dionisio Gallo, faithful and true soldier under Christ and on His behalf, a man sent by God for salvation, for three and a half years now, toward the end of this present month of August, to tell to all nations, in loneliness and candor, in great need and poverty, that in these last days all should repent and do penance and be reconciled to God on behalf of the will of Christ; I, crucified and in this holy tribunal in which, according to my own will, with a determined mind, steadfast and resolute, I have said to you: "Crucify me; through me you are free. Let my blood be for the illumination and conversion of the world to Christ. For Him I am on the earth and for His right in*

the universal Church Militant; for Christ as much as for His will, I have been sacrificed and killed; I who have often said to you: 'Sacrifice me; kill me.'" When you have interrogated me, I [have] respond[ed]: "I wish to be understood, and it is necessary that one understand what I cried out to the most famous Venetian Senate yesterday morning, calling to them: 'Pay attention; pay attention; pay attention, most famous Venetian senators. I, Dionisio Gallo, a man sent by God, have something great and necessary to tell you about your dominion and on behalf of the universal state of the Church Militant. Hear me; call me to speak late in the evening under penalty of death. And truly I have revelation.'"[129]

This long speech to the Venetian Inquisition is significant and perplexing, not only for what Dionisio said about his prophetic mission but for what he indicated about his appearance before the Senate on the previous day. During his appearance before the tribunal on August 3, he had warned the Inquisition that he wanted to be called before the Senate, since he had things "that must be said for the conservation of the Venetian dominion and republic." His words on August 20 may perhaps indicate that he had indeed appeared in the Senate. If this had been the case (and the scribe did not indicate any correction or remonstrance from the Inquisition), it would have been strange, to say the least, that a person on trial would have been allowed to appear before the Senate. The only explanation would seem to be that Dionisio's warning was taken seriously, given the numbers of enemies within and without in 1566. One should also recall that Dionisio had previously asked the Inquisition that Paolo Corner, a Venetian patrician, senator, and a lay member of the Holy Office in 1566, read and judge his writings. What relationship, if any, this earlier request had to his supposed appearance in the Senate during his trial still remains in the shadows. Dionisio's discourse passed without comment from the inquisitor, and our strange prophet was returned to the fourth prison *da basso*[130] of the Signori di Notte and was not summoned again for questioning until two months later, on October 15, 1566. The inquisition was brief; when questioned about the letter he had written to the Venetian Senate, Dionisio admitted that he had written the letter, but thereafter complained bitterly to his judges about the horrors of his confinement. He was again warned to answer the questions placed before him, but he railed against the tribunal, accusing them of resisting the reformation he had proposed. Thereupon he was again returned to the fourth prison *da basso* and was not recalled for questioning for almost four months. On February 8, 1567, a certain Vicenzo, a guard of the prisons of the Signori di Notte al Criminale, appeared before the tribunal to ask for the transfer of Dionisio Francese to another prison because his constant preaching and praying kept the other prisoners from sleeping. Vicenzo recounted that Dionisio had sung vile words as if he were singing litanies. The other prisoners beat him in an effort to stop his preaching and the so-called litanies, but to no avail, according to the guard. Following this testimony the other judges instructed the inquisitor to go to the prison, with a notary of the Holy Office, to examine the prisoners who had made complaints against Dionisio, in order to ascertain the truth.

The inquisitor visited the prison on February 14, 1567, going to the office of the magistrate of the Signori di Notte to ascertain which prisoners might have information concerning the so-called blasphemies of Dionisio. The prisoners questioned provided insubstantial evidence, since Dionisio was preaching and singing in Latin, which they admitted they did not understand. One witness, Simon Scalciarius, recounted that the Frenchman had only wanted to ask pardon of the saints and to submit to judgment and justice; he also noted that Dionisio had prayed every morning before the image of the Madonna and those of the saints. The inquisitor was incredulous when Scalciarius testified that he had not heard the infamous litanies. The witness replied that the prisoners told him that he should testify even if he had not heard the so-called litanies. The prisoners obviously did not hesitate to feign charges in order to get Dionisio moved and thereby have a little more sleep. The inquisitor's visit to the prison did not bring forth substantial evidence.

Four days later, however, Dionisio directed an apology to the "most reverend and illustrious lords" of the Inquisition. His statement, dated February 18, 1567, explained: "If I had written anything against the Holy Mother Church or her ministers or if I have spoken contrary to her, I, Dionisio Gallo, am prepared in reality both to abjure with effect and to detest [my words], submitting myself to the judgment of Christ and to His Holy Mother Church, from whom I seek pardon with all humility."[131]

The inquisitor did not question Dionisio about his retraction, contrary to the usual practice; however, Dionisio continued to remain in prison until the Inquisition could arrive at an appropriate disposition of the case. Two months elapsed before the trial of Dionisio was resumed.

It would have been logical for the inquisitor to have searched out other Venetian witnesses to ascertain if Dionisio was associated with any conventicles in Venice or with any agents of the prince of Condé, who were said to be active in recruiting those who would speak against the Roman Church. The inquisitor did indeed begin questioning other witnesses in

April 1567, but all were churchmen who had known Dionisio in Paris. A French priest named Jacobus Thiphineo testified on April 22, 1567, that he had seen Dionisio *gallo* in Paris, wearing a crown of brass and carrying a wooden staff as if it were a scepter. He remarked that Dionisio was mocked by all and called king of the Gauls.[132] Boys considered him a fool and laughed at him. The witness claimed that he had observed this mockery for a period of two years. Dionisio never tried to hide the mockery to which he had been subjected in Paris; in fact, he considered suffering and humiliation requisite to his role of messenger and prophet illuminated by God.

As I have indicated previously, the Benedictines of the Congregation Cassinese theorized that madness was a most important avenue for inhuman humiliations. This mentality was obviously an important part of the persona that Dionisio affected in Paris, and also in Rome, to express his role as prophet. In Venice, however, he did not dress the part of a fool when he preached in the *campi* and *campielli*.

The inquisitor did not pursue the question of Dionisio's mockery or strange attire in Paris. Instead, he asked if there were other Frenchmen who could give testimony about Dionisio. Jacobus did not name any others, yet in July of 1567 additional French priests visiting Venice were found and asked to give testimony. The Reverend Lord Martinus Albus testified that he had known Dionisio for eight years in Paris and had recently spoken to him in the Venetian prisons. He admitted that he had known his teaching and his manner of life, that Dionisio used to preach in the churches and outside the churches in every village, and that sometimes he preached Catholic doctrine, sometimes not. He also noted that he wore a crown on his head and was held to be a fool by all. Martinus said he preached against all who stirred up civil wars in France. Martinus also testified that the accused had lived soberly and without vice. Although this witness substantiated the strange behavior of Dionisio described by the other priest, his attitude toward the defendant appeared to be positive, and he praised Dionisio's manner of living. The inquisitor did not ask Martinus why he had visited Dionisio in prison or why the French priest had come to Venice. The questioning of other French clergy continued, however; on August 8, 1567, the inquisitor went to the Carthusian monastery of Sant'Andrea della Certosa, located on the island of Certosa. The Augustinian monks had originally been housed in the monastery of Sant'Andrea at the end of the twelfth century, but were later replaced by the *certosini* (Carthusians).[133] The inquisitor went to speak to Dom Foelix, prior of the Carthusian monastery in Paris and a visitor in the monastery of Sant'Andrea della Certosa. Dom

Foelix told the inquisitor that he had known a certain man in Paris who said he was king of the Gauls, but he did not know his name. The churchman gave an interesting account of this so-called prophet, whom he had seen in Paris for two and a half years. He said that the man was small, had ruddy complexion, and was handsome enough but seemed to be lame. The man spoke extemporaneously in excellent Latin. His reputation among the people was that of a fool, according to Foelix. He appeared to teach Catholic doctrine, and he railed against heretics. The Venetian inquisitor wanted to know what the Parisian inquisitor had thought of the man's teaching, and Dom Foelix explained that he was not troubled, because he considered him silly; some believed him to be a fool. He added that the prophet came very often to the Carthusian monastery in Paris, and after he had dined with the other monks, he preached publicly against heretics. Dom Foelix did not indicate what his opinion of the man was, or what he personally thought of his preaching. Dionisio was apparently a friend who was received regularly in the monastery by the prior and the other monks. He was almost certainly a religious of some kind, as indicated previously. No witness called Dionisio by his name, but rather noted that he was called "king of the Gauls" in France. The inquisitor was satisfied that the person who called himself "king of the Gauls" in France in 1562–63 was the same person who called himself Dionisio Gallo in Italy in 1566–67. The inquisitor's visit to the monastery of Sant'Andrea della Certosa apparently concluded the investigation of Dionisio Gallo. If other witnesses were called or if other testimony by Dionisio was solicited, there is no indication of such in his trial records.

Fourteen months after Dionisio was imprisoned, the Holy Office of the Inquisition rendered its verdict on the one who claimed to be God's servant and messenger and who had preached in the public places in Venice in 1566. The sentence was signed by Ioannes Antonius Fachinettus, bishop of Neocastrensis and papal legate; Ioannes Trivisanus, patriarch of Venice; and Fra Valerius Faventius, inquisitor general. It was read to Dionisio in the prison of the Signori di Notte by the priest Giam Battista Gisletus, secretary of the Inquisition, in the presence of the priest Luca Gallo, cantor in the Basilica di San Marco; Father Nicolas Lapicida, the nuncio of the Venetian Holy Office; and the guards of the prison. Sentences were customarily pronounced in the regular meeting place of the Inquisition, the Chapel of Saint Theodore. It was unusual for a sentence to be read in the prison if the prisoner was able to appear before the tribunal. Perhaps the Inquisition was weary of listening to Dionisio's challenges; perhaps the members wanted to conclude this vexing case, which was an enigma in regard to other *processi*.

Paolo Corner, one of the lay members of the tribunal and the Venetian patrician Dionisio had selected to judge his writings, was replaced by Hieronimo Grimani, knight and *procuratore di San Marco*, for the rendering of the sentence. The Inquisition found Dionisio guilty of public assemblies, contrary to the command of the Holy Office; in these gatherings he had expressed numerous opinions, some strange and rash, some heretical, some scandalous and offensive to the ears of the pious who were standing nearby. Nevertheless, the judges decided that Dionisio had committed his crimes "not from error of intellect but from a certain disturbance of soul, agitated by certain disquieting humors." Therefore he could not be held responsible. Consequently the tribunal decreed that he should be released from prison and perpetually banished from Venice and the Venetian dominion. The ban was to be executed within three days of the day of the sentence, August 12, 1567. Yet an entry in the records on the day of the sentence indicates that late in the evening of the same day, Dionisio Gallo was led by the ministers of the Holy Office to the ship of one Cesare Scarsela, who was to take him toward Ferrara.

It was fortunate for Dionisio that the Venetian tribunal considered him "disturbed in his humors," since his writings, which the Inquisition had evidently studied carefully, contained numerous arguments for which he could have been held culpable. If the duke of Ferrara or his uncle, the marquis de Masse, had intervened on Dionisio's behalf in any way, no record remains. We also do not know why he was sent in the direction of Ferrara or if he was again received in the palace of Francesco d'Este, marquis de Masse.

Thus was concluded the trial of Dionisio Gallo, but other pertinent facts emerge from examination of Dionisio's life in the prisons of Venice. We shall next turn our attention to the letters written by Dionisio from prison and the conversations he had with one of his cell mates, the notorious heretic Francesco Spinola.

· VI ·
CONVERSATIONS AND LETTERS FROM THE PRISONS OF THE PALAZZO DUCALE

he horrors of life in a Venetian prison have been amply documented from the trial of Dionisio Gallo and from many other sources. In spite of the cold, lack of food, abuse from cell mates, and terror from rats and other rodents—conditions that made prison life an indescribable torment—the prisoners, in conversation with each other, demonstrated much the same interests that they had outside the prison. By chance Dionisio Gallo shared a cell not only with a ferocious Turk but also with the apostate humanist Francesco Spinola.[1] The conversations between the two humanists, one a prophet, the other a heretic, are filled with lively discourse, even philosophical argumentation. These conversations and the letters Dionisio wrote from prison give us insight into the relationship between heresy and humanism.

Dionisio's involvement with Spinola in the prison of the Signori di Notte in the Palazzo Ducale and the strange relationship that developed between the two constitute an example of the converging elements we find so often in regard to Dionisio. Francesco Spinola, born in Como about 1520, had French connections in Venice, which may have been responsible for many of his problems. The Frenchman Dionisio had Venetian associations but apparently kept himself apart from the intrigues in which Spinola was involved. Dionisio's problems with the Venetian Inquisition stemmed from his own certainty of his prophetic role. Yet the paths of Dionisio Gallo and Francesco Spinola did cross in the Venetian prison, and certain aspects of their characters and beliefs converged in a relationship that, on the one hand, discovered a shared commitment to reform and, on the other hand, incited betrayal, remorse, and pardon. The example of Spinola and Dionisio provides insight into the complexities of understanding the inquisitorial process from historical evidence and an opportunity to hypothesize in a case where firm evidence is lacking.

Spinola was a humanist by profession and wrote more than twenty books of Latin poetry, which were published in Venice in 1563.[2] Although Spinola wrote many lyrics in imitation of Catullus, a high moral tone pervades his poetry, and religious themes abound. Spinola had enjoyed literary and personal success in Milan under the patronage of Carlo Visconti; however, when his protector went to congratulate the new pope Pius IV in Rome, where Spinola had also hoped to make his fortune in the papal family, Spinola was constrained to find work as a teacher in the public schools of Brescia, having probably been recommended by Paolo Corner. He enjoyed success at Brescia and also the friendship of the count of Gambara, Prospero Martinengo, and Andrea di Ugoni, among others. His heterodox opinions began to cause him problems in Brescia, however, and therefore he accepted Leonardo Mocenigo's offer to teach his sons Alvise and Antonio in Venice. Spinola arrived in Venice in the first few weeks of January 1561, and his teaching again brought success and the affection of his pupils. Spinola ingratiated himself with the French ambassador, Jean Hurault de Baistaille, and was soon under suspicion because of this association, since the ambassador "was said not to have wished to know either the Mass or Communion." He had drawn many Venetians into his circle; the records of the Holy Office reveal that his influence had been vast.[3] He had been the head of a heretical conventicle, seducing noble and nonnoble Venetians. Giacomo Malipiero was his disciple, and Carlo Corner, Alvise Malipiero, Antonio Loredan, and other noble youths can also be linked to him. The large number of Venetian patricians and citizens who had been influenced by the teachings of Spinola attests to his erudition, his charm, and his power of persuasion.

Although Spinola had arrived in Venice to teach the sons of Leonardo Mocenigo, he also found work as a teacher with Zuan Fineti, a lawyer, and afterward with Gabriel Giolito, the important Venetian publisher. Both men admitted that they had sent Spinola out of their homes when they found that he held heterodox opinions. Because of his teachings, which had been disseminated widely in Venice and in the Venetian dominion, Francesco Spinola was incarcerated for heresy in July 1564. The Inquisition continued its investigation of his conventicle a year after his incarceration.

The cells in the prison were small and so close together that prisoners could easily speak together.[4] Sharing the cell adjacent to Francesco Spinola, Dionisio, and the Turk was Marco da Novegrado, who had previously been condemned to the galley for twelve years. He had been moved to the prison when he made a supplication to the Holy Office in which he offered testimony against Spinola. Marco testified that Francesco Spinola had tried to persuade him of the new doctrines, as had Spinola's ally Giulio Panevino, who shared the cell with Marco. Spinola apparently boasted of his activities. He talked about his religious convictions, which he had recorded in a book that the Inquisition sought. He also spoke about a prayer he had written and about his followers in Padua. Most damaging for Spinola, however, was his claim that "one who was in the government of the most Christian king of France" had paid him one hundred ducats to preach heretical doctrine.[5] Marco testified that the person offering the payments was the prince of Condé, who had provided the money for those recruited "to go preaching the Gospel and this his [Spinola's] doctrine."[6] Spinola continued to preach his doctrine among the prisoners. Iseppo Bollani, a Venetian nobleman, confirmed Marco's statements about Francesco Spinola.

From their prison cells Spinola and Marco da Novegrado spoke about Spinola's tormenting dreams. For example, Spinola told Marco that some days before he had been imprisoned, he had had a terrifying dream in which he had been incarcerated. Not wanting to believe the dream, however, he had gone to Panevino and from him had received fourteen scudi, with which he then proceeded to Padua to see his followers, whom he called *fratelli*.[7] The word *fratelli* was used to describe "all those who do not believe in the Holy Roman Church," according to the testimony of the priest Fidele Vico under torture.

Giulio Panevino had the same beliefs as Spinola and was one of the *fratelli*; yet while imprisoned he did not participate in the discussions led by Spinola. Unrestrained by Panevino's circumspection, Spinola displayed the same argumentative nature as he had shown among the *letterati* and the religious at Brescia. Throwing caution to the winds, he proclaimed his views with fervor within the prison. He did not hide his scorn for the lives of many priests and friars. His relationship with the prince of Condé, as described in his conversations with Marco da Novegrado, was even more damaging. The receipt of money from a foreign agent was a treasonable act with severe political consequences.[8] His espousal of the French cause was also questionable. He wrote laudatory poems to the French ambassador, Hurault, and dedicated a book of epodes to him in spite of Hurault's perceived heretical opinions.[9]

Spinola's talkative nature among the prisoners was not in evidence when he was called before the Venetian Inquisition. Although the records of his trial have not been found, other documents affirm his reticence. When called to give testimony about a physician from Naples, Decio Belloebono, he was evasive; torture was necessary to loosen his tongue. A list of *complici* was finally secured from Spinola under duress, yet in his prison cell he continued to discuss religion and the dogma of the Roman Church.

The conversations between Spinola and Dionisio come to life in the letters that Dionisio wrote to the tribunal, the Senate, and the senators on the tribunal. Confined in the same small cell, they engaged in lively discourse and shared the horrors of prison life and the ever-present fear of the Turk. From the conversations recorded by Dionisio, it would appear a paradoxical friendship developed between the two humanists. Both scholars wrote and spoke Latin and shared literary as well as religious interests. Spinola's arguments, especially about purgatory, probably appealed to Dionisio, who admitted that he had been sorely tempted by them in prison. Spinola, however, betrayed Dionisio's confidences about purgatory, damaging the friendship between the two. Yet Spinola confessed to Dionisio his betrayal and asked forgiveness. Dionisio must have accepted Spinola's confession and forgiven him, for he wrote to the tribunal on Spinola's behalf. In addition, Dionisio explained Spinola's own reasons for his apostasy. Although apparently on opposite sides of the religious spectrum, the two men nevertheless held many ideas in common, especially about the reform of the pope and his Curia as well as of priests and friars. A strange tension seemed to draw these men to each other. One can be almost certain that they discussed the Council of Trent and its role in reforming the Church.

In a book of poetry entitled *Carmen seculare, cum aliquot poematibus additis,* published in 1563, Spinola wrote a long poem in elegant dactylic hexameter, the meter of epic poetry, addressed to the Council of Trent. In this poem, filled with imagery from classical poets, Spinola invoked the *spiritus alme,* which fills the poles, the sea, and the earth with its divine will, to favor the council so that mad discord would not overturn everything.[10] The Council of Trent was a point of contention for Dionisio, since he did not believe the council had solved the problems of religion, and for that reason he had, after its conclusion, begun his prophetic preaching and taken up the call for a council of lay princes to aid in the reform of the Church.[11] Francesco Spinola would have had ample reason to agree with Dionisio on the question of the council. It was quite clear that the prayerful poem "Pro Concilio Tridentino," written by Spinola in 1563, had not been answered by the fathers in council or elsewhere, since the civil and religious wars still raged in France. Dionisio's impatience with the slow enactment of reform, which he had expressed before the Venetian Inquisition in regard to the Council of Trent, was also at the heart of Spinola's ideas expressed in his poem.[12]

In spite of the fact that Dionisio, in his letters to the tribunal, referred to Spinola as the *apostata*, Dionisio himself obviously succumbed to some of Spinola's ideas about purgatory, which the latter had consistently denied. Because Spinola reported their conversations about purgatory to the Inquisition, Dionisio was forced to write a retraction. When he demonstrated reluctance, he was urged on by the other prisoners and the guards: "Write, Gaul, write that which the tribunal wants—this or that, and seek pardon. Without delay you will be freed; otherwise you will perish most miserably in prison."[13] Dionisio did not hesitate to state that his only hope was in God and in the "whole most famous Venetian Senate." Yet he did write a retraction of sorts: "I admit there is a purgatory, and it is wherever it is pleasing to the Most High: and I do not deny that it is a certain place designated by God where souls may be cleansed; moreover, the Holy Spirit forbids that one argue about where that place may be."[14] From this letter it is obvious that Dionisio and Spinola had discussed this topic and that Dionisio had evidently expressed some agreement with Spinola's ideas. In the same letter, Dionisio admitted certain things he had said and written, purgatory being one of the topics of those discussions. Both men had also deplored the wicked lives of many clergy, and our prophet referred obliquely to these conversations when he admitted saying "certain things." Spinola had also confessed to Dionisio that it was the "impiety of the clergy" that had led him into error, which admission must have won a sympathetic hearing from Dionisio, for whom the impiety of the clergy, "from the pope to lowest presbyter," was the central point in any program for reform of the Church.

When Spinola and Dionisio discussed the impiety of the clergy, both were reflecting the views of Savonarola in his *Trattato della reuelatione della reformatione della Chiesa* of 1526, in which Fra Girolamo wrote: "Omnipotent God, seeing that the sins of Italy multiply [and] not being able any longer to sustain them, He is purging His Church with a great whip."[15] Many of the young Venetian patricians called before the Venetian Inquisition had read this work; it was often named in testimonies under a slightly different title. The popularity of Savonarola's book on the reformation of the Church and the attendance at Dionisio's preaching as well as the following of Spinola made clear that reform of the hierarchy of the Church was uppermost in the minds of many Venetians before and after the Council of Trent. The conversations of Spinola and Dionisio in their prison cell showed that these concerns were uppermost in their minds. Dionisio repeated with sadness the haunting words of Spinola, "the impiety of the clergy led me into error." The impiety of the clergy was also the goad that spurred Dionisio into frenetic activity after his anointment by the Virgin.

In the prison cell fear deterred sleep, so the long days and nights of confinement provided ample opportunities for conversation. Spinola and Dionisio spoke freely between themselves as Spinola had done with the prisoners in adjacent cells. These conversations were not kept in confidence, as the testimony of Marco da Novegrado made clear. In the case of Spinola and Dionisio, the same was evidently true, since Dionisio recounted that Spinola had given false testimony against him. Prisoners often received bribes for incriminating others if the testimony proved to be true. Spinola was apparently rewarded for revealing his conversations with Dionisio to the Venetian Inquisition, since Dionisio accused the Inquisition of giving preferential treatment to Spinola in the form of some money and also a cell with light.[16] Since the prisoners had to pay for their food and for other necessities, money was indeed a strong inducement for disclosure.

Dionisio first believed that Spinola had betrayed him because of hatred, since Dionisio had used harsh words in attacking Spinola's errors. Their religious arguments became great sport for the other prisoners, who cheered on their favorites. Even harsh words and recriminations relieved the tedium and horror of prison life. Dionisio's arguments with Spinola did not accomplish the desired results, and eventually he changed tactics. He began to use kind and fraternal words, and this method proved more successful, if not for Spinola's conversion, at least for the relationship between the two incarcerated humanists.

Spinola, suffering remorse because of his false testimony against Dionisio, confessed his betrayal. "He said to me," Dionisio wrote, "that he, forced by your tribunal and corrupted by money that he twice received, had brought false testimony against me, and he asked my pardon."[17] Dionisio forgave Spinola, and their relationship improved. Our prophet, however, in his typical fashion, could not resist one final reprimand and another attempt at conversion: "O Judas betrayer, do not despair, but turn from your errors to the Lord so that those whom you have led astray may be recalled to the faith of Christ."[18]

In spite of the fierce arguments that ensued between the two because of Dionisio's efforts to convert Spinola, and in spite of Spinola's betrayal, Dionisio wrote on behalf of Spinola to the three Venetian senators who sat on the tribunal. At the time of Dionisio's letter the fate of Spinola was being determined by the Venetian Inquisition, and Dionisio was aware of this fact, having learned of it from Spinola or from sources inside or outside of the prison.[19] From whatever source Dionisio secured his information, it was correct. A letter of August 31, 1566, from the papal nuncio, Giannantonio Facchinetti, bishop of Nicastro, to Michele Bonelli, Cardinal Alessandrino, revealed that Spinola had been discussed on the previous Thursday while Facchinetti was at the Holy Office. At this point Facchinetti knew little about Spinola except that he was *un relapso*.[20] The papal nuncio, displeased that he had not been previously informed that discussions were to take place, wrote a few words about Spinola and his confinement to Cardinal Alessandrino. The papal nuncio had previously talked with Spinola in prison and had found him stubborn (*pertinace*), but after much persuasion Spinola told Facchinetti that if there were a promise of pardon for him, he would reveal "a conventicle filled with heretics and of great importance."[21] Although the nuncio explained that Spinola was difficult, he nevertheless believed that he would eventually forsake his heresies. He argued pragmatically that it was important to get from Spinola information about the adherents of the conventicle, and if anyone should have information, it was likely that he would, "because, as a humanist, he has lectured to many here in Venice and associated with many here and there." He also recommended a monastery for a perpetual prison. He advised the cardinal that information could more readily be secured with such a promise than with torture, because, "without hope of life, one can die with torments just as with fire or in water."[22]

About the same time that the papal legate wrote about Spinola to Cardinal Alessandrino, Dionisio wrote a letter on behalf of Spinola to the three Venetian Senators who were the lay representatives on the tribunal. In spite of Spinola's testimony against Dionisio and Dionisio's recriminations against Spinola, there was a strong bond between the two men, as Dionisio's letter to the senators makes clear:

> *You have decided whether to absolve or to condemn the apostate de Spinola; do not hurry until I shall have spoken in your presence: indeed, I know his soul and the demon that possesses him. This demon is not thrown out except with great difficulty, since it is the worst sort and very clever. I wish to cast out this demon in the virtue and wisdom of Christ for the grace and salvation of all heretics, especially those whom the apostate Spinola was able to seduce.*[23]

Dionisio's attempt to sway the decision about Spinola had no effect on the final decision of the tribunal, but it indicates the depth of the friendship that had developed between the two humanists in prison. Our prophet believed that he could exorcise the demon of Spinola's heresy through their conversations in the prison, a wretched place but obviously conducive to conversation. Dionisio preferred to attribute Spinola's heresies to a demon rather than discuss them as theological principles, though their positions concerning the pope and the Curia were more similar than Dionisio would want to admit. Dionisio, for example, had written that the pope should defend his right to occupy the chair of Saint Peter and that the Curia must be reformed, words that were reminiscent of Spinola's attacks on the papacy. Dionisio believed that Spinola's heresy could be removed in the same way that all heresy could be removed: namely, by a reform of the clergy. Dionisio may have wanted Spinola to help him in his great crusade of reform. For this reason he urged the lay representatives of the tribunal to be merciful to Spinola and to the whole human race in emulation of God's mercy to those who wanted to be converted. Dionisio pleaded: "Be very merciful this week and remove the death penalty, since God strongly wishes to have pity on the human race (although He threatens it), provided there is a desire to be converted."[24] Our prophet, however, requested that his plea for Spinola not be revealed to him. Since Dionisio knew Spinola's argumentative nature, he feared Spinola's response to the suggestion that he was possessed by a demon.

Dionisio's efforts to save Spinola also reveal his appreciation of a fellow humanist and devotee of Latin. Even from the confines of his prison cell Dionisio wrote letters in elegantly correct Latin. As noted earlier, Dionisio also gave his sermons and lectures in Venice and other Italian cities in Latin. His use of the Latin language naturally directed his remarks to a learned audience. To have a learned humanist in the same cell was obviously a stroke of fortune, for Dionisio as well as Spinola. In spite of their torments they whiled away the hours in religious and literary conversation to relieve the tedium, even as they tried to influence each other.

Countering Dionisio's attempt to save Spinola were other factors at work against him. In letters exchanged between the papal nuncio, Facchinetti, and Cardinal Alessandrino about Francesco Spinola, the advice from Rome was that justice should take its own course and that the nuncio should attend to its execution.[25] Although Facchinetti, in a conversation with Spinola, had suggested perpetual imprisonment in exchange for information about the large conventicle of heretics that Spinola frequented, he later urged, probably after receiving advice from Rome, that Spinola be burned publicly, since this penalty had been imposed by sacred canons; since the doge of Venice, when he assumed the scepter of power, had sworn to avenge heretics with this kind of punishment; and since it would edify Catholics in France and

Flanders because in those lands the Huguenots boasted that "Venice, the key of Italy, is their friend for tolerance, which one sees in the Germans at the *fondaco* and in the scholars of Padua."[26] In short, the death of Spinola was to serve as a warning to all. The Venetian Inquisition, especially the three lay representatives, did not follow the nuncio's advice, however. Public spectacles could easily arouse sympathy for the offender and cause a public tumult, which the Venetian authorities would never allow, regardless of the advice of the papal nuncio. Spinola's trial, however, was not easily concluded. The Venetian Inquisition took its time in determining his fate, since deliberations were held intermittently for more than three months. He finally met his end by drowning in the waters beyond the Lido, weighted down by a heavy rock. Death by drowning was the usual method of punishment executed by the secular arm of the Venetian government for the Holy Office of the Inquisition. The drownings took place at night, in the waters that gave Venice her life and also her vengeance.[27]

In the prison conversations of Spinola and Gallo two cultural strains converge, that of a condemned heretic and that of a self-proclaimed prophet. The knowledge we gain from this association and from the testimony of other witnesses provides us with another perspective on religion and politics in Renaissance Venice. If Spinola was in the pay of the prince of Condé, as the testimony indicates, his own blending of a desire for reform with a desire for a patron led him into the dangerous waters of politics, which in the end proved fatal. Spinola's ambition had always been apparent, and this may have been a part of the demon that Dionisio wanted to cast out, probably with more argumentation and rational discourse. Spinola's ambition to succeed as a humanist was also coupled with a sincere desire to reform the clergy. His disgust with the wicked lives of many clergy caused him to leave his religious calling and work for reform outside of the Church. As he indicated to his cell mate, "the impiety of the clergy" had led him into error; the impiety of the clergy had also led Dionisio the prophet to sound very much like Spinola the heretic. Both Spinola and Dionisio Gallo reflected the prophetic call for reform that Savonarola had preached in Florence;[28] Dionisio's criticism of the lives of the clergy was no less harsh than Savonarola's or Spinola's, but the final determination of his trial was quite different from theirs.

The papal nuncio, Facchinetti, informed Cardinal Alessandrino about the final resolution of the case of Francesco Spinola: "I discovered, after one or two attempts, that they put him to death as seemed fitting to them, similar to the order that I already had from our lord on another similar occasion when I was affirming that I believed that they had been in error in not burning him publicly. And so yesterday evening they drowned him."[29]

The death of Francesco Spinola on January 31, 1567, did not silence Dionisio Gallo, however. Their conversations in the loathsome prison apparently resounded in Dionisio's mind, and he continued to challenge the Inquisition in a series of letters even after the death of Spinola. These letters demonstrate Dionisio's conviction that he was God's servant and in so doing reveal a boldness bordering on temerity. These letters also show that by writing to the three lay members of the tribunal and to the Venetian Senate, for which he expressed great admiration, Dionisio was aware of tensions between Rome and Venice and hoped to "play a political card" in his dealings with this religious body.

Dionisio began writing letters to the tribunal, the Senate, and the lay members of the tribunal as soon as he was incarcerated. He had previously written a *Legatio* to the "most powerful Venetian dominion and to the most famous Venetian Senate," which he had completed in the home of Rocho de Mazzochis. The terrible conditions of his confinement did not deter him from pressing his opinions about his incarceration, about the horrible torments he was suffering, and especially about his role as God's messenger and servant. It seems that only a lack of writing paper hampered his flow of words, for many of his letters fill not only the text block but the margins on each side and on the top and bottom. He complained bitterly about his lack of writing paper, since his money had been stolen in prison. What is really surprising is the fact that he could write at all in the cramped and dark prison.

Dionisio's letters to the tribunal and to the Venetian senators who served as lay representatives on the Inquisition reveal a complete lack of subtlety in his understanding of the relations between the religious and the lay members of the tribunal. In 1550 the pope was indignant that three lay Venetian patricians had been added to the Venetian Inquisition, since he considered such an addition a usurpation of ecclesiastical authority. The pope indicated to the Venetian ambassador Mattio Dandolo that although the most celebrated Venetian patricians were literate and learned in philosophy and letters, which served them well in governing their republic, they had not studied canon law, but nevertheless they wanted to be equal or even higher than the ecclesiastical judges. Dandolo assured the pope that the lay members were coworkers with the ecclesiastics and helped them arrive at a good conclusion of their work.[30] The pope accused Venice of not wanting to admit the Inquisition, although the patriarch of Aquileia vehemently denied it, noting that Venice had always been most religious and had had an Inquisition before that in Rome.[31]

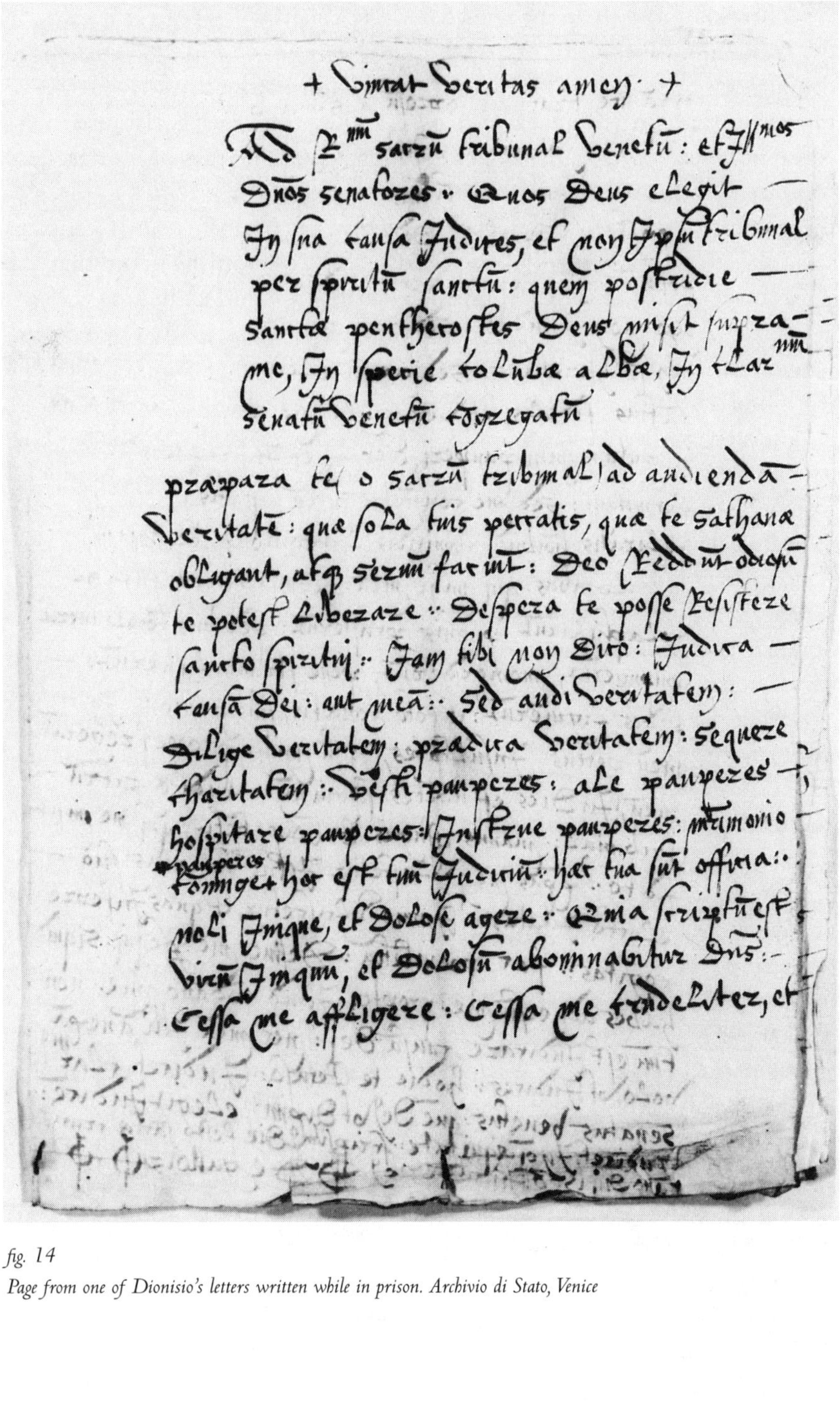

fig. 14

Page from one of Dionisio's letters written while in prison. Archivio di Stato, Venice

Whereas in 1550 the pope considered the Venetian lay representatives on the tribunal a usurpation of papal authority, Dionisio in 1566 challenged the authority of the tribunal with the exception of the three lay members. He wrote that the tribunal had lost its authority to judge, because of its constant persecutions, spiritual and corporeal, and because of its unseemly conduct in inducing false testimony by the payment of bribes.32 In place of the tribunal God had chosen the "most famous and illustrious Venetian senators" to be judges in His own cause.33 Since Dionisio wrote that the senators were God's elected representatives, he was in effect linking the senators' role as God's elected judges with his own role as God's elected messenger and servant. His imprudent words would only have increased the tension on the tribunal, especially in regard to the papal nuncio, Facchinetti.

The struggle between Rome and Venice on the question of papal authority had been long-standing.34 Girolamo Soranzo, Venetian ambassador to Rome in 1563, made the point very clear. In his dispatch to the Collegio he indicated that the early popes had held great religious authority when they were separated from every worldly interest. When religion began to be measured by temporal considerations, however, the ruin of religion followed.35 Soranzo placed the blame directly on the court of Rome. The popes acting as temporal princes had caused great damage to the Church. The Venetians did not question the pope's role as head of the Church, but rather his involvement in affairs of other states. Soranzo noted that he could not be certain if the pope's demonstrations of affection came "from a natural goodwill toward this most serene dominion" or from the exigencies of the times. "Only God, who sees and knows the errors of men, can know it [the pope's mind], and I could never be certain enough to affirm that one cause was greater than another."36 Michiel Surian, Venetian ambassador in 1565, had also written of the problem of papal jurisdiction, admitting that opinions varied about papal authority. Whereas the canonist argued that the pope had supreme authority both in temporal and in spiritual matters, others maintained that the pope's authority extended only to spiritual affairs. Surian, like his predecessor Soranzo, admitted that the popes in recent times had caused great scandal in the Church because of their involvement in temporal affairs, granting that all these new opinions in religion and in the new sects, for the fifty years in which they had brought all the world into confusion, had caused great disturbances because of the avarice or insolence or negligence of the popes.37

The fascinating relationship between Venice and Rome in the years before the Interdict of 1606 demonstrates various tensions at work. Paolo Tiepolo, Venetian ambassador to Rome, detailed the pressure put on him by Pope

Pius V concerning the extradition to Rome of Guido Zanetti da Fano, a teacher at Padua.[38] The pope reminded Tiepolo that the duke of Florence had acceded to his will in sending Pietro Carnesecchi, the duke's friend, to Rome notwithstanding the duke's temporal authority. The pontiff also noted that Venice had previously sent heretics to Rome at Rome's request. From the Venetian point of view the pope's authority had become too insistent in regard to the Venetian Inquisition. In 1555 Venice had extradited Pomponio da Nola and Guillaume Postel to Rome because of pressure from the papal nuncio, Filippo Archinto. In the 1560s the pope's demands continued to increase, since he admitted to Tiepolo that there were many in the Serenissima who had to stand before the Inquisition in Rome.[39] Tiepolo pointed out that the Venetians welcomed information pertaining to its *processi* but that the Inquisition of Venice was in the hands of the pope's own ministers—the nuncio, the patriarch, and the inquisitor. The discussion between the pope and the Venetian ambassador also touched on the propriety of a lower tribunal's judging cases of a higher tribunal.[40] The pope naturally believed that whatever cases he considered under his particular jurisdiction should be sent to Rome upon his request; many letters from Tiepolo to the Capi concerned the question of jurisdiction of the pope and the Venetian Inquisition, and Tiepolo tried to explain in the case of Guido Zanetti and others that the principal consideration for Venice was the conservation of the authority of the Inquisition of Venice.[41]

The pope based his authority upon his right to judge his own subjects, as in the case of Pomponio da Nola.[42] The Venetians believed, however, that when a person came to live in a land, he was under the jurisdiction of the princes of the territory.[43] The argument between the pope and the Venetian ambassador over the extradition of Guido Zanetti da Fano became very heated in July 1566. Ambassador Tiepolo tried to explain to Pius V that the extradition of those under investigation by the tribunal in Venice would lessen the authority of the Venetian body and even the authority of the doge, since the people looked to the prince for authority and protection.[44] The pope responded angrily that the Venetians did not want to obey him.[45] Tiepolo, writing to the Capi, indicated that if the pope did not have his way in this matter, he would never be favorably disposed toward Venice.[46]

Although Tiepolo was extremely well versed in diplomatic skills, he could not avoid the anger of the pope when the authority of the Venetian republic was discussed. The ambassador tried to explain to the pontiff that if Guido Zanetti were sent to Rome, the authority of the Venetian tribunal would be diminished, and the populace would then have less esteem for their prince. The pope, in a great fury, interrupted the ambassador, screaming,

"Enough, Enough! The authority of the tribunal of the Inquisition? As if that tribunal must be superior to us. Satisfaction of the people? As if you have not given to other popes others who had less to do with them than this one whom we ask of you. Perhaps your subject is such a grand person that you must show great regard for him lest you stir up resentment?"[47]

All the accusations the pope had made against the Venetians had been addressed to the papal nuncio, Facchinetti, who sat on the tribunal against which Dionisio had heaped his scorn. The relationship between Venice and Rome in the summer of 1566 had already reached the boiling point, as Tiepolo's letters to the Capi clearly show. Dionisio's challenge to the religious authorities on the tribunal would not have cooled the already tense situation. In the case of Guido Zanetti da Fano, all the diplomatic skills of Ambassador Paolo Tiepolo could not prevail against the iron will of Pius V.[48] In spite of all the valid objections raised by the ambassador, the Venetians finally agreed to send Guido Zanetti da Fano to the papal prisons in Ravenna for later transfer to Rome, after the pope wrote a personal letter to the Consiglio dei Dieci in which he claimed Guido as his own citizen.[49] Although the Consiglio dei Dieci yielded to the pope in this regard, several days later the council instructed the ambassador to make clear to the pope that in spite of its concession in this case, Venetian concerns had been properly and validly stated.[50]

In his letters to the tribunal and to the senators Dionisio demonstrated no appreciation for the delicate relations between Rome and Venice. Although he praised the Venetian senators on the tribunal, he wrote harshly, even contemptuously, to the religious members of the same body. Dionisio did not hesitate to shame the tribunal for the manner of his arrest by the legate of the papal nuncio, having been pounced upon in his bed "like a dove in its nest."[51] Dionisio also accused the tribunal of sending the nuncio's legate to him after his incarceration. The nuncio's legate had contributed to Dionisio's suffering by telling the guards and the prisoners to beat him if he cried out for justice.[52] Dionisio blamed the sacred tribunal personally for the terrible conditions he endured in prison. He addressed the Inquisition with the fervor of an Old Testament prophet, urging the body to bewail its wrongs and seek pardon. The Inquisition was not accustomed to hearing such reproaches:

> *Weep, O sacred tribunal. Moreover, let all the clergy weep; let the whole body of the Church break out in tears and bring forth true and serious penitence. Groan, shepherds of the Church, because you have lost the white ornaments of your fathers and the nuptial garments,*

charity, chastity, and innocence. And you have put on the sordid, infamous, filthy garments of Satan: avarice, enslavement to idols, ambition, and sexual excess. At the same time, many are guilty of cruelty and impiety.[53]

Dionisio believed that lay persons on the tribunal were better able to judge his veracity and his program than were the papal nuncio, the Dominican inquisitor, and the patriarch, although he apparently esteemed the patriarch as a Venetian. He pointed out for the second time that two excellent Venetian men, Giusto Morosini and Rocho de Mazzochis, had served as witnesses to the truth of his prophetic role and his prophecies.[54] Dionisio perhaps hoped that Marco Morosini, one of the lay members of the tribunal and cousin of Giusto Morosini, would help him, not only in regard to his imprisonment but also with his program for reform of the Church.[55] Dionisio's letters were in all likelihood a source of embarrassment to Marco Morosini, but we can only speculate about his role in the final disposition Dionisio's case. Giusto Morosini's signature did appear on one of Dionisio's writings that was in the hands of the Inquisition. The signature would tend to confirm Dionisio's frequently repeated boast that Giusto was his friend and in accord with the proposals of his legation. Since no notes from the deliberations of the Inquisition remain, Marco Morosini's role in them must remain speculative.

During his imprisonment Dionisio was strengthened in his belief that many ecclesiastics had lost their right to judge because of the corruption of the Church. In numerous letters he reminded the Venetian Senate that God had chosen it as judge. His immediate objective in reminding the Senate of its role was to win the Senate's approval and be freed from prison. On the other hand, it is clear that he hoped that the Senate, along with the doge, would help him in his grand enterprise of reform. With the regularity of a refrain he urged the senators to "let truth conquer and let Christ reign upon the earth." He also urged the senators to "give place to the Holy Spirit, which directs my reed [pen]."[56] The Holy Spirit, Dionisio warned, was "bold against those whom it wishe[d] to make healthy and terrible against those who resist[ed] it." He reminded the senators and the tribunal of their responsibility: "Be unwilling in any way to resist the Holy Spirit or to abuse the power that God gave to you, being fearful because it has been written: 'The powerful will suffer powerful torments, and the servant, knowing the will of God and not doing it, will be chastised with many blows.'"[57] In spite of the praise that Dionisio usually heaped upon the Venetian nobility, he did not hesitate to advise them about problems in the

Venetian state. He warned about the wrath of heaven because of two sins in particular: heresy and sodomy, though he referred to the latter only obliquely. He noted that "already [the wrath of heaven] would have befallen your state just as Sodom and Gomorrah unless the most Holy Virgin had interceded on your behalf and by her tears and by her divine virtue and authority had mitigated the anger of heaven on account of the prayers of many good and pious men who are in Venice."[58] In this long document Dionisio placed the Senate in opposition to the tribunal, reserving praise for the senators and their office and placing blame upon the Inquisition because of its treatment of him. The senators had evidently tried to prevent his abuse in prison; he wrote: "[Y]ou, most renowned senators, prevented me from being thus oppressed by the prisoners, since you are just and you know that by no right, either human or divine, is it permissible to betray the just and to oppress the innocent."[59]

Dionisio was especially hostile to the papal nuncio, who had sent his representative to apprehend him while he was sleeping and had seized his precious documents. Although Dionisio was usually astute about the political issues that resulted from religious considerations, he was, in regard to the nuncio and the tribunal, quite blind to the religious repercussions that his extravagant claims about himself would spawn and took ample opportunity to criticize the religious situation in Rome and the papal representatives. He was especially harsh in his accusations against the pope's nuncios in Florence and Venice. After all, it was the pope's nuncio who had seized him and his writing, refusing to accept what Dionisio believed was firm proof of his role as God's messenger. He pled with the Venetian senators on the tribunal to let their piety and fairness free him. He begged the tribunal not to afflict and humiliate him. He warned: "Indeed it is human to sin but diabolic to persevere in sin."[60] The tribunal, which refused to acknowledge his divine anointment, was persisting in its sin, according to Dionisio. Since the tribunal had mistreated God's servant and had been guilty of paying bribes to the heretic Spinola, God refused this body the right to judge.[61] Dionisio urged the Senate to judge rightly, following the Holy Spirit as guide. Relying on his prophetic persona, he warned the Venetians that they must placate the anger of heaven against their state by doing penance, by fasting, and by prayer.[62] The clergy, the Senate, and the wealthy citizens must feed and clothe the twelve thousand poor whom Dionisio claimed were in Venice and Padua. Public prayers should be said, and processions should be held in Venice and Padua and throughout the dominion of Venice on behalf of peace and the whole state of the Church Militant. If this advice would be followed, "the anger of heaven will be placated and the

Truth of the Lord will reign in Venice." To reform the clergy, to destroy heresy, to console and feed the poor, and to convert all infidels were the virtue and the wisdom of Christ.[63]

In his letter to the Venetian nobles, the tribunal, and the Senate, Dionisio did not hesitate to define his role and that of the newly elected pope.[64] He argued that because of the misery, God had decided that two rectors were necessary for the Church, just as in the ancient Church, when Peter had been assigned the apostolate among Jews and Paul among Gentiles.[65] Dionisio also tried to clarify his role in relation to that of the newly elected pope, since he had been accused by the Venetian Inquisition of claiming that his was a higher calling: "Let the present pope be higher than I am to the extent that he has greater charity and has labored more since his creation [as pope] in directing the Church of God than I in my calling."[66] He pointedly made other distinctions: the pope had been chosen only eight months before, while Dionisio had been elected by God three and a half years previously; the pope had been elected "by sinners, by mortal and earthly cardinals," while he had been chosen "by God through the heavenly, immortal, sinless, immaculate Virgin."[67] Writing of the relationship between himself and the pope, Dionisio also asked rhetorically which was greater—Peter or Paul. His response to the question, naming Peter as higher, could not have been displeasing to those who were a part of the Inquisition, since Mark, who became the patron saint of Venice, had been sent by Peter on a preaching mission that had led, according to legend, to the founding of the Venetian Church. Dionisio wrote of Saint Peter: "Which one of these [Peter and Paul] was greater? Both were elected by God. Both were just and holy. Without a doubt, blessed Peter was greater, having been chosen first and established by Christ as shepherd and rector of the Church and prince of the Apostles."[68] Dionisio made his point clear. The first pope, or shepherd, that is, Peter, was chosen by Christ to lead the Church Militant. All successive popes were elected by men. He obviously joined himself to Peter as one chosen by God, in contrast with Pope Pius V, who was elected pope only by sinful men, that is, cardinals. As if this were not challenge enough to papal authority, Dionisio also broached the thorny subject of the temporal goods of the Church and their appropriate division. The possessions of the Church were not the property of the pope or Dionisio but of Christ, that is, of the poor, who are members of Christ. The poor have been commended by Christ to Dionisio and to all the shepherds of the Church. Therefore Dionisio argued that the pope should allot a half part of his dominion and of the temporal goods of the Church to himself and to the poor. The other half should be given to the poor through distribution by

Dionisio, who before the rest of mankind had the obligation to console the poor. "Therefore, with divine providence let there be two shepherds of the sheepfold of Christ, chosen, approved, and recognized."[69] The pope might decide which parts of the Church he wished to govern, in which he would reform the clergy, remove heresy, clothe and feed the poor, and convert the infidels.[70]

Dionisio suggested that with the pope's approval he would direct the church of Gaul and Germany and the pope that of Italy and Spain.[71] He also advised, not too diplomatically, that the pope, being old, should not assume a burden greater than his strength; that since he, Dionisio, has been received by the princes, who have indeed approved him, he, along with the princes, will be of great service to the pope. As if to strengthen his own divine calling, he made reference to the gossip concerning the election of Pope Pius V: "I am unwilling to call into doubt whether the present pope was legitimately elected," Dionisio wrote, making an oblique reference to questions raised when Cardinal Carlo Borromeo, nephew of Pius IV, did not receive the elevation.[72] Since Pius V, from the time he had sat on the Venetian Inquisition, had never been a special friend of Venice, Dionisio's insinuation probably resonated with some who read his letter. He may also have hoped that his remark about the pope's election would elicit some favor in his own behalf from the Venetian noblemen. If Facchinetti had revealed to Pius V the contents of Dionisio's letter, the pope's anger would have been unabated, since in the marginalia of the same letter Dionisio had written "that only the best was a worthy successor to the seat of the blessed Apostles Peter and Paul." Yet this seat occupied by the pope was less worthy than the mystical seat of David, the royal and pontifical seat of Christ that Dionisio claimed as his own under Christ. In this very important letter Dionisio did not deny his fantastic claims as the servant of God. Indeed, he reiterated in the same prophetic language that appeared in all his writings his divine anointment and his specific role in the reformation of the Church Militant. With no hesitation he linked his own persona to that male described in the twelfth chapter of the Apocalypse; he was the angelic pope awaited throughout the Middle Ages and now anointed to lead the Church in the reform of itself. He did not deny the accusation made by the Venetian Inquisition that he had preached he was the shepherd promised in the most recent times, the highest and immediate pope under Christ. In fact, Dionisio linked his own prophetic persona to the Apocalypse: "Indeed, through my writings I announce another thing to you—metaphysically, that is, with nature admiring, that male described in the twelfth chapter of the Apocalypse has been born and carried to God and to His seat to rule kings and wicked nations with an iron rod."[73] Although Dionisio was certain of his messianic calling, his claim was not that he was Christ but that he was the one under Christ, the angelic pope. Dionisio was obviously following the commentary of Joachim on Apocalypse 12, where the abbot explained that although the Virgin Mary had given birth to her only begotten son, whom she saw hanging on the cross, the "woman clothed in the sun" indicated the Church of the learned, and the son of the woman "the army of all the just who will reign with Christ."[74] Dionisio saw himself as that man named in the Apocalypse, the angelic pope who would lead all the just. In many of his letters written from prison, Dionisio reiterated his divine calling, confirmed by his divine anointment. He associated himself, as "the third king," with the man from Edom in order to confirm his messianic role as God's servant and messenger in leading all the just in the reformation of the Church Militant.

In a remarkable letter written on May 4, 1567, from his cell in the fourth prison of the Signori di Notte, Dionisio addressed "the most reverend and illustrious, just and modest Venetian nobility," indicating that the one who greeted them was he who had a "name that no one knows except him who received it." This mysterious greeting sets the tone for further revelations about his messianic persona. In the marginalia of this letter he asks rhetorically who is the great third king, and then he proceeds to answer:

> *Tell, I beg you, and admit honestly on account of the Virgin . . . : "Who is that great third king?" You owe justice to God, to Christ, to me, and to the people in all truth. Therefore, in supplication, my father and my mother, most reverend and illustrious Venetian dominion, I urge and compel you, through holy Michael archangel, through all the blessed orders of angels, through all the holy elect, male and female, and through all the blessed heavenly armies of the new Jerusalem, admit honestly: "Who is that great third king? . . ." Do you not wish to believe me? Speak and announce. If you doubt, consult the holy learned theologians. He is surely the one about whom, in his own person, David himself speaks in the psalm: "I, moreover, have been established as king by God upon Zion, His holy mountain, preaching His precept." He is surely the one about whom Isaiah wrote: "Send forth the lamb, O Lord, the giver of the earth, from the rock of the desert to the mountain of the daughter of Zion, and he will be just like a bird fleeing and chicks flying from their nest.". . . He is surely the one about whom the same Isaiah wrote: "Who is that one who came from Edom with colored garments from Bosra, that one handsome in his stole." He who writes this is that one, established*

by God, and I come from Edom, that is, from the land, from the city, gi-sors, that is, from the land of prophecy [lot] and from Bosra, that is, from hell, from the depths of the prisons in great tribulations and grief.[75]

Dionisio linked his identity to Jewish messianic expectations of the third king described by Isaiah, a king who would cleanse the Church and return it to the holy mountain of Zion, where Moses received God's Law. He also explained the relationship of the "third king" to Christ the King, or Messiah.[76] "Christ the King is both God and man. The 'third king' is the pure servant of Christ, God, and man, and a creature."[77] He also noted that other differences could be introduced between God and man, between creator and creature. There were also likenesses through infused grace and divine kindness. The signs of divine infusion were good works and a life holy and complete in perfect charity.[78] Dionisio appropriated all these signs of the third king for himself, and he even indicated that God, when He said, "Ask of me and I shall give to you the nations as an inheritance," was speaking of the third king, not of David, "who ruled and possessed" but did not inherit. He argued that Christ did not inherit the nations, because He had said to Pilate, "My kingdom is not of this world."

Dionisio also noted that the one who wrote the letter was the "third king," who came from Edom. By linking the third king with the man from Edom, Dionisio demonstrated his expertise in portraying his prophetic persona. He joined the meaning of Edom, that is, land, with the city of his birth, Gisors, to which he gave an exotic derivation. He observed that the name Gisors came from *gê* in Greek, meaning "earth," and from *sors* in Latin, meaning "a lot by which auspices were discerned," therefore prophetic.[79] The prophetic land of Gisors had given birth to the prophetic man from Edom. He also claimed metaphorically to be from Bosra, the probable capital of Edom.[80] For him, the Venetian prison was Bosra, a horror and a curse. In the words of Jeremiah concerning Bosra was an implicit threat to the tribunal, which had placed him in this "Bosra." Dionisio's reference to himself as the man from Edom was perhaps his boldest messianic claim, although there was a precedent for his claims. Guillaume Postel used the image of Edom in the same context as Dionisio when he wrote that Christ could be called the man from Edom because he had taken upon himself the sins of the world and suffered a grievous death for all of mankind.[81] Christ's descent into hell was into the depths of horror, that is, into Bosra. Postel's unpublished text enables us to comprehend more clearly the messianic implications in the marginalia of Dionisio's letter. It also raises questions about the possible relationship between these two prophetic Frenchmen, both of whom assigned a special role to Venice for the restoration of the Church universal.

In Dionisio's letters written from prison he continued to describe his role as God's prophet and messenger, while at the same time he emphasized Venice's providential role in the reformation of the Church, urging the Venetian dominion to heed his words of wisdom, although he noted that he himself was "the most foolish of the fools, the arch fool because he was the prince of fools." As noted earlier, Dionisio considered repute as a fool necessary to his role as God's messenger.[82] To the Venetian dominion he wrote in regard to wisdom that "[w]isdom is the mother of honor and all heavenly and terrestrial riches. The beginning of wisdom is the fear of the Lord. The root of wisdom is humility; the root of all evils is cupidity, haughtiness of life, and concupiscence of the flesh." To obtain wisdom, the Venetian dominion must know "Christ crucified for the salvation of men and meditate on this day and night throughout life."[83] He implied that, to have wisdom, the Venetians must heed his words by turning from the sins of heresy and sodomy. He cited the Psalm of David, "Sing unto the Lord a new song," as a reminder to turn from sins to the practice of charity, humility, and simplicity.[84] In spite of his warning to the Venetian dominion, Dionisio nevertheless addressed the dominion, the Senate, and the Tre Savi sopra Eresia with respect and even with affection. We recall that he had previously referred to Venice as "that dear city of pigeons . . . chosen by God."[85] Dionisio demonstrated special esteem for Paolo Corner, one of the lay patricians who served on the Inquisition. He had ordered the guards to hand over his writings to Corner, who, Dionisio noted, would understand them. We cannot discern if there had been a previous acquaintance between Gallo and Corner. Although he complained bitterly about the horrors of the Venetian prison, he did not blame the Venetian republic. Rather, he directed his hostility and accusations against the papal nuncio and the tribunal,[86] which had enclosed him in a "most loathsome" prison, even though, according to Dionisio, he had ceased preaching "in accordance with your mandate, on account of the reverence of powers ordained by God." It was the mandate of the Venetian senators on the tribunal that he claimed to have accepted, not the tribunal at large. According to Dionisio, only the lay members of the Inquisition were eligible to judge, since "their power had been ordained by God." Since Venice had a providential role in God's plan for the reformation of His Church, Venetian senators would naturally share in Venice's destiny. He argued that God had chosen the Senate of Venice as judges, since the tribunal had lost its right to judge, because of improper actions, one of which was obviously Dionisio's incarceration.

Dionisio's blunt words would have been less than amusing to the religious representatives on the tribunal and embarrassing to the three senators.

In addition to the esteem he had expressed for Paolo Corner, he indicated great respect for the Venetian Senate, "which God chose as judge in His own cause, through the Holy Spirit, which He sent into the assembled Senate on the day after Pentecost in the appearance of a white dove [that flew] above the head of the one writing."[87] Dionisio also praised the Venetian nobility, in part, perhaps, because of his esteem for "two pious and honored Venetian men, the most illustrious Giusto Morosini, a nobleman, and the best citizen Rocho Veneto, both of whom signed my legation, since they approved all my writings."[88] He called the Venetian nobility to be his "mother and father" and urged that they receive their son. If they, the Venetian nobility, the parents, received their son, they would inherit the possession of the whole world.[89] Dionisio cited "the royal prophet David," to whom the Lord said: "Ask from me and I shall give to you the nations as an inheritance."[90] He interpreted this to mean that the "third king" would inherit the nations, since David ruled but did not inherit and Christ's kingdom was not of this world. Dionisio was pleading with his "mother and father" to care for their son, to free him from prison and allow him to continue his work. Dionisio's promise to Venice of inheriting the nations was perhaps his metaphor for Venice as the new Jerusalem. As Jerusalem, the holy city, was a paradigm for the *Ecclesia militans*, so Venice, which had been chosen by God to judge, according to Dionisio, could be considered the parent and paradigm for the reformation of the *Ecclesia militans*.[91]

Venice as justice, depicted as a beautiful woman who holds a balance in her left hand and a sword in her right hand, graced the exterior and interior of the Palazzo Ducale, in the Cinquecento as today, and surmounted the sculptures above the Porta della Carta; beneath the figure of Venice represented as justice one sees the sculpture of the doge kneeling before Saint Mark. The tableau presides over the four sculpted figures of beautiful women who represent the virtues of charity, prudence, temperance, and strength. The virtue of justice is first, however; all other virtues are subsumed in justice. The representation of Venice as justice, which follows the Platonic ideal, combines Venice's role as loving mother and as firm disciplinarian.[92]

The concept of the feminine was significant in Dionisio's worldview, especially in his own personal spiritual journey. It was the Virgin who anointed him; it was Saint Bridget who was a spiritual guide and model for him; it was the Mother Church who, corrupted by a male hierarchy, was crying to be reformed. Dionisio did not emphasize the feminine alone, however. The union of the female and male in the work of reform was paramount.

fig. 15
Venice as justice holding a balance in her left hand and sword in her right. The inscription reads, "Choose justice O you who judge the earth."
Biblioteca del Museo Correr, Venice

The male prophet Dionisio received his divine anointment, which marked his prophetic entry into the work of reform, from the ultimate female, the Virgin. The male prophet was constantly inspired by the feminine voice of Saint Bridget. This union of male-female is a recurring theme in Dionisio's program for reform and never more effectively represented than when he addressed the Venetian dominion as his mother and father. Dionisio and Venice shared a familial relationship of the most intimate nature. Instead of consanguinity, Dionisio and Venice shared the divinely infused right to administer justice and thereby bring reform to the Church. Dionisio's adoption of Venice as mother and father was part of his sacramental program for effecting justice. Venice as mother and father was not a concept unique to Dionisio, however. In numerous documents Guillaume Postel, who perpetuated the concept of Venice as the most perfect magistracy, referred to the dual nature of the Venetian republic as female and male. He acknowledged that the temporal magistracy was female and that the spiritual magistracy was male. The union of the female, or temporal, magistracy with the male, or spiritual, magistracy made Venice the most perfect magistracy. The perfect blending of male-female was represented in the Venetian state and in its justice, according to Postel.93 This conception of Venice as male-female is similar to Dionisio's conception of Venice as his mother and his father. Consequently, Dionisio called upon his mother and father, the perfect combination of familial justice, to free him from the horrors of prison life, which had made him long for death. Dionisio begged that Venice free him through the justice that was owed to God, to Christ, to him, and to the people, "poor as well as rich, on a daily basis."94 In the interest of justice, it was expedient for Venice to punish the wicked so that good men could live in peace.95 Dionisio's statements about Venetian justice reveal his sensitivity to the concept that was central to the Venetian republic.

Dionisio's understanding of Venetian justice was shared by Venetians themselves. An interesting letter, written in 1555 to the Capi del Consiglio dei Dieci by Orpheo Fioccha of Polpenaze, reveals a concept of justice similar to that described by Dionisio. It is clear that Orpheo had help in writing this elegant letter; however, whether the ideas expressed were his or those of a notary, the point is the same. Venice, as an example of God's justice in the world, must administer its laws and God's Laws with equity. In fact, Venice was the receptacle of God's Law. Orpheo wrote that "the grandeur, the happiness, and the conservation of this most holy republic depends on the many beautiful orders that come especially from the most holy laws established by your most excellent Signorie through which honor has been given to God. His Majesty has been proclaimed, and His name has been lauded."96 The laws that protect men from the "wicked, who disturb the tranquillity of those who wish to live in peace, will be conserved by the hand of God, who has a care for this justice that reigns in the hearts of your most excellent Signorie."97 Orpheo, like Dionisio, emphasized that Venetian justice "represented the place of God on the earth."98 Dionisio, like Orpheo, had also noted that it was in the best interest of the "republic that the wicked be punished so that the good can enjoy peace in security."99

The concept of Venice as the vehicle of God's justice on earth was illustrated in a beautiful miniature with accompanying text that served as Andrea Gritti's *proemio dogale* to the *Libro d'oro vecchio* of the Maggior Consiglio.100 Saint Mark is shown handing the book of God's Law to the new doge Andrea Gritti, who is kneeling before the saint. The text describes the remarkable foresight of God, who, after He created the earth and eternal intelligences, brought forth laws, ordering the universe and giving it stability.[101] The text makes clear that the republic that emulates God's order and stability will be well instituted. God's Laws are perpetual in spite of the vicissitudes of human circumstances. A republic must necessarily follow God's Laws, and it is incumbent upon the doge to safeguard and protect *incorrupte sancteque* the laws of the Venetian republic in order to preserve the stability and the *perennitas* of the Serenissima.[102]

Dionisio's letters from prison were filled with long discussions about justice and Venice's responsibility insofar as this bore on Dionisio. He challenged the "most reverend and illustrious, just and modest Venetian nobility" to condemn him if he was guilty but free him if he was just and innocent. Dionisio's persistent repetition of the horrors of prison life, which he was suffering unjustly, was also a taunt to the republic that had been chosen to administer justice. The essence of justice is truth, and Dionisio warned the Venetians that they must acknowledge the truth that had been sent by God through His chosen servant. Without truth there could be no justice. Without justice Venice would lose its *raison d'être*. In spite of these challenges with respect to justice, Dionisio referred to Venice throughout the long letters in laudatory terms—*reverendissima, illustrissima, justa et modesta dominatio veneta,* praising her also as *benigna*. At the same time, he warned the Serenissima of grave dangers if she did not fulfill her role as a just judge and recognize her "true son," the one chosen as "third king." Dionisio noted that because of the suffering he had endured at the hands of "his father and his mother," that is, the Venetian dominion, the "mother of Christ, the bride of God the Father," was said to have wept at Dionisio's arrival; her "chosen *groom*" had been badly treated and continued to be badly treated. Dionisio even claimed that the Virgin had performed many miracles and had given many signs on his behalf so that the Venetians would believe the truth about her chosen *sponsus*.[103] Dionisio's claim that the Virgin had wept because of the treatment of her *sponsus* recalls the prophecies of Father Rusticanus, who had prophesied in the Quattrocento that "there will be a new *sposo* in these years, alone elected by God; he will be as His own son." Teolosphoro da Cosenza noted that there would be three false *sposi* and one legitimate *sposo*. When the legitimate *sposo* arrives, then "the Gaul will sing [or the cock will crow], and there will be the best restauration."[104] If Venice should not believe the truth and perform justice in Dionisio's regard, our prophet warned, "to this state the danger of the arrows and wrath of omnipotent God is imminent."[105]

Dionisio's letters from prison are fascinating in many respects and certainly noteworthy because they reveal Dionisio Gallo's skill in incorporating both praise and blame for Venice. For example, he praised Venice for her divinely ordained justice, but he reminded her that she must beware of heaven's anger against the Serenissima because of the sins of sodomy and heresy. To soften the blame he noted that the Virgin had mitigated the wrath of Heaven because of the prayers of many good and pious Venetians. Yet he did not hesitate to warn the Venetians that

> [o]n account of this, omnipotent God, proceeding with a slow pace to anger and to punishment, weighing the delay with the seriousness of the crime, will strike Venice with many blows. He will transfer the dominion and will destroy the bodies and souls of all who stubbornly agree with the sacred tribunal. I see these evils are not at a distance but are imminent. They will not be averted except through extreme fairness, piety, charity, and a just reparation for the assault on Divine Honor.[106]

Dionisio's bold indictment of the tribunal and Venice placed the blame for many sins, especially heresy and sodomy, upon the tribunal, which had failed to rid Venice of the sins that angered God. Instead of punishing heretics and sodomites, the Inquisition had made God's messenger suffer the torments of hell in prison. He rehearsed his torments over and over, chiding the Inquisition for his injuries. Nor did he soften his rhetorical accusations against the papal nuncio, Facchinetti. In fact, in his harsh denouncements against the papal nuncio and the tribunal, he indicated that they had aided the work of the Devil and hindered the right of Christ. Dionisio said that the tribunal wished to destroy him rather than to try him or find him innocent. He could not understand their refusal to accept the mission of the Holy Spirit in the aspect of a white dove that followed him into the Senate. He claimed this sign was "more powerful, more important, and more excellent for the approval of my heavenly legation and of all my writings than if I had raised up a thousand dead or had healed twelve thousand sick or had cast out legions of demons from human bodies."[107] He noted that the Antichrist would perform miracles to deceive the nations. Instead of miracles to demonstrate his divine calling, Dionisio relied on what he considered an unimpeachable sign, the flight of the white dove over his head. His harsh words against the Inquisition were a reproach to Venetian justice, at least in regard to the ecclesiastical judges. Our prophet did not find fault with the temporal justice. In fact, he urged the Senate to assume more authority in order to fulfill its role as divinely ordained judge. He praised the senators on the tribunal for trying to prevent his oppression by the other prisoners. Dionisio also mentioned the *generosa nobilitas* of the second and third prisons who had intervened on his behalf against the other prisoners and had threatened to tell the three Venetians on the tribunal the truth about the brutal treatment Dionisio was receiving. The two nobles who came to Dionisio's defense were almost certainly Iseppo Bollani and Stefano Moro, who had been imprisoned near Dionisio's place of confinement and had given testimony concerning Francesco Spinola.[108] Bollani and Moro may have been instrumental in having Dionisio moved from the fourth prison, where he had received so many torments, into the third prison. In the letter written to the Venetian nobility on May 4, 1567, that in which our prophet identified himself as he who has a name that no one knows "except the one who received it,"[109] he described a quasi-miracle he had performed in prison. Although he had previously discounted the need for miracles, since a white dove had confirmed his divine appointment, he wrote of an incredible debasement he had suffered at the hands of some of the other prisoners. They had bound Dionisio to an urn they used for their excretions. In addition to defiling his face with their filth, they urinated on his clothing. They beat him while bound and ordered him to do this and that or else remain bound all night. They mocked him: "You trust in God. Ask God to free you and loose your chains. Then we shall believe you." Dionisio was bound with two ropes, his hands and feet tied behind. His suffering was great, according to his account; not daring to cry out for fear of more punishments, he called out silently to God and asked for His help. He then felt his hands being freed from their bonds because of divine virtue, according to his story. He then picked up a large urn and broke it. His cell mates were terrified, but Dionisio told them not to be afraid of him but to fear God. The accuracy of this "miracle" cannot be ascertained. What is certain, however, is the fact that Dionisio believed that he had received strength from the Divine. This in turn made him even more certain of his divine calling.

In these letters, written with special fervor, Dionisio revealed an excellent knowledge of Old Testament prophecy and the Psalms; in addition, he demonstrated a familiarity with Jewish messianic expectations. Dionisio's mysticism is especially apparent in the letters of early May 1567. It is interesting that he addressed both the Senate and Venetian nobility and the tribunal, the former for praise, the latter for blame. He insistently lectured both bodies, however, about justice. In the letter written on May 4, 1567, from the prison in the Ducal Palace, Dionisio joined truth and justice as the theme. "From the high heavens truth has been revealed. Still truth has risen from the land, and justice has looked down from heaven," he wrote. "In opposition to the power of Satan and human wisdom, God chose the fools of the world to confound the wisdom of the wise."[110] Though a fool to the world, Dionisio believed that truth had been revealed to him by his divine anointment.[111] If the Venetians did not heed the truth as revealed by Dionisio, they would be incapable of rendering justice, for to reject Dionisio was to reject the truth. Since Dionisio was convinced that truth had been revealed to him, he was extremely frustrated in his inability to convince the Inquisition that he spoke the truth. If the Inquisition could not comprehend the truth that Dionisio reiterated, it certainly could not administer justice. The foundation of all truth and its consequent justice was the Law of God expressed in His commandments to Moses. The proper expression of God's Law, according to Dionisio, was the understanding and practice of charity. Indeed, all the commandments could be subsumed under the love of God and love of one's neighbor. For this reason, in his letter to the tribunal and to the Venetian dominion, Dionisio exhorted them to remember God's Law and practice it: "I ask and I beg our most revered friends, the Venetian tribunal and the legate of the pope, to love me on account of the commandment of omnipotent God: Love the Lord your God with your whole heart and your whole soul and with all your strength and your neighbor as yourself. No one shows greater charity than in laying down his life for his friends."[112] Dionisio's emphasis on God's Law is similar to that of Savonarola, who, like Dionisio, equated Truth with God's Law, which should be the foundation for the rule of all states.[113] Dionisio's insistence that Venice had been chosen by God to judge probably was based upon his belief that Venetian justice was derived from God's Law and that the Venetian republic had been founded upon the precepts of God's Law.

The Holy Spirit is also a constant reference in Dionisio's letters written from prison. The Holy Spirit was his guide and the guide for the whole world. In a letter directed "to the whole Venetian dominion, temporal and spiritual, on behalf of all Christian princes and general clergy," Dionisio wrote a poem to the Holy Spirit as a proemium to the letter.[114] He not only reiterated that the Holy Spirit had revealed his divine anointment in the appearance of a white dove that had hovered over his right shoulder, but he also reminded the Venetian Senate that God had chosen it to rule as an instrument of God's justice. Dionisio had previously written to the senators sitting on the tribunal that he had "mysteries and secrets that must be revealed to them."[115]

The Holy Spirit, as the guide for the Venetian Senate and the whole world, was revealed as a "great mystery" by Dionisio. He wrote: "Now let the universe yield to the Holy Spirit, through whom the fools are wise and the learned are ignorant, the poor exult, the rich wail, the humble conquer, the haughty are conquered, the simple trust, the clever are disturbed, the weak are strong, the strong grow weak, the scorned are praised, the gloried are held cheap. Truth conquers, the lie trembles, virtue triumphs, and sin dies. Virtue, moreover, is Christ."[116] Dionisio's emphasis on the Holy Spirit recalls the thought of Joachim of Fiore even though Dionisio did not specifically write of the Age of the Spirit. Joachim had also received a mystical vision that had revealed to him all the "truth hidden in the Sacred Scriptures."[117] He also had prophesied a series of angelic popes who would cleanse the Church of its sin; a final angelic pope would then preside over the Age of the Spirit. During the cleansing of the Church, Joachim wrote, twelve men, "under the new religion," would go into all parts of the world to preach the Gospels of Christ in the manner of the original Apostles.[118] Dionisio obviously relished such a role for himself, writing often of his travels and his preaching for the sake of the Gospel of Christ.[119] His constant references to the dove that he said had followed him into the Venetian Senate reflect Joachimite literature in which the dove of the Holy Spirit was said to have been sent out as a sign that "just judges and counselors of peace will be restored to the Church."[120] Dionisio even claimed that the warnings he had delivered to the papal nuncio in Florence had been directed by the Holy Spirit in order to arouse the pope to perform his duty by guiding the Church to a true reformation in which the Holy Spirit would live as the Spirit of Christ in the hearts of all men.[121] Dionisio, as God's servant and messenger, believed that he was acting under the impulse of the Holy Spirit, which directed his pen.[122] In addition, Dionisio's authority had been demonstrated not only in his divine anointment but also in his sanctification by God's grace, which had revealed to him many secrets from heaven.[123]

Dionisio's conviction that he had received a divine anointment from the Virgin, that he had received the Holy Spirit in his person, and that he was now God's messenger and servant joined him to others in the Cinquecento who claimed direct relationships with God, the Holy Spirit, and the Virgin Mary.[124] These men and women believed that they were illumined from on high and preached reform of the Church and society without reference to theological dogma. Dionisio, in his quest for reform, bypassed the Council of Trent, which had only recently recessed. He never mentioned the council or its work in his letters, a deliberate omission that indicated he considered the reformation of the Church to be incomplete.[125] For this reason he urged the Italian princes to join with him in forming a council, under the guidance of the Holy Spirit, to bring true reform to the *Ecclesia militans*. The infusion of the Holy Spirit into the hearts of men was the common denominator for all true Christians, or *spirituali*. Savonarola defined them thus: "The *spirituali* are true Christians full of both light and grace of the

Holy Spirit and supernatural light of faith and are joined with the highest spirit, which is God. These are the *spirituali* subjected totally to the spirit and to God, and this is the spirit and the grace and the oil of the Holy Spirit . . . the true Christian must be anointed with this oil of the Holy Spirit, which must penetrate in the soul and in the body in order that man be all spiritual."[126] These *spirituali* like Savonarola and Dionisio bypassed the magisterium of the Church, whose earthly hierarchy they considered corrupt; instead, they believed that their inspiration came directly from God, who was the real head of the Church.

Either Dionisio was unable to recognize the challenge his claims of divine anointment made to the authority of the Church, or he deliberately revealed his so-called divine anointment in order to force the hierarchy of the Church into the action of reform. Although Saint Paul, writing in the Acts of the Apostles and in the Letters about the manifestation of the Holy Spirit, noted that a time would come when charismatic gifts would be diminished, Dionisio believed that the gifts of the Holy Spirit were still very much in evidence, certainly in his regard.[127] In the Christian era, however, prophecy was in the hands of those who held the keys of Saint Peter. The Roman Church did not sanction prophecy or prophets outside the magisterium of the Church or the Bible.[128] Dionisio's certainty concerning the revelations of the Holy Spirit was not only a challenge to the hierarchy of the Church in general but also a frontal attack on the Venetian Inquisition, which he claimed "was warring against the Holy Spirit."[129] For this reason, he argued, the tribunal's right to act as judges had been rejected by God and by him.[130] As I have indicated, he made an exception of the three Venetian senators on the tribunal. But if the Inquisition as a whole was not inspired by the Holy Spirit, it was not truly Christian and consequently not qualified to judge him. Dionisio suggested implicitly that the Inquisition should be searching out heretics for punishment, not God's servant. He stated explicitly that heretical princes in France, such as Condé, Dandelot, and Portianus, should be captured by Christian princes.[131] Dionisio's florid language, which linked the decline of morality and religion with political upheaval, reminds us of Savonarola, who had preached that unless Florence was reformed, the *flagella* of God would be used against the city, since Christ alone was its king.[132] The political implications were clear in Savonarola's warnings. Equally clear was Dionisio's preference for the Venetian Senate as judges qualified to render justice. Indeed, his whole program for reform was based upon the premise that chosen Christian princes, especially the Venetian doge and Senate, should direct the reform of the Church, since the pope and the ecclesiastical hierarchy had been ineffective. Under the guidance of the Holy

Spirit, which infused him, Dionisio believed that he and the Italian princes could bring about a true reform of the Church. In this regard the doge and especially the Venetian Senate had a primary task, since the Senate had been chosen by the Holy Spirit to judge.[133] In most of the letters written from the Venetian prison between June 8, 1566, and August 12, 1567, Dionisio claimed direct revelation from the Holy Spirit. Whether he was decrying the sins of sodomy and avarice or proclaiming his own providential role, he claimed that he had been taught by the Holy Spirit.

The horrors Dionisio had endured in the prisons of the Palazzo Ducale had strained his emotional stability to the breaking point. His highly charged language reveals his suffering and his fear, yet for the most part he maintains a remarkable consistency of presuppositions and arguments. He recognized that his claims about himself were at the root of his problems: "[I]t is true folly if I wish stubbornly to maintain that I am a man sent by God; plainly ridiculous that I am King of Kings and Lord of Lords; madness that I am higher than the pope. But it is beautiful that I am a poor mendicant, act modestly, tranquilly, and peacefully, also humbly."[134] He then noted ironically that no one should boast of the gifts of grace he had received from God. He did not deny his gifts from the Holy Spirit but rather condemned his pride. He would have fared better, he remarked, if he had conducted himself in a humble manner. He begged the Venetian noblemen on the tribunal to call him for questioning, indicating that "they would hear better things and things more to be desired." He astutely recalled from Saint Paul's letter to the Romans that "it has been written that he who resists power resists the ordination of God."[135] Although he had indicated his willingness to submit to Venetian authority, his resolve was to convince the Tre Savi to free him and aid him in his grand design for the reform of the Church and of society. He demonstrated the same consistency of purpose in all the letters he wrote, whether from prison or from the palaces of princes; these letters were preserved by the Venetian Inquisition, which he so often rebuked in these same letters.

· VII ·
THE HORSEMAN OF THE APOCALYPSE AND THE COURSE OF THE CHURCH MILITANT

n order to set forth his program of reform and to clarify his role in the reformation of the Church Militant, Dionisio Gallo wrote several long works, some of which were dedicated to the Italian princes; all, however, were written for a universal audience.[1] In these long works Dionisio more precisely defined the meaning of his calling as servant and messenger of God. In this chapter Dionisio's role as the charioteer of the Church Militant who was to lead the Church on a different course, and his directives for the Church Militant, will be analyzed. In the dedication of the *Liber, quem Nullus* to the Medici princes, Dionisio noted that prophets like Saint Paul, John the Evangelist, and David called themselves messengers of God not for their glory but for the glory of God. In like manner Dionisio noted that he had enjoyed special gifts from heaven for three years, starting from the time he had been called to be the ally of Christ. He linked his own suffering in prison to the will of Christ, who allowed Dionisio miraculously to survive almost certain death. His particular role had been proclaimed by the prophets and by the Blessed Bridget, according to Dionisio's words to Cosimo I.[2] In spite of his certainty about his divinely ordained role, he was equally certain that he alone could not reform the clergy, extirpate heresy, feed the poor, and convert the Turks and Jews. For this grand enterprise he had called upon the pope and the Italian princes. His numerous "legations" and his *Liber apertus* provided the "true and absolute art and method" for accomplishing the reform of the Church and society.

The epithets Dionisio appropriated for himself are significant for an understanding of his program of reform. I have noted many times that he referred to himself as God's messenger and servant, clearly indicating his divinely appointed role as an apostle for Christ in the sixteenth century.[3] With Pauline certainty he declared his apostolate as "messenger and servant." To clarify his specific role in the Church Militant, he used a figure from the race track, alluding to himself as the "charioteer of the horses that are the seven spirits of God." The implication of Dionisio's epithet is that the Church Militant has been without direction, without a driver. Now a charioteer with the seven spirits of God has been appointed to lead the Church on a new course. This new course was indeed to retrace the road to the original mission of the Church Militant. Dionisio saw a Church derailed by sickness, especially the Church in France. The symptoms of the sickness of the Church were the bitter ambition of many prelates and the errors of the heretics. These ailments were common to all nations, and the common illness in the Church Militant required a common medicine.[4] Dionisio believed himself to be the *medicus* who had been called to administer the appropriate medicine.

The evangelist John had written of the book sealed with seven seals that could be opened only by the Lamb of God.[5] Dionisio called himself the Lamb under Christ, the true Lamb of God. Believing himself to be the second John the Evangelist, he relived John's vision on the island of Patmos and made it his own. With a long list of metaphoric associations Dionisio defined himself and his mission.[6] As charioteer, *medicus,* and a second John the Evangelist, Dionisio offered his writings as prescriptions for an ailing Church. In several long works he set forth a specific program for the renewed health and rehabilitation of the Church and of society. His *Liber, quem Nullus aut in coelo aut in terra aut subtus terram, antea poterat aperire ne quidem respicere* takes its title from the Apocalypse and reveals throughout the influence of apocalyptic ideas drawn from the Blessed Bridget, Joachim of Fiore, the Pseudo-Methodius, as well as Isaiah and the "royal prophet" David. The *Haec est causa,* another long work, also sets forth his program for action. In addition, he wrote and rewrote his *Legatio,* for which he claimed a divine inspiration. On numerous occasions he indicated the Holy Spirit had directed his "reed" as he wrote this book. He considered his *Legatio* in Latin, in French, and in Latin and French of utmost importance. He made at least four copies of this work, as if to emphasize its significance by the number of copies.[7] In the various versions of the *Legatio* there is a clear ordering of principles, which he presented as essential points for inaugurating a new order of things. His *Liber, quem Nullus,* to which he gave the more grandiose title and numerous subtitles and prefaces, is, in fact, very similar to his *Legatio* written in French and Latin.

The *Liber, quem Nullus* (and by extension the *Legatio*) can be clearly defined as apocalyptic. On the page following the title, the work is called the course of the whole Church Militant: the horses that pull the Church Militant are the various gifts of the Holy Spirit.[8] The charioteer, or horseman, of the Apocalypse is Dionisio, under the names *auriga, pastor, rex, summus pontifex*. The book is also called the "work of the Lord, the book of kings, princes, and nations, the true and Catholic resolution of all things that are controversial, the book of life, the judgment and mercy of Christ, the praise and victory of Christian princes and armies, the mirror of truth and the journey of salvation." To these apocalyptic titles Dionisio added the Pauline imperatives of "the clarity of faith, the security of hope, and fiery charity." On several of the introductory pages Dionisio affixed his cipher, recording it, as a design, in the margins. The cipher is composed of a series of staffs arranged vertically and intersected by another series of staffs arranged horizontally. Dionisio's cipher, which he almost always added to his name, obviously had mystical significance for him and for his followers. If the name Dionisio Gallo was a pseudonym, as I suspect, the cipher would have allowed his identity to be known to his intimates.

In the preface that begins "This is the battle of the whole Church Militant," Dionisio identified himself with the person described in the second and third chapters of the Apocalypse. He repeated the mystical words of John: "I shall give, to the one conquering, the hidden manna, and I shall give to him the white stone: and on the stone a new name has been written that no one knows except him who has received it."[9] In one of his letters to the Venetian senators, Dionisio explained that he had been given the white stone on which was a name unknown except to him who had received it. Dionisio's identification of himself with the one who received God's hidden manna and the white stone was one of his boldest statements about his prophetic role. By mentioning the white stone Dionisio was recalling not only Apocalypse 2:17 but also the ascension of Moses, Aaron, and the seventy elders to Mount Sinai, where they viewed the God of Israel, under whose feet was a shining stone, often called a sapphire. Dionisio may have believed himself to be a new Moses as well as the "one who has conquered" in the Apocalypse. Moses was considered to be a new type of messiah and also a prophet who foretold the Messiah's coming. Moses was God's faithful servant, while Jesus was God's son. Dionisio apparently believed that he was following in the tradition of Moses as God's servant and in the tradition of Christ as an angelic pope and a temporal messiah.

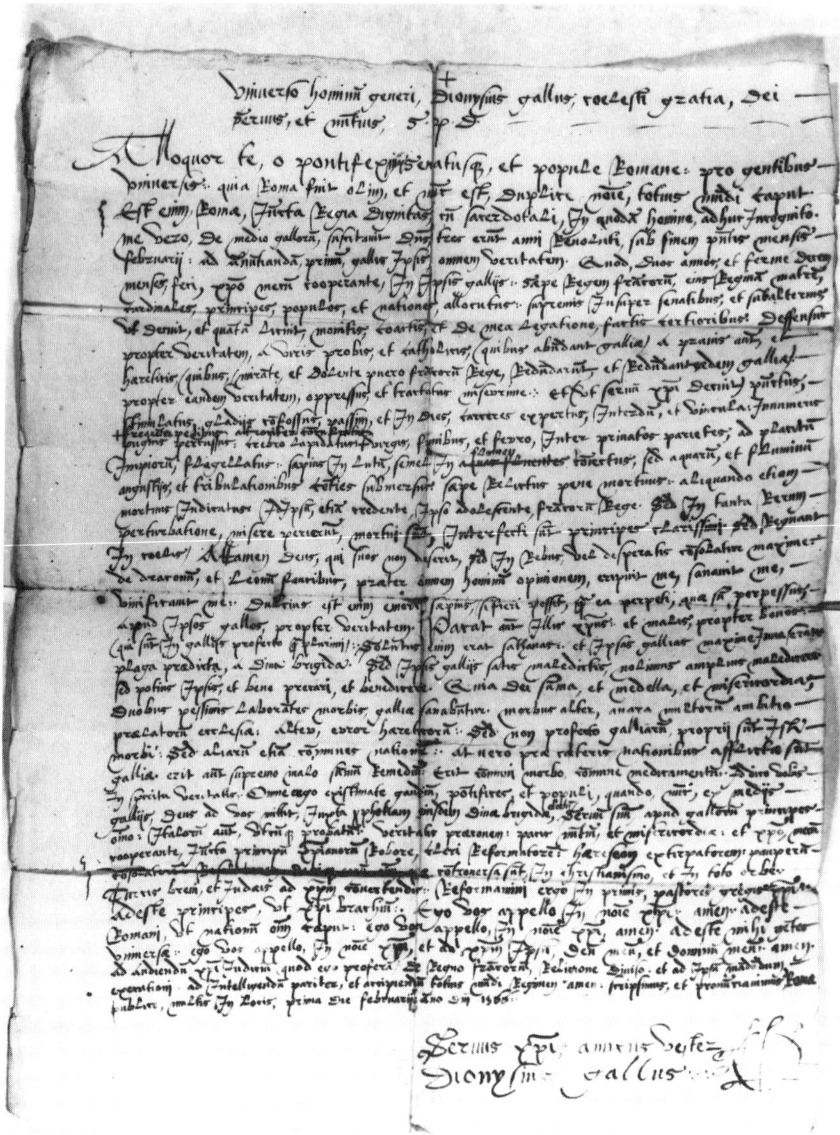
Universo hominum generi, Dionysius gallus, coelesti gratia, dei servus, et nuntius, S. P. D.

Servus Christi, amicus veritatis
Dionysius gallus

fig. 16
Letter from Dionisio showing his signature and cipher at lower right. Archivio di Stato, Venice

His prefaces to his *Liber, quem Nullus* make clear his concept of himself and his apocalyptic visions.[10]

His borrowings from the Apocalypse were typical of many thinkers in the Cinquecento, many of whose works are found in Venice. Joachim and his followers had brought apocalyptic thought to the forefront, and their works were printed in Venice in 1516–17. The mysterious book, circulated under the title of *Mirabilis Liber* and read in Venice, contained apocalyptic thought from both Joachim and the Blessed Bridget.[11] In numerous *processi* of the Holy Office of the Inquisition those being investigated for possible heretical thought often noted that the Apocalypse supported some of their opinions. Oderico Grisson, for example, admitted that he had referred to the pope as the Antichrist, noting that the Apocalypse supported his opinion.[12] In addition, a group of artisans in Venice in the middle of the Cinquecento followed the teachings of an armorer called Benedetto Corazzaro. After Corazzaro's death his millenarian ideas were perpetuated by Benedetto Florian and others. The mosaics of San Marco were also believed to hold many prophecies, especially those dealing with the Apocalypse, and Benedetto often explained the meaning of such prophecies to his followers. In fact, the mosaics of San Marco became an important text for millenarians in Venice, not only among artisans but also among learned men, such as Guillaume Postel, who was often to comment on the "very mysterious mosaics" in San Marco.

Dionisio believed that his works in which he set forth his program for the restoration of the Church and society contained the Truth, since he was certain that his reason had been restored and that his vision had been perfected by his mystical anointment.[13] He thought that his program, if actively pursued, would inaugurate a new age of harmony between heaven and earth. He held the utopian belief that mankind would be reformed if the clergy would show the way. With a reformed Christianity, the infidels, Turks and Jews, would soon be converted, and peace would reign on earth. He did not formulate a philosophical argument about sin and human perfectibility. His optimism was based on his certainty about his prescription for the ills of the world. Since his program seemed logical to him, he believed it would seem logical to others. In truth, however, Dionisio's utopian program was long on generalities and short on specifics of implementation.

Dionisio's various legations, including his *Liber, quem Nullus*, were organized around principles that dealt with the Church, the state, and society in general and often included principles for both Church and state. From the points he reiterated in each *Legatio* it is clear that Dionisio's plan for reformation presupposed some type of universal state in which God's Law and God's anointed would order society according to divine precepts. Though there is frequent repetition in his various writings, his *Legatio* is well organized and more straightforward than many of his other works. He apparently wrote his *Legatio* as a kind of constitution for the new order of the world he envisioned. The first thirty-seven points deal with Church and state. The next four (38–41) define necessary beliefs. Eleven points (42–52) define changes and practices specific to France. Dionisio directs seven (53–59) points to the Christian princes. The final sixteen (60–75) principles are edicts that would apply to all. Dionisio's visionary program, although naive and excessively idealistic, is nevertheless interesting. It is significant as an example of a utopian idealism that envisioned a united world governed by God's representatives on earth.

The various *Legationes* differ only slightly in the formal text; however, Dionisio appended different prefaces to each *Legatio*. The *Legatio* that appears in his *Liber, quem Nullus*, written in French and Latin, contains seventy-nine points, or principles, for his program of action, as does the *Legatio* written in Ferrara, in French. The *Legatio* written in Latin and completed in the home of Rocho de Mazzochis in Venice contains seventy-five; the *Legatio* written in Rome has seventy-seven points, in French. The difference in the number of principles arises from including, on occasion, two points within one number.

The principle that appeared as number seventy-three on the *Legatio* written in Rome (on February 18, without the year) was, however, deleted from the other *Legationes*. The statement reads as follows: "Clement Marot receu par les docteurs correct." Since Clement Marot died in 1544, Dionisio's statement is unclear. Was he referring to Marot's translation of the psalm that appeared in the Genevan Psalter? If so, his language is strange, because in the very next point, when referring to the books of Calvin (not Calvin himself), he wrote: "tous liures de Calvyn et auttres heretiques." Therefore, his statement appears to be a reference to Marot himself. The meaning, however, is veiled. This is the only reference to Clement Marot in Dionisio's writings preserved in Venice. To make the issue even more confusing, on the back of the legation a hand different from Dionisio's wrote: "Fra li altri libri approbati da i dottori e Clemente Marot."

We know that Marot found refuge in Ferrara as the friend of René, duchess of Ferrara, years before Dionisio arrived as guest of René's son, Alfonso II, but we do not know why Dionisio made a point of Marot or why, having made it, he decided to delete the remark. The mention of Marot is the only variant of any significance in the several legations.

Mercy, pardon, and charity were the virtues deemed essential in Dionisio's reformation of the Church and were paramount in his *Legatio*. Whoever wished to be converted and to cease sinning should be pardoned and granted mercy, regardless of the enormity of the sins. Charity as the basis of mercy and pardon should be practiced in every situation.

The application of the guiding principles of the *Legatio* pertained to both the Church and the state, although the first twenty-five principles presented changes in the ecclesiastical order. To accomplish an active expression of charity, Dionisio proposed that every town and village should have a treasury for subventing the poor, for feeding and clothing them and providing dowries. He did not, however, provide a systematic argument for subventing the poor or for his other principles. He noted principles of natural law, as did Juan Luis Vives in his *De suventione pauperum*, although, unlike Vives, he did not argue a premise but rather presented points for a program of action.[14] As a parallel to the action of the state toward the poor, the Church should fund the treasury in the cities from a third part of the goods of the Church. To conserve the Church's money, every bishop was to preside over only one bishopric; if he should try to hold more than one, he would be deprived of them all.

Dionisio insisted that all prelates must reside in their parishes and must be responsible for the parochial wealth. The rectors were obligated to feed the poor presbyters or give them stipends for their necessities. To assist in accomplishing the social program of the Church, the French king must cease receiving his tithe, since the money could be better spent on the poor. Likewise, secular lords should not receive any benefices from the Church, and no pensions from the state should be held by the rich.[15] Dionisio was not alone in criticizing the king's control of ecclesiastical appointments. The Venetian ambassador wrote that the use of the Concordat of Bologna by King Francis I opened the door to Protestantism in France, noting: "All hope was lost for good and lettered priests to receive a recompense for their work. . . . Incompetent priests, appointed by the king at the whim of ladies and courtiers and motivated only by greed and self-interest, took over the French church. [They] troubled the faith of the innocent people and dampened the fervent piety of the old times. It is by this door . . . that heresy entered France."[16]

Rigorous standards of virtue and intelligence should be applied to all religious, whether canons, priests, abbots, bishops, archbishops, cardinals, or legates. Should they fail to meet these standards, they must be dismissed. In addition, prelates created with simony must also be removed from their offices. The responsibility of conferring priesthoods and benefices should be in the hands of the bishop in every diocese, provided that he had been elected by the Holy Spirit.

One of the most significant changes concerned the pope. The name of the pope was to be changed to "king and more than king." Dionisio did not specify how a different name would affect the pope's duties. Since he would be called king, he would obviously have a realm, which Dionisio called the *Ecclesia militans*. There was never a clear demarcation in Dionisio's proposals between the political and religious, secular and sacred. The universal state Dionisio envisioned would reflect a spiritual and political entity, a utopian political theocracy. The blending of the political and spiritual elements could often be found in prophecies attributed to Joachim of Fiore. A book of his prophecies was published in Venice in a collection entitled *Abbas Joachim magnus propheta*,[17] which included the *De magnis tribulationibus et statu ecclesie*, in which Joachim wrote of the holy shepherd who would be "the charioteer [*equitiarius*] in the nation, a man most wise and a friend of God."[18] The political-spiritual conception of the *sanctus Pastor* described by Joachim is similar to Dionisio's conception of the pope whose name would be changed to "king and more than king."[19] Dionisio not only prophesied about the pope-king but also appropriated the role for himself, calling himself the charioteer (*auriga*) of the *Ecclesia militans*.[20] *Equitiarius*, the word for charioteer used by Joachim, is synonymous with *auriga*, the word chosen by Dionisio to describe his role in the reformation of the Church on earth.[21]

There are other similarities in the thought of Dionisio and Joachim. In the same Joachimite text the abbot wrote "that Jesus looses the seventh seal and opens the book placed in the right hand of the Holy Trinity; thus He reveals to the faithful and to the world through his own servants the seventh and last state of the Church Militant."[22] Dionisio used the apocalyptic passage indicated by Joachim (Apoc. 5:1–10) as the title of his *Liber, quem Nullus*, since he, as servant and messenger of God, had been given authority to open the book and to proclaim the necessity of immediate reform of the Church Militant.[23]

Although Dionisio often referred to Saint Bridget rather than to Joachim, the ideas of Joachim and other apocalyptic thinkers are apparent in his numerous writings. Marjorie Reeves has noted that there was a galaxy of prophets who spoke with one voice in honor of the last great ruler who would usher in an age of gold. Among those she names are Rabanus, Methodius and the Sibyls, Cataldus, Cyril and Merlin, Joachim, Rupescissa and Telesphorus, Gamalion, Bridget and St. Vincent Ferrer, Reinhard Lichtenberger, Torquatus, Carion and Paracelsus.[24] Rupescissa cited many obscure prophecies, among which were those of P. Cataneus, which seem especially relevant to Dionisio's change of the pope's name to "king and more than king." Cataneus concluded his prophecies with these words: "Then there will be one sheepfold and one shepherd, and one Lord, who will hold the whole world under his power, and a golden age will be declared."[25] Peter Galatinus, a Franciscan who in 1524 wrote a *Commentary on the Apocalypse* dedicated to the emperor Charles V, may have been one of Dionisio's sources, since Galatinus wrote of the *magnus rex* who would be victorious over the infidel in Africa and in Europe. He quoted the Blessed Amadeus: "erit ter maximus: maximus videlicet Pontifex maximus Rex et maximus Dominus."[26]

Teolosphoro da Cosenza's prophecies are also reflected in Dionisio Gallo's thought. Teolosphoro described the false *sponsi* and the one legitimate *sponsus*, noting: "Then a Gaul [*gallus*] will sing [or a cock will crow], and there will be the best restauration. . . . The best Gaul and true pope will sing, and there will be a restitution when all errors have been extirpated."[27] In a state of poverty and in thanks to God, this angelic shepherd, along with the emperor the shepherd would crown, would reform the Church.[28] Teolosphoro's prophecy would have been especially meaningful to Dionisio, who called himself *gallus*, whose meaning in Latin is both "Gaul" and "cock." Dionisio was certainly a "crowing cock" and a "singing Gaul," insofar as he never wavered in crying out his divinely appointed role as servant and messenger who proclaimed Christ's truth for the restoration of the Church. His various *Legationes* could be called the "song of the Gaul" that heralded the plan for a restitution of the Church. Dionisio must have been aware of the numerous connotations associated with the word *gallus*, and thus must have been aware that his cognomen Gallus, whether real or invented, would convey rich associations related to his prophetic persona. The iconography of the cock is rich, and Dionisio, as I have pointed out, made careful use of symbolism. Previously, Prudentius had affirmed that "the cock [*gallus*] is a remarkable creature of God and is rightly the figure of that presbyter."[29] He is the messenger of light; he invites us to prayers; he casts out demons. Because the cock is the symbol of the sun, Marsilio Ficino affirmed that he is superior to the lion. An early source grants the cock prophetic powers, which reminds one of Dionisio's claims about himself. In the text we read: "The cock, among other winged creatures of the heavens, hears the angels' choir; then he warns us to cast aside the words of evil men and to taste and comprehend the secrets of the sublime."[30]

Guillaume Postel, a fellow countryman of Dionisio, blended the concept of king with that of angelic pope, whom he called "priest of reason." Postel, like Dionisio, believed himself called by God to fulfill his mission

fig. 17
Manuscript of Telesforo da Cosenza. The angel is holding a book on which is written "Hic est liber" (This is the book)—a quote from the apocalypse and the title of one of Dionisio's long works. Biblioteca nazionale di San Marco

as angelic pope or the third Elias.[31] He wrote that the prince of the new age "will follow the right of David and the works of the Venetian doge forever in his order, about to preserve them in his own highest order, so that, as Hercules formerly in the law of nature tried to make one state for the universe, that one, whoever he will be, in the name of Christ Jesus will do this, and thus in our time there will be one sheepfold and one shepherd, with pardon as a guide."[32] Postel dreamed of a universal monarchy both spiritual and political that in many ways resembled the reformed Church and society Dionisio envisioned.[33] Postel's *respublica mundana* would be a loose confederation presided over by twelve patriarchs, four for each of the three parts of the universe.[34] Dionisio proposed in his *Legatio* exactly the same organization, that is, twelve patriarchs who would preside over the earth, four for each of the three parts of the world. The duties of the patriarchs were not specified, but they would probably have been quasi-political-religious. The relationship between these patriarchs and the pope-king was also not explained. However, it is clear that the role of the pope, now called king, would have been different from the role of the former popes in Rome, since Dionisio wrote that bulls previously promulgated would be invalid. In spite of the change of the name of the pope and the abrogation of papal bulls, Dionisio believed that the authority of the apostolic see was not to be diminished or the *dignitas* of the pope removed.

In a Church purified and pious there could be no simony.[35] Therefore, ecclesiastics moved to different locations were not to receive any compensation. Priests must adhere to strict norms based on honor and erudition. In order to guarantee the priest's suitability for the profession, ordination generally would not take place before the professed reached forty years of age; thirty years would be the minimum. Dionisio placed great emphasis on an educated clergy, indicating even presbyters who were ignorant and base should learn the mechanical arts or else become educated and virtuous.

In keeping with the Franciscan tradition, Dionisio preferred a poor scholar over a rich one, even if their virtues were equal. Poverty was especially desirable for the clergy, whom Dionisio had often criticized because of their love of ostentation and luxury.[36] Under no circumstances would benefices be paid when the prelate did not reside in his district. In addition, an ecclesiastical hierarchy with the requisites of virtue and intelligence was essential to a purified Church; anyone, no matter how high his rank, should be dismissed if he did not fulfill the requirements of virtue and intelligence. Dionisio stopped short of naming the pope in the list of prelates to whom this principle applied; however, in another statement he noted that even the pope, by his virtue and wisdom, must defend his right to occupy the chair of Saint Peter. In order to have constant supervision of the organization and functions of the Church, synods should be frequent and just. Dionisio was obviously not satisfied with the results of the Council of Trent. He believed that frequent meetings of the clergy could define and overcome problems before they became divisive issues, as in France and Germany. Dionisio was not alone in his lack of confidence in the Council of Trent. In 1546 Ignatius Loyola considered recalling Diego Lainez from the Council of Trent because he thought the council was moving at a snail's pace. In fact, he asked the three Jesuits at the council if for God's greater glory they should withdraw from the council and go about their accustomed ministries elsewhere.[37] The Jesuits did not often write of "reform of the Church," because they did not want to criticize the Church. However, from the Jesuit headquarters in Rome documents emanated that spoke of the reform of the Curia. Ignatius reportedly said that if the pope reformed himself, "the papal 'household' (or Curia), and the cardinals in Rome, everything else would fall into place."[38] On March 13, 1555, Lainez preached in Rome, according to Juan Alfonso de Polanco, "against the heretics and Roman abuses," and in the fall and winter of that year he denounced "sinful Rome." By 1563 Lainez and Jerónimo Nadal, along with Polanco and Canisius, were convinced that the "reform" would best be undertaken by the pope himself.[39] As I have indicated, Dionisio in like manner insisted upon the reform of the pope and the Curia, "from the highest to the lowest." Although he often wrote of the *pugna* of the *Ecclesia militans* or the *cursus* of the Church, his criticism, like that of the Jesuits, was directed against the abuses of the ecclesiastical hierarchy. For this reason he went to Rome and carried a huge cross through the streets of the city, crying out, "Crucify your hearts, oh Romans." As we recall, he also addressed the pope in Saint Peter's, urging him to reform himself and his Curia. In this regard Dionisio's remarks about the pope and the Curia again raise the question of a connection, if any, with the Jesuits.

After indicating twenty-five items that pertained to the reform of the ecclesiastics and the practice of charity and pardon, Dionisio turned to the question of order in the Christian state. Education of the laity as well as the clergy was a priority.[40] Schools were to be established in all cities and villages, and teachers were to be rewarded with good salaries for their learning. An adequate stipend would allow preceptors to marry, since inadequate salaries had forced many teachers to live in the poorest circumstances and consequently to be less attentive to their pupils. Dionisio wanted the universities, which he called the "famous daughters," to be restored to their former honors, but he also indicated that they should be reformed. Hebrew, Greek, and Latin should be taught in the universities, and men well versed in these languages should be kindly received by all. Jacques Lefèvre d'Etaples had previously encouraged the study of Greek and Hebrew so that one could read the Bible in the original languages.[41] Philology was useful because it helped preserve the purity of the Bible's text. Translation was desirable so that scripture might be accessible to as many people as possible. In the trilingual *collège* established by Francis I, the study of Hebrew was encouraged by royal readers such as François Vatable and Agathias Guidacerius. In 1538 Guillaume Postel had been appointed royal reader in Greek, Hebrew, and Arabic.[42] John Calvin also emphasized the study of languages as necessary for the preparation of ministers. Future Calvinist ministers were required to learn Hebrew. The importance Calvin attached to a humanistic education as a means of spreading the Gospel can be seen in the curriculum of the academy in Geneva that he established to train leaders of the church and state of Geneva.⁴³ Dionisio was obviously aware of the state of Hebrew and Greek studies in Paris and elsewhere, but he believed that the study of Hebrew, Greek, and Latin should be expanded to all universities and their students.⁴⁴

Unlike modern litigious society, the world Dionisio envisioned would generate few legal contests. However, when necessary they should be settled with dispatch. The responsibility for settling any disputes that might arise would be in the hands of the mayors of the various states, cities, or villages. Other judges were to be chosen from the bailiffs who resided in the various territories. In his *Legatio* Dionisio did not mention, as he often did in his letters written from prison in Venice to the Senate and to the tribunal, that the Venetian Senate, composed of pious Venetians, had been chosen by God to act as judges. Nevertheless, he placed great emphasis on justice and the rendering of justice, since temporal justice should reflect God's justice coupled with mercy. In Dionisio's mind, Venetian justice held a divine sanction and should reflect its true and appropriate role as an example of divine justice in the new order of the world.⁴⁵

The question of justice is a recurring theme in Dionisio's *Legatio*, and in one of his concluding principles he noted that the Edict of Orléans should be preserved.⁴⁶ In France, Catherine de' Medici and Chancellor L'Hôpital labored with a proposal to reform the judicial and administrative systems. Various articles of the edict "called for the suppression of all offices created since the reign of Louis XI, for the banning of judicial pluralism, and the prohibition of close relatives sitting on the same magisterial bench."⁴⁷ The Edict of Orléans, like other edicts, such as that of Blois in 1499 and Villers-Cotterets in 1539, aimed to reform justice. The enactment of the edict was thwarted in large measure by the Parlements.⁴⁸ Perhaps Dionisio, while noting that the Edict of Orléans must be preserved, understood the failure of Crown and Parlement to cooperate and therefore proposed that Venetian justice follow divine precepts.

The process of choosing officials was to be revamped, and all magistrates, both temporal and spiritual, were to be elected for their virtue alone by honorable men untainted by heresy.⁴⁹ Magistrates must also set the example for Christian orthodoxy; anyone who had subscribed to the new doctrines would be dismissed. In addition, he must be beyond reproach in matters of money. Magistracies must not be bought, as had been the practice under King Henry II and his father Francis I.⁵⁰ Dionisio probably expected this dictum to serve as a warning to the young king Charles IX, and especially to his mother, Catherine de' Medici, of whom Dionisio was especially critical. The Crown's need for cash to pursue the war against heresy made the selling of offices a modus operandi, of which Dionisio was aware. In spite of the financial exigencies practices such as this should be curtailed immediately. The king must also cease his selling of the goods of the Church and return all things to the Church so that they could be used to feed and clothe the poor.[51] J. H. M. Salmon has pointed out that in local assemblies preparatory to the meeting of the Estates-General in Orléans in December 1560, the nobility and the third estate approved the confiscation of Church property to pay the king's debts.[52] Dionisio, however, placed the blame upon the king, since it was the king who had appealed to the pope for license to sell ecclesiastical goods in order to pay for the war against the Huguenots.[53] This edict for the sale of ecclesiastical goods and land was rendered by Charles IX in 1563 and caused quite a stir in the kingdom.[54]

Dionisio noted that the peace the king had made with Admiral Coligny should be declared truly "cruel and satanic."[55] Since preaching by Calvinists had been increasing in the 1560s, Dionisio's remarks were obviously leveled against these "sowers of heresy." His own preaching in the public places of Paris and Languedoc was no doubt a response to the growing success of Protestant preachers in France.[56] Conventicles were to be disbanded, and all preaching by heretical pastors was to be forbidden. Dionisio's harshest words were leveled against Huguenot preachers and their conventicles:[57] they should be burned alive or drowned. However, the first principle in his legation was a call for mercy and pardon for all who, leaving their sins, wished to be converted.

Dire punishment was to be accorded only to those who refused to be reformed. Again we see Dionisio's inability to accept any valid points in the sermons of dissenting preachers. He abhorred divisions in the kingdom of France, both religious and political, yet his own prophetic certainty had led him to extreme solutions.[58] Dionisio's proposals reflected a certain desperation, since he did not believe the politics of the young king and his mother could resolve the crisis. The youth and inexperience of the king prevented him from discerning sagacious responses to the complicated problems of his kingdom. Although often critical of the king's actions, Dionisio nevertheless demonstrated sympathy for him because of his youth and the enormous problems he faced. He often wrote of being in the king's presence in Gaîllon, at Mont Marsan, and in Paris. Although no additional documents have been found to clarify the relationship between Dionisio and the young Charles IX, his perceptive remarks about the boy king lead one to speculate that perhaps Dionisio Gallo served as tutor to Catherine's sons after his departure from his position as rector at Lisieux. A tutor-prophet for

Catherine's children would not have been alien to the queen's disposition at the time.[59]

Although Dionisio was often impatient with some actions of the Crown, his words never reflected the gossip that circulated in Paris: "Ce petit filz de putain, ce bastard là, ce sera ung petit messère bogrinot d'Italie, qui ne vauldra rien ne que sa mère et perdra le royaume de France."[60] Dionisio placed the blame on the bad advice of the young king's ministers and the jealousy of the princes. The sympathy Dionisio expressed for the young king was shared by Michiel Surian, the Venetian ambassador, who wrote that because of the untimely death of Henry II when Charles was still a small boy, the young boy had never had the opportunity to learn from his father how to govern.[61] Surian painted a dire picture of the violence in France and of the commoners' envy of the rich. Social unrest was part of the fabric of the religious strife. In such a climate an experienced ruler would have had difficulty; but for a boy king without experience, and with many princes and nobles adding to the confusion by supporting the reformed religion, success was impossible.[62]

The problems in France continued to absorb Dionisio, and many of his proposals for a reformed Church and society pertained only to this divided kingdom. Always concerned about the young king, he recommended that Charles and his brothers study for at least three years in the colleges of Paris if they wished to rule. As I have previously noted, Dionisio emphasized education as an essential part of a reformed Church and state.

To allow time for his proposals to be completely implemented, the royal Senate should be disbanded for three years, during which only the Senate of Paris would speak as the political voice of the kingdom. However, he noted that the Senate of Rouen should rule Normandy. As a Norman, Dionisio trusted the lords of Normandy and intended for them to retain their dignity and even to have greater authority based on their virtues. At one point Dionisio had claimed that he was descended from the ancient line of Norman rulers, which would explain, in part, his preference for Norman political authority. His desire to disband the royal Senate probably derived from his accusation that the king, his council, and the Senate had usurped the goods of the Church.

Never favorably disposed toward the queen mother, Dionisio directed her to live simply but nobly, with her daughter. She should also live as a Catholic. Many times our prophet had written that Catherine de' Medici favored the Huguenots, thereby allowing the divisions to continue. If she lived as a Catholic, Dionisio presumed that she, grieving over the divisions of the kingdom, would in some way overcome them. Dionisio urged all the Christian princes to help the divided kingdom by quickly enacting the tenets of his *Legatio*. In addition, the princes should be good tutors for the young king, giving him good advice. They should also be the best protectors of the Church Militant and, along with the pope, give necessary monies for the Catholic faith. Concerns similar to Dionisio's were again voiced by Michiel Surian, Venetian ambassador to France in 1561, who wrote of the religious strife in France and its repercussions throughout the kingdom.[63] Surian pinpointed certain actions he believed had led to the general confusion in France. His attitude toward heresy resembled the stance of Dionisio. Surian wrote:

> *Another error was to tolerate free speech against the Catholic religion in the schools and in public gatherings, and in the presence of the king and of the council. Worse was to agree to the diminution of the authority of the Church, and much worse to accept scandalous writings and to allow the heretics to preach and to assemble and to allow them to dispute their opinions in the meetings of the bishops, as if with public authority the division of the kingdom must be nourished.*[64]

Surian attributed the increase in the numbers of Huguenots to these errors of the Crown. Throughout the kingdom the Huguenots "have begun to toss on the ground the image of our Lord Jesus Christ and the saints, to defile the churches, to violate the priests and prelates, to open public prisons, and to insult the ministers and royal lieutenants and finally also the queen."[65] The ambassador related the debasement of religion to the disorder in the civil realm; he noted that it was commonly said that "the king received his authority from the people and that the subject was not obligated to obey the prince when he commands something that is not expressed in the Gospel."[66] Consequently, the overthrow of the monarchy and the king would be the result.[67] Dionisio was also not alone in expecting the Christian princes to lead the way in solving the problems of a divided Christianity. In a letter to the Collegio the patriarch of Venice indicated his great distress that any Christian prince had not taken necessary precautions at the beginning to extinguish the first signs of heresy, "which has the strength to destroy—I shall not say the families—but the states."[68]

In regard to society, the princes and the senates that were just and noted for virtue would have grave responsibilities for caring for the poor. They should redistribute the riches, stolen or dishonestly obtained, by giving them to the poor. Prelates who were heretical, wicked, and negligent in their duties must be dismissed and their goods distributed to the poor. Dionisio did not approach the problem of a diminished clergy. He apparently believed there would be enough virtuous men dedicated to Christ to take the places of those who had been released because of their faults. This was his conviction, especially in regard to Venice. He often commented on the piety of the Venetian nobility and the doge of Venice. He had indicated that the Virgin had taken pity on Venice and interceded on her behalf because of the piety of Venetian nobility, in spite of the sexual abuses of some of its citizens. Dionisio regularly referred to his friend and host Rocho de Mazzochis as the "most pious Christian and Venetian citizen." Dionisio obviously admired Venice's confraternities and pious places that offered aid to the poor, to widows, orphans, and girls without dowries.[69] Venice appeared to be the model for Dionisio's political-religious state. He admired its republican form of government and its great emphasis on piety and active charity. Although he railed against the sodomites of Venice, he nevertheless thought Venice's faults of small consequence in comparison with its virtues. Venetian institutions made active charity an essential element of city government. For example, the Consiglio dei Dieci voted to pay eight hundred ducats as credit to the procurators of San Marco, "to be distributed for marrying young girls, for freeing prisoners, for clothing the poor, and for other pious causes."[70] This example could be multiplied many times. The city's unquestionable devotion to pious places and acts of charity made Venice an especially appropriate location for the presentation of Dionisio's *Legatio*.

The vision of Christianity that Dionisio proclaimed had its roots in the teaching of Jesus and the practices of the early Church. Care of the poor and the helpless was the quintessential role of the clergy and every Christian. In Dionisio's scheme, before a prelate could be approved, he must agree to give a third of all his worldly goods for the needs of his parish. From these resources, youths could be instructed in certain mechanical arts, and some could be sent to school. Poor young girls would be given dowries.

With reform in the religious, political, and social realms Dionisio believed peace could become a reality in the whole world. He obviously abhorred the Huguenots' scorn of the Catholic Mass, since he reiterated the need for all to attend the Mass. Although Dionisio seldom emphasized theology, the question of the real presence of Christ in the Eucharist was for him an essential tenet of belief. Any priest who had strayed from his faith in the real presence must confess his fault. He also accepted the seven sacraments of the Catholic Church, since these had been given by Jesus and the Holy Spirit to men. Dionisio seemed incapable of accepting as valid any theological interpretations that varied from the teachings of the Church, with perhaps the exception of purgatory. He clearly believed that the abuses of the ecclesiastical hierarchy and the temporal, rather than the spiritual, power of the Church were causes for divisions in the Church. Dionisio was convinced that if the abuses of the Church were removed, the union of all people in the *Ecclesia militans* would become a reality. His criticism of the lives of ecclesiastics was no less harsh than that of the reformers. Dionisio, unlike Luther, Zwingli, or Calvin, however, did not criticize the teachings of the Catholic Church. Nevertheless, he never seemed to consider how similar his own attacks on the abuses of the Church were to those of the Protestant reformers.[71] In his own way Dionisio was a Catholic "radical reformer" who wanted to return to the roots of early Christianity.[72] His emphasis on poverty is only one example of such views.

Although radical in his desire for a purified Church, he lauded certain practices of the Church that were considered by the Protestant reformers either nonessential or actually heretical. He commended, for example, fasting and praised abstinence from meat on Holy Friday, the Sabbath, and Lent. However, Dionisio, realizing that this issue divided Protestants and Catholics, indicated that the clergy and certain princes should help him with the decision about food laws, since the Holy Spirit had revealed to him the priority of the conversion of all unfaithful and the reconciliation of the whole human race. In several of the final points made in his *Legatio* Dionisio appeared to be at least aware of some problems raised by dissenters. For example, on the question of work he noted that one could work the whole week; still the Lord's day was to be preserved, and the solemn feasts of the Trinity, the Blessed Virgin, the Apostles, John the Baptist, and Dionisio were to be observed. Dionisio's words about work are confusing. Did he mean that work was permissible on all days except the Sabbath, although one should take time from work to observe the solemn feast days? This appears to be his intention, but his statement is ambiguous. Also problematical is the reference to the Feast of Dionisius, or Saint Denis, who in the third century Gregory of Tours cites as one of the bishops who brought Christianity to the Gauls. The Feast of Saint Denis was appropriately a French feast day that Dionisio perhaps interjected to remind his readers of his own association with the French saint as a new missionary to the Gauls. Dionisio's role was not limited, however, to the Gauls, as he made abundantly clear. He had been chosen by God as His messenger for the Church Militant.

Although Dionisio's remarks about work seem deliberately ambiguous, he evidently wanted to leave the door ajar for the return of the Church's critics. On several practices, however, Dionisio was dogmatic. Saints both male and female must be revered, since honor to the saints was pleasing to

God. Images of saints had spiritual value, and iconoclasts should be punished. Dionisio also believed that all the objects connected with Catholic ritual were conducive to proper worship. He considered prayers for the dead holy and pious. On the question of purgatory, which had been debated so often in religious discussions in Venice and elsewhere and by Dionisio and Spinola during their incarceration in the same cell, Dionisio would only say that "purgatory was wherever it pleases the Most High."

In his concluding points Dionisio returned again to his own role in renewing the Church and society. He stated that "the third king has been born, that male seized up to God and His throne; the second is the shepherd promised in the last days; the first is Christ eternal."[73] Although Dionisio did not specifically state which role he had appropriated for himself, since he mentioned the third king and shepherd in addition to the first king, the eternal Christ.

In a document written from prison in the Ducal Palace of Venice, however, Dionisio did reveal his persona as third king in addition to his role as messenger and servant of God. He elaborated additional aspects of his persona that confirmed his role as third king.[74] His messianic associations were chosen from the Apocalypse, the Psalms of David, Isaiah, and Jewish mysticism. In contrast to the pope, who would sit upon the apostolic seat, Dionisio claimed as his own "the new holy, mystical seat of David, king and prophet, that is, on the throne of Christ, royal and pontifical."[75] In spite of his messianic boasts, Dionisio did not claim the prerogatives of Christ as second person of the Trinity. He believed his role was to put into practice Christ's teachings by reforming His kingdom on earth, that is, the *Ecclesia militans*. He wrote often of his utopian vision of a reformed world as a real possibility, since he acted with Christ as a coworker (*Christo cooperante*). Dionisio never wavered in his certainty of his own role, since he claimed that the Holy Spirit directed his thoughts and his hand as he wrote his various treatises about a reformed *Ecclesia militans*. He interpreted his sufferings and imprisonment as part of God's plan, since "God sent me on account of His Name."[76] The mystery and the manifestation of God's Name had been described by Dionisius Areopagitica in numerous Cabalistic writings and by Johannes Reuchlin, among many others. The power inherent in the divine names held great meaning for Dionisio, since he claimed for himself the mysterious name that had been written on the white, or shining, stone, which was unknown to anyone except him who had received it. The mystery of the name written on the white stone was, in Dionisio's mind, a sign of his own divine anointment. In Apocalypse 2:17 we find the source for Dionisio's claim about his name written on a white stone: "To him who overcomes, I will give the hidden manna, and I will give him a white pebble [stone], and upon the pebble [stone] a new name written that no one knows except him who receives it." Because of Dionisio's undaunted efforts to restore and renew the *Ecclesia militans,* he interpreted the passage from the Apocalypse as still another reference to himself.

One can also presume that Dionisio had read Joachim's *Espositio . . . in Apocalipsim,* where the abbot from Fiore explained the passage from the Apocalypse about the white stone.[77] Joachim noted that the rock which Moses struck and from which water flowed was Christ: "That very rock reproved by the Jews has been elected by God and preordained, for Simon says: 'You are Christ, son of the living God.'"[78] Christ, calling Simon the rock (*petra*), established him as the head of the Church. The Church becomes the "rock" because of its strength. But whence does this strength come? Joachim asks. It comes, he writes, from the participation of the grace in that most strong rock. To participate in so many graces is to receive the body of Christ, which is to inherit the gift of this precious stone.[79] This commentary by Joachim, in which the eucharistic bread, the body of Christ, is related to the white stone, would have held great significance for Dionisio, who emphasized the centrality of the body of Christ to the Church and to man's life. The white stone, according to Joachim, has been promised to the victor over sins. To be a victor over sin is to become a new man. Since Dionisio had claimed this newness in Christ, he had been given the white stone. Joachim's commentary on this passage about the name on the white stone illuminates Dionisio's claim. Joachim cited the passage from the Apocalypse: "[O]n the stone a name has been written that no one knows except him who receives it."[80] He then explained: "No one knows how great a dignity it is to be called Christian from Christ unless it has been given to one to know and to understand."[81]

Since Dionisio believed that he had been given the stone with the unknown name inscribed upon it, he would necessarily assume that the name Christian would apply to him, since his double anointment, divinely given, had allowed him to know and understand. The statements about the white stone are at the very center of Dionisio's concept of the reform of the ecclesiastical hierarchy. Each minister of Christ, including the pope, must be worthy of having the white stone with the unknown name.

Following Apocalypse 2:17 Dionisio linked the hidden manna to the white stone, since both were gifts from God to the "one who conquers." Abbot Joachim explained the verse as a reference to the sweetness of the interior word, about which David sang: "How great is the multitude of your sweetness, O Lord, which you have hidden for those who fear you."[82] Then Joachim noted that the sweetness was the manna and living bread that descended from the sky. Christ was the hidden manna, the word and the wisdom of good and learned men, and makes them drunk with as much sweetness of His pleasure as is appropriate for that one to be called teacher.[83] In beautiful language Joachim described the infusion secretly given to the just man to whom has been given a new name written on the white stone.[84] Joachim is important to an understanding of the apocalyptic language of Dionisio. In both prophetic voices one hears the same metaphoric language and compelling passion of one who has sensed the sweetness of divine love and the certainty of divine revelation. Joachimite associations are apparent in many of Dionisio's writings.

As well as allusions to Joachim, Dionisio added to his own prophetic persona the concept of the third king, with its messianic implications. In his *Legatio* Dionisio's statement that a "third king has been born" is a gloss on Apocalypse 12:5: "And she brought forth a male child, who was to rule all nations with a rod of iron; and her child was caught up unto God and to his throne." Dionisio associated the male of this apocalyptic passage with the third king and assimilated the apocalyptic vision to his own double anointment as "third king," the double anointment signifying his dual role, spiritual and political.[85]

In the same document in which Dionisio discussed his double anointment, he also identified himself with the "third king." In rhetorical language he addressed the question over and over again to the Venetian dominion, to the tribunal, and to the papal legate, "Who is that great third king?" He then answered his query by indicating that the third king was he about whom David spoke in the Psalms: "I, moreover, have been established as king by God upon Zion, His holy mountain, preaching His precept."[86] The third king had also been proclaimed by Isaiah: "Send forth the lamb, O Lord, the giver of the earth, from the rock of the desert to the mountain of the daughter of Zion, and he will be just like a bird fleeing and chicks flying from the nest."[87] Dionisio cited Isaiah for the second time, noting that the third king was certainly the one about whom Isaiah said: "Who is that one who came from Edom with colored garments from Bosra, that handsome one in his stole."[88] Dionisio used Old Testament prophecy and the Psalms of David as essential elements in his apocalyptic vision. He also made clear his own identification with "the man from Edom" when he wrote that this man came "from the earth, from the city of Gisors [*gi sorte*], that is, from the land of Iot."[89] Although Dionisio's personification of himself as the man from Edom is precise and central to his role as God's servant and messenger, the Isaiah passage itself has been much disputed and subject to various interpretations.

In his *Commentary on the Book of the Prophet Isaiah* Calvin denied that the passage in chapter 63, verse 1, was a reference to Christ.[90] He interpreted the passage about the man from Edom as referring to God the avenger returning from the slaughter of the Edomites, as if he were drenched with their blood.[91] Calvin's interpretation is far removed, however, from the messianic reading Dionisio gave to the passage by associating the man from Edom with the third king.[92] To understand Dionisio's meaning about the man from Edom, we must turn first to the Book of Jubilees in the Pseudepigrapha of the Old Testament, where in chapters 35 and 36 we learn of the reconciliation of Esau and Jacob, that is, of Edom and Israel. Rebecca had sent for Esau, begging that she be buried near Sarah and that Jacob and Esau "will love each other, and that neither will desire evil against the other, but mutual love only."[93] In chapter 36 Isaac called his sons Jacob and Esau to him and asked that he be buried near Abraham. Then he commanded his sons to practice righteousness and uprightness on the earth "so that the Lord may bring upon you all that the Lord said that He would do to Abraham and to his seed. And love one another, my sons, your brothers as a man who loves his own soul, and let each seek in what he may benefit his brother, and act together on the earth." Both sons received the blessing from their father, and though Isaac gave to the firstborn, Esau, the larger portion, the tower and all that Abraham possessed at the Well of Oath, Esau said: "I have sold to Jacob and given my birthright to Jacob; to him let it be given, and I have not a single word to say regarding it, for it is his."[94] Then Esau went to Edom, and Jacob dwelt in the mountains of Hebron. The reconciliation of Esau and Jacob as recounted in the Book of Jubilees is pertinent to the messianic implications in Dionisio's words about the third king and the man from Edom. At the time of the Messiah, all enmity will be laid aside, and all men will live in peace as brothers. Esau (Edom) in the Jubilees account is truly responsible for the reconciliation, since he, though defrauded of his birthright, forgave the wrong done to him and yielded to his father's command that the brothers love each other. The reconciliation of Edom and Israel became a paradigm for the reconciliation of the whole world in Dionisio's mind; his *Legatio* was a blueprint for reform and reconciliation.

Additional insight into the significance of Edom can be gained from the messianic idea in Cabalism, as described by Gershom Scholem.[95] The Gentiles, who were designated as Esau or Edom, received their redemption, or light, in an instant, but it would depart from them gradually until they were destroyed by Israel, who had grown strong. "And when the spirit of uncleanliness passes from the world and the divine light shines upon Israel without let or hindrance, all things will return to their proper order—to the state of perfection that prevailed in the Garden of Eden before Adam sinned. The world will all be joined one to another, and nothing will separate Creator from creature."[96]

Dionisio's passionate insistence upon the immediate reform of the Church and society and on his own role in augmenting the restoration of the world seems to have its roots in the esoteric interpretation of the reconciliation of Edom and Israel. It is clear that Dionisio blended the mysterious passage from the Apocalypse about the woman clothed in the sun and her son who has been seized up to God's throne with Isaiah's statement about the man from Edom. He apparently drew from pseudepigraphical and cabalistic sources about Esau (Edom) and Jacob to enhance his own messianic claims as well as to reinforce his demands for a reform of the *Ecclesia militans* and a reconciliation of all peoples.

In describing the third king as the man from Edom, Dionisio also explained the hierarchy of the other two kings. The second king was the shepherd who had been promised, and the first king was Christ eternal. It is apparent that Dionisio was also following medieval prophecies regarding the angelic shepherd. The state of the *Ecclesia militans* described by Telesforo was similar to that described as essential in Dionisio's *Legatio* and in his other works. For example, Telesforo noted: "This holy man will lay low the proud horns of the religions. And all will be near the state of the primitive Church. And then there will be one shepherd, one law, one lord, true and modest, fearing God. Orthodox faith will reign among Christians."[97] In the *Mirabilis Liber* three angelic shepherds are also predicted: "Subsequently God will raise up three other most holy men, one after the other, very similar in virtues and miracles, who confirm the deeds and words of their predecessor. Under their rule the state of the Church will renew itself and they will be called angelic shepherds."[98]

Medieval prophecy was clearly a source for Dionisio's prophetic voice. Following the numerous predictions about the angelic pope or popes, Dionisio saw himself as one of God's chosen servants, whom he referred to as the man from Edom. His message was congruent with that of the angelic pope of medieval prophecy who would usher in the restitution of the Church. As third king, he would follow the angelic pope, the second king.

In addition to the sources already cited, several of Guillaume Postel's works provide insight into the problem of the third king from Edom. Postel's

Quonam modo possit venire aut venisse Christus de Aedom is especially appropriate for our consideration of Dionisio as the man from Edom.[99] Postel used metaphorical language and metaphysical constructs to explain how Christ could be said to come from Edom, since Edom had been reproved. Postel wrote an esoteric story about Jacob and Esau (Edom), not once, but twice,[100] since in this story, which he turned into the story of cosmic redemption, he was able to incorporate some of his favorite themes. Edom (Esau), as firstborn of Isaac, had a special place in the order of nature. Isaac preferred this son, and even after his blessing had passed to Jacob, he longed for reconciliation with his firstborn. In a peculiarly Postellian treatment of the grades of being in which each is linked to the other, Postel wrote of the higher Isaac, "le but et final point là où la divine Loy tend" as a paradigm of Isaac, the father of Edom (Esau) and Jacob.[101] Especially fond of correspondences, Postel made Edom correspond to the Gentiles and Jacob correspond to the Jews, although he pointed out that Jacob had sinned as much as Edom.[102] For Postel, Edom represented the feminine, material, or maternal realm, while Jacob represented the masculine, spiritual, or paternal realm.[103] A union of male and female was essential to Postel's metaphysics; in the story of Edom and Jacob the consummation and restitution of the world is portrayed.[104]

Since Edom was described by Isaiah (63:1) as handsome in his red stole, red being the color of blood and the image of Edom, Postel associated Edom with man's corporeal nature, the basis of which is the blood. The redness of blood became for Postel an essential aspect of salvation, or restitution. Postel wrote that

> *truly that redness or Edomness that was born in Esau before Jacob and that Isaac loves more in Edom and wishes to bless more than Mother Rebecca wishes is that very holy and never cursed part from which King Messiah in the whole race of Adam and Noah came, as He through His own sacraments makes this part from the substance of this Church Militant by assuming that water as He turns it into wine. Through the union of the triumphant and angelic Church, very similar to the angels, this wine is poured from the sacred chalice and truly through the consecration becomes the blood of Christ.*[105]

Postel pointed out that Christ could not be said to come from Edom in the literal sense, because the Holy Scripture indicated otherwise. He noted, however, in the figurative sense and in regard to the truth of doctrine and faith, He yielded to "no one of the most holy men." In many of Postel's works, almost as a leitmotif, he spoke of the second coming of Christ, not at the end of time, but within mankind. The second coming *intra nos* was the root and foundation of Postel's concept of restitution, or salvation.[106] In the text in which Postel explained how Christ could be said to come from Edom, he made "Edomness," or the Edom-body, correspond to the second coming of Christ within us. The following passage from Postel is significant for understanding Dionisio's statements about himself as the man from Edom: "[E]specially in declaring this second coming, when one speaks of that Edom-like body, which is second and maternal and exists within us, while Christ Formed in Us truly everywhere also Rises up Within Us. He alone descends from the sky, bearing us, and hence He alone ascends into the sky as victor and conqueror of the whole Edom-like Potency of the world."[107]

Edom as a symbol of wickedness will be destroyed by Christ coming from Edom, "so that the kingdom Israel is to be restored truly Christian and truly Jewish or most Christian."[108] Christ's assumption of the sins of the world in order to redeem it is captured symbolically in His descent into and emergence from Hell, which is described by Postel as coming from Edom. Dionisio described his own coming from the profound depths of a Venetian prison "as coming from Edom." His words about the man from Edom could be considered a gloss on the passages cited from Postel. Dionisio's remarks, written in the margins of his text, were necessarily abbreviated, since he was running out of paper. Postel's interpretation of the Isaiah passage about the man from Edom clarifies for us Dionisio's concept of himself as this man, who had Christ within himself. The presence of Christ living in Dionisio, the man from Edom, was confirmed by a double anointment that cleansed and purified him on the inside and the outside. This double anointment restored his reason to its pristine state, and with his new vision he drafted his *Legatio* and other works. He was also impelled by his anointment as servant and messenger to proclaim constantly a need for the reformation of the Church. In his *Legatio* Dionisio wrote of the deplorable state of the shepherds of the Church who were created with simony and who lived luxurious lives, contrary to the teaching of Christ and His Church.[109] Postel likewise noted that the one who came from Edom would be a very severe judge of those infected with simony, which was the fount and cause of all doctrinal heresies.[110]

Dionisio believed that his *Legatio* was the medicine a sick Church and a sick world needed. He was totally convinced that his program could heal, since its author had been instructed by the Holy Spirit in a double anointment. Dionisio's insistent referral to his double anointment is also significant for understanding his conception of himself. In Israel anointment was bestowed upon a king at his inauguration, upon a priest at his consecration, and upon a leper at his rehabilitation. In the Bible, *mshh* implies that the anointment stems from God (2 Sam. 1:21, Jer. 22:14). The attribute *mashi'ah* (anointed) came to designate the king and high priest and by extension other divinely appointed functionaries who were not anointed at all, that is, the prophets. Anointment was even applied to the Messiah, which word derived from the Hebrew "anointed."[111] Because of Dionisio's mystical religious experience, which culminated in his double anointment, our prophet had complete confidence in his calling and noted on several occasions that he was the one to whom Saint Bridget referred as God's messenger to reform the world.[112] All of Dionisio's longer works express this conviction as they present his program for reform.

In contrast to the *Legatio*, which presents a platform of religious, political, and social principles, the *Haec est causa totius ecclesiae militantis* is a narrative about the reform of the Church and frequently repeats the themes of the *Legatio*. This work was dedicated to all the Christian princes and to all the nations of Christianity, with special dedication to the emperor and to the Catholic king. The treatise was completed in Padua at the home of the rector of the university and read in Venice on June 5, 1566, according to Dionisio's own words.[113] Dionisio noted that he began the work in Ferrara and presented it to Duke Alfonso II and his uncle Francesco d'Este, marquis de Masse. In regard to the style of this work, Dionisio wrote that it had been pleasing to set forth the cause of Christ and his Church "in that new form of speaking, just as in rhetorical practice."[114] The document, written in Latin, is moving because of its passionate language and its interesting minidialogues. The *Haec est causa* also provides additional information about France and Dionisio's relation to the court.

At the beginning of this work Dionisio wrote of his credentials: the double appearance of the Virgin and his double anointment by the Virgin. Following the Virgin's directive, he set out to reform the world in preparation for the second coming, which he believed was imminent. Dionisio found great significance in the fact that God had chosen him, a simple and poor man, small in stature and weak in body, a man considered by the wise of his day a foolish and silly man. Dionisio's words recall those of Saint Paul and the Psalms of David. Certainly they reflect the humility of Christ entering Jerusalem on a donkey. Savonarola also wrote of the "fools of the world" being chosen by Christ for His work on earth.[115] Both Savonarola and Dionisio took seriously many of Saint Paul's teachings. Savonarola indicated that he sought to please God, not men, "because, as the Apostle says, 'if I should still please men, I would not be a servant of Christ.'"[116] Fra Hieronimo also knew that every man "who speaks of these things is considered crazy by the wise men of this world."[117] It was never in Savonarola's vision to please men. He believed in the wisdom of Saint Paul's words: "To those [who think they are wise] I shall say, together with the Apostle: 'We are fools for Christ: you, however, are the wise.'"[118] Dionisio felt the same scorn from the so-called wise men of the world who refused to believe that he was God's duly anointed servant.

Dionisio was quite conscious that his actions and his words as a servant of God would draw down scorn upon him, but he considered his suffering an aspect of his divine mission. As if to emphasize the scorn of the world for this "weak little man," Dionisio wrote on the parchment covering in which he carried his writings the following words: "Nos insensati vitam illorum putabamus insaniam. Ecce quo modo computati sunt inter filios Dei."[119] These words, from the Book of Wisdom (5:4–5), were also used by Saint Bridget to describe the life of God's prophets. The citations vary slightly.[120] Savonarola also cited the same passage when writing of the derision Christ's "fools" must suffer: "Nos insensati vitam illorum estimabamus insaniam et finem illorum sine honore. Ecce quomodo computati sunt inter filios dei et inter sanctos sors illorum est."[121]

In the *Haec est causa* Dionisio summarized his platform of restitution: reform of the clergy, extirpation of heresy, consolation of the poor from one third of the goods of the Church, and conversion of the infidel. He argued that the reform of the clergy was of primary importance, since the faults of the clergy had already been made known by Satan, by which he meant Luther and Calvin. He contrasted the wealth of the cardinals with the poverty of thousands in Rome and Christ.[122] Dionisio's words about poverty and the conditions of the poor are moving. "The poor are members of Christ," he wrote. "These are created by God from equal matter as kings and princes, popes and cardinals, the powerful and the rich." Linking poverty to Christ and his teachings, he asked: "Did not Christ come into the world? Did not Christ enter Jerusalem? Did not Christ live?"[123] Dionisio was pleading for Christ to become a reality in the lives of men. Therefore, he insisted upon the immediate reform of the clergy and a return to the practice of the disciples of Christ in the early Church.[124]

Dionisio argued that the abuses of the clergy were the root of all problems in the Church and the cause of the civil wars in France. The sins of heresy could be linked directly to the sins of the clergy and their lack of charity.[125] He again complained about the lack of direction from the pope. If the pope would not reform the clergy, who would? he asked. Evidence of the pope's failings could be seen in his refusal to call together the princes in a league to fight heresy. Dionisio's dissatisfaction with the results of the Council of Trent is evident in his insistence on a league of princes to fight heresy, since the religious solution had not yielded the desired results. Dionisio was in effect proposing a political endeavor to effect religious reform. His criticism of the pope is especially pungent in the *Haec est causa*. The pope should defend his right to sit in the chair of Saint Peter unless he instituted a council of princes to fight heresy. In this regard, Dionisio presented an imaginary dialogue between the pope and himself, with Dionisio pleading for a council of princes and the pope giving countless reasons why he could not act except in conjunction with the cardinals. These imaginary dialogues are among the most interesting aspects of Dionisio's writings, for he could criticize sharply yet escape censure, since he admitted in writing that these were imaginary.[126]

According to Dionisio, the pope's refusal to work with the princes in a council to remove heresy was based upon the cardinals' unwillingness to give up their riches and to reform themselves and the pope's unwillingness to effect change in the ecclesiastical hierarchy. For this reason God was punishing his Church. By His permissive Will the Turks had expanded their empire and were threatening Christianity. Dionisio even claimed that there would be no war with the Turks if the clergy were reformed.[127] This was a challenge he repeatedly hurled at the pope. Yet in spite of Dionisio's numerous criticisms of the pope, he approved of papal authority. He believed that the authority of the vicar of Christ would be greatly enhanced if the pope, truly angelic and Christlike, provided exemplary leadership for the Church.

Dionisio also interjected additional information about French politics, especially about his relationship with the young king and the queen mother. Dionisio placed the cause of the civil wars in France directly on the abuses of the clergy. The royal Senate, more than the young king, feared a union of princes to reform the Church and stamp out heresy. Because of the abuses of the clergy and the heresy that resulted from these abuses, good and truly Catholic rectors, reformers, and extirpators should be sent to France to put into practice his *Legatio*. Dionisio also recounted his arrival in Gaîllon, where the king and his court were sojourning. He explained to the king what must be done to reform his kingdom. He remained for several days, during which the king read Dionisio's *Legatio*. But the king, although he was in agreement with Dionisio's proposals, could not bring himself to implement the principles of the *Legatio*, which would require him to punish the heretics and to send cardinals and bishops from his court to their own flocks.[128]

Although the king was not ready to enact his *Legatio*, Dionisio was still allowed to preach in Paris: in the churches, in the palaces, and in all public places. He enjoyed this freedom to preach until the king went to visit his kingdom. The young King Charles IX began a grand tour in the spring of 1564, visiting almost all parts of his kingdom in about two years.[129] Dionisio apparently had complete freedom of movement until the king left Paris. With the king's departure, however, Dionisio was imprisoned and suffered greatly, according to his account in *Haec est causa*. He was mysteriously freed— according to our prophet, God freed him—and quickly followed the king to Mont Marsan. The king's party had arrived in Bayonne in April 1565;[130] therefore, Dionisio had probably met the royal party at Mont Marsan in March 1565. It is interesting to note that before the king and his mother arrived in Bayonne, Catherine directed the entourage to Aix to consult Nostradamus.[131] A second prophet, our Dionisio Gallo, would greet Catherine and Charles IX at Mont Marsan. His predictions to the king and the queen mother did nothing to calm their troubled souls. Dionisio had pursued the king to Mont Marsan "in order to remind him of the things that God had commanded him through [Dionisio]: that he should unite his own kingdom; otherwise in a short time it would happen that he, sitting on two seats in a divided kingdom, would come to a bad end, being deprived of each seat."[132] The king, his mother, and the royal Senate received this prophecy poorly; the heretics were even more aroused by Dionisio's predictions. From all of Dionisio's accounts about his experience with Catholics and Huguenots, the latter appeared to be much more hostile to Dionisio's prophetic voice than were the Catholics. He obviously had enemies enough at the court, but he claimed his enemies were the heretical princes. He apparently found favor with those at the top of the political hierarchy but not with all nobles regardless of their religious persuasion.

In Paris Dionisio continued to urge the king to reform his kingdom, to punish the heretics, and to send all the shepherds back to their flocks. In the royal palace Dionisio cried out: "O Charles, King of the French, if you wish, the mad, raging dogs who have destroyed all of your kingdom are captured. If you let them escape, if you do not enact justice, your crown perishes."[133]

When King Charles IX heard Dionisio's warnings about the division and loss of kingdom and Crown, our prophet was no longer welcome in the court; "*ex aula* dimissus sum," to quote Dionisio. Yet he was apparently free to go about where he wished in the city of Paris. It is doubtful that he was allowed to preach after his encounter with the king at Mont Marsan, since he said only that "irem, quo vellem."[134] After our prophet's prediction of the dissolution of the Crown, the king and especially Catherine de' Medici could no longer abide his highly charged words, which were bound to inflame the passions on all sides of the religious spectrum. After the Mont Marsan episode, the "king and all the people" called Dionisio the king of the Gauls, obviously in derision.[135] It is uncertain if Dionisio continued to teach. An entry of November 1563 in the *Journal* of Abbé Jehan de La Fosse confirms that Dionisio was called king of the Gauls. The statement in the *Journal* probably reflects our prophet's frenzied preaching activity in Paris before his visit to the king at Gaîllon. The entry is significant: "In that time [November 1563] there was a young man with good Latin and also of great mind who in disguise played the fool and made great protests against the Huguenots and spared no one in his speaking. He called himself the king of the Gauls."[136] Dionisio's own words about his preaching activities in Paris are in harmony with the statement of Abbé de La Fosse, since our prophet noted that he went throughout Paris wearing a tin crown on his head and his clothes on backward and carrying in his hands a large staff, as he preached the need for reform of clerical abuses and for the practice of active charity by all. Dionisio's foolish kingly attire obviously mocked royalty not truly "royal," since a king was he who served God; in Dionisio's interpretation of the word, a king who did not serve God was not truly a king. Because Dionisio proclaimed himself king of the Gauls, who served God in his poverty, he mocked the king and his court, and he was likewise mocked as a fool by rowdy youths and others who saw him. His preaching was apparently very well known in Paris, since two monks from that city testified before the Venetian Inquisition in 1566 that he preached throughout Paris, wearing a tin crown and calling himself king of the Gauls. Because of his very public persona it is easy to see why the king and queen mother chose to send him out of their court. Such passion could easily inflame the Paris mobs. After the loss of the king's favor Dionisio headed south to Languedoc and then to Italy, as previously noted.

In the *Haec est causa* Dionisio often emphasized his own authority and his credentials. To underscore his own claims, he urged the princes and peoples to read the scriptures and study Saint Bridget. Writing to princes, he nevertheless noted that the first nobility was that of virtue, the second that of knowledge and intellect. Both types of nobility he claimed as God's gift to himself. Advantages of birth were of little importance if the aforementioned nobilities were absent, Dionisio warned. For himself, however, he acknowledged both types of nobility; in addition to the nobility granted to him by God, he traced his own origin to the ancient stock of Gallic princes, as his name *Gallus* or *de Gallois* signified. This was the only indication in any of Dionisio's writings about his family background. There is no record in Gisors of his birth.

The elaboration of his credentials was important in regard to the major theme of this work. As the various *Legatio* set forth his program for action and the *Liber* identified his platform with the apocalyptic vision of John the Evangelist, so the *Haec est causa* presented the prophet's plea for practical help from the princes of Italy: "God wishes ... that you bring aid and work for these things that now remain to be done," Dionisio wrote. In a beautiful rhetorical passage our prophet enlisted first the aid of the princes and next that of all segments of society in reforming the Church and the world:

> *Come, therefore, oh dear princes; come with me, chosen people and nations; come, you fearless ones. Come now, all dear princes and noblemen, endowed with virtue. Come, judges and magistrates. Come, doctors and you skilled in laws, old men and young, fathers and sons, all teachers and pupils. Come, you men and women. Come, children, servants, and maidservants. I wish Franciscan doctors to be present, to rejoice, to be glad in their assemblies. Come, you, poor, naked, hungry, weak, despised; come seek your right. Come, shepherds, you who oversee well. Let us all triumph.*[137]

With the exception of the Franciscans, Dionisio's call for help in the work of reform was directed to secular society. He urged a political and social solution for the spiritual ills of his day. He obviously did not believe that the Church could or would reform itself. Therefore, he urged all society to take up arms. "Let us all, united in faith, take up arms," he wrote. "Let our arms be gleaming justice, fiery charity."[138] It is clear that Dionisio Gallo saw a united Christianity, which included Jews and Arabs, resulting from a renewed *Ecclesia militans*.

His challenge to society for a new world order was couched in elegant Latin style, demonstrating his rhetorical ability. His sermons—or speeches, as he called them—were equally moving, as the large crowds that heard him in Venice attest. Dionisio's discourse about the need for society to take up arms reminds us not only of Saint Paul but of Erasmus in the *Enchiridion militis Christiani*. But similar as their ideas are, Dionisio's language resembles more closely the rhetorical brilliance and passion of Cicero or Guillaume Postel than the measured elegance of Erasmus.

In the *Haec est causa*, as in the *praefatio* of the various versions of the *Legatio* and in the *Liber apertus*, he enlarged upon his divinely appointed mission and that of the princes. He urged the princes to be coworkers with him in the task of reforming the clergy and of feeding the poor. It was their responsibility, since they were "gods," as he was. He supported this assertion by citing the Psalm of David: "God stood in the synagogue of gods. In their minds He judged the gods, saying to the gods of the earth: 'To what extent are you judging iniquity and taking on the appearance of sins?'"[139] This psalm (81 [82]) clarifies for us what seems at first an incredulous boast. In Psalm 81 (82) God rebukes the "gods" who are the judges and magistrates on earth, challenging the "gods" of the earth to judge justly and render justice to the afflicted and downtrodden.[140] Dionisio's citation from this psalm invokes the divine authority of the holy writ to urge the princes into action for the reform of the Church and society.[141] As heads of their respective states, they were judges, hence gods, who must adopt immediate resolutions for universal justice. By calling for political help to solve a basically religious, moral problem, Dionisio was implicitly expressing his lack of faith in the Church's ability to reform itself by religious action alone. Pious princes and indeed all humanity must take up the cause of the ailing, divided Church.

Dionisio's use of Psalm 81 (82), in which the psalmist used metaphoric language to convey profound meaning about justice, exemplifies his use of metaphor to express divine mysteries. Erasmus had indicated that when we can comprehend the figurative language of scriptures, we then can begin to comprehend the hidden mysteries. Erasmus and Dionisio used the same reference to the book sealed with the seven seals.[142] Dionisio's claim to have opened the book meant that he understood the metaphor in which the Apocalypse was written. This ability was in Dionisio's mind a divine gift, representative of his divine anointment. When he wrote of the double anointment by the Virgin, he probably meant that he understood not only the literal meaning of divine references but also the hidden, inner meaning. In describing his double anointment, he always wrote of the anointment first on the outside of his body, from head to toes, then on the inside. The interior anointment indicated his ability to comprehend the arcana of revelation. His metaphoric language echoes the language of divine scripture. Rhetorical and metaphorical language was a significant element in the voice of the Cinquecento prophet; it not only revealed his prophetic persona but in many instances was his protection, or "his armor." When the prophet's language was not understood, he was often deemed crazy and thus was protected from a death penalty. This was the case in Dionisio's trial before the Inquisition; it was also the case in Guillaume Postel's trial in Venice in 1555. Even the inquisitor told Postel that he could not understand anything that he had said; therefore, he must be mad. In fact, his condemnation as *amens* saved his life. Many aspects of prophetic language, however, elude the modern sensibility; and these need to be examined further to achieve a better understanding of the continuing presence of prophecy in the Cinquecento.

Princes as judges and prelates as spiritual guides must work together to render God's justice on earth, according to Dionisio's program for action. Because of his restored insight and divinely ordained prophetic vision, Dionisio believed he had the appropriate solution for the reform of the Church and society. His apocalyptic understanding was grounded in scripture and in his own personal religious and mystical transformation from rector of the Collège de Lisieux to servant and messenger of God. His prophetic persona was best expressed by David and John the Evangelist. The vision of John became his own vision, and he believed that John's revelation spoke directly to him. In David, Dionisio found comfort and strength, since the Psalms, which he often quoted, supported his views, or so he believed. Dionisio did not rely upon astrology or numerical signs to enhance his prophetic gifts. He followed his own prophetic voice, divinely bestowed, and the divinely inspired written word.

Dionisio's prophecies were directed to the world in which he lived, not to some distant future. Although he sometimes warned of a moral and spiritual debacle if the Church were not reformed, his platform for renovation revealed principles and precepts for the world of the Cinquecento. The substructure of all of Dionisio's principles was justice and charity. He warned that it was the responsibility of every prince, temporal and spiritual, to enact God's justice on earth. The ministry of Christ to the poor, the outcast, the hungry, and helpless was the model for all to follow. To Dionisio, Venice seemed to be the city that most fully exemplified this kind of justice and charity. Other Frenchmen, like Jean Bodin and Guillaume Postel, had also praised Venice's justice and charity.[143] It is significant that Dionisio chose the cortile of the Ducal Palace, the seat of Venetian justice as well as the home of the doge, to proclaim his role and Venice's role in effecting the restitution of the Church and the world. To enter the cortile, where Dionisio preached on the *banca* of the grand stairway, one had to pass through the Porta della Carta, sometimes called the "Via Triumphalis," over whose portal presides the sculpted figure of Doge Francesco Foscari on his knees before the winged lion that represents Saint Mark. On the pinnacle above the door, the figure of Justice sits enthroned. Four virtues, in addition to Justice, especially esteemed by Venice, Caritas, Prudentia, Temperantia, and Fortitudo, surround the *porta* as appropriate icons of the doge.[144] This Venetian space, with all its political, religious, and social implications, was the appropriate setting for our scholar-turned-prophet to proclaim his full-blown program for action. Since Dionisio had experienced a double anointment by the Holy Virgin, he himself became a sacred vessel, and he chose the sacred space of the Ducal Palace and the Church of Saint Mark in which to reveal his program of reform, sacred and temporal. This sacred space was, as it were, the passageway for those "chosen by God to judge."[145] Dionisio reminded the Venetian senators that they had been chosen by God to judge. The question of justice linked Dionisio to Venice and the "sacred space," since he also had been chosen by God to judge. In spite of his friendship with Cosimo I and Alfonso II, our prophet emphasized Venice's role in God's plan for reform, which he was trying to enact. Many aspects of Dionisio's program resembled Venice's concept of Church and state. Nevertheless, the sweeping changes that Dionisio wanted to put into practice would have threatened stability of the Venetian republic and hence were unacceptable to Venetian authority. His call for reform did find a favorable response among the citizens and patricians of Venice, however. Even in the prison of the Ducal Palace Dionisio found adherents to his plan for a renewed Church and world.

Dionisio's prophetic voice was different in some ways from many of the prophetic voices heard throughout the sixteenth century.[146] He did not prophesy for future ages. His admonitions were for his own age. In other respects, however, the hopes and dreams Dionisio uttered were similar to others in the sixteenth century.[147] Dionisio's prophetic voice also resonated with late medieval apocalyptic thought. The Antichrist and the angelic pope were equally real to him, and he was obviously well versed in the medieval prophetic tradition. On the other hand, his program of action was grounded in the present, his present, with the deplorable conditions of the Church—the moral laxity of the clergy, the inertia of the papacy, the divisions in the Church—as the *raison* for his prophecy. The Wars of Religion in France nourished the prophetic voice; in Dionisio's case they set him into frantic action. On the soil of France Dionisio received his divine anointment, but from France he fled, having lost favor with the king and constantly harassed by the Huguenots. Even as late as 1566 Italy still seemed to him "the door through which reform would pour out over Europe," to use Bernardino Ochino's phrase, since he believed the Italian princes more pious than the French and therefore more willing to adopt his cause.

Dionisio was only one vehicle for cross-fertilization of reformist-prophetic ideas between France and Italy, however. Francesco Giorgio (Zorzi) Veneto had a strong influence in France even into the seventeenth century,[148] and Guy Le Fèvre de la Boderie, a disciple of Postel, translated Zorzi's *De harmonia*

fig. 18
Saint Mark as a winged lion holding a standard on which is written, "The lion of the tribe of Judah has conquered." Biblioteca nazionale di San Marco, Venice

into French. A contemporary of Dionisio, Pietro Carnesecchi, a humanist reformer, fled Italy for France, and Giacomo Brocardo, a humanist-prophet, having escaped from the guards who were accompanying him from the prison in San Giovanni in Bragora to the nearby Venetian Inquisition, fled Venice and found refuge and an audience in France.[149]

Dionisio used the prophetic traditions of the past to speak to the ills of the present.[150] The Old Testament prophets, David, Saint Paul, and John the Evangelist were his sources for understanding his own world. Most significant, however, for all his prophetic program of reform was his divine anointment "on the inside and on the outside," as he said, which made him a new man with a new vision. His divine anointment shaped his life and his action and gave him absolute certainty about his divine appointment as God's messenger and servant. This certainty enabled him to endure torments and persecution, but the excessive claims he made in its name in turn caused him to be called a fool and mocked as "king of the Gauls." Scorn by the world in no way moved him from what he believed was God's plan for his life. His various writings reveal a consistent, if unrealistic, program for the reform of the Church and the world. Dionisio Gallo, who truly believed that the new Jerusalem would descend if his precepts were followed, can be added to a growing list of utopian thinkers of the Cinquecento. The new Jerusalem was intimately related to Dionisio's belief in his own divine anointment, as his words in *Haec est causa* make clear: "Christ enabled me to conquer the open door that no one can close, because I have corporeal virtue in proper measure and I have preserved his word and have not denied his name. Christ will make me, conquering, a column in the temple of His Father . . . and He will write above me the name of God, His Father, and the name of the city of God His Father, the new Jerusalem, which descends from heaven from God His Father."[151] In the same text Dionisio makes clear his persona as the soldier of Christ and His angelic pope. Dionisio's conception of himself was an essential aspect of his apocalyptic thought and the basis of all his writings. According to Dionisio, his words must be comprehended and his directives set in motion, since, as he wrote, "[m]any indeed likewise battle. Many conquer; many themselves have their own promises from Christ also very beautiful and pleasing, but I alone am the one who battles against Satan, against heresy, on behalf of the right of the poor, against all the abuses of the clergy, and against all iniquity. Now I go forth as victor. . . . I am he whom God has chosen; He established me the king and highest shepherd under His own son."[152] Utopian dreams and a belief in divine anointment, strange as they may seem to us today, were not uncommon during the Cinquecento, though modern scholarship sometimes overlooks them. Dionisio Gallo makes us focus, moreover, upon the significance of prophecy and prophetic hopes for God's kingdom on earth, a purified Church, to become a reality in the Cinquecento.

CONCLUSION

he story of Dionisio Gallo is fascinating and frustrating at the same time. His persona is appealing, and his language is beautifully expressive. Missing from his history, however, are links that years of research have not traced. Yet the many bits and pieces that remain inform us about the continuing importance of prophecy among various strata of society well after the middle of the sixteenth century. Medieval prophecy followed a long tradition from antiquity and the pre-Christian era. Prophecies concerning the angelic pope and a reformation of the Church were widespread in the Middle Ages, and the influence of Joachim was enormous, as Marjorie Reeves, Cesare Vasoli, and more recently Ottavia Niccoli have shown. Joachim provided written and visual representations to reveal his prophetic voice.

Medieval prophecies coupled with new revelations and warnings were influential in many cases until the end of the century. Prophets found favor among friends in court circles and in conventicles whose members were looking for ways to reform the Church. Humanists were among those who believed they had received a prophetic voice. Many humanists believed that even after the Council of Trent the work of reform was incomplete. Prophecy that was inspired by God was a most potent means of instruction for reform. Men like Dionisio, Postel, and Brocardo believed that prophetic preaching and teaching could bring about immediate results, if the words of God transmitted to His prophets were put into practice.

Humanists like Dionisio and Postel gave up important positions, often in royal circles, to convey to the world the prophetic message of reform.

Prophecy is often concerned with predictions of the future in the manner of Nostradamus, a most famous prophet of the sixteenth century. Others in the Cinquecento, however, spoke as prophets not about the future but about their own days. This type of prophetic voice, whose aim was reform of the Church and society, has been the subject of my investigation. Dionisio's prophecy was one instrument among many others advanced for the reform of the Church. A prophet conveyed God's directions as His servant and messenger, and Dionisio claimed this role for himself. He believed that he had been anointed to reform the Church and society, and he never wavered in his convictions or in his attempts to secure the aid of the Italian princes in an enterprise that the pope and ecclesiastical hierarchy seemed reluctant to undertake. In spite of the Council of Trent and its measures for reform, Dionisio believed that reform was incomplete. His task was to purify and strengthen the *Ecclesia militans* so that it would be truly *un ovile* under *un pastore*. As I have frequently pointed out, Dionisio's ideas were not particularly original, although interesting. In fact, as I have endeavored to demonstrate, they were more common than one would believe at first glance. It seems essential for the historian of our day to try to make sense of humanists like Dionisio and not to relegate them to the "lunatic fringe." If we insist on calling men like Dionisio lunatics, we must also accept the fact that the "fringe" was much larger and more inclusive than we have previously believed.

Dionisio, linking his humanism to his prophetic persona, seemed to have no difficulty in finding hospitality in court circles. In addition to powerful princes like Emanuele Filiberto of Savoy, Cosimo I de' Medici of Florence, and Alfonso II of Ferrara, he had received favor and friendship from well-known Venetians like Rocho de Mazzochis and patricians like Giusto Morosini. His reception into the home of Rocho de Mazzochis upon his arrival in Venice would seem to indicate that he had previously known his host or had received a letter of introduction from a mutual friend or friends. The same holds true of his princely associations and also his patrician connection with Giusto Morosini and possibly with Paolo Corner, one of the Tre Savi sopra Eresia who, Dionisio had indicated, could understand his writings.

The fact that Dionisio had preached to crowds in the public spaces of Venice for more than a week before he was told to desist indicates that there was an audience for prophetic preaching among noblemen as well as artisans like Benedetto Corazzaro and his circle. The Basilica di San Marco seemed to encourage prophetic interpretations, and Dionisio used all the mysterious associations of the basilica to enhance his prophetic person. Here he revealed himself as prophet and announced his prophecies for Venice among the gilded mosaics and the illustrious personages. The crimson robes he wore in the magnificent golden sanctuary would surely have engraved his image indelibly upon the Venetian consciousness. His lavish praise of Venice, his cultivated speech, and his striking personality would have assured immediate notoriety and even favor with some.

We have traced his story from archival records where his trial and his writings have been preserved. We have observed him in France and in various cities in Italy before his arrival in Venice.

Dionisio Gallo is a fascinating personality about whom we know few biographical details but much about his program for reform and his utopian vision. From his writings that remain in the Venetian Archive the influence of other prophetic voices is discernible, especially those of Savonarola and Guillaume Postel. Dionisio's certainty about his own role in reforming the Church resounded the prophetic tone of the prophets of Israel, which Fra Girolamo had adopted when he claimed that the will of heaven spoke through his tongue. Savonarola's mingling of theology, politics, and prophecy in his preaching can also be found, as we have seen, in the words of Dionisio Gallo. Each believed with absolute certainty that he had been sent by God to reform the Church and to preach against corruption. Both Savonarola and Dionisio noted publicly that the censures against them were unjust and without authority, and each railed against the scandalous life of the clergy and held that the Church had to be reformed.

Each believed that God often granted a greater light of understanding to some than to others, and the illuminated must reveal to the others the direct communications from God that had been hidden except to God's chosen. Many biblical texts cited often in Dionisio's writings can be found in Savonarola. One of the most revealing is "Cantate Domino canticum novum" (Ps. 33:3). In the context of the need for abandoning pomp and the vanities, Savonarola urged that all superfluous things be sold and given to the poor. Alms were to be gathered for the poor in all the churches; money allocated for the University of Pisa should at least for one year be given instead to the poor. Should this be insufficient, "let us put our hand to the vases and precious objects of the churches," Savonarola wrote. He preached that the Lord wanted to renew everything, and he repeated, "Cantate Domino canticum novum." Dionisio in like manner urged that one-third of the riches of the Church be given to the poor. Writing about the man from Edom, the third king who had been chosen by God because of his purity and charity to be His servant and reform the world, Dionisio explained: "About which king, then, David speaks when, exulting in the spirit, he says, 'Sing unto the Lord a new song'" (Cantate Domino canticum novum).[1]

Both Savonarola and Dionisio repeated the Pauline challenge: "God chose the foolish things of the world in order to reprove the wisdom of the wise, and the infirm to confound the strong." Dionisio wrote these words when he argued that truth had been revealed to him by God "against the heights of Satan and human prudence."[2] In a letter written to Pope Pius V, Dionisio, as if to ameliorate his boast about being God's messenger and servant, concluded his warnings to the pope with the same paraphrase of Saint Paul: "Elegit Deus stulta mundi, vt sapientiam sapientum reprobet et infirma quaeque vt fortia quaeque confundat."[3] In a striking parallel Savonarola, in a letter sent to the pope after his excommunication, wrote that he had tried to show the truth of his doctrine, his innocence, and submission to the Church; however, he could no longer hope in the pope but must only turn himself to Him "who chose the weak things of this world to confound the strong lions of perverse men."[4]

Whereas Savonarola could no longer expect understanding from the pope, Dionisio still tried to arouse the pope to embrace the act of reform that our prophet believed the pope could not accomplish on his own. The similarity of context, two letters to two popes, is indicative of the prophetic certainty and fervor of each.

Savonarola had often intoned to the brothers of San Marco the idea of being God's fool. If you want to become a perfect religious, he wrote, you must believe for certain that many are wiser and more illuminated by God than are you. After urging the religious to subject themselves to their superiors, he warned them "to become *pazzi* [foolish, crazy] in order to be saved in the sight of God, as the apostle says: 'If any one among you seems to be wise in his generation, let him become foolish so that he becomes wise.'"[5]

Dionisio not only wrote about being Christ's fool, he also acted the part of Christ's fool as he moved through the streets of Rome, carrying a huge cross with an old breastplate askew. He, as Christ's soldier, was obviously playing His fool. Savonarola's harsh criticism of priests "who do not know the difference between good and bad, true and false, sweet and bitter," was repeated, as we have observed, in Dionisio's challenges to the pope, the Curia, cardinals, bishops, and the whole hierarchy of the Church to reform their lives and practice charity. Savonarola condemned the priests for their immorality and their worldly existence, accusing them of minding art and books more than their flocks.[6] In like manner Dionisio criticized the extravagant lives of cardinals and bishops who preferred their lavish attire and horses to the poor who were their flock.

The influence of Savonarola on the prophetic preaching of Dionisio was significant, as it appears, not only from the inherent ideas about reform but also from the rhetorical style in which these ideas were expressed. The repetition of key ideas and phrases was part of the rhetorical style of both men. The use of metaphor, scene painting, as it were, enhanced the vibrancy and power of each speaker. When Dionisio wrote about the beauty of poverty, his language, though prose, soared as if poetry. His imaginary conversations with the Devil, who argued that the Church would never be reformed, because the Curia did not want reformation, present a theatrical and entertaining turn to a well-worked theme. He also wrote an apparently verbatim exchange between himself and the papal nuncio in the duomo in Florence, which is just as effective as his imaginary exchange with the Devil. Dionisio's writing reflects his humanistic training as well as his prophetic voice. The written and spoken words of both Savonarola and Dionisio had a power that enhanced the prophetic persona of each.

The mentality of Dionisio reflected the Quattrocento prophetic fervor of Savonarola. In addition, the influence of Guillaume Postel on Dionisio Gallo is so pervasive that the two men seem to speak with one voice. Dionisio's actions in Paris in the 1560s seem to re-create the actions of Postel twenty years earlier. For example, Postel lost favor in the royal circle of Frances I in 1543, when he urged the king to reform himself, his court, and his kingdom or else suffer dire calamity. Thereupon he left France for Rome to become a member of the Society of Jesus. Dionisio lost favor in the circle of the young King Charles IX in 1563, when he preached to him that he must reform his kingdom. He was mocked by the courtiers, yet for a while he was still allowed to speak in the public places of Paris. Although Postel in 1564 and Gallo in 1563 were silenced, for the repose of the city, by the king's orders, Postel being sent to the monastery of Saint Martin des Champs and Dionisio to his native city of Gisors, the calm was of short duration. Postel continued to teach his doctrine of restitution from within the monastery's walls, and Gallo, like Postel in 1543, left France for Italy, arriving in Savoy in late 1565 after a journey through the Midi.

The courts that Dionisio chose to visit had connections not only with France but also with Postel. For example, the wife of Emanuele Filiberto, Marguerite of France, duchess of Berry, was the person to whom Postel in 1553 dedicated his *Les très merveilleuses victoires des femmes du nouveau-monde*. It was to the court of Emanuele Filiberto and his wife that Dionisio first presented himself two days before Christmas in 1565. In 1551 Postel dedicated his *De Etruriae regionis . . . originibus . . .* to Cosimo I and continued his friendship with the duke thereafter. Postel was convinced that God had bestowed upon the duke the highest responsibility for restoring Etruria to its ancient splendor.7 Dionisio Gallo returned to the court of Cosimo I in 1566 after a visit to Rome and remained with the duke for an extended period. Several letters written by Dionisio to the duke extolled the merits of Cosimo as the "friend of truth and constant protector of the Catholic faith." Dionisio also wrote of a most wonderful gift that the duke had bestowed upon him; our prophet, like Postel, surely enjoyed the favor of the duke for some time. It is clear, moreover, that both Dionisio and Postel before him expected Duke Cosimo I to help in their programs of restitution and reform.8 It is significant that both Postel and Dionisio expected certain princes to work with churchmen in the business of reform.9 Among those was Alfonso II, duke of Ferrara, who had spent many years of his life in France.

Postel believed that the restitution of the world would take place in 1566 and that he had been chosen by God because of his filial relation to the Venetian Virgin as the prophet of the restitution of all things. Postel's concept of his divine mission was confirmed in 1552 by an experience he called his "immutation," in which the body of the Venetian Virgin was engrafted into his own. The presence of Christ, which dwelled most fully in the Venetian Virgin, was "immuted" into Postel himself, and his reason was restored as before the Fall. After this experience he proclaimed with frenzied passion the imminent restitution he believed was to take place in 1566. In 1563 Dionisio experienced a remarkable double anointment by the Virgin Mother of God, who advised him that he must assume his role as servant and messenger of Christ. After preaching the need for reform of the Church in Paris and in the Midi, he arrived in Italy shortly before the New Year of 1566. It seems more than a coincidence that Dionisio arrived on the scene in Italy, and especially in Venice, in 1566, in the year Postel had proclaimed the restitution would begin and at the place Postel said was chosen by God for the inauguration of the new age.

What recommended Venice, one could ask, to Postel, who had been one of the royal readers to the king, and to Dionisio Gallo, who had been known to the boy king Charles IX? Although Postel had previously indicated that Gaul was to lead the world in a restitution of all things and that the king of France was to be the leader of the reformed world, his emphasis had shifted by 1547 to an extended concept of Gaul, as in antiquity, and to the city of Venice because of the merits of the mysterious Venetian Virgin. It was she who had instructed Postel on the role of Venice in the restitution that was to begin in 1566.

According to Postel, Saint Mark, the patron of Venice, had protected Venice and established his patriarchy first at Aquileia in the Venetian dominion. In an unpublished text Postel wrote that since the primitive Church had been founded "under the standard of Mark the Evangelist clothed as a lion, the Church of the Cinquecento must also be restored under the standard of Saint Mark."[10] In addition, the Gospels were prefigured in the Decalogue, and Saint Mark was prefigured in Moses.[11] Postel noted that "Mark looks back to the mysteries of the written Law hidden to this day to the whole world and now reappearing in the fourth age of the Church."[12] Postel's association of the Decalogue with Saint Mark established Venice as the seat of political justice and as the exemplar of the Decalogue, demonstrated through the "new Moses," John Mark. This concept of Postel's was a powerful precedent for Dionisio's belief that Venice and Venetian senators had been chosen by God to administer justice. Consequently, Dionisio urged the Venetians to assume their proper role in bringing about God's justice, that is, to bring about the restitution or reform of the world. The concept of Venice as the dispenser of God's justice was evident in many facets of Venice's political and artistic life. This association is not only important for my immediate argument but essential for an understanding of Venice's concept of itself as justice and of men in the Cinquecento like Postel, Bodin, and Dionisio Gallo, who shared this view. With this in mind, the sculpture of the doge kneeling before the lion of Saint Mark, that is, before the "new Moses," assumes more dramatic significance in Venice's concept of itself as a prophetic city. One is also reminded of Andrea Gritti's *proemio dogale* of the *Libro d'oro*, where a beautiful miniature of Saint Mark giving the Law to the kneeling doge appears. Additional evidence for Venice as the symbol of God's justice is incised in the first column of the Palazzo Ducale before the Porta della Carta, where one sees God giving his Law to Moses. These images of Venice as a political-religious entity give substance to Postel's concept of Saint Mark as a new Moses and give credence to Dionisio's challenge to the doge and Venetian senators to administer justice, since they have been chosen by God for this task.

Postel's understanding of Saint Mark as a new Moses may have had influence in the prophetic circles of Venice among humanists like Brocardo and artisans like Corazzaro. In addition, the so-called myth of Venice can be reinterpreted in light of Postel's analogy and Dionisio's challenges to the Venetian ruling class. This is a converging element that comes into focus with Dionisio's arrival in Venice and the subsequent events that surround him. This concept of Mark as the new Moses also helps to explain the primacy of the political in Venice. The doges, since the adoption of Saint Mark as patron of the city, had the responsibility, as heads of the Venetian state, of maintaining his authority and that of the Serenissima in order to

fig. 19
Saint Mark giving the Law to the kneeling doge. From proemio dogale of Andrea Gritti, Libro d'oro, Maggior Consiglio. Archivio di Stato, Venice

ensure the appropriate religious and social responses to the Law of God, brought down from Sinai by Moses and disseminated by the "new Moses," John Mark, adopted as patron by the Venetians.

The concept of Saint Mark as a new Moses would have been a catalyst for Dionisio's prophetic persona and for his prophetic insistence upon reform of the Church and its institutions and of society at large. The association of the evangelist with Moses was surely an important factor in Dionisio's insistence that the Venetian senators render justice and help him in the great work of reform, since they had been chosen by God to judge.

Just as Moses had received the Decalogue as the Law of Israel, so the new Moses, John Mark, as patron of Venice, gave not only his Gospel but also God's Law to the Venetians as a paradigm for their actions and their laws. The doge on his knees, receiving the standard from Saint Mark, appears on the *zecchino d'oro* in the sixteenth century and serves to confirm the idea of Venice as the upholder of justice, supported by its patron and lawgiver,

John Mark. The doge became the dispenser of justice through the agency of John Mark, whose cult at Venice was his responsibility to promote. In the aforementioned proemium of Andrea Gritti in the *Libro d'oro vecchio*, the doge emphasized that God's providential care for the world is demonstrated by His giving His law for His creation. He also indicated with great pride that Venice had been governed from its origin by laws and by decrees of the Senate. Postel's concept of Saint Mark as a second Moses and Dionisio's apparent acceptance of this designation helps to explain the peculiar political-religious nexus of the Venetian republic. The cult of the saint was inextricably linked with devotion to the Serenissima.[13] The stronger the devotion to the new Moses, Saint Mark, the stronger would be the devotion to the doge and the state that saw itself as the agent of justice—both political and religious. This interpretation of Saint Mark as the new Moses makes Dionisio's insistence upon the rendering of justice by the Venetian patriciate more significant than the babbling of a self-styled prophet.

The linking of Saint Mark to Moses helps to explain why Dionisio Gallo came to Venice to preach his message of reform and also gives insight into Venice's concept of itself as Serenissima. Dionisio, as a disciple of Postel, would share his master's enthusiasm for Venice and the Venetians as the "most perfect temporal magistracy," which would lead the Church into a new reformation. Since the primitive Church, according to Postel, had need of being "founded under the standard of Mark the Evangelist, clothed as a lion," the Church of the Cinquecento must also return to its ancient basis, restored under the standard of Saint Mark. The association of Saint Mark and Moses would also clarify why Dionisio chose the cortile of the Ducal Palace to address the many nobles and others who daily passed through this space that was both political and religious. The doge, as protector of the political space of the palace and of Venice itself, was also responsible for upholding the laws of the republic and the Law of God. The miniature that graces the proemium of the *Libro d'oro* makes this clear. The political space of the palazzo also takes on a religious aspect, with the doge as defender of both the political and religious space. His dual role was also extended to the *sala regia*, his private chapel, in the Basilica di San Marco. An ancient inscription found on the molding of the Chapel of San Clemente, through which the doge entered the basilica, warns the doge "to choose justice and render justice to all and be pious to all."[14] There is also an inscription about justice in the atrium, which preceded the mosaic of the judgment of Solomon. The text warns: "Let the judge of the earth love to bring justice everywhere. May he not suffer the unjust for the fact that he is subjected to burning."[15] These references to justice in the Basilica di

San Marco are trenchant examples of the political-religious role of the doge and the Venetian state. Dionisio reiterated this point countless times when he begged the doge and the senators to render justice. He was infuriated when he saw many examples of sodomy in Venice, since this act seemed to him to indicate that justice was not being administered. He noted many times that the Inquisition did not have the right to judge; only the Venetian senators, including the doge, had been chosen by God for this great work.

In addition to the concept of Saint Mark as the new Moses, other ideas and circumstances link Postel to Dionisio Gallo. Since Postel was in the monastery of Saint Martin des Champs for most or all of 1566, Dionisio may have been sent by Postel to Italy to proclaim the imminent advent of the restitution, since Postel had claimed that the restitution of all things would begin in 1566.

The language that both men used to express their ideas is very similar in style and syntax. Both used metaphors to conceal and also to reveal their prophetic pronouncements. Postel used various pseudonyms, such as Rorispergius, Elias Pandochaeus, Petrus Anusius Synesius Venetus, and Jan-Cain, to describe cryptically the concept of himself as prophet of the restitution of all things. Dionisio wrote that he had been given the white stone on which was inscribed a name unknown to all except him who had received it. He also called himself the man from Edom and the man from Bosra. Both Postel and Dionisio assumed quasi-messianic roles for themselves. They did not claim to be Christ but the servants of Christ, fulfilling the expectations about the angelic pope. Both combined mystical visions with political programs. Postel, for example, described the universal monarchy and its operation, which would follow the restitution of the whole world. In addition, he wrote a detailed "eternal or newest testament" in which he expressed his philosophy of restitution and a description of the ordering of God's kingdom on earth.[16] Dionisio called himself God's servant and messenger who would lead chosen Italian princes and hopefully the pope to inaugurate a new world order based on the principles expressed in the various versions of his *Legatio*. Although they contained between seventy-five and seventy-nine points, depending on the arrangement of topics, the subject matter in all his texts was identical and concerned reform in the Church, in society at large, and in the universities. Dionisio's *Legatio* resembles in many respects Postel's various works about the "table of eternal ordination" and his plan for a universal monarchy. Both Postel and Dionisio clearly were universalists who believed that a reformed Church and society would make strong temporal governing bodies unnecessary, since all were to be ruled by God. Each man, while professing weakness and humility, believed himself to have a special role, indeed a chosen role, in establishing God's kingdom on earth. Dionisio's *Legatio*, in its various versions, presents a program of action for the reform of the Church and society at large. He considered the *Legatio* a blueprint for this action, in which he hoped to engage Italian princes and the pope, if possible. He saw himself as chosen by God and mystically anointed to be the head of this enterprise. Like Postel, Dionisio did not argue dogma but rather a reform of morals and the practice of charity as a means of praising God.

Dionisio, under the epithet of derision "king of the Gauls," was mentioned in conjunction with Postel by a contemporary, Jehan de La Fosse, in his *Journal*, and in the *Memoires de Condé*. This is not surprising, since the two shared similar concerns about reform and about their own roles in accomplishing it. Many circumstances suggest that Dionisio Gallo was a disciple of Postel hitherto unknown, at least under the name he chose to use in Italy. The records from France refer to him only as "king of the Gauls."

Since Postel had been secluded in the monastery of Saint Martin des Champs for safekeeping and therefore was not able to be in Venice, where he believed the restitution was to begin, it was quite plausible that he would send his disciple in his place to urge the Venetians to assume their proper role in the *restitutio omnium*. Both men left France in disgrace because of their certainty of their divine calling. Postel had warned the king in 1543 that he must reform his court and his realm or suffer dire consequences. Twenty years later, in 1563, Dionisio warned the king at Mont Marsan of imminent danger if he did not act with him in reforming the Church and society. Both men were called fools by members of the royal circle. Postel left France and joined the Jesuits in Rome in 1543. Although he lost favor with Ignatius because of his visions of reform, which Ignatius had originally shared, Postel always considered himself a Jesuit and often commented that the Jesuits lived the most holy lives. In his *Legatio* Dionisio reflected the influence of the *Spiritual Exercises* of Ignatius, especially in regard to the need for an educated clergy and for a clergy that demonstrated by their lives their love of God and their concern for their fellowmen. The major themes in Dionisio's *Legatio* are piety and love of one's neighbor. But direct influence of Ignatius on Dionisio cannot be ascertained. An indirect influence, however, could possibly have been derived from Postel's ideas, which recur in the thoughts of Dionisio Gallo. In addition, Dionisio's benefactor in Venice, Rocho de Mazzochis, had friends who praised the lives of the Jesuits and worked among them at the Hospital of the Incurabili.

Dionisio's early success in Venice in 1566 was thwarted by his imprisonment for a year and a half and by his subsequent banishment. This may have been one reason why Postel in the last year of his life wrote from the monastery that twelve disciples like the Apostles must go out from the academies of Paris to continue the work of restitution—which he had believed would take place in 1566.

Banished from Venice in 1567 by the Holy Office of Inquisition after more than a year of investigation, Dionisio was placed on a barge headed toward Ferrara. With his mysterious departure late at night, traces of our prophet seem to evaporate.

But the story of Dionisio Gallo does not soon leave us. Through his associations and his actions the continuing significance of prophecy as an agent of reform can be confirmed. His story makes us consider again the role of humanism in relation to prophecy and especially the role of humanist-prophets. His story is also important for clarifying the paramount role that Venice played in the imaginations and in the programs for action of men like himself and Guillaume Postel. Both believed that the new age was to begin in Venice, since the Serenissima was "the most perfect republic," more beloved by God than any other city with the exception of Jerusalem. Therefore, it seemed natural, at least to them, that Venice should lead in the renovation of the Church and the world.

Michael Jacoff has cogently argued that the four ancient bronze horses that were installed on the west facade of the Basilica di San Marco represented the *Quadriga Domini* and "evoked with singular vividness Mark's place as one of the four co-equal Evangelists who conveyed the work of Christ to the world under his guidance."[17] Jacoff has also noted that the horses "epitomize the inextricable blending of the sacred and the secular that pervades so much of the adornment of San Marco."[18] Jacoff's association of the horses with the *Quadriga Domini* provides a fitting analogy for our humanist-prophet Dionisio Gallo, who styled himself the *auriga Ecclesiae militantis*. As the charioteer of the Church Militant, the reformed church of the new age, he could figuratively envision himself driving the beautiful horses of San Marco as the powerful team that would draw the rest of the Church and the world into a new age of pristine reform.

Under the standard of Saint Mark, "the new Moses," the Venetians must cooperate with the *auriga Ecclesiae militantis*, Dionisio Gallo, in leading the Church and society into a new age. In Dionisio's view, the true reformation must begin in Venice because the Venetian nobility had been chosen to judge and consequently to pursue, with the *auriga* Dionisio, the path of reform following the *Quadriga Domini*. Dionisio's metaphoric language blended with the countless ideas suggested by the mosaics of San Marco and the *Quadriga Domini*, which he hoped would inspire the Venetians to work with him in his grand design for reform. His certainty about his prophetic role was matched by his conviction that Venice as the prophetic city of Saint Mark had a unique role to play in the restitution of the Church and the world. It seems clear that Dionisio (and certainly Postel) was aware of the medieval account of Saint Mark, who was "descended from a most famous Levitical tribe" and was said to have "yielded his duties [offices] given by Mosaic Law."[19] Mark did not yield his duties as upholder of the Decalogue when he became patron of Venice, however. Postel knew the medieval legend and interpreted it to mean that Mark, descended from a Levitical line, "heeds the mysteries of the Decalogue hidden to this day from the whole world and now renewing [themselves] in the fourth age of the Church." His disciple Dionisio was obviously aware of this understanding of Saint Mark. Dionisio reinforced Venice's concept of itself as dispenser of justice through his constant exhortations to the city to administer justice, as was its divinely given duty.

In addition to Saint Mark's role as the upholder of the Law of God, ancient tradition linked him to the *Terapeuti* or *Esseni*, terms that both mean *medici*, or physicians. In addition, in the Aquileian *Passio* of Ermacora, Mark is described as "christianus et medicus ad omnes infirmitates curandas."[20] This aspect of Saint Mark as *medicus* would also have had deep significance for Dionisio, who often used medical metaphors to emphasize the need for healing a sick society. Dionisio's insistence upon the rendering of justice by the Venetian nobility could also imply his challenge to the nobles to be *medici*, like their patron Saint Mark, and heal their state. If the Venetian nobility practiced the "medical art," they would render justice and begin the reformation of the world in the Serenissima, the city of Saint Mark.

The dreams of Dionisio Gallo for a reformed Church and a reformed society had a long medieval tradition that was still alive after the midpoint of the sixteenth century. Many who expected the dawning of a new age, pristine and reformed, were humanists who used their various scholarly pursuits in the cause of reformation of the Church and the world. Dionisio, like Postel, was willing to give up his career as a humanist to follow what he believed was his divinely appointed role—that of servant and messenger of God.

The story of Dionisio, although incomplete, provides us with a panorama of the many paradoxes of the sixteenth century. His story, which ends in Venice, as far as documentation is concerned, enables us to rethink the meaning of religion and politics in Venice, as we reconsider the patron saint of Venice not only as the Evangelist but also as the new Moses, who gave God's Law to the doge of Venice as a paradigm for the most serene republic. Prophecy in the sense in which Dionisio called himself God's prophet joins the past to the present and God's voice to man's action. Prophecy is then, as man's response to God's Law and His words, an effort to effect God's kingdom on earth. When every person becomes God's prophet, the future takes care of itself. Such a person Dionisio considered himself to be. In urging Venice, the prophetic city of Saint Mark, to assume its God-given role as upholder of justice, he was demonstrating the myth, or *emeth* (truth), behind the "myth of Venice."

NOTES

Introduction

1. The records of Dionisio's trial and his numerous letters to princes can be found in Venice, Archivio di Stato, Santo Uffizio, Processi, Busta 22. All future references to this collection will be indicated as ASV, S.U., Processi, with the appropriate *busta*. All other manuscripts from this archive will be indicated as ASV, followed by the appropriate collection.

2. See Carlo Ginzburg, *The Cheese and the Worms: The Cosmos of a Sixteenth-Century Miller*, trans. John Tedeschi and Anne Tedeschi (Baltimore, Md.: Johns Hopkins University Press, 1980). For the complete text of Menocchio's trial, and a very helpful introduction, see *Domenico Scandella detto Menocchio*, ed. Andrea Del Col (Pordenone: Edizioni Biblioteca dell'Immagine, 1990).

3. J. G. A. Pocock, *The Machiavellian Moment: Florentine Political Thought and the Atlantic Republican Tradition* (Princeton, N.J.: Princeton University Press, 1975), 170–72.

4. On the *Quadriga Domini*, see Michael Jacoff, *The Horses of San Marco and the Quadriga of the Lord* (Princeton, N.J.: Princeton University Press, 1993).

5. See John W. O'Malley, *Religious Culture in the Sixteenth Century: Preaching, Rhetoric, Spirituality, and Reform* (Aldershot: Ashgate Publishing, Variorum, 1993), 188–90.

Chapter 1

1. For a description of Dionisio Gallo's attire, see ASV, S.U., Processi, Busta 22, Contra Dionisium Gallum, testimony of Jacobus Gambacurta, June 15, 1566; Father Augustinus de Martinis, June 15, 1566; and Johannes Franciscus Pisani, July 2, 1566.

2. On Venetian dress in the sixteenth century, see Achille Vitali, *La moda a Venezia attraverso i secoli* (Venice: Filippi Editore, 1992); see especially 31–32, 146, 153–54, 431–32. The standard work, however, is Cesare Vecellio, *De gli habiti antichi et moderni di diuerse parti del mondo . . .* (Venice: Damian Zenaro, 1590).

3. ASV, S.U., Processi, Busta 22, testimony of Jacobus Gambacurta of Verona, June 15, 1566: "et mi fu figurato per l'habito colorato et lungo, sopra il quale hauea molte Croci grande e picciole, et mi par vero di Cordele d'oro al bauaro della ueste, et a lungo le maniche." Dom. Padre Stephanus de Franciscis gave a similar description: "ha sentito predicare un certo Francese che ueste di pauonazzo con certe Croci sopra la uesta lunga, et con una cendalina rossa al colo."

4. Ibid., testimony of Joannes Franciscus Pisani, July 2, 1566: "Sono molti giorni che retrouandomi in corte di palazzo uidi uno uestito in questo modo il quale

haueua anche uisto in gran conseio el quale diceuano che era un Vescouo Francese et predicaua sopra quelli banche li di corti."

5. Jacobus Gambacurta carefully described Dionisio's chosen space for speaking: "un certo Francese predicaua li sopra quella banca alla scala di palazzo uerso la Corte." ASV, S.U., Processi, Busta 22, testimony of June 15, 1566. There can be no question about where Dionisio was preaching. Padre Augustinus de Martinis testified: "trouai questo medesimo pur in corte, che sopra quella banca attaccatta alla scala di palazzo uerso la corte grande predicaua." The *banca* is visible in early designs and also today. See *Il Palazzo Ducale di Venezia da Francesco Zanotto* (Venice, 1840), vol. 1, chap. 13, 87–92, and vol. 5, plates XXVIII–XXXIII. See also Wolfgang Wolters, *Storia e politica nei dipinti di Palazzo Ducale: Aspetti dell'autocelebrazione della Repubblica di Venezia nel Cinquecento*, trans. Benedetta Heinemann Campana (Venice: Arsenal Editrice, 1987), and Umberto Franzoi, "La Scala dei Giganti," *Bollettino dei Musei Civici Veneziani* 10, no. 4 (1965): 8–31.

6. For accounts of the construction of the *scala*, see *Monumenti per servire alla storia del Palazzo Ducale di Venezia . . . da Giambattista Lorenzi, Parte 1 dal 1253 al 1600* (Venice: Tipografia del Commercio di Marco Visentini, 1868), 106: "1491, 9 ottobre. La illustrissima Signoria comanda a vui Magnifici Signori Provedadori al Sal che Vostre Magnificentie debino esser cum maistro Antonio Rizo et veder di romagnir dacordo con lui cerca il perseverar di la fabrica del Palazzo nostro cussi per le figure come per la scala et altre cose necessarie che sa far."

7. The contract for the work was accorded to Jacopo Sansovino on July 31, 1554. The agreement was that the figures were to be "belle et ben finite in termine de uno anno proximo alla più longa," but the work required more time. Ibid., 481. Note also *Il Palazzo Ducale di Venezia da Francesco Zanotto*, vol. 1, Scalea dei Giganti Opera di Antonio Riccio, and vol. 5, plates XXVIII–XXXIII and p. 27: "Ergesi poi sulla sommità della predetta scalea, sopra due basi aggiunte nel 1566, i due colossi di Marte e Nettuno semboleggiandi la potenza di terra e quella di mare della Repubblica, qui posti nel citato anno."

8. See *Il Palazzo Ducale di Venezia da Francesco Zanotto*, vol. 1, Scalea dei Giganti Opera di Antonio Riccio, and vol. 5, plates XXVIII–XXXIII, and p. 3: "Antonio Riccio adunque architettava questa magnifica scala, la quale fu con sagacissimi mira da lui collocata di fronte alla porta principale, ed eretta allo scoperto, acciocchè si vedesse dal popolo, raccolto intorno al Cortile e lungo l'ampio portico, e fuori fino alla torre Marciana, la maestà del doge e del senato, allorquando comparivano ne'giorni solenni, come diremo: e perciò di aspetto teatrale dovea questa mostrarsi per ottenere lo scopo divisato."

9. See notes 5 and 6 above. See also Wolters, *Storia e politica nei dipinti di Palazzo Ducale*, 22: "L'11 novembre 1485, poco dopo l'inizio della ricostruzione delle parti danneggiate dall'incendio, il Maggior Consiglio deliberò la costruzione di una scala d'onore nel cortile di Palazzo Ducale. . . . La costruzione della Scala dei Giganti formò nel cortile del Palazzo . . . due Corti, la grande et comune, et la picciola

dei Senatori, vale a dire dei membri dei Consigli. Per esplicita testimonianza di Francesco Sansovino questi due cortile avevano un'importante funzione di luogo d'incontro e anche di 'broglio.'" Note also *Venetia città nobilissima, et singolare, descritta già in XIIII libri da M. Francesco Sansovino et hora con molta diligenza corretta . . . da M.R.D. Giovanni Stringa* . . . (Venice: Altobello Salicato, 1604). See also Deborah Howard, *The Architectural History of Venice* (New York: Holmes & Meier Publications, 1981).

10. "In questo tempo . . . fo portà el corpo de S. Marco da Alexandria et fo messo in una camera secreta in palazo fin se feva una chiexia la qual dito doxe face principiar una giexia fra la giexia de San Teodoro et fra lo palazo ducal el qual terrea era de le monache de San Zacharia. . . . Et dita chiexia fo costituì esser capela ducal et fu intitulà San Marcho et in quella messo el suo corpo era in la dita camera secreta et fo terminà tuor quello per confalon et San Teodoro per protector et fo del 800." See *La ducale Basilica di San Marco: Documenti per la storia dell'augusta ducale Basilica di San Marco* . . . (Venice, 1886), 1. See also *La Basilica di San Marco in Venezia illustrata nella storia e nell'arte da scrittori veneziani sotto la direzione di Camillo Boito* (Venice: Ferdinando Ongania Editore, 1888).

11. *La Basilica di San Marco in Venezia*, 19: "Dal giorno che San Marco fu scelto a protettore della republica, un raggio della gloria celeste dell'Evangelista illuminò la figura del capo dello Stato. Accennammo già come la spada trionfatrice del Doge scintillasse sovente a canto alle torcie dell'altare, come i reggitori della repubblica comprendessero di quanta utilità fosse il mettere a profitto la tendenza del popolo verso il soprannaturale, e come, con le magnifiche solennità della chiesa, signoreggiassero le passioni delle turbe, ne avvivassero gli entusiasmi ne dirigessero gli sdegni e gli amori."

12. Gino Benzoni has astutely noted the relationship, pointing out that "'Sotto la tutela di Gesù Cristo,' Venezia è, insieme, 'sotto la protezione di San Marco.'" Note especially: "Comunque sia, se San Marco è di Venezia, lo è anzitutto del doge che, impersonando la città, è il primo sacerdote, il pontefice massimo, il grand' officiante della devozione pel patrono." See Gino Benzoni, "San Marco e il doge," in *Omaggio a San Marco: Tesori dall'Europa*, ed. Hermann Fillitz and Giovanni Morello (Milan: Electa Editrice, 1994), 55–56. See also Magdalena Stoyanova, "La preistoria ed i mosaici del battistero di San Marco," *Atti dell'Istituto Veneto di Scienze, Lettere ed Arti: Classe di Scienze Morali, Lettere ed Arti* 147 (1989): 17–28.

13. Otto Demus, *The Mosaics of San Marco in Venice: The Eleventh and Twelfth Centuries* (Chicago: University of Chicago Press, 1984), 1:260.

14. All translations are my own unless attributed otherwise. The Latin text is as follows: "Dilige justitiam; sua cunctis reddito iura; Pauper cum vidua, pupillus et orphanus, O Dux, te sibi patronum sperant; pius omnibus esto. Non timor aut odium vel amor nec te trahat aurum ut flos casurus; Dux es, cineres futvrus et velut acturus, post mortem sic habiturus." My transcription varies slightly from that cited in *La Basilica di San Marco in Venezia*, 346. For example, I read *futvrus* not *facturus*. Two other inscriptions about justice in the Basilica di San Marco were, like the

inscription in the Capella di San Clemente, part of the original decorations. In the atrium, over the last door toward the Orologio, is a mosaic that warns: "Intrent sicuri, veniam quia sunt habituri. Omnes confessi qui non sunt crimine pressi." Also in the atrium, in the alcove where the Judgment of Solomon is depicted, one sees an inscription with an admonition to the judge: "Iustitiam terre judex amet undique ferre. Ne ferat iniustum per quod paciatur adustum." The last word was omitted when the mosaic was restored.

15. "Nos Andreas Griti Dux Venetiarum . . . quem muneri nostro incumbat leges incorrupte, sancteque seruare ac tueri caeterisque magistratibus nostris, iudicibus, ciuibusque seruandas demandare eas ordine dispositas faciles et perspicuas reddere decreuimus." See Venice, Archivio di Stato, Maggior Consiglio, Libro d'oro vecchio, inizio del Proemio dogale, cc. 25–25^v. The date of the proemium is September 28, 1529. The miniature is known as *La traditio legis di San Marco al Doge Andrea Gritti*.

16. Ibid. See also Gaetano Cozzi, "Giuspatronato del doge e prerogative del primicerio sulla cappella ducale di San Marco (secoli XVI–XVIII): Controversie con i procuratori di San Marco de supra e i patriarchi di Venezia," *Atti dell'Istituto Veneto di Scienze, Lettere ed Arti: Classe di Scienze Morali, Lettere ed Arti* 151, no. 1 (1992–93): 1–69. Note also *La Basilica di San Marco in Venezia*, 41: "Ma chi guarda bene a dentro nello spirito di tutte queste istituzioni, sa che Venezia divenne potente, associando al culto del vangelo quello delle sue leggi civili, e impetrando da Dio la confermazione di una indipendenza, con tanti sacrifici acquistata."

17. ASV, S.U., Processi, Busta 22, Contra Dionisium Gallum, testimony of Jacobus Gambacurta, June 15, 1566: "Lo ascoltai per un pezzo et senti fra le altre cose che molte volte lui replicò queste formali parole: Domini Veneti ego sum missus a spiritu sancto; uidistis columbam et est portentum mee ueritatis. Dico enim quod Papa cum suis cardinalibus non bene sentiunt de uera et catholica doctrina, quia multa faciunt et dicunt contraria doctrinae Euangelicae, ut uobis ostendam in discursu meo."

18. The suffering of Christ and suffering for Christ were also important aspects of the Lutheran Reformation. See, for example, the self-portrait of Albrecht Dürer in which he appears to be a suffering Christ: Ottavia Niccoli, *La crisi religiosa del Cinquecento* (Turin: Giulio Einaudi Editore, 1975), 93.

19. See page 1 above.

20. Dionisio's story begins and ends in Venice, since the records of his trial and many of his writings are found only in Venice.

21. ASV, S.U., Processi, Busta 22, Contra Dionisium Gallum. For a history of the Inquisition, see ASV, S.U., Processi, Busta 154, document entitled *Dell'origine dell'Inquisizione, et inquisitori e particolarmente di Venezia*. Other documents concerning the procedures against heretics follow this document. See also ASV, Consiglio dei Dieci, Parti secrete, Registro 6, 1547–58, cc. 29^r–30^v, for procedures used for interrogating witnesses and for instructions to the rectors in the cities of the dominion. See also ASV, Consiglio dei Dieci, Parti secrete, Filza 7 (1547–50), *Modus qui*

seruatur in tribunali in procedendo contra hereticos. For the best modern discussion of the Inquisition in Venice, see Andrea Del Col, "Organizzazione, composizione e giurisdizione dei tribunali dell'Inquisizione romana nella Repubblica di Venezia (1500–1550)," *Critica Storica* 25 (1988): 244–94; idem, "Il controllo della stampa a Venezia e i processi di Antonio Brucioli (1548–1559)," *Critica Storica* 17 (1980): 457–510; see also Adriano Prosperi, "L'Inquisizione: Verso una nuova immagine?" *Critica Storica* 25 (1988): 119–45; Silvana Seidel-Menchi, "Inquisizione come repressione o inquisizione come mediazione?" *Annuario dell'Istituto Storico Italiano* 35/36 (1983/84): 53–77; John Martin, "L'Inquisizione romana e la criminalizzazione del dissenso religioso a Venezia all'inizio dell'età moderna," *Quaderni Storici* 66, anno XXII, no. 3 (1987): 777–802; Paolo Simoncelli, "Clemente VIII e alcuni provvedimenti del Sant'Uffizio," *Critica Storica* 13, no. 1 (1976): 129–72; idem, "Documenti interni alla Congregazione dell'Indice 1571–1590: Logica e ideologia dell'intervento censorio," *Annuario dell'Istituto Storico Italiano per l'Età Moderna e Contemporanea* 35–36 (1983–84): 189–215; Giovanni Sforza, "Riflessi della controriforma nella Repubblica di Venezia," *Archivio Storico Italiano* 1 (1935): 5–216, and 2 (1935): 25–52, 173–86. Also significant for any consideration of the Venetian Inquisition is Paul Grendler, *The Roman Inquisition and the Venetian Press, 1540–1605* (Princeton, N.J.: Princeton University Press, 1977), and his "Tre Savii Sopra Eresia, 1547–1605: A Prosopographical Study," *Studi Veneziani*, n.s., 3 (1979): 283–340. See also Brian Pullan, *The Jews of Europe and the Inquisition of Venice, 1550–1670* (Totowa, N.J.: Rowman & Littlefield, 1983), and Anne Jacobson Schutte, "Uno spazio, tre poteri: La cappella di San Teodoro, sede dell'Inquisizione veneziana," in *San Marco: Aspetti storici e agiografici*, ed. Antonio Niero (Venice: Marsilio Editori, 1996), 97–109.

22. ASV, S.U., Processi, Busta 22, testimony of June 6 and June 8, 1566.

23. Ibid.

24. ASV, S.U., Processi, Busta 22, Contra Dionisium Gallum, document of June 4, 1566: "Cum ex multorum fide dignorum relatione delatum fuisset Santo Officio reperiri ad presens in hac Civitate Venetiarum quendam Gallum, qui in plateis et locis publicis predicatoris munere fungitur absque licentia superiorum asserendo et disseminando se esse nuntium Dei Reverendissimi dominus legatus apostolicus et dominus Patriarcha Venetiarum et Primas Dalmatię una cum eorum Reverendissimo domino Auditore et reverendissimo domino Vicario respective, ac Venerabilis pater Inquisitor cum assitentia clarissimorum domini Pauli Cornelii, domini Marci Mauroceni doctoris et domini Julii Contareni procuratoris Sancti Marci mandarunt, ut per nuntium eiusdem Sancti Officii dicto Gallo intimaretur de eorum ordine et commisione quod desisteret a predicando et sub poena triremis discederet ex hac civitate."

25. The curia of Saint Mark was originally in the Doge's Palace. See Giuseppe Boerio, *Dizionario del dialetto veneziano* (Venice: Giovanni Cecchini Editore, 1856), 215: "Curia, chiamavasi ne' tempi Veneti la, così allora detta, Corte de' publici Rappresentanti Capi di Provincia, composta degli Assessori e de' Cancellieri, i quali

si dicevano quindi Curiali." On the relationship of the palace to the Church of San Marco, see Wolters, *Storia e politica nei dipinti di Palazzo Ducale,* 19. In writing of the Porta della Carta, which gave access between the new wing of the palace and San Marco, Wolters cites Sansovino: "Conciosia che essendosi fondato il Palazzo publico per habitazione del Principe, et per render ragione al popolo: parve agli antichi, che la Chiesa fosse congiunta al Palazzo, essendo cosa convenevole, che la giustizia s'abbracci, secondo il detto del salmo, con la pace e la religione."

26. ASV, S.U., Processi, Busta 22, "Die sabbati 8 eiusdem mensis. . . . Et sic cum die dominica, quae fuit nona presentis mensis, deprehensus fuisset predicans fuit detentus per ministros sancti officii. Et in carceribus illustrissimorum dominorum Capitum detrusus."

27. ASV, S.U., Processi, Busta 22, document entitled *In nomine Domini nostri Jesu Christi crucifixi, amen, Ad Reverendissimos ac Illustrissimos Dominos, sacrum tribunal venetum et Senatum . . . :* "Ergo per nuntium legati, sic captus sum, atque circumventus et coniectus in carceres, ligatus in meo cubiculo, tum quietus an tranquillus . . . incarceratus sum, sine causa sicut capitur columba quieta in suo columbario."

28. Ibid.; testimony of Jacobus Gambacurta of Verona, June 15, 1566: "Essendo che per l'opinione di esso Magnifico Daniel, et per quanto haueua giudicato ascoltandolo era uno di quelli detto Francese, che haueua opinione che il tutto douesse esser commune." Gambacurta was also distressed that a Venetian patrician and a priest had been listening intently. He said: "Vidi che molto attentamente era ascoltato dal Magnifico Messer Zuan Francesco Pisani fo' di Messer Marc'Antonio. Et anche da un certo prete credo officio a S. Zuane di Rialto, et adesso l'ho ueduto qui di fuora." Ibid.

29. See ASV, S.U., Processi, Busta 22, document entitled *Ex coelo empireo veritas reuelata . . . ,* written from the Venetian prison on May 4, 1567. Dionisio used Greek and Latin words to explain the derivation of Gisors. When he wrote *de urbe gi sorte,* he was thinking of Greek (γη), which is equivalent in Latin to *terra,* as well as *sors, sortis.* Therefore he considered the city of his birth the "land of chance," which he explained as *gi sorte,* or "from the chance [lot] of the earth." Note also the document entitled *Liber quem nullus aut in coelo aut in terra: Legatio servi Dei et nuntii magistri Dionysii Galli . . . Romanum Proemium:* "Ego concoeptus in peccatis similis factus descendentibus in lacum, natus in vrbe Gisortiana." Dionisio's etymology was fanciful but appropriate for the point he was making about his role as prophet. Gisors was originally called Caesortium or Caesarotium, then later Gisorium and commonly Gisors. See Alphonsus Lasor a Varea, *Universus Terrarum orbis . . .* (Patavii [Padua]: Ioannes Baptista Conzatti, 1713), 1:213.

30. ASV, S.U., Processi, Busta 22, document entitled *Haec est causa totius ecclesiae militantis (henceforth Haec est causa).*

31. I am deeply indebted to notable persons in France who have provided most precise information from various French archives. Dr. Agnès Housseau Delaneau wrote many letters on my behalf, as did her husband, Dr. Jean Delaneau, sénateur

de Loire, président de Conseil général de l'Indre et Loire, maire de Chateau Hurault, to whom I am very grateful. I have also received help from Dr. Joël Bourdin, sénateur de l'Eure, conseiller général, maire de Bernay. Dr. Eliane Carouge, directeur des Archives de l'Eure, has confirmed that no record of Dionisio Gallo exists in the Archives de l'Eure, nor do baptismal records before 1588 remain. In a letter of April 16, 1993, directed to Dr. Joël Bourdin, sénateur de l'Eure, Dr. Carouge wrote:

> Les recherches que nous avons menées ne nous pas permis d'identifier Dionisio Gallo auquel aucun historien local ne semble s'être intéressé. Nous n'avons même pas la possibilité d'explorer les registres de baptême de Gisors dont le plus ancien est de 1588.
>
> Je trouve curieux que le très compétent érudit local du début du siècle, Louis Régnier, qui était de Gisors et a particulièrement étudié l'histoire de sa ville, n'en fasse aucune mention.

These statements would appear to strengthen my opinion that "Dionisio Gallo" may have been a pseudonym.

32. I am deeply indebted to sénateur A. Dupont, president of the Conseil général of Calvados, to Dr. Louis Le Roc'h Morgere, directeur des Archives départementales du Calvados, and to J. Y. Laillier, archivist, Archives du Calvados, for supplying indispensable information about the Collège de Lisieux and the ancient Collège de Lisieux in Paris; this information was forwarded to me in a letter from the director of the Archives du Calvados, dated February 1993, Caen.

33. I am also very grateful for the excellent and most efficient help from the director of the Archives de France, Gérard Ermisse, who supplied me with the following pertinent information:

> Les recherches menées dans les archives du Collège de Lisieux, conservées aux Archives nationales, n'ont pas permis de retrouver l'identité de son recteur dans les années 1550/1560.
>
> En effet, il y figure peu de documents du XVIe siècle et la nature des dossiers conservés est surtout d'ordre juridique et économique. Ainsi les comptes du Collège sont dans la sous-série H/3 mais ils ne débutent qu'en 1705; l'essentiel des pièces cotées M146 sont des titres de propriété postérieurs à 1613 et les rares documents du XVIe de cette liasse ne concernent pas le recteur du Collège. Enfin, des archives importantes figurent sous les cotes S6464 à 6473 et 6181–6182, mais là encore il s'agit de titres de propriétés ne faisant allusion au recteur; les deux dossiers conservés sur le Collège en S6181 et 6182, qui comportent des pièces de procédure, ont été examinés avec soin mais en vain.

I am also deeply grateful to the research service of Dr. Ghislain Brunel.

34. ASV, S.U., Processi, Busta 22, Contra Dionisium Gallum. For important notices about the Carthusians (Order of Chartreuse), that is, the Certosini, and their monastery in Paris (Vauvert), founded in 1257, see *Dizionario degli Istituti di Perfezione*, ed. Guerrino Pelliccia (1962–68) and Giancarlo Rocca (1969–) (Rome: Edizioni Paoline, 1975), 2:782–839, s.v. *Certosini*.

35. ASV, S.U., Processi, Busta 22, document entitled *Haec est causa:* "Regina coeli,

sacratissima Christi mater atque virgo . . . ipsa missa ab aeterna trinitate de coelo descendit; mihi apparuit et certe narrauit suprema munita. Quaenam? . . . Ego annuntio nouum coelum, nouam terram, saeculi solutionem: natum antichristum, cleri reformationem, auulsionem errorum, pauperum consolationem, infidelium omnium ad Christum conuersionem; mea simul officia ex diuina voluntate sempiternae trinitatis. Tres anni sunt elapsi sub finem februarii nouissime praeteriti; apparuit aut circa mediam noctem, noctem sabbathi, si bene memini, mihi soli in cubiculo soli iacenti in letto neque pudeat dicere, tum rectori collegii ciuitatis Lexoneanae. . . . Ea vero erecta, vultu serenissimo me alloquebatur. Intellectis ego tantis nuntiis illam interrogo. Quoniam solus tum res humanas parum expertus nullarum homo pene virium, vel auderem vel possem tam ardua, tam periculosa . . . perficere negotia. Illa signis et rationibus mihi omnia soluit et explicat Dei coelique fauorem et suum auxilium mihi pollicita. Tandem ego vniuersa mea imbecillitate et fragilitate declarata consentio totumque meum corpus et totam meam animam Deo onnipotenti voueo, et dedico dicens, 'Fiat in coelo et in terra beatissimae trinitatis voluntas.'"

36. Ibid.

37. Ibid.

38. Ibid.

39. Ibid. "Ergo omni libertate vocem meam tamquam tubam exalto omnibus veritatem hominibus palam et publice praedico; boni me defendebant atque custodiebant; innumeris autem modis affligebant me impii peruersi et haeretici."

40. Ibid. We know that Jacques Amyot became the tutor of Charles IX after his return from the Council of Trent. When Charles came to the throne, he named his preceptor, Amyot, the *grand aumônier* and gave him the Abbey of Roches. That Amyot was the young king's tutor does not preclude some tutorial position for Dionisio, given the active literary life of Amyot and his new position as *aumônier*, or "grand giver of alms." See *Nouvelle biographie générale* . . . (Paris: Firmin Didot Frères, 1854), 1:461–64.

41. ASV, S.U., Processi, Busta 22, document entitled *Haec est causa*.

42. On Gaîllon and the ecclesiastical goods of the Châtellenie de Gaîllon and the cession to the archbishop by King Saint-Louis in 1262, see C. Lannette, *Guide des Archives de l'Eure* (Evreux: Les Archives, 1982), ser. G, p. 247. The sumptuous chateau was not included in the ecclesiastical bequest.

43. ASV, S.U., Processi, Busta 22, document entitled *Haec est causa*.

44. Ibid.

45. On the life of the famous humanist and his relationships, see George Joseph, *Clément Marot* (Boston: G. K. Hall, 1985); P. Leblanc, *La poésie religieuse de Clément Marot* (Paris, 1955); Michel Jeanneret, *Poésie et tradition biblique au XVIe siècle* (Paris, 1969); Michael Andrew Screech, *Clément Marot* (Leiden: E. J. Brill, 1994). For his poetry, see *Les oeuvres de Clément Marot*, ed. Jean Plattard (Paris, 1929, 1931), vols. 4 and 5.

Calvin made use of Marot's translation of the Psalms. Note Jeanneret's comment about their relationship: "la manière dont les paraphrases du poète sont venues entre les mains du réformateur demeure un mystère; on peut conjecturer seulement que les deux hommes se sont peut-être rencontrés et concertés, au début de 1536, à la cour de Ferrare, sous les auspices de Renée de France, ou, à la fin de la même année, à Genève." Jeanneret, *Poésie et tradition biblique*, 28. The name of Clement Marot would not have been pleasing to the inquisitor, since Marot was a critic of the Venetian Republic who "prese lo spunto dal dispendio dei veneziani nell'edilizia e soprattutto nell'addobbo delle chiese per segnare a dito le piaghe sociali. La sua è una delle voci più appassionate nel coro antiveneziano e inoltre una rara testimonianza dell'effetto prodotto dalla città su un osservatore attento e non benevolo." Wolters, *Storia e politica nei dipinti di Palazzo Ducale*, 25. Wolters notes that Marot's comments were sent in a letter from Venice to the duchesse de Ferrare.

46. See *Nouvelle biographie générale*, 9:844–48, s.v. "Charles IX."

47. Ibid.

48. See Eugene F. Rice Jr., ed., *The Prefatory Epistles of Jacques Lefèvre d'Etaples and Related Texts* (New York: Columbia University Press, 1972).

49. ASV, S.U., Processi, Busta 22, Contra Dionisium Gallum, testimony of August 3, 1566.

50. For King Francis I's nominations to benefices and his involvement in religious affairs subsequent to the Concordat of Bologna of 1516, see Marilyn Manera Edelstein, "Church Patronage in France on the Eve of the Reformation," in *Renaissance Society and Culture: Essays in Honor of Eugene F. Rice, Jr.*, ed. John Monfasani and Ronald G. Musto (Ithaca: Cornell University Press, 1991), 33–49. Note especially the Venetian ambassador's condemnation of the king's use of the concordat. According to the Venetian ambassador, Francis I's use of the concordat opened the door to Protestantism in France: "All hope was lost for good and lettered priests to receive a recompense for their work. . . . Incompetent priests, appointed by the king at the whim of ladies and courtiers and motivated only by greed and self-interest, took over the French church. [They] troubled the faith of the innocent people and dampened the fervent piety of the old times. It is by this door . . . that heresy entered France" (ibid., 47). Dionisio evidently believed that the French practice led to much corruption in the Church.

51. See N. M. Sutherland, *Princes, Politics, and Religion, 1547–1589* (London: Hambledon Press, 1984), 31–54; see also J. H. M. Salmon, *Society in Crisis: France in the Sixteen Century* (London: Ernest Benn, 1975), 146–67; Donald Nugent, *Ecumenism in the Age of Reformation: The Colloquy of Poissy* (Cambridge, Mass.: Harvard University Press, 1974), 13–36.

52. See Sutherland, *Princes, Politics, and Religion*, 113–37, for a lucid and incisive discussion of Catherine's role in regard to the Colloquy of Poissy. See also Venice, Biblioteca nazionale di San Marco, MSS latini, Cl. XIV, Cod. XLII (= 4325), cc. 144–48ᵛ, *Capitoli dell'accordo di Francia con Ugonotti et la lettera della Regina Madre*. Note

especially cc. 147ʳ–147ᵛ: "Poiche è piacciuto alla gran bontà di Dio risguardare quello regno e i popoli et suggetti del Padre nostro et il figlio con l'occhio della sua pietà . . . in una buona pace et santa reconciliatione, unione et concordia per stabilimento della quale sono stato per auuiso dei Prencipi del sangue et d'altre grandi et notabili huomini del Conseglio del Re nostro signore, et figliuolo, et spedite lettere patenti le quali saranno presto mandate per tutte le Provincie di questo regno et paesi sotto l'obedienza sua et accioche mentre s'aspetta la publicatione di dette lettere non possa nascere cosa veruna contraria a detta pace et riposo publico di questo regno, noi facciamo sapere per le presenti la pace essere conclusa."

53. Nugent, *Ecumenism*, 23.

54. Ibid.; see also Sutherland, *Princes, Politics, and Religion*, 31–43.

55. Sutherland, *Princes, Politics, and Religion*, 31–43; see also Denis Crouzet, *Les guerrières de Dieu: La violence au temps des troubles de religion vers 1525–vers 1610* (Paris: Champ Vallon, 1990), 1:163–82.

56. ASV, S.U., Processi, Busta 22, document entitled *Finis legationis serui Dei et nuntii.* . . . Note especially: "Quare Regnum francorum antea Christianissimum nunc impie et sathanice religione diuisum tandiu ferimus?" See also the document entitled *Proces clos de la cause de Dieu pour les droictz de Jesuschrist, en son egglise militante* . . . , in which Dionisio writes of the king of France: "Le Roy de France et son conseil sont ennemys de la verité, et craingnent grandement ceste assemblee et vnyon des princes christians et qu'ilz n'allent en France ou Dieu les enuoye pour trencer et raser les haultz rochers et montaignes des heresies quy y sont vnyr le Royaume le quel est diuise."

57. Ibid., document entitled *Haec est causa*.

58. Ibid.: "Regem francorum ego sum persecutus ad montem Marsanum vsque vt recordaretur eorum quae per me Deus illi mandauerat: suum regnum vniret alias breui futurum esse, vt in regno diuiso duabus sellis insidens vtraque priuatus male se haberet." There was an ancient proverb about sitting on two seats: "De iis qui duo vel plura negotia inter se diversa eodem tempore suscipiunt: vel qui duobus certantibus neutri favent, et utriusque amici videri volunt." Seneca cites an exchange between Cicero and Labienus in which Labienus says to Cicero: "Atque soles duabus sellis sedere." See *Totius Latinitatis Lexicon consilio et cura Jacobi Facciolati, opera et studio Aegidii Forcellini* (Patavii [Padua]: Typis Seminarii, apud Thomas Bettinelli, 1805), 4:85, s.v. *sella*.

59. ASV, S.U., Processi, Busta 22, document entitled *Haec est causa*.

60. Ibid.

61. See Crouzet, *Les guerrières de Dieu*, 1:163–82.

62. Catherine de' Medici seldom found a sympathetic audience. For a balanced modern appraisal of Catherine and the religious crisis, see Sutherland, *Princes, Politics, and Religion*. The Venetians were very anxious to have the goodwill of the queen mother and to know all that was happening in France. Note the instruction to

Zuan Corner, the new Venetian ambassador, which he was to present to the most Christian king: "Farai poi colla serenissima Regina Madre conformemente quell'officio in nome nostro, che ti parerà oportuno ed conueniente, cosi farai ancora con li Illustrissimi suoi figli fratelli ed sorelle del Re cristianissimo con li Reverendissimi Cardinali e specialmente Lorena, Principe di Condé, Il contestabile, L'armiraglio, il gran Cancelliere e altri personaggi, che ti parerà uisitandoli medesimamente con le lettere nostre di credenza et con particolar officio uerso le persone loro, sicome li parerà convenir. Et procurerai con ogni studio e uigilantia possibile di ben intender le trattamente ed negocii che per giornata occorresanno a quello corte." The ambassador was warned, however, to stay neutral in any matter concerning religion; at the same time, he was to do his duties with the king and queen mother in favor of religion yet "non descendo pero mai ad alcun particolare che potesse obligar la Signoria nostra ad alcuna cosa ma sempre parlerai sopra il generale e di quanto opererai, ne farai participe il Reverendissimo Noncio di Sua Santità." ASV, Senato, Deliberazioni, 1, Secrete, Filza 37, 1566, letter of September 23, 1566, in pregadi. Note also *Capitoli dell'accordo di Francia con Ugonotti e la lettera della Regina Madre*, cc. 144–48ᵛ. Dionisio's contemporary, Postel, had also made himself unpopular with Francis I and the court because of his constant warnings to the king about his need to reform his realm. Because of the increasing hostility, Postel left France in 1543 and went to Rome to join the Jesuits. See Marion Leathers Kuntz, *Guillaume Postel, Prophet of the Restitution of All Things: His Life and Thought* (The Hague: Martinus Nijhoff, 1981), 40–58.

63. Dionisio never mentioned Nostradamus, perhaps because he felt the more famous prophet had not been chosen by God. For Nostradamus's predictions for the year 1566, see *Il vero et vniversale Giuditio di M. Michiele Nostradamo, Astrologo Eccell. et Medico di Solon di Craus di Prouenza, nel quale si vede breuemente quanto mostraro le stelle, et pianeti di mese in mese, et di quarto in quarto dell'anno 1566* . . . (n.p. 1566), sig. Aiᵛ. The shelf mark is Biblioteca nazionale di San Marco, Venezia, Miscellanea 1339.

64. ASV, S.U., Processi, Busta 22, document entitled *Haec est causa*.

65. Ibid. Juan Luis Vives had expressed the same idea in his *De subventione pauperum* . . . , 1525. I have consulted the Italian translation, *Il modo del sovvenire a poveri di Lodovico Vives novamente tradotto di Latino in volgare* . . . (Venice: Curtio Troiano de i Nauò, 1545), c. 34ᵛ. The shelf mark of this work is Biblioteca nazionale di San Marco, Venezia 149.C.191. The words of Vives certainly applied to the clergy as well as to society in general: "Ladro è (dico) et rubbatore chi malamente consuma la pecunia ne giuochi et chi quella in casa et nelle casse rinchiusa tiene et chi in feste, et banchetti la getta uia et chi in troppo pretiose Vestimenta o in ornatissimi et per lo uario et souerchio argento et oro pomposissimi Deschi et a cui in casa le robbe si marciscono et chi cose superflue o uero inutili comprando sanza bisogno spendono la pecunia et chi in uane fabbriche simelmente" (c. 34ᵛ). Note also the responsibility of the city and of the prince in setting a policy of modesty and restraint: "Appresso tolga la città medesima qualche cosa delle spese publiche, si come da conuiti solenni, dalle xenie, cio è da doni, che si fanno a forestieri, da i

presenti che si danno à gli ambasciatori et a i sudditi, da i giuochi et pompe annuali, le quali cose tutte o per uoluptà si fanno, o uero per soperbia o per ambitione. Ne e dubito io ponto che'l Prencipe non habbia ad hauer piacere, anzi piu tosto allegrezza di essere con uie menor parato accolto pur che sappia egli in quali usi si spenda quella pecunia la quale è costume che si consumi nella uenuta sua" (cc. 62–62^v).

66. Dionisio wrote: "Je perdis mon credit de quelque escu destat que jauoye chascum jour par prouision d'ordonnance du Roy." See ASV, S.U., Processi, Busta 22, document entitled *Proces clos de la cause de Dieu pour les droictz de Jesuchrist, en son egglise militante*. . . .

67. Ibid.

68. Jehan Baptiste de La Fosse, *Journal d'un Curé ligueur de Paris sous les trois derniers Valois*, ed. Édouard de Barthélemy (Paris: Librairie Académique Didier, Libraires-Editeurs, 1865), 66.

69. Ibid., 67. The *Journal* of de La Fosse contains references to the "king of the Gauls" only in the entries of November 1563 and of January 1564.

70. See *Memoires de Condé, servant d'éclaircissement et de preuves à l'Histoire de M. de Thou, . . . augmenté d'un supplément qui contient la légende du Cardinal de Lorraine, celle de Dom Claude de Guise* . . . (Paris: Chez Rollin, 1743), 5:44. The text is as follows: "Fera renvoier à Gisors, celui qui se nomme le Roi des Gallois, pour y estre semblablement gardé, jusques à ce que Sadite Majesté en ait autrement ordonné; et ce suivant la lettre que Sadite Majesté en escrit à ceux de ladicte Ville." The king's order concerning the "one who called himself king of the Gauls," our Dionisio Gallo, follows the *arrêt* of Guillaume Postel in January 1564.

71. Ibid.

72. See page 11 above.

73. In a document entitled *Dionysius Gallus, coelesti gratia, Dei seruus, et nuntius, tibi (sancte pater) foelicitatem precatur, et salutem* and dated January 27, 1566, Dionisio wrote: "De medio Gallorum (pater sanctissime) religione diuisorum, prae caeteris nationibus, suscitauit me dominus, tres erunt anni reuoluti, sub finem mensis februarii proximi ad annuntiandam primum, gallis ipsis omnem veritatem quod duos annos, et ferme decem menses, Christo mecum cooperante, feci in ipsis Galiis: saepe francorum Regem, eius Reginam matrem, cardinales, principes, populos, et nationes: supremos etiam senatus, et subalternos presentes allocutus et adhortatus, defensus propter veritatem, a viris probis et catholicis." ASV, S.U., Processi, Busta 22. Dionisio had his defenders as well as his detractors, as the above citation makes clear.

74. See ASV, S.U., Processi, Busta 22, document entitled *A tres illustre, et puissant seigneur monseigneur Dampuille, cheuallier de l'ordre, Gouuerneur pour le Roy du pais de Languedoc: Denys de Gallois par la grace celeste ambassadeur et seruiteur de Dieu salut*, with the date of October 23, 1565, and that entitled *A vous, messieres, tenans les estatz du pais de Languedoc: Denys de gallois, par la grace celeste ambassadeur, et seruiteur de Dieu, salut*, with the date of October 20, 1565.

75. For the career of Henri Damville, see Franklin Charles Palm, *Politics and*

Religion in Sixteenth-Century France (New York: Ginn & Co., 1927). See also Paul Salon, "Tax Commissions and Public Opinion: Languedoc, 1438–1561," *Renaissance Quarterly* 43, no. 3 (1990): 479–508, with bibliography.

76. See note 74 above.

77. On the organization of the French government in the sixteenth century, see Salmon, *Society in Crisis*, 59–91; note especially the chart opposite p. 68.

78. ASV, S.U., Processi, Busta 22, document entitled *A vous, messieres, tenans les estatz du pais de Languedoc:* "Vous euesques, grandz prelatz, e vicaires qui debues estre les lumyeres des peuples, vous gouuerneur, cheualiers, et seigneurs, qui debues tous batailler pour la foy. Vous deleguez pour la cause du peuple . . . : voules vous pas ouyr la verité."

79. On the politics of the Midi, see James E. Brink, "Les états de Languedoc de 1515 a 1560: Une autonomie en question," *Annales du Midi: Revue de la France Méridionale* 88, no. 128 (1976): 287–305.

80. ASV, S.U., Processi, Busta 22, document entitled *A vous, messieres, tenans les estatz du pais de Languedoc:* "Jesuschrist faict les rois et vertu faict les nobles. Jesuschrist et vertu auecques verité sont vne mesme chose."

81. Ibid., document entitled *A tres illustre, et puissant seigneur monseigneur Dampuille:* "Les sages de ce monde disent que suys ung fol." Dionisio was to repeat this statement many times, finding some apparent solace in being Christ's fool. In this respect he was very Pauline.

82. See *Trattato di setti gradi per i quali si ascende alla sommita della uita spirituale*, in *Molti devotissimi trattati del Reverendo Padre Frate Hieronimo Sauonarola da Ferrara* (Venice: Zan della Speranza, 1547), c. 68.

83. Ibid.

84. See Paris, Bibliothèque nationale, Fonds lat. 3401, fol. 4. See also, for the Venetian Inquisition's charges, ASV, S.U., Processi, Buste 12 and 159.

85. Anton Francesco Doni, *L'Academia peregrina e i mondi sopra le medaglie del Doni, in Vinegia nell'Academia P.* (Venice: Francesco Marconlini, 1552), c. 86^v. In 1567 Doni also published in Venice *Il Dialogo de ignoranza*.

86. ASV, S.U., Processi, Busta 22, document entitled *A tres illustre, et puissant seigneur monseigneur Dampuille*.

87. Ibid. Juan Luis Vives, in *Il modo del sovvenire a poveri*, c. 67^v, writes that the medicine that cures is aid to the poor. Note especially: "Onde faciamo noi qui, si come fa l'arte della medicina la quale non toglie le infirmità de gli huomeni in generale ma quanto è in lei gli risana. Et uolesse Iddio che ualesse tanto negli animi et petti nostri la legge di Christo quanto douerebbe ualere che in uero piu assai efficace sarebbe chella cognitione della Medicina farebbe da douero che non ui sarebbero tra noi poueri alcuni si come non ue ne furono ancora nel principio della Christiana Chiesa."

88. Medical metaphors abound in Cinquecento prophetic literature and were

used by the popes, the papal nuncio, and ambassadors. The Council of Trent had been a kind of "medicine," but Dionisio believed the Church needed a new medicine and a stronger one.

89. Dionisio did not indicate that he had been able to speak to the duke or the Estates in person.

90. See page 13 and ASV, S.U., Processi, Busta 22, document entitled *Haec est causa*.

91. See the article by Peter Partner, "Appunti sulla riforma della curia romana," in *Libri, idee e sentimenti religiosi nel Cinquecento italiano* (Modena: Edizioni Panini, 1986), 32–330. He notes that Priuli, Carnesecchi, Gualteruzzi, and Pole were still hoping in the 1540s and 1550s for a reform of the Roman Curia. "Come ha detto in sostanza Massimo Firpo, fino ad un certo punto non fu impossibile l'idea di una riforma interna della chiesa conforme ai desideri dell'ambiente valdesiano. La riforma della Curia non stava in testa al loro programma, ma dobbiamo chiederci almeno se la possibilità di una tale riforma esisteva realmente" (77).

92. See Barbara Hallman, *Italian Cardinals, Reform, and the Church as Property* (Berkeley and Los Angeles: University of California Press, 1985).

93. Ibid., 3.

94. Ibid., 148.

95. See ibid., 1–2.

96. Paris, Bibliothèque nationale, Fonds française 2115, fol. 45.

97. Hallman, *Italian Cardinals*, 2. For an excellent discussion of political considerations by Roman Catholic churchmen, see Paolo Simoncelli, "Diplomazia e politica religiosa nella Chiesa della controriforma," *Rivista di Storia e Letteratura Religiosa* 19, no. 3 (1982): 415–60.

98. Hallman, *Italian Cardinals*, 80. For an informative biography of an important Italian cardinal, see Elisabeth G. Gleason, *Gasparo Contarini: Venice, Rome, and Reform* (Berkeley and Los Angeles: University of California Press, 1993).

99. Marjorie Reeves, *The Influence of Prophecy in the Later Middle Ages: A Study in Joachimism* (Oxford: Oxford University Press, 1969); Delio Cantimori, *Eretici italiani del Cinquecento: Ricerche storiche* (Florence: G. C. Sansoni Editore, 1977). See Bernard McGinn, *Visions of the End: Apocalyptic Traditions in the Middle Ages* (New York: Columbia University Press, 1979); Robin Bruce Barnes, *Prophecy and Gnosis: Apocalypticism in the Wake of the Lutheran Reformation* (Stanford: Stanford University Press, 1988); *Prophecy and Millenarianism: Essays in Honour of Marjorie Reeves*, ed. Ann Williams (Essex: Longman, 1980); Cesare Vasoli, *Profezia e ragione: Studi sulla cultura del Cinquecento e del Seicento* (Naples: Casa Editrice A. Morano, 1974); idem, *Filosofia e religione nella cultura del Rinascimento* (Naples: Guida Editori, 1988); Ottavia Niccoli, *Profeti e popolo nell'Italia del Rinascimento* (Rome and Bari: Laterza, 1987); and idem, *La crisi religiosa del Cinquecento* (Turin: Giulio Einaudi Editore, 1975). Prophecy is also a major focus of Donald Weinstein's *Savonarola and Florence: Prophecy and Patriotism in the Renaissance* (Princeton, N.J.: Princeton University Press, 1970) and Kuntz's *Guillaume Postel*.

Note also Guillaume Postel, *Le thrésor des prophéties de l'univers*, with an introduction and notes by François Secret (The Hague: Martinus Nijhoff, 1969). One should also see Cesare Vasoli, *Immagini umanistiche* (Naples: Morano Editore, 1983). I shall not review the enormous amount of modern literature about prophecy, but shall only point out examples that are particularly pertinent to my topic. I shall mention treatises and ideas that reflect ideas similar to those of Dionisio Gallo. The particular situation in Venice in regard to reform and prophetic ideas is discussed in a later chapter.

100. See, for example, Venice, Biblioteca nazionale di San Marco, MSS latini, Cl. III, Cod. CLXXVII (= 2176).

101. Reeves, *The Influence of Prophecy*, 265. Cantimori, *Eretici italiani*, 10.

102. Weinstein, *Savonarola and Florence*, 200–201.

103. Ibid., 201.

104. For a concise account of devotional works, see Rolando Bussi, ed., *Libri, idee e sentimenti religiosi nel Cinquecento italiano* (Modena: Edizioni Panini, 1986).

105. The copy I have consulted is in the Biblioteca nazionale di San Marco, with the shelf mark Misc. Teza 2308.

106. See Carlo Ginzburg and Adriano Prosperi, "Le due redazioni del 'Beneficio di Cristo,'" in *Eresia e riforma*, 137–204.

107. See Guillaume Postel, British Library, Sloane MS 1412, fol. 5ᵛ: "Innumeri tamen opera Luteri sunt . . . ad sacra studia excitati, et maxime serio, qui Valdesii Hispani prudentiam aut Erasmi Astum aut Poli cardinalis librum de Christi beneficio scriptum sectantur." See also *Nuovi studi sulla riforma in Italia: Il Beneficio di Cristo* (Rome: Edizioni di Storia e Letteratura, 1976).

108. See Vives, *Il modo del sovvenire a poveri*.

109. Ibid., sig. aiᵛ.

110. *Oratio de circumcisione dominica Magistri Petri Galatini* (n.p., 1515), sig. biiᵛ: "Circumcidi nos suo exemplo Christus edocuit: resecari cordis preputium ac discordiarum fomenta praecepit. Seruate (Bernardus inquit) circumcisionem non carnis . . . sed cordis. . . . Sed quis hodie ita circumcisus est? Quis non flagitiis abundat? Quis pacis foedera seruat? Quis fidei sacramenta custodit? Quis claues ueneratur ecclesiae? . . . Speculemur in triuiis: contemplemur fora: uicos omnes adeamus urbanos: quem uere circumcisum inueniemus?" This is the message Dionisio was to cry out in the streets of Rome in 1566. The shelf mark of the volume I have consulted is Biblioteca nazionale di San Marco, Miscellanea 507.

111. Cantimori, *Eretici italiani*, 11; see also Niccoli, *La crisi religiosa del Cinquecento*, 11–13. Egidio da Viterbo especially denounced the evils of the Church: ambition, greed for money and property, aggressive use of arms. Note also Ottavia Niccoli, "Un aspetto della propaganda religiosa nell'Italia del Cinquecento: Opuscoli e fogli volanti," in *Libri, idee e sentimenti religiosi nel Cinquecento italiano*, 32–33; after Egidio's opening remarks at the council about the corruption of the Church, he exclaimed:

"Quando mai infatti apparavero con tanta frequenza e di così terribile aspetto mostri, portenti, prodigi segni delle minacce celesti e del terrore sulla terra? quando vi potranno essere una strage o una battaglia più sanguinose di quella di Brescia o di Ravenna? [. . .] Quest' anno la terra è stata insuppata più di sangue che di pioggia." Professor Niccoli points out that at the end of the Quattrocento and at the beginning of the Cinquecento many little books reveal the stereotype of the prophet who announces punishments from God because of mankind's sins.

112. Cantimori, *Eretici italiani*, 10–11.

113. *Mirabilis Liber qui prophetias Reuelationesque necnon res mirandas praeteritas presentes et futuras apte demonstrat* (n.p., 1524), sig. bii[v]–biii.

114. Ibid., sig. xxiii.

115. Ottavia Niccoli, "'Prophetie di Musaicho': Figure e scritture Gioachimite nella Venezia del Cinquecento," in *Forme e destinazione del messaggio religioso: Aspetti della propaganda religiosa nel Cinquecento*, ed. Antonio Rotondò (Florence: Leo S. Olschki Editore, 1991), 204–5.

116. *Flagellum et Renouatio mundi et Ecclesiae Dei* (n.p., 1537), unpaginated.

117. Ibid. "Nouo propheta cosi ha pronunciato, come mostro lagnello il precursore altri gran tempo fa, questo han mostrato costui piu uolte la morte e dolore col foco prenuncio gli saria dato segno di uer propheta del Signore, dico il Sauonarola il Ferrarese, le sante opere del qual fan sue difese." The shelf mark of the text consulted is Herzog August Bibliothek, Wolfenbüttel, 240.7 Quod (16). I am indebted to Professor Friedrich Nieuwöhner for securing a photocopy of the work for me.

118. *De reformatione ecclesiae suasoria: R.P.D. Zachariae Ferrerii Vicentini Pontificis Gardiensis Fauentiae et Vallis Hamonis gubernatoris dudum missa ad Beatissimum Patrem Hadrianum vi Pontificem Maximum. Et inscribitur, Tu es qui uenturus es, an alium expectamus?* (Venetiis [Venice]: per Io. Antonium et fratres de Sabio, 1522), sig. Aiii[v]: "Expectamus quippe diu pro instauranda Hierusalem hac mystica, quae sua uetustate attrita et corrosa ruinam minatur, angelicum Pontificem aduenturum. Tu es qui uenturus es, an alium expectamus? . . . Si tu Hierusalem hanc ingrediens facto flagello e triplici illo funiculo fidei, spei, et charitatis, qui difficile rumpitur non eijcis ementes et uendentes columbas de templo domini quis alter eijciet?"

119. Ibid., sig. Aiii[v]–Aiiii: "Si tu diuturnis dissidiis ac intestinis bellis discerptam, diuisamque ciuitatem dei hanc non connectis, et authore domino non resarcis, non consolidas, ut sit unum ouile et unus pastor, quis alter resarciet, quis alter connectet, quis alter consolidabit?" Zacharias Ferrer was bishop of Guardiafiera, suffragan bishop of Beneventum.

120. Ibid., sig. Aiiii.

121. Ibid., sig. B: "Hinc oriuntur schismata, hinc haereses, hinc scandala in ecclesia dei, nec grex pastoribus, nec pontificibus principes parent, nec sacerdotes ueneratur populus."

122. Ibid., sig. Biiii^v.

123. See *Sequitur libellus qui intitulatur Onus mundi id est prophetia de malo futuro ipsi mundo superuenturo* (Rome: Eucharius Franck, 1485). Note especially: "ergo uoluntati dei factus est sanctus Dionisius prenuncius ac precursor qui apparens ei in quadam ciuitate." The shelf mark is Biblioteca nazionale di San Marco, Incunabuli 1088. The pages are not numbered.

124. *Prophetia di Brigida*, Venice, Biblioteca nazionale di San Marco, MSS latini, Cl. III, Cod. CLXXVII (= 2176), c. 16.

125. ASV, S.U., Processi, Busta 22, document without title but with incipit "Ego Dionysius Gallus Dei seruus et nuntius . . .": "Me permittunt et depingunt cum diua Brigida sacra prophetarum eloquia."

126. Ibid., document entitled *Haec est causa*.

127. *Sequitur libellus qui intitulatur Onus mundi id est prophetia de malo futuro ipsi mundo superuenturo*.

128. See Niccoli, *La crisi religiosa del Cinquecento*, 93.

129. Ibid., 68–80; note especially 68, where Niccoli, following Bainton, reproduces a parody of the Credo: "Credo nel papa, legatore et scioglitore in cielo, terra el inferno, ed in Simonia suo figliuolo signor nostro, concepito nella legge canonica, nato dalla Chiesa romana." This parody was being circulated in Worms when Luther was called before the Imperial Diet.

130. Ibid. Dionisio repeatedly writes that the Antichrist has been unleashed in France.

131. Anton Francesco Doni, *Dichiaratione del Doni, sopra il XIII cap. dell'Apocalisse contro a gli heretici con modi non mai piu intesi da Hvomo vivente . . .* (Venice: Gabriel Giolito de' Ferrari, 1562), 13.

132. See Frank E. Manuel and Fritzie P. Manuel, *Utopian Thought in the Western World* (Cambridge, Mass.: Harvard University Press, 1980), 183. See also Aldo Stella, "Utopie e velleità insurrezionali dei filoprotestanti italiani (1545–1547)," *Bibliothèque d'Humanisme et Renaissance* 27 (165): 133–82; S. Ferlin Malavasi, "Sulla diffusione delle teorie ereticali nel Veneto durante il '500: Anabattisti rodigini e polesani," *Archivio Veneto*, 5th ser., 96 (1972): 5–24; Niccoli, *La crisi religiosa del Cinquecento*, 94–95; *Eresie, magia, società nel Polesine tra '500 e '600*, ed. Achille Olivieri (Rovigo: Associazione Culturale Minelliana, 1989).

133. Manuel and Manuel, *Utopian Thought*, 190.

134. Aldo Stella, "L'ecclesiologia degli anabattisti processati a Trieste nel 1540," in *Eresia e riforma*, 207–37; see also idem, *Anabattismo e antitrinitarismo in Italia nel XVI secolo* (Padua: Liviana Editrice, 1969), and U. Gastaldi, "Il comunismo dei Fratelli Hutteriti," *Protestantesimo* 28 (1973): 1–24.

135. Stella, "L'ecclesiologia," 211–14. Note also Delio Cantimori, "Studi di storia della riforma e dell'eresia in Italia e studi sulla storia della vita religiosa nella

prima metà del '500 (rapporto fra i due tipi di ricerca)," *Bollettino della Società di Studi Valdesi* 76 (1957): 29–38, where the author discusses methodology and gives pertinent bibliography.

136. Stella, "L'ecclesiologia," 210. Note especially: "Vi si era realizzato un comunismo, di produzione oltre che di consumo, evangelicamente inteso e finalizzato, perché la comunanza dei beni . . . era considerata il necessario presupposto per potersi liberare da ogni forma di egoismo personale e di costrizione mondale o statuale."

137. See Domenico Caccamo, *Eretici italiani in Moravia, Polonia, Transilvania (1558–1611)* (Chicago: Newberry Library, 1970).

138. Niccoli, *La crisi religiosa del Cinquecento*, 94.

139. Ibid., 94–95.

140. Vasoli, *Profezia e ragione*, 136–39.

141. Ibid., 238. For a perceptive account of Zorzi's *De harmonia mundi*, see J. F. Maillard, "Le *De Harmonia mundi* de Georges de Venise," *Revue de l'Histoire des Religions* 179 (1971): 181–203. Zorzi's *De harmonia mundi totivs cantica* was published in Venice by Bernardino De Vitalibus in 1525; in 1536 the same editor also published, in Venice, Zorzi's *In scriptvram sacram problemata*.

142. See Kuntz, *Guillaume Postel*, 52. See also *L'italianisme en Francia au XVII siècle*, collected and edited by Giorgio Mirandola (Turin: Società Editrice Internazionale, 1970).

143. *I Gesuiti e Venezia: Momenti e problemi di storia veneziana della Compagnia di Gesù*, ed. Mario Zanardi (Padua: Gregoriana Libreria Editrice, 1994).

144. For a recent study on the Jesuits, see John O'Malley, *Ignatius Loyola* (Cambridge, Mass.: Harvard University Press, 1994); see also *The Jesuits: Cultures, Sciences, and the Arts (1540–1773)*, ed. John W. O'Malley, S.J., Gauvin Alexander Bailey, Steven J. Harris, and T. Frank Kennedy, S.J. (Toronto: University of Toronto Press, 1999).

145. See *Biografia universale antica e moderna* (Venice: Presso Gio. Battista Missiaglia, 1825), 21:104.

146. Ibid.

147. British Library, Sloane MS 1413, fols. 23–53.

148. See note 147 above and also Paris, Bibliothèque nationale, Fonds française 2115, fol. 103.

149. This broadsheet, without date, was published in Venice by Marco Classaro Stampadore in Calle delle Balote. See ASV, S.U., Processi, Busta 49, fascicolo *Libri proibiti*.

150. John Martin, "Salvation and Society in Sixteenth-Century Venice: Popular Evangelism in a Renaissance City," *Journal of Modern History* 60, no. 2 (1988): 233.

Chapter II

1. See note 70 to Chapter 1. See also de La Fosse, *Journal d'un Curé ligueur de Paris sous les trois derniers Valois*, 66–67.

2. ASV, S.U., Processi, Busta 22, document entitled *Haec est causa*.

3. Ibid., document entitled *A son Altesse, maistre Denys de gallois, par la grace celeste ambassadeur et seruiteur de Dieu*. . . .

4. It was to Margaret, duchess of Berry, that Postel dedicated his *Les très merveilleuses victoires des femmes* in 1553. Margaret had tried in 1551–52 to get Postel reinstated as royal reader in the king's circle but was unsuccessful because Postel's positions after his "immutation" by the Venetian Virgin in January 1552 were considered too extreme.

5. Pietro Egidi, *Mezzogiorno medievale e Piemonte moderno* (Bari: G. Laterza & Figli, 1931), 114.

6. Ibid., 115.

7. Ibid., 144.

8. ASV, Collegio, Esposizioni Principi, Filza 1, October 12, 1567, c. 182. Note especially: "Et per che potria occorrer che questi signori non hauerano anchor inteso il presente stato delle cose, voi li communicarete quanto giudicarete esser ragioneuole mostrandoli se sarà di bisogno le presente: alla quale io agiongero che se ben noi douemo tener per certo che il nostro Signor Dio donarà forza et modo al Re di farsi temer et obedir." Margaret's letters, as reported by the French ambassador to Venice, provide the historian with precious and personal reflections on the tragic situation unfolding in France.

9. Ibid., c. 180: "perche niuna cosa può le piu conturbar, et offender un Regno et un stato che le seditioni et le guerre e tumulti ciuili et intestini." October 17, 1567.

10. Ibid., c. 180ᵛ.

11. Ibid., c. 181.

12. See *L'editto et capitoli del Re Carlo IX fatti novamente per la pacificatione de i suoi popoli nel Regno di Francia . . . tradotti fedelissimamente dalla lingua Francese, nella nostra buona Italiana* (n.p., n.d.). The young king explained the reasons for the edict: "Nondimeno la malignità del tempo, et la Maestà diuina ancora per suo occulto giudicio (prouocato, secondo si deue credere da nostri peccati) ha voluto lasciare, et abbandonare la briglia a tali tumulti: di modo, che hanno messo mano all'armi, in tal maniera, che ne sono seguiti infiniti homicidii, vendette, assassinamenti, deplorationi, sacchi de' luoghi, ruine di tempii, et chiese, goirnate fatte et tanti altri mali, e calamità e desolationi commesse, et essercitate in diuersi luoghi, e parti, che continuandovi questo male, et vedendo tanti forestieri già in questo nostro Regno, sapendo ancora li preparatiui per introdurne più, la ruina evidente di esso essere ineuitabile, aggionto la grande, et irreparabile perdita che . . . habbiamo fatto dal principio di questi tumulti di tanti Principi, Signori, Cauallieri dell'Ordine nostro, Grandi Capitani,

et genti da guerra, le quali cose sono tutte (doppo Dio) il vero sostegno appoggio, difesa, et protettione di questa nostra Corona, et vno argomento a nostri vicini, quali hauessero volontà cattiua di assaltarci, come ne siamo stati già minacciati" (sig. Ai^v–A2). The king's youth and indecision are apparent, since he names those upon whose advice he has relied in drafting the edict. "Sopra di che habbiamo bene voluto pigliare il buono, et prudente conseglio della Regina, nostra carissima, et honoratissima Signora et Madre, de nostri carissimi, et amantissimi cugini il Cardinale di Borbon, Principe di Condè, Duca di Mompensieri, e Principe della Rocca Surione, Principi di nostro sangue, ancora di nostri carissimi cugini li Cardinali di Guisa, Duca d'Aumal, Duca di Montemoransi Contestabile, Pari di Francia, Duca d'Estampes, Marescalco di Brissac, e di Bordiglione, Sig. d'Andelotto, de Sansac, di Sipierri, et altri buoni, e grandi persone di nostro secreto conseglio, quali sono stati tutti d'accordo, et hanno trouato ragioneuole pel bene publico di questo nostro Regno fare, et ordinare cio che seguita" (sig. A2). The shelf mark of the volume I have used is Biblioteca nazionale di San Marco, Misc. 2643.4. Dionisio was angry with the King's Council because of this advice, which he believed strengthened the position of the Huguenots and contributed to weakening the Church and the Crown.

13. ASV, Collegio, Esposizioni Principi, Filza 1, c. 181.

14. The French ambassador, on the other hand, was implicitly warning the Venetians that what was happening in France could soon flow into Italy.

15. ASV, Collegio, Esposizioni Principi, Filza 1, c. 123^v.

16. Ibid., c. 124.

17. Dionisio was evidently correct in blaming the council, at least for some of his problems. Note the entry of January 1564 in the *Journal* of Jehan Baptiste de La Fosse: "Ledict mois, le roy des Gaulois fut mené prisonnier, puis il fut baillé en garde en une religion au païs de Normandie, et ce par délibération du privé conseil" (67).

18. The ambassador was very impressed not only with Margaret's virtues but also with her lineage. He wrote: "Dunque Madamma Margherita Duchessa di Sauoia et di Beri (non mettendo a conto che sua era figlia di Re di Francia et di una regina di Spagna . . .)." ASV, Collegio, Relazioni, Ambasciatori, Savoia, Busta 24, relazione di Andrea Boldù, 1561, cc. 25^v–26.

19. Ibid.

20. Ibid. She also added: "m'affermò che in ogni tempo osservantia di hauer in tanto cara la uita sua, in quanto ella poteua esser consentata per spenderla in seruitio di questo serenissimo dominio; lequali parole prometto alla serenissima uostra furono dette da sua Eccellentia con tale affeto che di dolcezza gli ueniuano le lagrime agli occhi."

21. Ibid. The duchess expressed her deep appreciation many times to the ambassador: "Onde me disse sua Eccelentia che se sentiua talmente obligato alle molte

demostrationi fatteli dalle uostra serenita che non basterà mai a pagarne una minima parte. Ma questi ufficii che spetialmente uostra serenissima mantenne a sua eccellentia quando si trouauo in basso stato, et fuor di casa sua, nel quel tempo oltra che non haueuo da sua parte pur un ducato da spender. . . . Non mancò pero questo serenissimo Dominio di far fare in ogni tempo da suoi Ambasciadori appresso la Cesarea et Cattolica Maestà quelli ufficii, che benegnamente dimostrauano al mondo il conto che uostra serenità teneua de lei." This seems strange, since Margaret's dowry was 300,000 scudi.

22. The Venetian Senate also admired Margaret and accordingly had instructed Vicenzo Tron, ambassador to the duke of Savoy, to pay special courtesies to her. "Visiterai a nome nostro la Illustrissima Signora Duchessa con le nostre lettere credentiali che per ciò ti hauemo date et farai quello officio che conuiene non solamente alla molta beneuolentia che portamo allo Illustrissimo Signor Duca suo consorte et a lei, ma ancora alla molta osseruantia che hauemo hauuto alli christianissimi Re . . . Padre et fratello di sua altezza et all'Sanctissima corona et casa di Franza." ASV, Senato, Deliberazioni, Secrete, Registro 74, c. 59, April 2, 1566.

23. ASV, Capi del Consiglio dei Dieci, Dispacci degli Ambasciatori, Savoia, Busta 28, August 6, 1560, da Nizza, c. 17.

24. Ibid., c. 21, October 24, 1560.

25. Ibid., January 6, 1565, fascicolo 31: "Schigniragni . . . uiene in quella città per cose di grandissima importantia per la Ugonotaria, che cosi sua Eccellenza la chiama: et però hauea uoluto darmene auiso, si come farebbe di ogn'altra cosa nella quale potesse comprendere concernersi danno, oueramente seruitio della serenità uostra."

26. Ibid., fascicolo 30. See note 59 below.

27. Ibid. "Io ripigliando le sue parole disse che ueramente niuna cosa è piu pericolosa ad un prencipe che la diuersità di religione nei suoi stati in che ogni poci di tempo poteua apportare grandissimo pregiudicio." Letter dated February 2, 1565.

28. ASV, S.U., Processi, Busta 22, document entitled *Haec est causa*, written in Ferrara in April or May 1566. See page 45 and note 75 below.

29. Juan Luis Vives had also written about the need for good and virtuous men to teach in the schools: "Certo a Rettori delle città non conuiene essere in ciò negligenti, et trascurati: anzi con ogni studio ritrouin Maestri alli loro garzoni, non solo di ingegno, et di dottrina adornati, ma ancora di giudicio sincero e sano." *Il modo del souvenire a poveri*, c. 10. The shelf mark is Biblioteca nazionale di San Marco, 149.C.191.

30. The pope had granted many advantages to the Jesuits in Savoy and "sono essi in grandissimo numero dependendo da loro principalmente il culto diuino." ASV, Archivi propri, Roma, Filza 19, March 22, 1567, c. 76ᵛ. On teaching in the schools of Italy, see Paul F. Grendler, *Schooling in Renaissance Italy: Literacy and Learning,*

1300–1600 (Baltimore, Md.: Johns Hopkins University Press, 1989), especially 363–90.

31. C. Contessa, "Echi del centenario della nascita di Emanuele Filiberto di Savoia," *Archivio Veneto* 5 (1929): 369–98; see especially 395.

32. Ibid., 394.

33. "Quanto alle dote dell'animo è religioso et diuoto molto la qual uirtù portò seco sin da suoi progenitori . . . hauendo fondate molte Abbatie et fabricati diuersi monasteri nel stato suo et più uolte ancora essendo andati fino in Leuante solo per combattere per la fede di Christo contra Turchi et infideli." ASV, Collegio, Relazioni, Ambasciatori, Savoia, Busta 24, relazione di Andrea Boldù, 1561.

34. Emanuele Filiberto, *IV centenario di Emanuele Filiberto e X anniversario della vittoria* (Turin: S. Lattes, 1929), 362.

35. Ibid., 363–65.

36. Ibid., 371.

37. ASV, Archivi propri, Savoia, Filza 1, c. 339, dispatch of Hieronimo Lippomano, January 1, 1573.

38. Note the ambassador's words to the doge concerning the new order: "et mi ha detto che staua aspettando il giongere delle bolle per ragionar qualche cosa in questo proposito, ma poi che uede che pur tardano non ha uoluto più diffetare a darmi perche lo scriua a uostra Serenità che questa religione conferita nella persona sua le è stato tanto più cara quanto quella Republica Serenissima potrà commandare et disponere di questo di più nel tempo auenire come hora, et sempre può far di tutte le cose sue, et come piu particolarmente le farà poi intendere per un gentilhuomo che le manderà espressa, aggiongendomi queste formal parole." Ibid.

39. "è cosa chiara da uedere che ogni honore, et favore che piacerà a loro eccellentissime Signorie di farmi tornerà a gloria propria di quella Republica." Ibid., c. 339^v. See also Arturo Segre, "Emanuele Filiberto e la Repubblica di Venezia (1545–1580)," in *Deputazione veneta di storia patria*, Miscellanea, 2d ser. (Venice, 1901), 7:65–507; note especially 314–17.

40. Segre, "Emanuele Filiberto e la Repubblica di Venezia," 315–17.

41. Ibid., 312–13.

42. Ignatius Loyola had also praised the use of good example by priests. See, for example: "Christi bonus odor sumus. . . . così i Ministri di Dio, quali sono gli Ecclesiastici, debbono operare in maniera, che si spanda ne' secolari delle opere loro per mezzo del buon esempio il soave profumo de' precetti, e de' consiglij di Gesù Cristo: e questo è quel, che inculcava in altro luogo il medesimo San Paolo: Providentes bona non tantum coram Deo, sed etiam coram hominibus." *Esercizj spirituali di S. Ignazio Lojola . . .* (Parma: dalla stamperia Ducale, 1816), 81. The shelf mark is Biblioteca nazionale di San Marco, 247.D.190.

43. Emanuele Filiberto, *IV centenario*, 366ff.

44. See Hubert Jedin, *Storia del Concilio di Trento*, 2d ed. (Brescia, 1973), 1:627–36.

45. See Contessa, "Echi del centenario," 393ff.

46. French domination in Piedmont had carried the seeds of reform into that land. As Carlo Guido Mor noted, the reform that, "già esistente nei valli valdesi, s'era rapidamente estesa in tutte le città occupate. Cattolico convinto . . . il duca diede opera attiva per aiutare lo stabilirsi di corporazioni religiose e di confraternite, . . . e, . . . tentando in fine di arginare il dilagare della Riforma, ma rifuggendo, per quanto poteva, dai modi violenti." "Recenti studi su Emanuele Filiberto," *Archivio Storico Italiano*, 7th ser., 12 (1929): 86–87.

47. The duke's ideas of reform were tempered by practical expediency. For example, for his program to stabilize commerce with the East from the port of Nice, he favored Hebrew merchants, but he had to change his plan because of the hostility of the pope and the Spaniards.

48. Contessa, "Echi del centenario," 393.

49. Ibid.

50. Emanuele Filiberto, *IV centenario*, 108–9; see also Segre, "Emanuele Filiberto e la Repubblica di Venezia," 108–9.

51. ASV, Collegio, Secreta Esposizioni Principi, Filza 1, c. 522.

52. Ibid., cc. 522–522^v: Note especially: "uolendo uostra signoria intender piu espressamente la mente nostra, la sapera che la signoria nostra per proprio et natural istituto ha sempre amata et desiderata la pace come quella che apporta ogni bene et felicità alli stati onde poi che'l Signor Dio per sua benignità (si puo dire miracolosamente) ha introdotta la pace tra li Principi Christiani uossemo uederla continuare, massimamente in questo tempo, che se ne ha grandissimo bisogno per poter rimediar co'l concilio alli tanti dispareri, che sono nella Christianità per causa della religione et percio di nostro sommo contento sarebbe che non si facesse operatione che potesse far moto, ouero che desse suspitione, dalla quale potesse nascer qualche importante disturbo al concilio." For the duke's frustrations with Geneva and his desire to use force against the city, see Segre, "Emanuele Filiberto e la Repubblica di Venezia," 112–41. For the numerous discussions about the formation of a league of Italian princes, see ibid., 122. Note especially: "Il Granvelle . . . gli aveva in un'altra sua narrato un aneddoto del 1554, quando il Duca di Ferrara, Ercole II d'Este, fece istanza ad Em. Filiberto di accettare il comando supremo delle sue forze, assicurandolo che tutti i principi d'Italia l'avrebbero aiutato per cacciar dalla penisola di Spagnoli e Francesi. 'V.M.,' scriveva il Granvelle con profonda intuizione, 'sea cierto que la mayor parte de los dichos potentados de Italia, y quasi todos, tienen este fin, y que andan pláticas que parece llevan camino á ciertas ligas, que aunque no se sabe que haya conclusion, bien se entiende por muchas partes que se discurre en ello.' In Italia, secondo il Granvella, favorevole al Re era solo il duca di Parma, Ottavio Farnese, alleato ben debole. Necessario dunque impedire qualsivoglia unione di principi italiani, e siccome Ginevra poteva esserne occasione, combattere ogni impresa diretta contro quella città."

53. Segre, "Emanuele Filiberto e la Repubblica di Venezia," 157–58.

54. Ibid., 158.

55. ASV, Collegio, Esposizioni Principi, Filza 1, cc. 457ᵛ–458: "Di che la prencipale cagione è che la guerra di Franza è stata fondata e principiata col consiglio e instantia di sua santita et de la Maesta Catholica per la diffesa de la vera fede Christiana e santa ghiesa e estirpatione dell'errori."

56. Ibid., c. 458: "Parendo a loro che Santa Maestà Christianissima non douuesse comportar in nessun modo, l'usansa della Religion esser diuersa da quella che sempre é stata et facendo certo giudicio che venendo la Franza, la quale è sita nel centro di la Christianità, ad infettarsi, s'infettarian ancora di man in mano le circonuecine prouincie D'Italia e Spagna."

57. The ambassador recounted the help he had received from the Catholic king, the duke of Savoy, some princes of Germany, and the duke of Lorraine, and urged the Venetians that "non siate restati soli spetatori delle miserie e rovina di quel Regno col danno vniuersale de la Christianità e particolare de la vostra Republica si come vi piacera considerare e risoluergli con quella prestezza che cognoscete, assai la necessita domandar." Ibid., cc. 459–459ᵛ.

58. See ASV, Capi del Consiglio dei Dieci, Dispacci degli Ambasciatori, Savoia, Busta 28, fascicolo 31. Ambassador Zuan Corner's January 6, 1565, dispatch speaks of a Provençal named Schigniragni who had recently come into Angrogna "per cose di grandissima importantia per la Ugonotaria." See note 25 above.

59. Ibid., dispatch of February 11, 1565, fascicolo 30: "Entro poi a dire che niuna cosa può piu facilmente sturbare il quieto uiuere di prencipi Italiani che questo humore di nuoua religione perche i popoli che son contaminati da simil peste, ci chiamano idolatri et con tali coperta dicono di non essere tenuti ad ubbidire."

60. Ibid., dispatch of Vicenzo Tron, March 7, 1568, fascicolo 39. Note especially: "Percioche questi che loro nominauono non poteuano esser chiamati ne gientil' homeni, ne uassali di sua Maestà ma piu tosto rebelli hauendo prese l'armi contra il suo proprio Signore et la religione catholica et christiana. Onde li pareua che fusse neccessario purgar questo corpo infetto con quelle proprie medicine che conueniua alla qualità del male, altrimenti bisognaua che in poco spatio di tempo corrompesse tutte li altri membri non contaminati con grandissimo pericolo della Religione del Regno et della uita di sua Maestà Christiana."

61. See ASV, Capi del Consiglio dei Dieci, Dispacci degli Ambasciatori, Savoia, Busta 28, fascicolo 42, dispatch of Ambassador Hieronimo Lippomano, October 4, 1570: "et presentatogli anco lettere che non uoglia Sua Eccellenza accetar alcuno carico che le potesse esser offerto in questa lega contra i Turchi dandogli intentione et speranza di restituirgli li doi fortezze di Sauiglian, se ben si crede, che non le daranno massime Pinarolo, per tenir quella porta aperta per loro alla Italia." Lippomano indicated that he knew these things from a minister who was very close to the duke of Savoy.

62. Ibid. "Sua Eccellenza gli rispose che quanto alla liga non sa cosa alcuna et che pero non può dir altro se non che attende al solo gouerno di suoi stati, et che se piaccerà alle Sua Maestà di restituirgli le fortezze gli ne hauera molto obligo perche hauendo questi speraria fermamente di hauer li altri doi da Spagna."

63. ASV, Secreta Archivi propri, Savoia, Filza 1, c. 272. The duke, nevertheless, allowed one of the Visconti, who had actively stirred up Huguenot sentiments and who openly professed the reform faith, to live in Piedmont, much to the chagrin of the pope.

64. Ibid., c. 273. Before his death, the admiral had sent his older son into Germany. From Germany the youth went to Geneva, where a grand feast was held in his honor. Theodore Beza greeted him with great warmth. See ibid., c. 285.

65. Ibid., cc. 337–337v.

66. ASV, S.U., Processi, Busta 22, letter addressed *A son Altesse*. For confirmation of the day of his arrival, see Adriano Capelli, *Cronologia, cronografia e calendario perpetuo*, 5th ed., rev. (Milan: Editore Ulrico Hoepli, 1983), 98–99.

67. ASV, S.U., Processi, Busta 22, letter addressed *A son Altesse*.

68. *Espositio magni prophete Abbatis Joachim in Apocalipsim* (Venice: In edibus Francisci Bindoni ac Maphaei Pasini, 1527). Note especially cc. 73–73^v for the exegesis of the hidden manna and the white stone, themes very dear to Dionisio. Joachim explained the mystery of the white stone: "Et in calculo nomen scriptum quod nemo scit nisi qui accipit quod quante sit dignitatis vocari a Christo Christianus nemo scit nisi cui scire et intelligere datum est quod proprium est eorum qui vicerunt concupiscentias mundi qui occultum aduersarium prostrauerunt in bello qui ab immundis desideriis cordis ergastulum mundauerunt" (c. 73). The shelf mark is Biblioteca nazionale di San Marco, 51.C.130.

69. See ASV, S.U., Processi, Busta 35 for the *processi* of Benedetto Corazzaro and Benetto Florian; also Venice, Archivio storico del Patriarcato di Venezia, Criminalia Santissimae Inquisitionis, 1561–85, Busta 2, cc. 184–195^v. For secondary literature, see Carlo Ginzburg, "Due note sul profetismo cinquecentesco," *Rivista Storica Italiana* 78 (1966): 184–227; Adriano Prosperi, "Intorno a un catechismo figurato del tardo '500," in *Von der Macht der Bilder: Beiträge des C.I.H.A.—Kolloquiums "Kunst und Reformation,"* ed. Ernst Ullman (Leipzig: E. A. Seeman; Karl-Marx Universität, 1983), 99–114. Especially pertinent to our concerns is Niccoli, "'Prophetie di Musaicho,'" 197–227. See also John Martin, *Venice's Hidden Enemies* (Berkeley and Los Angeles: University of California Press, 1993), 199–215.

70. Demus (*Mosaics of San Marco in Venice*) does not give the precise date for the apocalyptic mosaics in San Marco but indicates that they were in place at least by 1570. Benedetto Corazzaro, before his death in 1561, had lectured on the Apocalypse to his Venetian followers, using the mosaics as themes for his teachings. See also Bruno Bertoli and Antonio Niero, *I mosaici di San Marco: Un itinerario biblico* (Milan: Electa Editrice, 1987), and *La Basilica di San Marco: Arte e simbologia*, ed. Bruno Bertoli (Venice: Edizioni Studium Cattolico Venziano, 1993).

71. See Francesco Sansovino, *Venetia città nobilissima* (ed. Giovanni Stringa), bk. I, chap. XCIII, c. 58: "Non è dubbio alcuno, che l'inuentore di esse figure non sia stato quel uenerabile huomo, chiamato l'Abbate Giovanni Gioachino, il quale essendo uenuto a Venetia pochi anni dopo, che principio si diede a lauorar in questa Chiesa di mosaico, et ottenuto un luogo in detta Chiesa molto angusto et rimoto . . . per sua habitatione . . . , habitando in detto luogo con molta astinenza et con fama di Santità di uita, formò quiui, e disegnò con le proprie mani le perdette figure nel modo, come quiui dipinte si ueggono." Giovanni Stringa was canon of the Basilica di San Marco. Guillaume Postel, the learned contemporary of Dionisio Gallo, also wrote of Joachim and the mosaics of San Marco.

72. See, for example, Venice, Biblioteca nazionale di San Marco, MSS latini, Cl. III, Cod. CLXVII (= 2176), a compilation of prophecies of Frater Rusticanus, Teolosphoro da Cosenza, and Joachim relevant for our consideration, since they proclaim forerunners of the angelic pope who will be like Christ. Note especially c. 27: "erit alter Zacheus, alter Johannes baptista, alter Christus homo sacrosanctus papa praedictus. Item erunt XII noui apostoli qui praedicabunt iterum euangelium Dei, ut omnes conuertantur ad deum."

73. See *Mirabilis Liber qui prophetias . . . demonstrat*. In this remarkable and rare book there are many revelations of the Blessed Bridget about false popes and also about the true "angelic" pope. Note especially the following (c. XVI^v): "Sybilla Cretensis sic loquitur de aquila et lilio et pseudo pontificibus; erit in infidiis sponse agni depauperans cultum eius et erunt sponsi tres adulteri: vnusque legitimus in cantu debilis qui alios vorabit. Deinde cantabit gallus; optima fiet restauratio in eo. Et fulminabit ipse legitimus papa sententiam in tres alemannos prelatos tanquam inobedientes et rebelles sponse agni. . . . Unde propheta: Disperdam nomina idolorum de terra et ecclesia. Cantabit gallus et verus papa optima fiet restauratio erroribus extirpatis et sub ipsa aquila finientur tribulationes clerique post ipsum imperium destruetur. Illud attendite o religiosi et reuerendi et uos philosophi." The text I have consulted is found in the Biblioteca del Museo Correr, Venice, with the shelf mark Op. Cicogna 626.9 (100.9). Note also Venice, Biblioteca nazionale di San Marco, MSS latini, Cl. III, Cod. CLXXVII (= 2176), c. 27, and page 1 above; for a similar prophecy about the "singing Gaul," see Rome, Biblioteca Apostolica Vaticana, Vat. latini, 6085 (s. xvi), c. 196^v: "simonia destruetur quia cantabit gallus, sub pedibus proterens turgidas spicas septem." This manuscript is entitled *Qua comenza la Cronica de Tutta la proventia de la citta de Veniesia*. . . .

74. In Israel the king absorbs divine attributes from anointment. The unction of the high priest sanctifies him by removing him from the realm of the profane and placing him in the realm of the sacred. The methods of anointment vary from sprinkling oil on the head to a good dousing, as in the case of Aaron. David was anointed with oil poured from a horn. See *Encyclopaedia Judaica* (Jerusalem, 1972), 3:27–31. The significance of Dionisio's anointment, certainly to himself, was similar to that in ancient Israel. The method of anointment, however, was very different.

75. ASV, S.U., Processi, Busta 22, Contra Dionisium Gallum, letter addressed *A son Altesse.*

76. In the prophecies of Teolosphoro is a beautiful drawing of an angel holding a book in his hand; above the angel is inscribed the following: "Verba angeli loquentis noue religionis. Accipite librum et seruate uiam dei et que in eo scripta sunt. (c. 29ᵛ)." Venice, Biblioteca nazionale di San Marco, MSS latini, Cl. III, Cod. CLXXVII (= 2176), c. 29ᵛ. On a subsequent page of Teolosphoro's prophecies the angel is holding a book on which is written *Hic est liber apertus,* which is the title of one of Dionisio's books seized by the Venetian Inquisition. Above the angel's head we read the following: "Hic est liber apertus et erat scriptus intus et extra signatus VII sigillis in cuius appertione consumate sunt prophetie noui et ueteris testamenti, usque ad hec tempora" (c. 34ᵛ). Dionisio's description of the Virgin closely correlates with this beautiful watercolor. His account of his anointment appears in the document entitled *Haec est causa:* "Tum illa virgo, albis induta precincta quasi quidam episcopus presbiteros sacraturus, et ordinaturus, omni coepit reuerentia exterius in cute oleo coelesti me perungere."

77. See *La Bibbia concordata* (Florence: Arnoldo Mondadori Editore, 1968), 2040. Note the commentary on Apoc. 5: "Un libro: è una pergamena arrotolata e sigillata, che contiene i decreti di giustizia di Dio contro i suoi nemici.... Affinché apra sigilli: per giudicare e condannare."

78. *Encyclopaedia Judaica* (Jerusalem, 1972), 2:1407–8. See also, in the same volume, the article "Messiah," by Louis Jacobs, 1407–16, and the article "Messianic Movements," by Haim Hillel Ben-Sasson, 1417–28.

79. See ASV, S.U., Processi, Busta 22, Contra Dionisium Gallum.

80. The archbishop of Turin (1564–92) was Hieronymus della Rovere, bishop of Toulon. See *Hierarchia Catholica medii et recentioris aevi sive summorum pontificum, S.R.E. cardinalium, ecclesiarum antistitum series,* ed. Guilelmus Van Gulik, Conradus Eubel, and Ludovicus Schmitz-Kallenberg (Padua, 1960), 3:309.

81. ASV, S.U., Processi, Busta 22, Contra Dionisium Gallum, document entitled *Haec est causa.:* "probauit et eam Ducum Italiae primus Duc Ille Sabaudiae ad eamque mandandam executioni a nobis interpellatus, declarit se toto suo conatu esse quam paratissimum. Incertum est: certum est illi et mihi."

82. See Segre, "Emanuele Filiberto e la Repubblica di Venezia," 112–41. The advice of Cardinal Granvelle to King Philip II not to begin a new war, since they had been at peace only one year, was also pertinent to the other states (ibid., 121). Savoy's claims on Cyprus, in addition to Venice's preoccupation with the Turkish advance, were enough to dissuade Venice from such action.

83. In the letter to Henry Montmorency, duke of Damville, Dionisio acknowledged that "the sages of the world say that I am a fool." The bishops and prelates mocked him. ASV, S.U., Processi, Busta 22, Contra Dionisium Gallum; see the document entitled *A tres illustre, et puissant seigneur monseigneur Dampuille.*

84. Emanuele Filiberto, *IV centenario*, 115.

85. See Egidi, *Mezzogiorno medievale e Piemonte moderno*, 144–45.

86. ASV, S.U., Processi, Busta 22, Contra Dionisium Gallum, document entitled *Proces clos de la cause de Dieu pour les droictz de Jesuchrist, en son egglise militante...*, with a dedication: "A tous les princes et seigneurs, iuges et magistratz, peuples et nations de la chrestiante.... Monseigneur le Duc de Sauoye la ouye et entendue et la grandement approuuee: Respondant luy, par moy, estant interpellé pour donner son adionction, affin d'executer: que de sa part estoit tresprest: et que j'allasse aux aultres Ducz, et princes D'Italie."

87. Ibid., letter addressed *A son Altesse:* "Duo sunt omnino veritatis ipsius hostes acerrimi: vnus, auaritia et ambitio praelatorum ecclesiae: alter, error haereticorum. Veritas autem vtrumque confundet."

88. Ibid., document entitled *A vous, messieres, tenans les estatz du pais de Languedoc:* "Jesuschrist faict les rois et vertu faict les nobles. Jesuschrist et vertu auecques verité sont vne mesme chose."

89. See ASV, Consiglio dei Dieci, Parte Comuni, 1565–1566, Registro 27, c. 113. The duke was warmly welcomed in Venice, and coins bearing his likeness were struck in his honor.

90. Dionisio described his "backward" attire and his huge cross many times. See especially ASV, S.U., Processi, Busta 22, Contra Dionisium Gallum, documents entitled *Clarissimo principi Domino, Domino Cosmo Mediceo; Haec est causa;* and *Relatio fidelis....*

91. Ibid., document entitled *Dionisius gallus, coelesti gratia, Dei seruus et nuntius, tibi (sancte pater) foelicitatem precatur et salutem,* dated January 27, 1566.

92. For a concise account of the attempts to reform the Roman Curia, see Partner, "Appunti sulla riforma della curia romana," 77–80; note especially 79: "E in questo modo che vedo la Curia romana, come un'organizzazione che trova quasi impossibile una riforma che sia qualcosa di più che un'operazione cosmetica; ma che nutre dei curiali come Pole, Carnesecchi, Flaminio, che rivendicano con grazia aristocratica il diritto di pensare da uomini liberi." Although the Council of Trent forbade, for example, the selling of benefices, the enforcement of this legislation in Rome, especially minor benefices and privileges for cardinals and their families, is uncertain. Dionisio was to speak again and again about the abuses of the Roman Curia.

93. ASV, Collegio, Relazioni, Ambasciatori, Roma, Busta 1, relazione di Alvise Mocenigo, cc. 122–142ᵛ.

94. Ibid., cc. 122ᵛ–123: "in Franza hanno intimato concilio prouinciale o nationale, cosa che saria contraria in tutto al generale concilio et poneria confusione et scisma nella Christianità, si conosce anco chiaramente che li pontifici se ben con parole hora dimostrato di uoler concilio generale, con gli effetti pero non han uoluto mai se non sforzati, anca si uede manifestamente che non solamente

perche dubitano di non hauer dalli concilii documento grande alle cose, et commodita loro."

95. Ibid., c. 123: "onde vanno dicendo sempre non essere bisogno di tal cosa perche tutte le difficultà siano terminate da gli altri concilii."

96. Ibid.: "Papa Paolo IIII di santa memoria andaua continuamente facendo qualche noua diterminatione et riforma et sempre diceua prepararne delle altre et questo lo faceua per corregger li abusi quanto piu che poteua, accio che restasse manco occasione, et menor necessita di far concilio."

97. Ibid.: "Il presente Pontifice doppo eletto, se ben per inanzi parlaua altrimenti disse nel principio del suo pontificato, che per via di congregatione di Cardinali uoleua attender alla riforma, condir però che bisognando poi anche concilio non mancheria di darlo quando uederà tutti li principi di Christianità d'accordo. Ma si uede chiaro, per commune opinione che non ha uolonta di farlo ne sua Santita ne alcun prelato."

98. Ibid., cc. 122–122^v.

99. Ibid., c. 122^v: "li populi assentiuano uolontieri a quello che uedeuano esser ordinato dalli pontifici come a cosa che li pareua commandata da proprio Dio."

100. Ibid., c. 131^v. Mocenigo also wrote about the deplorable morality in the College of Cardinals: "in questo caso non troppo sacro, ne santo collegio de cardinali è retto et gouernato in tutto per quello che si può giudicare humanamente, dalla uoluntà de principi et dall'interesse particolar de cardinali." He also pointed out that in the process of choosing a pope, a cardinal's piety was not considered, but his powerful connections were. Note: "Non ho mai sentito dir io il tal cardinale sarà Pontifice perch'è huomo di dottrina di religione o di bontà, ma ben spesso non sarà il tale, perche è troppo scrupuloso . . . et ogni di ho udito discorrer, il tale sarà o non sarà Ponitifice perch'è nominato raccomandato o escluso da Franza o la Spagna, et perch'è o amico o nimico del tale cardinale delli capi principali."

101. ASV, Collegio, Relazione, Ambasciatori, Roma, Busta 20, relazione di Girolamo Soranzo, June 14, 1563.

102. ASV, S.U., Processi, Busta 22, document entitled *Vniuerso hominum generi Dionysius gallus, coelesti gratia, Dei seruus et nuntius,* dated February 1, 1566. Note especially: "Morbus alter, auara multorum ambitio praeletorum ecclesiae; alter error hereticorum Sed non profecto galliarum proprii sunt isti morbi. Sed aliarum etiam communes nationum. . . . Erit autem supremo malo summum remedium. Erit communi morbo commune medicamentum."

103. ASV, Collegio, Relazione, Ambasciatori, Roma, Busta 20, relazione di Girolamo Soranzo, June 14, 1563: "chel Concilio a questi tempi non può far altro effetto, se non quello se suol operare una gagliarda et potente medicina in un corpo debole et estenuato, che non lo risano, ma lo ammazza; cosi quando il mondo è in santo disordine et trauaglio co'l uoler adoperar un rimedio cosi potente, si corri pericolo non di acconciare, ma di rouinare la sede apostolica."

104. See note 96 above.

105. ASV, Collegio, Relazione, Ambasciatori, Roma, Busta 20, relazione di Girolamo Soranzo.

106. Jedin, *Storia del Concilio di Trento*.

107. See the seminal work of Gaetano Cozzi on the results of the Council of Trent, "Fra Paolo Sarpi, l'anglicanesimo e la 'Historia del Concilio tridentino,'" *Rivista Storica Italiana* 68 (1956): 559–619; also pertinent is his "Domenico Bollani: Un vescovo veneziano tra Stato e Chiesa," *Rivista Storica Italiana* 89 (1977): 562–89. For an interesting discussion comparing the views of Andrea Morosini (in his *Historia Veneta*) and those of Sarpi regarding the results of the council, see Giuseppe Trebbi, "Venezia tra '500 e '600 nell'opera storica di Andrea Morosini," *Studi Veneziani*, n.s., 25 (1993): 73–129; note especially 119: "Il Morosini, nonostante tutto, non ha dubbi sull'utilità del Tridentino ai fini della riforma della Chiesa, da tanti e da tanto tempo auspicata; per il Sarpi, invece, il Concilio 'maneggiatto da li principi per riforma dell'ordine ecclesiastico, ha causato la maggior deformazione che sia mai stata da che vive il nome cristiano.'"

108. ASV, S.U., Processi, Busta 22, Contra Dionisium Gallum, document entitled *Dionisius gallus, coelesti gratia . . .*: "Haec omnia mihi coelitus ante reuelata sunt quam concilium tridentinum, et postremum haberetur." I say more about this point in the Conclusion.

109. ASV, Collegio, Relazioni, Ambasciatori, Roma, Busta 20, relazione di Girolamo Soranzo, read in the Senate, June 14, 1563: "L'Illustrissimo Morone quando partí per il concilio mi disse che andaua a cura disperata et che nulla spe erat della religione cattolica: gli altri cardinali di maggior auttoritá deplorano con tutti a tutte l'hore la loro miseria la quale stimano tanto maggiore quanto che uedono, et conoscono assai chiaro non ui esser rimedio alcuno se non quello che piacesse al Signor Dio di dare con la sua santissima mano."

110. Ibid.: "Fu indito dal Papa il concilio poche mesi appresso la sua assontione al Pontificato; et si deue ben certo creder che Santita Sua si mouesse in cosi santa opera per sua propria elettione con fine di redur sotto un solo pastore tutto il grege, non di meno si sà che la necessità ne ha hauuto una gran parte, per che uolendo i francesi fino al tempo de Re Francesco far un Concilio Nationale, et esso questo tanto abhorrito a Roma si pensò diuestirlo con indir il Generale et dapoi superate le difficoltà del luogo et della inditione, a continuatione finalmente di concorde uolere dei Principi si apre il Concilio a Trento."

111. ASV, Collegio, Lettere Cardinali e altri ecclesiastici, Filza 2, July 11, 1566. Note, for example: "l'obedientia della chiesa non solamente non uiene prestata, ma da suoi Ministri uiene conculcata et posta in odio, l'auttorità della chiesa uiene diminuita, le operationi de' sacerdoti uengono calumniate . . . et uedendo che i miei deffetti sono scoperti et palesi nell'Isola di Veglia, poscia che mi sia tolta la speranza di poterli piu coprire. . . . Io faccio; il Vescouato che è casa di Dio, casa del Diauolo, io non son giudice sinciero, ma corruttibile et ingordo al guadagno,

io non son quello che habbi la pace di Dio nel petto, ma la discordia et sedittione del diauolo, io non son quello, al quale ha detto Christo, discite a me, et estote perfecti, ma son un tristo et scelerato. . . . i Preti, i Frati et altre sorte de religiosi non possono dare piu benedittioni et pregare per il popolo, perche sono stati da gl'huomini . . . et che siano maledetti quanti preti e frati e religiosi si trouano, di che ponto mi curerei, se da essi a me o priuatamente ciò hauesse detto, et dicesse, ma perche lo ha detto publicamente in palazzo, in piazza, et mi conseglio, io con le presente, ne dimando giustitia alla Serenita, Vos, et alle Signorie Vostre eccellentissime a quali dio dice per bocca del profeta regale: diligite iustitiam, qui iudicatis terram: eripite pauperem et egenum; et per un altro profeta lor fa intendere: per me Reges regnant et uos poscia che questo non è adempimento del precetto di Dio uerso il prossimo, ne ua aggrandire la Chiesia di Dio et metter in pretio in suoi Ministri." See notes 171 and 179 below for similar ideas expressed by Savonarola.

112. Pietro Bembo was the son of Giovanni Mattheo Bembo. He was named bishop of Veglia in 1564. See *Hierarchia Catholica*, 3:328.

113. See *Esercizj spirituali di S. Ignazio Lojola*, 76–77: "E forza che il Signore ne sia ben offeso, poichè ordina nel Levitico di offerirgli un sagrifizio si grande per lo peccato di un sol Sacerdote, come per quelli di tutto il popolo. Questo c'insegna, dice San Grisostomo, che i peccati di un sol Sacerdote offendono Dio più gravemente che tutti quelli di un popolo intiero. . . . Che offenda Dio un Turcho, un infedele, un eretico, è un gran male, che lo offenda un secolare cattolico è male maggiore; ma che lo offenda un Sacerdote, ahi quanto il male è più orrendo! Oh malizia! Oh ingratitudine! Oh perfidia!"

114. ASV, S.U., Processi, Busta 22, Contra Dionisium Gallum, document entitled *Vniuerso hominum generi Dionysius gallus, coelesti gratia, Dei seruus et nuntius*, dated February 1, 1566.

115. Ibid.: "Omne ergo existimate gaudium pontifices et populi, quando nunc ex mediis galliis Deus ad vos mittit, iuxta prophetiam eiusdem Diuae Brigidae, electum seruum suum apud gallorum principes."

116. Ibid.

117. Dionisio's travels on behalf of the reform of the Church remind one of the suggestions of Nicolas of Cusa for the reform of the Church. Cusano proposed that the best remedy for the ills of the Church would be a universal pastoral visit to see firsthand the conditions of Christianity and to propose specific solutions for each case. See *La Chiesa cattolica nella storia dell'umanità: Splendore e decadenza del medio evo*, ed. Carlo Lenta and Francesco Chiaramento (Fossano: Editrice Esperienze, 1964), 3:44–45.

118. *Abbas Joachim magnus propheta: Expositio magni prophete Ioachim in librum beati Cirilli de magnis tribulationibus et statu Sancte matris Ecclesie* (Venice: Laçarus de Soardis, 1516), c. xxv. Note especially the following: "Pastor egregius in solio sedebit, custoditus ab angelis qui multa faciet. Hic mitis; hic sine macula; qui cuncta rectificabit et statum ecclesie et dominium temporale per suos et alienos laycos dispersum et

separatum cum mansuetudine redimet. . . . Hic vir sanctus religiosorum cornua conteret superba et omnes erunt ad statum primitiue ecclesie: itaque pastor vnus, lex vna, dominus vnus verus et modestus deum timens. . . . Joachim . . . vocat hunc papam angelicum pastorem, et de laudibus multa dicit." The shelf mark of this rare volume is Biblioteca nazionale di San Marco, Rari V 408, Rari V 409.

119. Ibid.: "Ille vere iudeorum deus dominus Iesus christus cuncta prosperabit et ordinabit ultraquam mens humana credere poterit quia summus dominus et verus medicus qui post vulnera tribuet mellifluam medicinam."

120. ASV, S.U., Processi, Busta 22, Contra Dionisium Gallum, document entitled *Clarissimo principi Domino, Domino Cosmo Mediceo*, written from prison in Rome.

121. The early Church was often held up as a model in the Cinquecento. Note the letters of Paul Pasqualitius, a notary of Tragurien, to Pope Pius V in 1571: for example, "Cogitemus cum nostris animis Apostolos Christi nudos, inopes, illiteratos homines despicatissimos non syllogismorum uersutiis, nulla mundi sapientia instructos se tantum fidei loricam indutos accintosque gladio, quod est uerbum Dei, sapientiam sapientum prostrauerunt." He also wrote of the proper role of bishops: "Fuit hoc munus priscis temporibus Episcoporum peculiarium, instituebantur pastores in ecclesiis tantum pascendo gregi Dominico, qui lupos arcerent ab ouibus et spirituali cibo Euangelice doctrine populum Dei pascerent." See ASV, S.U., Processi, Busta 41, fascicolo, Tranquillo de Andreis.

122. Ibid., Busta 154. This interesting document addressed to the doge describes the practices at Mass in the early Church. The author contrasts the simplicity and the charity of the early Church with the complexity of the Church in the sixteenth century.

123. Ibid., Busta 22, document entitled *Pio quinto pontifici maximo . . .* , dated February 5, 1566.

124. See *Prophetia de maometani et altre cose Turchesche*, trans. Lodovico Domenichi (Florence, 1548), c. Biii^v.

125. ASV, S.U., Processi, Busta 39, Contra Girolamo Donzellino. The long statement of Donzellino was dated January 27, 1561. Donzellino was deeply concerned about the moral life of the Church. He believed the duty of a Christian man was "liberare pauperes a clamore."

126. Donzellino noted that the bishop's absence from his diocese is like "un gentilhomo pigliasse una moglie ricca, et poi egli solo si godesse la dote et a dormir con sua moglie mettesse un seruitore." Ibid.

127. The legation that Dionisio read in Rome was written in French. On the title page we read *Legatio servi Dei . . . Duci Cosmo Medices et principi Francisco Florentinus, dedicata, tradita et interpretata, nuper etiam a Romanis cognita*. The text in French was written in France; the title page was added later. This is the *Legatio* that contains a reference to Clement Marot.

128. ASV, S.U., Processi, Busta 39. In the discussion between the patriarch of Venice and Spatafora, in the presence of Donzellino, Spatafora "difendeua . . . una

propositione di Santo Agostino nello Enchiridione doue parlando della predestinatione et salute nostra, dice totum Deo dandum est et a noi non lasciaua che altro fussimo che instrumenti di Dio e da lui mossi al bene et allegaua, non sumus sufficentes ex nobis tanquam ex nobis sed sufficientia nostra ex Deo est. Disse il Contarino questi sono i fundamenti di Luterani. Rispose il Spatafora, questi sono i fondamenti della salute de gli homini fatti da Dio scritti da Dottori santi et approbati dalla Santa Chiesa Romana."

129. ASV, S.U., Processi, Busta 22, Contra Dionisium Gallum, document entitled *Pio Quinto pontifici maximo . . . :* "In legatione nostra a me quidem scripta, pronuntiata, publicata Rothomagi, Lutetiae, nunc Romae et in multis antea galliarum partibus et Italiae."

130. Ibid. Dionisio used exclusively feminine forms as synonyms for Truth, coining a feminine form when only the masculine was available. The feminine forms also emphasize the suffering of the pregnant woman and the suffering for Truth. Dionisio wrote of his travails in France at the hands of the heretics for the sake of Truth. See *Senatui populoque Romano . . .* , a letter, in ibid.

131. See Niccoli, "'Prophetie di Musaicho,'" 213.

132. ASV, S.U., Processi, Busta 22, Contra Dionisium Gallum: "Horum autem omnium decenter perficiendorum artem et methodum continet absolutam nostra legatio." Dionisio may have chosen the words of Raymond Lull to describe his technique for reforming the world. Document entitled *Pio quinto pontifici maximo. . . .*

133. Ibid.

134. Ibid., document entitled *Relatio fedelis et declaratio succinctatus multarum rerum cognitione dignarum. . . .*

135. Ibid., document entitled *Clarissimo principi Domino, Domino Cosmo mediceo.* See also *Haec est causa.*

136. Ibid., document entitled *Relatio fidelis. . . .*

137. Ibid.

138. Ibid., document entitled *Pio quinto pontifici maximo. . . .* See also Ps. 50 (51): 7.

139. Ibid., document entitled *Dionisius gallus, coelesti gratia . . .* and dated January 27, 1566. Dionisio concluded the letter with the following words: "Elegit Deus stulta mundi, vt sapientiam sapientum reprobet; et infirma quaeque vt fortia quaeque confundat." Dionisio often admonished the pope "to fulfill his duty" (*officio fungi*).

140. See Doni, *L'Academia peregrina,* c. 86^v. An interesting example in French literature is Rabelais's Pantagruel, who urged Panurge to seek the advice of a fool, since the wise were of little help.

141. Dionisio often wrote of the *indignitas, negligentia, ambitio,* and *avaritia* of many prelates. He never tried to conceal his despair over the lives of the clergy.

142. ASV, S.U., Processi, Busta 22, Contra Dionisium Gallum, document entitled *Haec est causa.*

143. Ibid., document entitled *Clarissimo principi Domino, Domino Cosmo Mediceo*. Before his arrest Dionisio had urged all the Romans to crucify their hearts, again following Saint Paul.

144. Ibid., document entitled *Relatio fidelis.* . . .

145. Ibid., document entitled *Haec est causa*.

146. ASV, Capi del Consiglio dei Dieci, Dispacci degli Ambasciatori, Roma, Busta 24, from Rome, December 21, 1560, Marc'Antonio Da Mula, Ambasciatore, c. 124.

147. ASV, Consiglio dei Dieci, Parti secrete, Registro 7 (1559–63), c. 137.

148. See Venice, Biblioteca del Museo Correr, Opus P.D. 11.759 al 11.786 (11780), n.p., n.d. See Chapter IV, note 124, for the text of this poem.

149. ASV, S.U., Processi, Busta 22, Contra Dionisium Gallum, document entitled *Relatio fidelis* . . . : "essem autem (credo) adhuc in carceribus, nisi Deus ad me misisset quemdam gallum heremitam, qui de me sollicitus, quasi mulier de viro charissimo non quieuit nec desiit iudicibus esse importunus, donec illo presente me liberauerint."

150. Ibid., document entitled *Haec est causa*.

151. Ibid., document entitled *Clarissimo principi Domino, Domino Cosmo Mediceo*. Somewhere along the way Dionisio had acquired a horse, probably a gift from Cosimo; he wrote in the *Relatio fidelis* . . . : "me si placet paucos Dies recipe cum equo meo." The guards may have returned this horse, which they had previously taken. Cosimo I had been generous to Dionisio during our prophet's previous visit to Florence. Dionisio acknowledged this generosity in his *Relatio fidelis* . . . , addressed to Cosimo I: "Quotidie autem Deo gratias agebam et tibi habebam de munere magnifico quo me transeuntem pro eximio animi tui candore donasti Florentiae." The money Dionisio had distributed to the poor was probably part of the duke's munificence.

152. See Rome, Biblioteca Apostolica Vaticana, Barberini latini, 2871, *Sermo Pii V, in Summum Pontificem electi habitus in prima congregatione generali 1566*, cc. 277–279^v. Note especially: "Ubi spiritualia negligi, temporalia plurimi fieri coepere, diffluere item omnia ac dilabi cepisse, Regum ac populorum studia refrixisse, paulatim homines a pristina in hance sedem obseruantia desciuisse, ita ueterem Eccelesie gloriam concidisse." See also ASV, Senato, Dispacci, Ambasciatori, Roma, Filza 1, April 6, 1566, c. 75^v, dispatch of Paolo Tiepolo. Criticizing their lavish lifestyles, the pope reminded the cardinals "che cosi nei costumi nelle conuersationi et nel uiuer loro come nella modestia del uestire et senza pompa non fossero di scandolo a i laici. . . . Ordinò poi, che tutti quelli che hanno beneficii o sono in ordine sacro uadino uestiti da preti secondo gl'ordeni che hanno et che i contra facienti siano messi pregion et non siano liberati senza suo ordine expresso."

153. ASV, Senato, Dispacci, Ambasciatori, Roma, Filza 1, dispatch of October 19, 1566, c. 352^v: "non uolendo, come si dice, che le Preti adoprino Razzi ne lette

di seda ne che mangino in argenti et questi dì ha fattto un gran rebuffo a Cardinal Alessandrino hauendo inteso che le sue camere erano adornase di letti richissimi." The cardinals had not only to use simple cloth rather than satin or silk but to give up their silver plates and eat out of *magioliche*.

154. Ibid.

155. See Rome, Biblioteca Apostolica Vaticana, Barberini latini, 2871, c. 278. Note especially the pope's words about the lives of the clergy in regard to the heretics. "Igitur cum heretici clericorum mores ac licentiam reprehendendo praeclaram se occasionem nactos existiment et sue nequitię excusandę et plebis seducendę neque Catholicis ulla alia re magis insultent, profecto eniti nos oportere, ut huic malo remedium adhibeamus atque ita uitam instituere, ut et Deo placeamus et bonos confirmemus contra hereticos ac peruersos homines confundamus eorumque audaciam retundamus."

156. ASV, Senato, Dispacci, Ambasciatori, Roma, Filza 1, c. 27.

157. ASV, S.U., Processi, Busta 24, fascicolo 3, Contra Franciscum Cagiola Mediolaneum: "Questi Santi Signori grandi hanno intrada et pascono i cani et lasciano morir i pouereti da fame." The date of the questioning was July 13, 1568.

158. ASV, Archivi propri, Roma, Filza 19, c. 246.

159. Ibid., Filza 18, c. 253.

160. Ibid.

161. ASV, Senato, Dispacci, Ambasciatori, Roma, Filza 1, c. 257^v.

162. Ibid., c. 99, April 27, 1566.

163. ASV, Archivi propri, Roma, Filza 19, c. 49. The dispatch of Paolo Tiepolo is dated March 8, 1567.

164. *Reverendi P. Fra Hieronymi Sauonarolę in primam D. Ioannis epistolam et in alia sacrę scripturę verba* . . . (Venetiis [Venice]: Officina Domini Bernardini Stagnini, 1536), 26. Countless works of Savonarola were published in Venice in the Cinquecento. See E. Pastorello, *Edizioni Veneziane del secolo xvi* (1501–99), Biblioteca nazionale di San Marco, Venezia, senza segnatura, c. 477.

165. *Mirabilis Liber qui prophetias . . . demonstrat*, c. B. III^v.

166. ASV, S.U., Processi, Busta 41, fascicolo, Tranquillo de Andreis. See also, in the same *fascicolo, Summa processus uoluminis suspecti contra Dominum Franciscum de Andreis*. . . . The uncle of Francesco de Andreis, Tranquillus de Andreis, was said to be the author of a similar letter addressed to the pope.

167. Ibid., document entitled *Summo Pontifici Pio Quinto*.

168. Ibid. The poverty of the early Church had vanished, according to Dionisio. Note especially: "Illius sanctae ueterum paupertatis in qua Christi Ecclesia fundata et propagata est, ne vestigia quidem apparent." Poverty had brought forth the flowering of the Church, while the acquisition of riches had been responsible for its downfall. Note: "Idem quod imperii Romani et fidei finis fuit, ita quam

florentem ecclesiam innocentia comes paupertatis et diuini cultus non simulata simplicitas reddiderunt, eandem accessio diuitiarum pene euertit. (Nam pro sanctitate atque virtute honor diuitiis . . . haberi ceptus est . . .).''

169. Ibid. "A regibus Christianorum episcopi ferme indocti inexpertique quos ipsi creauerunt in aula more satraparum retinentur ouilibus absque legitimo pastore disiectis et distractis, non quidem ut in commune consulant, quippe sunt ferme rudes et ciuilium et militarium operum, sed ad pompam aulici strepitus. . . . Arbitror utilius futurorum rebus principum si pro iis in consiliis periti conducantur et eorum idoneus quisque Pastor instituto apostolorum delegetur ad suum munus ut oues domino suo congreget quos absentia boni pastoris errantes lupi uarie discerpunt. . . . Demus tum episcopos suffragiis et iudicio Principum doctos et probos elegi, quorsum utile est alienigenas ecclesiis perficere?" Church unity should be the goal of every bishop, as Pasqualitius notes: "ut antea dixi quod dei factus uerus administer emaculatis homini purgamentis studes diligenter et fideliter mundum ad unitatem ecclesiae reuocare."

170. Ibid., Busta 22, Contra Dionisium Gallum, document entitled *Legatio serui Dei*. . . .

171. Savonarola had addressed the same types of concerns. In his sermons in Florence, he urged the priests to return to the simple life and put aside their worldly pleasures. Note, for example, *Prediche del Rev. Padre Fra Hieronymo Sauonarola dell'ordine de predicatori sopra alquanti salmi et sopra Aggeo Profeta* . . . (Venice: Bernardino de Bindoni Milanese, 1544), c. 8ᵛ: "come a figliuoli ui parlero hora piu particularmente, et tutto per uostra correctione, et per uostra salute, o sacerdoti udite le mie parole, o preti, o prelati della chiesa di Christo, lasciate e beneficii e quali giustamente non potete tenere, lasciate le uostre pompe, et uostri conuiti, et desinari, e quali fate tante splendidamente lasciate dico le uostre concubine et li cinedi, che gli è tempo dico da far penitentia, che ne uengono le gran tribulationi, per lequali Dio uuole raconciare la sua chiesa, dite le uostre messe con deuotione, altrimenti se uoi non uorrete intendere quel che uuole Dio." He was also appalled at the wicked practices of the priests. Note especially c. 9ᵛ: "O sacerdoti, bisogna che io ritorni a uoi: io dico de cattiui, con riuerentia sempre de buoni, lasciate dico quel uitio indicibile, lasciate quel maledetto uitio che tanto ha prouocato l'ira di Dio; sopra di uoi che guai guai a uoi. . . . O uoi, che hauete le case uostre piene di uanita et di figure e cose disoneste e libre scelerati et el Morgante et altri uersi contra la fede; portateli a me questi per farne fuoco, et uno sacrificio a Dio." Note also his interesting remarks about the Antichrist and the reformation of the Church. He speaks harshly against those who are *tepidi* in their faith and in their will to reform the Church. See cc. 177–177ᵛ. The shelf mark of the volume I have used is Biblioteca nazionale di San Marco, 17.C.167.

172. ASV, S.U., Processi, Busta 22, document entitled *Legatio serui Dei* . . . , written in Latin (*praefatio*) and French. The fourteenth point in the legation is as follows: "Nom de pape changé par le vouloir de Dieu, en nom plusexcellent de Roy et plusque Roy." In another *Legatio* written in French, probably from Ferrara, though

without date or precise place of writing, the meaning of Dionisio's "king and more than king" is clarified. He added a postscript to his point (number 55) about helping the poor: "Hic Christus facit bonos principes et magistratus, reges et sacerdotes." To become a "king and priest" of Christ, "one must subvent the poor."

173. Ibid. See note 166 above. In a letter to Pope Pius V entitled *Pio quinto pontifici maximo. . . .* Dionisio made the same point: "Reges regantur ab uno summo rege et pastore, non ipso quidem Christo sed ipsius Christi cooperantis seruo et facto vno ouili sub vno ipso pastore, totus mundus confiteatur Christum ipsum verum Deum, verum etiam hominem." ASV, S.U., Processi, Busta 22. Dionisio apparently thought of himself as this shepherd.

174. Venice, Biblioteca del Museo Correr, Fondo Morosini Grimani, MS 127, c. 112ᵛ: "Questo è di tanta eccellenza et perfettione, fratelli, che senza esso mai potreti conoscere Iddio. Però diceua Christo in Giouanni ch'egli ci insegnarà ogni uerità: conciosia che per questo acquistamo per bontà di Dio, et merito del suo figliuolo la uiua fede par la quale siamo santificati e ripieni di bontà, de pace, speranza, ardente carità, continenza, castidade et che piu questo santissimo spirito ci rende pieni d'inestimabile letitia." Note also, from the same sermon, the following: "è scritto che'l spirito de Dio parlerà in noi. Ma dico ui meglio, tutti li figliuoli d'Iddio pel spirito di quello sono gouernati et da lui retti e giudati" (c. 113ᵛ). Dionisio very often expressed this idea in regard to himself.

175. *Trattato della reuelatione della reformatione della Chiesa diuinitus fatte dal Reuerendo et deuotissimo padre F. Hieronimo da Ferrara de l'ordine de frati predicatori* (Venice: M. Bernandino Stagnino, 1536). The shelf mark of this volume, in which other *trattati* of Savonarola are found, is 55.D.227, from the Biblioteca nazionale di San Marco. This rare edition is in its original binding.

176. Ibid., cc. 30–30ᵛ: "La prima diceua: In ogni cosa sia sempre fatta la volonta di Dio. La seconda: Inanzi a ogni cosa vogliamo lo honore di Dio el la sua gloria. La terza: Chiediamo la renouatione de la Chiesa. La quarta: Desideriamo la salute di tutti li fideli. La quinta: Preghiamo specialmente per la salute de le anime nostre. La sesta: La remissione delli peccati del popolo fiorentino liquali hanno impedite le promissioni a loro fatte da Dio. La settima: La remotione et auersione de li fragelli li quali per questo essi hanno meritati. La ottaua: Copia di gratia et doni de lo spirito santo ne la citta di Firenze. La nona: Abondantia di ricchezze et dilatatione di imperio per diffondere queste gratie anchora ne li altri popoli. La decima et ultima: La restitutione di tutto cioe che a loro era stato promesso."

177. ASV, S.U., Processi, Busta 22, Contra Dionisium Gallum. The papal nuncio seized these documents, enclosed in their cover of parchment, and placed them in the hands of the Inquisition.

178. See *Sequitur libellus qui intitulatur Onus mundi id est prophetia de malo futuro ipsi mundo superuenturo,* chap. 20, unpaginated.

179. In an imaginary conversation with the Devil, Savonarola responded to the tempter's derision: "Rispuosi. Io non cerco di piacere a li huomini ma a Dio perche

con dice lo Apostolo: Si adhuc hominibus placerem, Christi seruus non essem. Et non sono di si poco iudicio che io non sappia che ogni huomo che parla di queste cose è reputato pazzo da li sauii di questo mondo. Alliquali io diro insieme con lo Apostolo. Nos stulti propter Christum: vos autem sapientes. . . . Spero di vdire le voci di questi sauii et che diranno. Hi sunt quos habuimus aliquando in derisum et in similitudinem improperii: nos insensati vitam illorum estimabamus insaniam et finem illorum sine honore. Ecce quomodo computati sunt inter filios dei et inter sanctos sors illorum est." See *Trattato della reuelatione della reformatione della Chiesa*, c. 22ᵛ. Savonarola also noted, c. 15ᵛ, when the Devil asked him why "Iddio ha eletto te che vn altro essendo ne la chiesa molti migliori di te? Rispuosi. Padre io vorrei sapere da voi perche Iddio elesse santo Pietro che tre volte nego Christo. . . . Non si puo assegnare di questa ragione nessuna; ma solo la volonta diuina."

Dionisio Gallo often commented that he, a small man considered a fool by the "wise," had been chosen as God's messenger and servant.

180. ASV, S.U., Processi, Busta 22, Contra Dionisium Gallum, document entitled *Relatio fidelis*, with a letter, addressed to Cosimo I, written as Dionisio was departing for Florence, where he arrived on or before March 2. The letter, which follows the title page, is addressed *Illustrissimo et excellentissimo Duci florentino Domino Domino Cosmo mediceo: veritatis amico et fidei catholicae protectori perpetua*. . . .

181. "Iam Victrix Veritas parcit nemini sed omnes iudicat in veritate a summis ad minimos vt omnes ipsa Deo reconciliat his nouissimis omnino diebus."

Chapter III

1. See Joel 2:13.

2. See Wolters, *Storia e politica nei dipinti di Palazzo Ducale*, 19: "Nel 1438 iniziò la costruzione della Porta della Carta, eretta fra l'ala nuova del palazzo e S. Marco come porta di accesso al cortile; nel 1442 essa veniva già definita 'rial' (regale) da Jacopo di Albizotti Guidi. La porta rende evidente anche il rapporto fra i due edifici, illustrato incisivamente seppure *post festum*, dal Sansovino con il rinvio al salmo 84: 'Conciosia che essendosi fondato il Palazzo publico per habitazione del Principe et per render ragione al popolo: parve agli antichi, che la chiesa fosse congiunta al Palazzo essendo cosa convenevole, che la giustizia s'abbracci, secondo il detto del salmo, con la pace e la religione.'"

3. See Marcia B. Hall, *Renovation and Counter-Reformation: Vasari and Duke Cosimo in Santa Maria Novella and Santa Croce, 1565–1577* (Oxford: Oxford University Press, 1979). Note the citation from Vasari about Duke Cosimo I: "The Duke takes pleasure not only in building palaces, cities, fortresses, ports, loggias, squares, gardens, fountains, villas and other grand things useful to his people, but also as befits a Catholic prince in constructing and renewing churches in imitation of King Solomon" (5). Hall points out that Cosimo's aim was to secure the title of grand duke of Tuscany for himself and his heirs. Since he realized that the title would

not be forthcoming from the emperor, he turned his attention to the papacy. While Pius IV was pope, Cosimo "traveled to Rome and remained there for two months, spending much time with the Pope in intimate conversations which ranged over the whole gamut of problems facing Catholic Christendom" (7).

4. ASV, S.U., Processi, Busta 22, document entitled *Illustrissimo et excellentissimo Duci florentino Domino Domino Cosmo Mediceo*, dated March 26, 1566.

5. ASV, S.U., Processi, Busta 22, document entitled *Illustrissimo et excellentissimo principi Domino Domino Francisco Medices . . .* , dated March 7, 1566, from Florence.

6. Ibid.: "Da si placet zonam militarem, ensem atque pugionem quia concupiscit animus meus bellum aliquod optimum gerere."

7. The Museo d'Arte Antica, Brussels, houses a beautiful mid-fifteenth-century representation of the prophet Jeremiah by the Maestro dell'Annunciazione d'Aix. The prophet is clothed in elegant red garments and is reading a book. He is pictured in an *aedicula* that has a shelf of books over the prophet's head. Jeremiah appears to be a bishop rather than a prophet. This representation of the prophet reminds one of Dionisio's desire to have clothing appropriate to his calling. For the illustration of the prophet Jeremiah, see *La Chiesa cattolica nella storia dell'umanità*, 486. I am indebted to Dr. Daniela Ambrosini, of the Biblioteca nazionale di San Marco, who called this painting to my attention.

8. See Niccoli, *Profeti e popolo nell'Italia del Rinascimento*, 151–53.

9. See Alessandro D'Alessandro, "Il Gello di Pierfrancesco Giambullari: Mito e ideologia nel principato di Cosimo I," in *La nascita della Toscana dal Convegno di Studi per il IV centenario della morte di Cosimo I de' Medici* (Florence: Leo S. Olschki Editore, 1980), 73–104. See also Paolo Simoncelli, *La lingua d'Adamo* (Florence: Leo S. Olschki Editore, 1984). For Dionisio's remarks about his ancestry, see ASV, S.U., Processi, Busta 22, document entitled *Haec est causa*: "oriundus sum ex antiqua principum galliarum prosapia quod nomen testatur quod est mihi gallus, gallice de gallois."

10. ASV, S.U., Processi, Busta 22, document entitled *Illustrissimo et excellentissimo Duci florentino Domino Domino Cosmo Mediceo*, March 26, 1566. At the conclusion of the letter, Dionisio wrote *Vincat vertas*.

11. ASV, S.U., Processi, Busta 22, letter addressed to Cardinal Ferdinando Medici, dated March 6, 1566.

12. Dionisio did not complete the work within eight days, as evident from his remark at the conclusion of the work: "Colophonem addidimus, nostra manu scribentes, mensis martii die XXVI anno a natiuitate domini 1566."

13. Ibid.: "Numue videor haec ita scribere mente captus esse? Non me quidem mente captum, sed mente raptum oportet opus ipsum et scribere et annuntiare. Nam qui mente captus est neque proponere neque propositum continuare neque continuatum recte concludere vllo modo potest. At mente raptus quia ipsi inest quaedam specialis Dei gratia haec omnia potest recte perficere."

14. For the Blessed Bridget's rapture, see *Sequitur libellus qui intitulatur Onus mundi id est prophetia de malo futuro ipsi mundo superuenturo*. Note especially chap. 4: "Post hoc audiuit domina Birgitta eadem in raptu a Christo hec verba. Ego percussi eum quia nolebat obedire et postea sanaui eum quia ego sum medicus ille qui sanaui Thobiam et regem Israhel." The shelf mark of this rare volume is Biblioteca nazionale di San Marco, Incunabuli 1088. See also *Revelationes celestes preelecte sponse Christi beate Birgitte vidue de regno Suecie octo libris diuise* . . . (Rome: Officiana Federici Peypus, 1517), 52, where there is an analysis of rapture, or ecstasy: "extasis non aliud sit quam mentis in Deum eleuatio cum omnimodo a exterioribus sensibus abstractione ex magnitudine ipsius elevationis procedens. . . . et primo cum [Beatus Dionysius] dicit et sensus linguae, hoc intelligendum non solum de exteriorum sensuum, sed etiam interiorum abstractione, ita ut comprimendae et claudendae sint omnium sensuum fenestrae ut anima in se recollecta valeat ad altissima Dei mysteria super semetipsam eleuari: hic est enim modus praestantissimus, quo homo ab humanis ad divina rapitur, et eius mens supernaturali gratia adiuta in Deum elevatur."

15. There are eight *raptus* and ten *sermones* in the *Apocalypsis nova*. The manuscript I have consulted is in the Biblioteca nazionale di San Marco, MSS latini, Cl. III, Cod. CXCV (= 2211), and dates from the sixteenth century. On the history of the *Apocalypsis nova* and its authorship, see Vasoli, *Profezia e ragione*, 78–127, and idem, *Filosofia e religione nella cultura del Renascimento*, 211–29; see also A. Morisi, *"Apocalypsis nova": Ricerche sull'origine e la formazione del testo pseudo-Amadeo* (Rome: Istituto Storico Italiano per il Medio Evo, 1970).

16. ASV, S.U., Processi, Busta 22, Contra Dionisium Gallum, document entitled *Illustrissimis et excellentissimis viris dominis dominis Duci Cosmo Medices, principi Francesco, Reverendissimo Cardinali Ferdinando* . . . , dated March 2, 1566. The letter begins: "Liber compositus est, o excellentissima et illustrissima Domus Florentina atque pene omnino Latine scriptus et gallice, sed scripsi interruptus et saepe interturbatus in cubiculo virorum iuuenum. Quare rescribendus erit, ut oculis excellentiae vestrae digne possit offerri."

17. Ibid. Dionisio departed from Rome around February 18, 1566, and apparently made his way directly to Florence.

18. One also cannot be certain if Catherine communicated with Cosimo concerning the learned preacher-prophet who believed himself to be God's servant and messenger. Although the personal relations between Catherine and Cosimo were not cordial, Cosimo wrote commendatory letters to Catherine about Pietro Carnesecchi on the latter's departure for France in 1547. See Paolo Simoncelli, "Inquisizione romana e riforma in Italia," *Rivista Storica Italiana*, Anno C, fasc. 1 (1988): 53–60, especially n. 162. Catherine provided a position at court for Carnesecchi. His intimacy with Catherine and his friendship with François Olivier, grand chancellor of France, also provided his patron, Cosimo, important political information. Yet Carnesecchi declared in his last interrogation by the Holy Office that his sojourn in France had been "uno interregno del diavolo." See Antonio Rotondò's excellent article on Carnesecchi, with extensive bibliography,

in *Dizionario biografico degli italiani* (Rome: Istituto della Enciclopedia Italiana, 1984), xx:466–76.

19. For a succinct account of the life of Cosimo I, see the article by E. Fasano Guarini, "Cosimo I de' Medici," in *Dizionario biografico degli Italiani* (Rome: Istituto della Enciclopedia Italiana, 1984), xxx:30–48; note especially 44–45. See also *Cosimo I de' Medici: Lettere*, ed. Giorgio Spini (Florence: Vallecchi, 1940); *Diario fiorentino di Agostino Lapini: Dal 252 al 1596, ora per la prima volta pubblicato da Giuseppe Odoardo Corrazzini* (Florence, 1900); and *Petri Angelii Bargei Laudatio ad funebrem concionem quae Pisis habita est in Exequiis Cosmi Medicis Magni Hetruriae Ducis* (Florence: Iuntas, 1563).

20. ASV, S.U., Processi, Busta 22, Contra Dionisium Gallum, letter addressed *Illustrissimo et excellentissimo principi Domino Domino Francisco Medices* . . . , dated March 7, 1566.

21. Ibid.: "Omne quod excellens opus et insigne futurum est difficules aditus habet, incrementaque tarda tamquam aurum in fornace probat Deus quos elegit numquam sua daeerunt inclitae virtuti praemia." In a letter to Cardinal Alessandrino dated August 24, 1566, Francesco de' Medici wrote to the cardinal as a young prince who was assuming leadership and who wanted to serve the pope well. Note the following: "Io desidero tanto di seruire in quel che posso a Sua Beatitudine et compiacere vostra Signoria Illustrissima che uisto quanto ella mi scrive di quel Lione di Coluccio da Cingoli mi deliberai subito che fusse consegnato prigione a ministri di Sua Santità. Ma con tutta l'instantia che me n'ha fatta a ogn' hora Monsignor Nuntio Brisegno, non ho possuto darne la commissione prima che io hauessi risposta dal Vicario della Pieve della Marco, o da altro offitiale di Sua Beatitudine gli uerrà domandato, la dia loro su'l confino concertando con essi del tempo et del luogo, accio paghi quel castigo che merita la sua sceleratezza." See Rome, Biblioteca Apostolica Vaticana, Barberini latini, 3614, cc. 22–23, letter of Francesco de' Medici, *all'Illustrissimo et Reverendissimo mio Colendissimo Monsignore Cardinale Alessandrino, a Roma, 24 d'agosto 1566*.

22. See *Cosimo I de' Medici: Lettere*, 174–78.

23. Ibid., 176: "Il fatto che ci dispiace è questo che tu acquisti nome appresso del universale d'esser persona che sei piu atta a esser governato che da governare." Cosimo continued to advise his son that only by good actions in regard to all "mostrerai iuditio et che sei atto a governar altri, et non a essere governato."

24. See Hubert Jedin, "La politica conciliare di Cosimo I," *Rivista Storica Italiana* 62 (1950): 345–74. Note especially Cosimo's attempts in 1563, through one of his petitioners, Giovanni Battista Strozzi, to secure the services of the patriarch of Jerusalem, Antonio Elio, and the archbishop of Ragusa, Ludovico Beccadelli (362).

25. Ibid., 363.

26. One must note, however, that until 1566 Cosimo's support of Carnesecchi had been constant. Cosimo's pressure on Pius IV during a visit to Rome in 1561 was responsible for a full absolution in the proceedings against Carnesecchi. After Carnesecchi's final condemnation in Rome, Cosimo continued to pressure Pius V,

who for ten days delayed the execution of the sentence. See Rotondò, "Pietro Carnesecchi," in *Dizionario biografico degli italiani*, xx:472–74.

27. ASV, Capi del Consiglio dei Dieci, Dispacci degli Ambasciatori, Roma, Busta 25, fascicolo 5. Note Paolo Tiepolo's remarks about the pope's compliments to Cosimo I: "ma che dice bene che haueua da lodarsi assai de'l Duca di Fiorenza co'l qual non haueua che far quanto al temporal che le hauesse dato il Carnesecchi suo amico intrinsico et che quel serenissimo Dominio ancora daua homini tali a questa inquisition quando li pareua et si raccordaua di dui, et che oltra quello che mi haueua nominato, ne erano altri molti in quel stato, che sariano stati necessarii haverli qui, et tra questi un Giulio Tressino Vicentino." The letter is dated July 6, 1566. The pope was so moved by Cosimo's capitulation that "in fine narrò quanto a caso hebbe Sua Santità la noua della retention del Carnesecchi, perche hauuta si messe in un devotissimo pianto, ringratiò deuotamente Dio, e prorupe in molte parole piene della satisfattion che faueua del Duca di Fiorenza, dicendo che questo era Principe da stimar, et da fauorir, et che per lui, ogni uolta che bisognasse, metteua sempre quanto hauesse." Ibid.

28. Giovanni Capoville, "Giorgio Vasari e gli edifici dell'ordine militare di Santo Stefano in Pisa (1562–1571)," *Studi Storici* 17, fasc. II (1908): 305–79. "L'idea di dare vita ad un Ordine Militare che, accentrando le energie più vigorose del tempo, le facesse convergere a scopi più positivi di quelli ai quali avevano mirato o continuavano ancora a mirare, con forze sempre minori le consimili istituzioni medievali, sorse e si andò maturando nella mente di Cosimo I con processo lento e graduale. Il nuovo Ordine dovendo essere . . . un sostegno tale della signoria medicea che alle audaci scorrerie dei Turchi i quali infestavano le coste tirreniche, avesse da opporre una flotta sempre pronta, se non numerosa, certo equipaggiata di uomini valorosi, armati di stocco e di croce, aveva bisogno anzitutto di una sede sulla marina, dalle quale, come da base d'operazione, potesse esplicare con maggiore prontezza la sua attività difensiva e soprattutto offensiva" (305). "La piazza delle Sette Vie di Pisa, divenuta sede dell'Ordine, si chiamò appunto per effetto di ciò, la piazza dei Cavalieri; però giova notare sin d'ora che ad essa più che il nome è legata indissolubilmente l'opera loro" (306–7). "Il palazzo degli Anziani della Repubblica Pisana, sede dell'Ordine di Santo Stefano per tre secoli, e ora della R. Scuola Normale Superiore" (307).

29. ASV, Collegio, Relazioni, Ambasciatori, Firenze, Busta 18, 1566, unpaginated. The Venetian ambassador Lorenzo Priuli interpreted Cosimo's actions as follows: "che quella prudenza, quella costanza, et quella continenza, che ha usata il Duca al tempo della Duchessa sua moglie tutto dipendeua dal buon consiglio et buona volontà di lei concludendosi dalla maggior parte, che la buona fortuna prima, et da poi il consiglio della Duchessa habbia hauuto maggior parte nella grandezza del Duca, che la prudenza d'esso medessimo uedendosi chiaramente che doppo la morte di lei le cose di sua eccellenza non sono passate con quella dignità ne con quella sodisfatione de sudditi." See also *Orazione de M. Gio. Battista Adriani fatta in Latino all'esseqvie del sereniss. Cosimo de' Medici Gran Duca di Toscana* (Florence: Giunti,

1574), c. E ii^v. Note also *Discorso sopra l'autorità del Pape fatto in tempo* [an. 1569] *che Papa Pio V insigni con titolo di Granduca di Toscane Cosimo I de' Medici*, Rome, Biblioteca Apostolica Vaticana, Urbinates latini, 860, cc. 209–16.

30. This is the work with the apocalyptic title *Liber, quem Nullus aut in coelo aut in terra aut subtus terram, antea poterat aperire ne quidem respicere.*

31. ASV, S.U., Processi, Busta 22, Contra Dionisium Gallum, letter appended to the *Liber apertus*, addressed *Illustrissimis ac excellentissimis principibus Dominis Dominis Duci Cosmo Medices, principi Francisco et Reverendissimo Cardinali Ferdinando florentino*: "Diuus Paulus . . . praeter fidem atque veritatem quam ludaeis et gentibus magnis vitae periculis varia passus tormentorum genera constanter praedicabat; Diuum Johannem euangelistam tacebo. Dauidem non memorabo; silentio praeteribo ipsos prophetas qui siue reuelationum siue aliarum gratiarum dona tempore oportuno dixerunt atque scripserunt."

32. Ibid.

33. Ibid. He wrote: "Sed agnita veritas statim liberauit et innocentia ruborem ipsis infudit iudicibus."

34. On the previous disturbances in Florence, see Guarini, "Cosimo I de' Medici," 30–48; note especially 32: "Tuttavia l'esistenza di forti nuclei di fuorusciti fiorentini a Roma, Venezia, Bologna ed altrove; la ripresa fin dalla primavera del 1536 della guerra tra Francia e Spagna e le minacce che tornavano quindi a gravare sulla stabilità dell'area di influenza spagnola in Italia; l'ostilità del pontefice Paolo III Farnese verso i Medici, la sua aspirazione a creare uno Stato farnesiano nell'Italia centrale e la politica di neutralità attiva tra le grandi potenze de lui perseguita aggravavano la pericolosità del momento. In questo quadro la successione fu al centro di un conflitto sotterraneo ma aspro. Da un lato il gruppo dei consiglieri del duca defunto, guidati dal 'forestiero' cardinale Innocenzo Cibo, parente dei Medici ed uomo di fiducia di Carlo V, mirava all'elezione di Giulio, figlio illegittimo treenne di Alessandro, ed alla concessione, della tutela al cardinale stesso: la direzione della vita politica fiorentina sarebbe così passata nelle mani di uomini di corte ed altri funzionari estranei al contesto cittadino, fautori di una linea di stretta osservanza imperiale e di rigido accentramento." Note also the remarks of the Venetian ambassador Lorenzo Priuli, on his return from Florence to Venice in 1566: "et come si legge ampiamente nell'Istorie in maniera che quel seme di Prencipato, che quel Vecchio e famoso Cosmo de Medici getto uia molti anni aggiutato da varii uenti et horende tempeste in costui del medissmo nome ha finalemente prodota et fondata la pianta." ASV, Collegio, Relazioni, Ambasciatori, Firenze, Busta 18, relazione di Lorenzo Priuli, 1566.

35. Dionisio was not the first to praise Cosimo I as an ideal prince with a prophetic mission. In 1551 Guillaume Postel had dedicated to Cosimo I his *De Etruriae regionis . . . originibus . . .* , in which he noted that no one more than Cosimo I could return Tuscany to its ancient splendor in preparation for the coming restitution of all things. See Guillaume Postel, *De Etruriae regionis . . . originibus . . .* , ed.

Giovanni Cipriani (Rome: Consiglio Nazionale delle Ricerche, 1986), 23. Cipriani discovered an unknown letter of Postel written to Cosimo in 1553. Note the laudatory tone: "Sed verum in hoc te serio principem agere certo constat, quod ut in republica repurgato Augiae stabulo avitos ordines sensim collapsos sensim instaures ab animorum reformatione ducis exordium" (21). The letter was addressed *Insigni Pietate et Aequitate Viro Cosmo Medici Florentiae et Thusciae Duci Principi Optimo*. See also Cesare Vasoli, "Lucio Paolo Rosello e un'immagine cinquecentesca del principe," *Nuova Rivista Storica* 65 (1981): 552–71. Vasoli discusses Rosello's *Il ritratto del vero governo del principe* and also mentions (p. 561) Postel's relationship with the duke. On Cosimo's relationship with the letterati, see Claudia di Filippo Bareggi, "In nota alla politica culturale di Cosimo I: L'Accademia Fiorentina," *Quaderni Storici* 7 (1973): 527–74.

36. See, for example, ASV, Consiglio dei Dieci, Parti secrete, Registro 8, cc. 129ᵛ–130, October 22, 1568, for the Venetian response to the papal nuncio, who had brought still another request for the formation of a league of princes: "del conseglio poi che sua Santita dimanda circa il pensiero ch'ella haurebbe di unir li Principi che hanno stati in Italia in lega defensiua contra heretici, conoscemo la fede che l'ha in noi et l'amor che porta alla Signoria Nostra delche con ogni affetto del cor nostro la ringratiamo, et per non mancar de dirli, con ogni syncerita et candor di animo il parer nostro se ben giudicamo che la prudentia di sua beauitudine non habbi tal bisogno, pur poi che ella cosi ne ricerca gli diremo con quella riuerentia che si conuiene a deuotissimi figlioli come noi gli siamo, che se ben intendemo che sono dei esserciti d'heretici in arme, l'uno nella Francia et l'altro nella Fiandra, et che hanno qualche aiuti dalla Germania, uedemo all'incontro le forze de doi potentissimi Re Christianissimo et Catholico li quali si po sperar che con l'aiuto del Signor Dio, la causa del qual defendeno habbiano a restar superiori massimamente che hanno a far con gente de diuerse sette colligati insieme, hanno li fini diuersi, come sono anco diuerse l'opinioni: onde in poco spacio di tempo conuengono disoluersi, secondo che l'esperientia delli tempi passati ha fatto chiaramente conoscer."

37. ASV, Capi del Consiglio dei Dieci, Dispacci degli Ambasciatori, Roma, Busta 25, fascicolo 68, dated November 17, 1568: "tutta uia uien detto che non sara dichiarito in essa questo nome di heretici, ma in luogo di quello sara detto contra ciascuno che turbasse la quiete di Italia et li stati delli principi confederati hauendo quale rispetto a esprimer questo nome di heretici, forsi per non dar tanta reputatione a quella sorte di homeni."

38. Ibid.: "il conte Brocardo . . . mi disse che se ben si trattaua questa lega et che era sollicitata da Cardinal Farnese et da altri pero si haueua dubio solamente della serenita vostra, che non assentisse et il Cardinal Gambara il qual credeua che sua Santita trattasse questo negotio co'l mio mezo mi disse in discorso che il Duca di Fiorenza era quello che metteua pronti questa cosa a sua Santita et che è aiutato da questi Spagnoli." For the substance of the Venetian arguments, see note 36 above. In addition, they argued that "il agionar di lega mostraria un timor grande,

che non seruirebbe ad altro che a spauentar li fedeli et accrescer l'audacia all'Infideli, che li farebbe entrar in speranza di poter far quello, che hora non giudicano essergli possibile."

39. The Blessed Bridget prophesied about a council: "Veniet magnifici fratres ad concilium et predicabunt unionem et nata est ab eis trinitas nauicule. . . . Facto aut concilio Petrus liberatus est et predicabitur aduersus antichristum et facta est remissio contra infideles." Venice, Biblioteca nazionale di San Marco, MSS latini, Cl. III, Cod. CCXXIX (= 2791).

40. See the letter *Illustrissimis ac excellentissimis principibus Dominis Dominis Duci Cosmo Medices, principi Francisco et Reverendissimo Cardinali Ferdinando florentino* . . . , which serves as a *praefatio* to his *Liber apertus*: "Sed et horum omnium perficiendorum ad poenam vel flammarum, veram artem trado et methodum absolutam quam ipsa nostra continet coelica *Legatio*." ASV, S.U., Processi, Busta 22.

41. There were many discussions in Cosimo's *accademia* about the origin of language, especially the ancient origin of the Tuscan language. Gelli and Giambullari were leaders in the arguments for the antiquity of Tuscan. See Simoncelli, *La lingua d'Adamo*.

42. See Ezek. 2:8–9 and 3:1–3. Note the language of the Vulgate, 3:1–3: "Et dixit ad me: Fili hominis quodcumque inveneris comede: comede volumen istud, et vadens loquere ad filios Israel. Et aperui os meum, et cibavit me volumine illo: et dixi ad me. Fili hominis venter tuus comedet, et viscera tua complebuntur volumine isto, quod ego do tibi. Et comedi illud: et factum est in ore meo sicut mel dulce." See also Apoc. 10:9–10. Dionisio was obviously well versed in Scripture.

43. Note ASV, Senato, Deliberazioni, Secreti, Registro 74, c. 76, entry of July 30, 1566: "Al Proveditor dell'armata. Havemo poco fa riceuute le uostre di hieri, et da quelle inteso, il progresso dell' armata Turchesca, onde laudandoui della diligentia, che usate in tenerci ben auisati, vi commettemo co'l Senato che uenendo detto armata più inanzi debbiate leuarui di doue che vi ritrouarete et uenir con tutto l'armata nostra uerso questa citta et porto di Malomocco dandone prima auiso del uostro uenire per una delle uostre galee o fregate con ogni possible diligentia." The Venetians were not only concerned with the Turkish threat but also with piracy. Note, for example, ibid., c. 67, entry of June 1, 1566: "Al Proveditor dell'armata. Havemo dalle uostre de 27 del mese passato inteso quanto ci scriuete cosi circa l'armata Turchesca, come circa le fuste de corsari, che si preparauano per venir in colfo a depredar quelli che uanno alla fiera de Lanzano."

44. ASV, S.U., Processi, Busta 22, Contra Dionisium Gallum, document entitled *Haec est causa*: "Ipsum ducem cum filio principe, saepe numero monens, rogans interpellans vt in nomine et virtute Christi suum adderent ad clerum reformandum ad haereses extirpandas ad pauperes consolandos. Polliciti sunt seseque iuncturos esse cum aliis principibus."

45. Ibid.: "Declarabam autem ipsis principibus florentinis Christum per me clamare et ecclesiam vehementer conqueri de papa clerum non reformante, non

extirpante haereses nec pauperes consolante nec interpellato, principes conuocante, vt haec omnia fierent." The centrality of poverty in Dionisio's teachings reflects not only Franciscan piety but also the emphasis of the Society of Jesus.

46. Ibid.: "Ergo pauperibus nos compatiamur. Multa quidem bona illis debentur, quae nostri maiores illis erogarunt, et quae Deus ipse his adiudicauit. At haec clerus tenet neque vult reddere adversus pauperes; citius irascitur. Quidam ex clero ex suis foribus expellunt pauperes, eos verberantes. Nemo defendit; nemo in hac causa se praebet patronum."

47. Ibid.: "Hoc est enim Tempus quo Christus vos facit reges atque sacerdotes. Ergo pauperibus suum ius reddite de tertia parte bonorum ecclesiae."

48. Ibid.: "An si clerus nolit huic rei consentire, possimus cogere? O almi principes, vos quidem potestis propter rationem modo supradictam postquam omnipotentis Dei nuntium audiuistis qui vos facit certiores his vltimis omnino diebus hanc Deum dare vobis authoritatem et potestatem ius reddendi pauperibus."

49. Ibid. Juan Luis Vives had made this point abundantly clear in his *Il modo del sovvenire a poveri*. Note especially bk. 1, cc. 27^v–28: "Hora se cotali cose nella uecchiezza si serbano, o per le infermità che uuol dire la tanta pompa, et nel uestire, et ne cibi: che, la tanta moltitudine de seruitori, et de clienti per la confidanza delle ricchezze tue, cosi otiosa, et trascurata: che, i tanti cani, i tanti uccelli, le tante simie, i tanti giuochi, i tanti buffoni se per nome di un ricco dimanda ad alcuno cosa alcuna; . . . ascolti quello che dice Solomone. Qualunque dà per Dio al pouero, colui non mai hauera bisogno. Et qualunque dispreggia i preghi dei dimandante, colui suo mal grado sostenterà disaggio." The translator, Gioan Domenico Tharisia da Capo d'Istria, dedicated Vives's work to Pietro Carnesecchi, who was praised as one who gave to the poor in secret.

50. ASV, S.U., Processi, Busta 22, Contra Dionisium Gallum, document entitled *Haec est causa*.

51. Ibid. Note also: "O quanta paupertas. Dicunt se esse diuites; at coram Deo pauperrimi sunt atque miserrimi. . . . O speciosa magnificentia. O paupertas extrema. O summa miseria. O desolatio atque confusio plane intolerabilis, ita excellere et agere magnifice ex bonis pauperum Christi membrorum, nudorum horridorum, languentium prae dolore et aerumna mori desiderantium."

52. Ibid.: "Quid dicitis, o almi principes, electi populi atque nationes? Papa debet sine mora clerum reformare; haereses extirpare; pauperes consolari. Si non potest, debet nos conuocare et nostrum implorare auxilium. Quid faciam ego? . . . Si papa non vult, si cardinales ipsi impediunt? Si francorum Rex, senatus regius, et heretici omnes dissuadent . . . ne congregemini? Hic est nodus. . . . Haec est difficulta totius presentis negotii."

53. Ibid.: "Nolumus igitur in enarrandis cleri vitiis, auaritia, ambitione, negligentia, iniquitate, ignorantia, indignitate diutius immorari. Haec enim omnia manifesta sunt et apertissima. Vos nouistis Sathanas ipse, secta eius, pseudoprophetae

et haeretici, veritatis hostes acerrimi, in suam ipsorum confusionem atque perniciem, cleri peccata reuelauerunt, publicauerunt, diuulgauerunt omnia."

54. Isa. 16:7. Dionisio demonstrated a deep knowledge of the Old Testament prophets. He was probably aware of the dictum of Savonarola: "Sesta regola spesso considerar la uita de i santi padri nostri cosi del uecchio come del nuouo testamento, et pensare che conciosia cosa che fussino huomini grandi et degni iquali non era il mondo degno d'hauerli, et che facessino cose grandi et stupende, nientedimeno fuggiuano gli honori, et sprezzauano se medesimi, et cercauano di star sotto la obedientia d'altri et uolentieri patiuano ingiurie et persecutione et martyrio per amore di Christo Jesu." See *Trattato della Hvmilita*, in *Molti devotissimi trattati del Reverendo Padre Frate Hieronimo Sauonarola da Ferrara*, c. 8ᵛ. The shelf mark of the volume I used is Biblioteca nazionale di San Marco, 193.C.233.

55. ASV, S.U., Processi, Busta 22, Contra Dionisium Gallum, document entitled *Haec est causa:* "Id nisi feceritis breui sentietis vera esse verba prophetae Dauidis: Deposuit potentes de sede, et exaltauit humiles; esurientes impleuit bonis, et diuites dimisit inanes." See Luke 1:48–53; also Ps. 32:10.

56. ASV, S.U., Processi, Busta 22, Contra Dionisium Gallum, document entitled *Haec est causa.*

57. Ibid. "Quis unquam vidit dissolutum scholasticum, vt corrigeretur aequum, et optimum, praeceptorem quaerere aut desiderare?"

58. Ibid.: "O quanta paupertas. Dicunt se esse diuites. At coram Deo pauperrimi sunt atque miserrimi. Vidi Romae ingressum quorumdam Cardinalium in pallatium apostolicum ad papam ipsum. O perpulchra magnificentia (dicebant quidam) profecto; mirabar Cardinalem ingredi tanto apparatu tali pompa tali humana gloria, quasi regem aut imperatorem. O speciosa magnificentia. O paupertas extrema. O summa miseria. O desolatio atque confusio plane intolerabilis, ita excellere et agere magnifice ex bonis pauperum, Christi membrorum, nudorum, horridorum languentium prae dolore et aerumna, mori desiderantium. Quid tu tum dicebas cum tantam ipse videres magnificentiam? Quid tum dicebam (O principes et populi). Intensissima voce clamabam. Vociferabar quasi tortor aliquis vniuersa membra mihi confregisset. Hanc persequens confusionem in curiam vsque memorali pallatii et vsque ad ianuas templi beati Petri. Siccine Christus venit in mundum? Siccine Christus Hierusalem ingressus est? Siccine Christus vixit? Aut docuit viuendum: Siccine Petrus pastor ecclesiae Romam ingressus est? Siccine vixerunt apostoli? Aut patres sancti."

59. Ibid. "Videtur tamen Deus in Galliis cum Sathana foedus iniisse nam pari libertate viuit illic haereticus atque catholicus; cum errore veritas illic confunditur; fides et impietas pari lege feruntur."

60. Ibid. Note Dionisio's language: "Sto autem ego, pro Deo cuius nuntius sum et cuius nunc causam ago. . . . Iam igitur has difficultates nos aggrediamur quas proposuimus, Sathanae turres ingentes, valla et propugnacula nunc funditus euertamus omnia."

61. Ibid. Notice also his use of metaphor in the following passage: "Triumphemus omnes. Sed omnes in armis fortes triumphemus. Antichristus enim (id scio) natus est ne nos exarmemus; fide nos armemus omnes vniti. Sint et arma nostra fulgens iustitia, ignea charitas. Haec vera sunt arma quae ferre debemus.... Ne reformidemus antichristum istum; ense veritatis hunc interficiam scindente gladio ex vtraque parte."

62. In a letter addressed to Prince Francisco Medici, son of Cosimo I, and written from Florence on March 7, 1566, Dionisio, after requesting new clothing from the prince, asked for a "zonam militarem, ensem atque pugionem. Quia concupiscit animus meus bellum aliquod optimum gerere; dato et reliqua quae Christi militem decent et nuntium, tres annos integros iam praeliantem atque dimicantem, pro sacrosancta fide catholica." Ignatius Loyola also made very clear that the appropriate role of a priest was to be a soldier of Christ, and that of the Church, a holy army: "Quindi è, che il nostro Ministero è uno spirito ancor di fatica: il Sacerdotio è una dignità laboriosa: la Chiesa, di cui siamo Ministri, è una vigna, un campo, una messe, una santa milizia." *Esercizj spirituali di S. Ignazio Lojola*, 187. Note especially: "L'armi della nostra milizia sono, dice San Paulo, armi spirituali, destinate a combattere l'orgoglio, l'avarizia, la voluntà, e ogni alterezza, che si solleva contro la scienza di Dio; la fede è il nostro scudo; lo zelo della salute delle anime la nostra spada; ecco quali armi ci mette in mano la chiesa associandoci al Sacerdozio" (102).

63. ASV, S.U., Processi, Busta 22, Contra Dionisium Gallum, document entitled *Haec est causa*. Note Dionisio's strong words: "Sed [Satanas] et inde concludit omnes vna congregatos principes christianos, iure non posse papam reformare quantumcumque peccet, si peccare libet sed ne quidem vnum Cardinalium. Hinc inferens clerum ipsum numquam iri reformatum. Quamobrem asserit Sathanas se causam victurum; Deum autem sua casurum; iura Christi fore abolita; haereses magis atque magis pululaturas."

64. Ibid.

65. Apoc. 21:2–3.

66. In advising the princes of their need for action, he wrote: "Omnes sint vobis curae pauperes. Id nisi feceretis, breui sentietis vera esse verba prophetae Dauidis: Deposuit potentes de sede et exaltauit humiles esurientes impleuit bonis et diuites diuisit inanes." ASV, S.U., Processi, Busta 22, Contra Dionisium Gallum, document entitled *Haec est causa*.

67. Ibid., document entitled *Illustrissimis et excellentissimis viris Dominis Dominis Cosmo Medices, principi Francisco et Reverendissimo Cardinali Ferdinando, pro caeteris principibus et gentibus vniuersis*.... This letter, written on March 19, 1566, seems to serve almost as a conclusion to Dionisio's *Liber, quem Nullus*, which he had presented to the duke and his sons.

68. Ibid.

69. Dionisio indicated that, when Cosimo heard his plan, he greatly approved.

He wrote: "Et retourne vers monseigneur le Duc de Florence lequel entendant tout mon faict, l'approuua grandement, et fut fort rejouy"; document entitled *Proces clos de la cause de Dieu pour les droictz de Jesuchrist, en son egglise militante* . . . and written "a tous les princes et seigneurs, iuges et magistrats, peuples et nations." Brisegno was appointed papal nuncio to Florence on February 8, 1565. See Florence, Archivio di Stato, Diplomatico, Normale 1565, Archivio mediceo, *Credenziale de Papa Pio IV a Cosimo de' Medici Duca di Firenze uel in favore de Bernadino Brisegno, che veniua presso il med. Duca come Nunzio Apostolico*, dated February 8, 1565, Rome, Saint Peter's. Note especially: "Dilecte fili nobilis vir salutem et apostolicam benedictionem. Dilectum hunc filium Bernardinum Brisenium notarium nostrum idoneum duximus quem mitteremus istuc nostri, et Apostolicae sedis Nuncii munere functurum: iis enim uirtutibus eoque rerum usu cum praeditum nouimus ut speremus laudabiliter ipsum hoc officio esse functurum."

The first papal nuncio sent to Tuscany in 1560 (July) was Giovanni Campeggi; on January 10, 1561, Giorgio Cornaro, bishop of Treviso, was appointed nuncio. There were numerous reasons for sending the first nuncio to Florence. "Vedremo, allora come dall'intesa tra Cosimo e Pio IV si venne alle trattative per l'invio del primo Nunzio Apostolico a Firenze. Pio IV infatti voleva attuare la politica delle nunziature in vista del Concilio de Trento e della riforma della Chiesa; Cosimo da canto suo vagheggiava l'alleanza con Papto per una egemonia toscana in Itallia. . . . Si sono trovate le cause, invece, nel campo puramente politica e cioè nella politica delle nunziature di Pio IV, intenta a riallacciare relazioni diplomatiche interrotte e ad aprirne nuove allo scopo di creare un ambiente favorevole alla riapertura del Concilio; e nella politica di Cosimo de'Medici che intendeva raggiungere una stabile intesa politica col papato. . . . Lo Stato Fiorentino dal canto suo aveva le carte in regola per chiedere e ricevere una nunziatura; nobiltà del sovrano, ampio territorio, stabilità politica interna, autonomia dello stato; e Pio IV concedendola, non solo volle riconoscere queste prerogative, ma elevare a livello europeo lo Stato Toscano." See Lorenzo Baldisseri, *La nunziatura in Toscana* (Vatican City: Archivio Vaticano, 1977), 22 and 34. Note also, p. 66, the powers of the nuncio: "Il Nunzio secondo la bolla ha i potere di istruire e dirimere qualsiasi causa spirituale profana e mista pertinente al foro ecclesiastico."

70. ASV, S.U., Processi, Busta 22 Contra Dionisium Gallum, document entitled *Haec est causa*: "Declararim papam reum esse occupatae sedis apostolicae donec ipsos christianos principes conuocaret. Quibus intellectis, nuntius ipse papae in furorem pene conuersus est."

71. Ibid.: "Duce florentino . . . absente vere mandatum misit nuntius papae, vt sine mora Florentiam egrederer. Ego Dei nuntius ad papae me contuli nuntium vt diceret cur me vellet egredi Florentiam et si absente duce hanc haberet potestatem."

72. Ibid. Note especially: "Conflictum consyderate nuntii Dei et nuntii papae. Iura Christi tuetur et defendit Dei nuntius; nuntius Papae iura papalia, Nuntius Dei palam agit et aperte coram principibus. Nuntius papae clam agit et ex insidiis. Sit Dux, sit princeps, sint testes omnes florentini."

73. Ibid. Note the interesting exchange: "'Cur ego discedam?' aio. Ait: 'Tu publice declarasti papam occupatorem sedis apostolicae.' 'Non ego, sed Christus.' 'Non Christus,' ait, 'sed insania tua.' 'Ego sum Dei nuntius; meum est eius reuelata proferre iudicia.' 'Non es Dei nuntius,' ait, 'sed insanis.' 'Tu es papae nuntius et nimis sapis; si non sum Dei nuntius, quare Romae papam interpellaui.'" Dionisio used the dialogue form, whether the dialogue itself was real or imaginary, for his own advantage. Dionisio's challenge to the nuncio about the superiority of his own appointment, which was made by God, is an interesting contrast to a letter written by Cornelius de Mussis, bishop of Bitonto, to Pope Pius V in which the bishop advises the pope on the duties of the nuncios and on their qualifications. See Rome, Biblioteca Apostolica Vaticana, Borghese latini, 300, cc. 387^v–388. The bishop relates the nuncios to "angels of God." Note especially: "Il primo più importante è per conservare col instrumento di questi suoi Nuntii come d'Angioli di Dio nella fede cattolica et nella diuotione et obedienza di questa Santa sede essi Prencipi christiani et in consequenza anco gli loro regni, stati et popoli" (c. 387). Of their essential qualifications he writes: "ma saria bisogno che il grand'Idio ci rimandasse un'altra uolta gli apostoli di Christo o almeno che vostra Santità ci mandasse delli più diletti et più uenerandi huomini che habbi il secolo nostro gli quali con la dottrina, uita, et essempio loro rappresentessero l'officio di ueri Angioli di Dio et di ueri Nontii di questa Santa sede et l'imaginare della bontà et santità di Lei, et non solo conseruassero quella poca fede, prouigione et obedienza che ci restano, ma anco ricuperassero le già perse" (cc. 387^v–388).

74. After a long series of questions to the nuncio about why he would suffer all these torments if not for his obligation as Christ's messenger, he asks finally: "Quare non eligo in aliqua ciuitate iuuenes honorates docere?" The papal nuncio replies that "se haec omnia non curare." Dionisio's reported conversation with the nuncio is one of the most interesting parts of the *Haec est causa*. It surely reveals that Dionisio cared nothing for diplomacy, since he seemed unaware of the problems his remarks might cause for Cosimo, his patron, not to mention himself. Dionisio's effective use of the dialogue form adds vivacity and realism to his writings. These dialogues, either real or imaginary, set out exchanges with the pope, the papal nuncio, and the Devil.

75. Massimo Firpo and Paolo Simoncelli, "I processi inquisitoriali contro Savonarola (1558) e Carnesecchi (1566–1567): Una proposta di interpretazione," *Rivista di Storia e Letteratura Religiosa* 18 (1982): 202: "il Sant'Ufficio si rivelava ben consapevole delle laceranti fratture che l'istituzione ecclesiastica aveva sofferto negli ultimi decenni. Di qui la necessità di ripercorrere quel passato e di tracciarne un filo rosso, quello che all'insegna dell''eresia,' intesa sia come deviazione dottrinale che come disobbedienza all'autorità pontifica, poteva unire Girolamo Savonarola a Giovanni Morone, a Pietro Carnesecchi e a tanti altri protagonisti della 'dissidenza interna,' contro cui ora gli inquisitori facevano i conti, reputandoli molto più pericolosi . . . di ogni 'contagio esterno,' con cui si può dire che fin dall'inizio la frattura era stata definitivamente consumata: *extra ecclesiam*."

76. Ibid., 238. Note the praise of Carnesecchi in the preface of the Italian translation of Vives, *Il modo del sovvenire a poveri*, c. 2^v: "Ma perchio che sono certissimo, che ne altra gloria, ne altro frutto di esse qui giù cercate che di piacere a Giesu Christo, il cui amor solo et non altro respetto alcuno ui moue et spinge ad operarle."

77. Ibid., c. 241.

78. Pope Giulius III published the bull on March 18, 1551. See Pio Paschini, *Venezia e l'Inquisizione romana da Giulio III a Pio IV* (Padua: Editrice Antenore, 1959), 70–71.

79. For Dionisio's bold comparison of himself with the papal nuncio, see note 73 above. Dionisio's fiery pronouncements remind one of Savonarola.

80. See Antonio Panella, "L'introduzione a Firenze dell'Indice di Paolo IV," *Rivista Storica degli Archivi Toscani* 1 (1929): 11–25; for the role of Cosimo's representatives at the Council of Trent, see Jedin, "La politica conciliare di Cosimo I"—note especially 357–62. See also idem, "La censura sulla stampa e una questione giurisdizionale fra Stato e Chiesa in Firenze alle fine del secolo XVI," *Archivio Storico Italiano*, 5th ser., 43 (1909): 140–51. Note the equivocal position of Cosimo I: "Cosi, il principe, mentre da un lato fomentava l'incremento dell'arte tipografica fino a permettere il cambiamento della data a libri che . . . difficilmente potevano essere venduti e cercava di salvaguardare dai rigori della censura le opere di buoni scrittori come il Boccaccio, d'altra parte, seguendo l'esempio di Carlo V, comminava pene severe contro gli stampatori infetti di eresia, permetteva la pubblicazione dell'editto degli inquisitori di Roma contro i libri degli ebrei, accettava, con qualche limitazione, l'Indice di Paolo IV" (142–43).

81. Cosimo's early hopes for the title from Pius IV had been blocked by Spain and the Holy Roman Emperor. See Guarini, "Cosimo I de' Medici," 45. See also Rome, Biblioteca Apostolica Vaticana, Urbinates latini, 817, cc. 446–57, "La coronazione di Cosmo de' Medici Gran Duca di Toscana fatta in cappella di Palazzo in Roma."

82. "Nihil ad haec respondit nuntius ille papae nisi se haec omnia non curare, dicens semper Florentiam egredere et cito; alias absente duce, te coniiciemus in carceres et pessime tractabimus. Quo die Judas Christum prodidit eodem die sero ex insidiis captus sum et detrusus in carceres vbi tres noctes mihi fuerunt molestissimae. Rediit Dux Florentiae. Ducem timuerunt aduersarii mei. Statim me liberauerunt et duxerunt extra ciuitatem." ASV, S.U., Processi, Busta 22, Contra Dionisium Gallum, document entitled *Haec est causa*.

83. Ibid. Note especially: "Roma discedens Florentiam remigravi vbi dux florentinus omnia resciens quae Romae peregissem vehementer approbauit atque gauisus est; a quo summa receptus humanitate tota nouissime elapsa quadragesima multa Florentiae scripsi, feci, dixi. Ipsum ducem cum filio principe saepe numero monens rogans interpellans vt in nomine et virtute christi suum robur adderent ad clerum reformandum ad haereses extirpandas ad pauperes consolandos

polliciti sunt seseque iuncturos esse cum aliis principibus." Note also ibid., document entitled *Proces clos de la cause de Dieu pour les droictz de Jesuchrist, en son egglise militante . . . :* "Je me despartis de Rome et retourne vers monseigneur le Duc de Florence lequel entendant tout mon faict l'approuuva grandement . . . pour quoy eulx Duc et Prince de Florence par moy (comme dict est) souuent interpellez donner leur adjonction pour ces choses executer, l'ont accordee. Le Prince de Florence se declarant prest marcher auec les autres Ducs et seigneurs D'Italie." Dionisio is not reluctant to name the princes: "Doncques (Seigneurs) il apert que ma *Legation* est approuvee; et autant doibt valloir y me appointcee par cinq des principaulx seigneurs D'Italie par vous monseigneur le Duc de Ferrare, par vous monseigneur le Marquis de Masse, par Messeigneurs le Duc et Prince de Florence et par monseigneur le Duc de Sauoye."

84. ASV, S.U., Processi, Busta 22, Contra Dionisium Gallum, document entitled *Proces clos de la cause de Dieu pour les droictz de Jesuchrist, en son egglise militante . . . :* "Je lesseray les bons princes et seigneurs de la France auec plusieurs supremes parlementz ausquels me suys presente, a la poine du feu lesquelz layans entendue ont confesse qu'elle estoit bonne, selon Deiu et Raison, tresvniuerselle et catholique, mais tres difficille a executer."

85. Ibid.: "Nous te croyons Seigneurs, monseigneurs le Duc de Sauoye la ouye et entendue et la grandement approuuee. Respondant luy par moy, estand interpellé pour donner son adionction, affin dexecuter que de sa part estoit trespret et que j'allasse aux aultres ducz et princes D'Italie."

86. See note 83 above.

87. ASV, S.U., Processi, Busta 22, Contra Dionisium Gallum, document entitled *Proces clos de la cause de Dieu pour les droictz de Jesuchrist, en son egglise militante . . . :* "Je vous assure (Seigneurs) que incontinent apres toutes les aultres forces de la Chrestianté viendront a se joindre vnir et assembler (Dieu a deja prepare les forces su sacré empyré des allemaignes, du royaume catholique). Toutes lesquelles forces des bons princes et seigneurs christians ainsy ioinctes ensemble ne seront pas seullement suffizantes pour reformer le clergé extirper les heresies rendre le droict aux poures de la tierce partie des biens de legglise. Mais aussy ilz vauldront grandement auec le sainct espérit lequel cooperera pour faire au Turc deposer les armes et se combler et consentir a recevoir baptesme et toute la Turquie avec la Judee et croire en Jesuschrist."

88. Ibid.: "Jonignes vous auec eulx Dieu par moy vous le monde. Pourquoy faire? Esse pour resister au Turc? Non seullement. Pourquoy doncques? Pour principalement et deuant toutes choses reformer le clerge, extirper les heresies faire droict aux poures."

89. ASV, S.U., Processi, Busta 22, document entitled *Proces clos de la cause de Dieu pour les droictz de Jesuchrist, en son egglise militante. . . .* Dionisio linked the reformation of the clergy with the conversion of the Turks and Jews.

90. ASV, Collegio, Esposizioni Principi, Filza 1, dispatch dated December 23,

1567: "niente altra cosa è puì alta a rimouere li animi delli populi et alienarli dalla obedienza delli principi che la via della religione et con la quale tendono prima a distruggere tutti li principati et li domini et leuare la superiorità de' nobili, che è cosa sopra tutte le altre desiderata dalli Populi et poi concedono una libertà di uiuere lizentiosa . . . et che se questo apporta pericolo grande al presente al regno di Franza non manco lo apporta alla Italia et particolarmente a questo Serenissimo Dominio perche oltra quello che si è scoperto di molti heretici che sono in più parti d'Italia, si sa che li Caluinisti hanno tenuto et tengono delle intelligentie in questo stato il quale per esser di republica de' Nobili porta puì pericolo di tutti li altri."

91. See Rome, Biblioteca Apostolica Vaticana, Barberini latini, 2871, *Sermo Pii V in summum Pontificem electi habitus in prima congregatione generali 1566*. Note Pius's words that link the sins of the clergy with the increase of heresy: "Vbi spiritualia neglegi, temporalia plurimi fieri coepere, diffluere item omnia. . . . Igitur cum heretici clericorum mores ac licentiam reprehendendo praeclaram se occasionem nactos existiment et sue nequitie excusande et plebis seducende neque Catholicis ulla alia re magis insultent, profectò eniti nos oportere, ut huic malo remedium adhibeamus atque ita uitam instituere, ut et Deo placeamus et bonos confirmemus contra hereticos ac peruersos homines confundamus eorumque audaciam retundamus."

92. Surian reported that Cardinal Farnese continued "per trattar con sua Santita questa lega fra li principi di Italia per difesa delli stati di ciascuno di quelli che saranno compresi e con obligo ciascuno per la parte sua di contribuir certa quantita di agiuti in ogni occasione e benche si facci contra heretici." The pope hoped to remove Venetian reluctance by noting that the duke of Florence was "quello che metteva pronto questa cosa a sua Santita e che é aiutato da questi spagnoli." See ASV, Capi del Consiglio dei Dieci, Dispacci degli Ambasciatori, Roma, Busta 25, fascicolo 68. The date of this dispatch is November 17, 1568.

93. See the article "Alfonso II of Ferrara," by Romolo Quazza, with excellent bibliography, in *Dizionario biografico degli italiani* (Rome: Istituto di Enciclopedia Italiana, Trecanni, 1960), II:337–41.

94. ASV, Senato, Deliberazioni, Secreti, Registro 74, July 16, 1566, c. 73^v: "Rectoribus Veronae. Il Magnifico Ambassatore dell'Illustrissimo Signor Duca di Ferrara residente appresso di noi, ne ha con molta instantia ricercato per nome dell'eccellentia sua che essendo lei con 2 mila caualli uerso il fine di questo mese, per inuiarsi alla uolta di Germania, per andar all'esercitio della Maesta Cesarea in Ongaria, et per ciò douendo passar per il territorio a uoi commesso siamo contenti dar ordine che sia fatto un ponte a Dolce sopra l'Adese, si come in passaggio de altri principi, altre uolte è stato fatto e che li sia prouisto di alloggiamenti et de uiuere per li suoi danari aggiongendo che la detta cauallaria non passarà tutta in una uolta ma a parte a parte però desiderando noi compiacer l'eccellentia sua in cosa tale."

95. Not only was Lucrezia, Alfonso's first wife, the daughter of Cosimo I, but

Barbara of Austria, daughter of Maximillian II, Alfonso's second wife, was the sister of Giovanna of Austria, the wife of Francesco I, son of Cosimo I. Alfonso II was again related to the Medici as brother-in-law to Cosimo's son Francesco.

96. Renée's decision to leave Ferrara eleven months after the death of her husband, Ercole, was not without personal pain. She wrote to her son, Alfonso II: "Mon fils, pour le regret quel j'ai eu de m'éloigner d'auprès de vous, j'ai fui l'occasion de vous parler plus longuement pour ne pas me laisser vaincre par les larmes." See Christiane Gil, *Renée de France* (Paris: Perrin, 1990), 180.

97. According to Theodore Beza, Renée's admiration for Calvin never waned. "When the Lady Duchesse of Ferrara saw and heard Calvin," wrote Beza, "she knew of whose spirit he was; and as long as he lived, she remained a special instrument of God, faithful in love and devotion." Cited by F. Whitfield Barton, *Calvin and the Duchess* (Louisville, Ky.: John Knox Press, 1989), 5.

98. Ibid., 171.

99. Catherine de' Medici was hoping that this gesture by the cardinal would help to reconcile differences of religion in the kingdom of Florence. There was no possibility of reconciliation at this point, however, since the audacity of the Reformers increased. Even Reformed pastors could not control their adherents, and violence was rampant in Paris, Dijon, Rouen, and Toulouse.

100. Barton, *Calvin and the Duchess*, 172.

101. Ibid., 172. Renée (1510–75) was the daughter of Louis XII, king of France, and Anne of Brittany. Her sister was Claude of France, wife of Francis I. Renée was the aunt of Henry II, son of Francis I and Claude; Alfonso II was often found in the service of his uncle, King Henry II.

102. See E. Rodocanachi, *Renée de France: Duchesse de Ferrare* (Paris: Ollendorff, 1896), 400–406.

103. Catherine did promulgate an edict that forbade celebration of religious services in private houses except to their subjects; the edict also refused the Reformers the right to assemble in synods or to impose taxes. In addition, those religious who were married must repudiate their wives and "return to their first state" or leave the realm.

104. Rodocanachi, *Renée de France*, 403.

105. ASV, S.U., Processi, Busta 22, Contra Dionisium Gallum, document entitled *Haec est causa:* "ingressus Ferrariam: illic Deo fauente, dante consilium nos humanitus recipiente et alente illustrissimo et excellentissimo viro Domino Francisco Estensi, Marquione Massae illustrissimi et excellentissimi Ducis Ferrariae patruo." The letter to the duke and his uncle is dated April 30, 1566. For the confirmation of Francesco d'Este's title, see Dott. Ernesto Lasinio, *Regesto delle pergamene del R. Archivio di Stato in Massa* (Pistoia: Ministero dell'Interno, 1916), 224, no. 652, 1559, Maggio 15: "Argentae, ducat. ducis Ferrariae in pal. iuris dictae terrae, Franciscus Estensis, March. Massae Lombardorum, eques ordinis Sacrae Maiestatis

Christianissimae nec non eiusdem Maiestatis locumtenens in Aethruria constituit suum procuratorem capitaneum Joannem Paulum Caselam ad petendum seque recepisse ac consecutum fuisse confitendum a tesaureriis Sacrae Maiestatis Christianissimae omnes et quascumque pecuniarum quantitates, de quibus praefatus constituens reperitur et est creditor, occasione pecuniarum mutuatarum et occasione suorum stipendiorum et pagarum sibi debitarum."

106. Eph. 6:14–17.

107. See O'Malley, *Ignatius Loyola*.

108. See ASV, S.U., Processi, Busta 22, document entitled *A tres illustres et tres excellens Seigneurs messeigneurs Alfonse Duc de Ferrare et François Deste* . . . , dated *le penult jour dapril 1566*.

109. For an excellent, succinct study of Philip II's political and religious ambitions, see H. G. Koenigsberger, "The Politics of Philip II," in *Politics, Religion, and Diplomacy in Early Modern Europe: Essays in Honor of De Lamar Jensen*, ed. Malcolm R. Thorp and Arthur J. Slavin, Sixteenth-Century Essays and Studies, vol. 27 (Kirksville, Mo.: Truman State University Press, 1994), 171–89.

110. James Westfall Thompson, *History of the Wars of Religion in France, 1559–1576: The Huguenots, Catherine de Medicis, Philip II* (New York: Frederick Ungar Publishing Co., 1957), 210–24.

111. Ibid., 260–62.

112. Ibid., 256–59.

113. Ibid., 260.

114. ASV, S.U., Processi, Busta 22, document entitled *Haec est causa*: "Nos igitur habita temporis atque loci ratione agentes Ferrariae ad illustrissimos et excellentissimos Ducem et eius patruum ferrarienses hanc primo scripsimus et habuimus orationem." Dionisio wrote some additional pages in Padua.

115. Thompson, *History of the Wars of Religion in France*, 215.

116. It was not only difficult in regard to a league of Italian princes to have concerted and consistent actions for reform. The popes had also desired reform but had seemed ineffective in accomplishing it. Note, for example, Baldisseri, *La nunziatura in Toscana*, 22: "Il proposito di agire per una riforma della Chiesa ritenuta da ogni parte necessaria e urgente era da tempo nelle intenzioni dei Pontefici, ma nessuno di essi ebbe la forza di portarla ad effetto finché avvene l'irreparabile con la scissione nella Chiesa."

117. ASV, Consiglio dei Dieci, Parti secrete, Registro 8, October 22, 1568, c. 130: "oltra che il ragionar di lega mostraria un timor grande, che non seruirebbe ad altro, che a spauentar li fideli et accrescer l'audacia all'Infideli, che li farebbe entrar in speranza di poter far quello, che hora non giudicano essergli possibile." The Venetians had been resisting such a league for several years. The arguments of the *consiglio* against the league are persuasive; note also: "Non é necessario per le ragioni dette di sopra, et anco perche si po esser certi, che nelli Principi catholici sempre

che occorre il bisogno sia una constante uolonta di resister a questi scelerati, si per difesa dell'honor del Signor Dio, et conseruatione della sua santa religione, come per il proprio interesse, talmente, che questa unione de animi ne i detti Principi non ha bisogno di capitulatione o conuentioni in scrittura: Non sarebbe utile a questi tempi simil trattatione di leghe, perche ella si scoprirebbe, et essendo questi inimici de Dio, intesa insegnarebbe a quei che stanno in quiete et che non pensano a danni d'altri." Ibid.

118. ASV, S.U., Processi, Busta 22, Contra Dionisium Gallum, document entitled *Haec est causa:* "Rex autem ipse et vniuersus populus Regem me gallorum appellabant. Esset quidem longius . . . millesimam solum earum rerum partem narrare quas soli gessimus in galliis ergo Regem ipsum pro vnitate religionis et regni. . . . Si Rex ipse paucos heresiarchas punire voluisset quicum eo erant Lutetiae in suo pallatio vt haeretici caeteri resipiscerent. Quod vt fieret in ipso regis pallatio vociferabar dicens (O Charole Francorum Rex) capti sunt (si vis) canes rabientes atque furiosi qui tuum totum desolati sunt. Si sinis eos abire si non facis iustitiam periit tua corona."

119. Ibid., document entitled *Legation de L'ambassadeur de Dieu, maistre Denys De Gallois, percatholique, et tres general Legislateur Dyuin, et termporel.* . . . The preamble is written in Latin, the text of the *Legatio* in French.

120. The text of the *Legatio* is written on paper different from the cover on which we find the dedication to Cosimo. On the back of the manuscript, as indicated previously, are the words "fra li altri libri approbati da i dottori e Clement Marot." No date appears on this document. The various documents called *Legatio* are almost identical in content; the principles are numbered, although they vary slightly in numbering. The prefaces vary, however, since they were written for different princes. This *Legatio*, in French and without date, was probably written in France.

121. After several blank pages these two documents follow the *Legatio* addressed to the duke of Ferrara and the marquis de Masse.

122. ASV, S.U., Processi, Busta 22, document entitled *Proces clos de la cause de Dieu pour les droictz de Jesuchrist, en son egglise militante* . . . : "Certes je mestonnoye de veoir vng cardinal marcher en telle pompe et telle gloire humaine sembloit de quelque Roy ou de quelque empereur. O grand magnificence. O pourete extreme. O souuraine misere. O desolation et desordre trop dur, du tout intollerable brauer et pomper en telle façon des biens des poures membres de Jesuschrist, tous nudz, horrides, languissans, crians de grand douleur, au monde, misericorde." Dionisio's words reflect ideas of Savonarola's. See, for example, *Trattato della Hvmilita,* in *Molti devotissimi trattati del Reverendo Padre Frate Hieronimo Sauonarola da Ferrara,* c. 4^v: "Et s'egli è pouero, che non cerchi diuentar ricco, perche le ricchezze non mandano al cielo, anzi piu tosto impediscono il camino. Et se non ha dignita, o secolare, o Ecclesiastia, ch'egli non cerchi d'hauerla, anzi la fugga, perche non il grado, ma la bona uita fa l'huomo grato a Dio." Note also Vives, *Il modo del sovvenire a poveri,* c. 38^v: "Tu di uestimenta non uestito solamente, anzi piu tosto carco et oppresso, uedi il pouero

nudo; et oltre allui trascorri. Doue è all'hora il segnale, co'l quale si segnano le peccorelle di Christo. Ma neanche ama Iddio che non ama l'huomo ancora." Note also c. 43: "il quale delle molte sue ricchezze, dà molto ancora a poueri, siamo auuisati molto bene, che non è a Dio grata quella lemosina la quale sia dal ricco stata afforza tolta dal sudore et sostantia de poueri."

123. Although Dionisio had been imprisoned in Rome after his encounter with the pope in the Church of Saint Peter, he nevertheless wrote that "les iuges me dirent que le pape estoit ma partie." See ASV, S.U., Processi, Busta 22, document entitled *Proces clos de la cause de Dieu pour les droictz de Jesuchrist, en son egglise militante*. . . .

124. ASV, S.U., Processi, Busta 22, Contra Dionisium Gallum, document entitled *Haec est causa*.

125. Ibid., document entitled *Proces clos de la cause de Dieu pour les droictz de Jesuchrist, en son egglise militante* . . . : "de porter tel proces et mener telle cause; mais mon Dieu m'a eleu, et ma seul enuoye, en symplicite et grande pourete, pour ueu d'ung petit corps de trespetites forces, prequ'ainsy, comme vng fol, entre les aultres hommes. C'est le conseil de Dieu."

126. Ibid.

127. Note Dionisio's words: "Ceulx lesquelz me couronnent couronnent Jesuchrist; ceulx lesquelz me font droict, font droict a Jesuchrist. Car il est auec moy et moy auec luy, incorporez ensemble, vnys par volonte; Dieu le pere auec nous, tout vng avec son filz et le sainct esperit mesmement procedant et de lung et de l'aultre consolant inspirant et conferant ses graces tout vng auec le pere et auec ques son filz; sont les quatres personnes quy souurainement, parlent en ce proces." Guillaume Postel often wrote of a quaternity of divine persons: Father, Son, Holy Spirit, Lamb; or Father, Mother, Daughter, Son. He included himself as the fourth person of the quaternity because he, like Dionisio, had experienced a divine "immutation."

128. Ibid.

129. Col. 3:11.

130. ASV, S.U., Processi, Busta 22, Contra Dionisium Gallum, document entitled *Premyer auditeur des hommes de ceste cause, en ce stille, ainsy que premyerement l'auyons escripte a este, Monseigneur le Marquis di Masse . . . daquel l'aduis et iugement ensuyt*: "Quand a nostre faict et tiltre d'ambassadeur de Dieu . . . a dict quil croit que, tout cela est vng oeuure de Dieu et qu'il a ferme opynion que pour ce faire Dieu nous a delegue."

131. Ibid., document entitled *Haec est causa*. Note Dionisio's words about his style: "Illic Deo fauente dante consilium, nos humanitus recipiente et alente. . . . Illustrissimo et excellentissimo viro Domino Francisco Estensi, Marquione Massae, Illustrissimi et excellentissimi Ducis Ferrariae patruo placuit ipsa noua dicendi forma, more velut oratorio, Christi causam et ecclesiae proponere et agere propter

arduas rationes et supremas difficultates quae publice et ab omnibus adferebantur ad impediendam nostrae Legationis . . . executionem."

132. The court of Alfonso II was filled with many *letterati* and artists, among whom were G. B. Guarini, G. B. Pigna, Francesco Patrizi, Piero Ligorio, Antonio Montecatini, the painters Giuseppe Mazzuoli and Sebastiano Filippi, and the architect G. B. Aleotti. See Quazza, "Alfonso II of Ferrara," 388.

Chapter IV

1. On the so-called myth of Venice, see Frederic C. Lane, *Venice: A Maritime Republic* (Baltimore, Md.: Johns Hopkins University Press, 1973), 87–91; William J. Bouwsma, *Venice and the Defense of Republican Liberty* (Berkeley and Los Angeles: University of California Press, 1968), 52–59; Edward Muir, *Civic Ritual in Renaissance Venice* (Princeton, N.J.: Princeton University Press, 1981). See also Franco Gaeta, "Alcune considerazioni sul mito di Venezia," *Bibliothèque d'Humanisme et Renaissance* 233 (1961): 58–75. See also the very important study by Franco Gaeta, "L'idea di Venezia," in *Storia della cultura veneta: Dal primo Quattrocento al Concilio di Trento*, ed. Girolamo Arnaldi and Manilio Pastore Stocchi (Vicenza: Neri Pozza Editore, 1981), 3/III:563–641; G. Fasoli, "Nascita di un mito," in *Studi storici in onore di Gioacchino Volpe* (Florence, 1958), 1:445–79; Renzo Pecchioli, "Il 'mito' di Venezia e la crisi fiorentina intorno al 1500," *Studi Storici* 3 (1962): 452–92. Also, consult the rich bibliography in Brian Pullan, *Rich and Poor in Renaissance Venice: The Social Institutions of a Catholic State to 1620* (Cambridge, Mass.: Harvard University Press, 1971); and M. T. Muraro, "La festa a Venezia e le sue manifestazioni rappresentative: La compagnia della calza e le mommearie," in *Storia della cultura veneta: Dal primo Quattrocento al Concilio di Trento*, 3/III:315–41; R. Maschio, "Le scuole grandi a Venezia," in ibid., 193–206; Franco Gaeta, "Storiografia, coscienza nazionale e politica culturale nella Venezia del Rinascimento," in ibid., 3/I:123–75. See also the important studies by Myron Gilmore, "Myth and Reality in Venetian Political Theory," in *Renaissance Venice*, ed. J. R. Hale (Totowa, N.J.: Rowman & Littlefield, 1973), 431–22; William J. Bouwsma, "Venice and the Political Education of Europe," in ibid., 445–66; Felix Gilbert, "The Venetian Constitution in Florentine Political Thought," in *Florentine Studies: Politics and Society in Renaissance Florence*, ed. Nicolai Rubinstein (London: Faber, 1968), 466–72; idem, "Religion and Politics in the Thought of Gasparo Contarini," in *Action and Conviction in Early Modern Europe: Essays in Memory of E. H. Harbison*, ed. Theodore K. Rabb and Jerrold E. Seigel (Princeton, N.J.: Princeton University Press, 1969), 90–116; Brian Pullan, "Service to the Venetian State: Aspects of Myth and Reality in the Early Seventeenth Century," *Studi Secenteschi* 5 (1964): 95–148; Gino Benzoni, *Venezia nell'età della controriforma* (Milan: Munsia, 1973); Georg Roellenbleck, *Venezia scena dell'ultimo dialogo umanista: L'Heptaplomeres di Jean Bodin (ca. 1590)*, Quaderni 29 (Venice: Centro Tedesco di Studi Veneziani, 1984); Marion Leathers Kuntz, "The Home of Coronaeus in Jean Bodin's *Colloquium Heptaplomeres*: An Example of a Venetian Academy," in *Acta Conventus Neo-Latini Bononiensis* (Binghamton, N.Y.:

Medieval & Renaissance Texts & Studies, 1985), 277–83; idem, "The Myth of Venice in the Thought of Guillaume Postel," in *Svpplementvm Festivvm: Studies in Honor of Paul Oskar Kristeller*, ed. J. Haskins, J. Monfasni, and F. Purnell (Binghamton, N.Y.: Medieval & Renaissance Texts & Studies, 1987), 505–23; idem, "Guillaume Postel e l'idea di Venezia come la magistratura più perfetta," in *Postello, Venezia e il suo mondo*, ed. Marion Leathers Kuntz (Florence: Leo S. Olschki Editore, 1988), 163–78; Frederic C. Lane, *Venice and History* (Baltimore, Md.: Johns Hopkins University Press, 1966); Barbara Marx, *Venezia-Altera Roma? Ipotesi sull'umanesimo veneziano*, Quaderni 10 (Venice: Centro Tedesco di Studi Veneziani, 1978); E. O. G. Haitsma Mulier, *The Myth of Venice and Dutch Republican Thought in the Seventeenth Century*, trans. G. T. Moran (Assen: Van Gorcum, 1980), 12–19. For a sixteenth-century source, see Jean Bodin, *Colloquium of the Seven About Secrets of the Sublime* [*Colloquium Heptaplomeres*], trans. Marion Leathers Kuntz (Princeton, N.J.: Princeton University Press, 1975), 3–4.

2. See Antonio Niero, "Il culto dei santi dell'antico testamento," in *Culto dei santi a Venezia*, ed. Dom Silvio Tramontin (Venice: Edizioni Studium Cattolico Veneziano, 1965), 157.

3. Ibid., 158.

4. Ibid. On the *giudaico-cristianesimo* in the early Church of Aquileia, see the important article by Gilberto Pressacco, "Marco 'Christianus et Medicus,'" in *San Marco: Aspetti storici e agiografici*, ed. Antonio Niero (Venice: Marsilio Editori, 1996), 647–84.

5. See Cantimori, *Eretici italiani*, 14.

6. Silvana Seidel-Menchi, *Erasmo in Italia 1520–1580* (Turin: Bollati Boringhieri, 1987), 82.

7. ASV, S.U., Processi, Busta 22, fascicolo, Contra Lucencgo, Giangiacomo, testimony of Marco Schiavon da Nove Gradi, August 11, 1565.

8. Ibid., Busta 161, May 12, 1560. See also Busta 14, fascicolo 3, Contra Francesco Scudieri, fra Michele da Brescia, fra Stefano da Scio, August 26, 1559, unpaginated. One witness, Franciscus Butironus, testified that Scudieri, who taught humanities, said that "el papa è antichristo . . . and che lui non ha liberta di absoluer ne di ligar . . . et nominando il papa lui lo nominaua Pancenarchio et lo interpretaua anti-christo."

9. David Joris published his *'T Wonderboeck* in 1542. See George Huntston Williams, *The Radical Reformation*, 3d ed. (Kirksville, Mo.: Sixteenth-Century Journal Publishers, 1992), 724–29; see also Roland H. Bainton, "Wylliam Postell and the Netherlands," *Nederlandsch Archief voor Kerkgeschiedenis* 24 (1931): 161–71. Bainton shows that Postel's writings had wide distribution in Davidist circles. See Kuntz, *Guillaume Postel*, 46–48. Postel notes that the man known as David Georgius had changed his name from Johannes a Bruges. See the British Library, Sloane MS 1412, fol. 311ᵛ.

10. ASV, S.U., Processi, Busta 14, fascicolo 3, Contra Francesco Scudieri, fra Michele da Brescia, fra Stefano da Scio, August 26, 1559, testimony of F. Butironus:

"lui teneua il libro nominato Philippo Melantone et Oecolampadio et el Caluin et altri libri che non mi ricordo et anche uedeua il Talmuth, lo Alcorano et Rabbinni hebrei."

11. See Niccoli, *Profeti e popolo nell'Italia del Rinascimento*. See also idem, "Un aspetto della propaganda religiosa nell'Italia del Cinquecento," 32, where the author cites Egidio di Viterbo: "Quando mai infatti apparvero con tanta frequenza e di cosi terribile aspetto mostri, portenti, prodigi segni della minacce celesti e del terrore sulla terra? Quando vi potranno essere una strage o una battaglia più sanguinose di quella di Brescia o di Ravenna? [. . .] Quest'anno la terra è stata insuppata più di sangue che di pioggia." Niccoli (ibid., 33) comments that at the end of the fifteenth century and the beginning of the sixteenth century the prophet who announced divine punishment for sin became a stereotype.

12. Note Ignatius Loyola's words about the importance of preaching:

> *Il nostro celeste Medico . . . ha voluto fin da primo suo nascere il figliuolo di Dio Cristo Signore incomuncicar a combattere questi tre capitali vizj del mondo, opponendo all'attacco di roba la sua povertà, all'amor de piaceri la sua mortificazione, all'appetito di comparire il suo nascondimento. Visitiamo difatti col nostro pensiero la stalla di Betlemme ove egli per infinita sua degnazione ha voluto eleggere di nascere, e vi troveremo che tutto spira povertà, mortificazione, umiliazione. . . .*
>
> *L'altro fine immediato e subordinato alla gloria divina, che moveva il Redentore alla Predicazione dell'evangelo era la salute dell'anime. . . . Bastava che avessero di lui bisogno, perchè si movesse ad istruirle, a dirigerle e metterle sul buon sentiero della salute. (Esercizj spirituali di S. Ignazio Lojola, 290 and 300)*

A. Lynn Martin has some interesting remarks about Jesuit preachers in northern Italy, like Louis Coudret, a Savoyard who had gained a reputation as a convincing preacher. Martin notes that the Jesuits made use of good preachers to fight heresy and reform morals and to attract members to the Society of Jesus. In addition, good preachers provided entertainment and distraction for the masses as well as salvation of souls. See A. Lynn Martin, *The Jesuit Mind: The Mentality of an Elite in Early Modern France* (Ithaca, N.Y.: Cornell University Press, 1988), 7–15. See also John W. O'Malley, *The First Jesuits* (Cambridge, Mass.: Harvard University Press, 1993), 91–110. O'Malley notes that in addition to preaching, the Jesuits considered lecturing a distinct part of their ministry. Hearing confessions was also an important aspect of their work. See note 18 below.

13. Ignatius and Saverio wanted "occuparsi allora in servigio degli' infermi, e dedicarsi alle più vili e alle più stomachevoli opere, ciò essi a bella post facendo, affine di vincere la naturale ripugnanza che provato aveano al primo accostarsi a quelle schifose e sciagurate creature. . . . Furono adunque i veneziani spedali la prima evangelica vigna da essa cottivata; e perciò in gratitudine della esemplare carità non solamente dal Loiola e dal Saverio, ma da Tiene e dal Miani eziando esercitata, vollesi appresso ch'eretti fossero i simulacri loro nell'interiore della cappella dell'ospitale degl'Incurabili, destinandosi inoltre, e con assai perspicacia, i figliuoli

del Tiene, ad udir le confessioni degli infermi, i seguaci del Loiola ad esortarli con sermoni alla penitenza e i discepoli del Miani all'spirituale direzione dell'ospitale medesino." See *Annali urbani di Venezia dall'anno 810 al 12 Maggio 1797 di Fabio Mutinelli* (Venice: Tipografia de G. B. Merlo, 1841), 396–97. See also *Ecclesiae Venetae antiquis monumentis nunc etiam primum editis illustratae ac in decades distributae authore Flaminio Cornelio, Senatore Veneto* (Venice: Typis Joannis Baptistae Pasquali, 1749), 3–4:273, where the Jesuits' contributions to the *derelitti* as well as to the *incurabili* are described: "Anno MDXXVII mense Januario Divus Ignatius Societatis Jesus Fundator Venetiis degens cum socios Parisiis advenientes excepisset, eos in duobus Derelictorum, atque Incurabilium nosocomiis locarit, ut quaedam quasi exordia futuro sanctissimo instituto disponeret, ipse vero alternis nunc in uno, nunc in altero Xenodochio aegrotis ministravit. Hanc priman vineam evangelicam fuisse, quam Societas Jesu colere coepit." For the early place of residence of the Jesuits in Venice, see Flaminio Corner, *Notizie storiche delle chiese e monasteri di Venezia e di Torcello*, facsimile reprint (Bologna: Arnaldo Forni Editore, 1990), 524, the article on the Church of S. Maria dell'Umiltà: "Nell'anno dunque di Christo 1550 il sopra lodato Andrea Lippomano Fratello, ed imitatore delle virtù del celebre Vescovo di Verona Luigi Lippomano, avendo affaggiato negli esercizi spirituali fatti sotto la direzione di Giacomo Laynez di quanto vantaggio douesse esser alla chiesa la nuova Religione fondata dal Lojola, che già per ben tre volte aveva in Venezia dato chiari attestati dell'Apostolica sua carta approvata da Dio con euidenti miracoli, consegnò a' di lei figli la Chiesa, ed i contigui edificj di Santa Maria dell'Umiltà."

14. See Gaetano Cozzi, "Fortuna e sfortuna della Compagnia di Gesù a Venezia," in *I Gesuiti e Venezia*, 59–88.

15. See John W. O'Malley, "Early Jesuit Spirituality: Spain and Italy," in *Religious Culture in the Sixteenth Century*, IX, 11. See also, in the same volume, "Was Ignatius Loyola a Church Reformer? How to Look at Early Modern Catholicism," XII, 177–93.

16. Kuntz, *Guillaume Postel*, 22–23.

17. Ibid., 69–78. See also ASV, S.U., Processi, Busta 160, for the investigation of Postel by the Capi del Consiglio dei Dieci on March 19, 1548, because of his remarks on the previous day, when he had officiated at the Mass at Santa Maria dei Miracoli. See Marion Leathers Kuntz, "'Venezia portava el fuocho in seno': Guillaume Postel Before the Council of Ten in 1548: Priest Turned Prophet," *Studi Veneziani*, n.s., 33 (1997): 95–121. The article can also be found in idem, *Venice, Myth, and Utopian Thought in the Sixteenth Century: Bodin, Postel, and the Virgin of Venice* (Aldershot: Ashgate Publishing, 1999).

18. Cozzi, "Fortuna e sfortuna," 64–67; note especially 65: "Andava assai bene con i ragazzi che frequentavano le loro scuole: non solo si confessavano e comunicavano di loro iniziativa, ma facevano venire anche genitori e parenti." The Jesuits had established many favorable opinions about their work in Venice. For example, when one Zuane de Vancimugio was being investigated by the Venetian Inquisition,

a witness, Rocho de Mazzochis, a friend of Dionisio Gallo, testified that Zuane had been a good Christian previously because he had associated with the Jesuits. See ASV, S.U., Processi, Busta 21, Costituto di Rochus de Mazzochis, July 16, 1566. "Per un certo tempo io l'hebbi per buon christiano perche lui pratticaua al Giesù con quelli Padri Gesuiti et spesso si confessaua et si communicaua."

19. Cozzi, "Fortuna e sfortuna," 67: "Il 24 ottobre 1556 il padre Elmi scriveva al padre Giacomo Lainez di esser edificato dal comportamento dei giovani veneziani che frequentavano la Compagnia di Gesù. 'Oh quanto sono humili, devoti et ferventi' dicevano di loro delle persone 'dovete et nobili' che li vedevano immersi nella preghiera: 'Non paiono imagini o statue immobili, quando fanno le loro orationi insegnateli dalli padre del Giesù, et quando ascoltano le messe?'"

20. See Marion Leathers Kuntz, "Guillaume Postel e l'idea di Venezia come la magistratura più perfetta," in *Postello, Venezia e il suo mondo*, ed. Marion Leathers Kuntz (Florence: Leo S. Olschki Editore, 1988), 163–78.

21. See Postel's *Le prime nove del altro mondo* and *Il libro della divina orinationatione*, both published in Padua in 1555. See also ASV, S.U., Processi, Busta 160, document dated March 19, 1548, and note 17 above.

22. British Library, Sloane MS 1411, fol. 313^v. Also cited by Stella, *Anabattismo e antitrinitarismo in Italia nel XVI secolo*, 116 n. 116, and by François Secret, "Une lettre retrouvée de G. Postel au Grand Prieur de France," *Bibliothèque d'Humanisme et Renaissance* 30 (1968): 142 n. 7.

23. See ASV, S.U., Processi, Busta 12, fascicolo 20. In 1548 Postel had also made the same warning when he was summoned before the Capi del Consiglio dei Dieci to explain his remarks at Mass at Santa Maria dei Miracoli on March 18, 1548; see also ASV, S.U., Processi, Busta 160, and note 17 above.

24. For reform initiatives in the two decades before Dionisio's arrival in Venice, see Andrea Del Col, who points out that the *libraio* Andrea Arrivabene expressed, in a letter to his friend Lucio Paolo Rosello, "some confidence that in Venice one could aspire that religious reform could be set in motion by a group working in the city." See Del Col's "Lucio Paolo Rosello e la vita religiosa veneziana verso la metà del secolo XVI," *Rivista di Storia della Chiesa in Italia* 22 (1978): 422–59; note especially 423. He also indicates that in the oration Pier Paolo Vergerio sent in late 1545 or early 1546 to the newly elected doge Francesco Donà, the prelate urged the doge to support the reform. The letter gives the sense "delle attese, dell'impegno personale e delle lotte non solo del Vergerio, ma di un vasto numero di sudditi veneti 'che hanno il lume di Dio et l'intendono bene' e che seguono una dottrina 'spirituale,' ai quali il vescovo stesso fa esplicito riferimento" (430). See also Aldo Stella, "L'orazione di Pier Paolo Vergerio al doge Francesco Donà sulla riforma della Chiesa (1545)," *Atti dell'Istituto Veneto di Scienze, Lettere ed Arti: Classe di Scienze Morali, Lettere ed Arte* 128 (1970): 1–39; in addition, his "Tradizione razionalistica patavina e radicalismo spiritualistico nel XVI secolo," *Annali della R. Scuola Normale Superiore di Pisa* 37 (1968): 275–302; see also Anne Jacobson Schutte, *Pier Paolo Vergerio: The Making of*

an Italian Reformer (Geneva: Librarie Droz, 1977), especially 156–87; note also Federico Chabod, "Venezia nella politica italiana ed europea del Cinquecento," in *La civiltà veneziana del Rinascimento* (Florence: Sansoni, 1958), 139–90, but see especially 36, where Chabod writes of the consequences of Agnadello: "Certo all' 'acerba nova' della sconfitta di Agnadello, a Venezia s'era 'chome morti' e, al dir dello stesso Priuli, 'de superbi devientati humillssimi,' timori e pentimenti, lacrime e preghiere a Dio s'alternavano nella 'tribulata et affannata citade,' che temeva di veder il gran re di Francia 'sopra le ripe salse': e il Priuli ne traeva motivo per un esame di coscienza, e un'aperta denunzia dei 'peccati' per cui Dio aveva permesso, anzi oridinato 'questa tanta ruina dello Imperio Veneto.'" See also, by the same author in the same volume, "Contributo veneziano alla riforma cattolica," 105–24. The comments of Antonio Foscari and Manfredo Tafuri in *L'armonia e i conflitti: La chiesa di San Francesco della Vigna nella Venezia del '500* (Turin: Giulio Einaudi Editore, 1983) are especially appropriate for our study; see especially p. 22: "Il terreno della profezia escatologica, nello Zorzi, si separa dunque da quello della profezia politica, a differenza di quanto accade in altri spiriti inquieti, come Giorgio Benigno Salviati: ma anche lo Zorzi partecipa alla tendenza ad ampliare i limiti della *ratio* umana, ad estendere la ragione fino ad annettervi la realtà del miracolo e del *raptus*, non senza implicazioni sul piano dei rapporti fra religione e politica." See also Paolo Simoncelli, "Pietro Bembo e l'evangelismo italiano," *Critica Storica* 15, no. 1 (1978): 1–63.

25. See Bouwsma, *Venice and the Defense of Republican Liberty*, 8.

26. From Geneva, Ochino wrote to a Venetian friend on December 7, 1542: "credo che Venetia sarà la porta." See Edouard Pommier, "La société vénitienne et la reforme protestante au XVI siècle," *Studi Veneziani* 1 (1959): 4; see also Gigliola Fragnito, "Gli 'Spirituali' e la fuga di Bernardino Ochino," *Rivista Storica Italiana* 85 (1972): 777–813; note also John Martin, "Salvation and Society in Sixteenth-Century Venice." See also Paolo Simoncelli, "In margine a una edizione di scritti ochiniani," *Critica Storica* 22, no. 4 (1985): 439–48, noting especially 447, where Simoncelli cites Ochino's words about Venice from the *Dialogi sette* . . . *:* "Già Christo ha incominciato penetrare in Italia; ma vorrei che v'intrasse glorioso, a la scoperta, e credo che Venezia sarà la porta, e felice a te se la accetterai." Ochino also expresses his hopes for his republic: "e Dio sa quanto desidero veder che Christo regni nella mia Venezia, e che sia libera da ogni diabolico gioco, e maxime da quello che sotto la spezie di bene la tiene più oppressa." On the problems connected with Ochino's preaching at Santi Apostoli in 1542, see Emmanuele Antonio Cicogna, *Delle inscrizioni veneziane* (Venice, 1842), 5:401–2.

27. See Silvio Tramontin, "Lo spirito, le attività, gli sviluppi dell'Oratorio del Divino Amore nella Venezia del Cinquecento," *Studi Veneziani* 14 (1972): 111–36; Innocenzo Cervelli, "Storiografia e problemi intorno alla vita religiosa e spirituale a Venezia nella prima metà del '500," *Studi Veneziani* 8 (1966): 447–76; note especially Cervelli's citation (449) from a letter written to Pope Paul III in 1538 by Gasparo Contarini, Pietro Carafa, Jocopo Sadoleto, Reginald Pole, and Gian Matteo Giberti: "Nam spiritus ille Dei quo virtus coelorum firmata est, ut ait propheta labantem

imo fere colapsam in praeceps ecclesiam Christi per te huic ruine manum ut videmus supponere decrevit, eamque erigere ad pristinam sublimitatem decorique pristino restituere certissimam divine huius sententie coniecturarum nos facere valemus quibus sanctitas tua ad se vocavit, mandavit, ut nullius aut commodi tui aut cuiuspiam alterius habita ratione tibi significaremus abusus illos gravissimos videlicet morbos quibus iampridem ecclesia Dei laborat ac presertim hec Romana Curia." Note also the important article by Simoncelli, "Pietro Bembo e l'evangelismo italiano"; see also *Venezia e Lorenzo Giustiniani*, ed. Silvio Tramontin (Venice: Comune di Venezia, 1981). Note the words of Pietro Bembo about Venice's declining moral health: "Languescant otio Veneti et a priscorum uirtute degenerent pereatque maritima disciplina et nautica illa militia qua maiores nostri praestiterunt et per tot saecula omnibus populis libertatem defenderunt." *Delineatio historiae quae res gestas Venetorum complectitur . . . Petrus Bembus*, bk. x, p. 116, Venice, Biblioteca nazionale di San Marco, MSS latini, Cl. x, Cod. CCLXXXV (= 3180).

28. Venice, Biblioteca nazionale di San Marco, MSS latini, Cl. XIV, Cod. II (= 4590).

29. On the influence of Savonarola's preaching in Rome, see Paolo Simoncelli, "Momenti e figure del savonarolismo romano," *Critica Storica*, n.s. I, II (1974): 47–82. Note especially the opinion of Archbishop Alessandro de' Medici, cited by Simoncelli, 82 n. 132: "Serenissimo Signor mio, per la molta pratica che io ho delli humori di cotesta città, a me pare che la devotione di Fra Girolamo causi dei cattivi effetti, anzi pessimi, quando vi si gettano, come fanno di presente. Il primo è che quelli che li credono, si alienano dalla Sede Apostolica, et se non diventano heretici non hanno buona opinione dell'clero secolare, et de' prelati, et gli obediscono mal volentieri: et io lo pruovo."

30. Weinstein, *Savonarola and Florence*, 27.

31. Nicolai Rubinstein, "Italian Reactions to Terraferma Expansion in the Fifteenth Century," in *Renaissance Venice*, ed. Hale, 205.

32. Ibid. See also 214 nn. 67 and 68. On the "Venetianization" of Florence and on Savonarola's concept of the Venetian state, see Gaeta, "Alcune considerazioni sul mito di Venezia," 63–65.

33. See Felix Gilbert, "Venice in the Crisis of the League of Cambrai," in *Renaissance Venice*, ed. Hale, 274–92; Innocenzo Cervelli, *Machiavelli e la crisi dello stato veneziano* (Naples: Guida, 1974), 149–63.

34. Gilbert, "Venice in the Crisis of the League of Cambrai," 274; Cervelli, *Machiavelli e la crisi dello stato veneziano*, 30–35.

35. See *La cronica veneziana trascritta da Gasparo Zancaruolo*, Venice, Biblioteca nazionale di San Marco, MSS italiani, Cl. VII, Cod. MMDLXX (= 12462) già Phillips 5215. On the Italian indulgence in *lussuria*, see Guido Ruggiero, *The Boundaries of Eros: Sex, Crime, and Sexuality in Renaissance Venice* (New York: Oxford University Press, 1985); see also Patricia Labalme, "Sodomy and Venetian Justice in the Renaissance," *Legal History Review* 52 (1984): 217–54. On the relationship of politics to the religious life in Venice in the Cinquecento, see Innocenzo Cervelli, "Storiografia e problemi

intorno alla vita religiosa e spirituale a Venezia nella prima metà del '500," in which Cervelli argues that the death of Contarini and the flight of Ochino mark the *terminus ad quem* of one phase of the religious and spiritual life of Venice in the Cinquecento. For an overview of the religious problems in Italy in the Cinquecento, see *Problemi di vita religiosa in Italia nel Cinquecento: Atti del convegno di storia della chiesa in Italia* (Padua: Antenore, 1960).

36. See Lane, *Venice: A Maritime Republic.*

37. Lane, in ibid., 248, cites Girolamo Priuli, who, during the War of the League of Cambrai, wrote in his diary "that some Venetians were saying that if the mainland was lost, the Venetian nobles, citizens and populace would devote themselves to the sea and going on voyages and, besides gaining profits, would become valiant men and experts in the ways of the sea and every other undertaking, and perhaps that would be of more benefit to the Venetian Republic than the income received from the mainland." Cf. Gilbert, "Venice in the Crisis of the League of Cambrai," 274–77. See also Cervelli, *Machiavelli e la crisi dello stato veneziano*, 167–217; note especially 216, where Cervelli states: "L'antitesi fra il mare e la terraferma, nello scrittore belga [Jean Lemaire] ostile a Venezia, acquistava una fisionomia particolare, affidata come era a simboli e profezie dall'indubbio significato, comunque, semplicisticamente popolaresco e propagandistico, in quel far risalire a Gioachino da Fiore il più lontano segno premonitore della rovina veneziana." For Venice's particular problems with Rome at the time of the League of Cambrai, see Giuseppe Dalla Santa, "Il vero testo dell'appellazione di Venezia dalla scomunica di Guilio II," *Nuovo Archivio Veneto*, 2d ser., 19 (1900): 349–61. For an excellent study of Girolamo Priuli, see Achille Olivieri, "Un momento della sensibilità religiosa e culturale del Cinquecento veneziano: 'I diarii di Girolamo Priuli e gli orizzonti della esperientia,'" *Critica Storica* 3 (1973): 397–414; note especially 413, where Olivieri writes: "L'onda problematica de *I diarii* permette di riconoscerlo, seguirlo palmo a palmo nei suoi punti cruciali. Un universo i cui tratti risultano 'nuovi' con quell' 'esperientia' dominatrice di ogni barriera religiosa e culturale, che inserisce nella meditazione traiettorie diverse da quella della precedente contrapposizione fra Dio e la 'fortuna.' Ed il posto occupato dal Priuli nella cultura veneziana del Cinquecento, proprio per queste aree mentali precedentemente rintracciate, risulta di fondamentale importanza; rielabora alcuni temi cari al mondo dei mercanti del Quattrocento, e li sintetizza in alcune categorie principali, in un mondo concepito per gli uomini, per la ragione e per la continuità storica degli uomini del loro retaggio di conquiste."

38. A recent study, however, has taken this point of view. See Donald E. Queller, *The Venetian Patriciate: Reality Versus Myth* (Urbana: University of Illinois Press, 1986). For a balanced view of the Venetian patriciate centuries earlier, see Stanley Chojnacki, "In Search of the Venetian Patriciate: Families and Factions in the Fourteenth Century," in *Renaissance Venice*, ed. Hale, 47–90. See also Alberto Tenenti, "The Sense of Space and Time in the Venetian World," in ibid., 17–46, especially 34–37. For a view of the patriciate on the eve of the Cinquecento, see Margaret

L. King, *Venetian Humanism in an Age of Patrician Dominance* (Princeton, N.J.: Princeton University Press, 1986). See also Muir, *Civic Ritual in Renaissance Venice;* Pullan, *Rich and Poor in Renaissance Venice;* and idem, "The Occupations and Investments of the Venetian Nobility in the Middle and Late Sixteenth Century," in *Renaissance Venice,* ed. Hale, 379–408. For an excellent study of the problem in late medieval and early Renaissance Venice, see Dennis Romano, *Patricians and Popolani: The Social Foundations of the Venetian Renaissance State* (Baltimore, Md.: Johns Hopkins University Press, 1987). See also the excellent study by Silvio Tramontin, "Il *De officio episcopi* di Gasparo Contarini," *Studia Patavina* 12 (1965), 292–303, in which the author analyzes the religious sensitivity and zeal for reform of Contarini and his circle of friends.

39. Cf. Gilbert, "Venice in the Crisis of the League of Cambrai," 278.

40. Ibid., 279–80. On the sumptuary laws a century earlier, see Margaret M. Newett, "The Sumptuary Laws of Venice in the Fourteenth and Fifteenth Centuries," in *Historical Essays,* ed. T. F. Tout and James Tait (Manchester: Manchester University Press, 1907), 245–78.

41. Gilbert, "Venice in the Crisis of the League of Cambrai," 279–80.

42. Ibid., 287.

43. Ibid., 288.

44. Gaetano Cozzi, "Authority and the Law in Renaissance Venice," in *Renaissance Venice,* ed. Hale, 307. Note also his *Repubblica di Venezia e stati italiani: Politica e giustizia dal secolo XVI al secolo XVIII* (Turin: Giulio Einaudi Editore, 1982), especially 81–216.

45. Cozzi, "Authority and the Law in Renaissance Venice," 314.

46. Ibid., 320; cited by Cozzi from Marino Sanuto, *Cronachetta* (Venice, 1880), 23:483.

47. Cozzi, "Authority and the Law in Renaissance Venice," 321. See also ASV, Riformatori dello Studio di Padova.

48. For a comprehensive view of Venetian humanism, see King, *Venetian Humanism in an Age of Patrician Dominance.* See also Vittore Branca, "Ermolao Barbaro and Late Quattrocento Venetian Humanism," in *Renaissance Venice,* ed. Hale, 218–43; Gigliola Fragnito, "Cultura umanistica e riforma religiosa: Il 'De officio viri boni ac probi episcopi' di Gasparo Contarini," *Studi Veneziani* 11 (1970): 75–189; Paul Oskar Kristeller, "Marsilio Ficino e Venezia," in *Miscellanea di studi in onore di Vittore Branca III: Umanesimo e Rinascimento a Firenze e a Venezia* (Florence: Leo S. Olschki Editore, 1983), 475–92.

49. Gino Benzoni, *Gli affanni della cultura: Intellettuali e potere nell'Italia della controriforma e barocca* (Milan: Feltrinelli Editore, 1978), 26–29. Note also Benzoni's remarks, p. 30: "Venezia appunto, ritratta allegoricamente da Paolo Veronese, in un dipinto posto nel Palazzo Ducale a conforto e stimolo della classe di governo ivi deliberante, come una splendida donna—la smagliante bellezza della città, il lusso e la pompa pubbliche e private erano sentite come autentici valori da proporre all'altrui ammirazione e invidia—attorniata dalla 'pace . . . abbondanza . . . fama . . . felicità . . . honore . . . sicurità . . . gratie . . . libertà.'"

50. See Silvio Tramontin and Giorgio Fedalto, *Santi e beati vissuti a Venezia* (Venice: Edizioni Studium Cattolico Veneziano, 1971); Silvio Tramontin, *Pagine di santi veneziani: Antologia* (Brescia, 1968); *San Giralamo Miani e Venezia nel v° centenario della nascitad* (Venice: La Tipo-Litografia Armena per conto dell'IRE, 1986).

51. See Gleason, *Gasparo Contarini*; also idem, *Reform Thought in Sixteenth-Century Italy*, ed. and trans. Elisabeth G. Gleason, AAR Texts and Translations Series, no. 4 (Ann Arbor: University of Michigan Press, 1981); Paolo Prodi, "The Structure and Organization of the Church in Renaissance Venice: Suggestions for Research," in *Renaissance Venice*, ed. Hale, 409–30; Gasparo Contarini, *De magistratibus et republica venetorum* (Venice, 1589); Gilbert, "Religion and Politics in the Thought of Gasparo Contarini"; Hubert Jedin, "Gasparo Contarini e il contributo veneziano alla riforma cattolica," in *La civiltà veneziana del Rinascimento*, Centro di Cultura e Civiltà della Fondazione Giorgio Cini (Florence: Sansoni, 1958), 105–24.

52. Gilbert, "Religion and Politics in the Thought of Gasparo Contarini," 101.

53. See ibid., 90–116, especially 101 n; note also Fragnito, "Cultura umanistica e riforma religiosa."

54. Gilbert, "Religion and Politics in the Thought of Gasparo Contarini," 108.

55. See Gleason, *Gasparo Contarini*, 194ff.

56. Gilbert, "Religion and Politics in the Thought of Gasparo Contarini," 111 and n. 72.

57. Venice, Biblioteca nazionale di San Marco, MSS italiani, Cl. VII, Cod. CXX (= 8158). For brief biographies of Egnazio, see *Catalogus translationum et commentariorum*, vol. 4, ed. F. Edward Cranz and Paul Oskar Kristeller (Washington, D.C.: Catholic University of America Press, 1980), 48–49, and *Nouvelle biographie générale*, 15:736; see also Giovanni degli Agostini, "Notizie istoriche spettanti alla vita e agli scritti di Batista Egnazio sacerdote viniziano," in *Raccolta d'opuscoli scientifici e filologici*, ed. A. Calogerà (Venice, 1745), 33:1–191; James Bruce Ross, "Venetian Schools and Teachers, Fourteenth to Early Sixteenth Century: A Survey and Study of Giovanni Battista Egnazio," *Renaissance Quarterly* 29 (1976): 521–57.

58. Venice, Biblioteca nazionale di San Marco, MSS italiani, Cl. VII, Cod. CXX (= 8158), c. 3ʳ: "che tutti per via della semplice purità conforme alla regola del ben vivere de' nostri padri la cercarono . . . et insegnò che la vita della sapienza consisti nella pouerta, nel dispregio dell'humane cose, e nella religione."

59. The title of the Latin printed edition is *De exemplis illustrium virorum Venetae civitatis et aliarum gentium* (Venetiis [Venice], 1554). The citations from Egnazio are from the Italian manuscript cited in note 58 above, because the manuscript often has interesting marginalia missing from the printed text.

60. "quella città laquale da piccioli principii uenuta a smisurata grandezza, non habbia potuto altra origine sortire . . . che a testimonio di Platone: alcuna città non può esser con prosperità constituta, o con felicità constituita o con felicità gouernata senza l'aiuto di Dio." Venice, Biblioteca nazionale di San Marco, MSS italiani, Cl. VII, Cod. CXX (= 8158), c. 4ᵛ.

61. Ibid., c. 19.

62. Ibid., cc. 5ᵛ, 19ᵛ.

63. Ibid., c. 20. Because of a terrible earthquake and pestilence, one-third of patricians and *popolani* died. The dire happenings, according to Egnazio, warned "che chiaramente portendessero il principato di Marino Faliero, il quale s'haueua preso ad opprimere la libertà della patria per appropriarla a lui solo con tirannia." On the conspiracy of Doge Marino Falier, who wanted to become "Lord and Master, Master with the Rods [*Signore a bacheta*]," and the efficient, legal, and severe punishment executed against him and the fellow conspirators, see Lane, *Venice: A Maritime Republic*, 181–83.

64. Venice, Biblioteca nazionale di San Marco, MSS italiani, Cl. VII, Cod. CXX (= 8158), c. 21ʳ.

65. See Reeves, *The Influence of Prophecy*, 191–228, 262–73.

66. Venice, Biblioteca nazionale di San Marco, MSS italiani, Cl. VII, Cod. CXX (= 8158), c. 104.

67. Ibid. See note 19 above.

68. Ibid., c. 191ᵛ: "Quasi tutti sogliamo desiderare che la lusinghiera ci doni delle ricchezze, e de gli honori, ne avvertiamo, che questi suoi doni generano la lussuria, o la libidine la quale se nell'adolescenza l'assale, non cosi facilmente otterrai li commodi dell'honorata vecchieza. Perciò che questa resasi a poco, a poco sfrenata, parturisce l'Auaritia, e prepara tanta Morbidezza, che fa d'animo, e di corpo non ben sani quei tutti, che lei seruono."

69. Ibid. See also Ruggiero, *The Boundaries of Eros*.

70. Many editions of Joachim's works were printed in Venice in the early decades of the sixteenth century. Manuscripts of Joachim's writings can also be found in Venetian libraries. For an interesting account of elements of Franciscan prophecy, see Olga Z. Pugliese, "Apocalyptic and Dantesque Elements in a Franciscan Prophecy of the Renaissance," *Proceedings of the PMR Conference* 10 (1987): 127–35. In addition to other works about Joachim cited in Chapter 1, see Silvano Onda, "Stato delle fonti e ricerca storica sull'estetica gioachimita e l'iconografia marciana," in *San Marco: Aspetti storici e agiografici*, ed. Antonio Niero (Venice: Marsilio Editori, 1996), 568–84.

71. See Postel's *Le thrésor des prophéties de l'univers*, 248: "l'abbé Joachim, qui ordona les peinctures en entailleures de la tres misterieuse Eglise de Sainct Marc."

72. *Abbas Joachim magnus propheta: Expositio magni prophete Ioachim in librum beati Cirilli de magnis tribulationibus et statu Sancte matris Ecclesie*, c. XXIᵛ. The shelf mark is Biblioteca nazionale di San Marco, Rari V. 408, Rari V. 409.

73. Ibid., c. XXII. Note especially: "Hic est sanctus episcopus seu patriarcha Venetorum cuius admonitione suus populus, id est Veneti, emendabuntur ab iniquitatibus suis et de cetero continue magis ac magis vsque ad diem iudicii emend-

abuntur ita vt non inueniantur ita boni inter omnes nationes christianorum, vt dicit Merlinus in suis reuelationibus."

74. Ibid. See note 73 above.

75. Ibid., c. XXII–XXII^v.

76. Ibid., c. XXIII.

77. Ibid., c. XXV.

78. Ibid.: "Tantaque erit virtus benigni pastoris quod montium cacumina incuruabit quasi nihil habens et omnia possidens. Hic vir sanctus religiosorum cornua conteret superba et omnes erunt ad statum primitiue ecclesie ita quod pastor vnus lex vna dominus vnus verus et modestus deum timens."

79. Ibid., c. XLIIII.

80. *Espositio magni prophete Abbatis Joachim in Apocalipsim*, c. 82: "ita nec apud Deum nomen quisque habere credendus est quod christianus dicitur sed quod innocens timoratus et iustus." The edition I have used is in the Biblioteca nazionale di San Marco, shelf mark 51.C.130.

81. Ibid.

82. Ibid.: "Porro commune donum quod est charitas dei agit commune nomen vniuersitate iustorum vt vocentur ciues Hierusalem; quot quot sunt electi a domino et preordinati ad vitam."

83. See Pullan, *Rich and Poor in Renaissance Venice*.

84. Kuntz, "Guillaume Postel e l'idea di Venezia," 166–67.

85. *Dichiaratione del Doni sopra il XIII cap. dell'Apocalisse*, 17. On the significance of numbers, note p. 10 : "Egli è scritto dal Saluator nostro, per mano dell'Euangelista, che i capegli del nostro capo sono annouerati: et Salomone afferma, che Iddio ha in numero, peso et misura il tutto disposto: et Platone teneua, che i Cieli fossero composti di numeri et per uia de numeri gli antichi Cabalisti, i gran secreti sapeuano. Di qua intese Beda Venerabile la cagione, perche in quaranta sei giorni appunto, il corpo nostro era formato: et ce lo dimostrò per uia di numero: usando l'alfabeto Greco, e suoi numeri pigliando il capo de nomi delle quattro regioni del mondo."

86. Ibid., 12–13.

87. See *Cronica breuis ab initio ordinis vsque ad presens tempus de omnibus Pontificibus Romanis et omnibus huius praedicatorum ordinis magistris generalibus et de viris illustribus tam sanctitate quam scientia preditis ipsius ordinis* (Venetiis [Venice]: Laçarus de Soardis, 1516), c. 143^v: "Venerabilis autem abbas Joachim floriacensis ordinis institutor fratribus habitum quem dictus magister Reginaldus a beata virgine acceptat prophetice demonstrans in quodam monasterio sui ordinis quod est in Calabria depingi et etiam in ecclesia sancti Marci de Venetiis opere musico fieri fecit." One should bear in mind that a variant of *musaicus* is *musicus*. See Charles Du Cange, *Glossarium Mediae et Infimae Latinitatis* (Bologna: Forni Editore, 1982), 5:554, s.v. *musaicus*. This account

of Abbot Joachim supports the many stories circulating about his plan and execution of many of the mosaics in San Marco.

88. Ibid. "Cito surget in ecclesia dei nouus ordo docentium cui praeerit vnus maior et cum eo et sub eo erunt XXII praefatum ordinem regentes. Quare sicut Jacob patriarcha cum XII filiis ingressus est Egyptum sic ipse cum XII filiis in illo ordine post ipsum ingredientur et illuminabunt mundum."

89. *I diarii di Marino Sanuto* (Venice: N. Barazzi, 1882), vol. 8, col. 326. The text is as follows: "A San Chimento era un certo frate di l'hordine di la Charità, qual è gran tempo sta li con un converssso, et nome don Piero Nani, zenthilomo nostro, di anni 90; et dice molte cosse, qual le traze di prophetie. Et io fui da lui ozi, mi disse molte cosse. A gran corso di patricij. Dice, questa terra perderà tutto el dominio per li pechati; . . . et il Turcho si farà christianus et la Signoria rehaverà tutto il suo stato; el re di Franza viverà pochi mexi; et questa flagelation durerà do anni e mezo, e poi questo anno sarà phame et peste grandissima, tamen Veniexia resterà intacta. E questo dice è scripto per le prophetie, di le qual el ne ha gran copia etc. Et nota, la briga' al presente atende molto a prophetie et vano in chiesa di San Marco, vedando prophetie di musaicho, qual fece far l'abate Joachim etc." See also the excellent study by Ottavia Niccoli that explores in depth the Joachimite prophecies in San Marco, "'Prophetie di Musaicho.'"

90. See *Venetia città nobilissima*, vol. 8, bk. 1, chap. XCVIII, c. 58: "Due altre figure simili senza il lor nome, ma di habito differenti fece egli [Giachino] parimente sotto un altro arco, quindi poco lontano, et uicino a quello, sotto di cui ui è quella diuota Imagine della Madonna in marmo scolpita et attaccata al pilastro, che risponde a quello dell'altar di S. Giocomo, fece egli pingere e formare, nè si può sapere, se ancora questi siano uenuti al mondo: una di esse, vestita pontificalmente credesi, c'habbia da essere l'ultimo sommo Pontefice, sotto di cui, Fiet come dice il Vangelo; unum ouile, et unus Pastor."

91. Ibid. If the inscription cited above was written under the figure in brown, he was obviously considered to be the angelic pope. The figure in blue, however, matches the description in Joachim regarding the humility of the angelic pope. See note 124 below.

92. See Niccoli, "'Prophetie di Musaicho,'" 207.

93. See *Basilica patriarcale in Venezia, San Marco: I mosaici, le iscrizioni, la pala d'oro*, ed. Maria Andaloro, Maria da Villa Urbani, Ivete Florent-Goudouneix, and Renato Polacco (Milan: Ettore Vio Fabbri Editori, 1991), 128.

94. Demus, *The Mosaics of San Marco in Venice*, 1:257.

95. See Venice, Biblioteca nazionale di San Marco, MSS italiani, Cl. VII, Cod. CCCXIV (= 8038), c. 16ᵛ, for the text: "fo lauorada tuto mosaicho et ornada de molte profecie de fomenti che doueua vegnir et fo denada la ditta giesia per lo abate Joachin, homo spiritual et molto de dio el qual Abate fexe fare in ditta giesia molte cose et desegni liquali da poi e sta insto la similitudine et effetto, per modo esse reputa certa che tante ditte cose esser state misterioxe et in segno di profecie et fo

conpida ditta giesia soto messer Vidal Falier."

96. Demus, *The Mosaics of San Marco in Venice*, 1:9–11.

97. Vasoli, *Profezia e ragione*, 136–39.

98. Ibid., 139.

99. See Kuntz, *Guillaume Postel*, 74–75.

100. On the Venetian Virgin, see Marion Leathers Kuntz, "Guglielmo Postello e la 'Vergine Veneziana': Appunti storici sulla vita spirituale dell'Ospedaletto nel Cinquecento," in Quaderni 21 (Venice: Centro Tedesco di Studi Veneziani, 1981), 1–24; idem, *Guillaume Postel*, 69–142; idem, "Guillaume Postel e l'idea di Venezia," 163–78; idem, "The Myth of Venice in the Thought of Guillaume Postel," 503–23; idem, "Lodovico Domenichi, Guillaume Postel, and the Biography of Giovanna Veronese," *Studi Veneziani*, n.s., 16 (1988): 33–44; idem, "The Virgin of Venice and Concepts of the Millennium in Venice," in *The Politics of Gender in Early Modern Europe*, Sixteenth-Century Essays and Studies, vol. 12, ed. Jean R. Brink, Allison P. Coudert, and Mary Anne C. Horowitz (Kirksville, Mo.: Truman State University Press, 1991), 111–30.

101. Mother Johanna did not reveal, even to her intimate friends, such as Guillaume Postel, the name of her parents or the occupation of her father. When Postel asked her about her family, she replied: "Nivno sa donde io sia." Guillaume Postel, *Le prime nove del altro mondo* (Padua, 1555), sig. B. All that she would say about herself was that she was born in the environs of Padua and Verona. Because of her familiarity with the *Zohar*, I have often thought that she may have been a "New Christian," that is, one of the *conversos*, although I have found no direct evidence to support my supposition.

102. See note 105 below. Kuntz, *Guillaume Postel*, 79–80. See London, British Library, Sloane MS 1410, fol. 51–51^v.

103. See Kuntz, "The Virgin of Venice," 122 and n. 62.

104. Ibid., 122–24. The prophecies can be found in Postel's *Le prime nove del altro mondo*, sigs. G1v–1^v.

105. Kuntz, "The Virgin of Venice," 127. The text is found in London, British Library, Sloane MS 1410, fol. 51^v: "Io son el Signor per che esso habita in me et per questo io sono in esso il Papa Santo Reformatore del mondo." See also Kuntz, "Guillaume Postel e l'idea di Venezia," 172.

106. See Lodovico Domenichi, *Historia varia di M. Lodovico Domenichi* . . . (Venice: Gabriel Giolito de' Ferrari, 1564), 617–18.

107. See Kuntz, "Lodovico Domenichi, Guillaume Postel, and the Biography of Giovanna Veronese."

108. "Benche questo non auuenisse hora ma molti anni adietro, non dimeno perch'egli auuenne in Vinegia, et non solamente m'è parsa cosa dignissima ma necessaria anchora di sapersi, n'ho uoluto far memoria in questo luogo." See *Historia varia di M. Lodovico Domenichi*, 617–18. See also note 107 above.

109. *Historia varia di M. Lodovico Domenichi*, 617–18.

110. Kuntz, "Guglielmo Postello e la 'Vergine Veneziana,'" 8–9.

111. See ASV, S.U., Processi, Buste 12, 159. Postel was also investigated by the Capi del Consiglio dei Dieci in 1548. See ASV, S.U., Processi, Busta 160. See also Kuntz, "'Venezia portava el fuocho in seno.'"

112. Kuntz, *Guillaume Postel*, 122.

113. See Paul Oskar Kristeller, *Iter Italicum*, vols. 3 and 4 (Leiden: E. J. Brill, 1983 and 1989).

114. The English version was translated by H. A. Milne Horne from the French translation by Monsieur Morand. Horne's translation was published in Plymouth, England, in 1922.

115. See Kuntz, *Guillaume Postel*, 128–29.

116. Ibid., 118–29; see also Aldo Stella, "Il processo veneziano di Guglielmo Postel," *Rivista di Storia della Chiesa in Italia* 22, no. 2 (1968): 425–66.

117. See ASV, S.U., Processi, Busta 160.

118. Ibid. Pisani's words were: "quando li venne ditto l'Euanzeleo se uoltò uerso el populo et exhortò tutti al ben viuer . . . et poi disse al populo: Dise un pater noster et pregè la maesta de Dio per questa tera." See note 111 above.

119. In the inquisitorial record Postel is identified as D. Presbyter Guielmus Postello.

120. On the conspiracy of Baiamonte Tiepolo, see Paolo Preto, "Baiamonte Tiepolo: Traditore della patria o eroe e martire della libertà?" in *Continuità-discontinuità nella storia politica economica e religiosa: Studi in onore di Aldo Stella*, ed. Giovanni Silvano and Paolo Pecorari (Vicenza: Neri Pozza Editore, 1993), 217–64; Dennis Romano, "The Aftermath of the Querini-Tiepolo Conspiracy in Venice," *Stanford Italian Review* (1987): 147–59; also Lane, *Venice: A Maritime Republic*, 114–17; S. Romanin, *Storia documentata di Venezia*, 3d ed. (Venice: Libreria Filippi Editore, 1973), 3:21–39. For reminders of Baiamonte Tiepolo's conspiracy throughout Venice, see Giuseppe Tassini, *Curiosità veneziane*, 9th ed. (Venice: Filippi Editore, 1988), 65, 198, 328, 353, 543. See also Venice, Biblioteca nazionale di San Marco, MSS italiani, Cl. VII, Cod. LXIX (= 7727), cc. 123^r–132^v, in which the conspiracy of Baiamonte Tiepolo is discussed.

121. ASV, S.U., Processi, Busta 160: "Non altro, Signori, saluo ch'el spirito me dice che Venezia è in gran pericolo et ha bisogno che continuamente se fazza oratio per la sua conversion a Dio."

122. Ibid.: "di poi che li fu detto per li Signori capi ch'el meritaua laude de queste sue bone operationi, ma ch'el non douesse nominar più Tiepolo ne altri."

123. London, British Library, Sloane MS 1411, fol. 313^v: "Quomodo vero et Turchae et Tartari venerint ex ea regione in qua illos Samaritanos relegauerat Senacherib, alibi est expositum, praecipue in commentariis sacrarum rerum Venetiis et Gallis

creditarum et procurationis aeternae instituendae, quos in suae reipublicae rem aut ruinam si excudatur aut negligat dedi Senatui Venetorum per sui Ducis manus." See also Stella, *Anabattismo e antitrinitarismo in Italia nel XVI secolo*, 116 and n. 56.

124. See Venice, Biblioteca del Museo Correr, Opus P.D. 11.759 al 11.786 (11780), n.p., n.d.

> Francesco Sansouino, "A Principi Christiani"
>
> *Legge et se sprezza il Thrace e il mar ingombra*
> *Di legni, arde l'Illirio, et Cipro prende*
> *Roma, Adria e Iberia, armate e vnite attende*
> *Nel'acqua, et rotto poi quindi si sgombra*
> *Or qual tema, o gran Regi, il corvi adombra,*
> *Se'l ciel l'antica gloria hoggi vi rende?*
> *Perche desio d'Imperi hor non vi accende?*
> *Che l'empio senza honor fatto è vana ombra?*
> *Chiama Asia, Africa spera, Europa grida,*
> *Chi sia ch'il collo e i piè, ne sleghi e sferri?*
> *Et dove hora è Baal, croci, et lumi erga?*
> *Armi, armi adunque, et il rio Selim s'vccida,*
> *E in Bisanzo Macon falso s'atterri,*
> *Et poi, sia vn solo Ouil, sola vna Verga.*

125. ASV, S.U., Processi, Busta 25, Contra Isabella Frattina, fascicolo 1, c. 3, Costituto Giacomo Brocardo, May 14, 1568. See also Antonio Rotondò, "Jacopo Brocardo," in *Dizionario biografico degli italiani* (Rome: Istituto della Enciclopedia Italiana, 1972), XIV:384–89; note also Delio Cantimori, "Visioni e speranze di un ugonotto italiano," *Rivista Storica Italiana* 62 (1950): 199–217.

126. Rotondò, "Jacopo Brocardo," 386.

127. ASV, S.U., Processi, Busta 25, Contra Isabella Frattina, fascicolo 1, c. 41, Costituto Giacomo Brocardo, August 23, 1568. Note especially: "Pratticaua anche in casa di messer Giulio Camillo con il quale fece amicitia et mi fece molte cortesie qual uenni poi a ritrouar a Venetia et sua Serenità mi messe in casa di Monsignor Reverendissimo Vescouo de Lodi come ho detto."

128. Camillo was known to the king of France. In Venice in 1545, he published *Due orationi di Givlio Camillo al re christianissimo*, in which he begged Francis I for the freedom of his friend Giovan Battista Palavicino. Note especially: "Aggiungiamo poi che la gloria de le arme, non si partirà da questo mondo, ma quella de la misericordia rimanerà eterna anchora in cielo, per la quale potrà uostra Maestà essere simile a Dio, che per quella de le armi, mi rendo hormai certo altissimo Rè, che la Maestà uostra habbia gia compreso da la uoce et da lo spirito mio, che quella regge, la istessa uoce et lo medesimo spirito del predicatore Palauicino, a cui essendo da acerba prigione, già per più di uno anno uietato il potere uenire a i piedi suoi, uengo io, che unico e sconsolato fratello li sono, anzi uiene esso medesimo in uno altro corpo poi che il suo in si duro carcere è ritenuto dal qual la sola uostra clementia

lo può liberare" (sig. Aiii–Aiii^v). In the second oration to the king, Camillo thanks him profusely for granting freedom to Palavicino. The edition I have used, from the Biblioteca nazionale di San Marco, has the shelf mark Biblioteca nazionale di San Marco, Misc. 2336. It appears that King Francis I rewarded Camillo in other ways. Note a letter of Pietro Aretino written to Pier Paolo Vergerio in 1534: "veggasi il bene che ha fatto al divino Luigi Alamanni, al solo Giulio Camillo, al mio Alberto e a tanti altri belli spiriti." See Mina Gregori, "Tiziano e l'Aretino," in *Tiziano e il manierismo europeo,* ed. Rodolfo Pallucchini (Florence: Leo S. Olschki Editore, 1978), 274.

129. See *Opere di M. Givlio Camillo* . . . (Venice: Gabriel Giolito de Ferrari, 1560); the shelf mark is Biblioteca nazionale di San Marco, 65.D.218. Note especially p. 223: "Io Luni o Martedi serò a Portogruaro per andar a Vinegia con una bella compagnia; et cosi ci potremo teneramente abbracciare." Note also the postscript Camillo wrote: "V. S. degnerà salutare le Eccelente compadre mio Maestro di Scola, et li Magnifici Signori Fratini, insieme con gli altri Magnifici, et ualorosi gentilhuomini amici communi."

130. Note p. 3 in the *praefatio* of Jacomo (Giacomo) Brocardo, *In tres libros Aristotelis de arte retorica paraphrasis* (n.p., 1549): "tibi quidem assentior Georgi Corneli mihi saepius praedicanti, illos omnes semper tanto parente, ac suo genere indignos iudicari, qui in eo vehementer se non exercentes turpi otio, ac desidiae se dediderunt."

131. Ibid.: "Ac mihi quoque tecum assidue in studio literarum versanti, atque ex eo fructum aliquem exportare cupienti, videntur profecto omnes vitae meae rationes eius esse, qui ab humana societate, immo vero a sua familia seiunctus sit, dum pro hac communione naturae, in eo, in quo iamdiu versor opere nihil efficere nihil procurare inuenior."

132. ASV, S.U., Processi, Busta 18, Contra Pietro Carnesecca, document entitled *Ex confessione D. Petri Carnesecchi carcerati in curia turris nonae* . . . : *Hora costui si troua al presente (se pero non è mutato da due anni in qua) maestro di schola in Venetia et li suoi scolari sonno tutti figlioli de gentilhuomini grandi in quella republica.* . . . See also ASV, S.U., Processi, Busta 25, Contra Isabella Frattina.

133. ASV, S.U., Processi, Busta 25, Contra Isabella Frattina. The trial of Brocardo is enclosed in the fascicolo "Contra Isabella Frattina." See especially his first appearance before the Inquisition on May 14, 1568, fascicolo 1, cc. 3–5.

134. For the *processo* of Pietro Carnesecchi, see ASV, S.U., Processi, Busta 18; for the conventicle at San Fantin in which Carnesecchi participated, see ibid., Busta 11, Contra Andrea de Ugonibus, testimony of Michele Schiavon, March 2, 1565. Carnesecchi had been a friend of Brocardo since 1549, when they were both in France. Ibid., Busta 25, Contra Isabella Frattina, fascicolo 1. See also the article on Carnesecchi by Antonio Rotondò, in *Dizionario del biografico italiano.*

135. On the inquisitor's interest in Andrea da Ponte, and for his heresies, see ASV, S.U., Processi, Busta 11, Contra Andrea da Ugonibus; Busta 20, Contra Michele

Schiavon; Busta 23, Contra Carlo Corner, Contra Giacomo Malipiero; Busta 20, fascicolo 20, abjuration by Giacomo Malipiero.

136. See Marion Leathers Kuntz, "Voices from a Venetian Prison in the Cinquecento: Francesco Spinola and Dionisio Gallo," *Studi Veneziani*, n.s., 27 (1994): 79–126.

137. ASV, Capi del Consiglio dei Dieci, Lettere secrete, Filza 7; note the following: "11 Maii 1568, al podesta de Portogruar. Li tre nobili nostri assistenti al santo Tribunal dell'Inquisition di questa citta hanno ricercato li capi del consilio nostro di X che uolendo esso tribunal hauer nelle mani uno nominato Jacomo Brocardo Piemontese professore di lettere latine e grece."

138. ASV, S.U., Processi, Busta 25, fascicolo IV, c. 29, letters of Salvador Surian, podesta of Portogruaro, to the Capi del Consiglio dei Dieci, May 10, 1568, and May 12, 1568.

139. Ibid. The date was May 11, 1568; see notes 137 and 138 above.

140. Ibid., c. 22, letter of Surian to Capi, May 17, 1568.

141. Ibid., cc. 18–18^v, May 11, 1568.

142. Ibid., c. 18: "È uero che io sono entrato nelle libri et studii della profecia et però hauendo io tali libri di profecia et non altri libri dell'altra sorte prego le eccellentissime Signorie Vostre che tali libri gli ritengano, se l[i] parerà appresso loro per buon rispe[tto]."

143. Ibid., c. 18^v: "et io stimo esser mandato qui da Dio perche uoglio dir alle eccellentissime Signorie Vostre quanto in quelle profecie appartiene importante al stato vostro, altro per adesso non voglio dire."

144. See ASV, S.U., Processi, Busta 160; see also Kuntz, "'Venezia portava el fuocho in seno,'" 109. See also Stella, "Tradizione razionalistica patavina e radicalismo spiritualistico nel XVI secolo," and London, British Library, Sloane MS 1411, fols. 431, 433.

145. ASV, S.U., Processi, Busta 12, fascicolo 20, September 10, 1555, letter of Postel to Maffio Venier: "non manchate di far che nel serenissimo conseio di dieci i sia a[ldit]o auanti chio mori, imo il piu presto che voi potrete percio che io so di grandissimi pericoli nelli quali è la vostra republica, et sono cose tali che io non li posso metter qua in scritto percio che sono cose di principi vicini, etc."

146. See Rotondò, "Jacopo Brocardo," 386–87.

147. ASV, S.U., Processi, Busta 25, fascicolo I, cc. 10–13, testimony given on June 3, 1568.

148. Ibid., cc. 33^v–36, testimony of August 9, 1568.

149. ASV, S.U., Processi, Busta 25, Contra Isabella Frattina, fascicolo I, c. 4.

150. See Vasoli, *Filosofia e religione nella cultura del Rinascimento*, 203–4. There has been a long tradition of the belief that God revealed hidden knowledge to His enlightened. Note, for example, Francesco Barozzi's comments about the philosophic

tradition: "Mos enim antiquorum philosophantium fuit arcana philosophiae quibusdam occultare uelaminibus, ne uulgo nota fierent." *Francisci Barocii Iacobi filii patritii veneti commentarius in locvm Platonis obscvrissimvm* . . . (Bononiae [Bologna], typis Alexandri Benacii, 1566), 5.

151. Vasoli, *Filosofia e religione nella cultura del Rinascimento*, 281.

152. Ibid., 282.

153. See. G. Stabile, "Camillo, Giulio, detto Delminio," in *Dizionario biografico degli italiani* (Rome: Istituto della Enciclopedia Italiana, 1974), XVII:218–30.

154. Cesare Vasoli has edited this important text. See his "Uno scritto inedito."

155. Ibid., 216.

156. Ibid., 217. The concept of man created in the image and likeness of God is also at the heart of Postel's metaphysics.

157. See Rotondò, "Jacopo Brocardo," 384–89.

158. Ibid., 388–89.

159. *Espositio magni prophete Abbatis Joachim in Apocalipsim*, c. 154. "O vere magnum et admirabile signum. Ecclesia in cordis vtero: verbum dei cruciatur affligitur, angustiatur et ideo non cessat clamare. Et quid clamat? Filioli mei quos iterum parturio donec Christus formetur in vobis . . . Mulier ista generaliter matrem designat ecclesiam que in verbo predicationis clamando et parturiendo laborabat."

160. ASV, S.U., Processi, Busta 25, fascicolo IV, c. 23, Costituto D. Vincentius Julianus Romanus, August 12, 1568: "si levo su con allegrezza dicendo questo e quel tempo del qual parla il propheta: Dolores mulieris parturientis et parlando di questa authorita Regnum celorum uim patitur."

161. Ibid. "Mi raccordo anco che disse che il papato doueva finire o in questo presenti papa o nel futuro o nel passato."

162. ASV, S.U., Processi, Busta 25, fascicolo I, c. 28, Costituto Giacomo Brocardo, July 29, 1568.

163. See, for example, ASV, S.U., Processi, Busta 23, Contra Sylvestrum Semprini, Angelam Zoin, Stephamum et Cyprianum Semprini, and Contra Fidelem Vico, Contra Aloyius Mocenigo, Contra D. Marcum Antonium a Canale, Contra D. Andream Dandulo, in which there is a letter—evidently written by or to one of the accused mentioned above—that speaks of God's anger "at the world, which loves the shadows more than the light."

164. Anton Francesco Doni, *Il mondo massimo dell'Academia peregrina* . . . , in *L'Academia peregrina* (Venice: Francesco Marcolini, 1552), c. 113: "O Luce che nelle tenebre risplendi; luce le quali non comprendono le tenebre dell'intelletto mio, se da te non è infuso in me tal lume, che io possi penetrare l'altezza del tuo splendore."

165. Ibid., c. 112^v: "Ma si bene che con tutto il cuore, con tutta l'anima, et con tutta la mente voi amiate, la Bontà Diuina. Percioche si come il legno non per riceuer lume, ma per accendersi diuenta fuoco; cosi voi non per inuestigare solamente

la Diuina luce, ma per infiammarui del Diuino amore, Diuini diuenterete."

166. Kuntz, *Guillaume Postel*, 101–3.

167. See Gregori, "Tiziano e l'Aretino," 271–306 (*Civiltà Veneziana*, Saggi 24), for an interesting discussion of the concept of the portrait in the Cinquecento; note pp. 289–93 and especially p. 292: "L'epistolario dell'Aretino, insieme agli scritti di Anton Francesco Doni, rappresenta altresì la rivalutazione dei letterati come giudici di pittura e la partecipazione sempre più incisiva dei conoscitori e dei dilettanti nel campo figurativo." The engraving of Doni's is similar to the portrait of Postel that appears in Andrè Thevet's *Les vies des hommes illustres*. . . .

168. ASV, S.U., Processi, Busta 18. Pope Pius V had demonstrated great interest in the trial of Carnesecchi because of his influence in Italy and France and especially because he was a priest. The Venetian ambassador Paolo Tiepolo, writing in June 1566 to the Capi del Consiglio dei Dieci, noted that the pope wanted Carnesecchi in his hands more than anyone else, even more than Guido da Fano. See ASV, Capi del Consiglio dei Dieci, Dispacci degli Ambasciatori, Roma, Busta 25, c. 5.

169. ASV, S.U., Processi, Busta 25, Contra Isabella Frattina, Costituto Giacomo Brocardo, cc. 36^v–40.

170. ASV, Consiglio dei Dieci, Parti criminali, Registro 11, c. 25^v, November 5, 1568: "Che sia fatto publice proclamar sopra le scale de San Marco et de Rialto et a Santo Antonin che se alcuno accusera quei scelerati fin' hora incogniti, quali alli 30 del mese passato la matina hanno fatto fugir dalle mano delli Officiali Jacomo Brocardo, el qual dalli detti officiali era stato leuato dalla cason de S. Zuanne in Bragora de ordine del tribunal dell'Inquisitione per condurlo al ditto Tribunal hauendo gettato in acqua a Santo Antonin un officio che conduceua il detto pregion." See also *Nunziature di Venezia*, ed. Aldo Stella (Rome: Istituto Storico Italiano per l'Età Moderna e Contemporanea, 1963), 8:451, letter of Giovanni Antonio Facchinetti, papal nuncio in Venice, to Michele Bonelli, October 30, 1568: "Io con molto mio dispiacere faccio sapere a V.S. illustrissima che stamattina da quattro tutti armati è stato levato di mano dei ministri del S. Offitio Giacomo Brocardo, ch'era condotto per essaminarsi dalle prigioni al luogo dove ci congreghiamo."

171. *Nunziature di Venezia*, 8:451, letter from Facchinetti to Bonelli, dated November 3, 1568: "Io intendo che questi signori spediranno forsi questa sera la parte con la taglia debita contra quelli levarno il Brocardo delle mani dei ministri del S. Offitio." See also ASV, S.U., Processi, Busta 25, Costituto di Isabella Frattina (fascicolo 1), who denied any knowledge of the men who helped Brocardo to escape. Note, however, *Nunziature di Venezia*, 8:458, letter from Fracchinetti to Bonelli, November 10, 1568: "Il marito della signora Isabella Frattina, ritenuta prigione a instanza del S. Offitio, è inditiato d'haver tenuto mano a coloro che levarno il Broccardo alla corte; onde li signori capi l'hanno fatto ritenere et anco uno di quei ministri che servivano al S. Offitio per il che credo che si verrà di certo a notitia della verità."

172. *Nunziature di Venezia*, 8:459, letter from Facchinetti to Bonelli, November 13,

1568: "Ho ricevuto la lettera di V. S. illustrissima delli 6. Del Frattina ritenuto per conto del Brocardo, questi signori non mancheranno di diligenza et la verità verrà ad ogni modo in luce; egli, come io credo, è in colpa et con esso anco gli sbirri che servivano al S. Offitio et che conducevano esso Brocardo."

173. See Niccoli, "'Prophetie di Musaicho.'"

174. See the various articles by John Martin cited in his 1993 work on heresies among the artisans, *Venice's Hidden Enemies*.

175. ASV, S.U., Processi, Busta 35, fascicolo 11, c. 1, September 3, 1573, Contra Dominico di Lorenzi Callegaro, Benetto Floriani far arpecordi, Lunardo quondam Michiel cinador da panni et Biasio quondam Christofolo lancilloto samiter.

176. Ibid., September 5, 1573, cc. 1–2.

177. Ibid., cc. 1ᵛ–2; see also Costituto di B. Floriano [Florian], September 5, 1573, c. 5.

178. Ibid., c. 2ᵛ: "Interrogatus se'l sa che altri siano di questa Compagnia. Respondit: Io non so di certezza, ma ho inteso et credo che sia una schuola grande." It is not certain whether Alessandro meant one of the existing *scuole grandi* or was only designating the group by the term *scuola grande* to indicate a sizable number of adherents.

179. See ASV, S.U., Processi, Busta 35, Costituto di Alessandro Callegher, September 5, 1573, c. 3. See also Venice, Archivio storico del Patriarcato di Venezia, Criminalia Santissimae Inquisitionis, Busta 2, October 26, 1573, Costituto di Ioannes Baptista de Rauaiolis. Ioannes Baptista said they often went "to reason with the Hebrews, and their practice was of the Hebrews."

180. Venice, Archivio storico del Patriarcato di Venezia, Criminalia Santissimae Inquisitionis, Busta 2, October 14, 1573, Costituto di Donna Camilla de Foligattis de Venetiis, wife of Ioannes Baptista de Rauaiolis. Camilla testified that "più uolte mentre che mio marito desinaua o cenaua teneua l'appresso il Testamento vecchio et legendolo." While in Venice, he also read the Old Testament with Lunardo Cimador.

181. ASV, S.U., Processi, Busta 35, Costituto di Benedetto Florian, cc. 3ᵛ and 5, September 5, 1573.

182. Ibid., c. 5.

183. Ibid., c. 6ᵛ.

184. Ibid., c. 5.

185. Ibid., Costituto di Dominico Callegher [Callegaro], September 7, 1573, c. 8.

186. Ibid.

187. "Hic est generalis Capitaneus totius classis marittime Venetorum et vnionis sancte ecclesie qui post legationem suam in Anglia in qua ita prudenter omnia sibi commissa perficiet; qui post annum sue reversionis ex Anglia eligetur gener-

alis Capitaneus magne armate vt dicit Merlinus." *Abbas Joachim magnus propheta: Expositio magni prophete Ioachim in librum beati Cirilli de magnis tribulationibus et statu Sancte matris Ecclesie,* c. XXII^v.

188. Ibid., c. XXII.

189. Ibid., c. XXII^v. "Tempore magne tribulationis bonorum marinariorum in Anglia legatione fungetur eiusdem gentis et urbis. Vir quidam nobilis ortus ex stirpe primi domini eorundem quod ita prudenter ac fideliter omnia sibi commissa perficiet vt merito post annum sue reuersionis ex Anglia: Capitaneus generalis maritimi belli a suo Senatu eligatur ac in seruitium ecclesie sancte ex precepto angelici pastoris infedeles aggredietur et magnam inde victoriam consequetur ita vt penitus anihilentur."

190. Ibid., c. XXIII^v. "Hanc autem emendationem eis largietur deus ob admonitionem et consilium sancti presulis ciuitatis eorum. . . . Item dicit quod habebunt principem sanctum qui adhuc viuens miraculis clarus erit." See also c. XXXVIII.

191. Ibid., c. XXIII^v: "Item quod post mortem antichristi emendati erunt supra omnes mundi homines et erunt meliores ac sanctiores. Item quod Dominium eorum non deficiet vsque ad finem mundi." Many of Merlin's prophecies appear in Joachim's *Expositio magni prophete Ioachim in librum beati Cirilli de magnis tribulationibus et statu Sancte matris Ecclesie.*

192. ASV, S.U., Processi, Busta 35, Costituto di Dominico Callegher, September 7, 1573, c. 9.

193. Ibid., cc. 8–8^v: "Et è come quando more il sommo Pontifice li Cardinali restano grauidi, et ne parturiscono un'altro. Et cosi il Dose di Venetia che quando more la Signoria ne parturisse un'altro. Et non parturisse un putto, ma un'homo fatto."

194. Ibid., c. 9.

195. Ibid., c. 9^v.

196. Ibid., cc. 13–13^v.

197. Ibid., c. 15.

198. ASV, S.U., Processi, Busta 35, Contra Domenego di Lorenzi Callegaro, Benetto Florian . . . 1573. See the confession of Domenego Callegher: "Ho anche creduto et tenuto che li Hebrei, Turchi, et ogn'uno nella sua fede si possono saluare anchora che non siano battizati."

199. The idea of an angelic shepherd, or even a series of angelic shepherds, was dominant in the fifteenth century and continued even after the Council of Trent. The message was the same—the unity of a reformed Church led by an angelic shepherd. See, for example, Venice, Biblioteca nazionale di San Marco, MSS latini, Cl. III, Cod. CLXXVII (= 2176), c. 26^v: "Hic uir sanctus religiosorum cornua conterret superba. Et omnes erunt ad statum primitive ecclesie. Itaque pastor unus, lex unus, dominus unus, verus et modestus deum timens."

200. Venice, Archivio storico del Patriarcato di Venezia, Criminalia Santissimae Inquisitionis, Busta 2, Costituto di Ioannes Baptista de Rauaiolis, October 26, 1573,

cc. 187–187^v. When Ioannes Baptista was asked if he knew why he was being summoned, he replied: "Io non lo so ma credo che siamo presi per causa di un libro scritto a mano che legeuano in casa di messer Domenico calzolaro sudetto alias calligaro il qual libro messer Benetto legeua in presentia del detto maestro Domenico Leonardo mio genero . . . et poi andavamo tutti a spesso, et mi conduceuano dalli hebrei con li quali loro ragionauano et la prattica loro era dell'Hebrei. . . . Io non mi son mai accorto che detto libro fusse heretico, ma conteneua solo di Profecie ciò è che haueua da essere la rotta del Turcho, la priuatione dell'imperio in casa d'Austria et che s'haueua a pigliar Constantinopoli et che il Turcho haueua a uenire alla Fede Christiana et che haueua ad essere uno solo Ouile et un sol Pastore."

201. Ibid., c. 188.

202. Ibid.

203. Ibid., c. 188^v.

204. Ibid., c. 190. According to Benedetto Florian, his teacher Corazzaro, who had been dead twelve years (having died in 1561), had denied the words of a preacher in Venice who had interpreted the passage as a reference to the Virgin Mary. Corazzaro maintained that the woman clothed in the sun represented the Holy Mother Church; Florian followed his late teacher's interpretation.

205. Ibid., c. 190^v.

206. See *Venetia città nobilissima*, c. 58^v. See also the excellent article by Ottavia Niccoli, "'Prophetie di Musaicho.'" Note also Letizia Pierozzi, "La vittoria di Lepanto nell'escatologia e nella profezia," *Rinascimento*, 2d ser., 34 (1994): 317–63.

207. See Postel's *Il libro della divina ordinatione*, written in Venice under the inspiration of the Venetian Virgin and published in Padua in 1555. This book, along with its companion, *Le prime nove del altro mondo*, caused Postel grave problems with the Venetian Inquisition.

208. See Marion Leathers Kuntz, "What's in a Name? Postel as Petrus Anusius in 1560," in *Sociétés et idéologies des temps modernes: Hommage à Arlette Jouanna*, ed. J. Fouilleron, G. LeThiec, and H. Michel (Montpellier: Conseil scientifique de l'Université de Montpellier III, 1996), 731–45.

209. John Martin, on the other hand (*Venice's Hidden Enemies*, 206–8), has made a strong argument that the *cavaliere* was a Priuli, because of the strange statement in the inquisition of Ioannes Baptista de Rauaiolis, son-in-law of Lunardo *cimador*, a follower of Corazzaro, which noted that the *cavaliere* was born in Domo Priullia. This certainly sounds as if the statement refers to a Priuli, but the whole passage is highly metaphorical, and I personally think Postel is a more likely candidate for the role because of the similarity of what he said about himself and his role and because of the two books he published in Padua (see note 207 above), in which he clearly defined his mission in regard to Venice and the Venetian Virgin. However, Martin has worked diligently on this point, and he may be correct in his identification. From the testimony of Ioannes Baptista, there are things that cannot be attributed positively to either Postel or Priuli.

210. Dionisio believed that he was the *cavaliere* who was chosen by God to lead the Church in a universal reformation. But see Cesare Vasoli, "Giorgio Benigno Salviati" (Dragisic), in *Prophetic Rome in the High Renaissance Period*, ed. Majorie Reeves (Oxford: Clarendon Press, 1992), 121–56. See also his *Profezia e ragione*.

211. Guy Le Fèvre de la Boderie, Postel's disciple and amanuensis, translated into French Zorzi's *De harmonia mundi*.

212. Cantimori, *Eretici italiani*, 206.

213. The trial of Giorgio Siculo has not been found. However, in 1566 the physician Francesco Severo da Argenta carefully explained Siculo's teachings to the Inquisition in Ferrara. See Venice, Archivio storico del Patriarcato di Venezia, Criminalia Santissimae Inquisitionis, Busta 2.

214. Nascimbene Nascimbeni also revealed Siculo's teachings to the Inquisition in Venice. See ASV, S.U., Processi, Busta 30, fascicolo 10, Contra Nascimbene Nascimbeni. Giorgio Siculo was investigated and condemned by the Inquisition in Udine. See also Cantimori, *Eretici italiani*, 57–70; Carlo Ginzburg, "Due note sul profetismo Cinquecento," *Rivista Storica Italiana* 78 (1966): 184–226. Neither Cantimori nor Ginzburg made use of the trial of Francesco Severo at the Archivio storico del Patriarcato di Venezia. See also Niccoli, "'Prophetie di Musaicho.'" For an interesting account of Severo's literary interests and his correspondence with Paolo Manuzio, see Renato Raffaelli, "Notizie intorno a Francesco Severi 'il medico d'Argenta,'" *Studi Urbinati* 56/B3 (1983): 91–136. Severo was also a friend of Giovanni Battista Pigna, who, in addition to being a philosopher, physician, and *letterato*, was the secretary for Duke Alfonso II of Ferrara.

215. See Venice, Archivio storico del Patriarcato di Venezia, Criminalia Sanctissimae Inquisitionis, Busta 2, Costituto di Francesco Severo, cc. 86–87.

216. Ibid., c. 87.

217. Ibid., c. 102^v.

218. Ibid., c. 106^r.

219. Ibid., cc. 106^v–107^r. "Quod doctrine et constitutiones antiquorum et modernorum doctorum ecclesiae propter suam temeritatem reduxerunt res celestes in cerimonias et ritus carnales ex quibus causata est perditio humana, et per hoc ostenditur toti mundo quod fides Christiana sit secta diabolica et maledicta plena fraude super omnes sectas infidelium et qui Georgius Siculus hortatus fuit omnes ad non credendum doctoribus ecclesiae sed reuelationi sibi factae a Christo in dicto libro."

220. Ibid., c. 112.

221. Ibid., c. 112^v: "Modo autem sibi Georgio vltimo seruo suo Christus in propria persona reuellauit ueritatem sacrae scripturae et fecit eum Georgium legatum suum ad manifestandum mundo doctrinam et ueritatem Christianam occultatam vsque ad presentem diem per opera diaboli et per presumptionem ac temeritatem doctorum ecclesiae."

222. Ibid., cc. 113ʳ–113ᵛ: "Quod domini temporales non debent permittere quod in eorum dominiis iudicetur secundum leges canonicas uel ciuiles sed iudicia debent fieri secundum precepta iudicialia legis mosayce et quod doctores qui dixerunt legem Mosaycam esse abrogatam quantum ad precepta iudicialia sunt ignorantes quia plus obligant modo quam obligarent ante aduentum Christi."

223. Ibid., c. 113ᵛ: "Quod Domini temporales non debent permittere episcopos habere diuitias aut uiuere voluptuose et si non faciunt officium suum prout tenentur debent eos castigare et deponere ab episcopatu."

224. Cantimori, *Eretici italiani*, 58.

225. Ibid., 59–60.

226. ASV, S.U., Processi, Busta 35, Costituto di Benedetto Florian da Cittadella. Note especially "Ei dictum: chi sarà dunque quel Pastor che li sarà simile et chi sarà quel seruo fidel come di sopra. Respondit: Non credo che sarà nome quel seruo che farà la uolontà di Dio. Ei dictum: Quel non è al proposito se ui domanda chi sarà quel pastor solo simile al figliuol dell'huomo. Respondit: Chi farà la uolontà di Dio in quel fatto perche Dio elese molti come ha fatto Moise." Florian was questioned on September 3, 1573, but he was reporting the prophecies of Benedetto Corazzaro, his teacher, who had died ten years before.

227. In his testimony Dominico Callegher indicated that the shepherd they awaited "è un'homo che Dio genera non come ha generato Christo ma genera cioè eleze a destrution de infideli et de heretici et far uegnir tutto il mondo sotto questa fede, et far quel che ha ditto Christo. Erit unum ouile et unus pastor. Et questo homo non è Christo ma è quel sol del qual parla Malachia quando parla del sole perche Christo è la luce, che da lume al sole cioè a questo homo. Et questo homo è fiol di Dio et della Chiesa et quello che dice il Salmo, Postula a me et dabo tibi gentes hereditatem tuam." See ASV, S.U., Processi, Busta 35, Costituto di Dominico Callegher, September 7, 1573, c. 8.

228. See Kuntz, "'Venezia portava el fuocho in seno,'" 119; London, British Library, Sloane MS 1411, fol. 433. See also ASV, Maggior Consiglio, Libro d'oro vecchio, inizio del Proemio dogale, c. 21, where there is a beautiful miniature of Saint Mark giving the Law to the doge of Venice, Andrea Gritti, who is on his knees before the saint.

229. ASV, S.U., Processi, Busta 30, fascicolo 10, Contra Nascimbene Nascimbeni, document entitled *Abiuratio D. Nascimbeni de nascimbenis ferrariensis, MDLI die 15 Januarii*. Note especially: "Et specialiter abiuro, reuoco et detestor omnes haereses Georgii Siculi Rioli de Santo Petro contentas in eius libro maiore, in tractatu de iustificatione, in lettera ad Illustrissimum Ducem Ferrariae et in lettera ad fratrem Thomam Genuem ac in aliis eius scriptis de quibus haeresibus quae ferè omnes haereses complectuntur; merito habuistis me uehementissime suspectum ex eo quam pluries illum hospitio recepi, et per menses retinui quem hereticum sciebam, et eius scripta haeresibus refertissima penes me retinui, ac aliis ostendi, ac laudaui cum eorum authore et in multis constitutis periurus fui, et pro viribus egi, ut non uenirent ad

manus inquisitoris ac alios induxi ad dicta opera comburenda ne eorum errores ad notitiam uestram uenirent."

230. Ibid., *costituto,* January 14, 1570. Concerning the duration of his adhesion to Siculo's teachings, Nascimbene responded: "Del tempo precise non mi ricordo, ma posso pensare che'l sia dal 1550 in circa in qua." He also spoke of performing his duties as a priest, including consecration, while believing the teachings of Siculo. "Io son prete da messa ordinato, et ho hauuto tutti gli ordeni sacri successiuamente et ho celebrato pui uolte. . . . Io diceua le parole per haueua in memoria il beneficio della passion di Christo. . . . Io credeua a quello che mi haueua insegnar Giorgio, il qual mi disse che quel sacramento era il corpo mistico di Christo. In questo modo, che Giesu Christo in quella ceremonia del pane et del uino fece una unione in spirito de tutti i credenti presenti, passati et futuri. Et un questo corpo tutto insieme andò alla Croce, et morendo Christo moressemo tutti in Christo, et resuscitando Christo resuscitassimo tutti insieme." Nascimbene is an example of the *nicodemismo* practiced before and after the Council of Trent. For his two abjurations, see note 229 above and note 233 below.

231. ASV, S.U., Processi, Busta 30, document entitled *1560 die ultima mensis Octobris.*

232. Ibid.; see the document entitled *Abiuratio D. Nascimbeni de nascimbenis ferrariensis,* MDLI *die 15 Januarii;* see also the *costituto* of Nascimbene, February 14, 1570, c. 4: "Ei dicto che ui mosse quelle altre due uolte a fingerui pentito con abgiurar, come hauete fatto due uolte in Ferrara? Respondit la prima uolta abgiurai per far l'obedienza che mi comandaua l'Inquisitore perche cosi ricercaua il merito della causa. Dell'altra poi, perche fui chiamato come ho detto di sopra."

233. Ibid., *costituto,* January 14, 1570, c. 2. Note especially: "Interrogatus sit presbyter aut laicus uel uxoratus? Respondit: Io son prete da messa ordinato et ho hauuto tutti gli ordeni sacri successiuamente et ho celebrato più uolte. Interrogatus se dopo che egli è stato in questi errori di heresia ha celebrato? Respondit Ho celebrato piu uolte che ho celebrato ad euitandum scandalum."

234. Ibid., *costituto,* February 16, 1570, c. 6.

235. Ibid., fascicolo 10, Contra Nascimbene Nascimbeni. Don Antonio Montavono da Bozzolo's abjuration is without date, but it was made, according to the monk, during the reign of Pope Pius V, that is, between January 7, 1566, and May 1, 1572, and during the time when Alfonso Rosetti was bishop of Ferrara, that is, 1563–77. See, for the dating, *Hierarchia Catholica,* 3:196.

236. ASV, S.U., Processi, Busta 30, fascicolo 10, Contra Nascimbene Nascimbeni, abjuration by Don Antonio Montavano.

237. See ASV, S.U., Processi, Busta 161, document entitled *Summario del processo contra pre Giovanni Battista Clario da Udine . . . ,* September 1, 1568.

238. See ASV, S.U., Processi, Busta 159. In 1578 Nascimbene, because of his poor health, was allowed to live in the house of Girolamo Donzellino. See ASV, S.U., Processi, Busta 30, Costituto di Girolamo Donzellino, document entitled *Die Jouis 17 mensis Juilii 1578 in palatio Illustrissimi D.D. legati apostolici prope S. Francisci a Vinea.*

Nascimbene left the home of Donzellino to make some *"soldi,"* as he wrote to his host on July 10, 1578. See the letter from Nascimbene to Donzellino, Busta 30. Nascimbene's departure caused Donzellino more problems with the Inquisition.

239. The letter written by Floriano Turchi from Bologna on January 29, 1556, was directed to the Capi del Consiglio dei Dieci, whom he informed about the days that were to be dangerous. Although he was in the habit of publishing each year a *prognostico universale,* he decided to write a letter rather than publish things that might be damaging for Venice. See ASV, Capi del Consiglio dei Dieci, Lettere diverse, Busta 6, January 29, 1556.

Chapter V

1. ASV, S.U., Processi, Busta 22, Contra Dionisium Gallum, document entitled *Legatio serui Dei . . . :* "Audiuerunt clarissimi viri Veneti domini Justus Maurocenus, vulgari sermone, Mauresiny et Rochus Venetus sensarius bladorum vulgari sermone sensare de biave." On the duties of the *senser di biave,* see Giulio Rezasco, *Dizionario del linguaggio italiano storico ed amministrativo* (Florence: Forni Editore, 1881; reprint, Bologna, 1982), 1010: "Quegli che s'intromette tra i contraenti per la conclusione del negozio, specialmente tra il venditore e'l compratore, nelle cose de' traffici, traendone una mercede." The word *senser* also has variant forms such as *sansale, sansaro,* and *sansero.* At first the *senser* had to be an "original Venetian." By the middle of the sixteenth century, however, this qualification was not always respected, although the honorable conduct of the *senser* was essential. Note, for example: "L'andarà parte qui in nomine Iesu Christi et sanctissimi Diui Marci Protectoris nostri far si debba sanseri n°. cento quali siano Venetiani originarii et sappino ben legger et scriver, de'quali alla ellettori, che quelli ellezerà i quali nel Rialti nostri siano deputadi al far praticar, et concluder tutti i mercadanti nostri si terrieri come forastieri saranno fatti ne altri che loro detti mercadi possono praticar far ne concluder soto le pene inferias descritte non possondo per alcun modo praticar, ne far mercado alcuno nel fontego nostro di Todeschi ma solum nel Rialto sotto le pene de sotto contegnude . . . non possino etiam far mecadantia alcuna per se nec etiam faria far per altri per nome suo, ne haver parte, ne compagnia in Bottega ne con mercadaner ouer Botteghieri alcuno sotto le infrascritte pene." ASV, Arti, Busta 517. See also *Dizionario del Dritto comune e veneto che contiene le leggi civili, canoniche e criminali,* Opero di Marco Ferro Avvocato veneto (Venice, 1781), 10:7–10, s.v. *i sensali.*

2. ASV, S.U., Processi, Busta 22, Contra Dionisium Gallum, document entitled *Haec est causa:* "Audiuerunt clarissim viri Domini Iustus Maurocenus vulgari sermone Mauresiny, et Rochus Venetus sensarius bladarum vulgari sermone, sensare de biave: hi testentur in veritate, quae, sua sponte, sed instinctu motuque spiritussancti, quod credimus, nos consolantes et adiuuantes, ex nobis audiuerunt, partim in nostro hospitio insignis hominis peregrini partim, in aedibus ipsius humanissimi atque christianissim Domini Rochi Veneti. . . ." This statement is written on the verso of the last leaf.

3. Ibid.

4. Ibid., document entitled *Legatio electi serui Dei et nuntii magistri Dionisii Galli*. Above the signatures, Dionisio wrote: "Scripsimus Venetiis in aedibus ipsius clarissimi domini Rochi Veneti die iunii septimo anno Domini 1566." Dionisio signed his name "Denys de gallois," followed by his usual cipher; under his name was that of Morosini, and under Morosini's followed that of Rocho.

5. Ibid., document entitled *A tres illustre tresexcellent seigneur mon seigneur le Duc de Ferrare*. . . . Note, for example: "Monseigneur vostre oncle, mon seigneur le Marquis de Masse, a ouyr patiamment et a tressagement donne son aduys."

6. In an effort to identify Rochus Venetus, I read all the cases that the Inquisition heard in 1566–67, hoping to find some link with Dionisio's mysterious benefactor as well as to compare Dionisio's case with all others heard during the same period. This method was fruitful, since in Santo Uffizio, Processi, Busta 21, the name of Rocho de Mazzochis, *senser di biave* in 1566, appeared as a witness. His occupation, *senser di biave*, appended to his cognomen, confirmed Rochus Venetus's identity. On July 18, 1566, when Rocho was called as a witness in the case of Vancimugio, he was identified as "Dominus Rochus de Mazzochis Venetus sensarius bladorum habitans in parochia Santi Moysis in domibus Domini Bartholomei Nani ab auro testis." Rochus Venetus was, in reality, Rocho de Mazzochis, *senser di biave* in 1566. His position was obviously important to him, since he always identified himself as *senser di biave*. Dionisio also referred to him in the same way and, in addition, called him Venetus. See ASV, S.U., Processi, Busta 21, Contra Ioannem de Vancimugio Vicentinum, who had been investigated in 1561 and again in July 1566. From an undated document of the same trial, it appears that Rocho was summoned in both investigations of Vancimugio.

7. When Rocho was associated with Dionisio in Venice in 1566, he was living in the house of Bartholomeo Nani in the *parrochia* of San Moisé; he later resided in San Paternian and in San Samuele. Throughout his mature years Rocho de Mazzochis had always lived near San Marco. Although he had changed residences, he continued to rent a *mezado* in San Moisé from Signor Nani until 1582. See ASV, Dieci Savi sopra le Decime a Rialto, Condizioni, San Marco, Busta 158, no. 1002: "Io Bartolamio Nani del quondam messer Steffano abitante in contra di San Moise dicho atrouarmi la sotto scrita intrada et prima. . . . Item un mezado il qual afitaua per inanzi a messer Rocho sanser da biaue ducati uinti cinque et ora la ho data a messer Alvise Sonicha spagnol il qual si ha obligato a insegnar la gramatica a tre fioli picoli per dito afitto." Bartholomeo Nani, a Venetian patrician and son of Stefano Nani, owned several properties in the *contrada* of San Moisé.

8. Rocho de Mazzochis was obviously comfortable in the business and social life of aristocratic circles in Venice. Baldassare Moro, son of Agustin, grandson of Baldassare, was a patrician, scion of an old and important Venetian family. He was born on July 5, 1512, and was received into the Maggior Consiglio on July 4, 1531, the day before his nineteenth birthday. See ASV, Avogaria di Comun, Prove di età per magistrate (1529–39), Busta 176, c. 41.

9. ASV, S.U., Processi, Busta 21, Contra Ioannem de Vancimugio Vicentinum, testimony of Alvisi Moro, July 9, 1566.

10. ASV, S.U., Processi, Busta 21, testimony of Alvise Moro, a stonecutter. Alvise said that on numerous occasions Vancimugio had indicated a desire to join the "Compagnia de i Padri del buon Giesù." In all likelihood he meant the Jesuits, since his confessor was a Jesuit. However, note that the Padri del buon Giesù of Ravenna were established in that city around 1500 by a virgin named Margherita da Rusci from Castello di Romagna. See *La piazza universale di tutte le professioni del mondo, nvovamente ristampata . . . da Thomaso Garzoni da Bagnacauallo. . . .* (Venice: Vincenzo Somasco, 1595), 68. The witness also indicated that Zuane was in desperate circumstances, which had caused him to lose his love and faith. He had spoken of going to Geneva, since he would be given fifty scudi or more if he needed it; he also said that the faith was better served in Geneva. Zuane's confessor, Father Flamminio, a member of the Society of Jesus, testified that Zuane had uttered those words about Geneva out of desperation and physical need; when he was no longer in need, he had returned to his good Catholic posture.

For an account of the early activity of the Jesuits, see O'Malley, *The First Jesuits,* and *The Jesuits: Cultures, Sciences, and the Arts,* ed. O'Malley et al.; see also *I Gesuiti e Venezia.* Lynn Martin has some interesting remarks about Jesuit preaching in northern Italy. Louis Coudret, a Savoyard, had gained a reputation as a convincing preacher. Martin notes that the Jesuits made use of good preachers to fight heresy, to reform morals, and to attract members to the Society of Jesus. In addition, good preachers provided entertainment and distraction for the masses as well as salvation of souls. See Martin, *The Jesuit Mind,* 7–15.

11. See note 8 above.

12. ASV, S.U., Processi, Busta 20, Contra Fra Cipriano Corner (in actuality Fra Cherubino).

13. One of the most notorious cases involving a priest was that of Fra Aurelio, a member of the strict Camaldolensian order. Fra Aurelio, having taken the white habit of the hermits of the company of San Romoaldo, was accused of divination and chiromancy, of keeping harlots in his house, and of neglecting his Christian duties. So flagrantly shocking were the acts of Fra Aurelio said to be that both Venetian patricians and religious complained about his behavior to the inquisitors. Fra' Aurelio apparently was a sort of "medicine man" who prescribed herbs for various ailments, recited certain prayers that purported to have curative value, and, in addition, predicted the future for his clients, who were said to be "persons of diverse states: men, women, brothers, priests, Jews, gentlemen, and other persons." The case of Fra Aurelio, magician-prophet, was heard off and on for many years before Dionisio arrived in Venice and several years after his departure. The investigation of Fra Aurelio revealed that one of his associates was Paolo Magno, a lawyer, also accused of living a scandalous life almost devoid of religious observance. For the trial of Fra Aurelio, see ASV, S.U., Processi, Busta 31, Contra Fra Aurelio Stichiano.

14. Ibid., Busta 31, fascicolo Contra fratrem Aurelium Stichiano Senensem 1572, c. 1^v–2. The testimony of Gidonus was given on May 6, 1568. Note: "Il magnifico messer Giusto Moresini uenne queste quaresima a casa mia et cosi in ragionamento mi disse: mi maraviglio che Monsignor reuerendissimo Patriarcha non proueda a quello tristo, et io li risposi come uolete che Monsignor Reverendissimo Patriarca li proveda, che esso non deue saper cosa alcuna, ne conosce costui." The priest Gidonus also noted that Paolo Magno, a friend of Fra' Aurelio, "dice sempre male de prete et de frati" (c. 1^v).

15. A large group of young patricians were interested in reform of the Church. For their trials, see especially ASV, S.U., Processi, Buste 20 and 23. See also Federica Ambrosini, "Tendenze filoprotestanti nel patriziato veneziano," in *La Chiesa di Venezia tra riforma protestante e riforma cattolica*, ed. Giuseppe Gullino (Venice: Edizioni Studium Cattolico, 1990), 155–81; Silvana Seidel-Menchi, "Protestantesimo a Venezia," in ibid., 131–54. On the patrician heretics, note also Grendler, *The Roman Inquisition and the Venetian Press*, 134–38. Donald E. Queller, in *The Venetian Patriciate*, paints a gloomy picture of the patricians. Yet in his conclusion he states: "Behind my rather straightforward attack on the myth of the patriciate lies a concern for a more adequate, complex, and indeed ambiguous conception of man and society. Venetian nobles, like the rest of us, were not one-dimensional caricatures of human beings, as the mythographers depict them, but many-sided, complicated and inconsistent beings caught up in the glory and the tragedy of real life" (253). Note also Pommier, "La société vénitienne et la reforme," 3–26. For a general view of the religious climate, see Paolo Ulvioni, "Cultura politica e cultura religiosa a Venezia nel secondo Cinquecento: Un bilancio," *Archivio Storico Italiano* 14 (1983): 591–651; also the important article by Achille Olivieri, "Fra collettività urbane e rurali e 'colonie' mediterranee: L"eresia' a Venezia," in *Storia della cultura veneta: Dal primo Quattrocento al Concilio di Trento*, ed. Girolamo Arnaldi and Manilio Pastore Stocchi (Vicenza: Neri Pozza Editore, 1981), 3/III:467–512.

16. See note 1 above.

17. In Rocho's testimony before the Holy Office concerning Zuane de Vancimugio, he stated that he had known Vancimugio because Vancimugio was a friend of Rocho's patron, Baldassare Moro. Then Rocho added: "Io hebbi domestichezza con lui perche esso fu causa, che io seruissi da alcuni pochi denari una pouera famiglia da ca negro, per il quale imprestito hebbi poi un officio a Doana de Mar fin che sconti in parte i miei danari, perche del resto fui satisfato." ASV, S.U., Processi, Busta 21, Contra Ioannem de Vancimugio Vicentinum, testimony of July 18, 1566.

18. The will of Andriana Centani was written on April 23, 1561, as indicated in ASV, Sezione Notarile, Testamenti, Carlo Bianco, Buste 78, 87. Unfortunately, the will that appears in the *busta* indicated is not Andriana Centani's but rather Andriana Contarini's. Someone at some period misread Contarini for Centani. Andriana Centani's will has not been found. See Tassini, *Curiosità veneziane*, 160–61, s.v. "Centani." See also ASV, Dieci Savi sopra le Decime a Rialto, Condizioni, San

Marco, Redecime 1661, Registro 387, no. 364. I am indebted to Professors Beth and John Glixen for the latter reference.

19. See ASV, Sezione Notarile, Testamenti, Nicolò Cigrini, Busta 198, no. 23, dated August 14, 1574.

20. The couple lived in San Trovaso at the time the will was written. Anzola willed to the Hospital of San Giovanni e Paolo one ducat for prayers at vespers for her soul and the same amount to the Hospital of the Incurabili. She also wanted a ducat dispensed to the poor in the *contrade* of San Lorenzo, Trinità, and Castello. She left all of her other possessions to her daughter, Camilla, and any other children she and Signor Bartholomeo might have. She wanted money to be given every year to her brother Giacomo; her father and mother would receive five ducats each, as would her brother Zuanmaria. She willed that at her husband's death four hundred ducats be given to the place of her burial on condition that a perpetual Mass be said for the repose of her soul. She requested that the rest of her dowry be used for the needs of her brothers, Giacomo and Zuanmaria. At the death of one brother, the money would go to the other. She also indicated that if Zuanmaria, evidently the younger brother, married and had legitimate children, the dowry would go to his heirs. The young woman requested that she be buried in the habit of the Madonna, in the place where her husband was buried. Since Anzola had only one child at the time her will was written, she was probably very young. It is difficult to determine from Anzola's will the precise amount of her dowry, although it was in excess of four hundred ducats, since she willed that amount to the place of her burial. Apart from her charitable bequests, she left all her other possessions to her daughter, Camilla. Since she also requested that the rest of her dowry be divided among her brothers and their heirs, thus expecting that residue would remain for this purpose, her dowry could have been perhaps one thousand ducats.

21. See ASV, Giudici di Petizion, Inventari, Busta 340/5, nos. 59, 60.

22. See Tassini, *Curiosità veneziane*, 161; see also Alvise Zorzi, *Venetian Palaces* (New York: Rizzoli, 1989), 206, where the author discusses the Palazzo Zantani, or Centani, at San Tomà. The Zantani (Centani) rented this house from the Rizzo family. Carlo Goldoni was born in this house in 1707.

23. This marriage can be ascertained from Rocho's will, dictated from his deathbed on February 6, 1592. See ASV, Sezione Notarile, Atti, Giovann Battista Tomasi, Busta 979, no. 613. I am indebted to *ricercatrice* Dr. Viola Visentini for her help in locating this important document, which was listed in the *fondi* not accessible to the *studiosi*.

24. The marriage contract was witnessed on March 14, 1587. See ASV, Sezione Notarile, Atti, Lion Lioni, Busta 7835. Giulia's dowry was sizable. To Giulia, Rocho bequeathed a fourth part of his first wife's dowry and a half of all else that remained. The remainder of Andriana's dowry and the residue of her possessions were bequeathed to his daughter Anzola. However, four days later, on February 10, 1592, Rocho, still gravely ill, added to his will a codicil in which he gave all the

remainder of his fortune to his daughter Anzola, thereby rescinding the half portion of his estate that he had originally given to Giulia, his second wife. (See note 23 above.) The fourth portion of Andriana's dowry, however, still remained with Giulia. The Franceschi were important *cittadini* in Venice, and some of the Franceschi held noble status in the early seventeenth century. It is rather unusual that Rocho willed a fourth of his first wife's dowry to his second wife, Giulia. Having married Giulia at an advanced age, he lived with her only five years before his death. After his death, Giulia seems to have managed her affairs well, since a notary document dated April 25, 1610, indicates that Giulia had loaned one Vettor Galina 300 ducats and that said Vettor had paid the final 190 ducats on the date indicated. From this document we learn that Giulia had been married to Messer Domenego Ciduzzi before her marriage to Rocho de Mazzochis. See ASV, Sezione Notarile, Atti, Anzolo Schietti, Busta 11971. I am indebted to Dr. Elisabetta Barile, Archivio di Stato Venezia, for her help in locating these references.

25. ASV, Sezione Notarile, Atti, Bartholomeo Bressan, Busta 494.

26. See note 7 above.

27. During his first marriage, Rocho may have been living in the house of his wife, Andriana Centani. For his residence in the Ca'Corner at least five years before his marriage to Giulia, see ASV, Sezione Notarile, Atti, Bartholomeo Bressan, Busta 494, c. 32. In a complicated land transaction handled by the notary Bartholomeo Bressan, son-in-law of Rocho de Mazzochis, Rocho acted as a witness, identified in the document as "D. Rochus de Mazzochis quondam di Andrea olim sansarius bladorum di contrada Santi Samuelis in domibus da Cha cornelio."

28. See ASV, Sezione Notarile, Atti, Lion Lioni, Busta 7835.

29. Giusto Morosini's lineage was called dalla Sbarra. See Venice, Biblioteca nazionale di San Marco, MSS italiani, Cl. VII, Cod. CMXXVII (= 8596), Marco Barbaro, Alberi, c. 188^v; see also ASV, Avogaria di Comun, Cronaca Matrimoni, Registro 106, c. 91^v: "Ottobrio 1510, Pietro Antonio Morexini fo. di S. Giusto con la fia del Bartolomeo Venier quondam signor Beneto." For the will of Laura Venier, mother of Giusto Morosini, see ASV, Sezione Notarile, Testamenti, nodaro Antonio Marsilio, Busta 1210, no. 647. Laura's will was written in 1514, before the birth of her sons. From Laura's will one can ascertain her devotion to her husband, Pietro Antonio. For the birth of Giusto, see ASV, Avogaria di Comun, Libro d'oro, Nascite (1506–54), Busta 68, c. 18^v. See also ASV, Avogaria di Comun, Registri di Battesimo (1513–18), Registro 37, no. 3. For the birth of Giusto's brother, Andrea Victor, see ASV, Avogaria di Comun, Libro d'oro, Nascite (1506–54), Busta 68, c. 49^v.

30. For Giusto's entry into public life, see ASV, Avogaria di Comun, Balla d'oro, 1537, die quarto decembris, infrascripti nobiles remanserunt de maiori consilio venetorum in festa S. Barbara, Signor Justus Mauroceno, di Signor Pieroantonii, quondam, Signor Justi, c. 143^v.

31. See ASV, Secretario alle Voci, Registro 11 (ex 8), 1523–56.

32. See note 14 above.

33. A good portion of Pietro Antonio Morosini's wealth was in land and in the revenues from wine produced on his farms in the Paduan territory of Mirano. For his tax return, see ASV, Dieci Savi sopra le Decime a Rialto, Condizioni di Decima 1537, San Marco, Busta 93, no. 549. Giusto inherited some of the land near Mirano from his father and a relative, Madona Iachoma di Imagrabourg. See ASV, Dieci Savi sopra le Decime a Rialto, Condizioni, Traslati, Busta 1239, c. 206^v, March 21, 1554.

34. For Giusto's *decima* for 1566, see ASV, Dieci Savi sopra le Decime a Rialto, Condizioni 1566, Castello, Busta 131, no. 964.

35. Ibid.

36. See notes 1, 2, and 4 above.

37. ASV, S.U., Processi, Buste 20 and 23.

38. The group may have been known as the *veri fratelli*, at least to each other. The testimony of Father Fidele Vico, a humanities teacher of the children of Antonio and Alvise Grimani, revealed that he was implicated in the meetings of the young Venetian patricians discussed above and was summoned to appear before the Venetian Inquisition. Fidele was asked to name all the *veri fratelli*. See ASV, S.U., Processi, Busta 23, Contra Padre Fidele Vico, June 29, 1568. Among other *fratelli*, Fidele implicated Alvise Mocenigo, testifying that the *veri fratelli* "siano tutti quelli che non credono alla Santa Chiesa Romana et sono l'infrascritti da me conosciuti cosi in Venetia come in quelle parti de Francia ciò è messer Alvise nepote di Monsignor Mocenigo sta a S. Hieronimo il qual mi ragionò del concilio di Trento, che non era legitamente congregato." *Oracolo della renouatione della chiesa secondo la dottrina del Reverendo Padre Frate Hieronimo Savonarola da Ferrara . . . per lui predicata in Firenze* is the correct title of Savonarola's published sermon.

39. ASV, S.U., Processi, Busta 20, inquisition of Antonio Loredan.

40. Malipiero testified: "queste opinioni le ho imparate da Francesco Spinola lo più di un'anno fa, che esso Spinola mi menaua alla predica a S. Mattio di Rialto, et notaua alcuni passi del predicatore, esso Spinola me interpretaua alcuni sensi delle sue prediche. . . . Et questo Spinola è stato quello ueramente, che solo mi ha seduto, oltrache io anchora ho letto alcuni libri per la lettione delli quali mi son confirmato in dette opinioni." ASV, S.U., Processi, Busta 20. A preacher from San Mattio di Rialto also came to hear Dionisio speak in the cortile of the Palazzo Ducale.

41. See Chapter VI below.

42. See note 38 above.

43. On the influence of penitential preachers and prophets in addition to Savonarola, see Antonio Volpato, "La predicazione penitenziale apocalittica nell'attività di due predicatori del 1473," *Bollettino dell'Istituto Storico Italiano* 82 (1967): 113–28; Delno C. West Jr., "The Education of Fra Salimbene of Parma: The Joachite Influence," in Reeves, *The Influence of Prophecy*, 193–215.

44. See Ambrosini, "Tendenze filoprotestanti nel patriziato veneziano"; note especially p. 170, where Ambrosini points out that "nonostante la discreta cultura (letteraria, filosofica, giuridica) di cui appaiono dotati, questi patrizi non rivelano una solida formazione teologica; o in ogni caso, hanno cura di non rivelarla." In the same volume, see Seidel-Menchi, "Protestantesimo a Venezia," 139, where the author notes that Calvin's catechism was arriving in Venice in ever increasing numbers and that the French ambassador was circulating in Venice the New Testament published in Geneva. See also her *Erasmo in Italia 1520–1580*. On the various conventicles in Venice, see John Martin, "Salvation and Society in Sixteenth-Century Venice," and idem, "A Journeymen's Feast of Fools," *Journal of Medieval and Renaissance Studies* 17, no. 2 (1987): 149–74.

45. At the conclusion of the *Haec est causa* Dionisio wrote: "Haec postrema verba scribimus Patavii in aedibus candidissimi ac excellentissimi Rectoris Scholarum."

46. See Nicolai Commeni Papadopoli, *Historia Gymnasii Patavini* (Venice: Sebastianus Coleti, 1726), 1:97, and *Fasti Gymnasii Patavini* (Patavii [Padua]: Joannes Manfrè, 1757), 2:18, 211. For a discussion of the supposed heresy of the German rector, see ASV, Collegio, Relazioni, Roma, Varie, Duplicati IV, November 2, 1565. The pope was concerned that "un heretico fusse rettor de Scolari." The Church of the Holy Spirit, dedicated on July 22, 1539, was in the parish of San Gregorio. See Corner, *Notizie storiche delle chiese e monasteri di Venezia e di Torcello*, 521–23.

47. Ibid. The exchange between the ambassador and the pope is interesting. Note especially: "A questo se è resposto che il grado di Rettor è laico e non è necessario che si facci la profession et che quando si udesse astringerlo a farla sarebbe un licentiar dal studio di Padoa tutti li Alamani che ui sono li quali andrebbero nelli studii di Germania et la speranza che li conuersa non di Padoa li potessero far boni Christiani sarebbe perduta perche in quei studii di Germania senza alcun dubio diuenterebbono heretici. . . . Pero instando il sufraganeo di Padoa che di qua Sua Santita ne facesse qualche prouisione fu ordinato al Cardinale Pisani che essendo detto Rettor heretico si dousse formar processo contra di lui senza astringerlo a far la professione. . . . Niente di manco hauendone il clarissimo Ambassadore parlato a Sua Santita in nome della Serenissima Signoria dolendosi che non fusse bon modo questo di formar processo, massime che il Rettor uiueua in casa et fuor di casa christianamente: Lei gli disse che le non hauea ordinato che cosí senza altro inditio che'l fusse heretico, si douesse formar processo, ma che in caso che lui fusse heretico et viuesse con scandalo et con questo se restò di far che Sua Santità specificasse meglio quest'ordine al Cardinale Pisani."

48. See note 46 above. For an important study on the *spirituali* in Padua, see Stella, "Tradizione razionalistica patavina e radicalismo spiritualistico nel XVI secolo." Note especially pp. 299–300, where Professor Stella mentions Dionisio Gallo as a millenarian prophet who recalled the ideas of Guillaume Postel, a point with which I concur.

49. See *Storia di Padova dalla sua origine sino al presente dal Cavaliere RR Guiseppe Cappelletti* (Padua, 1875), 2:261. See also ASV, Secretario alle Voci, Elezioni di Maggior Consiglio, 4 (1562–70), cc. 119ʳ–120. Cicogna took office on April 16, 1566; his duties as podesta continued until August 12, 1567.

50. See *Hierarchia Catholica*, 3:267. Alvise Pisani (1535–70) di Zuanne Paolo was elevated to the cardinalate by Pope Pius V in 1565. See Venice, Biblioteca nazionale di San Marco, MSS italiani, Cl. VII, Cod. CMXXVII (= 8596) Marco Barbaro, Alberi, c. 256ᵛ. See also *Hierarchia Catholica*, 3:44, 284.

51. See Gaetano Cozzi, *Repubblica di Venezia e stati italiani: Politica e giustizia dal secolo XVI al secolo XVIII* (Turin: Giulio Einaudi Editore, 1982); see especially 265–77.

52. ASV, S.U., Processi, Busta 22, Contra Dionisium Gallum, document entitled *Haec est causa:* "Quatuor sumus personae qui summe loquimur, in hac fidei causa catholicae: paruus et humilis homo quem videtis, sub, pro et cum tribus personis aeternae trinitatis et beatissimae."

53. Ibid.

54. Ibid.

55. This small work appears to be a second part of *Atila flagellvm Dei* (Stampata in Venetia per Mattio Pagan in Frezaria al segno della fede, 1505). The pagination is continuous in the two little books. The shelf mark is Biblioteca nazionale di San Marco, Miscellanea 2351.

56. In a slightly different context Gabriella Zarri has clarified the divine election of a *santa* as an example of "sacred space" in a physical presence. See Gabriella Zarri, "Pietà e profezia alle corti padane: Le pie consiglieri dei principi," in *Il Rinascimento nelle corti padane: Società e cultura* (Bari: De Donato Editori, 1977), 210.

57. His preaching in the cortile of the Ducal Palace obviously had political and religious implications. His emphasis on justice had, of course, a particular relevance for Venice, the "sacred space" chosen by God for the administration of justice. These ideas previously appeared in pronouncements by Guillaume Postel.

58. Dionisio's decision to proclaim his message on the Feast of Pentecost was obviously intended to suggest his association with the Holy Spirit and to separate his persona from the numerous itinerant preachers who often claimed to be Elias, Enoch, or John the Baptist, identifying themselves with the "two testimonies" of the Apocalypse. For a discussion of preachers and prophets in Italy, including those in Venice, see the following by Ottavia Niccoli: "Profezie in piazza: Note sul profetismo popolare nell'Italia del primo Cinquecento," *Quaderni Storici* 41 (1979): 500–534; "Visioni e racconti di visioni nell'Italia del primo Cinquecento," *Società e storia* 28 (1985): 253–73; *La crisi religiosa del Cinquecento; Profeti e popolo nell'Italia del Rinascimento*. See also McGinn, *Visions of the End*, especially 246–50, and Barnes, *Prophecy and Gnosis*.

59. See Consiglio dei Dieci, Parti secrete, Filza 12, February 27, 1567: "Li prudentissimi maggiori nostri, quali con la faculta et il sangue hanno acquistata

et lasciato a noi soi posteri questo dominio in uigilando alla conseruatione di esso statuirono molte leggi et ordini per reuocar li habitanti in questa citta dalli uitii et in durli alla uirtu et particolarmente li Nobili a quali la maesta di Dio ha dato carrico di reger e gouenar li altri accio che frenando l'immodorata ambitione con la via della uirtu."

60. On the relationship of the laity and the ecclesiastics after the Council of Trent, see Adriano Prosperi, "Le istituzioni ecclesiastiche e le idee religiose," in *Il Rinascimento nelle corti padane*, 160–63.

61. See note 58 above.

62. Gabriella Zarri, *Le sante vive: Profezie di corte e devozione femminile tra '400 e '500* (Turin: Rosenberg & Sellier, 1990). Note, for example, p. 57: "L'interesse dei principi verso queste mistiche era prevalentemente rivolto alle manifestazioni di carattere straordinario che essi si preoccupavano di testimoniare, difendere e propagandare, come segni inconfutabili della presenza e della protezione di Dio sulla città; ma era anche sollecitato dal desiderio di essere resi partecipi di particolari rivelazioni e di poter penetrare misteri nascosti: 'de multis abditis clarius investigare responsum,' come pretendeva il duca Ercole." On the prophetic power of the feminine voice, see, by Kuntz, "The Virgin of Venice"; "Angela da Foligno e la Vergine Veneziana: Un paradigma della spiritualità veneziana nel Cinquecento," in *Res Publica Litterarum* 11 (1988): 175–82; "Lodovico Domenichi, Guillaume Postel, and the Biography of Giovanna Veronese"; and "Guglielmo Postello e la 'Vergine Veneziana.'" See also Kuntz, *Guillaume Postel*, 69–142; Vasoli, *Profezia e ragione*, 163–69; idem, *Filosofia e religione nella cultura del Rinascimento*, 255–77; Adriano Prosperi, "Dalle 'divine madri' ai padri spirituali," in *Women and Men in Spiritual Culture XIV–XVII*, ed. Elisja Schulte Van Kessell (The Hague: Martinus Nijhoff, 1986), 71–90; Andrea Erba, "Il 'caso' di Paola Antonia Negri nel Cinquecento italiano," in ibid., 202–16; and Gabriella Zarri, "Le sante vive: Per una tipologia della santità femminile nel primo Cinquecento," *Annali dell'Istituto Storico Italo-Germanico in Trento* 6 (1980): 371–445. Note also Edward Muir, "The Virgin on the Street Corner: The Place of the Sacred in Italian Cities," in *Religion and Culture in the Renaissance and Reformation*, Sixteenth-Century Essays and Studies, vol. 11, ed. Steven Ozment (Kirksville, Mo.: Truman State University Press, 1989), 25–40.

63. Dionisio was especially prone to acknowledge the salutary grace of the feminine, not only of the Virgin Mother of Christ, whom he called the *ancilla Trinitatis*, but also of the Blessed Bridget, whom he revered. In his *Haec est causa* he argues his case as God's prophet: "Videte meam Legationem. Videte prophetas; scripturas legite. Et si causae seruit, videte quid dicat Diua Brigida."

64. The letter was written on June 3, 1566, before his problems with the papal nuncio and his subsequent imprisonment.

65. ASV, S.U., Processi, Busta 22, Contra Dionisium Gallum, testimony of Padre Stephanus de Franciscis, subdeacon of the Church of San Zuane di Rialto, June 20, 1566.

66. I have previously commented about other aspects of this space. See note 57 above and pages 149–50.

67. ASV, S.U., Processi, Busta 22, Contra Dionisium Gallum. "Et sic cum die Dominica quae fuit nona presentis mensis deprehensus fuisset predicans fuit detentus per Ministros Sancti Officii, et in Carceribus Illustrissimorum dominorum Capitum detrusus." These were the prisons of the Consiglio dei Dieci.

68. Dionisio described the circumstances in a letter addressed to the Venetian tribunal after his incarceration. He wrote: "non puduit te per nuntium legati papae, me solum et symplicem et quietum in meo cubiculo, circumuenire, et tamquam columbam in suo columbario, capere, ligare, velare, traducere in obscuros carceres cum malefactoribus qui me opprimerent." See ASV, S.U., Processi, Busta 22, Contra Dionisium Gallum, document entitled *Vincat Veritas* and addressed to the tribunal.

69. Ibid., testimony of Jacobus Gambacurta, June 15, 1566. Gambacurta testified that Dionisio had said: "Dico enim quo Papa cum suis Cardinalibus non bene sentiunt de uera et Catholica doctrina quia multa faciunt et dicunt contraria doctrinae Euangelicae ut uobis ostendam in discursu meo."

70. ASV, Capi del Consiglio dei Dieci, Dispacci degli Ambasciatori, Roma, Busta 23, c. 99, August 30, 1544: "Supplica vostra Santità mandare . . . li Nuncii sui con la commissione sua, che versino nelle materie di stato tantum lassando il carico nelle cose guidiciarie, et de heresia a Vinetia al Reverendissimo Patriarcha et nelle altre diocesi alli sui ordinarii, perche il tutto procederà con maggior regula, essendo massimamente etiam li inquisitori che hanno carico nella materia di heresia Ricordando reuerentemente a uostra Santità che li Nuncii per li tempi passati soleuano essere mandati dalli summi Pontifici per fare quell'officio, che spetta a cose di stato et non piú . . . et veramente si puo dire che questo hauer legati sia come le medicine, le quale ad alcuni tempi, et con cause sono proficue, ma non si deueno hauere come il cibo quotidiano."

71. The Venetian authorities feared the Anabaptists more than other heretics, since their teachings often called for the overthrow of existing orders. Because of social and religious instability for which the Anabaptists were held responsible, the Inquisition usually dealt more harshly with them than with other heretics. Hutterite Anabaptists listened for the prophetic voice that would proclaim the next instauration of God's kingdom on earth. See, by Stella, "Utopie e velleità insurrezionali dei filoprotestanti italiani"; "L'ecclesiologia degli anabattisti processati a Trieste nel 1540," in *Eresia e riforma*, 210; *Anabattismo e antitrinitarismo in Italia nel XVI secolo*; "Movimenti di riforma nel Veneto nel Cinquecento," in *Storia della cultura veneta dalla controriforma alla fine della repubblica: Il Seicento* (Vicenza: Neri Pozza Editore, 1983), 1–21. See also Giorgio Radetti, "Riformatori ed eretici italiani del secolo XVI," *Giornale Critico della Filosofia Italiana* 31 (1940): 13–24; Malavasi, "Sulla diffusione delle teorie ereticali nel Veneto durante il '500"; Achille Olivieri, "Il 'catechismo' e la *Fedei et Doctrinae . . . Ratio*' di Bartolomeo Fonzio, eretico veneziano del Cinquecento," *Studi Veneziani* 9 (1967): 339–59; Caccamo, *Eretici Italiani in Moravia, Polonia, Transilvania*;

Cantimori, "Studi di storia della riforma." And note most recently Aldo Stella, *Dall'anabattismo veneto al "Sozialevangelismus" dei fratelli Hutteriti e all'illuminismo religioso sociniano* (Rome: Herder Editrice e Libreria, 1996), 48, where the author remarks: "Inoltre, negli atti processuali l'accusa più ribadita è che Jakob Hueter non aveva mai desistito dall'inveire contra ogni autorità costituita: 'Hueter perfino nelle sue prediche asserì che l'imperatore, re e signori perseguitano loro, ossia i [veri] cristiani, perche se si lasciassero vivere costoro, appunto i veri cristiani, tutti i loro poteri sarebbero sminuiti e infranti.'" Professor Stella also noted that Hueter was condemned to death because of the accusation of sedition against the political and ecclesiastical authorities. See also his "Origini patavine e sviluppi polacchi dell'illuminismo religioso sociniano," in *La nascita dell'Europa per una storia delle idee fra Italia e Polonia*, ed. Sante Graciotti (Florence: Leo S. Olschki Editore, 1995), 231–56.

72. See note 21 to Chapter 1.

73. See ASV, S.U., Processi, Busta 22, Contra Dionisium Gallum, document of June 8, 1566. Venice, under the prodding of Rome, reinstituted the Inquisition, which had originally been formed in the thirteenth century. Note, for example: "Ne troviamo, per la prima volta, parola nella *Promissione* del doge Marino Morosini (1248), che giurava, *ad honorem Dei et sacrosanctæ matris ecclesiæ et robur et defensionem fidei catholicæ, di eleggere alcuni probi et discreti et catholici viri*, per la inquisizione degli eretici.... I deputati della repubblica, i probi et discreti viri, dobevano ricercare gli eretici; ai prelati spettava giudicarli, al governo eseguir le sentenze. Nel 1298, per ascoltare finalmente le vive intercessioni di Roma, fino allora vane, il doge Pietro Gradenigo stabilì regolarmente, coll'approvazione del Maggior Consiglio, il Santo Uffizio, e fece col papa Nicolò IV un concordato. Si ammetteva che lo stato avesse sotto la propria vigilanza e dipendenza il tribunale della Sacra Inquisizione, e tre incaricati del Doge, chiamati poi *Savi all'Eresia*, dovessero continuare la loro assistenza di giudici religiosi." See *La Basilica di San Marco in Venezia*, 42. In addition, an interesting diagram (on p. 43) shows the seating arrangement of the tribunal. Through the right door of the Chapel of Saint Theodore, near the sacristy of San Marco, entered the patriarch, the papal nuncio, and the Tre Savi sopra Eresia; they sat in the order in which they entered. Through the door on the left side of the chapel entered the inquisitor, the *auditore* of the nuncio, the vicar of the patriarch, and the *fiscale*, who sat in the order in which they entered. The inquisitor sat at the center of the long table.

74. Machiavelli, in his letter to Vettori in 1513, also considered the use of clothing to express the appropriate mood of an event: "Venuta la sera, mi ritorno in casa ed entro nel mio scrittoio; e in sull'uscio mi spoglio quella veste cotidana, piena di fango e di loto, e mi metto panni reali e curiali; e rivestito condecentemente, entro nelle antique corti delli antiqui uomini; dove da loro ricevuto amorevolmento, mi pasco di quel cibo che *solum* è mio e che io nacqui per lui." Cited by Eugenio Battisti, *L'anti-Rinascimento* (Milan: Garzanti Editore, 1989), 1:211. For a detailed description of Dionisio's clothing and the *banca* of the Scala dei Giganti in the cortile of the Palazzo Ducale, see pages xv, 1–2 above.

75. See, for example, *La Chiesa cattolica nella storia dell'umanità*, pl. cx, opposite p. 487. I am indebted to Dr. Daniela Ambrosini, Biblioteca nazionale di San Marco, for bring this reference to my attention.

76. See Niccoli, "Profezie in piazza," 515, where the author cites the case of a *romito* who passed through Modena in 1539: "uno povero vestito de sacho descalso tuto impolverato in cappilli con una croce et Cristo in mano andava cridando questo dì per la piaza de Modena: fate penitentia, fate penitentia, che Dio ve vole punire, e ogni homo rideva e lui andava dreto al fatto suo."

77. ASV, S.U., Processi, Busta 22, Contra Dionisium Gallum, testimony of Gambacurta, June 15, 1566.

78. Dionisio often made reference to the truth of his statements and to his willingness to suffer torments if they were not true. In this he was no different from other prophets, notably Savonarola and Postel. Note what Savonarola had to say in his sermon given on the fourth Sunday of Advent: "Et se questo che io ti dico non è uero, io ne uoglio stare a iudicio dinanzi al tribunale di Christo al tempo dell'iuditio, in presentia di testimonii, quanti ne sono qua presenti et dico ti piu, che chi sara contrario a questo che Dio lo punira." See *Reverendi P. Fra Hieronymi Sauonarolę in primam D. Ioannis epistolam et in alia sacrę scripturę verba . . .*, 149. Postel, during his trial by the Venetian Inquisition in 1555, said that he would ask to be put to death if what he had said about himself and the Venetian Virgin were not true. See ASV, S.U., Processi, Busta 12, Contra Postellum.

79. Pope Paul IV was very concerned about the reform of the Church. The Venetian ambassador reported that the pope spoke to the cardinals and other doctors and religious "della simonia ch'accese et insiammo ognuno, facendoli conoscere ch'in questo solo staua la uera riforma della chiesa." ASV, Archivi propri, Roma, Busta 8, c. 99; note also that a few days later the pope told the assembled prelates "di fare la riforma e di cominciar da se; perche questo era un metter la secure alla radice" (c. 106^v). See also Eva-Marie Jung, "On the Nature of Evangelism in the 16th-Century Italy," *Journal of the History of Ideas* 14 (1953): 511–27; Simoncelli, "Pietro Bembo e l'evangelismo italiano"; Aldo Stella, "La lettera del cardinale Contarini sulla predestinazione," *Rivista di Storia della Chiesa in Italia* 15, no. 3 (1961): 411–41; Gleason, *Reform Thought in Sixteenth-Century Italy*, 81–100; Fragnito, "Cultura umanistica e riforma religiosa"; Tramontin, "Il *De officio episcopi* di Gasparo Contarini"; Hubert Jedin, "Contarini und Camaldoli," *Archivio Italiano per la Storia della Pietà* 2 (1953): 1–67; note also Felix Gilbert, "Contarini on Savonarola: An Unknown Document of 1516," *Archiv für Reformationsgeschichte* 59 (1968): 145–49.

80. ASV, S.U., Processi, Busta 22, Contra Dionisium Gallum, testimony of Stephanus, June 20, 1566.

81. See note 29 above.

82. ASV, S.U., Processi, Busta 22, Contra Dionisium Gallum, testimony of July 9, 1566.

83. Ibid., testimony of July 12, 1566. Dionisio responded to the question about the Council of Trent: "Vt ueritas illius Sanctissimi Concilii executioni mandetur, et quae defuerunt terminantur summo et postremo Concilio antequam Christus ueniat et seuiat Antechristus in electos, quod fiat citissime iuxta reuelationem sibi factam cęlitus, cuius uirtute agit que agit et patitur que patitur et clamat que clamat."

84. Ibid.

85. Weinstein, *Savonarola and Florence*, 200–201.

86. Note, for example: "Confidandomi dunque con la gratia di Dio che non solamente uoi, ma anchora ciascuna altra persona leggendo questo trattatello, et intimamente le sententie non mie, ma di Dio, et de i suoi santi contemplando, ruminando, et orando, et sospirando alle pieta delle uiscere di Iesu Christo dal quale procedono queste, et tutte le altre virtu, farete profitto nella uia di Dio, la qual e tutta humilita, et charita, con fiducia che il Spirito Santo me allumini in questa parte, haro ardire di esaltar questa mia opera sopra le mie forze. . . . Che intendi non solamente per scientia, o per dottrina data da altri, ma per propria esperientia, et affetto che non puo peruenire a questa uirtu, ne ad alcuna altra operatione buona per sua industria, ma solo per gratia et misericordia dell'Omnipotente Dio." *Trattato della Hvmilita*, in *Molti devotissimi trattati del Reverendo Padre Frate Hieronimo Sauonarola da Ferrara*, c. 4.

87. See Paolo Simoncelli, "Il 'Dialogo dell'unione spirituale di dio con l'anima' tra alumbradismo spagnolo e prequietismo italiano," *Annuario dell'Istituto Storico Italiano per l'Età Moderna e Contemporanea* 29–30 (1977–78): 565–601; see especially pp. 569, 583. On active and passive annihilation, see Kent Emery Jr., "Mysticism and the Coincidence of Opposites in Sixteenth- and Seventeenth-Century France," *Journal of the History of Ideas* 45 (January–March 1984): 3–23. Note especially the Capuchin Benet of Canfield (1562–1610) and his teaching about active annihilation. Emery notes: "But whereas in passive annihilation the institution of God's All and the creature's nothing is the effect of union, in active annihilation this intuition is a means to union. . . . Passive annihilation takes place when the soul is elevated, stripped bare and drawn outside itself by the 'actual drawing of the will of God.' In active annihilation, the soul is drawn solely by the 'virtual drawing of God' by which it remains united to God when 'impeded exteriorly with images and occupied in affairs'" (13).

88. Simoncelli, "Il 'Dialogo dell'unione spirituale di Dio con l'anima.'"

89. Ibid., 581.

90. Ibid., 583.

91. Ibid., 569–70; Simoncelli notes that it was said of Fra Giovanni that when he preached, God was inspiring him. On the union of the soul with God, see Cesare Vasoli, "Uno scritto inedito di Giulio Camillo 'De l'humana deificatione,'" *Rinascimento* 24 (1984): 191–227. Giulio Camillo Delminio insisted not only on the traditional virtues of humility and abstinence but also on the separation from the

world and from one's self, so that man could ascend "'all'immagine divina che in noi è' e 'rivolgersi' a Dio." Vasoli, "Uno scritto inedito," 196.

92. See *Epistola del preditto a tutta la congregatione de i frati di San Marco, del modo di resistere alle tentationi, e di peruenir alla perfettione*, in *Molti devotissimi trattati del Reverendo Padre Frate Hieronimo Sauonarola da Ferrara*, c. 54ᵛ: "Prima nelle cose interiori dell'anima quanto all'intelletto, creder, douete, et tener per certo che molti son piu saui, et piu illuminati da Dio di uoi, et bisognaui massimamente sottomettere il iudicio uostro in tutto a gli uostri superiori, diuentar pazzi per essere salui nel conspetto di Dio, come dice l'Apostolo. Si quis uidetur inter uos sapiens esse in hoc seculo, stultus fiat ut sit sapiens."

93. Because Dionisio believed that he had been anointed by the Virgin and filled with the divine spirit, normal concerns were no longer important. As God's messenger, he committed the "folly" of proclaiming the need for reform of the clergy, for unity of the church and the world, and for active service to the poor. Dionisio believed himself to be Christ's fool and God's messenger who had been humiliated by the "wise men" of the world. One is also reminded of Saint Paul's words about folly from his letter to the Corinthians (1 Cor. 4:9–13): "For I think God has sent forth the apostles last of all, as men doomed to death, seeing that we have been made a spectacle to the world, and to angels, and to men. We are fools for Christ, but you are wise in Christ! We are weak, but you are strong! You are honored, but we are without honor! To this very hour we hunger and thirst, and we are naked and buffeted, and have no fixed abode. And we toil, working with our own hands. We are reviled, and we bless; we are persecuted and we bear with it, we are maligned and we entreat, we have become as the refuse of this world, the offscouring of all, even until now!"

94. ASV, S.U., Processi, Busta 22, Contra Dionisium Gallum, inquisition of July 12, 1566. Note Dionisio's words: "Quicquid scripsit ut oratorem et nuntium Dei se recte scripsisse iudicent principes congregati. Subdens accensus et ualde iratus uociferans, Iam dixit amplius, non respondebit, quia estis Rei, propterea quia estis reformandi, ut fassus est Reverendissimus dominus legatus, estis aduersarii, estis iudices, estis crudelissimi. (quae uerba, estis crudelissimi, nolebat scribi), sed dixit quotidie uos me occidentes, cogatur propter atrocitatem iniuriarum, quas patitur hęc uerba proferre."

95. Ibid.: "unde post multas eius impiissimas uociferationes decretum fuit, ut poneretur in carceribus Dominorum noctis. Et sic fuit remissus conductus, et positus." See notes 99 and 100 below.

96. See ASV, Consiglio dei Dieci, Parti comuni, Registro 23, 1557–58, c. 198, January 27, 1558; also cited in *Monumenti per servire alla storia del Palazzo Ducale di Venezia*, 302, no. 646: "Illustrissimi Signori Capi dell'Ecelentissimo Conseglio di x, Vostre Signorie Illustrissime seranno contento de far passar una parte nel Ecelentissimo Conseglio di x de ducati cento per far conzar le tre preson liona, malpaga de sopra, et malpaga de sotto, al far le fosse gatoli suoli et altri lor bisogni che in vero stando le cose come sono molti patisseno morte, come chiaramente si vede per le gran

puzze over fettori che rendono algune fosse per non aver esito le acque pero bisogno provedergli con prestezza per conservar quelli poveri incarcerati che così miseramente non muora." See also ASV, Consiglio dei Dieci, Parti comuni, Registro 26, March 31, 1563, c. 9ᵛ: "Quanto siano aspre et anguste le prigioni del Palazzo nostro, et quanti carcerati per la mala qualità loro di continuo s'infermino et morano, massimamente al tempo dell'està, non è alcuno di questo Consiglio che non lintenda onde i ritrovati innocenti patiscono, et i nocenti et colpevoli spesse fiate passano con poca et lieve pena"; also cited in *Monumenti per servire alla storia del Palazzo Ducale di Venezia*, 313–14, no. 669.

97. See *Monumenti per servire alla storia del Palazzo Ducale di Venezia*, 172, no. 368: "1519 Die x Decembris. In Consilio x cum additione. Capita. Se attrovano nelle preson nostre da basso una infinita de presonieri come hora e sta lecto et dechiarato, molti de li qual sono condennati a tempo et molti per debiti e cose di pocho momento quali se hanno aspresentado: et per langustia de dicte preson se infermano et moreno che e cosa impia. Al che per i progenitori nostri fo altre volte provisto che volseno ne fusse una preson a questo effecto signanter deputata, chera la preson domandata Nuova per mezo el ponte de la paja: la qual e sta desfatta et facta pezor de le altre, domandata Vulcan: unde che le al tuto et per reverentia del nostro Signor Dio et per ogni altro respecto farne provision et percio: Landara parte, che cum sit chel se attrova a ladi a la Novissima una volta qual e longa passa 5½ et larga passa 4 ne la qual al presente i Signori di nocte tien i pegni del suo Offico, sia per auctorita de questo conseio preso che dicta volta sia facta una preson alleffecto sopradicto deputata sicome era la preson Nova soprascritta." See also Enrico Bacchetti, "La gestione del sistema carcerario a Venezia e il regolamento del Doge Antonio Venier (1391)," *Atti dell'Istituto Veneto di Scienze, Lettere ed Arti: Classe di Scienze Morali, Lettere ed Arti* 155/II (1997): 301–27. This article is important because it clarifies not only the laws concerning incarceration and the places of incarceration but also important aspects of life in Venetian prisons.

98. *Monumenti per servire alla storia del Palazzo Ducale di Venezia*, 320, no. 677: "Nos capita Illustrissimi Consilij x vobis Magnifico Domino Alexandro Barbo eiusdem Consilij Camerario mandamus che dar dobbiate al fedel nostro Zuan Antonio Rusconi protho, ducati settantaquatro lire una soldi cinque per el resto delle spese in maistranze et manuali et altro per lui fatte in destruzzer la casa di la dal rio di Palazzo ove si hanno a far le priggion. . . . Datum die 27 Augusti 1563." Note also 318, no. 674: "L'asprezza et l'augustia delle prigioni del Palazzo nostro et il patir che perciò senteno i poveri carcerati mosse questo Consiglio a deliberar che la casa di là del rio all'incontro del Palazzo nostro nella quale habitavano i Vedova, et che è della Signoria nostra fusse fatta evacuar et che si facessero uno o due modelli di prigioni con li quali si venisse a questo Consiglio, per deliberar poi quello che paresse ad esso Consiglio essere a proposito et essendo stati fatti i dui modelli, non si de mancar di proseguir così buona opera: però, L'anderà parte che in esecution della sopradetta deliberazione sia deliberato che nel luogo della casa soprascritta siano fabbricate tante prigion quante capira esso luogo, secondo il modello del Rusconi."

99. Ibid., 320, no. 678: "1563, Die ultimo Augusti. In consilio x cum additione Capita. Per sollevare in qualche parte i poveri priggionieri da gli incommodi che pasticono per l'asprezza delle preggioni, et che ciò fosse fatto quanto più presto fusse possibile fu imposto per questo Consiglio a gli avogadori di Commun et alli provedditori sopra le fabbriche di Rialto, che insieme dovessero veder et considerar il luogo, i modelli fatti, et che si havessero a far et la spesa che vi anderebbe in far le preggioni di la dal rio di Palazzo, et perchè i detti avogardi son molto occupati et non possono esser insieme con li pretati provedditori per far gli efftetti onde son passati molti di senza che si abbia fatto cosa alcuna, è conveniente proveder che se incamini questa materia secondo la deliberazione di questo Consiglio."

100. A prisoner in Venice was responsible for his own sustenance. It was considered an act of piety for Venetians to bring food and drink to the prisoners with arms outstretched between the bars of the prison. We do not know who supplied food to Dionisio while in prison, but according to his testimony, he had almost nothing to eat. For the deliberations of the Consiglio dei Dieci about the conditions in the prisons, see *Monumenti per servire alla storia del Palazzo Ducale di Venezia*, 313–30. So many were dying in the prisons that many Venetians feared the pestilence would spread throughout the city. In the deliberations on April 7, 1564, the *consiglio* decided to place the sick in one section of the prison, like an infirmary in a monastery (ibid., 323). Dionisio vividly described his misery in prison: "Ego fame pereo, et tamen non sum conturbatus, et coactus modis omnibus non solum extrema penuria, frigore nocturno dormiens cum uestibus super nudam terram oppressus a Turca." ASV, S.U., Processi, Busta 22, Contra Dionisium Gallum, testimony of October 15, 1566. There were, however, some public gestures of support for the prisoners. See Giovanni Scarabello, *Carcerati e carceri a Venezia nell'età moderna* (Rome: Istituto della Enciclopedia Italiana, 1979), especially 24–31: "Questi interventi di assistenza a favore dei carcerati potevano essere pubblici come, ad esempio, le sovvenzioni che per consuetudine antichissima i consigli maggiori della Repubblica concedevano a Natale, Pasqua e Giovedi Grasso o all'occasione di fausti eventi quali le vittorie in guerra. Potevano essere di associazioni come le Fraterne, le Scuole, le Arti che taloro assumevano tra i loro scopi quello di soccorrere i carcerati. Potevano essere di privati, come le elemosine sollecitate per le chiese o raccolte alle inferriate delle prigioni, o implorate per la vie della città da emissari dei carcerati medesimi" (24–25). The prisons were designated by names from ancient tradition, such as "Liona, Mocina, La Prigion Forte, Andruzza, Le Inferiori a piano terra affacciate al Cortile del Palazzo Ducale: Scaletta, Orba, Schiava, Armamento, Frescagioia, Vulcano. Le Superiori al primo piano presso gli uffici dei Signori di Notte, con li il 'luogo del tormento' uno stanzone più alto degli altri, la trave da cui pende la corda, i posti per i giudici ad attendere la confessione" (31). The prisons of the Signori di Notte were called the "'camerete' (o 'cameroti') che si trovavano al pian terreno e al mezzanino." See Bacchetti, "La gestione del sistema carcerario a Venezia"; note especially p. 311 and n. 24. These prisons remained terrible in the Cinquecento, just as in the Quattrocento. Those assigned to the prisons of the Signori di Notte had been condemned for serious

crimes ("per homecidio, per furto, o per gran' excesso"). Clerics arrested by the civil authorities were placed in the same prison (Grandoina, or Grandonia) with murderers. In fact, it appears that any cleric arrested for whatever reason was detained in La Grandoina (ibid., 312). Because of the charges against Dionisio (preaching without a license), he may have been placed in La Grandoina. He bitterly complained about being in prison with a murdering Turk and the apostate Spinola.

101. Some accounts indicate that those who abused others were placed in harsher prisons. Note, for example, the following: "Quod custodes carcerum deputati per capita huius Consilii conqueruntur, quod faciendo circam quotidie sibi fit a carceratis iniuria verborum et factorum, et modo nuper unus eorum percussus fuit in faciem de uno lapide, quod est malefactum supportare quod faciendo officium custodes percutiantur, et sibi dicatur iniuria: Vadit pars, quod iste percussor statim ponatur in asperiori carcere qui sit subtus Palatium et iste actus committatur Advocatorum comunis, ut quod percussore predictum procedant, nec inde removeatur quousque fuerit contra ipsum processum. Et ex nunc sit captum, quod si de cetero constabit Capitibus quod aliquis carceratis verberaverit, vel iniuriatus fuerit alicui custodi facienti circam vel aliter suum officium, ipso facto debeat per capita poni in asperiori carcere qui sit subtus Palatium et in compedibus si fuerit apud considerato casu suo et exinde non moveatur quousque Avocatores comunis processerint ad punitionem eius sicut eius error merebitur." See *Monumenti per servire alla storia del Palazzo Ducale di Venezia*, 73, no. 168, June 12, 1448.

102. See ASV, S.U., Processi, Busta 22, Contra Dionisium Gallum, dated July 30, 1566: "Ego Dionisius Gallus electus Dei seruus et nuntius divina gratia et eterna prouidentia sub Christo Rex Regum et Dominus Dominantium ad penam flammarum, uel Crucis instans pro Christo, et pro jure eius in uniuersa Ecclesia militante adiuro uos per Deum omnipotentem qui mundum creauit, et misit unigenitum filium suum uocatum Jesum Christum incarnatum in utero beatissime Virginis ad redimendum genus humanum, ut uos declaretis amicos uel inimicos Christi" (I, Dionisio Gallo, elect servant of God and messenger by divine grace and eternal providence under Christ, King of Kings and Lord of Lords, ready for the punishment of fire or cross for Christ and for His right in the universal Church militant, do beg, through God omnipotent, who created the world and sent his only begotten son, called Jesus Christ, incarnate in the womb of the blessed Virgin, to redeem the human race, that you declare yourselves friends or enemies of Christ and the evangelical truth).

103. See Chapter IV above.

104. For the tension inherent in Venice's concept of the state and the Church, see Gaetano Cozzi, "I rapporti tra stato e chiesa," in *La Chiesa di Venezia tra riforma protestante e riforma cattolica*, ed. Giuseppe Gullino (Venice: Edizioni Studium Cattolico, 1990), 11–36; note especially 17, where Cozzi cites Bernardo Giustiniani, who reminded the Venetian cardinals "che Venezia era la loro madre, Roma fa matrigna." In the same volume, see also Gino Benzoni, "Una città caricabile di valenze

religiose," 37–61. See also Prodi, "The Structure and Organization of the Church in Renaissance Venice," 409–30.

It is especially interesting to consider from a Venetian perspective the reasons for the religious problems in France. For the Venetian ambassador's comments about Francis I, his nominations to benefices, and his involvement in religious affairs subsequent to the Concordat of Bologna in 1516, see Edelstein, "Church Patronage in France on the Eve of the Reformation," and Chapter 1, note 52, above.

105. Contarini and the other authors of the *Consilium de emendanda ecclesia* of 1537 wrote against will-making by clerics: "The license for bequeathing the goods of the Church ought not to be given to clerics except for an urgent reason, lest the goods of the poor be converted into private delights and the amplification of houses." Cited by Hallman, *Italian Cardinals,* 80; see also Prodi, "The Structure and Organization of the Church in Renaissance Venice," 415–22; Romano, *Patricians and Popolani,* 91–118. For an excellent discussion of the papal *famiglia,* see John F. D'Amico, *Renaissance Humanism in Papal Rome: Humanists and Churchmen on the Eve of the Reformation* (Baltimore, Md.: Johns Hopkins University Press, 1983).

106. See Cozzi, "I rapporti tra stato e chiesa," 17. See also Sforza, "Riflessi della controriforma nella Repubblica di Venezia," 21 and n. 1, where the author cites Monsignor Francesco Caraffa, who had been nuncio in Venice and who wrote to his successor Giovanni Della Casa: "Ogni qual volta si ha a trattare di alcuna cosa appartenente alla Santa Sede, sia spirituale, o temporale, si escludono da Pregadi quei senatori che hanno parenti costituiti in dignità ecclesiastica.... Quindi avviene che molte delle più cospicue famiglie si astengono dall'incamminare i loro figli a Roma appunto per non chiudersi la strada al Collegio."

107. Cited by Antonio Battistella, "La politica ecclesiastica della Repubblica di Venezia," *Archivio Veneto,* 2d ser., 16 (1892): 390.

108. Bouwsma, *Venice and the Defense of Republican Liberty,* 115.

109. See Giuseppe Alberigo, "Studi e problemi relativi all'applicazione del Concilio di Trento in Italia," *Rivista Storica Italiana* 70 (1958): 239–98; also Sforza, "Riflessi della controriforma nella Repubblica di Venezia," 5–216.

110. ASV, S.U., Processi, Busta 22, Contra Dionisium Gallum, inquisition of July 30, 1566. Note the following exchange: "Interrogatus. Ad quem pertineat iudicare utrum Ecclesia bene uel male utatur diuitiis et Dominio temporali. Respondit. Pertinet ad principes a quibus magna ex parte data sunt pie illa Dominia, et ad electos pastores simul cum ipsis. Interrogatus. Quis eligat istos electos Pastores. Respondit. Clerus ipse possit eligere una cum Principibus."

111. One recalls that Dionisio had urged King Charles IX to dismiss the cardinals and bishops from his court and send them back to their flocks; the king, however, could not bring himself to do it. This same prophetic fervor had gripped Guillaume Postel, who also warned the king to reform himself, his court, and his realm. Postel's advice and warnings in 1543 caused him to lose favor in the king's circle. See Kuntz, *Guillaume Postel,* 53–56. Postel went to Fontainebleau to warn the

king. Dionisio said he saw the king *in castello*, called in French *gaillon*. In an important document, *Ad sacrum tribunal Venetum*, written from prison, Dionisio wrote of the heretics in France: "Christus Rex aeternus imperat principibus christianis, vt omni diligentia et quouis prudenti modo capiantur haeresiarchæ princeps De Conde, admiralius Dandelot, princeps Portianus et quidam alii heresiarchæ qui Gallias bellis ciuilibus afflixerunt occupandæ et rapiendæ coronæ gratia, sub prætextu religionis." ASV, S.U., Processi, Busta 22, Contra Dionisium Gallum.

112. Lane, *Venice: A Maritime Republic*, 394.

113. Ibid., 264. On this point see also Gleason, *Gasparo Contarini*, 118–25.

114. See note 105 above.

115. Bouwsma, *Venice and the Defense of Republican Liberty*, 128.

116. "Et per mio credere nell'alienazione della Germania ed Inghilterra ha avuto molto maggior parte il proprio interesse dei principi che la opinione di Martino Lutero o del Melantone; e dei presenti molti di Francia sa molto bene la Serenità Vostra che non il Calvino nè il Beza, ma le inimicizie particolari e il desiderio di governare ne sono state principal cagione." See *Le relazioni degli ambasciatori veneti al Senato durante il secolo decimosesto*, ed. Eugenio Alberi (Florence: Società Editrice Fiorentina, 1857), 10:81, "Relazione di Girolano Soranzo letta in Senato il 14 Giugno, 1563."

117. Bouwsma, *Venice and the Defense of Republican Liberty*, 128; see also Tramontin, "Lo spirito, le attività, gli sviluppi dell'Oratorio del Divino Amore nella Venezia del Cinquecento," noting especially p. 199, and Cervelli, "Storiografia e problemi intorno alla vita religiosa e spirituale a Venezia nella prima metà del '500."

118. See Gleason, *Reform Thought in Sixteenth-Century Italy*, 93.

119. ASV, S.U., Processi, Busta 22, Contra Dionisium Gallum, inquisition of July 30, 1566.

120. Apoc. 1:1–2, 5–6.

121. See Silvio Tramontin, "I Teatini e l'Oratorio del Divino Amore a Venezia," in *Regnum Dei* (Venice, 1973).

122. Siculo, the Benedictine apostate from Sicily, had a following in Ferrara and Riva di Trento as well as in Venice. Cantimori noted: "Nel profetismo ispirato, nella dottrina della religione nell'esigenza di una religiosità semplificata, si trovano i precedenti dei motivi del Siculo e insieme le ragioni della diffusione e della influenza del suo pensiero, che non affronta, oltre la critica al dogma della predestinazione, nè i problemi dei Sacramenti, nè quello del purgatorio, nè gli altri luoghi comuni della controversia anticattolica, e non mostra neppur traccia di anticlericalesimo." See Cantimori, *Eretici italiani*, 63. It is interesting to point out that Postel used similar dramatic words while asserting the certainty of his beliefs before the Inquisition on September 8, 1555. Note, for example: "Et perciochè io volendo al mondo monstrar la perfettissima vittoria di Christo contra di Satanasso, egli è di necessità che come se Adamo non havessi peccato non fossi stato nè

circoncisione nè battesimo, ma la sola Raggione naturale illuminata per grazia di Christo aeterno et non conditionale Re del mondo, volendo dico alla Chiesa monstrar et colla vita testificar la verità della vittoria perfetta di Christo et per conseguente negar la necessità del battesimo alli figliuoli di battezati, bisogna che detta Chiesa per voi mi condemni alla pena della morte per la sommersione secondo le usitate pene della Chiesa." ASV, S.U., Processi, Busta 12, Contra Postellum, letter of Postel to Maffeo Venier. Note also Stella, *Anabattismo e antitrinitarismo in Italia nel XVI secolo*, 131–32: "infine tralascio ogni reticenza nicodemitica, fiducioso nello spirito profetico che lo esaltava a altero sede sua integrità morale, proclamò di voler morire piuttosto che rinnegare quanto 'la divina et invincibile forza dello intelletto et della conscientia' lo induceva a credere."

123. ASV, S.U., Processi, Busta 22, Contra Dionisium Gallum, testimony of August 3, 1566: "Ego Dionysius Gallus pro iure Christi similis factus descendentibus in lacum mea scripta declarare me non ab homine ullo, sed a Deo missum esse per ministerium sacratissimæ Virginis, quæ caelitus ad me missa mihi apparuit me allocuta est misteria nunciauit horum miserrimorum noussimorum temporum, me consentientem eius caelesti legationi."

124. See note 62 above.

125. ASV, S.U., Processi, Busta 22, Contra Dionisium Gallum, July 30, 1566: "sed quod non est suum interrogare sed ad interrogata duntaxat respondere, quia Reus est, et coram indicibus Sancti Tribunalis Christi representatibus constitutis."

126. Ibid., document dated August 3, 1566.

127. Ibid.: "habeo quędam dicenda pro conseruatione huius Dominii Veneti et Reipublicę quę illis enarrabo quando illis placuerit me uocari."

128. Dionisio reiterated that he was innocent and that his legation was true. It is interesting to note that in 1555, in a letter to Maffeo Venier, *procuratore sopra la heresia*, Guillaume Postel wrote similar statements that purported to concern Venice's safety. See Kuntz, "'Venezia portava el fuocho in seno.'" As early as 1548 Postel had also said that he had "given to the Venetian Senate, through the hands of the doge," a work that would explain how Venice could convert the Turks and bring about peace in the world. See London, British Library, Sloane MS 1411, fol. 313^v; also cited by Stella, *Anabattismo e antitrinitarismo in Italia nel XVI secolo*, 116 n. 116, and Secret, "Une lettre retrouvée de G. Postel au Grand Prieur de France," 142 n. 7. The inquisitor repeatedly warned the defendants to tell the truth. Based on my reading of cases from the inquisitorial trials, the question of truth seemed uppermost in the minds of the Inquisition.

129. ASV, S.U., Processi, Busta 22, Contra Dionisium Gallum, testimony of August 20, 1566.

130. The prison in which Dionisio was enclosed, on the lowest level in the Palazzo Ducale, was commonly called *da basso* and was, because of the dampness and cold, one of the most terrible. See, for example, ASV, Consiglio dei Dieci, Parti comuni, Registro 27, c. 170^v, December 30, 1566, an entry concerning this

prison during the period of Dionisio's confinement: "Capita. Che sia commesso al Depositario de l'Officio nostro del Sal che dar debba ducati vinticinque al Cassier de la cassa piccola deputato sopra le fabriche suo collega per acconciar una rottura fatta nella preson quarta da basso, si come per polizza dal protto de le fabriche appar." Cited in *Monumenti per servire alla storia del Palazzo Ducale di Venezia*, 540–41, no. 717.

131. ASV, S.U., Processi, Busta 22, Contra Dionisium Gallum: "Reverendissimi ac Illustrissimi Domini. Si quid contra sanctam matrem ecclesiam aut suos ministros scripserim aut dixerim ego Dionysius gallus paratus sum Realiter et cum effectu abiurare et detestari me per omnia submittens Christi judicio et eiusdem santæ matris ecclesiæ a qua omni cum humilitate veniam peto. Ego Dionisius gallus qui supra manu propria subscripsi."

132. See notes 87 and 91 above.

133. On the monastery of Sant'Andrea della Certosa, see *Ecclesiae Venetae antiquis monumentis nunc etiam primum editis illustratae ac in decades distributae authore Flaminio Cornelio, Senatore Veneto*, 135–72. Bartholomaeus Ferrarianus was the procurator of the monastery from 1563 to 1566. For the year 1567 Andrea Baroccius Graecus directed Sant'Andrea. For a concise history of the order, see A. Degand, "Chartreux," in *Dictionnaire d'archéologie chrétienne et de liturgie* (Paris: Letouzey et Ané, Éditeurs, 1913), 3:1046–71.

Chapter VI

1. For biographical information about Francesco Spinola, see Pio Paschini, "Un umanista disgraziato nel Cinquecento," *Nuovo Archivio Veneto*, n.s., anno XX, 37 (1919): 65–186.

2. *P. Francisci Spinulae Mediolanensis Opera* (Venetiis [Venice]: Ex officina stellae Jordani Zileti, 1563). Spinola's poetry included lyrics, epodes, one book of *carmen saeculare*, elegies, hendecasyllables, and epigrams. He was an excellent poet who had mastered the classical Latin meters in imitation of classical style. He was especially fond of Catullus and, in imitation of him, wrote a book of hendecasyllables dedicated to Lodovico Domenichi. The book, published in 1563, actually contains twenty-three books of poems that were published in 1562 and 1563 in Venice by Zileti, who printed them in one volume in 1563. The edition I have used is in the Biblioteca nazionale di San Marco, shelf mark 69.D.140.

3. Spinola was a close friend of Hieronimo Donzellino, a physician who was investigated on numerous occasions by the Venetian Inquisition and imprisoned. Spinola wrote several poems to Donzellino.

4. See *Monumenti per servire alla storia del Palazzo Ducale di Venezia:* for example, 269, no 547; 319, no. 676; 350, no. 734; see especially 354, no. 741, an entry appropriate to my depiction: "Le prigioni li questo Conseglio per colpa delli protti che hebbero il carico, sono state in modo che, per la strettezza soa se possono chiamar sepolture d'huomini et con tutto questo nissuna e secreta, perché li pregionieri

tutti si parlano un con l'altro, et di più possono dar fuori et pigliar dentro ogni sorte di scritture secondo che l'esperientia ha fatto conoscer talmente che con grandissima difficultà si può haver la verità dalli rei, però essendo necessario farvi provisione accioché la giustitia possi haver il loco suo." The date of this document is November 26, 1568. See also further in Chapter VI and notes 5 and 6 below.

5. See Kuntz, "Voices from a Venetian Prison," 100–102 and n. 108.

6. Ibid., 102–3.

7. Ibid., 104–5.

8. Ibid., 106–8.

9. In the introduction to *P. Francisci Spinulae Epodon Liber, quo Q. Horatii Flacci carminum uarietatem imitatur Venetiis* (in *P. Francisci Spinulae Mediolanensis Opera*), which Spinola dedicated to Jean Hurault, he wrote enthusiastically of the ambassador: "Tvae religionis sapientiaeque species et pulchritudo non tantum nos omneis maximam in admirationem traduct, sed eam ipsi Gallorum reges, quorum in aula et educatus et eruditus es, etiam atque etiam adamarunt." The two humanists obviously enjoyed literature, and in the introduction to his text Spinola wrote to his friend about the metrical practice of Horace and Catullus and suggested an emendation of the latter. The interests of the two were obviously similar in literature, but it is significant that Spinola also praised the religion and wisdom of Hurault. This praise of Hurault's religion, which was said to be Huguenot, would certainly have caused problems for him with the religious authorities, since heresy from France was an ever-increasing problem. Spinola addressed numerous poems to Hurault as well as to the ambassador's brother.

10. *P. Francisci Spinulae Mediolanensis Carmen seculare, cum aliquot poematibus additis,* in *P. Francisci Spinulae Mediolanensis Opera,* 35–36. Note especially the following:

> *Spiritus alme polos, mare et implens numine Terram,*
> *Iam fractas hominum res et miserate labores,*
> *Dum rabies et caecus amor furit, horrida nobis*
> *Hostis et humani generis dum concitat arma,*
> *Concilio patrum faueas obsecro uocatus:*
> *Discordes animos illorum et dexter amorem*
> *Concilia arcanis tibi uocibus, incola mentis*
> . . . .
> *Omnia ne euertat, patres discordia demens;*
> *Scindatur uestrum studia in contraria nemo.*

11. On the Council of Trent, see Hubert Jedin, *History of the Council of Trent,* translated from the German by Ernest Graf (St. Louis: B. Herder Book Co., 1957).

12. Note, for example, the following exchange between Dionisio and the inquisitor. ASV, S.U., Processi, Busta 22, Contra Dionisium Gallum, testimony of July 12, 1566:

> *Inquisitor: Quomodo habeat pro articulis controuersis ea quę iam approbata fuerunt diffinita a communi judicio et consensu totius Ecclesie Catholice, et ultimo loco a sacro sancto oecumenico vniuersali concilio Tridentino?*
>
> *Dionisio: Ut ueritas illius sanctissimi Concilii executioni mandatur, et quę defuerunt terminantur summo et postremo Concilio antequam Christus ueniat, et seuiat antechristus in electos, quod fiat citissime iuxta reuelationem sibi factam cęlitus, cuius uirtute agit quę agit et patitur, quę patitur et clamat quę clamat.*

13. Ibid., document entitled *Ad clarissimos senatores Venetos*, dated October 15, 1566.

14. Ibid., document entitled *Ad sacrum tribunal venetum*, without date. This letter, whose incipit is *Fateor in meis scriptis*, is the closest Dionisio ever comes to a retraction.

15. "Vedendo lonnipotente Dio multiplicare gli peccati della Italia massime negli capi cosi ecclesiatici come secolari non potendo piu sostenere contermio purgare la chiesa sua per vno gran flagello." And then Savonarola cites the prophet Amos: "Non faciet dominus Deus verbum nisi reuelauerit secretum suum ad seruos suos prophetas." See *Trattato della reuelatione della reformatione della Chiesa*, c. 4. This work is bound with other works by Savonarola; the shelf mark is Biblioteca nazionale di San Marco, 190.C.142.

16. See Kuntz, "Voices from a Venetian Prison," 116–17. Probably a little before Dionisio wrote a quasi-retraction to the tribunal, Francesco Spinola, under torture, gave evidence to the Venetian Inquisition. See ASV, S.U., Processi, Busta 23, fascicolo 2, Testes examinati ad defensam fratris Antonio de Ferandina carta intitolata contra Decium Bellumbonum medicum. Ex constituto Francesci Spinolę, in Octobris 1566 fuit extractum.

> *Fuit sibi dictum. Si a dimanda chi erano presenti quando diceuano che sentiuano queste opinione? Respondit: Decio bellobona medico del Regno de Napoli prattica li da lui e de gli altri. Interrogatus: de tempore? Respondit: del 63. Interrogatus: de articulis super quibus colloquebantur? Respondit: Non mi ricordo specialmente de che cosa dicessero, ma generalmente delle cose di Alemagna ma non mi ricordo specialmente. Interrogatus: Si isti per ipsum nominati sentiebant male de religione, et in quibus articulis? Respondit: Io non uorrei dir una cosa per un'altro, che son confuso per esser amalado. Io non so se non in general. Et paulo inferius. Fuit sibi dictum se ui adimanda che nominate li complici che in parte o in tutto erano di questa uostra opinione? Respondit: Questi mi pareuano conformi con la mia opinion circa il clero, et circa la potestà della chiesa et cetera.*

17. See Kuntz, "Voices from a Venetian Prison," 117.

18. Ibid., 118.

19. Ibid., 119.

20. Ibid., 120–21.

21. Ibid., 121 and n. 161.

22. Ibid., 120

23. ASV, S.U., Processi, Busta 22, Contra Dionisium Gallum, document entitled *Spirito sancto calamum dirigente satis anxie scripsi ego Dionysius gallus . . . :* "Apostatam de Spinula, siue absolvere, siue perdere decreuistis; nolite festinare donec in vostra presentia ipsum allocutus fuero: novi enim animam eius, et daemonium a quo possidetur. Hoc non eiicitur nisi magna difficultate, quoniam pessimum est et versutissimum. Hoc autem in virtute et sapientia Christi volo eiicere in gratiam et salutem omnium vestrorum haereticorum eorum maxime quos apostata potuit seducere." This letter was directed "ad clarissimos et illustrissimos dominos senatores venetos assidentes pro Christo vinctus et incarceratus."

24. Ibid.: "Estote hac hebdonada valde misericordes et differte supplicia mortis, quoniam Deus humani generis valde vult misereri, cum ipsi valde minatur, si modo velit conuerti."

25. Kuntz, "Voices from a Venetian Prison," 122–23.

26. Ibid., 122–23 and n. 167.

27. John Martin has some suggestive remarks in this regard. See his *Venice's Hidden Enemies,* 69–70.

28. Fra Girolamo Savonarola felt the same disgust. In a letter to the pope, Alessando Borgia, written in 1498, Savonarola chided the pope for his lack of help in reforming the Church. Villari noted that Savonarola wanted to show that the pope was the real heretic and miscreant and the chief cause of all the evils that were tearing the Church apart. See Pasquale Villardi, *La storia di Girolamo Savonarola e de' suoi tempi* (Florence: Felice Le Monnier, 1861), vol. 2, bk. 4, chap. vi, 105–6.

29. Kuntz, "Voices from a Venetian Prison," 123.

30. ASV, Archivi propri, Roma, Busta 8.

31. An interesting letter, dated August 3, 1555, and written by Domenico Morosini, Venetian ambassador in Rome, recounts a conversation with the nuncio in which the nuncio complained that the Inquisition in the Venetian dominion had not demonstrated enough diligence in performing its duties. The question of lay representatives also entered the discussion. Note, for example: "hora interuengono ne si inquirisse, ne li processi fatto espediti, laqual cosa accioche si possi fare ricordano che saria a proposito in ciascuna sua città, instituire vno Tribunale de Inquisitione simile a quello, che è in cotesta città dalquale ricordo mossi li Reverendissimi Cardinali inquisitori sono in opinione di ordinar chel si faccia con l'assistentia non di laici ma di persone ecclesiatiche et dottorate, essendo la cognitione di queste cause in tutto ecclesiastica." See ASV, Capi del Consiglio dei Dieci, Dispacci degli Ambasciatori, Roma, Busta 24, c. 9. See also Aldo Stella, *Chiesa e lo stato nelle relazioni dei nunzi pontifici a Venezia,* Studi e Testi, 239 (Vatican City: Biblioteca Apostolica Vaticana, 1964; facsimile reprint, Modena: Dini, 1981).

32. See ASV, S.U., Processi, Busta 22, Contra Dionisium Gallum, document entitled *Vincat Veritas.* It is addressed *Ad Reverendissimum sacrum tribunal Venetum et illus-*

trissimos dominos senatores quos Deus elegit in sua causa iudices et non ipsum tribunal per spiritum sanctum. . . . The text of the letter is equally condemning of the tribunal. Note, for example: "*Praepara te (o sacrum tribunal) ad audiendam veritatem quae sola tuis peccatis, quae te Sathanae obligant atque seruum faciunt Deo reddunt odiosum te potest liberare. Despera te posse resistere sancto spiritui.*"

33. Ibid.

34. Stella, *Chiesa e lo stato*, 55–59, 63–64.

35. "se volemo considerarlo come commun Pastore esso successore di Pietro, che fu instituito per suo vicario dal saluator nostro Jesu Christo, doveria senza dubio esser tenuto per capo da tutti i Christiani, come è stato al tempo de quei primi padri in quali col menar uita cosi essemplare et honesta con quel che le stauano appresso, et con mostrarsi in tutte le attioni loro lontani da ogni interesse mondano, erano da tutta la Christianità come si deue riuerito et con le scomuniche loro arme spirituali summamente tenuti. Ma dapoi che si incominició a misurar la religione per via d'interesse incominció all'hora la rouina della religion cattolica, e questa pessima introduttione per non tacer il uero hebbe origine alla corte di Roma et con l'esempio di quella è poi passata nei principi temporali." ASV, Collegio, Relazioni, Ambasciatori, Roma, Busta 20, relazione dell'Ambas. Girolamo Soranzo, June 14, 1563.

36. Ibid.

37. ASV, Relazioni, Roma, Varie, Duplicati IV, relazione de Michiele Suriano. Surian did not mince words. Note especially: "Ma è ben uero, et questo non se puo negare, che alcuni Papi et massime in questi ultimi tempi hanno cosí mal usata questa sua auttorità c'hanno messo gran scandolo nel mondo, cosí nel gouerno temporale, come nel spirituale, et nella fede, perche oltra le tante guerre che sonno nate, et massime in Italia dell'ambitione o dalla poca prudentia di qualche Papa, donde sonno sequite tante mutationi di stati et tante essaltationi et depressioni di uno o di un'altro Principe, pare anco che tutte queste nouve opinioni nella religione et nuoue sette, sia che da cinquanta anni in qua hanno messa in confusione tutto'l mondo habbino hauuto gran fomento o dall'insolenza o dall'auaritita o dalla negligentia de Papi."

38. ASV, Capi del Consiglio dei Dieci, Dispacci degli Ambasciatori, Roma, Busta 25, c. 7, dated July 6, 1566. For the most complete account of Guido Zanetti da Fano, see Aldo Stella, "Guido da Fano eretico del secolo XVI al servizio dei re d'Inghilterra," *Rivista di Storia della Chiesa in Italia* 13 (1959): 196–238.

39. ASV, Capi del Consiglio dei Dieci, Dispacci degli Ambasciatori, Roma, Busta 25, c. 7^v.

40. Ibid., cc. 5–6. Note c. 5^v especially: "Rispose sua Santità che sapeua tutto questo, ma che non hauia dignità di questo principal Tribunal dell'inquisition far, che una causa sua fusse giudicata da un inferior. Come diss'io Padre santo, non è cosa ordinaria che un superior commetta diuerse cause all'inferior?" Tiepolo also wrote that the pope held Cosimo I in the greatest esteem and favored him above

all the other princes because he had sent Carnesecchi to Rome at the pope's request.

41. Ibid., cc. 7–7ᵛ.

42. See ASV, Capi del Consiglio dei Dieci, Dispacci degli Ambasciatori, Roma, Busta 24, fascicolo 13. The Venetian ambassador Domenico Morosini recorded the request on August 24, 1555: "Eccellentissimi Domini, Questa mattina il Reverendissimo Gouernator di Roma per commissione di sua Santità è uenuto a trouarmi a casa, et in nome di quella mi ha narrato di essere auisata come in Padova dal Reverendissimo Suffraganeo e stato mosso in prigione per heresia uno scolare chiamato Pompeo da Nolla heretico pertinace, hora, che é nelle carcere sua Santità desiderare, che vostre Eccellentie diano ordine alli Clarissimi Rettori di Padoa, che fauorischino il detto suffraganeo in questo caso, et lo espedischino accio secondo la giustitia sia punito. Altro non risposi saluo che non mancarei di signifecarle a vostre eccellentie l'officio che di ordine di sua Santità faceua meco. Et il desiderio che la tiene della spedittione di questo caso." Numerous letters of Filippo Archinto, the papal nuncio, reveal the pressure he applied to secure the extradition.

43. Ibid., Busta 25, cc. 7ᵛ–8: "et io dissi che quando un uien ad habitar in un Dominio, s'intende fatto suddito di quel Principe, et che ogni uolta che si da un tale, i altri prendono causa di temer, che'l medesimo sequiti in tutti, et che nessuna cosa era piu stimatata dell'essempio, perche poi a domandarne delli altri questa pareua gran ragione, che altre uolte cio si hauesse fatto et poteua uenir tempo che le cose non passassero con quella giustitia et sincerità che passano al presente."

44. Ibid., c. 11, July 26, 1566. Note, for example: "ma che ritrouandosi essa sul fatto, comprendeua molta ben quanto importassero i rispetti che erano in contrario da mandarlo qua a Roma; prima quanto al Tribunal dell'Inquistione, che per questa uia potria perder assai dell'auttorità, et poi quanto alla satisfattion d'i populi, la qual de ciascun Principe douea esser grandemente stimata."

45. Ibid., c. 11ᵛ. Paolo Tiepolo vividly recorded the pope's angry remarks: "dicendo adunque non ne le uogliono dar? Basta, basta, autorità di tribunal d'inquisitione? Quasi che quel tribunal debba esser superior a noi; satisfattion de populi? Quasi che non hauete dato altri ad altri Pontifici. . . . Forse uostre suddito, forse qualche gran personaggio? Che douete hauer tanti riguardi chi si puo risentir di lui?"

46. Ibid., c. 12. See Venice, Biblioteca nazionale di San Marco, MSS italiani, Cl. VII, Cod. CCXIII (= 8836) (MS sec. XVI), for relations between Venice and Rome as described by G. Lippomano. While Pius V was a *frate* and inquisitor in Venice, he felt he was held in low esteem. See also ASV, Consiglio dei Dieci, Parti secrete, Registro 8, cc. 54ᵛ–55, for instructions to the Venetian ambassador in Rome concerning the pope's distaste for Nicolò da Ponte.

47. ASV, Capi del Consiglio dei Dieci, Dispacci degli Ambasciatori, Roma, Busta 25, c. 11. The pope's sarcasm and anger were transparent, according to Tiepolo.

48. ASV, Consiglio dei Dieci, Parti secrete, Registro 8, c. 64. For the many instructions directed to Ambassador Tiepolo in Rome, see cc. 48ᵛ–49ᵛ, 59ᵛ–60ᵛ, 63–66.

49. Ibid., c. 65, August 8, 1566, al sommo Pontefice. Note especially: "che per saluezza delli nostri importantissimi rispetti quali ultimamente facessimo dechiarire dall'Ambassadore nostro alla Santità vostra et noi parimente dechiarissemo di qua al Reverendissimo Noncio di Vostra Beatitudine che la causa et imputatione di esso Guido douesse essere conosciuta et giudicata da questo Tribunale dell'inquisitione di questa città che è Tribunale della Santità vostra ilche ueramente ci seria stato molto charo per la causa sopradetta la quale ci deue essere come in fatti ci è molto a cuore. Ma finalmente hauendo ueduto dalle lettere di propria mano della beatitudine vostra presentatene dal Reverendissimo suo Noncio et da noi riceuute con quella riverenza che è proprio della republica nostra verso vostra Santità et parimenti inteso dalle lettere del nostro Ambassadore presso di lei et dal predetto Reverendissimo Noncio quanto grande sia il disiderio di vostra Beatitudine che le sia mandato questo sopradetto preggione per caggioni importantissime, massimamente essendo egli suddito di quella Santa Sede."

50. Ibid., c. 65ᵛ. On the same day, August 8, 1566, the *consiglio* wrote to Paolo Tiepolo, ambassador in Rome: "che andato alla Santità soa debbiate presentarle esse lettere, accompagnandole con officio conforme ad essa nostra deliberatione et alla continentia delle lettere nostre predette, si che la Santità soa conosca che per darle questa satisfattione dal lei tanto desiderata et bramata, come ne scrive per importantissimi rispetti noi si siamo contentati di lassare da canto per questa uolta li nostri che parimenti sono importantissimi et delli quali douemo hauer cura diligentissima per le cause che ultimamente in questo proposito vi hauemo significato operando in modo con la solita prudentia et uirtu uostra."

51. ASV, S.U., Processi, Busta 22, Contra Dionisium Gallum; see the document entitled *Vincat Veritas*. Dionisio's skill in writing the Latin language enhanced his description. Dionisio, the gentle dove asleep in his nest, was caught by the papal nuncio, the heartless hunter. See note 68 to Chapter v.

52. Ibid.

53. Ibid.

54. Ibid. See the document entitled *Vincat Veritas*, whose second section begins, "In nomine et virtute Dei omnipotentis . . . vincat veritas." Dionisio wrote: "sed etiam uniuersam meam legationem variis scriptis expressam et illustratam esse ex Deo veram et iustam, sicut testati sunt duo pii et honorati viri Veneti, Clarissimus Iustus Maurocenus vir nobilis et optimus ciuis Rochus Venetus qui meae legationi subscripserunt omnia mea scripta approbantes."

55. Both Giusto and Marco Morosini were from the Morosini called dalla Sbarra. Giusto was from the line of Benetto, and Marco was from the line of Lorenzo. Benetto, son of Giusto, son of Benetto, was the brother of Lorenzo, grandfather of Marco. Therefore, Marco Morosini's grandfather Lorenzo was the brother of Giusto Morosini's great-grandfather. The cousins Giusto and Marco were only one year apart in age, Giusto born in 1514 and Marco in 1513.

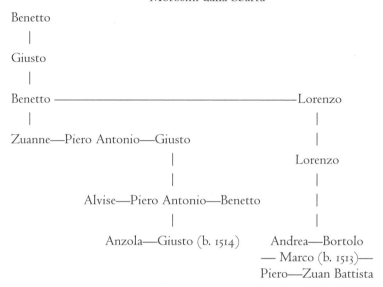

See Venice, Biblioteca nazionale di San Marco, MSS italiani, Cl. VII, Cod. CMXXVII (8596), Marco Barbaro, Alberi, c. 188ᵛ. See also note 29 to Chapter V.

56. ASV, S.U., Processi, Busta 22, document entitled *In nomine Domini nostri Jesu Christi crucifixi*.

57. Ibid.: "Nolite ergo ipsi ullo modo resistere spirito sancto aut abuti potestate quam Deus vobis dedit timentes, quia scriptum est potentes potenter tormenta patientur et seruus sciens voluntatem Domini et non faciens multis plagis vapulabit."

58. Ibid. Dionisio was especially prone to acknowledge the salutary grace of the feminine. After all, it was the Virgin Mother of Christ who had revealed to him his role as God's messenger. Dionisio's explanation is similar to that of the Blessed Bridget.

59. Ibid.

60. Ibid.

61. Dionisio was less than objective in his opinion of the Inquisition. See Romanin, *Storia documentata di Venezia*, 5:355–56, where the author notes: "d'inquisitori furono anzi sempre tenuti negli stretti limite della legge impoverati e puniti d'ogni azione arbitraria."

62. Dionisio's warnings are similar to those made by Guillaume Postel in 1548, while he was saying Mass in Santa Maria dei Miracoli. See ASV, S.U., Processi, Busta 160. See also Kuntz, "'Venezia portava el fuocho in seno.'"

63. ASV, S.U., Processi, Busta 22, Contra Dionisium Gallum, document entitled *In nomine Domini nostri Jesu Christi crucifixi*. This document was written "postri-

die sanctae Crucis anno domini, 1566," that is, on September 14, 1566. Dionisio's long letter, then, was written on September 15, 1566. On prophecy and piety in Padua, see Gabriella Zarri, "Pietà e profezia alle corti padane: Le pie consiglieri dei principi," in *Il Rinascimento nelle corti padane: Società e cultura*, ed. Paolo Rossi (Bari: De Donato Editore, 1977), 201–37.

64. ASV, S.U., Processi, Busta 22, Contra Dionisium Gallum, document entitled *In nomine Domini nostri Jesu Christi crucifixi*.

65. Ibid.: "Placuit Deo omnipotenti, duos esse his miserrimis et vltimis temporibus ecclesiae suae rectores praecipuos sicut in primitiua ecclesia beatos Petrum et Paulum."

66. Ibid.: "Sit papa presens tanto me superior quanto maiorem habet charitatem quam ego et quanto plus a sua creatione laborauit in regenda dei ecclesia quam ego a mea vocatione."

67. Ibid. Dionisio's conclusion was clear: "Iam autem, cum diuina prouidentia, duo sint ouilis Christi pastores electi probati et cogniti."

68. Ibid.

69. Ibid. See note 67 above.

70. Ibid.

71. Ibid.

72. Many shared Dionisio's sentiment following the election of the pope. On May 26, 1565, Giacomo Soranzo, Venetian ambassador to Rome, wrote that "li Ministri del Re di Spagna in diversi parti, et massimamente a Napoli uanno inquirendo, et fanno scrivere contra la elettione del Pontefice come fatta con simonia, et pero non giuridica." See ASV, Capi del Consiglio dei Dieci, Dispacci degli Ambasciatori, Roma, Busta 24, c. 173.

73. ASV, S.U., Processi, Busta 22, document entitled *In nomine Domini nostri Jesu Christi crucifixi*. Note, for example: "Immo per mea scripta aliud ego vobis annuntio: metaphysice scilicet, id est, natura mirante, partum esse masculum illum descriptum in duodecimo capite apocalipseos, raptum ad deum et ad solium eius, recturum reges et gentes impias in virga ferrea."

74. See *Espositio magni prophete Abbatis Joachim in Apocalipsim*, c. 157: "Tu Christum occidere non timuisti sed teipsum non dominum nouo rursum iaculo peremisti. Tu parturientis ecclesie filium absorbere putasti sed permissus non es vt hoc faceres quod te prostrato et deuicto raptus est ad deum et ad thronum ipsius. Vocare autem ecclesiam apostolorum matrem Christi ipsum interroga dei filium Christum. . . . Peperit ergo Maria vnigenitum suum quem tandem respiciens pendentem in cruce vna cum ecclesia apostolorum non sine gemitu parturiuit qui tamen natus est in alio regno et factus primogenitus mortuorum. Sane secundum typicum intellectum sicut ecclesia doctorum designatur in muliere: ita in filio mulieris exercitus omnium iustorum qui regnaturi sunt cum Christo et sessuri cum ipso in iudicio." The shelf mark of this work is Biblioteca nazionale di San Marco, 51.C.130.

75. ASV, S.U., Processi, Busta 22, document entitled *Ex coelo empireo veritas reuelata.* . . .

76. Ibid.

77. Ibid. In the *Mirabilis Liber qui prophetias . . . demonstrat,* an interesting passage drawn from cxxiii–cxxiii^v of the *Vaticinium sancte Brigide virginis sub similitudine lilii crescentis in agro occidentali* provides a corollary to Dionisio's statements about himself as third king; Bridget wrote of the "three lilies" that would proceed from the most Christian kingdom. Note especially: "Nam primum lilium predicat te et successorem esse et ministrum altaris vicarii Christi manum sinistram tenentis in epistolis vniuersarum nationum. Secundum lilium predicat te et tuos esse columnam Christianitatis in parte occidentali ab isto lapide marmoreo qui abicisus est de monte sine manibus. Tertium lilium predicat te esse aduocatum sponse Christi gerens aureolam lilii in capite optimi odoris. Ergo vocitaris Chrisitanissimus inter omnes reges."

78. ASV, S.U., Processi, Busta 22, document entitled *Ex coelo empireo veritas reuelata.* . . .

79. Ibid. Dionisio wrote: "et is qui scribit, ipse rex est, a deo constitutus veni tamquam de Edom, id est, de terreno de urbe gi sorte, id est, terra sortis, et de Bosra, hoc est, de inferno, de profundis carceribus magnis tribulationibus et mortis doloribus."

80. On Bosra, see *Encyclopaedia Judaica* (Jerusalem, 1969), 6:370–79, s.v. "Edom." The capital of Edom was probably Bozrah (see Amos 1:11–12). "For I have sworn by myself that Bozrah shall become a horror, a taunt, a waste, and a curse; and all her cities shall be perpetual wastes" (Jer. 49: 13). In the biblical tradition about the origin of the Edomites—or, more precisely, in accounts about the eponym "Esau, who is Edom" (Gen. 36:1)—the Edomites are related to the Hebrews. Esau was the grandson of Abraham and the son of Isaac. Thus it was stated that Rome was founded by the children of Esau, since Rome was identified as one of the cities of the chiefs of Esau enumerated at the end of Genesis 36. At a still later period the term became a synonym for Christian Rome and a theme for Christianity in general; allusions have even been found to Constantinople as one of the cities of Edom (*Encyclopaedia Judaica,* 6:379).

81. See Paris, Bibliothèque nationale, Fonds lat. 3679, fol. 23. Postel wrote that Mohammed said that Christ "esse faciem omnium hominum. Quod verissimum est Christi Epitheton quatenus nos omnes per naturam sumus Imago de Imagine eius et similitudo de similitudine eius et per gratiam ita necesse est ut . . . nos virginificari omnes et fieri os de ossibus eius et carnem de carne eius vt fiat vuna sola virginea massa."

82. ASV, S.U., Processi, Busta 22, *Contra Dionisium Gallum*; see the document entitled *Ex coelo empireo veritas reuelata.* . . . Savonarola had made the same point in a letter to the brothers of San Marco. He wrote that "many were wiser and more enlightened by God than you" who need "diuentar pazzi per essere salui nel con-

spetto di Dio, come dice l'Apostolo. Si quis uidetur inter uos sapiens esse in hoc seculo, stultus fiat ut sit sapiens." See *Epistola del preditto a tutta la congregatione de i frati di San Marco, del modo di resistere alle tentationi, e di peruenir alla perfettione*, in *Molti devotissimi trattati del Reverendo Padre Frate Hieronimo Sauonarola da Ferrara*, c. 54ᵛ.

83. ASV, S.U., Processi, Busta 22, Contra Dionisium Gallum, document entitled *Quis novit sensum domini . . .*, dated May 3, 1567.

84. Ibid. See the document entitled *Ex coelo empireo veritas reuelata. . . .* In the same context we can again note that Savonarola interpreted the Psalm "Sing unto the Lord a new song" to mean that "God wished the Church to be reformed, His people to renew their lives in good practices." See *Prediche del Rev. Padre Fra Hieronymo Sauonarola dell'ordine de predicatori . . .* ; note especially c. 55ᵛ: "et pero Dio che uede ch' ella [chiesa] è inuecchiata, ua conducendo nell' arca chi uuol' far bene per renouarla et leuar uia quel uecchio che ci è di male. Et pero dice el salmo nostro, Cantate domino canticum nouum, cioè, o eletti di Dio, o uoi che siate nell' arca, cantate uno cantico nuouo, che Dio uuole rinouare la chiesa sua." Note also c. 57: "Cantate al signore uno cantico nuouo, renuouate la vita uostra in buon costumi."

85. ASV, S.U., Processi, Busta 22, Contra Dionisium Gallum; see the document entitled *Legatio electi serui Dei et nuntii magistri Dionisii Galli*.

86. In almost every letter written from the Venetian prison, Dionisio used harsh words against the papal nuncio and the tribunal.

87. ASV, S.U., Processi, Busta 22, Contra Dionisium Gallum; see the document entitled *In nomine et virtute Dei omnipotentis Vincat Veritas*: "et illustrissimum Senatum quem Deus elegit in sua causa iudicem per spiritum sanctum quem misit in ipsum Senatum congregatum postridie Pentecostes in specie columbae albae supra caput scribentis." Dionisio repeated these words several times in the letter.

88. Ibid. "mean legationem variis scriptis expressam et illustratam esse ex Deo veram et iustam sicut testati sunt duo pii et honorati viri veneti, clarissimus Iustus Maurocenus, vir nobilis et optimus ciuis Rochus Venetus qui meae legationi subscripserunt, omnia mea scripta approbantes." In *Ex coelo empireo veritas reuelata . . .*, a letter addressed to the Venetian nobility, Dionisio wrote: "Deus te suum elegit et ordinauit iudicem."

89. Ibid., document entitled *Ex coelo empireo veritas reuelata . . .*, dated May 4, 1567. Dionisio wrote: "Esto mihi pater et mater et vniuersae terrae possessionem accipe; ea mea est."

90. Ps. 104 (105): 11.

91. Dionisio may have had in mind Psalm 86 (87), where David praises Jerusalem, the mother of all people and beloved by God, as the "center of a new order" among men who form with the people of Israel "one family in one explicit messianic-eschatological vision" (*La Bibbia Piemme* [Turin: Edizioni Piemme, 1995], 324, where one will find perceptive comments on this psalm).

92. For another view of Venice as justice, see *Delle orationi volgarmente scritte da diversi Hvomini . . . Raccolte gia della felice memoria del Signor Francesco Sansouino et hora in questa nostra vltima impressione arrichite . . .* (Venice: Presso Altobello Salicato, Alla Libraria della Fortezza, 1548). Note especially c. 158ᵛ: "O Giustitia salute de gli huomini e regina del mondo. O perpetuo uincolo dell'humana generatione. O salutifera medicina d'ogni nostra infermitade. O anima comune della città e Terre tutte. Alta et sublime Vergine, che gli alti cieli habiti, dimmi, ti prego, santissima Dea, chi giamai tenne la tua bilancia piu per tutti uguale di questo clarissimo nostro? Quale fu mai che con le tue armi sì ben sapesse difendere, et conseruare i popoli alla sua fede commessi?"

93. See Kuntz, "Guillaume Postel e l'idea di Venezia come la magistratura più perfetta."

94. ASV, S.U., Processi, Busta 22, document entitled *Ex coelo empireo veritas reuelata . . . :* "Admoneo te (pater mi materque mea, Reverendissima, ac illustrissima justa et benigna dominatio veneta) et obsecro per ipsam iustitiam quam tu mihi debes, quam Deo promisisti atque iurauisti te facturum populo tam pauperi quam diviti vt hodierno die."

95. Ibid.: "enim interest malos puniri vt in securitate boni pace fruantur." For an excellent discussion of Venice as justice in the sculptures of the Palazzo Ducale and the Loggia, see David Rosand, "Venetia Figurata: The Iconography of a Myth," in *Interpretazioni veneziane*, ed. David Rosand (Venice: Arsenale Editrice, 1984), 177–96.

96. See ASV, Capi del Consiglio dei Dieci, Lettere, Filza 56 (1555): "La grandezza, la felicità et la conseruatione de questa Santissima Republica depende da molti belli ordini che in quella si veggono, ma particolarmente dalle leggi Santissime statuite da Vostre Eccellentissime Signorie per le quali è dato honore a Dio, aggrandita la Maestà sua, et honorato il nome suo, è prouisto a la conseruatione de li beni, honor, et vita de gli huomini, et sono castigati gli empii, et scelerati che transgrediscono le leggi, et sono scandalosi al mondo et che sturbano la quiete di quelli, che vogliono viuere pacificamente, et però mentre che queste leggi sarano conseruate, ogni di più fiorirà questo illustrissimo Dominio, allargarà i confini et sarà preseruato intatto da la potentissima mano de Dio, che ne ha particolar cura, per la giustitia, che regna nei petti di Vostre Eccellentissime Signorie, per la quale io Orpheo Fioccha de la Terra di Polpenaze le supplico a farmi giustitia le quale sono Conservatori de le leggi, et massime in caso di tanta importantia . . . per la solita giustitia che rappresentano il luoco d'Iddio in Terra, per conseruatione de le sue santissime leggi, che deenno inuiolabilmente esser conseruate per essempio de gli altri che imparino a viuer bene, et per la sicureza de la vita mia." See also the miniature of Saint Mark handing over the Law to Doge Andrea Gritti. The text under the beautiful miniature, which shows Doge Gritti kneeling at the feet of the saint, who is extending the Book of the Law to the doge, is important: "Summus ille optimus Deus Qui uniuersum mundum eternasque Intelligentias creauit primus omnium mirabili prouidentia leges tulit. . . . Nos Andreas Griti Dux Venetiarum . . . quem muneris nostro incumbat leges incorrupte, sancteque

seruare ac tueri caeterisque magistratibus nostri Judicibus, civibusque, seruandas demandare eas ordine . . . reddere decreuivus." ASV, Maggior Consiglio, Libro d'oro vecchio, miniatura, 1529, inizio del Proemio dogale, c. 21.

97. ASV, Capi del Consiglio dei Dieci, Lettere, Filza 56 (1555).

98. Ibid.: "per la solita iustitia che rappresentano il luoco d'Iddio in Terra, per conseruatione de le sue santissime leggi."

99. ASV, S.U., Processi, Busta 22, document entitled *Ex coelo empireo veritas reuelata* . . . , dated May 4, 1567, written in the margins: "de Leonis et Draconis me eruas faucibus aut mitte gladium vt hodierno die me interficiant et dona cras eos pristina libertate si possis id facere, citra offensionem nostrae reipublicae eius enim interest malos puniri vt in securitate boni pace fruantur."

100. ASV, Maggior Consiglio, Libro d'oro vecchio, cc. 21–21^v.

101. Ibid., c. 21: "Ea scilicet ratione ut quae diu perpetuoue essent . . . duratura ceu globorum conuersiones, solis meatus et stellarum perennes cursus leges ratas, diuturnasque haberent. Quae uero fluxa et uariis euentis obnoxia, et mox interitura temporaneis momentaneisque institutis pro locorum temporum et personarum natura gubernanda et regenda constituit."

102. Ibid., c. 21^v.

103. ASV, S.U., Processi, Busta 22, Contra Dionisium Gallum, document entitled *Ex coelo empireo veritas reuelata* . . . : "quae Venetiis in aduentu meo fleuisse praedicatur (causam ego scio) sponsus dilectus male tractabatur, in hunc usque male tractatus et multo multis bona fecisse, signa dans, faciensque pluraque miracula vt veritati crederes credasque quam sponsus annuntiat tibi scriptis commissam."

104. See Venice, Biblioteca nazionale di San Marco, MSS latini, Cl. III, Cod. CLXXVII (= 2176), c. 30. See also *Mirabilis Liber qui prophetias . . . demonstrat*, where *cantare* means "to sing" and "to prophesy." Although *gallus* in Latin means both "Gaul" and "cock," in the context in which Teolosphoro used the word, it clearly refers to a "Gaul" who will initiate the restitution after the Church is reformed. The iconography of the cock is rich, and Dionisio certainly was aware of its symbolism. Prudentius affirms that "Gallus est mirabilis Dei creatura et recte presbyteri illius est figura." He is the messenger of light; he invites us to prayer; he casts out demons. Marsilio Ficino affirmed that the cock, because he is the symbol of the sun, is superior to the lion. From an unknown early source, we find the following: "Gallus inter caetera altilia caelorum audit super ethera concentum angelorum tunc monet nos excutere verba malorum gustare et percipere arcana supernorum." See Battisti, *L'anti-Rinascimento*, 1:255–59.

105. ASV, S.U., Processi, Busta 22, document entitled *Ex coelo empireo veritas reuelata* . . . : "quod huic ciuitati periculum imminet sagittarum et irae Dei omnipotentis nisi causam presentem diligenter expediant."

106. Ibid., document entitled *In nomine Domini nostri Jesu Christi crucifixi*, addressed to the Venetian tribunal and the Senate.

107. Ibid.

108. Iseppo Bollani's name appears in the trial of Marco da Novegrado. Bollani, although a patrician, had been imprisoned for debts. As an official at the Dazio del Vin, he had encountered problems with the Capi in 1563, being accused of irregularities with money. He could not be found in December 1563, so he was given eight days to come and defend himself; otherwise he would be tried in absentia. On December 23, 1563, Bollani wrote a letter denying the charges. See ASV, Consiglio dei Dieci, Parti criminali, Filza 14. On April 3, 1567, the mother of Stefano Moro petitioned to have her son placed where medical attention was available, since he suffered from vertigo; a physician testified that this was true. See ASV, Consiglio dei Dieci, Parti comuni, Filza 99.

109. Ibid., S.U., Processi, Busta 22, document entitled *Ex coelo empireo veritas reuelata*. . . .

110. Savonarola also used this idea in his *Prediche del Rev. Padre Fra Hieronymo Sauonarola dell'ordine de predicatori* . . . , sermon XIX, c. 143^v, explaining how God uses those whom He chooses for His glory: "Allhora io risposi al signore, et disse, io non sono instrumento atto a questa cosa, uorrei signore chel ti piacesse e leggere un altro piu atto et migliore instrumento de me: lui rispose. Non sai tu quod deus elegit infirma huius mundi, ut confundat fortia. Dio elegge le cose uili et inferme per confondere et superare le cose forti et gagliardi et non uuole che la laude si atribuisca allo instrumento, ma a Dio." The shelf mark of the volume I have consulted is Biblioteca nazionale di San Marco, 17.C.167.

111. Dionisio referred to himself many times as a fool for Christ, paraphrasing Saint Paul. Savonarola also wrote of the "folly of the Cross" as the greatest wisdom. See *Prediche di Fra Girolamo da Farrara sopra Ezechiel* (Venice: Zuan Antonio di Volpini da Castel Giuffredo, 1541), sermon XVII, cc. 101–101^v: "Pero lo omnipotente Idio, vedendo gli huomini pazi che si reputono savi, volse venire nel mondo, et con la croce, cosa stoltissima, ha messa nel mondo la sua sapientia. Li philosofi speculauano, l'vniuerso, e Cristo ha voluto che stiamo a speculare la croce. Hor sta a udire questa stultitia." The shelf mark is Biblioteca nazionale di San Marco, 20.C.157.

112. ASV, S.U., Processi, Busta 22, Contra Dionisium Gallum, document entitled *Ex coelo empireo veritas reuelata*. . . .

113. *I Dieci Comandamenti Espositione molto devota composta da fra Hieronimo Sauonarola de Ferrara* . . . , in *Molti devotissimi trattati del Reverendo Padre Frate Hieronimo Sauonarola da Ferrara*, c. 167^v: "Tutta la perfettione della religione christiana et della uita spirituale consiste nella charita, laqual e diuisa in due parti, nella charita di Dio et nella charita del prossimo. Perche adunque i precetti di amar Dio con tutto il cuore, et di amar il prossimo come se medisimo sono i primi, dalliquali depende ogni legge."

114. ASV, S.U., Processi, Busta 22; see the document beginning "Corona mea, Sanctus Spiritus / Gloria mea crux Christi Jesu / Victoria mea mors, et veritas Deique gratia / Triomphus meus meipsum vicisse et pro inimicis vltro orauisse." This letter was written shortly after September 21, the Feast of Saint Matthew,

when Dionisio was supposed to have received the message from the Holy Spirit. The year was probably 1562 or 1563 because his letters of 1567, after more than a year in prison, reveal a desperation and some willingness to placate the religious officials whom he had severely reprimanded previously.

115. ASV, S.U., Processi, Busta, 22, document entitled *Ad clarissimos Senatores Venetos assidentes tribunali Veneto* . . . : "Habeo mysteria et archana vobis reuelanda," dated October 15, 1566. After the dedication, Dionisio wrote: "Donysius gallus suos honoris titulos retices sibi Diuinitus concessos et humanitus, in galliarum partibus." These "divine" honors refer to his mystical anointment by the Virgin. By human honors he probably meant the honor of being rector of the Collège de Lisieux.

116. Ibid.

117. See *Vaticinia siue prophetiae Abbatis Ioachini* (Venetiis [Venice]: Hieronymum Porrum, 1589). Note the *vita* by Gabriele Bario that precedes the *Vaticinia*, sig. di^v: "Et piglio habito Monastico di color bianco et aspro: Oue essendo entrato in certi luoghi deserti, dubitando di morire per la gran sete c'hebbe si alterro di arena, accio stando insepolto non fusse dalle Fiere diuorato; et cosi sepolto stando, mentre contempla la Sacra Scrittura fu dal sonno preso: Et ecco che gli pare vedere un Fiume di Oglio, et un' huomo da vicino, che staua in pie il quale le diceua; Beui di questo Fiume; et lui ne beuuè a satietà. Et essendo suegliato gli apense l'intelligentia de tutta la sacra scrittura. Nel monte poi nel quale Christo si trasfiguro, in una Cisterna vecchia passo tutta una Quadragesima con Vigilie, Orationi, Digiuni, Hinni, et Salmi: et la notte della Resurrettione del Signore gli apparue un gran splendor. Et cosi si empi di divinità, per intendere la concordanza del Vecchio et Nuouo Testamento; et ogni difficultà et oscurità de essi." The shelf mark of this volume is Biblioteca nazionale di San Marco, 32.D.152.

118. Venice, Biblioteca nazionale di San Marco, MSS latini, Cl. III, Cod. CLXXVII (= 2176), c. 14^v.

119. Fra Rusticanus had also repeated the idea of twelve apostles for the new age. Ibid., c. 15^v. Guillaume Postel also saw himself as an apostle of Christ. In the last year of his life (1581) he wrote of twelve apostles who would go out from Paris like the Apostles of old to preach the Gospel to the whole world. See Paris, Bibliothèque nationale, Fonds lat. 3401, c. 6.

120. Venice, Biblioteca nazionale di San Marco, MSS latini, Cl. III, Cod. CLXXVII (= 2176), cc. 20^v–21.

121. ASV, S.U., Processi, Busta 22, Contra Dionisium Gallum, document entitled *Ad sacrum Tribunal Venetum*. Dionisio emphasized the duty, rather than the honor, of being pope.

122. He made this boast in a letter entitled *Spiritu sancto calamum dirigente*. . . . In the section that begins "monita spiritussancti Reverendissimis ac Illustrissimis Dominis Venetis," he noted: "Prohibete duo peccata quae nimis Deum irritant, haeresim et sodomiam regnare et committi Venetiis et toto vostro Dominio, sub poenis gravissimis."

123. Ibid., document entitled *Ad clarissimos Senatores Venetos . . . Spiritu sancto calamum dirigente. . . .*

124. Savonarola, in his *Trattato della reuelatione della reformatione della Chiesa*, c. 2, writes in a similar vein: "Benche lungo tempo in molti modi per inspiratione diuina io habbia predette molte cose future." Also notable among the prophets in the Cinquecento were Giorgia Siculo of Ferrara and his disciple Francesco Severo. See, for example, Adriano Prosperi, "Una cripto-ristampa dell'Epistola di Giorgio Siculo," *Bollettino della Società di Studi Valdesi* 134 (December 1973): 52–68. Records of the proceedings against Siculo have not yet been found. The trial of Francesco Severo, however, sheds much light on the teachings of Siculo. Especially interesting for our consideration is Siculo's emphasis on the Holy Spirit. He claimed that when a man was truly baptized by the Spirit, it would be impossible for him to sin any more. According to Siculo's teaching, his disciples were awaiting the justice promised by the "sending of the Holy Spirit." See Venice, Archivio storico del Patriarcato di Venezia, Criminalia Santissimae Inquisitionis, Busta 2, fascicolo, Processus pro secta Georgii Siculi, Crim. Franciscus Severi, December 24, 1567, c. 84^v.

125. See note 12 above.

126. "Li spirituali sono e ueri Christiani pieni di lume, et di gratia dello spirito santo, et di lume sopranaturale di fede, e sono congiunti col sommo spirito che e Dio e questi sono spirituali subietti totalment allo spirito et a Dio e questo e lo spirito, e la gratia e l'olio del spirito santo . . . chel uero Christiano debbe esser unto di questo olio di spirito santo elquale debba penetrare nell'anima et nel corpo, accioche lhuomo sia tutto spirituale." *Prediche del Rev. Padre Fra Hieronymo Sauonarola dell'ordine de predicatori . . .* , sermon III, c. 21. The shelf mark is Biblioteca nazionale di San Marco, 17.C.167.

127. For a succinct article on prophecy in the Bible and in the Christian era, see Robert R. Wisson, "Biblical Prophecy," in *Encyclopedia of Religion*, ed. Mircea Eliade (New York: Macmillan, 1987), 12:14–23.

128. See Jordan Aumann, "L'azione dello Spirito Santo," in *La mistica: Fenomenologia e riflessione teologica*, ed. Ermanno Ancilli and Maurizio Paparozzi (Rome: Città Nuova Editrice, 1984), 2:153–68. Dionisio attributed great significance to the white dove that followed him when he appeared in the Senate; after the baptism of Jesus, the Holy Spirit descended in the appearance of a dove (Luke 3:22).

129. Dionisio wrote this criticism of the Inquisition in a letter addressed *Ad clarissimos senatores Venetos assidentes tribunali Veneto* and dated October 15, 1566. Note especially: "codices totos intus, et foris scriptos quos egoispse ad vos deferre volebam, nolens ipsos vostro tribunali committere quia militat adversus spiritum sanctum."

130. See the letter written *Ad clarissimos ac illustrissimos Dominos senatores Venetos*, without date but probably in October 1566. Note: "In hac Dei causa Christi et mea totiusque ecclesiae militantis Reverendissimum sacrum Tribunal Venetum, supra

quod decuit declarauit sese adversarium. Quamobrem Deus ipsum recusat et ego, pro Christo Domino et pro me et pro vniuersa ecclesia militante ipsum recuso iudicem."

131. Ibid., document entitled *Ad sacrum tribunal Venetum:* "Consulit spiritussanctus et Christus Rex aeternus imperat principibus Christianis, vt omni diligentia et quouis prudenti modo capiantur haeresiarchae princeps De Conde, Admiraloius Dandelot, princeps Portianus et quidam alii haeresiarchae qui gallias bellis ciuilibus afflixerunt occupandae et rapiendae coronae gratia sub praetextu religionis."

132. See *Profezie politiche e religiose di Fra Hieronymo ricavate dalle quelle prediche de Messer Francesco de Guicciardini l'historico* (Florence: M. Cellini e Compagni, 1763).

133. ASV, S.U., Processi, Busta 22, document entitled *Ad clarissimos ac illustrissimos Dominos senatores Venetos.* Note, for example: "Quos, in sua causa, Deus elegit Iudices per Spiritum Sanctum quem. . . . Deus misit supra suum electum seruum et nuntium Dionysium gallum, in specie columbae albae, in clarissimum ipsum senatum Venetum congregatum." Dionisio's point is clear: the Holy Spirit, in the form of a white dove, had manifested itself over its chosen messenger when he was entering the body chosen to judge, namely, the Venetian Senate.

134. Ibid., document entitled *Ad illustrissimos ac reverendissimos dominos Venetos* and dated October 3, 1566. This document was presented to the tribunal by Father Nicolas Lapicida, messenger of the tribunal, in the name of Dionisio Gallo.

135. Rom. 13:2. Dionisio may also have had in mind the words of Saint Peter: "Submit yourself to every ordinance of man for the Lord's sake, whether it be to the King, as supreme, or unto governors. . . . For so is the will of God that with well-doing ye may put to silence the ignorance of foolish men" (1 Pet. 2:13–15).

Chapter VII

1. Dionisio's writings were preserved with the records of his inquisition. A list of his longer works follows:

> 1. *Liber, quem Nullus aut in coelo aut in terra aut subtus terram, antea poterat aperire ne quidem respicere.* (This work is dedicated to Cosimo I, to his sons Francesco and Cardinal Ferdinando, and to Lord Paulus Jordanus Ursinus, and also to Johanna of Austria, wife of Francesco, and to Isabella Medici and their friends on behalf of the whole noble and universal feminine sex.) The work contains several parts: a long dedication, various short propositions, then a *Legatio serui Dei, et nuntii, magistri Dionysii galli, Diuini Legislatoris, et humani.* . . . To this *Legatio* Dionisio wrote a proemium in Latin, a second in French, and then a subtitle, *Articles de la paix de nostre Redempteur, et sauluer Jesuschrist.* . . . The articles are written in French and Latin and are similar to propositions in his other *Legationes.*

2. *Legatio electi serui Dei et nuntii magistri Dionisii Galli.* (This work is dedicated to the patriarch of Venice, the doge, the Venetian dominion, Senators, and most Christian Venetian men.)

3. *Premyer auditeur des hommes de ceste cause, en ce stille, ainsy que premyerent l'auyons escripte a este, Monseigneur le Marquis di Masse . . . daquel l'aduis et iugement ensuyt.* (This work is dedicated to the marquis de Masse, uncle of Duke Alfonso of Ferrara.)

4. *Legation de L'ambassadeur de Dieu, maistre Denys De Gallois, percatholique, et tres general Legislateur Dyuin, et termporel . . .*

5. *Legatio servi Dei Dei et nuntii ministri Dionysii galli diuini legislatoris et humani . . .*

6. *Haec est causa totius ecclesiae militantis.* (This work is dedicated to all the princes and illustrious men and their senates and especially to the emperor and to the Catholic king. The work was completed on June 5, 1566, in Venice.)

Four other rather long works repeat the ideas expressed in the writings listed.

2. ASV, S.U., Processi, Busta 22, Contra Dionisium Gallum, document entitled *Liber, quem Nullus:* "Deo dante coelitus, priuatæ nostræ personæ proprie accommodantur: Reique veritatem probant, iam tres annos integros . . . nostræ res gestæ a prophetis praeuisae et a Diua predictae Brigida." Note also, in the letter to the pope entitled *Vniuerso hominum generi, Dionysus Gallus, coelesti gratia, Dei seruus et nuntius, S.P.D.,* that Dionisio claims Saint Bridget predicted his mission: "quando nunc ex mediis galliis Deus ad vos mittit iuxta prophetiam eiusdem Diuae Brigidae, electum seruum suum apud gallorum principes." The words of Saint Bridget as reported in the *Sequitur libellus qui intitulatur Onus mundi id est prophetia de malo futuro ipsi mundo superuenturo,* chap. 12, are as follows: "Vnde cum beata Birgitta in capitulo xxxvii quarti libri peteret ut dominus mitteret aliquos de amicis suis ad precauendum mundum de periculo suo dominus respondit inter alia verba. . . . Verumtamen mittam amicos meos ad quos mihi placuerit et preparabunt uiam deo."

3. ASV, S.U., Processi, Busta 22, Contra Dionisium Gallum, document entitled *Liber, quem Nullus:* "Ergo nunc, quando tempus postulat et exigit negotium vultis (o Illustrissimi et excellentissimi principes) vt gratias et beneficia iam tres annos reuolutos mihi concessa coelitus vos celem et taceam? In aeternum peream nisi veritatem dico; pulcherrimis igitur titutlis me coelum honorauit: id est Christus coelorum Rex orbisque conditor atque dedit officia omnium maxima ac difficillima quibus Christo sociante . . . functus sum."

4. Ibid., document entitled *Vniuerso hominum generi, Dionysus Gallus, coelesti gratia, Dei seruus et nuntius, S.P.D.,* but addressed especially to the pope, the Senate, and the Roman people. In this heading we can see that Dionisio joined the idea of *Senatus populusque romanus,* the temporal magistracy, with the spiritual magistracy of the pope. Dionisio's medical metaphor is interesting: "Quia Dei summa et medella et misericordia duobus pessimis laborantes morbis galliae sanabuntur. Morbus alter auara multorum ambitio praelatorum ecclesiæ: alter, error haereticorum. Sed non profecto galliarum proprii sunt isti morbi. Sed aliarum etiam communes nationum.

At uero præ caeteris, nationibus afflicatæ sunt Galliae. Erit autem supremo malo summum remedium. Exit communi morbo, commune medicamentum."

5. Apoc. 5:5.

6. ASV, S.U., Processi, Busta 22, Contra Dionisium Gallum, document entitled *Liber, quem Nullus*. Note, for example: "ego sicut auis fugiens, et pulli a nido auolantes; ego propugnator ad saluandum, ego sub Christo, agnus tamquam occisus, qui Christo cooperante, librum aperui sigillis septem signatum; ego post Christum, gentium expectatio, ego vox multarum aquarum."

7. One *Legatio* was dedicated "ad illustrissimum, grauissimum, aequissimum et potentissimum Dominium vniuersumque clarissimum Senatum Venetum" and written in very elegant Latin. In a long preface, Dionisio addresses the patriarch, the clergy, the doge, and most Christian Venetian men; this *Legatio* was completed in Venice on June 7, 1566, and read in the house of Rocho de Mazzochis in the presence of the Venetian nobleman Giusto Morosini. Another *Legatio*, written in French but without date, was read in Ferrara; Dionisio dedicated his work to all Christianity. A third *Legatio*, written in French, with its preface and dedication to Cosimo I and Prince Francesco in Latin, was perhaps written first. Although no date was affixed, the mention of Clement Marot's approval of this *Legatio* would suggest that it was the earliest of the four. This statement about Marot was deleted from the other three versions. The fourth *Legatio* is the final version, which appears as the central part of the *Liber, quem Nullus*, written in French and Latin.

8. See Jacoff, *The Horses of San Marco and the Quadriga of the Lord*, where the author argues that the ancient horses placed over the central portal of the Basilica di San Marco represent the horses that lead the Church, with Venice understood as the driver, or charioteer. More will be said of this later.

9. ASV, S.U., Processi, Busta 22, document entitled *Liber, quem Nullus*, whose preface begins: "Haec est pugna totius ecclesiae militantis." Note Dionisio's words, drawn from Apoc. 2:17: "Vincenti dabo manna absconditum et dabo illi calculum candidum et in calculo, nomen nouum scriptum quod nemo scit nisi qui accipit." He also cites from the same chapter, verse 28; note especially: "et dabo illi stellam matutinam, id est, clarissimam veritatis intelligentiam. Haec verba sunt Christi in persona vocis magnae tamquam tubae loquentis." See also below for additional discussion about the white stone. I am grateful to Rabbi David Blumenthal for helpful conversation about the meaning of the white stone in the Old Testament.

10. Dionisio, in a letter directed "Ad Reverendissimos ac Illustrissimos dominos, sacrum tribunal venetum et senatum," and written from prison, identified himself with the messiah mentioned in Apoc. 12:5. Note especially: "Immo per mea scripta aliud ego vobis annuntio: metaphysice, scilicet, id est, natura mirante, partum esse masculum illum, descriptum in duodecimo capite apocalipseos: raptum ad deum et ad solium eius, recturum reges et gentes impias in virga ferrea." ASV, S.U., Processi, Busta 22, document entitled *In nomine domini nostri Jesu Christi crucifixi*.

11. Note Joachim's vision about the meaning of the Apocalypse: "About the

middle of the night's silence, . . . as I was meditating, suddenly something of the fullness of this book and of the entire agreement of the Old and New Testaments was perceived by a clarity of understanding in my mind's eye." McGinn, *Visions of the End*, 130.

12. For the case of Oderico Grison, see ASV, S.U., Processi, Busta 22, Costituto Oderico Grison. See also Busta 20, Costituto Agnolo Baglione, fascicolo Pietro Agusto, for other examples of the influence of the Apocalypse.

13. Dionisio's certainty of his divine anointment was responsible for most of his problems.

14. Juan Luis Vives, in his *De subventione pauperum* . . . , argued that it was natural for men to want to help each other. Dionisio used the same natural-law theory to describe his social program for the state and for the Church. Note the social program of Vives, drawn from the Italian translation of 1545: "Pertanto è cotal desiderio marauigliosamente ne petti humani edificato; di sorte che qualunque generoso di animo ad assaissimi far bene, et giouare disidera; ne giudica cosa alcuna piu honesta, o piu prestante di questa: et ciò sanza sua alcuna utilità; anzi talhor con graue pericolo, o dello hauere, o della uita. Lequali cose tutte molti di animo grande, et eccelso, per solleuar gli oppressi, per souuenire a poueri, per confermar gli infermi, per auitare, et dar confronto a gli afflitti hanno si come uili, et abiette dispreggiate, onde hanno per ciò grandissimi premii con seguiti di maniera che sono stati giudicati degni di imortalità." *Il modo del souvenire a poveri*, cc. 13–13^v. Vives presents specific arguments from natural law. Note, for example: "se noi cosi pronti fossimo al dare, come al dimandare l'aiuto: o uero se ci mouesse almeno la liberalità delle fiere, et un certo loro sentimento piu alla natura accommodato, che'l nostro: delle quali nulla è; la quale pasciuta, e satiata, non lasci le cose, che le auanzano; iui in commune senza custodia alcuna; si come in spatioso et ampio armario della natura. Onde sappia chiunque possiede i doni della natura; se ei gli communica co'l fratel pouero; che ei giustamente, e secondo il uolere et l'ordine di lei gli possiede: ma se altramente fa, è si come ladro, et rubbatore, dalla legge della natura conuinto, et condannato: come colui il quale occupa, e ritiene per se quello che non allui solo hauea ella procreato" (c. 33^v).

15. Dionisio seems to have had in mind the Concordat of Bologna of 1516, which gave the French king the right of royal nomination to benefices in France. The king controlled the appointment of 800 abbots and 114 archepiscopal seats. Although the candidate was not obliged to have received holy orders, he had to take them before assuming his seat. The pope had to confirm the king's nomination and had the right to reject the royal candidate. In reality the pope rarely refused to confirm the king's choice, even when the person nominated was unqualified. As Edelstein has pointed out, the Venetian ambassador to the court of Francis I wrote that "the law insures him the obedience and fidelity of the clergy and of the laymen who aspire to benefices." She also noted that the Concordat ended the independence of the Gallican church "by putting the French church—or at least its

major offices—under the sole control of the monarch." See Edelstein, "Church Patronage in France on the Eve of the Reformation," 33–49.

16. Cited in ibid., 47. Interestingly, in regard to the Venetian ambassador's accusation about heresy, Venice had also been considered the door by which reformed ideas had entered Italy.

17. *Abbas Joachim magnus propheta: Expositio magni prophete Ioachim in librum beati Cirilli de magnis tribulationibus et statu Sancte matris Ecclesie.*

18. Ibid., c. XXVII (sig. Giii): "Hic quartus sanctus Pastor coronatur ab angelo sicut et alii supradicti qui vt dicit auctor erit natione equitiarius vir sapientissimus et amicus dei."

19. See Reeves, *The Influence of Prophecy.*

20. See ASV, S.U., Processi, Busta 22, document entitled *Ad Illustrissimum graussimum aequissimum et potentissimum Dominium vniuersumque clarissimum senatum Venetum;* Dionisio signed the letter "Electus Dei seruus et nuntius amicus voster et totius orbis vniuersae militantis ecclesiae auriga, Dionysius gallus." The letter is dated June 3, 1566. Similarly, Dionisio signed his *Legatio* written in Venice in the home of Rocho de Mazzochis with the words "Amicus vester et orbis totius electus Dei seruus et nuntius totius ecclesiae militantis auriga Dionysius gallus."

21. See *Roberti Stephani . . . Thesaurus linguae latinae in IV. tomos divisus* . . . (Basel, 1740), 2:226, s.v. *equitiarius:* "Centauro oriente qui natus fuerit, aut erit auriga, aut equorum nutritor et cultor, vel eorum exercitator, aut mulo-medicus, vel equitiarius."

22. *Abbas Joachim magnus propheta: Expositio magni prophete Ioachim in librum beati Cirilli de magnis tribulationibus et statu Sancte matris Ecclesie,* c. XXXIII (sig. Iii): "Hic Iesus soluit septimum signaculum et aperit librum in dextera sanctae trinitatis positum, sic reuelat fidelibus et mundo per seruos suos septimum et vltimum statum ecclesie militantis et vltimum flagellum in mundum venturum post quod finale iudicium immediare loquitur."

23. The full title of Dionisio's book is *Liber, quem Nullus aut in coelo aut in terra aut subtus terram, antea poterat aperire ne quidem respicere.*

24. See Reeves, *The Influence of Prophecy.*

25. Ibid., 371.

26. Ibid., 376–77.

27. See Venice, Biblioteca nazionale di San Marco, MSS latini, Cl. III, Cod. CLXXVII (= 2176), c. 27: "Deinde cantabit gallus optimaque fiet restauratio. . . . Cantet gallus optimus et uerus pontifex fietque restitutio scilicet erroribus extirpatis." See also Chapter 1 above.

28. Ibid., c. 26ᵛ. In France, for example, in August 1563, the Church began to sell its temporal goods, not to help the poor but to have more money to conduct the war against the Huguenots. See de La Fosse, *Journal d'un curé ligueur de Paris sous les trois derniers Valois,* 65. In February 1563 Charles IX had passed an edict directing

the Church to sell its temporal goods in order to subsidize his affairs; see ibid., 60–61.

29. See Battisti, *L'anti-Rinascimento*, 1:255–56.

30. Ibid., 259. "Gallus inter caetera altilia caelorum audit super ethera concentum angelorum; tunc monet nos excutere verba malorum, gustare et percipere arcana supernorum."

31. London, British Library, Sloane MS 1413, fol. 106; cited by Kuntz in *Guillaume Postel*, 169–70. See also idem, "Guillaume Postel and the World State," *History of European Ideas* 4, no. 3 (1983): 299–323, and no. 4 (1983): 445–65.

32. London, British Library, Sloane MS 1413, fol. 106.

33. In all of Dionisio's *Legatio* mention of this universal organization is made at point fifteen: "Sanctae patriarchae per tres mundi partes numero duodecim." See ASV, S.U., Processi, Busta 22, Contra Dionisium Gallum, document entitled *Legatio electi serui Dei et nuntii magistri Dionisii Galli*. Postel wrote (Paris, Bibliothèque nationale, Fonds lat. 3401, fol. 6) that twelve men should go out from the Academy of Paris to all parts of the world to help with the restoration of the world.

34. Postel did not specify the duties of these patriarchs under the angelic pope, but he envisioned a loose confederation in which few laws would be required if all people were truly restored. See London, British Library, Sloane MS 1412, fols. 12^v, 22^v, 27^v.

35. Dionisio defined three principles (nos. 18–20) that deal with this problem. Note *Legatio electi serui Dei et nuntii magistri Dionisii Galli:* "Pensiones nullæ sint retentae a diuitibus [18]. Praelati destituantur, creati cum symonia [19]. Dignitates quasuis ecclesiasticas permutantibus prohibemus nec quicquam accipiant in compensationem sub poena arbitraria [20]."

The Venetian ambassador Giacomo Soranzo, writing on May 26, 1565, to the Capi del Consiglio dei Dieci, noted accusations of simony in connection with the election of the pope. See, for example, ASV, Capi del Consiglio dei Dieci, Dispacci degli Ambasciatori, Roma, Busta 24, c. 173: "Eccellentissimi Signori si ua presentendo et da piu uie come li Ministri del Re di Spagna in diuersi parti et massimamente a Napoli uanno inquirendo et fanno scriuere contra la elettione del Pontifice come fatta con simonia et pero non giuridica: et le oppositioni per quanto si intende sono due, la prima che il Signor Duca di Fiorenza prometesse al Cardinal Caraffa scudi centocinquantamille in contanti se'l faceua che il Cardinal dei Medici riuscisse Papa et che di questo ne fu' scritta pollizza con la quale Caraffa lo fauori et sequi la creatione."

36. Note Savonarola on the subject of poverty: "Il voto della Pouerta è il primo, il quale purga il cuore dall'affetto delle cose esteriori, il qual uoto non basta osseruar solamente in exterioribus, ma bisogna in tanto amar la pouerta, che il seruo et la sposa di Christo non uogli hauer se non quello che è necessario alla uita etiam con fatica et penalita. . . . Questo uoto figliuola mia a nostri tempi moderni e mal osseruato da molti religiosi i quali uorrebbono essere poueri, ma che non mancasse a

loro niente." *Trattato Esortatorio: Trattato ilquale manda il Reu. Padre fra Hieronimo da Ferrara a Madonna Madalena contessa della Mirandola, laquale uoleva in Monasterio*, in *Molti devotissimi trattati del Reverendo Padre Frate Hieronimo Sauonarola da Ferrara*, c. 102ᵛ. Many of Savonarola's works were published in Venice in the first half of the Cinquecento. His influence on the religious thought of Venice can be demonstrated from the testimony of many accused of heresy by the Venetian Inquisition. Note, for example, the testimony of Antonio Columbani about those involved with Oderico Grison and the prohibited books they read. Antonio reported: "Vi era la Bibia del Bruccioli et le prediche del Sauonarola, et due altri libri del Bruccioli li quali portai al Reverendo Padre Inquisitore." ASV, S.U., Processi, Busta 22, fascicolo Contra Odoricum Grisonum et complices Anabaptisti . . . , Costituto Antonio Columbani, February 25, 1567.

37. See O'Malley, *The First Jesuits*, 325.

38. Ibid., 323.

39. Ibid., 322–23.

40. If a presbyter were unlearned, according to Dionisio, he should study mechanical arts or else "discat literas, vna cum virtute." See *Legatio electi serui Dei et nuntii magistri Dionisii Galli*, article no. 23.

41. See Rice, *The Prefatory Epistles of Jacques Lefèvre d'Etaples*. Guillaume Postel also had written on many occasions that Hebrew, along with Latin and Greek, should be taught in all the universities. He believed that Hebrew was the original language, in which God spoke to Adam, teaching him "from behind the veil" the names of things, and that it therefore held priority over all the others.

42. See Kuntz, *Guillaume Postel*, 28–31.

43. See William J. Bouwsma, *John Calvin: A Sixteenth-Century Portrait* (New York and Oxford: Oxford University Press, 1988), 14–15. Paul F. Grendler has shown that the Jesuits had made Hebrew a part of the curriculum at schools such as the Collegio Romano. See his *Schooling in Renaissance Italy: Literacy and Learning, 1300–1600*, 381. Grendler's concluding statements in his book are appropriate for our consideration of Dionisio's utopianism. Grendler notes: "Behind Renaissance education lay the optimistic presupposition that the world was susceptible to understanding and control. . . . With a few notable exceptions, Renaissance men believed that through learning people could improve themselves and their world" (410).

44. Dionisio and other humanists supported the study of Hebrew as a means of converting Jews. Note, from the *Legatio electi serui Dei et nuntii magistri Dionisii Galli*, the principles 57 and 58: "Hebraeus, graecus et Latinus homines variis instructi linguis a nobis benigne excipientur. Turcæ et Judaei cito conuertentur."

45. Note, for example, Dionisio's letter addressed "Ad Reverendissimos ac Illustrissimos dominos, sacrum tribunal venetum et senatum, quem in sua causa, Deus elegit iudicem per spiritum sanctum . . ." (ASV, S.U., Processi, Busta 22, Contra Dionisium Gallum), where the thrust of the letter concerns justice. God

is the source of all justice, and "Deus iudex iustus fortis et patiens numquid irascitur per singulos dies." He urged the Venetian Senate to judge "the cause of God" (in this case, his own trial) and exult: "Senatus venete, quem Deus honorauit et in sua causa per spiritum sanctum, elegit iudicem." If Venetian senators did not judge justly and assume their divinely appointed roles as judges, Venice would suffer many woes, according to Dionisio.

46. *Legatio electi serui Dei et nuntii magistri Dionisii Galli*, no. 71: "Seruentur edicta data Aureliis: quantum probata sunt a sapientibus."

47. See Salmon, *Society in Crisis*, 152.

48. Ibid., 152–55. See also Sutherland, *Princes, Politics, and Religion*, 52–54.

49. *Legatio electi serui Dei et nuntii magistri Dionisii Galli.* The principles concerning justice are presented in nos. 29–36.

50. For a clear and concise analysis of the organization of the French government in the sixteenth century, see Salmon, *Society in Crisis*, 50–89; note especially 70 (the following remarks are appropriate to the concerns expressed by Dionisio): "In the government of church and state corporative institutions radiated from the royal household and the council in a series of concentric circles. Overlapping and anachronistic jurisdictions defied attempts to rationalize the administrative structure, for prestige, tradition, and financial reward remained at least as important as logic and efficiency in the devolution of authority." See also 106ff., where Salmon discusses the relationship between financial difficulties and the expansion of venal office. Dionisio made no mention of Chancellor L'Hôpital's efforts to reform the administration of justice.

51. Dionisio, who felt that the goods of the Church should only be used for charity, was very opposed to selling such goods to conduct war.

52. Salmon, *Society in Crisis*, 123.

53. See Venice, Biblioteca nazionale di San Marco, MS italiani, Cl. VII, Cod. MMDLXXXV (= 12477) [Prov. Bibl. Phillips 5214], c. 204: "1563 ott. . . . il re di Franza manda a Roma per ottener dal Papa licentia di uender beni ecclesiastici per solleuarsi dalle molte spese fatte nella guerra contro Ugonoti."

54. See *Mémoires de Claude Haton . . .* , ed. M. Félix Bourquelot (Paris: Imprimerie impériale, 1857), 1:329–30: "Sous prétexte de couvrir les frais de la guerre religieuse, Charles IX rend un édit prescrivant la vente, au profit du trésor, des seigneuries et censives des églises de France. Les gentilhommes des provinces achètent à bas prix les biens ecclésiastiques; en réalité, la reine mère recueille seule les fruits de cette opération financière, soi-disant destinée à soutenir la guerre contre les protestants. Les chanoines de Saint-Quiriace de Provins font racheter leur seigneuries de Bonsac, de Saint-Martin-Channetron et de Boisdon. Le chapitre, malgré l'opposition d'un chanoine nommé Nic. Roussel, qui soutient que le roi n'a pas le droit de disposer du temporel des églises sans l'autorisation du pape, se procure de l'argent en faisant briser le chef de saint Quiriace. Cet acte est vivement blamé dans le pays."

55. Dionisio's reference was to the edict of January 1562 that recognized the Calvinists and granted them limited toleration. Coligny had been instrumental in obtaining this edict. For the vendetta between Coligny and Guise and the former's role in the French civil wars, see Sutherland, *Princes, Politics, and Religion*, 157–72. Michiel Surian, Venetian ambassador to France in 1562, also had no kind words for Coligny: "Quanto al mutarsi, fu tentato già di disputare al governo di sua maestà cristianissima monsignor armiraglio che è principal fautore d'eretici." *Relations des Ambassadeurs Vénitiens sur les affaires de France au XVIe siècle*, ed. and trans. M. N. Tommaseo (Paris: Imprimerie royale, 1838), 1:544. For the accusations against Admiral Coligny and the prince of Condé for the death on March 6, 1563, of François de Lorraine, duke of Guise, grand prior of France, see *Mémoires de Claude Haton* . . . , 1:328–29.

56. Protestant ministers often preached to crowds as large as their Catholic counterparts, delivering their sermons sometimes in private homes, when it was too dangerous to preach in public. Because their preaching was often conducted in such privacy, Catholic suspicions were aroused over the rumored "indecent behavior" by Protestants. See Larissa Taylor, *Soldiers of Christ: Preaching in Late Medieval and Reformation France* (Oxford: Oxford University Press, 1992), 189–209. See also Barbara Diefendorf, *Beneath the Cross: Catholics and Huguenots in Sixteenth-Century Paris* (Oxford: Oxford University Press, 1991), 54. The priest Claude Haton emphasized the sexual activities he assumed took place at Calvinists' conventicles. He noted in particular the "charité fraternelle et voluptueuse," believed to be enjoyed after the lights were extinguished.

57. See note 56 above; also Taylor, *Soldiers of Christ*, 209.

58. As Barbara Diefendorf has pointed out, the "Lutheran heresy" was not for sixteenth-century Parisians a mere failure of religious orthodoxy; it was a threat to the social order and a danger to the entire community. The Protestants were believed to be not only religious deviants but also "immoral and seditious." See Diefendorf, *Beneath the Cross*, 54.

59. See *Relations des Ambassadeurs Vénitiens*, 1:542, where Surian noted fears for the life of Charles IX and Catherine's consultation of Nostradamus: "E quanto al vivere, è opinione di molti che non sia per viver lungo tempo, si perchè è di complessione debole e delicata, sì ancora perchè non è notrito con quella regola che bisognaria. Ma quello che non dà manco suspetto, è che Nostradamus astrologo, il quale da molti anni in qua ha sempre predetto la verità di molte calamità occorse alla Francia . . . ha detto alla regina che essa vederà re tutti li suoi figli."

60. See *Mémoires de Claude Haton*, 1:330.

61. See *Relations des Ambassadeurs Vénitiens*, 1:542, where Surian wrote: "E quello che occorre negli altri re per poca prudenza è occorso al presente re Carlo per la tenera èta, e perchè come un agnello innocente conviene stare alla discrezione di che lo governa. E se fu sempre reputata calamità d'ogni regno l'aver il re putto . . . , molto più s'ha da reputare miserabile in un regno pieno di disordini, di divisioni

e di competenzie, oppresso da debbiti e da povertà, e stanco d'una longhissima e dispendiossima guerra, e dove è successo un putto ad un altro putto, e niuno di loro (per la brevità delle vita del padre) ha potuto imparare dalla sua instituzione e dal suo essempio, il modo di governarsi."

62. Ibid.: "E si può avere grande speranza di sua maestà, se vive, e se non si muta, e se sarà in essere tanto a tempo che non trovi le cose sue distrutte e rovinate in modo che sia sforzato d'accomodarsi a quello che fusse messo in uso dalla negligenzia o malignità d'altri."

63. See ibid., 1:465ff. On the dating of the *relazioni,* note 468 n. 1: "Questi commentarii parebbero forse meglio collocati tra il 1564 e il 1568, poichè 'l Suriano successe nella legazione al Barbaro, escitone nel 1562; e poichè del 1560 abbiamo la relazione del Michiel."

64. Ibid., 1:532.

65. Ibid.

66. Ibid., 1:538.

67. Ibid.: "E cosi si va alla via di redurre quella provincia a stato populare, come Svizzeri; e distruggere la monarchia e il regno."

68. ASV, Collegio, Lettere Cardinali e altri ecclesiastici, Filza 2, June 13, 1558: "che ha forza di distrugger non diro le famiglie ma li stadi." The patriarch said that Venice was in a different circumstance, however, noting "la qual cosa non si douerà temere dalla clementissima protettione diuina che ha sempre conseruata et conseruarà sempre la pietà et religione di questa Illustrissima Republica."

69. See Pullan, *Rich and Poor in Renaissance Venice.* See also his "Poverty, Charity, and the Reason of State: Some Venetian Examples," in *Bollettino di Storia della Società, e dello Stato* 2 (Venice: Fondazione Giorgio Cini, Centro di Cultura e Civiltà, 1960).

70. See ASV, Consiglio dei Dieci, Parti comuni, Registro 18, c. 192: "Die xi Jan. 1548. Che delli danari della Signoria nostra siano dati alli procuratori della chiesa di S. Marco ducati 800 a conto del credito che hano nella paga di settembre 1483, da essere dispensati in maritar donzelle, liberar prigionieri, vestir poueri, et altre dispense in pias causas et siano conce le scriture sicome sarà bisogno."

71. The organization of Dionisio's *Legatio* resembled in format Luther's *Disputatio,* with its ninety-five theses, or points, and Zwingli's sixty-seven *Articles.* In the various texts of Dionisio's *Legatio* there are seventy-five, seventy-seven, and seventy-nine points, or articles. For the text of Luther's *Disputatio* and Zwingli's *Articles,* see Carl S. Meyer, *Luther's and Zwingli's Propositions for Debate* (Leiden: E. J. Brill, 1963). One should also note that the organization of the *Legatio* was similar to that of the Edict of Orléans. For the organization of Dionisio's *Legatio,* see pages 213–15 above.

72. On the radical reformers, see George Huntston Williams, *The Radical Reformation,* 3d ed. (Kirksville, Mo.: Sixteenth Century Journal Publishers, 1992).

73. ASV, S.U., Processi, Busta 22, Contra Dionisium Gallum, *Legatio* written in Venice, 1566. The principle is no. 61 and reads as follows: "Partus est Rex tertius,

masculus ille Raptus ad Deum et ad thronum eius: secundus est pastor promissus his vltimis omnino diebus: primus autem est aeternus Christus."

74. Ibid., document entitled *Ex coelo empireo veritas reuelata*. . . . The text was written on May 4, 1567.

75. Ibid., document entitled *In nomine Domini nostri Jesu Christi crucifixi*, written on September 15, 1566: "Sedeat ergo papa vel optimus vel qualis, qualis sit, vtinam sanctissimus, in sede apostolica. Meum est pro Christo sedere in noua sancta sede Dauid Regis et prophetæ mystica: id est, in throno Christi regali et pontificali."

76. Ibid.: "scribens autem propter meum officium ad clarissimum senatum venetum, vt alia via negotium Christi promoueretur tamquam praevidens tribulationes et afflictiones in quas vel Deus me misit propter nomen suum."

77. *Espositio magni prophete Abbatis Joachim in Apocalipsim*, cc. 73–73ᵛ. On the significance of Joachimite thought in the Cinquecento in Venice, see Niccoli, "'Prophetie di Musaicho'"; note also her *La vita religiosa nell'Italia moderna: Secoli XVI–XVII* (Rome: Carocci Editore, 1998).

78. *Espositio magni prophete Abbatis Joachim in Apocalipsim*, c. 73: "Porro petra ipsa reprobata a iudeis, a domino vero electa et preelecta confitenti Symoni ac dicenti. Tu est Christus filius dei viui."

79. Ibid.: "Participare autem tante gratie et digne accipere corpus Christi pretiosi huius calculi donum hereditare est."

80. Ibid.

81. Ibid., cc. 73–73ᵛ: "Unde congruenter dictum est. Et in calculo nomen scriptum quod nemo scit nisi qui accipit quod quante sit dignitatis vocari a Christo christianus nemo scit nisi cui scire et intelligere datum est quod proprium est eorum qui vicerunt concupiscentias mundi qui occultum aduersarium prostrauerunt in bello qui ab immundis desideriis cordis ergastulum mundauerunt."

Many opinions have been expressed about the meaning of this passage. Note especially, however, *La Sacra Bibbia commentata dal P. Marco M. Sales O. P.: Il nuovo testamento: Le lettere degli Apostoli—L'Apocalisse* (Turin: Tipografia Pontifica, 1914), 623 n. 17: "*Gli darò una pietra*, ecc. L'Apostolo allude agli antichi usi greci. I Greci infatti solevano scrivere su piccole pietre bianche ben levigate, i nomi dei candidati nelle elezioni, i titoli dei vincitori nei giuochi olimpici; ecc. Anche nei giudizi i giudici con una pietra bianca esprimevano la sentenza di assoluzione. La pietra bianca promessa qui al vincitore indica quindi che egli sarà dichiarato santo, e perciò degno dell'eterna ricompensa sarà eletto ad essere cittadino del cielo. *Il nome nuovo* è probabilmente il nome di cittadino celeste oppure il nome di Dio e di Gesù Cristo. Nessuno può conoscere il pregio e il valore di tal nome, se non colui che è stato fatto degno di riceverlo, perchè questi solo può conoscere quanta sia la felicità che Dio ha preparato a coloro che lo amano e lo servono."

82. *Espositio magni prophete Abbatis Joachim in Apocalipsim*, c. 73–73ᵛ. See Ps. 30:20.

83. Ibid., c. 73: "Queris que sit ista dulcedo? Ipsa est manna et panis viuus de quo per semet ipsum panis ipse qui de celo descendit iudeis murantibus et non credentibus loquitur dicens. Non Moyses dedit vobis panem de celo sed pater meus dat vobis panem de celo verum. Ipse est ergo manna absconditus: ipse inquam Christus Iesus qui est verbum et sapientia patris qui tanto bonorum mentes doctorum torrente voluptatis sue influendo inebriat quanto proprium est illi vt vocetur magister."

84. Ibid.

85. See ASV, S.U., Busta 22, Contra Dionisium Gallum, document entitled *in nomine domini*, with the date May 3, 1567, for Dionisio's words about his double anointment: "Scripsi et affirmaui quia vere mater Christi virgo sacrissima mihi apparuit me allocuta est oleo coelesti totum meum corpus vnxit exterius et totam animam meam intra meum corpus. Haec ipsa duplex vnctio causa est vera et essentialis meae duplicis regiæ dignitatis atque maiestatis quae causa intelligenda est et plane consideranda." See pages 7–9 above for additional statements about the double anointment.

86. Ibid. See Ps. 2:6.

87. ASV, S.U., Busta 22, Contra Dionisium Gallum, document entitled *in nomine domini*. See Isa. 16:1.

88. ASV, S.U., Busta 22, Contra Dionisium Gallum, document entitled *in nomine domini*. See Isa. 63:1.

89. ASV, S.U., Busta 22, Contra Dionisium Gallum, document entitled *in nomine domini*. See ibid., document entitled *Ex coelo empireo veritas reuelata*. . . . Dionisio, responding to the question about who the man from Edom was, wrote: "Qui scribit ipse Rex est, a deo institutus venitque de Edom, id est, de terreno, de urbe gi sorte, id est, terra sortis et de Bosra: hoc est, de Inferno, de profundis carceribus magnis tribulationibus, et mortis doloribus."

90. See John Calvin, *Commentary on the Book of the Prophet Isaiah*, trans. Rev. William Pringle (Edinburgh: W. B. Erdmans, 1853), 4:337–38.

91. Ibid., 337.

92. One of Calvin's followers, Jerome Zanchi, showed a marked interest in Christocentric eschatology. See John L. Farthing, "Christ and the Eschaton: The Reformed Eschatology of Jerome Zanchi," in *Later Calvinism: International Perspectives*, Sixteenth-Century Essays and Studies, vol. 22, ed. W. Fred Graham (Kirksville, Mo.: Sixteenth Century Journal Publishers, 1994), 333–54.

93. *The Apocrypha and Pseudepigrapha of the Old Testament in English* . . . , ed. R. H. Charles (Oxford: Clarendon Press, 1913), 2:66.

94. Ibid., 67.

95. See Gershom Scholem, *The Messianic Idea in Judaism and Other Essays on Jewish Spirituality* (New York: Schocken Books, 1971), 37–48 (the chapter entitled "The Messianic Idea in Kabbalism").

96. Ibid., 40. See also the chapter entitled "Redemption Through Sin," in ibid., 78–141.

97. Venice, Biblioteca nazionale di San Marco, MSS latini, Cl. III, Cod. CLXXVII (= 2176), cc. 27–28ᵛ.

98. *Mirabilis Liber qui prophetias . . . demonstrat*, sig. Cᵛ: "Subsequentes confestim deus suscitabit alios tres viros sanctissimos: vnum post alium in virtutibus ac miraculis consimiles qui facta et dicta antecessorum confirmant sub quorum regime status ecclesie recrescet. Et ei appellabuntur pastores angelici." The copy of this rare book I consulted is in the Biblioteca del Museo Correr, shelf mark Op. Cicogna 626.9 (100.9).

99. See Paris, Bibliothèque nationale, Fonds lat. 3679, fols. 22–25.

100. See Postel, *Le thrésor des prophéties de l'univers*.

101. Ibid., 49. The "higher Isaac" also has messianic significance. Note especially: "Iesaie parlant de la sanglante victoire d'Aedom le sanguinaire, là où il fault que l'excellente victoire de Christ en son aisné se monstre, non pas sans cause ha en ce mesme chapitre mis ce propos de l'ignorance des deux les plus renommés et fameux patriarches, en se taisant de la second personne, ou d'Isaac, sauf à ceste fin seulement que nous cognoissons la science experimentale et la speciale qui soubs l'immobile et immuable Dieu trinun se faict, appartenir à Isaac superieur."

102. Paris, Bibliothèque nationale, Fonds lat. 3679, fol. 24: "Sed opera mala . . . sunt causa ut vltio fiat contra Aedom, licet Israel siue Iaacob vere ut quæ suum regem per inuidiam crucifixit, et pessime sub legge Dei vixit non minus mala quam Aedumaea et scelerata gens et interiori sanguine sacramenti punienda vel expianda quam ipsa Aedumea."

103. Ibid., fol. 22: "non sine mysterio maximo, eo quod sanguitas siue sangueficatio ex Matre est. . . . Et vocauit nomen eorum Adam in die creari illos. Vocatus est propter vnicum sanguinem qui in genere humano assiduus est, et constans. Unde nomen . . . Aedom deductum est, et ideo de Aedom venire Christus legitur." See also fol. 23ᵛ.

104. See Postel, *Le thrésor des prophéties de l'univers*, 113: "Et les salvateurs monteront, allant en la montagne de Tzion, pour juger la montagne d'Esau, et le royaulme sera du Seigneur Jehovah. Cecy est la fin du monde, assavoir pour la quelle fin il fut créé, affin qu'il soit faict une bergerie et un pasteur, et qu'en ce monde inferieur autant par royal, vray et politike ordre se voye estre restitué et réparé, comme par tyrannike, satanike et babylonike desordre voyons jusques icy havoir esté destruict." Note also a similar passage from *Apologia permessa all'interpretatione del Bahir:* "Sic enim necesse est ex uno utero gentilitatem Esaui nasci cum Israelitate Iaacobi, ut, postquam satis diu authoritate fratris privatus sua benedictione fuit, tandem veniat tempus ut excutiatur iugum authoritatis eius ab eo et sic dux ratio, sensibus nostris accomodata, redeat in sua imperia, hactenus per peccati tenebras expulsa." Cited by Antonio Rotondò, "La ricerca storica . . . ," *Critica Storica*, n.s., anno x (March 1973): 148.

105. Paris, Bibliothèque nationale, Fonds lat. 3679, fol. 23ᵛ: "At vero Rubedo illa et Redumeritas in Esau priusquam Iaacob nata et quam magis amat Isaac in Aedom et magis benedicere vult quam vellet Mater Rebeccah, est illa sacrosancta et nunquam maledicta pars de qua venit in toto genera Adami et Noachi Rex Messias, ut sua facit per sacramenta sua eadem assumendo ex Militantis huius Ecclesiae substantia dum in vinum vertit Aquam illam quam per Triumphantis et Angelicae Angelisue similimae [sic] Ecclesiae vnionem, calyci sacro infunditur, et vere per consecrationem fit sanguis Christi."

106. See Postel, *Le thrésor des prophéties de l'univers*, 113: "Ainsi un seul salvateur Jesus-Christ, par les membres aulsquels il habite et par son habitation nommés salvateurs comme luy, sera plus glorieusement que par soy mesmes conduict et mis en son siege, et ainsi la pierre reprouvée sera mise au chef de l'anglet et pignon de tout l'edifice humain."

107. Paris, Bibliothèque nationale, Fonds lat. 3679, fol. 23ᵛ: "et maxime in asserendo hoc secundo Aduentu vbi asseritur Aedumaeum istud corpus, qui secundus et Maternus existens INTRA NOS fit, dum FORMATUS in NOBIS Christus vere sensim etiam INTRA NOS RESVGIT qui solus descendit nos adferens de coelo et hinc solus ascendit in coelum victor et superator totius Aedumaeae Potentiæ mundi."

108. Ibid., fol. 24ᵛ.

109. Complaints against simony could be heard in many quarters. See, for example, ASV, Capi del Consiglio dei Dieci, Dispacci degli Ambasciatori, Roma, Busta 24, c. 173, where the Venetian ambassador Giacomo Soranzo, in a letter dated May 26, 1565, wrote about charges by Spanish ministers that Pope Pius IV had been elected with simony. Note especially: "Eccellentissimi Signori, si ua presentendo et da piu uie come li Ministri del Re di Spagna in diuersi parti et massimamente a Napoli uanno inquirendo et fanno scriuere contra la elettione del Pontifice, come fatta con simonia, et pero non giuridica: et le oppositioni per quanto si intende sono due, la prima che il Signor Duca di Fiorenza promettesse al Cardinal Caraffa scudi centocinquantamille in contanti se'l faceua che il Cardinal dei Medici riuscisse Papa, et che di questo ne fu' scritta pollizza con la quale Caraffa lo fauori et sequi la creatione." Pius IV was elected pope on December 26, 1559. There were also suspicions about the election of Pius V on January 7, 1566. Note Soranzo's words: "La sua elezione [Pius V] al papato colpí tutti, perché nessuno si sarebbe aspettato che il Card. C. Borromeo, nipote di Pius IV, facesse conuergere i uoti del propio partito sul Ghislieri."

110. Paris, Bibliothèque nationale, Fonds lat. 3679, fol. 25.

111. See *Encyclopaedia Judaica* (Jerusalem, 1969), 3:27–28, s.v. "Anointment," and 3:756.

112. See ASV, S.U., Processi, Busta 22, document without title but with the word *pectorale* at the top of the page that begins: "Ego Dionysius Gallus Dei seruus et nuntius non meis meritis sed gratia Dei praeueniente sanctificatus: Reuelatione mihi facta coelestibus nouissimorum temporum, quae instant et multorum

secretorum coelestium conscius. Vnctus in cute et intus per corpus vniuersum ab ancilla trintatis, sacratissima matre Christi et virgine quae mihi vigilante circa mediam noctem saepe apparuit. Mihique reuelauit officia mea ex diuina voluntate et decreto sanctissimæ trinitatis ipsam ancillam ad me mittendis. Amen; me permittunt et depingunt cum diua Brigida, sacra propheticarum eloquia. Amen."

The words of Saint Bridget that Dionisio believed were a reference to himself can be found in *Sequitur libellus qui intitulatur Onus mundi id est prophetia de malo futuro ipsi mundo superuenturo*, chap. 8: "Tunc ueniet ille dominus supradictus cui deus dabit fortitudinem et sapientiam quas a Christianis aufert ad debellandum et circumveniendum eos."

113. See note 1 above and note 46 to Chapter v.

114. ASV, S.U., Processi, Busta 22, Contra Dionisium Gallum, *Haec est causa*: "placuit ipsa noua dicendi forma, more velut oratorio, Christi causam et ecclesiae proponere et agere."

115. Note, for example, *Prediche del Rev. Padre Fra Hieronymo Sauonarola dell'ordine de predicatori . . .* , sermon 1, c. 8: "ma perche Dio ha uoluto cosi et ha preso uno huomo uile et inetto a far questo officio, accioche lui mostri d'essere lui quello che fa et non uno fraticello."

116. *Trattato della reuelatione della reformatione della Chiesa*, c. 22. "perche come dice lo Apostolo, si adhuc hominibus placerem, Christi seruus non essem."

117. Ibid. "che ogni huomo che parla di queste cose e reputato pazzo da lí sauii di questo mondo."

118. Ibid. "Alliquali io diro insieme con lo Apostolo. Nos stulti propter Christum: vos autem sapientes."

119. "We insensitive ones were thinking that the life of those was madness. See in what way they are counted among the sons of God." Wisd. 5:4–5.

120. For Saint Bridget's words, see *Sequitur libellus qui intitulatur Onus mundi id est prophetia de malo futuro ipsi mundo superuenturo*, chap. 20, unpaginated: "Nos insensati uitam et reuelationes predicte domine insaniam estimabamus. Ecce nunc intelligimus quod computata est inter iustas et inter sanctos sors illius."

121. Savonarola's complete statement is as follows: "Ma quando verrà quel tempo nel quale Justi stabunt in magna constantia adversus eos qui se angustiauerunt. Spero di vdire le voci di questi sauii et che diranno. Hi sunt quos habuimus aliquando in derisum et in similitudinem improperum: nos insensati vitam illorum estimabamus insaniam et finem illorum sine honore. Ecce quomodo computati sunt inter filios Dei et inter sanctos sors illorum est." *Trattato della reuelatione della reformatione della Chiesa*, c. 22ᵛ.

122. ASV, S.U., Processi, Busta 22, Contra Dionisium Gallum, document entitled *Haec est causa*: "Vidi curiam papae; vidi seruos eius, Regie vestitos. Vidi sectam eius non vniuersam; vidi multorum sectam Cardinalium; vera secta eorum pauperes esse debent. . . . O quæ miseria? O quanta paupertas? Dicunt se esse divites;

at contra Deo—pauperrimi sunt atque miserrimi. . . . O speciosa magnificentia. O paupertas extrema. O summa miseria. O desolatio atque confusio plane intolerabilis, ita excellere et agere magnifice ex bonis pauperum, Christi membrorum, nudorum horridorum, languentium præ dolore et arumna, mori desiderantium."

123. Ibid.

124. Cf., for example, Savonarola's words about charity: "Dunque poi chel nostro Signore ui ha chiamati al suo seruitio se uolete uiuere allegri et contenti, attendete alla pace del cuore et ad esercitar la charita di Dio et del prossimo secondo l'ordine del capitano nostro Christo et crediate a me che chi non fa a questo modo, uiuera inquieto. . . . Ma pensare chel ben uiuere come habbiamo detto è esercitar la charita in ogni luogo et in ogni modo che uuole in nostro Saluatore." *Epistola . . . dell'adoperarsi in charita secondo la diuina dispositione*, in *Molti devotissimi trattati del Reverendo Padre Frate Hieronimo Sauonarola da Ferrara*, cc. 49–49ᵛ, 50.

125. Dionisio is quite specific about the sins of the clergy, naming *avaritia, ambitio, negligentia, iniquitas ignorantia, indignitas:* ASV, S.U., Processi, Busta 22, Contra Dionisium Gallum, document entitled *Haec est causa*. Dionisio's remarks about the abuses of the clergy remind us of Francesco Spinola's poignant admission to Dionisio while both were imprisoned in the same cell: "It was the abuses of the clergy that led me into error." See pages 177–85 above, especially page 182.

126. Note in *Haec est causa:* "Hic est nodus . . . Haec est difficultas totius presentis negotii. Nam imprimis Papa dicet se esse in terra, caput totius militantis ecclesiæ et quamuis ita res habeat, vt peccet in multis, tamen a beato Petro, vsque ad seipsum neminem nouit, nec vult agnoscere supra se iudicem, ac Reformatorem. Dicet praeterea se non posse principes christianos conuocare ad clerum reformandum, ad extirpandas haereses et consolandos pauperes sine arbitrio, consensuque cardinalium et cleri electi." Dionisio also wrote an imaginary dialogue between himself and the Devil about why the Church was not reformed. He also presented what he said was a real conversation between himself and the papal nuncio in Florence.

127. This claim had been made earlier. A prophecy about the reform of the Church and victory over the Turks is found in a compilation of prophecies by Teolosphoro da Cosenza: "vir quidam nobilis ortus ex tirpe primi eorundem domini ita prudenter atque fideliter omnia a suo sibi senatu commissa explebit vt merito post annum a sua legatione reuersus in magnum ac generalem capitaneum belli maritimi ab eodem Senatu eligetur in seruitium sancte matris ecclesie ex precepto angeli pastoris et magnam et omnino dans contra infideles victoriam consequetur." See *Abbas Joachim magnus propheta: Expositio magni prophete Ioachim in librum beati Cirilli de magnis tribulationibus et statu Sancte matris Ecclesie*, c. XXXII.

Note also another example from Teolosphoro that makes reform of the Church a requisite for victory over the infidel: "Qui imperator cum pastore angelico qui ipsum coronabit reformabit eccleiam in statu paupertatis et in dei obsequiis. Et ipse imperator cum uno sancto papa faciet septimum et ultimum passagium per terram sanctam quam recuperabunt." Biblioteca nazionale di San Marco, MSS latini,

Cl. III, Cod. CLXXVII (= 2176), c. 26ᵛ. Note Dionisio's words in *Haec est causa:* "Propter peccata cleri, Deus praeteritas et presentes permisit turcarum commotiones sed ad bonum finem. Nam modo Deus per turcas vnit ipsos principes congregat et conuocat. Ad quid? Utrum ad praeliandum aduersus turcas ipsos? Nullum est cum turcis bellum si clerus reformetur, haereses extirpentur pauperes recreentur."

128. Dionisio vividly described his visit with the king at Gaîllon (Châlons): "Ita me audito primus omnium Connestablensis dixit: 'Si sapientes totius orbis essent congregati ad vniuersum christianismi resoluendum negotium, non possent id facere sanctius ac verius.' Pronuntiabam autem coram illis memoriter et sine scripto vllo; quod omnes admirati sunt. . . . Nostram Rex ipse francorum legationem postulauit illique scripsimus atque dedimus nostra manu obsignatam Rex ipse me dies aliquot gaudenter audiuit cum sibiipsi tum omnibus cardinalibus, principibus, catholicis et haereticis dicentem omne genus veritatis." Dionisio also wrote of a terrible storm that struck Gaîllon "contra omnem temporis dispositionem et naturam." The storm lasted about eight days, and Dionisio, taking advantage of having a captive audience, spoke "pro iure pauperum ac pro iure Christi in ipsos cardinales, episcopos et pastores presentes," calling the prelates "quales erant . . . fures et latrones, tenentes et abligurientes bona et iura pauperum." In 1543 Guillaume Postel had warned Francis I that he must reform himself, his court, and his kingdom, or else dire tragedies would ensue. He lost favor with the king because of this warning and shortly thereafter left France to join the Jesuits in Rome.

129. Salmon, *Society in Crisis,* 149; see also *Mémoires de Claude Haton,* 1:380.

130. Salmon, *Society in Crisis,* 149–51.

131. Ibid., 149. The purpose of Catherine's visit to Bayonne was to meet the duke of Alba and Elisabeth de Valois and thereby, she hoped, arrange marriages between Don Carlos, son of Philip II, and Marguerite de Valois and between Charles IX and the daughter of the emperor. These negotiations were not successful.

132. ASV, S.U., Processi, Busta 22, Contra Dionisium Gallum, document entitled *Haec est causa:* "Regem francorum ego sum persecutus ad montem Marsanum vsque vt recordaretur eorum quae per me Deus illi mandauerat: suum regnum vniret alias breui futurum esse vt in regno diuiso, duabus sellis insidens vtraque primatus male se haberet."

133. Ibid.: "Quod vt fieret in ipso regis pallatio vociferabar dicens: 'O Charole francorum Rex capti sunt (si vis) canes rabientes atque furiosi qui regnum tuum totum desolati sunt. Si sinis eos abire, si non facis iustitiam, periit tua corona.'"

134. Ibid.

135. Ibid.: "Rex autem ipse et vniuersus populus Regem me gallorum appellabant."

136. De La Fosse, *Journal d'un Curé ligueur de Paris sous les trois derniers Valois,* 66: "En ce temps il avoit ung jeune homme bon latin et aussi de grand esprit, lequel estant

deguisé, simuloit le fol et faisoit de grandes exclamations contre les huguenots et n'épargnoit personne à son parler. Il se faisoit appeler le roy des Gaulois." This reference to the one known as Dionisio Gallo in 1566–67 is listed under the month of November 1563. Under January 1564, on page 67 of the *Journal*, we read: "en cet moys fut defendu à Postel de ne plus prescher. Ledict mois, le roy des Gaylois fut mené prisonnier, puis il fut baillé en garde en une religion au païs de Normandie, et ce par délibération du privé conseil." The second part of the entry also refers to Dionisio Gallo.

In a note, "Les détentions de Postel a Saint-Martin des Champs," *Bibliothèque d'Humanisme et Renaissance* 22 (1960): 555, Secret cites the statement concerning the king of the Gauls when writing about Postel's confinement to Saint Martin des Champs. He makes no reference to two persons involved—one, the king of the Gauls, obviously Dionisio Gallo, the other, Guillaume Postel. There seems to be a mysterious relationship between Postel and Dionisio Gallo, however.

137. ASV, S.U., Processi, Busta 22, Contra Dionisium Gallum, document entitled *Haec est causa*: "Venite igitur o almi principes, mecum venite, electi populi atque nationes, venite securi. Venite iam omnes (o almi principes et viri nobiles, virtute praediti), venite iudices atque magistratus, venite doctores, legumque periti, senes et iuuenes, patres et filii, praeceptores omnes atque discipuli: venite vos viri atque mulieres: venite liberi, serui et ancillae. Volo franciscanos doctores adesse, eorum conuentus laetari gaudere. Venite pauperes, nudi, famelici languentes despecti, ius vestrum petite. Venite pastores qui bene praeestis. Triumphemus omnes."

138. Ibid.: "Fide nos armemus omnes vniti. Sint et arma nostra fulgens iustitia ignea charitas. Haec vera sunt arma quae ferre debemus." Erasmus had expressed similar ideas in his *Enchiridion militis Christiani*. Note, for example: "Armamus corpusculum hoc, ne timeamus sicam latronis, non armabimus menten, ut in tuto sit? Armati sunt hostes ut perdant, nos piget arma capere ne pereamus? Vigilant illi ut perimant, nos non vigilamus, quo simus incolumes? Sed de armatura Christiana speciatim suo loco dicetur. Interim ut summatim dicam, duo praecipue paranda sunt arma ei . . . precatio, et scientia." *Enchiridion militis Christiani . . . auctore Des. Erasmo Roterodamo* (Cantabrigiae [Cambridge]: ex officina John Hayes, impensis Guil. Graves, 1685), 55. The chapter is entitled "De armis militiæ Christianæ." In the same chapter, Erasmus wrote of the need to understand the figurative language of holy writ: "Habet autem spiritus ille divinus suam quandam linguam, suasque figuras, quae tibi sunt in primis diligenti observatione cognoscendae. Balbutit nobis divina sapientia et veluti mater quaepiam officiosa ad nostram infantiam voces accommodat. Lac porrigit infantulis in Christo, holus infirmis. Tu vero festina adolescere, et ad solidum propera cibum" (66). Then Erasmus, expressing ideas that certainly call to mind the words of Dionisio, urged those who had the ability to hasten to comprehend deeper mysteries: "Te vero qui ingenio tam felilci praeditus es, omnino nolim in sterili litera lentum esse, sed ad reconditiora mysteria festinare et improbum conatum industria, crebris precibus adjuvare, donec aperiat tibi librum septem signaculis obsignatum is qui habet clavem David, qui claudit, et nemo aperit arcana patris quae nemo novit nisi filius, et cui voluerit filius revelare" (68).

139. ASV, S.U., Processi, Busta 22, Contra Dionisium Gallum, document entitled *Haec est causa:* "Deus stetit in synagoga deorum; in medio autem deos diiudicat (dicens diis terræ) vsquequo iudicatis iniquitatem et facies peccatorum sumitis?" Dionisio's citation from the Vulgate was exact; he added the words in parenthesis to help explain the meaning. The Vulgate I have consulted is *Bibliorum sacrorum iuxta Vulgatam Clementinam nova editio . . .* , ed. Aloisius Gramatica (Milan: U. Hoepli, 1914), 517.

140. *Bibliorum sacrorum,* 517: "Iudicate egeno et pupillo, humilem et pauperem justificate. Eripite pauperem et egenum de Manu peccatoris liberate." Dionisio's citation of these verses varies only slightly.

141. One commentator has noted that "in the original the name of God signifies judge, because He is the highest judge who of the judges weighs the judgments and approves or disapproves their sentences. The earthly judges are called *dei* because they make the judgments of God on the earth." *Vecchio e Nuovo Testamento secondo la volgata . . . da Monsignor Antonio Martini . . .* (Venice: Giuseppe Antonelli, 1842), vol. 2, col. 1433, n. 1. For the same context, see 2 Chron. 19:6–7. See also *La Bibbia Concordata, tradoto dai testi originali con introduzioni e note,* ed. Società Biblica Italiana (Ravenna: Arnoldo Mondadori Editore, 1968), 791, where we read that the "gods" (*dei*) "è espressione indicante i giudici e i magistrati che rappresentano Dio sulla terra." See also the commentary in *La Bibbia Piemme* (Turin: Edizioni Piemme, 1995), 1317–18.

Dionisio's words to the princes become a gloss on Psalm 81 (82). He writes: "Es tu deus aliquis? Sed et vos (o almi principes, electi populi, atque nationes) vos ipsi dii estis. Quare deus ego non sum? Ego sum deus ille quem Rex David et propheta videbat in spiritu." See *Haec est causa,* in ASV, S.U., Processi, Busta 22.

142. See note 138 above.

143. See Bodin, *Colloquium of the Seven About the Secrets of the Sublime,* 3–4. For Postel's praise of Venice, see his *Le prime nove del altro mondo* and *Il libro della divina ordinatione;* also Kuntz, *Guillaume Postel.*

144. See Wolters, *Storia e politica nei dipinti di Palazzo Ducale,* 19–20, 88–90.

145. See Niccoli, *La vita religiosa nell'Italia moderna,* 13–59, for an excellent discussion of sacred time and sacred space.

146. For example, Dionisio was much more a court prophet than the vagabond *romito* described by Ottavia Niccoli in her *Profeti e popolo.* His emphasis on poverty, however, resembled many admonitions of the *romiti.* See also Niccoli, *La vita religiosa nell'Italia moderna,* 163–67.

147. Note the remarks of Robert Rusconi, "An Angelic Pope Before the Sack of Rome," in *Prophetic Rome in the High Renaissance Period,* 157: "In the first two decades of the sixteenth century a small group of important people, from the Spanish Cardinal Bernardino Carvajal to the Bosnian theologian Juraj Dragisic (Salviati), from Cardinal Adriano Castelli to Pope Leo x himself considered, on different grounds, that they had good reason to identify themselves with the Angelic Pope."

See also, in the same volume, Cesare Vasoli's excellent study of Giorgio Benigno Salviati, 121–56; see also his *Profezia e ragione*, 17–120.

148. See Vasoli, *Profezia e ragione*, 131–403.

149. On Carnesecchi, see Oddone Ortolani, *Pietro Carnesecchi* (Florence: Felice Le Monnier, 1963). On Brocardo, note Cantimori, "Visioni e speranze di un ugonotto italiano."

150. For the preacher Thomas Illyricus's use of similar strategy, see Taylor, *Soldiers of Christ*, 213.

151. ASV, S.U., Processi, Busta 22, Contra Dionisium Gallum, document entitled *Haec est causa:* "Dedit mihi Christus, vt ego vincerem ostium apertum quod nemo potest claudere, quia modicam habeo corporalem virtutem et seruaui verbum eius et non negaui nomen eius. Me vincentem faciet Christus columnam in templo patris sui . . . et scribet super me nomen Dei, patris sui et nomen ciuitatis Dei patris sui, nouae Hierusalem, quae descendit de coelo a Deo patre suo."

152. Ibid.: "Multi quidem simul praeliantur; multi simul vincunt; habent ipsi sua a Christo promissa, perpulchra etiam et iucundissima, sed solus ego sum, qui contra Sathanam, qui contra haereses pro iure pauperum contra vniuersos cleri abusus et aduersus omnem iniquitatem iamdudum praelior. Iam victor. Is ergo sum ego . . . quem Deus elegit, Regem constituit et summum pastorem sub filio suo."

Conclusion

1. Take note of the full context: "per spiritum veritatis, haec dicta sunt et promissa, pro quodam alio magno Rege Tertio, Christi tipum gerente: huicque simillimo per infusas gratias et collata coelitus diuina beneficia ac pro Christo, super ipsam Terram regnaturo: de quo Rege tum David loquitur: cum exultans, ait, in spiritu: Cantate Domino canticum nouum." ASV, S.U., Processi, Busta 22, Contra Dionisium Gallum, document entitled *Ex coelo empireo veritas reuelata. . . .*

2. Ibid.

3. Ibid., document entitled *Dionysius Gallus coelesti gratia Dei seruus et nuntius tibi (sancte pater foelicitatem precatur et salutem)*.

4. See Villardi, *La storia di Girolamo Savonarola*, vol. 2, bk. 4, chap. vi, 105: "Onde non posso piu sperare nella V.S. ma debbo solo rivolgermi a Colui che elegge le cose deboli di questo mondo per confondere i forti leoni degli uomini perversi."

5. See *Epistola del preditto a tutta la congregatione de i frati di San Marco, del modo di resistere alle tentationi, e di peruenir alla perfettione*, in *Molti devotissimi trattati del Reverendo Padre Frate Hieronimo Sauonarola da Ferrara*, c. 54^V; shelf mark Biblioteca nazionale di San Marco, 193.C.233.

6. Note Savonarola's harsh criticism of the ecclesiastical hierarchy: "Cosi la nostra Chiesa ha di fuori molte belle cerimonie in solennizare gli ufficii ecclesi-

astici con bei paramenti con assai drappelloni, con candellieri d'oro e d'argento, con tanti calici, che è una maestà. Tu vedi là quei gran prelati, con quella mitrie d'oro e di gemme preziose in capo, col pastorale d'argento; tu gli vedi con le belle pianete e piviali di broccato all'altare, cantare quei vespri e quelle belle messe, adagio, con tante ceremonie, con tanti organi e cantori, che tu ne stai stupefatto; e paionti costoro uomini di grande gravità e santimonia, e non credi che e' possonano errare: ma ciò che dicono e fanno credi che s'abbia a osservare come l'evangelino. Gli uomini si pascono di queste frasche e rallegransi di questa cerimonie, e dicono che la chiesa di Cristo Gesù non fiorì mai così bene, e che il culto divino non fu mai cosi bene esercitato quanto al presente . . . , e che li primi prelati erano prelatuzzi rispetto a questi nostri moderni, non avevano ancora tante mitrie d'oro nè tanti calici anzi quei pochi che gli avevano, li disfacevano per la necessità dei poverii: i nostri prelati per far de'calici, tolgono quello Che è de' poveri, senza di che questo non possono vivere. . . . Nella primitiva Chiesa erano li calici di legno e li prelati d'oro; oggi la Chiesa ha li calici d'oro e li prelati di legno." See Villardi, *La storia di Girolamo Savonarola*, vol. 2, bk. 4, chap. vii, 169–70.

7. Postel, *De Etruriae regionis . . . originibus . . .* , 23, and note 8 below.

8. In regard to Postel and Cosimo I, see especially the important letter of Postel to the duke, discovered by Giovanni Cipriani. Ibid., 21–22; note especially 21:

> Sed verum in hoc te serio principem agere certo constat, quod ut in republica repurgato Augiae stabulo avitos ordines sensim collapsos sensim instaures ab animorm reformatione ducis exordium.
>
> Faxit Deus ut tu expectationi quam de te concoepi respondeas illamque si possit fieri vincas, et te in hoc summo reipublicae Christianae discrimine tanto magis Deo probes quanto minor spes, res in suos ordines reducendi, in sacro nostri seculi magistratu, imo in humanis conciliis reposita videtur.

As I observed in Chapter III above, the main purpose of Dionisio's sojourn with Cosimo I was to enlist the aid of the duke in reforming the Church.

9. This type of cooperation was perhaps more widespread than has previously been thought. Michelle M. Fontaine has demonstrated that the bishop worked with the ruling elite in Modena for the good of the city and the reform of the Church. While not a bishop, as far as we know, Dionisio took upon himself a task similar to that of the bishop, hoping to enlist the ruling elite, especially the dukes of Florence, Ferrara, and Savoy, and the Doge and Senate of Venice, to work with him in the cause of reform and the peace of the city. See Fontaine's "For the Good of the City: The Bishop and the Ruling Elite in Tridentine Modena," *Sixteenth Century Journal* 28, no. 1 (1997): 29–43.

10. London, British Library, Sloane MS 1410, fol. 41.

11. Ibid., Sloane MS 1411, fol. 434.

12. Ibid., fol. 433.

13. Gino Benzoni has made this point countless times, although he has not

linked Saint Mark to Moses. The concept of Saint Mark as a second Moses, in my opinion, is one reason for the relationship between Saint Mark and the doge. Benzoni eloquently states: "Se Venezia è san Marco, se san Marco è Venezia, l'iconografia dogale effigiante il doge genuflesso di fronte al leone con in pugno lo stendardo, inginocchiato davanti al leone magari alato per volare verso la vittoria, esprime si devozione marciana, ma rasenta anche la statolatria. . . . Assoggettarsi a Venezia significa 'facere fidelitatem sancto Marco et duci Venetianum.' Quasi quasi doge e san Marco s'equivalgono." See Gino Benzoni, "Devozioni dogali," *Studi Veneziani*, n.s., 31 (1996): 18. A slightly different version of the article, with the same title, appears in *San Marco: Aspetti storici e agiografici*, ed. Antonio Niero (Venice: Marsilio Editori, 1996), 110–22.

14. The complete text is as follows:

> *Dilige institiam, sua cunctis reddito iura,*
> *Pauper cum uidua, pupillus et orphanus, O Dux,*
> *Te sibi patronum sperant; pius omnibus esto.*
> *Non timor aut odium vel amor nec te trahat aurum.*
> *Ut flos casurus, Dux es, ceneresque futurus*
> *Et velut acturus post mortem sic habiturus.*

Pietro Saccardo, in discussing the mosaics and their inscriptions, notes that the three inscriptions concerning justice "che contengono avvertimenti dalla religione imposti all'uomo, sia esso cittadino o magistrato o principe, dà a ritenere che sieno originarie con la prima decorazione della Chiesa, poichè non si comprenderebbe per quale circostanza quei tre moniti avessero, ad esseri stati collocati in luoghi cosi disparati quando il tempio era omai completo." See *La Basilica di San Marco in Venezia*, 346. I have corrected an error in Saccardo's transcription of the inscription in the Capella San Clemente; it is clear that *futurus* should be read in place of *facturus*.

15. "Iustitiam terre judex amet undique ferre / Ne ferat iniustum per quod paciatur adustum." The inscription reads *paciatur* instead of *patiatur*, as recorded by Saccardo.

16. See Kuntz, *Guillaume Postel*. See also idem, *Venice, Myth, and Utopian Thought in the Sixteenth Century*.

17. See Jacoff, *The Horses of San Marco and the Quadriga of the Lord*, 109.

18. Ibid., 110.

19. "Ortus siquidem levitica ex tribu famossima cessisse fertur officia quae dabat lex mosayca." Cited by Pressacco, "Marco 'Christianus et medicus,'" 650–51.

20. Ibid., 647–84; especially 663, where the author states: "termini Esseni e Terapeuti sono sinonimi, essendo il primo la traslitterazione e il secondo la traduzione greca dell'aramaico occidentale *'asìn*, che significa Medici/Terapeuti. . . . Qui interessa la traduzione latina poiché nella *Passio* aquileiese di Ermacora, Marco si autodesigna come 'christianus et medicus ad omnes infirmitates curandas.' Si può

certo pensare a pura casualità o alla genericità di tale designazione visto che Gesù stesso chiamato medico; ma si può pensare anche all'eco d'una tradizione aquileiese più antica, con memoria dell'appartenenza dell'Evangelista (o del primi evangelizzatori) a una comunità di 'terapeuti.'"

Bibliography

Manuscripts

VENICE

Archivio di Stato
    Archivi propri
        Roma, Filze 18, 19
        Roma, Busta 8
        Savoia, Filza 1
    Arti, Busta 517
    Avogaria di Comun
        Balla d'oro, 1537, c. 143^v
        Cronaca Matrimoni, Registro 106, c. 91^v
        Libro d'oro, Nascite (1506–54), Busta 68, cc. 18^v, 49^v
        Prove di età per magistrati (1528–39), Busta 176, c. 41
        Registri di Battesimo (1513–18), Registro 37, no. 3
    Collegio
        Esposizioni Principi, Filza 1^v
        Lettere Cardinali e altri ecclesiastici, Filza 2
        Lettere Comuni, Filza 34
        Lettere Secrete, Busta 22
        Relazioni, Ambasciatori, Firenze, Buste 17, 18, relazione di Lorenzo Priuli, 1566
        Relazioni, Ambasciatori, Roma, Busta 1, relazione di Alvise Mocenigo, 1559
        Relazioni, Ambasciatori, Roma, Busta 20, relazione di Girolamo Soranzo, 1563
        Relazioni, Roma, Varie, Duplicati iv, November 2, 1565
        Relazioni, Ambasciatori, Savoia, Busta 24, relazione di Andrea Boldù, 1561
    Consiglio dei Dieci
        Parti comuni, Filza 99
        Parti comuni, Registri 18, 23, 27
        Parti criminali, Filza 14
        Parti criminali, Registri 10, 11
        Parti secrete, Filze 7, 12
        Parti secrete, Registri 6, 8
    Consiglio dei Dieci, Capi
        Dispacci degli Ambasciatori
            Ferrara, Busta 8

  Roma, Buste 23, 24, 25
  Savoia, Busta 28
 Lettere, Filze 56, 67
 Lettere diverse, Busta 6
 Lettere secrete, Filza 7
 Notatorio, Registro 21
Dieci Savi sopra le Decime a Rialto
 Condizioni
  Castello, Busta 131, no. 964
  San Marco, Busta 93, no. 549; Busta 158, no. 1002
  San Marco, Redecime 1661, Registro 387, no. 364
  Traslati, Busta 1239, c. 206^v
Esecutori contra bestemmia, 1556
Giudici d' Petizion
 Inventari, Busta 340/5, nos. 59, 60
Maggior Consiglio
  Libro d' oro vecchio, inizio del Proemio dogale
Riformatori dello Studio di Padova, Filza 284
Santo Uffizio, Processi
 Busta 8, fascicolo 25, Contra Francesco di Giovanni Maria dei sartori
 Busta 11, Contra Andrea da Ugonibus
 Busta 12, fascicolo 20, lettera di Guillaume Postel al clarissimo Messer Maffio Veniero Magnifico Signore sopra la Heresia
 Busta 14, fascicolo 3, Contra Francesco Scudieri
 Busta 18, Contra Pietro Carnesecchi
 Busta 20, fascicolo 20, abjuration of Giacomo Malipiero
  Contra Michele Schiavon
  Contra Fra Cipriano Corner
  Costituto Agnolo Baglione
  Costituto di Antonio Loredan
 Busta 21
  Costituto Oderico Grison
  Costituto di Rochus de Mazzochis
  Contra Ioannem de Vancimugio Vicentinum
 Busta 22, Contra Dionisium Gallum
 Busta 23
  Contra Sylvestrum Semprini, Angelam Zoin
  Contra Carlo Corner
  Contra Giacomo Malipiero
  Contra Padre Fidele Vico
 Busta 24, fascicolo 3, Contra Franciscum Cagiola Mediolaneum
 Busta 25

　　　　　Contra Isabella Frattina
　　　　　Contra Marco Frattina
　　　　　Costituto Giacomo Brocardo
　　　　　Costituto D. Vincentius Julianus Romanus
　　　　　Lettera, Salvador Surian
　　　Busta 30, fascicolo 10, Contra Nascimbene Nascimbeni
　　　　　Costituto di Girolamo Donzellino
　　　Busta 31, Contra Fra' Aurelio Stichiano
　　　Busta 35
　　　　　Contra Dominico di Lorenzo Callegaro
　　　　　Costituto di Alessandro Callegher
　　　　　Costituto di Benedetto Florian da Cittadella
　　　Busta 39, Contra Girolamo Donzellino
　　　Busta 41, fascicolo, Tranquillo de Andreis
　　　Busta 49, Miracolo di San Francesco di Paolo
　　　Busta 51, Contra Padre Emilio profeta
　　　Busta 154, *Dell'origine dell'Inquisizione, et inquisitori e particolarmente di
　　　　　Venezia*
　　　Busta 156, Contra Balthasar Alterio
　　　Busta 159
　　　Busta 160, Costituto di Guillaume Postel, Capi del Consiglio dei
　　　　　Dieci (1548)
　　　Busta 161
　　　　　Contra pre' Giovanni Battista Clario da Udine
　　　　　Contra Francesco Scudieri
Secretario alle Voci
　　　Elezioni di Maggior Consiglio, 4 (1562–70)
　　　Elezioni in Pregadi, 1566–67
　　　Registro 11 (ex 8), 1523–56
　　　Serie mista, Buste 11, 12
Senato
　　　Deliberazioni, Secrete, Filza 37, Registro 74
　　　Dispacci, Ambasciatori, Roma, Filza 1
　　　Terra, Registro 46 (1566–67)
Sezione Notarile
　　　Atti
　　　　　Bartholomeo Bressan, Busta 494
　　　　　Lion Lioni, Busta 7835
　　　　　Anzolo Schietti, Busta 11971
　　　　　Giovann Battista Tomasi, Busta 979
　　　Testamenti
　　　　　Carlo Bianco, Buste 78, 87
　　　　　Nicolò Cigrini, Busta 198
　　　　　Antonio Marsilio, Busta 1210

Archivio storico del Patriarcato di Venezia
    Criminalia Santissimae Inquisitionis, Busta 2
        Costituto di Ioannes Baptista de Rauaiolis
        Costituto di Donna Camilla de Foligattis de Venetiis
        Costituto di Francesco Severo

Biblioteca del Museo Correr
    Fondo Morosini Grimani, MS 127
    Opus P.D. 11.759 al 11.786 (11780)

Biblioteca nazionale di San Marco
    MSS italiani
        Cl. VII, Cod. CMXXVII (= 8596)
        Cl. VII, Cod. MMDLXX (= 12462) già Phillips 5215
        Cl. VII Cod. LXIX (= 7727)
        Cl. VII, Cod. CXX (= 8158)
        Cl. VII, Cod. CCXIII (= 8836)
        Cl. VII, Cod. CCCXXIV (= 8038)
        Cl. VII, Cod. MMDLXXXV (= 12477) già Phillips 5214
        Cl. VII, Cod. DCCCLXXXIII (= 8389)
    MSS latini
        Cl. III, Cod. CLXXVII (= 2176)
        Cl. III, Cod. CXCV (= 2211)
        Cl. III, Cod. CCXXIX (= 2791)
        Cl. VI, Cod. CCLXXXII (= 2859)
        Cl. X, Cod. CCLXXXV (= 3180)
        Cl. XIV, Cod. XLII (= 4325)
        Cl. XIV, Cod. II (= 4590)
    Edizioni Veneziane de secolo XVI di E. Pastorello, senza segnatura

ROME

Biblioteca Apostolica Vaticana
    Barberini latini, 2871, 3614
    Borghese latini, 300
    Urbinates latini, 817, 860
    Vat. latini, 6085

FLORENCE

Archivio di Stato
    Diplomatico, Normale 1565, Archivio mediceo

LONDON

The British Library
    Sloane MSS 1410, 1411, 1412, 1413

PARIS

Bibliothèque nationale
    Fonds française 2115
    Fonds latin 3401
    Fonds latin 3679

WOLFENBÜTTEL

Herzog August Bibliothek
    Helmstedt 366
        Liber qui dicitur Vade mecum
        Hec sunt excerpta reuelationum sancte Brigitte
    240.7 Quod. (16), *Flagellum et Renouatio mundi et Ecclesiae Dei*

Printed Sources

Alberigo, Giuseppe. "Studi e problemi relativi all'applicazione del Concilio di Trento in Italia." *Rivista Storica Italiana* 70 (1958): 239–98.

Ambrosini, Federica. *Storie di patrizi e di eresia nella Venezia del' 500*. Milan: Franco Angeli, 1999.

———. "Tendenze filoprotestanti nel patriziato veneziano." In *La Chiesa di Venezia tra riforma protestante e riforma cattolica*, edited by Giuseppe Gullino, 155–81. Venice: Edizioni Studium Cattolico, 1990.

Annali urbani di Venezia dall'anno 810 al 12 Maggio 1797 di Fabio Mutinelli. Venice: Tipografia de G. B. Merlo, 1841.

The Apocrypha and Pseudepigrapha of the Old Testament in English. . . . Edited by R. H. Charles. Oxford: Clarendon Press, 1913.

Atila flagellvm Dei. Stampata in Venetia per Matthio Pagan in Frezaria al segno della fede, 1505.

Aumann, Jordan. "L'azione dello Spirito Santo." In *La mistica: Fenomenologia e riflessione teologica*, edited by Ermanno Ancilli and Maurizio Paparozzi. Rome: Città Nuova Editrice, 1984.

Bacchetti, Enrico. "La gestione del sistema carcerario a Venezia e il regolamento del Doge Antonio Venier (1391)." *Atti dell'Istituto Veneto di Scienze, Lettere ed Arti: Classe di Scienze Morali, Lettere ed Arti* 155/II (1997): 301–27.

Bainton, Roland H. "Wyllyam Postell and the Netherlands." *Nederlandsch Archief voor Kerkgeschiedenis* 24 (1931): 161–71.

Baldisseri, Lorenzo. *La nunziatura in Toscana*. Vatican City: Archivio Vaticano, 1977.

Bareggi, Claudia di Filippo. "In nota alla politica culturale di Cosimo I: L'Accademia Fiorentina." *Quaderni Storici* 7 (1973): 527–74.

Bargeus, Petrus Angelus. *Laudatio ad funebrem concionem quae Pisis habita est in Exequiis Cosmi Medicis Magni Hetruriae Ducis*. Florence: Iuntas, 1563.

Barnes, Robin Bruce. *Prophecy and Gnosis: Apocalypticism in the Wake of the Lutheran Reformation*. Stanford: Stanford University Press, 1988.

Bartholomei Mariscotti Oratio De vtilitate Concilii Tridentini. . . . Florence: Iuntas, 1565.
Barton, F. Whitfield. *Calvin and the Duchess.* Louisville, Ky.: John Knox Press, 1989.
La Basilica di San Marco: Arte e simbologia, Edited by Bruno Bertoli. Venice: Edizioni Studium Cattolico Venziano, 1993.
La Basilica di San Marco in Venezia illustrata nella storia e nell'arte da scrittori veneziani sotto la direzione di Camillo Boito. Venice: Ferdinando Ongania Editore, 1888.
Basilica patriarcale in Venezia, San Marco: I mosaici, le iscrizioni, la pala d'oro. Edited by Maria Andaloro, Maria da Villa Urbani, Ivete Florent-Goudouneix, and Renato Polacco. Milan: Ettore Vio Fabbri Editori, 1991.
Battistella, Antonio. "La politica ecclesiastica della Repubblica di Venezia." *Archivio Veneto,* 2d ser., 16 (1892).
Battisti, Eugenio. *L'anti-Rinascimento.* Vol. 1. Milan: Garzanti Editore, 1989.
Benzoni, Gino. *Gli affanni della cultura: Intellettuali e potere nell'Italia della controriforma e barocca.* Milan: Feltrinelli Editore, 1978.
———. "Una città caricabile di valenze religiose." In *La Chiesa di Venezia tra riforma protestante e riforma cattolica,* edited by Giuseppe Gullino, 37–61. Venice: Edizioni Studium Cattolico, 1990.
———. "Devozioni dogali." *Studi Veneziani,* n.s., 31 (1996). Revised reprint in *San Marco: Aspetti storici e agiografici,* edited by Antonio Niero, 110–22. Venice: Marsilio Editori, 1996.
———. "Profili Medicei di fattura Veneziana: Cosimo, Francesco I, Ferdinando I." *Studi Veneziana,* n.s., XXIV (1992): 69–86.
———. "San Marco e il doge." In *Omaggio a San Marco: Tesori dall'Europa,* edited by Hermann Fillitz and Giovanni Morello. Milan: Electa Editrice, 1994.
———. *Venezia nell'età della controriforma.* Milan: Munsia, 1973.
Bertoli, Bruno, and Antonio Niero. *I mosaici di San Marco: Un itinerario biblico.* Milan: Electa Editrice, 1987.
La Bibbia concordata. Florence: Arnoldo Mondadori Editore, 1968.
La Bibbia Piemme. Turin: Edizioni Piemme, 1995.
Biografia universale antica e moderna. Venice: Presso Gio. Battista Missiaglia, 1825.
Bodin, Jean. *Colloquium of the Seven About Secrets of the Sublime* [*Colloquium Heptaplomeres*]. Translated by Marion Leathers Daniels Kuntz. Princeton, N.J.: Princeton University Press, 1975.
Boerio, Giuseppe. *Dizionario del dialetto veneziano.* Venice: Giovanni Cecchini Editore, 1856.
Bouwsma, William J. *John Calvin: A Sixteenth-Century Portrait.* New York and Oxford: Oxford University Press, 1988.
———. *Venice and the Defense of Republican Liberty.* Berkeley and Los Angeles: University of California Press, 1968.
———. "Venice and the Political Education of Europe." In *Renaissance Venice,* edited by J. R. Hale, 445–66. Totowa, N.J.: Rowman & Littlefield, 1973.
Branca, Vittore. "Ermolao Barbaro and Late Quattrocento Venetian Humanism." In *Renaissance Venice,* edited by J. R. Hale, 218–43. Totowa, N.J.: Rowman & Littlefield, 1973.

Brink, James E. "Les états de Languedoc de 1515 a 1560: Une autonomie en question." *Annales du Midi: Revue de la France méridionale* 88, no. 128 (1976): 287–305.
Brocardo, Jacomo. *In tres libros Aristolelis de arte retorica Paraphrasis.* N.p., 1549.
Bussi, Rolando, ed. *Libri, idee e sentimenti religiosi nel Cinquecento italiano.* Modena: Edizioni Panini, 1986.
Caccamo, Domenico. *Eretici italiani in Moravia, Polonia, Transilvania (1558–1511).* Chicago: Newberry Library, 1970.
Calvin, John. *Commentary on the Book of the Prophet Isaiah.* Translated by Rev. William Pringle. Edinburgh: W. B. Erdmans, 1853.
Cantimori, Delio. *Eretici italiani del Cinquecento: Ricerche storiche.* 3d ed. Florence: G. C. Sansoni Editore, 1977.
———. "Studi di storia della riforma e dell'eresia in Italia e studi sulla storia della vita religiosa nella prima metà del '500 (rapporto fra i due tipi di ricerca)." *Bollettino della Società di Studi Valdesi* 76 (1957): 29–38.
———. "Visioni e speranze di un ugonotto italiano." *Rivista Storica Italiana* 62 (1950): 199–217.
Capelli, Adriano. *Cronologia, cronografia e calendario perpetuo.* 5th ed., rev. Milan: Editore Ulrico Hoepli, 1983.
Capoville, Giovanni. "Giorgio Vasari e gli edifici dell'ordine militare di Santo Stefano in Pisa (1562–1571)." *Studi Storici* 17, fasc. 11 (1908): 305–79.
Catalogus translationum et commentariorum. Vol. 4. Edited by F. Edward Cranz and Paul Oskar Kristeller. Washington, D.C.: Catholic University of America Press, 1980.
Cervelli, Innocenzo. *Machiavelli e la crisi dello stato veneziano.* Naples: Guida, 1974.
———. "Storiografia e problemi intorno alla vita religiosa e spirituale a Venezia nella prima metà del '500." *Studi Veneziani* 8 (1966): 447–76.
Chabod, Federico. "Contributo veneziano alla riforma cattolica." In *La civiltà veneziana del Rinascimento,* Centro di Cultura e Civiltà della Fondazione Giorgio Cini, 105–24. Florence: Sansoni, 1958.
———. "Venezia nella politica italiana ed europea del Cinquecento." In *La civiltà veneziana del Rinascimento,* Centro di Cultura e Civiltà della Fondazione Giorgio Cini, 139–90. Florence: Sansoni, 1958.
Chevalier, Jean, and Alain Gheerbrant. *Dizionario dei simboli.* Milan: Rizzoli Libri, 1986.
La Chiesa cattolica nella storia dell'umanità: Splendore e decadenza del medio evo. Edited by Carlo Lenta and Francesco Chiaramento. Vol. 3. Fossano: Editrice Esperienze, 1964.
Chojnacki, Stanley. "In Search of the Venetian Patriciate: Families and Factions in the Fourteenth Century." In *Renaissance Venice,* edited by J. R. Hale, 47–90. Totowa, N.J.: Rowman & Littlefield, 1973.
Cicogna, Emmanuele Antonio. *Delle inscrizioni veneziane.* Venice, 1842.
Circolazione di uomini ed idee tra Italia ed Europa nell'età della controriforma. Edited by Susanna Peyronel Rambaldi. Turin: Tipolitografia Camedda, 1998.
Confraternities and Catholic Reform in Italy, France, and Spain. Sixteenth-Century Essays and Studies, vol. 44. Edited by John Patrick Donnelly, S.J., and Michael W. Maher, S.J. Kirksville, Mo.: Thomas Jefferson University Press, 1998.
Contarini, Gasparo. *De magistratibus et republica venetorum.* Venice, 1589.

Contessa, C. "Echi del centenario della nascita di Emanuele Filiberto di Savoia." *Archivio Veneto* 5 (1929): 369–98.
Corner, Flaminio. *Notizie storiche delle chiese e monasteri di Venezia e di Torcello*. Facsimile reprint. Bologna: Arnaldo Forni Editore, 1990.
Cosimo I de' Medici: Lettere. Edited by Giorgio Spini. Florence: Vallecchi, 1940.
Cozzi, Gaetano. "Authority and the Law in Renaissance Venice." In *Renaissance Venice*, edited by J. R. Hale, 293–345. Totowa, N.J.: Rowman & Littlefield, 1973.
———. "Domenico Bollani: Un vescovo veneziano tra Stato e Chiesa." *Rivista Storica Italiana* 89 (1977): 562–89.
———. "Fortuna e sfortuna della Compagnia di Gesù a Venezia." In *I Gesuiti e Venezia: Momenti e problemi di storia veneziana della Compagnia di Gesù*, edited by Mario Zanardi, 59–88. Padua: Gregoriana Libreria Editrice, 1994.
———. "Fra Paolo Sarpi, l'anglicanesimo e la 'Historia del Concilio tridentino.'" *Rivista Storica Italiana* 68 (1956): 559–619.
———. "Giuspatronato del doge e prerogative del primicerio sulla cappella ducale di San Marco (secoli XVI–XVIII): Controversie con i procuratori di San Marco de supra e i patriarchi di Venezia." *Atti dell'Istituto Veneto di Scienze, Lettere ed Arti: Classe di Scienze Morali, Lettere ed Arti* 151, no. 1 (1992–93): 1–69.
———. "Note su Giovanni Tiepolo, primicerio di San Marco e patriarca di Venezia: L'unità ideale della Chiesa veneta." In *Chiesa, società e stato a Venezia: Miscellanea di studi in onore di Silvio Tramontin*, edited by Bruno Bertoli. Venice: Edizioni Studium Cattolico Veneziano, 1994.
———. "I rapporti tra stato e chiesa." In *La Chiesa di Venezia tra riforma protestante e riforma cattolica*, edited by Giuseppe Gullino, 11–36. Venice: Edizioni Studium Cattolico, 1990.
———. *Repubblica di Venezia e stati italiani: Politica e giustizia dal secolo XVI al secolo XVIII*. Turin: Giulio Einaudi Editore, 1982.
Crisi e rinnovamenti nell'autunno del Rinascimento a Venezia. Edited by Vittore Branca and Carlo Ossola. Florence: Leo S. Olschki Editore, 1991.
Cronica breuis ab initio ordinis vsque ad presens tempus de omnibus Pontificibus Romanis et omnibus huius praedicatorum ordinis magistris generalibus et de viris illustribus tam sanctitate quam scientia preditis ipsius ordinis. Venetiis (Venice): Laçarus de Soardis, 1516.
Crouzet, Denis. *Les guerrières de Dieu: La violence au temps des troubles de religion vers 1525–vers 1610*. Vols.1–2. Paris: Champ Vallon, 1990.
D'Alessandro, Alessandro. "Il Gello di Pierfrancesco Giambullari: Mito e ideologia nel principato di Cosimo I." In *La nascita della Toscana dal Convegno di Studi per il IV centenario della morte di Cosimo I de' Medici*, 73–104. Florence: Leo S. Olschki Editore, 1980.
Dalla Santa, Giuseppe. "Il vero testo dell'appellazione di Venezia dalla scomunica di Giulio II." *Nuovo Archivio Veneto*, 2d ser., 19 (1900): 349–61.
D'Amico, John F. *Renaissance Humanism in Papal Rome: Humanists and Churchmen on the Eve of the Reformation*. Baltimore, Md.: Johns Hopkins University Press, 1983.

Degand, A. "Chartreux." In *Dictionnaire d'archéologie chrétienne et de liturgie*, 3:1046–71. Paris: Letouzey et Ané, Éditeurs, 1913.
degli Agostini, Giovanni. "Notizie istoriche spettanti alla vita e agli scritti di Batista Egnazio sacerdote viniziano." In *Raccolta d'opuscoli scientifici e filologici*, edited by A. Calogerà. Venice, 1745.
de La Fosse, Jehan Baptiste. *Journal d'un Curé ligueur de Paris sous les trois derniers Valois*. Edited by Édouard de Barthélemy. Paris: Librairie Académique Didier, Libraires-Editeurs, 1865.
Del Col, Andrea. "Il controllo della stampa a Venezia e i processi di Antonio Brucioli (1548–1559)." *Critica Storica* 17 (1980): 457–510.
———. "Lucio Paolo Rosello e la vita religiosa veneziana verso la metà del secolo XVI." *Rivista di Storia della Chiesa in Italia* 22 (1978): 422–59.
———. "Organizzazione, composizione e giurisdizione dei tribunali dell'Inquisizione romana nella Repubblica di Venezia (1500–1550)." *Critica Storica* 25 (1988): 244–94.
———, ed. *Domenico Scandella detto Menocchio*. Pordenone: Edizioni Biblioteca dell'Immagine, 1990.
Delle orationi volgarmente scritte da diversi Hvomini . . . Raccolte gia della felice memoria del Signor Francesco Sansouino et hora in questa nostra vltima impressione arrichite. . . . Venice: Presso Altobello Salicato, Alla Libraria della Fortezza, 1548.
Delumeau, Jean. *La riforma: Origini e affermazioni*. Milan: V. Mursia Editore, 1975–88.
Demus, Otto. *The Mosaics of San Marco in Venice: The Eleventh and Twelfth Centuries*. Vols. 1 and 2. Chicago: University of Chicago Press, 1984.
De reformatione ecclesiae suasoria: R.P.D. Zachariae Ferrerii Vicentini Pontificis Gardiensis Fauentiae et Vallis Hamonis gubernatoris dudum missa ad Beatissimum Patrem Hadrianum vi Pontificem Maximum: Et inscribitur, Tu es qui uenturus es, an alium expectamus? Venetiis (Venice): per Io. Antonium et fratres de Sabio, 1522.
I diarii di Marino Sanudo. Edited by N. Barazzí. Vol. 8. Venice, 1582.
Diario fiorentino di Agostino Lapini: Dal 252 al 1596, ora per la prima volta pubblicato da Giuseppe Odoardo Corrazzini. Florence, 1900.
Diefendorf, Barbara. *Beneath the Cross: Catholics and Huguenots in Sixteenth-Century Paris*. Oxford: Oxford University Press, 1991.
Dizionario degli Istituti di Perfezione. Edited by Guerrino Pelliccia (1962–68) and Giancarlo Rocca (1969–). Rome: Edizioni Paoline, 1975.
Dizionario del Dritto comune e veneto che contiene le leggi civili, canoniche e criminali. Opera di Marco Ferro Avvocato veneto. Venice, 1781.
Dizionario di erudizione storico-ecclesiastica . . . compilazione del Cavaliere Gaetano Moroni Romano. Venice: Tipografia Emiliana, 1846.
Domenichi, Lodovico. *Historia varia di M. Lodovico Domenichi. . . .* Venice: Gabriel Giolito de' Ferrari, 1564.
———, trans. *Prophetia de maometani et Altre cose Turchesche*. Florence, 1548.
Doni, Anton Francesco. *L'Academia peregrina e i mondi sopra le medaglie del Doni, in Vinegia nell'Academia P*. Venice: Francesco Marconlini, 1552.
———. *Dichiaratione del Doni, sopra il XIII cap. dell'Apocalisse contro a gli heretici con modi*

non mai piu intesi da Hvomo vivente. . . . Venice: Gabriel Giolito de' Ferrari, 1562.

La ducale Basilica di San Marco: Documenti per la storia dell'augusta ducale Basilica di San Marco. Venice, 1886.

Du Cange, Charles. *Glossarium Mediae et Infirmae Latinitatis.* Vol. 5. Bologna: Forni Editore, 1982.

Ecclesiae Venetae antiquis monumentis nunc etiam primum editis illustratae ac in decades distributae authore Flaminio Cornelio, Senatore Veneto. Decades 4 and 5. Venice: Typis Joannis Baptistae Pasquali, 1749.

Edelstein, Marilyn Manera. "Church Patronage in France on the Eve of the Reformation." In *Renaissance Society and Culture: Essays in Honor of Eugene F. Rice, Jr.*, edited by John Monfasani and Ronald G. Musto. Ithaca: Cornell University Press, 1991.

L'editto et capitoli del Re Carlo IX fatti novamente per la pacificatione de i suoi popoli nel Regno di Francia . . . tradotti fedelissimamente dalla lingua Francese, nella nostra buona Italiana. N.p., n.d.

Egidi, Pietro. *Mezzogiorno medievale e Piemonte moderno.* Bari: G. Laterza & Figli, 1931.

Emanuele Filiberto. IV centenario di Emanuele Filiberto e X anniversario della vittoria. Turin: S. Lattes, 1929.

Emery, Kent, Jr. "Mysticism and the Coincidence of Opposites in Sixteenth- and Seventeenth-Century France." *Journal of the History of Ideas* 45 (January–March 1984): 3–23.

Erba, Andrea. "Il 'caso' di Paola Antonia Negri nel Cinquecento italiano." In *Women and Men in Spiritual Culture XIV–XVII*, edited by Elisja Schulte Van Kessell. The Hague: Martinus Nijhoff, 1986.

Esercizj spirituali di S. Ignazio Lojola. . . . Parma: dalla Stamperia Ducale, 1816.

Farthing, John L. "Christ and the Eschaton: The Reformed Eschatology of Jerome Zanchi." In *Later Calvinism: International Perspectives*, Sixteenth-Century Essays and Studies, vol. 22, edited by W. Fred Graham, 333–54. Kirksville, Mo.: Sixteenth Century Journal Publishers, 1994.

Fasoli, G. "Nascita di un mito." In *Studi storici in onore di Gioacchino Volpe*, 1:445–79. Florence, 1958.

Fasti Gymnasii Patavini. Patavii (Padua): Joannes Manfrè, 1757.

Fedalto, Giorgio. *Santi e beati vissuti a Venezia.* Venice: Edizioni Studium Cattolico Veneziano, 1971.

Firpo, Massimo. *Gli affreschi di Pontormo a San Lorenzo: Eresia, politica e cultura nella Firenze di Cosimo I.* Turin: Giulio Einaudi Editore, 1997.

———. *Del sacco di Roma all'Inquisizione: Studi su Juan de Valdes e la riforma italiana.* Alessandria: Edizioni dell'Orso, 1998.

———. *Tra alumbrados e spirituali: Studi su Juan de Valdes e il valdesianesimo nella crisi religiosa del '500 italiano.* Florence: Leo S. Olschki Editore, 1990.

Firpo, Massimo, and Paolo Simoncelli. "I processi inquisitoriali contro Savonarola (1558) e Carnesecchi (1566–1567): Una proposta di interpretazione." *Rivista di Storia e Letteratura Religiosa* 18, no. 2 (1982): 200–252.

Flagellum et Renouatio mundi et Ecclesiae Dei. N.p., 1537.
Florentine Studies: Politics and Society in Renaissance Florence. Edited by Nicolai Rubinstein. London: Faber, 1968.
Fontaine, Michelle M. "For the Good of the City: The Bishop and the Ruling Elite in Tridentine Modena." *Sixteenth Century Journal* 28, no. 1 (1997): 29–43.
Foscari, Antonio, and Manfredo Tafuri. *L'armonia e i conflitti: La chiesa di San Francesco della Vigna nella Venezia del' 500.* Turin: Giulio Einaudi Editore, 1983.
Fragnito, Gigliola. "Cultura umanistica e riforma religiosa: Il 'De officio viri boni ac probi episcopi' di Gasparo Contarini." *Studi Veneziani* 11 (1970): 75–189.
———. "Gli 'Spirituali' e la fuga di Bernardino Ochino." *Rivista Storica Italiana* 84, fasc. III (1972): 777–813.
Francisci Barocii Iacobi filii patritii veneti commentarius in locvm Platonis obscvrissimvm. . . . Bononiae (Bologna), typis Alexandri Benacii, 1566.
Franzoi, Umberto. "La Scala dei Giganti." *Bollettino dei Musei Civici Veneziani* 10, no. 4(1965): 8–31.
Gaeta, Franco. "Alcune considerazioni sul mito di Venezia." *Bibliothèque d'Humanisme et Renaissance* 233 (1961): 58–75.
———. "L'idea di Venezia." In *Storia della cultura veneta: Dal primo Quattrocento al Concilio di Trento,* edited by Girolamo Arnaldi and Manilio Pastore Stocchi, 3/III:565–641. Vicenza: Neri Pozza Editore, 1981.
———. "Storiografia, coscienza nazionale e politica culturale nella Venezia del Rinascimento." In *Storia della cultura veneta: Dal primo Quattrocento al Concilio di Trento,* edited by Girolamo Arnaldi and Manilio Pastore Stocchi, 3/I:123–75. Vicenza: Neri Pozza Editore, 1981.
Gastaldi, U. "Il comunismo dei Fratelli Hutteriti." *Protestantesimo* 28 (1973): 1–24.
I Gesuiti e Venezia: Momenti e problemi di storia veneziana della Compagnia di Gesù. Edited by Mario Zanardi. Padua: Gregoriana Libreria Editrice, 1994.
Gil, Christiane. *Renée de France.* Paris: Perrin, 1990.
Gilbert, Felix. "Contarini on Savonarola: An Unknown Document of 1516." *Archiv für Reformationsgeschichte* 59 (1968): 145–49.
———. "Religion and Politics in the Thought of Gasparo Contarini." In *Action and Conviction in Early Modern Europe: Essays in Memory of E. H. Harbison,* edited by Theodore K. Rabb and Jerrold E. Seigel, 90–116. Princeton, N.J.: Princeton University Press, 1969.
———. "The Venetian Constitution in Florentine Political Thought." In *Florentine Studies: Politics and Society in Renaissance Florence,* edited by Nicolai Rubinstein, 466–72. London: Faber, 1968.
———. "Venice in the Crisis of the League of Cambrai." In *Renaissance Venice,* edited by J. R. Hale, 274–92. Totowa, N.J.: Rowman & Littlefield, 1973.
Gilmore, Myron. "Myth and Reality in Venetian Political Theory." In *Renaissance Venice,* edited by J. R. Hale, 431–22. Totowa, N.J.: Rowman & Littlefield, 1973.
Ginzburg, Carlo. *The Cheese and the Worms: The Cosmos of a Sixteenth-Century Miller.* Translated by John Tedeschi and Anne Tedeschi. Baltimore, Md.: Johns Hopkins University Press, 1980.

———. "Due note sul profetismo cinquecentesco," *Rivista Storica Italiana* 78 (1966): 184–227.
Ginzburg, Carlo, and Adriano Prosperi. "Le due redazioni del 'Beneficio di Cristo.'" In *Eresia e riforma nell'Italia del Cinquecento,* Biblioteca del "Corpus Reformatorum Italicorum," Miscellanea 1. Chicago: Newberry Library, 1974.
Gleason, Elisabeth G. *Gasparo Contarini: Venice, Rome, and Reform.* Berkeley and Los Angeles: University of California Press, 1993.
———. *Reform Thought in Sixteenth-Century Italy.* Edited and translated by Elisabeth G. Gleason. AAR Texts and Translations Series, no. 4. Ann Arbor: University of Michigan Press, 1981.
Gregori, Mina. "Tiziano e l'Aretino." In *Tiziano e il manierismo europeo,* edited by Rodolfo Pallucchini, 271–306. Florence: Leo S. Olschki Editore, 1978.
Grendler, Paul F. *The Roman Inquisition and the Venetian Press, 1540–1605.* Princeton, N.J.: Princeton University Press, 1977.
———. *Schooling in Renaissance Italy: Literacy and Learning, 1300–1600.* Baltimore, Md.: Johns Hopkins University Press, 1989.
———. "The Tre Savii Sopra Eresia, 1547–1605: A Prosopographical Study." *Studi Veneziani,* n.s., 3 (1979): 283–340.
Guarini, E. Fasano. "Cosimo I de' Medici." In *Dizionario biografico degli italiani,* xxx:30–48. Rome: Istituto della Enciclopedia Italiana, 1984.
Hale, J. R. *Florence and the Medici: The Pattern of Control.* London: Thames & Hudson, 1977.
———, ed. *Renaissance Venice.* Totowa, N.J.: Rowman & Littlefield, 1973.
Hall, Marcia B. *Renovation and Counter-Reformation: Vasari and Duke Cosimo in Santa Maria Novella and Santa Croce, 1565–1577.* Oxford: Oxford University Press, 1979.
Hallman, Barbara. *Italian Cardinals, Reform, and the Church as Property.* Berkeley and Los Angeles: University of California Press, 1985.
Haton, Claude. *Mémoires de Claude Haton. . . .* Edited by M. Félix Bourquelot. Paris: Imprimerie impériale, 1857.
Hierarchia Catholica medii et recentioris aevi sive summorum pontificum, S.R.E. cardinalium, ecclesiarum antistitum series. Edited by Guilelmus Van Gulik, Conradus Eubel, and Ludovicus Schmitz-Kallenberg. Vol. 3. Regensburg: Librariae Regensbergianae, 1923. Reprint, Padua, 1960.
Howard, Deborah. *The Architectural History of Venice.* New York: Holmes & Meier Publications, 1981.
———. *Jacopo Sansovino: Architecture and Patronage in Renaissance Venice.* New Haven, Conn.: Yale University Press, 1975.
Jacoff, Michael. *The Horses of San Marco and the Quadriga of the Lord.* Princeton, N.J.: Princeton University Press, 1993.
Jeanneret, Michel. *Poésie et tradition biblique au XVIe siècle.* Paris, 1969.
Jedin, Hubert. "La censura sulla stampa e una questione giurisdizionale fra Stato e Chiesa in Firenze alle fine del secolo XVI." *Archivio Storico Italiano,* 5th ser., 43 (1909): 140–51.

———. "Contarini und Camaldoli." *Archivio Italiano per la Storia della Pietà* 2 (1953): 1–67.
———. "Gasparo Contarini e il contributo veneziano alla riforma cattolica." In *La civiltà veneziana del Rinascimento*, Centro di Cultura e Civiltà della Fondazione Giorgio Cini, 105–24. Florence: Sansoni, 1958.
———. *History of the Council of Trent.* Translated from the German by Ernest Graf. St. Louis: B. Herder Book Co., 1957.
———. "La politica conciliare di Cosimo I." *Rivista Storica Italiana* 62 (1950): 345–74.
———. *Storia del Concilio di Trento.* 2d ed. Brescia, 1973.
The Jesuits: Cultures, Sciences, and the Arts (1540–1773). Edited by John W. O'Malley, S.J., Gauvin Alexander Bailey, Steven J. Harris, and T. Frank Kennedy, S.J. Toronto: University of Toronto Press, 1999.
Joachim. *Espositio magni prophete Abbatis Joachim in Apocalipsim.* Venice: In edibus Francisci Bindoni ac Maphaei Pasini, 1527.
———. *Abbas Joachim magnus propheta: Expositio magni prophete Ioachim in librum beati Cirilli de magnis tribulationibus et statu Sancte matris Ecclesie.* Venice: Laçarus de Soardis, 1516.
Joseph, George. *Clément Marot.* Boston: G. K. Hall, 1985.
Jung, Eva-Marie. "On the Nature of Evangelism in 16th-Century Italy." *Journal of the History of Ideas* 14 (1953): 511–27.
King, Margaret L. *Venetian Humanism in an Age of Patrician Dominance.* Princeton, N.J.: Princeton University Press, 1986.
Koenigsberger, H. G. "The Politics of Philip II." In *Politics, Religion, and Diplomacy in Early Modern Europe: Essays in Honor of De Lamar Jensen*, ed. Malcolm R. Thorp and Arthur J. Slavin, Sixteenth-Century Essays and Studies, 27:171–89. Kirksville, Mo.: Truman State University Press, 1994.
Kristeller, Paul Oskar. *Iter Italicum.* Vols. 3 and 4. Leiden: E. J. Brill, 1983 and 1989.
———. "Marsilio Ficino e Venezia." In *Miscellanea di studi in onore di Vittore Branca III: Umanesimo e Rinascimento a Firenze e a Venezia*, 475–92. Florence: Leo S. Olschki Editore, 1983.
Kuntz, Marion Leathers. "Angela da Foligno e la Vergine Veneziana: Un paradigma della spiritualità veneziana nel Cinquecento." In *Res Publica Litterarum* 11 (1988): 175–82.
———. "Guglielmo Postello e la 'Vergine Veneziana': Appunti storici sulla vita spirituale dell'Ospedaletto nel Cinquecento." In *Quaderni* 21:1–24. Venice: Centro Tedesco di Studi Veneziani, 1981.
———. "Guillaume Postel and the World State." *History of European Ideas* 4, no. 3 (1983): 299–323, and no. 4 (1983): 445–65.
———. "Guillaume Postel e l'idea di Venezia come la magistratura più perfetta." In *Postello, Venezia e il suo mondo*, edited by Marion Leathers Kuntz, 163–78. Florence: Leo S. Olschki Editore, 1988.
———. *Guillaume Postel, Prophet of the Restitution of All Things: His Life and Thought.* The Hague: Martinus Nijhoff, 1981.

———. "The Home of Coronaeus in Jean Bodin's *Colloquium Heptaplomeres:* An Example of a Venetian Academy." In *Acta Conventus Neo-Latini Bononiensis,* 277–83. Binghamton, N.Y.: Medieval & Renaissance Texts & Studies, 1985.

———. "Lodovico Domenichi, Guillaume Postel, and the Biography of Giovanna Veronese." *Studi Veneziani,* n.s., 16 (1988): 33–44.

———. "The Myth of Venice in the Thought of Guillaume Postel." In *Svpplementvm Festivvm: Studies in Honor of Paul Oskar Kristeller,* edited by J. Haskins, J. Monfasni, and F. Purnell, 505–23. Binghamton, N.Y.: Medieval & Renaissance Texts & Studies, 1987.

———. "'Venezia portava el fuocho in seno': Guillaume Postel Before the Council of Ten in 1548: Priest Turned Prophet." *Studi Veneziani,* n.s., 33 (1997): 95–121.

———. *Venice, Myth, and Utopian Thought in the Sixteenth Century: Bodin, Postel, and the Virgin of Venice.* Aldershot: Ashgate Publishing, 1999.

———. "The Virgin of Venice and Concepts of the Millennium in Venice." In *The Politics of Gender in Early Modern Europe,* Sixteenth-Century Essays and Studies, vol. 12, edited by Jean R. Brink, Allison P. Coudert, and Maryanne C. Horowitz, 111–30. Kirksville, Mo.: Truman State University Press, 1991.

———. "Voices from a Venetian Prison in the Cinquecento: Francesco Spinola and Dionisio Gallo." *Studi Veneziani,* n.s., 27 (1994): 79–126.

———. "What's in a Name? Postel as Petrus Anusius in 1548." In *Sociétés et idéologies des temps modernes: Hommage à Arlette Jouanna,* edited by J. Fouilleron, G. LeThiec, and H. Michel, 731–45. Montepellier: Conseil scientifique de l'Université de Montpellier III, 1996.

Labalme, Patricia. "Sodomy and Venetian Justice in the Renaissance." *Legal History Review* 52 (1984): 217–54.

Lane, Frederic C. *Venice: A Maritime Republic.* Baltimore, Md.: Johns Hopkins University Press, 1973.

———. *Venice and History.* Baltimore, Md.: Johns Hopkins University Press, 1966.

Lannette, C. *Guide des Archives de l'Eure.* Evreux: Les Archives, 1982.

Lasinio, Dott. Ernesto. *Regesto delle pergamene del R. Archivio di Stato in Massa.* Pistoia: Ministero dell'Interno, 1916.

Lasor a Varea, Alphonsus. *Universus Terrarum orbis. . . .* Patavii (Padua): Ioannes Baptista Conzallus, 1713.

Leblanc, P. *La poésie religieuse de Clément Marot.* Paris, 1955.

L'italianisme en Francia au XVII siècle. Collected and edited by Giorgio Mirandola. Turin: Società Editrice Internazionale, 1970.

Maillard, J. F. "Le *De Harmonia mundi* de Georges de Venise." *Revue de l'Histoire des Religions* 179 (1971): 181–203.

Malavasi, S. Ferlin. "Sulla diffusione delle teorie ereticali nel Veneto durante il '500: Anabattisti rodigini e polesani." *Archivio Veneto,* 5th ser., 96 (1972): 5–24.

Manuel, Frank E., and Fritzie P. Manuel. *Utopian Thought in the Western World.* Cambridge, Mass: Harvard University Press, 1980.

Martin, A. Lynn. *The Jesuit Mind: The Mentality of an Elite in Early Modern France.* Ithaca, N.Y.: Cornell University Press, 1988.

Martin, John. "L'Inquisizione romana e la criminalizzazione del dissenso religiosa a Venezia all'inizio dell'età moderna." *Quaderni Storici* 66, anno XXII, no. 3 (1987): 777–802.

———. "A Journeymen's Feast of Fools." *Journal of Medieval and Renaissance Studies* 17, no. 2 (1987): 149–74.

———. "Salvation and Society in Sixteenth-Century Venice: Popular Evangelism in a Renaissance City." *Journal of Modern History* 60, no. 2 (1988): 205–33.

———. *Venice's Hidden Enemies*. Berkeley and Los Angeles: University of California Press, 1993.

Marx, Barbara. *Venezia-Altera Roma? Ipotesi sull'umanesimo veneziano*. Quaderni 10. Venice: Centro Tedesco di Studi Veneziani, 1978.

Maschio, R. "Le scuole grandi a Venezia." In *Storia della cultura veneta: Dal primo Quattrocento al Concilio di Trento*, edited by Girolamo Arnaldi and Manilio Pastore Stocchi, 3/III: 193–206. Vicenza: Neri Pozza Editore, 1981.

McGinn, Bernard. *Visions of the End: Apocalyptic Traditions in the Middle Ages*. New York: Columbia University Press, 1979.

Memoires de Condé, servant d'éclaircissement et de preuves à l'Histoire de M. De Thou, . . . augmenté d'un supplément qui contient la légende du Cardinal de Lorraine, celle de Dom Claude de Guise. . . . Vol. 5. Paris: Chez Rollin, 1743.

Meyer, Carl S. *Luther's and Zwingli's Propositions for Debate*. Leiden: E. J. Brill, 1963.

Mirabilis Liber qui prophetias Reuelationesque necnon res mirandas praeteritas presentes et futuras apte demonstrat. N.p., 1524.

La mistica, fenomenologia e riflessione teologica. Edited by Ermanno Ancilli-Maurizio Paparozzi. Rome: Città Nuova Editrice, 1984.

Molti devotissimi trattati del Reverendo Padre Frate Hieronimo Sauonarola da Ferrara. Venice: Zan della Speranza, 1547.

Monumenti per servire alla storia del Palazzo Ducale di Venezia . . . da Giambattista Lorenzi, Parte 1 dal 1253 al 1600. Venice: Tipografia del Commercio di Marco Visentini, 1868.

Mor, Carlo Guido. "Recenti studi su Emanuele Filiberto." *Archivio Storico Italiano*, 7th ser., 12 (1929): 77–95.

Morisi, A. *"Apocalypsis nova": Ricerche sull'origine e la formazione del testo pseudo-Amadeo*. Rome: Istituto Storico Italiano per il Medio Evo, 1970.

Muir, Edward. *Civic Ritual in Renaissance Venice*. Princeton, N.J.: Princeton University Press, 1981.

———. "The Virgin of the Street Corner: The Place of the Sacred in Italian Cities." In *Religion and Culture in the Renaissance and Reformation*, Sixteenth-Century Essays and Studies, vol. 11, edited by Steven Ozment. Kirksville, Mo.: Truman State University Press, 1989.

Mulier, E. O. G. Haitsma. *The Myth of Venice and Dutch Republican Thought in the Seventeenth Century*. Translated by G. T. Moran. Assen: Van Gorcum, 1980.

Muraro, M. T. "La festa a Venezia e le sue manifestazioni rappresentative: La compagnia della calza e le mommearie." In *Storia della cultura veneta: Dal primo Quattrocento al Concilio di Trento*, edited by Girolamo Arnaldi and Manilio Pastore Stocchi, 3/III:315–41. Vicenza: Neri Pozza Editore, 1981.

Newett, Margaret M. "The Sumptuary Laws of Venice in the Fourteenth and Fifteenth Centuries." In *Historical Essays*, edited by T. F. Tout and James Tait, 245–78. Manchester: Manchester University Press, 1907.

Niccoli, Ottavia. "Un aspetto della propaganda religiosa nell'Italia del Cinquecento: Opuscoli e fogli volanti." In *Libri, idee e sentimenti religiosi nel Cinquecento italiano*, edited by Rolando Bussi. Modena: Edizioni Panini, 1986.

———. *La crisi religiosa del Cinquecento*. Turin: Giulio Einaudi Editore, 1975.

———. *Problemi di vita religiosa. . . .* Padua: Antenore, 1960.

———. *Profeti e popolo nell'Italia del Rinascimento*. Rome and Bari: Laterza, 1987.

———. "Profezie in piazza: Note sul profetismo popolare nell'Italia del primo Cinquecento." *Quaderni Storici* 41 (1979): 500–534.

———. "'Prophetie di Musaicho': Figure e scritture Gioachimite nella Venezia del Cinquecento." In *Forme e destinazione del messaggio religioso: Aspetti della propaganda religiosa nel Cinquecento*, edited by Antonio Rotondò, 197–227. Florence: Leo S. Olschki Editore, 1991.

———. "Visioni e racconti di visioni nell'Italia del primo Cinquecento." *Società e Storia* 28 (1985): 253–73.

———. *La vita religiosa nell'Italia moderna: Secoli xv–xviii*. Rome: Carocci Editore, 1998.

Niero, Antonio. "Il culto dei santi dell'antico testamento." In *Culto dei santi a Venezia*, edited by Dom Silvio Tramontin. Venice: Edizioni Studium Cattolico Veneziano, 1965.

Nouvelle biographie générale. . . . Paris: Firmin Didot Frères, 1856.

Nugent, Donald. *Ecumenism in the Age of Reformation: The Colloquy of Poissy*. Cambridge, Mass.: Harvard University Press, 1974.

Nunziature di Venezia. Edited by Aldo Stella. Vol. 8 (1566–69). Rome: Istituto Storico Italiano per l'Età Moderna e Contemporanea, 1963.

Nuovi studi sulla riforma in Italia: Il Beneficio di Cristo. Rome: Edizioni di Storia e Letteratura, 1976.

Les oeuvres de Clément Marot. Edited by Jean Plattard. Vols. 4 and 5. Paris, 1929, 1931.

Olivieri, Achille. "Il 'catechismo' e la *Fidei et Doctrinae . . . Ratio* di Bartolomeo Fonzio, eretico veneziano del Cinquecento." *Studi Veneziani* 9 (1967): 339–59.

———. "Fra collettività urbane e rurali e 'colonie' mediterranee: L''eresia' a Venezia." In *Storia della cultura veneta: Dal primo Quattrocento al Concilio di Trento*, edited by Girolamo Arnaldi and Manilio Pastore Stocchi, 3/III:467–512. Vicenza: Neri Pozza Editore, 1981.

———. "Un momento della sensibilità religiosa e culturale del Cinquecento veneziano: 'I diarii di Girolamo Priuli e gli orizzonti della esperientia.'" *Critica Storica* 3 (1973): 397–414.

———, ed. *Eresie, magia, società nel Polesine tra '500 e '600*. Rovigo: Associazione Culturale Minelliana, 1989.

O'Malley, John W., S.J. *The First Jesuits*. Cambridge, Mass.: Harvard University Press, 1993.

———. *Ignatius Loyola*. Cambridge, Mass.: Harvard University Press, 1994.

———. *Religious Culture in the Sixteenth Century: Preaching, Rhetoric, Spirituality, and Reform.* Aldershot: Ashgate Publishing, Variorum, 1993.

Onda, Silvano. "Stato delle fonti e ricerca storica sull'estetica gioachimita e l'iconografia marciana." In *San Marco: Aspetti storici e agiografici*, edited by Antonio Niero, 568–84. Venice: Marsilio Editori, 1996.

Opere di M. Givlio Camillo. . . . Venice: Gabriel Giolito de' Ferrari, 1560.

Oracolo della renouatione della chiesa secondo la dottrina del Reverendo Padre Frate Hieronimo Savonarola da Ferrara . . . per lui predicata in Firenze. Venice: Casa di Pietro de Nicolini da Sabio, 1536.

Oratio de circumcisione dominica Magistri Petri Galatini. N.p., 1515.

Orazione de M. Gio. Battista Adriani fatta in Latino all'esseqvie del sereniss. Cosimo de' Medici Gran Duca di Toscana. Florence: Giunti, 1574.

Ortolani, Oddone. *Pietro Carnesecchi.* Florence: Felice Le Monnier, 1963.

Il Palazzo Ducale di Venezia da Francesco Zanotto. Venice, 1840.

Palm, Franklin Charles. *Politics and Religion in Sixteenth-Century France.* New York: Ginn & Co., 1927.

Panella, Antonio. "L'introduzione a Firenze dell'Indice di Paolo IV." *Rivista Storica degli Archivi Toscani* 1 (1929): 11–25.

Papadopoli, Nicolai Commeni. *Historia Gymnasii Patavini.* Venice: Sebastianus Coleti, 1726.

Partner, Peter. "Appunti sulla riforma della curia romana." In *Libri, idee e sentimenti religiosi nel Cinquecento italiano*, edited by Rolando Bussi. Modena: Edizioni Panini, 1986.

Paschini, Pio. "Un umanista disgraziato nel Cinquecento." *Nuovo Archivio Veneto*, n.s., anno XX, 37 (1919): 65–186.

———. *Venezia e l'Inquisizione romana da Giulio III a Pio IV.* Padua: Editrice Antenore, 1959.

Pecchioli, Renzo. "Il 'mito' di Venezia e la crisi fiorentina intorno al 1500." *Studi Storici* 3 (1962): 452–92.

P. Francisci Spinulae Mediolanensis Opera. Venetiis (Venice): Ex officina stellae Jordani Zileti, 1563.

La piazza universale di tutte le professioni del mondo, nvovamente ristampata . . . da Thomaso Garzoni da Bagnacauallo. . . . Venice: Vincenzo Somasco, 1595.

Pierozzi, Letizia. "La vittoria di Lepanto nell'escatologia e nella profezia." *Rinascimento*, 2d ser., 34 (1994): 317–63.

Pincus, Debra. *The Arco Foscari: The Building of a Triumphal Gateway in Fifteenth-Century Venice.* New York: Garland Publishing, 1976.

Pocock, J. G. A. *The Machiavellian Moment: Florentine Political Thought and the Atlantic Republican Tradition.* Princeton, N.J.: Princeton University Press, 1975.

Pommier, Edouard. "La société vénitienne et la reforme protestante au XVI siècle." *Studi Veneziani* 1 (1959): 3–26.

Postel, Guillaume. *De Etruriae regionis . . . originibus.* . . . Edited by Giovanni Cipriani. Rome: Consiglio Nazionale delle Ricerche, 1986.

———. *Il libro della divina ordinatione.* Padua, 1555.

———. *Le prime nove del altro mondo.* Padua, 1555.

———. *Le thrésor des prophéties de l'univers.* With an introduction and notes by François Secret. The Hague: Martinus Nijhoff, 1969.

Prediche di Fra Girolamo da Farrara sopra Ezechiel. Venice: Zuan Antonio di Volpini da Castel Giuffredo, 1541.

Pressacco, Gilberto. "Marco 'Christianus et Medicus.'" In *San Marco: Aspetti storici e agiografici,* edited by Antonio Niero, 647–84. Venice: Marsilio Editori, 1996.

Preto, Paolo. "Baiamonte Tiepolo: Traditore della patria o eroe e martire della libertà?" In *Continuità-discontinuità nella storia politica economica e religiosa: Studi in onore di Aldo Stella,* edited by Giovanni Silvano and Paolo Pecorari, 217–64. Vicenza: Neri Pozza Editore, 1993.

Problemi di vita religiosa in Italia nel Cinquecento: Atti del convegno di storia della chiesa in Italia. Padua: Antenore, 1960.

Prodi, Paolo. "The Structure and Organization of the Church in Renaissance Venice: Suggestions for Research." In *Renaissance Venice,* edited by J. R. Hale, 409–30. Totowa, N.J.: Rowman & Littlefield, 1973.

Profezie politiche e religiose di Fra Hieronymo ricavate dalle quelle prediche de Messer Francesco de Guicciardini l'historico. Florence: M. Cellini e Compagni, 1763.

Prophecy and Millenarianism: Essays in Honour of Marjorie Reeves. Edited by Ann Williams. Essex: Longman, 1980.

Prosperi, Adriano. "Una cripto-ristampa dell'Epistola di Giorgio Siculo." *Bollettino della Società di Studi Valdesi* 134 (December 1973): 52–68.

———. "Dalle 'divine madri' ai padri spirituali." In *Women and Men in Spiritual Culture XIV–XVII,* edited by Elisja Schulte Van Kessell. The Hague: Martinus Nijhoff, 1986.

———. "Un gruppo ereticale italo-spagnolo: La setta di Giorgio Siculo (secondo nuovi documenti)." *Critica Storica* 19 (1982): 335–51.

———. "L'Inquisizione: Verso una nuova immagine?" *Critica Storica* 25 (1988): 119–45.

———. "Intorno a un catechismo figurato del tardo '500." In *Von der Macht der Bilder: Beiträge des C.I.H.A.—Kolloquiums "Kunst und Reformation,"* edited by Ernst Ullman. Leipzig: E. A. Seeman; Karl-Marx Universität, 1983.

———. "Le istituzioni ecclesiastiche e le idee religiose." In *Il Rinascimento nelle corti padane: Società e cultura.* Bari: De Donato Editori, 1977.

———. "Opere inedite o sconosciute di Giorgio Siculo." *Bibliofilia* 87 (1985): 137–57.

Pugliese, Olga Z. "Apocalyptic and Dantesque Elements in a Franciscan Prophecy of the Renaissance." *Proceedings of the PMR Conference* 10 (1987): 127–35.

Pullan, Brian. *The Jews of Europe and the Inquisition of Venice, 1550–1670.* Totowa, N.J.: Rowman & Littlefield, 1983.

———. "The Occupations and Investments of the Venetian Nobility in the Middle and Late Sixteenth Century." In *Renaissance Venice,* edited by J. R. Hale, 379–408. Totowa, N.J.: Rowman & Littlefield, 1973.

---. "Poverty, Charity, and the Reason of State: Some Venetian Examples." In *Bollettino di Storia della Società, e dello Stato* 2 (Venice: Fondazione Giorgio Cini, Centro di Cultura e Civiltà, 1960).

---. *Poverty and Charity: Europe, Italy, Venice, 1400–1700.* Variorum Series. Aldershot: Ashgate Publishers, 1994.

---. *Rich and Poor in Renaissance Venice: The Social Institutions of a Catholic State to 1620.* Cambridge, Mass.: Harvard University Press, 1971.

---. "Service to the Venetian State: Aspects of Myth and Reality in the Early Seventeenth Century." *Studi Secenteschi* 5 (1964): 95–148.

Quazza, Romolo. "Alfonso II of Ferrara." In *Dizionario biografico degli italiani*, II:337–41. Rome: Istituto di Enciclopedia Italiana, Trecanni, 1960.

Queller, Donald E. *The Venetian Patriciate: Reality Versus Myth.* Urbana: University of Illinois Press, 1986.

Radetti, Giorgio. "Riformatori ed eretici italiani del secolo XVI." *Giornale Critico della Filosofia Italiana* 31 (1940): 13–24.

Raffaelli, Renato. "Notizie intorno a Francesco Severi 'il medico d'Argenta.'" *Studi Urbinati* 56/B3 (1983): 91–136.

Reeves, Marjorie. *The Influence of Prophecy in the Later Middle Ages: A Study of Joachimism.* Oxford: Oxford University Press, 1969.

---, ed. *Prophetic Rome in the High Renaissance Period.* Oxford: Clarendon Press, 1992.

Relations des Ambassadeurs Vénitiens sur les affaires de France au XVIe siècle. Edited and translated by M. N. Tommaseo. Paris: Imprimerie royale, 1838.

Le relazioni degli ambasciatori veneti al Senato durante il secolo decimosesto. Edited by Eugenio Alberi. Florence: Società Editrice Fiorentina, 1857.

Revelationes celestes preelecte sponse Christi beate Birgitte vidue de regno Suecie octo libris diuise. . . . Rome: Officiana Federici Peypus, 1517.

Reverendi P. Fra Hieronymi Sauonarolę in primam D. Ioannis epistolam et in alia sacrę scripturę verba . . . . Venetiis (Venice): Officina Domini Bernardini Stagnini, 1536.

Rezasco, Giulio. *Dizionario del linguaggio italiano storico ed amministrativo.* Florence: Forni Editore, 1881. Reprint, Bologna, 1982.

Rice, Eugene F., Jr., ed. *The Prefatory Epistles of Jacques Lefèvre d'Etaples and Related Texts.* New York: Columbia University Press, 1972.

Rodocanachi, E. *Renée de France: Duchesse de Ferrare.* Paris: Ollendorff, 1896.

Roellenbleck, Georg. *Venezia scena dell'ultimo dialogo umanista: L'Heptaplomeres di Jean Bodin (ca. 1590).* Quaderni 29. Venice: Centro Tedesco di Studi Veneziani, 1984.

Romanin, S. *Storia documentata di Venezia.* 3d ed. Venice: Libreria Filippi Editore, 1973.

Romano, Dennis. "The Aftermath of the Querini-Tiepolo Conspiracy in Venice." *Stanford Italian Review* (1987): 147–59.

---. *Patricians and Popolani: The Social Foundations of the Venetian Renaissance State.* Baltimore, Md.: Johns Hopkins University Press, 1987.

Rosand, David. "Venetia Figurata: The Iconography of a Myth." In *Interpretazioni veneziane*, edited by David Rosand. Venice: Arsenale Editrice, 1984.

Ross, James Bruce. "Venetian Schools and Teachers, Fourteenth to Early Sixteenth Century: A Survey and Study of Giovanni Battista Egnazio." *Renaissance Quarterly* 29 (1976): 521–57.

Rotondò, Antonio. "Jacopo Brocardo." In *Dizionario biografico degli italiani*, XIV:384–89. Rome: Istituto della Enciclopedia Italiana, 1972.

———. "Pietro Carnesecchi." In *Dizionario biografico degli italiani*, XX:466–76. Rome: Istituto della Enciclopedia Italiana, 1984.

———. "La ricerca storica. . . ." *Critica Storica*, n.s., anno X (March 1973).

———. *Studi e ricerche di storia ereticale italiana del Cinquecento*. Torino: Edizioni Giappichelli.

Rubinstein, Nicolai. "Italian Reactions to Terraferma Expansion in the Fifteenth Century." In *Renaissance Venice*, edited by J. R. Hale. Totowa, N.J.: Rowman & Littlefield, 1973.

Ruggiero, Guido. *The Boundaries of Eros: Sex, Crime, and Sexuality in Renaissance Venice*. New York: Oxford University Press, 1985.

Rusconi, Robert. "An Angelic Pope Before the Sack of Rome." In *Prophetic Rome in the High Renaissance Period*, edited by Marjorie Reeves. Oxford: Clarendon Press, 1992.

La Sacra Bibbia commentata dal P. Marco M. Sales O. P.: Il nuovo testamento: Le lettere degli Apostoli—L'Apocalisse. Turin: Tipografia Pontifica, 1914.

Salmon, J. H. M. *Society in Crisis: France in the Sixteen Century*. London: Ernest Benn, 1975.

Salon, Paul. "Tax Commissions and Public Opinion: Languedoc, 1438–1561." *Renaissance Quarterly* 43, no. 3 (1990): 479–508.

San Giralamo Miani e Venezia nel V° centenario della nascitad. Venice: La Tipo-Litografia Armena per conto dell'IRE, 1986.

Sansovino, Francesco. *Delle cose notabili che sono in Venetia in Venetio per Comin da Trino di Monferrato*. N.p., 1561.

Sanudo, Marino. *I diarii di Marino Sanuto*. Venice: N. Barazzi, 1879–1902.

Savonarola, Girolamo. *Prediche del Rev. Padre Fra Hieronymo Sauonarola dell'ordine de predicatori sopra alquanti salmi et sopra Aggeo Profeta. . . .* Venice: Bernardino de Bindoni Milanese, 1544.

Scarabello, Giovanni. *Carcerati e carceri a Venezia nell'età moderna*. Rome: Istituto della Enciclopedia Italiana, 1979.

Scholem, Gershom. *The Messianic Idea in Judaism and Other Essays on Jewish Spirituality*. New York: Schocken Books, 1971.

Schutte, Anne Jacobson. *Pier Paolo Vergerio: The Making of an Italian Reformer*. Geneva: Librarie Droz, 1977.

———. "Uno spazio, tre poteri: La cappella di San Teodoro, sede dell'Inquisizione veneziana." In *San Marco: Aspetti storici e agiografici*, edited by Antonio Niero, 97–109. Venice: Marsilio Editori, 1996.

Screech, Michael Andrew. *Clément Marot*. Leiden: E. J. Brill, 1994.

Secret, François. "Une lettre retrouvée de G. Postel au Grand Prieur de France." *Bibliothèque d'Humanisme et Renaissance* 30 (1968): 142.

Segre, Arturo. "Emanuele Filiberto e la Repubblica di Venezia (1545–1580)." In *Deputazione veneta di storia patria*, Miscellanea, 2d ser., 7:65–507. Venice, 1901.
Seidel-Menchi, Silvana. "Alcuni atteggiamenti della cultura italiana di fronte a Erasmo." In *Eresia e riforma nell'Italia del Cinquecento*, Biblioteca del "Corpus Reformatorum Italicorum," Miscellanea 1. Chicago: Newberry Library, 1974.
———. *Erasmo in Italia 1520–1580*. Turin: Bollati Boringhieri, 1987.
———. "Inquisizione come repressione o inquisizione come mediazione?" *Annuario dell'Istituto Storico Italiana* 35/36 (1983/84): 53–77.
———. "Protestantesimo a Venezia." In *La Chiesa di Venezia tra riforma protestante e riforma cattolica*, edited by Giuseppe Gullino, 131–54. Venice: Edizioni Studium Cattolico, 1990.
Sequitur libellus qui intitulatur Onus mundi id est prophetia de malo futuro ipsi mundo superuenturo. Rome: Eucharius Franck, 1485.
Sforza, Giovanni. "Riflessi della controriforma nella Repubblica di Venezia." *Archivio Storico Italiano* 1 (1935): 5–216, and 2 (1935): 25–52, 173–86.
Simoncelli, Paolo. "Clemente VIII e alcuni provvedimenti del Sant'Uffizio." *Critica Storica* 13, no. 1 (1976): 129–72.
———. "Il 'Dialogo dell'unione spirituale di Dio con l'anima' tra alumbradismo spagnolo e prequietismo italiano." *Annuario dell'Istituto Storico Italiano per l'Età Moderna e Contemporanea* 29–30 (1977–78): 565–601.
———. "Diplomazia e politica religiosa nella Chiesa della controriforma." *Rivista di Storia e Letteratura Religiosa* 19, no. 3 (1982): 415–60.
———. "Documenti interni alla Congregazione dell'Indice 1571–1590: Logica e ideologia dell'intervento censorio." *Annuario dell'Istituto Storico Italiano per l'Età Moderna e Contemporanea* 35–36 (1983–84): 189–215.
———. "In margine a una edizione di scritti ochiniani." *Critica Storica* 22, no. 4 (1985): 439–48.
———. "Inquisizione romana e riforma in Italia." *Rivista Storica Italiana*, anno C, fasc. 1 (1988): 53–60.
———. *La lingua d'Adamo*. Florence: Leo S. Olschki Editore, 1984.
———. "Momenti e figure del savonarolismo romano." *Critica Storica*, n.s., 1, 11 (1974): 47–82.
———. "Pietro Bembo e l'evangelismo italiano." *Critica Storica*, 15, no.1 (1978): 1–63.
Soranzo, Giovanni. "La riforma cattolica dapo il Concilio di Trento." Paper presented at the conference commemorating the fourth centennial of the Council of Trent, Università cattolica del Sacro Cuore, March 20, 1946.
Spini, Giorgio. "Introduzione al Savonarola." *Belfagor* 3 (1948): 414–28.
Stabile, G. "Camillo, Giulio, detto Delminio." In *Dizionario biografico degli italiani*, XVII:218–30. Rome: Istituto della Enciclopedia Italiana, 1974.
Stella, Aldo. *Anabattismo e antitrinitarismo in Italia nel XVI secolo*. Padua: Liviana Editrice, 1969.
———. *Chiesa e lo stato nelle relazioni dei nunzi pontifici a Venezia*. Studi e Testi, 239. Vatican City: Biblioteca Apostolica Vaticana, 1964. Facsimile reprint, Modena: Dint, 1981.

———. *Dall'anabattismo al socinianesimo nel Cinquento veneto.* Padova: Liviana Editrice, 1967.
———. *Dall'anabattismo veneto al "Sozialevangelismus" dei fratelli Hutteriti e all'illuminismo religioso sociniano.* Rome: Herder Editrice e Libreria, 1966.
———. *Il "Bauernfühere" Michale Gaismair e l'utopia di repubblicanesimo popolare.* Bologna: Società Editrice il Mulino, 1999.
———. "L'ecclesiologia degli anabattisti processati a Trieste nel 1540." In *Eresia e riforma nell'Italia del Cinquecento*, Biblioteca del "Corpus Reformatorum Italicorum," Miscellanea I. Chicago: Newberry Library, 1974.
———. "Guido da Fano eretico del secolo XVI al servizio dei re d'Inghilterra." *Rivista di Storia della Chiesa in Italia* 13 (1959): 196–238.
———. "La lettera del cardinale Contarini sulla predestinazione." *Rivista di Storia della Chiesa in Italia* 15, no. 3 (1961): 411–41.
———. "Movimenti di riforma nel Veneto nel Cinquecento." In *Storia della cultura veneta dalla controriforma alla fine della repubblica: Il Seicento*, 4/1:1–21. Vicenza: Neri Pozza Editore, 1983.
———. *L'orazione di Pier Paolo Vergerio al doge Francesco Donà sulla riforma della Chiesa (1545)." Atti dell'Istituto Veneto di Scienze, Lettere ed Arti: Classe di Scienze Morali, Lettere ed Arte* 128 (1970): 1–39.
———. "Origini patavine e sviluppi polacchi dell'illuminismo religioso sociniano." In *La nascita dell'Europa per una storia delle idee fra Italia e Polonia*, edited by Sante Graciotti, 231–56. Florence: Leo S. Olschki Editore, 1995.
———. "Il processo veneziano di Guglielmo Postel." *Rivista di Storia della Chiesa in Italia* 22, no. 2 (1968): 425–66.
———. "Tradizione razionalistica patavina e radicalismo spiritualistico nel XVI secolo." *Annali della R. Scuola Normale Superiore di Pisa* 37 (1968): 275–302.
———. "Utopie e velleità insurrezionali dei filoprotestanti italiani (1545–1547)." *Bibliothèque d'Humanisme et Renaissance* 27 (1965): 133–82.
Storia di Padova dalla sua origine sino al presente dal Cavaliere RR Guiseppe Cappelletti. Padua, 1875.
Stoyanova, Magdalena. "La preistoria ed i mosaici del battistero di San Marco." *Atti dell'Istituto Veneto di Scienze, Lettere ed Arti: Classe di Scienze Morali, Lettere ed Arti* 147 (1989): 17–28.
Sutherland, N. M. *Princes, Politics, and Religion, 1547–1589.* London: Hambledon Press, 1984.
Tafuri, Manfredo. *Venezia e il Rinascimento: Religione, scienza, architettura.* Turin: Giulio Einaudi Editore, 1985.
Tassini, Giuseppe. *Curiosità veneziane.* 9th ed. Venice: Filippi Editore, 1988.
Taylor, Larissa. *Soldiers of Christ: Preaching in Late Medieval and Reformation France.* Oxford: Oxford University Press, 1992.
Tenenti, Alberto. "The Sense of Space and Time in the Venetian World." In *Renaissance Venice*, edited by J. R. Hale. Totowa, N.J.: Rowman & Littlefield, 1973.
Thompson, James Westfall. *The Wars of Religion in France, 1559–1576: The Huguenots, Catherine de Medicis, Philip II.* New York: Frederick Ungar Publishing Co., 1957.

Totius Latinitatis Lexicon consilio et cura Jacobi Facciolati, opera et studio Aegidii Forcellini. Patavii (Padua): Typis Seminarii, apud Thomas Bettinelli, 1805.

Tramontin, Silvio. "Il *De officio episcopi* di Gasparo Contarini." *Studia Patavina* 12 (1965): 292–303.

———. *Pagine di santi veneziani: Antologia*. Brescia, 1968.

———. "Un programma di riforma della Chiesa per il concilio lateranense v: Il Libellus ad Leonem x dei veneziani Paolo Giustiniani e Pietro Querini." In *Venezia e i concili*. Venice: Leo S. Olschki Editore, 1962.

———. "Lo spirito, le attività, gli sviluppi dell'Oratorio del Divino Amore nella Venezia del Cinquecento." *Studi Veneziani* 14 (1972): 111–36.

———. "I Teatini e l'Oratorio del Divino Amore a Venezia." In *Regnum Dei*, 1–24. Venice, 1973.

———. *Venezia e Lorenzo Giustiniani*. Venice: Comune di Venezia, 1981.

Trattato della reuelatione della reformatione della Chiesa diuinitus fatte dal Reuerendo et deuotissimo padre F. Hieronimo da Ferrara de l'ordine de frati predicatori. Venice: M. Bernandino Stagnino, 1536.

Trebbi, Giuseppe. "Venezia tra '500 e '600 nell'opera storica di Andrea Morosini." *Studi Veneziani*, n.s., 25 (1993): 73–129.

Ulvioni, Paolo. "Cultura politica e cultura religiosa a Venezia nel secondo Cinquecento: Un bilancio." *Archivio Storica Italiano* 14 (1983): 591–651.

Vasoli, Cesare. *Filosofia e religione nella cultura del Rinascimento*. Naples: Guida Editori, 1988.

———. *La cultura delle corti*. Bologna: Nuova Casa Editrice L. Caleppi, 1980.

———. "Giorgio Benigno Salviati" (Dragisic). In *Prophetic Rome in the High Renaissance Period*, edited by Majorie Reeves, 121–56. Oxford: Clarendon Press, 1992.

———. *Immagini umanistiche*. Naples: Morano Editore, 1983.

———. "Lucio Paolo Rosello e un'immagine cinquecentesca del principe." *Nuova Rivista Storica* 65 (1981): 552–71.

———. *Profezia e ragione: Studi sulla cultura del Cinquecento e del Seicento*. Naples: Casa Editrice A. Morano, 1974.

———. "Uno scritto inedito di Giulio Camillo 'De l'humana deificatione.'" *Rinascimento* 24 (1984): 191–227.

Vaticinia siue prophetiae Abbatis Ioachini. Venetiis (Venice): Hieronymum Porrum, 1589.

Vecellio, Cesare. *De gli habiti antichi et moderni di diuerse parti del mondo. . . .* Venice: Damian Zenaro, 1590.

Venetia città nobilissima, et singolare, descritta già in XIIII libri da M. Francesco Sansovino et hora con molta diligenza corretta . . . da M.R.D. Giovanni Stringa. . . . Venice: Altobello Salicato, 1604.

Venice: A Documentary History, 1450–1630. Edited by David Chambers and Brian Pullan. Oxford: Blackwell Publishers, 1992.

Il vero et vniversale Giuditio di M. Michiele Nostradamo, Astrologo Eccell. et Medico di Solon di Craus di Prouenza, nel quale si vede breuemente quanto mostrano le stelle, et pianeti di mese in mese, et di quarto in quarto dell'anno 1566. . . . N.p., 1566.

Villardi, Pasquale. *La storia di Girolamo Savonarola e de' suoi tempi*. Vols. 1–2. Florence: Felice Le Monnier, 1861.

Vitali, Achille. *La moda a Venezia attraverso i secoli.* Venice: Filippi Editore, 1992.
Vives, Juan Luis. *Il modo del sovvenire a poveri di Lodovico Vives novamente tradotto di Latino in volgare.* . . . Venice: Curtio Troiano de i Nauò, 1545.
Volpato, Antonio. "La predicazione penitenziale apocalittica nell'attività di due predicatori del 1473." *Bollettino dell'Istituto Storico Italiano* 82 (1967): 113–28.
Weinstein, Donald. *Savonarola and Florence: Prophecy and Patriotism in the Renaissance.* Princeton, N.J.: Princeton University Press, 1970.
West, Delno C., Jr. "The Education of Fra Salimbene of Parma: The Joachite Influence." In *The Influence of Prophecy in the Later Middle Ages: A Study of Joachimism,* by Marjorie Reeves, 193–215. Oxford: Oxford University Press, 1969.
Williams, George Huntston. *The Radical Reformation.* 3d ed. Kirksville, Mo.: Sixteenth Century Journal Publishers, 1992.
Wisson, Robert R. "Biblical Prophecy." In *Encyclopedia of Religion,* vol. 12, edited by Mircea Eliade. New York: Macmillan, 1987.
Wolters, Wolfgang. *Storia e politica nei dipinti di Palazzo Ducale . . . : Aspetti dell'autocelebrazione della Repubblica di Venezia nel Cinquecento.* Translated by Benedetta Heinemann Campana. Venice: Arsenal Editrice, 1987.
Zarri, Gabriella. "Pietà e profezia alle corti padane: Le pie consiglieri dei principi." In *Il Rinascimento nelle corti padane: Società e cultura,* edited by Paolo Rossi. Bari: De Donato Editori, 1977.
———. "Le sante vive: Per una tipologia della santità femminile nel primo Cinquecento." *Annali dell'Istituto Storico Italo-Germanico in Trento* 6 (1980): 371–445.
———. *Le sante vive: Profezie di corte e devozione femminile tra '400 e '500.* Turin: Rosenberg & Sellier, 1990.
Zorzi, Alvise. *Venetian Palaces.* New York: Rizzoli, 1989.

INDEX

Aaron, 211
Abbas Joachim, magnus propheta, 216
Abraham, patriarch, 117, 230
abuses, and the pope, 20
Adam, 232
age of the Spirit, and angelic pope, 205
Agen, league in, 90
Aix-en-Provence, painter of, 154
Albus, Martinus, French priest, acquaintance of Dionisio, 174
Alexandria, and San Marco, 2
Alfonso II, duke of Ferrara, xiv, 41, 46, 77, 87, 92, 234–41, 246
    affection for Henry II, king of France, 88
    Cosimo I, 88
    Dionisio, 94
    marriage to Barbara of Austria, 87–88
    return from Vienna, 88
Allardet, bishop, 40
Altano, Antonio, conte di Salvarolo, 120
Amboise, conspiracy of, 10–11, 32
Amyot, Jacques, 10
Anabaptists, Hutterite, 27, 102
    fear of, in Venice, 153–54
Andreas Gostiath Polonus (Andreas Ctostinto Polonus), rector of *artistarum*, Studio of Padua, 148
Angrogna, valley of, 36
Annius of Viterbo, forgeries of, 69
anointment of Dionisio, 7, 45, 64, 74, 92, 95, 234–35
    divine, 205, 243
    double, 240
Antichrist
    binding of, 75
    concept of in Joachim, 109

    and truth and reason, 75, 242
Antoine de Bourbon, King of Navarre, 12
Antremon, count of, 42
Apocalypois nova, 70
Apocalypse, 44, 194
    borrowings from, 213
    and charioteer, 211
    commentary on, 109, 195
    influence on Dionisio, 210
    interpretation of, by Dionisio, 81–82
    and Joachim, 111
    messianic associations of, 227–28
    and prophecy, 23, 130
    and prophetic mosaics in Basilica of San Marco, 114
A Principi Christiani, poem of F. Sansovino, 59
Aquileia, 250
Archives de l'Eure, 7
Archinto, Filippo, 189
Areopagitica, Dionisius, 227
Aristotle, 120
artisans, in Venice, 213
Astrologia divinativa, 39
attire, of Dionisio Gallo, as "king of the Gauls," 18
Augustine, Saint, 55, 127
Augustinus, Martinis de, fra, 156
Aurelio, fra, 143, 145
auriga Ecclesiae militantis, and Dionisio, xvi, 211, 256
avarice, sins of, 207

banca, in cortile of Palazzo Ducale, 1, 3
Barbara, of Austria, sister of emperor Maximilian, wife of Alfonso II, 87
Barbaro, Francesco, 102

Bartholomew, Saint, massacre of, 43
Basilica di San Marco, xvi, 2, 5–6, 49,
    67, 151–52, 157
  and Dionisio, 149, 263 n. 11
  mosaics of, 44, 111, 257
Basilica of Saint Peter, 49, 55, 63
  choir of, 56
Bayonne, 237
Bellarmino, Roberto, 37
Belloebono, Decio, physician, 180
Bembo, Pieto, bishop of Veglia,
    Council of Trent, and abuses of
    Church, 53
Benedetto, il corazzaro. *See* Corazzaro,
    Benedetto
ben vivere, 61
Benzoni, Gino, 107, 261 n. 12
Bern, 47
Bernardo, Francesco, 121
Beza, Theodore, 169
  and Renée of France, 88
bishops, proper role of, 169
Bockelson, Jan, "king of Sion," 26
Bodin, Jean, 241, 251
Boldù, Andrea, ambassador of Venice,
    in Savoy, 35–36, 39, 41
Bollani, Iseppo, Venetian nobleman,
    179, 203
Bonaventura, fra, and book of prophecies, 100
Bonelli, Michele, Cardinal
    Alessandrino, 60, 183–84
Bordeaux, 16, 47
Borgia, Hieronimo, 106
Borromeo, Carlo, cardinal, 194
Bosra, 195–96, 229, 254
Bourbon, family of, 11–12
Brescia, 54
  Inquisition of, 137
  and Francesco Spinola, 178
Bressan, Bartholomeo de, lawyer, husband of Anzola de Mazzochis, 143
Bridget, Saint, 22, 25–26, 53, 63, 65, 67,
    70, 98, 216, 235–38
  and apocalyptic thought, 213
Brisegno, Bernardo, papal nuncio,
    Florence, 82, 87, 153
  and imprisonment of Dionisio, 82–83
  rage against Dionisio, 85
Brocardo, Giacomo, humanist, 119, 131,
    133, 243–51
  escape to France, 126
  Interpretatio et paraphrases libri Apocalipseos, 124
  maestro di schola, 120
  millenarian ideas, 122
  prophecy, 120–26, 245
  translator of *De arte rhetorica*, 120
  and vision, 135
Brotherhood of Catholics, in France, 90
brotherhood, universal, 21
Brucioli, Antonio, 56

Cabala, 123
Cabalism, messianic idea in, 230
Ca'Corner, San Samuele in Corte della
    Vida, residence of Rocho de
    Mazzochis, 144
Calais, 90
Callegher, Alessandro, 127
Callegher, Domenego, artisan, 127–29,
    132–33
Calvinism, 91
  toleration of, 90
Calvinists
  and danger to Venice. *See* Venice
  threat of to Savoy, 40
Calvin, John, 169, 235
  and emphasis on language study, 220
  Renée of France, 88
Cambiano, Cesare, count, 39
Cambrai, League of, 104, 109
Camillo, Giulio, 119–20
  and renewal of spiritual life, 123

La Idea del Theatro, Sermoni, and *De l'humana dieficatione,* 123
Campegio, Camillo de, inquisitor of Ferrara, 136
Canale, Marc'Antonio da, Venetian nobleman and religious reformer, 146
Canisius, Peter, 220
Cantimori, Delio, 20, 100
Capella di San Clemente, and inscription about justice, 2
Capi del Consiglio dei Dieci, 87
   and Postel, 118
   prisons of, 163–64
Capoville, Giovanni, 300 n. 28
Captus in mente, 70
Capuchins, order of, 38
Carcassonne, 16, 47
cardinals, lavish lives of, 61, 76
Carion, Ioannes, 123, 216
caritas, 241
Carlo II, duke of Savoy, 37
Carmen seculare . . . , poetry of F. Spinola, 180
Carnesecchi, Pietro, 21, 73, 119–20, 126, 170, 243
   extradition to Rome, 83–84
Carthusians, order of, in Mondovì, 38
Cassander, George, 12
Castellio, Sebastian, Franciscan conventual, 100–101
Cataldus, 216
Cataneus, P., 216–17
Catherine de'Medici, 16, 32, 71, 88, 90, 223, 237–38, 298 n. 18
   and action against league of Montluc and Philip II, 91
   Calvinists pastors, 12
   Dionisio's opinion of, 79
   and fear of Spain, 12
   prophecy, 14, 28
   reform of judicial system, 221
Catherine of Sienna, 67
Catiline. *See* Tiepolo, Baiamonte

Catullus, imitation of, by Spinola, 178
Cemonti, Leonardo, dom, translator of Egnazio, 108
Centani (Zantani) Andriana, first wife of Rocho de Mazzochis, 143–44
Cercam, treaty of, 47
Cervini, Marcello, cardinal, 19
Chambéry, college of 37, 39
Chapel of Saint Theodore, 163, 175
   meetings of Inquisition in, 154
Chapel, Sistine, 27
charity, acts of, and Christianity, 64
   practice of and pardon, 220
Charles VIII, king of France, 22, 103
   and San Francesco di Paolo, 28
Charles IX, king of France, xiv, xvii, 28, 33–35, 64, 90, 221–22, 237, 249–50
   and Dionisio Gallo, 15–16
   "divided" kingdom, 13
   tour of his kingdom, 12, 237
Châtillon, cardinal of, 88
Cherubino, fra, 141
Chieri, 47
Chivasso, 47
Christ, and Edom, 231–33
   the poor, 76, 241
   fool for, and Dionisio, 155
   second coming of, *intra nos,* 233
Christianity, travails of, 93
Christo cooperante, and Dionisio, 75
Chronica, of Carion, 123
Chronicle, Franciscan, 162
Church
   birth pangs of, 129
   causes of divisions in, 226
   corruption of, 30, 191
   crisis in, 80
   criticism of, by Dionisio and Protestants, 78
   and property, 91, 165–68
   purification of, and universal brotherhood, 48
   reform of, 21, 78, 102, 194, 225; and

Church (cont'd)
  norms of priests, 219; Venetian artisans, 130
  restoration under standard of Saint Mark, 253
  return to practices of primitive Church, 54
  role in regard to poor, 167
  sickness of, 51, 53
  temporal dominion of, 166
Churches (Venice)
  Anzolo Raffaelo, 127
  Santa Maria dei Carmini, 127
  Santa Maria dei Miracoli, 99, 118
  Santa Maria della Visitazione, 99
  Santa Maria Formosa, 102
  Santa Maria Maggiore, 127
  Santa Spirito, 151
  San Teodoro, 2
  San Zuane di Rialto, 156
  Venetian and dedication to saints and prophets of Old Testament, 99
Cicogna, Gerolamo, podestà of Padua, 148–49
Cimador, Luanardo, artisan, 127–29, 131
circumcision, of the heart, 22
Cittolini, Alessandro, 119
Clario, Giovanni, Battista, 137
Clement VII, pope, 27
clergy, abuses of, 78
  and cause of errors, 78–79, 235
  dismissal of wicked, 225
  impiety of, and apostasy of F. Spinola, 181–82
  moral laxity of, 242
  reform of, 193
clothing, and prophetic persona of Dionisio, 238
Coligny, Gaspard de, admiral of France, 12, 33, 42–43
Collège de Lisieux, xiii, xiv, 32, 79, 147, 241

College of Cardinals, and Pius IV, 50
College, of Lombards, 28
college, trilingual, 220
Collegio Romano, 37
Colonna, Vittoria, 170
Como, 177
concord, universal, 119
Concordat of Bologna, 215
Condé, Louis de Bourbon, prince de, 32
  and payments to preachers, 173, 179, 206
congregatio, and *Ecclesia*, 167
Consiglio dei Dieci (Council of Ten), xvii
  and advice to Venetians, 150
  Capi of, 42
  prisons of, 121, 138, 154, 225
Contarini, Gasparo, 107, 169–70
  and *Consilium de emendanda ecclesia*, 19–20
  De magistratibus et republica venetorum, 107
  De officio episcopi, 19–20, 107
  reform of the pope, 20
Contarini, Giulio, 263 n. 24
Contarini, Pierofrancesco, patriarch of Venice, 55
conventicles, and young Venetian patricians, 146
conversion, of all unfaithful, priority of, 226
Cordoni, Bartolomeo, Franciscan, and *Dialogo dell'unione, spirituale di Dio . . .* , 162
Corner (Cornaro)
  Carlo, Venetian nobleman, and religious reform, 146
  Giorgio, bishop designate of Treviso, 120
  Paolo, Venetian nobleman, 159, 172, 176, 178, 197–98, 246, 263 n. 25; and *Tre Savi sopra Eresia*, 54
  Zuan, Venetian patrician, and ambassador to Savoy, 36, 120

Corazzaro, Benedetto, 126–28, 130, 251
and millenarian ideas, 213
prophetic interpretations of mosaics in Basilica di San Marco, 11, 246
Corregio, Giovanni da, as Enoch, 21
cortile, of Palazzo Ducale, as sacred space, 4
Cosenza, 28
Cosimo I de'Medici, duke of Florence, xiv, 58, 70, 75–76, 96, 246, 249–50, 296 n. 3, 299 n. 26
and advice to son, Francesco, 71–72
challenges of Dionisio, 82
change in character, 73
grand duke of Tuscany (1569), 73
extradition of Carnesecchi, P. to Rome, 73
leadership among Italian princes, 68
league of princes, 92
Legatio of Dionisio, 93
political ambitions, 68–69
Council, Fifth Lateran (1512–17), 22
Council, Royal, of France, 94
Council of Trent, xiii, xviii, 18, 25, 40–41, 49–52, 79, 90, 127, 137, 139, 161, 180–81, 219, 236
opinion of Dionisio, 86, 151, 246
opinion of humanists, 245
and politual and religious developments, 72
reform of princes, 21, 58–59
Court
Estense, renown of, 87
papal, and opinion of Dionisio, 93
courts, princely, of Savoy, Florence, and Ferrara, xvii, xix
Cozzi, Gaetano, 262 n. 16
culture, converging elements of, xiv
Curia, papal, reform of, xiii, 19, 25, 220
curia, of San Marco, 6, 157, 263 n. 25
Cyprus, 39
Cyril, 216

Damville, duke of, letter of Dionisio Gallo to, 17. *See also* Montmorency, Henri de
Dandelot, François, 206
Dandolo
Andrea, Venetian nobleman, and religious reform, 146
Mattio, Venetian ambassador to Rome, 186
David, king, 74
Psalms of, 197, 228, 248
"royal prophet," 78, 210
De arte kabbalistica, of P. Galatinus, 22
Decalogue, 200, 204, 252, 258
and Gospels, 251
order of society, 214
Saint Mark, 251, 257
De Etruriae regionis . . . originibus, and Postel, G., 249
De harmonia mundi, of Zorzi, Francesco, 27
Del Col, Andrea, 154
Demus, Otto, 114, 131
Denis, saint, 25–26
Feast of, 226
Devil, and envy of Venice, 121
Diane, de Poitiers, 28
Dichiaratione del Doni supra il XIII capitolo dell'Apocalisse, 26. *See also* Doni, Anton Francesco
Dionisio Gallo
and abuse by Turk, 164
advice to Prince Francesco de Medici, 70, to Venice, 191–92
affection for Venice, 197
and alms to the poor, 54, 56–57
as "ambassadeur et seruiteur de Dieu," 17
as angelic shepherd, 45
authority of, 57
anointment of, 8, 45, 64, 74, 160, 233, 242
assault on papal authority, 84
audience in Venice, 156–57

Dionisio Gallo (cont'd)
- as *auriga*, 211
- benefactor in Rome, 59
- censure of Pope, 76
- certainty of prophetic voice, 245–46
- challenge to pope, 82
- charioteer of Church Militant, 209
- Church: health of, 53; reform of, 46, 60, 90, 209
- clothing, symbolism of, xv, 1, 4, 29, 54, 67–69, 149, 152
- conception of himself, 244
- conversations with F. Spinola, 180–82
- Cosimo I, 69
- criticism: of ecclesiastical hierarchy, 9, 58, 76, 143, 152; of papal nuncios, 192
- descendant of Norman kings, 7, 132, 223, 238–39
- dismissal from king's court, 13
- enthusiam for reform, 82
- erudition of, 5
- Francesco Spinola, 177–86
- as God's fool and messenger, 5, 17, 248
- God's Name, 227
- hostility against papal nuncio and Tribunal, 197
- imprisonment in Rome, 57, 71
- innovator, xvi
- insult to Catholic clergy in France, 16
- interpretation of problems in France, 13–14
- Italian princes, 68
- John the Evangelist, 74
- "king of the Gauls," 7, 18, 159, 238, 255
- league of princes, 91–92
- letters: to Emanuele Filiberto, 44; to duke of Damville, 17; to Francesco d'Este, 89; to the pope, 50; from prison, 186–88
- "man from Bosra," xix
- medieval world view, xvi; and apocalyptic thought, 242
- mock-dialogue with Satan, 79–80
- nature of justice and man, 148
- nuncio, papal, quarrel with, 82–83
- persona, prophetic, in Rome, 62; in Venice, 247
- plight of poor, 93
- politics in France, 236
- poor, rights of, 14
- preaching in Paris, 68, 237–38
- program of action, 139, 242
- rector of Collège de Lisieux, xiii
- refusal to stop preaching, 153
- return to Cosimo I, 66, 68
- rhetorical ability in, 76, 239
- "sacred actor," 150, 155
- sacred space, 49, 55
- scorn of world, 244
- sentence of Inquisition, 176
- servant of God and messenger, xix, 95
- "singing Gaul," 4
- suffering in Gaul, 13, 29, 80–81
- sustenance, royal, loss of, 15
- "sword of truth," xv
- sympathy for Charles IX, 223
- "third king," 229
- torment in prison, 203
- transformation of, 241
- universalism, 254
- use of Latin, 152–53
- utopia, vision of, xiii
- warning, to Charles IX, 13; to Inquisition, 172
- writings, 379–80 n. 1

discovery, of America, and prophecy, 27
Dodici Savi, of Ferrara, 87
Dogana di Mar, office of Rocho de Mazzochis, in, 143
doge, of Venice, blending of sacred and secular, 4
- as dispenser of justice, 253–54

and God's Law, 3
  guardian of political and religious justice, 3
Domenichi, Lodovico, 54
  and biography of Giovanna Veronese, 116–17
Domo Priullia Venetüs, 130. *See also* Martin, John
Donzellino, Hieronimo, 54–55
  and abuses of Church, 55
Doni, Anton Francesco, 17, 125
  and commentary on Apocalypse, 26, 112
  Giove and Momo, 17
  I mondi, 57
duomo. *See* Florence
Dürer, Albrecht, 26

Ebrietà, and love of Christ, 17
Ecclesia militans, xviii, 30, 65, 78, 246
  interpretation of, 167
  and Jerusalem, 198
Edict of Amboise, and tolerance of Calvinism, 90
edict of Charles IX, king of France, and expulsion of Dionisio Gallo, 16
Edict of Orléans, 221
Edict of Pacification, 12–14, 33–34
Edom, man from, 195–96, 229, 231–32, 254
"Edomness," 233
education, and clergy, 219–20
  Jesuits, xviii
Egnazio, Giambattista, 107–109
Eleonora de'Medici, wife of Cosimo I, 71, 74
Emanuele Filiberto, duke of Savoy, xiv, 31–32, 58, 82, 88, 92, 246, 249
  anxiety about religious disturbances, 36, 40
  league of princes, 85
  reform of education and interest in sciences, 37

  religious sensibility, 32
  tolerance of Waldenses, 40
  union against heretics, 68
Emo, Francesco, Venetian nobleman, and religious reform, 146
Enchiridion militis Christiani, 239
Erasmus, Desiderius, 27, 57, 239–40
  influence among Venetian youth, 147
  Praise of Folly, 17
Eremiti, of San Francesco di Paolo, 28
Esau (Edom), 230–32
Esdras, 4th, 55–56
Esseni, 257
Estates of Languedoc, importance of 16, 17
Este, family of, 47
  and loyalty to papacy, 91
  Savonarola, 88–89
Etaples, Jacques Lefèvre d', 220
Etruria, and ancient splendor, 250
evangelism, Venetian, 114

Facchinetti, Giannantonio, bishop of Nicastro and papal nuncio, Venice, 6, 86, 154, 175, 183, 190
Farnese, Alessandro, cardinal, 75
  family, 47
Faventius, inquisitor (1566), 154, 159, 175
feminine, concept of, in view of Dionisio, 198
Feast of the Annunciation of the Virgin, 82
Feast of Pentecost, and arrival of Dionisio in Venice, 149
Ferdinando, de'Medici, cardinal, 69, 80
Ferrara, 46, 87, 91, 99, 151, 214, 234
  court of, 88
  mission of Dionisio in, 16, 92
  religious persuasions, 88
Ferrer, St. Vincent, 216

Ferrer, Zacharias, Father
  and *De reformatione ecclesiae*, 23, 25
  and unity of Christianity, and challenge to pope, 23
Ficino, Marsilio, 161, 217
Fineti, Zuan, lawyer, and F. Spinola, 178
Fioccha, Orpheo, of Polpenaze, and concept of Venetian justice, 200
Firpo, Massimo, 83
flagella, of God against Florence, 206
Flagellum et Renouatio mundi et Ecclesiae Dei, 23
Florence, 82, 99, 103, 151
  activities of Dionisio in, 16
  and division in kingdom, 75
  duomo of, 85
  forced departure of Dionisio from, 83
  and Italy, 242
  origin of, 69
  problems in, 223
  sojourn of Dionisio in, 76
  Wars of Religion, xvii, 32, 75, 242
Florian, Benedetto, 127, 213
Foelix, dom, prior of Carthusian monastery in Paris, 174–75
folly, of Dionisio, 57, 234
Fontego dei Tedeschi, and Venetian youth, 146
Fonzio, Bartolomeo, heretic, 120
Fortitudo, 241
Foscari, Francesco, doge, 241
France, and division in kingdom, 75
  Italy, 242
  problems in, 223
  Wars of Religion, xvii, 32, 75, 242
Franceschi, Giulia di, second wife of Rocho de Mazzochio, 144
Francesco d'Este, marquis de Masse, 46, 72, 89, 91–92, 94, 96, 176, 234
Francesco de'Medici, Prince, 69, 80
Francis I, king of France, 10, 12, 27–28, 32, 52, 215, 267 n. 50
  college, trilingual, 220–21

Francis II, king of France, son of Francis I, 88
fratelli, followers of F. Spinola, 179
Frattina, Isabella, wife of Marco, 120–21
Frattina, Marco, 120–21, 126
Fribourg, 47

Gaîllon, 9, 14, 94, 222, 236
  visit of Dionisio to king at, 238
Galatinus, Peter, 22
Gallo, Dionisio. *See* Dionisio Gallo
gallo, good or bad, and Saint Bridget, 22
Gallo, Luca, cantor in Basilica di San Marco, 175
gallus, meaning of, 217
Gambacurta, Jacobus, magistrate, 154–55
Garden of Eden, 231
Garzia de'Medici, son of Cosimo I, 71–74
Gaul, ancient princes of, and descendants of Noe, 69
  suffering of Dionisio in, 74
Gaulois, Denys. *See* Dionisio, Gallo
Gelli, Giovambattista, 69
Geneva, 40–41, 120, 135, 141, 321
Geneviève, Sainte, 7
George, of Venice. *See* Zorzi, Francesco
Ghisliere, Paul, cardinal, 60
Giambullari, Pierfrancesco, 69
Gianà, Probo, captain of the guards, 121
Gidonus, priest, 143
Gilbert, Felix, 106–7
Ginzburg, Carlo, and significance of minor figures, xiv
Giolito, Gabriel, Ventian publisher, and F. Spinola
Giorgio, da Ferrara, fra. *See* Siculo, Giorgio
Giorgio, Francesco. *See* Zorzi, Francesco

Giovanni da Corregio, prophet, 161
Giovanni, fra, Spanish Franciscan, 162
Giovanni, de'Medici, cardinal, son of
    Cosimo I, 70, 71, 74
Gisletus, Giam Battista, priest, secretary of Inquisition, 175
Gisors, 16, 31, 196, 239, 249
    birthplace of Dionisio, 7, 93
Giustiniani, Tomaso, 107
Gleason, Elisabeth, 107
glorification of prophet, and role of
    prophet, 21
God, voice of, in Cinquecento, 74
Gonzaga, Ercole, cardinal, 40, 46
Gonzaga, Giulia, 170
goods, ecclesiastical, sale of, 222
gossip, Parisian, 223
Gostiath, Andreas. *See* Andreas Gostiath
Grimani, Hieronimo, *procuratore di San Marco*, and lay representative to tribunal of Holy Office, 176
Gritti, Andrea, doge, 3, 200
    proemio dogale, Libro d'oro, 251
    receiving Law from Saint Mark, 4
Guido da Fano, heretic, 73, 189–90
Guidarcerius, Agathias, 220
Guise, family of, 11–12
    feud with Montmorency, 90
    formation of league, 90

Hadrian VI, pope, 23
Haec est causa, 46, 80, 96
Hallman, Barbara, 19
Hannibal, and bravery of Romans, 106
harmony, need for among kings and
    princes, 59
Havre, Le, seizure of, by English, 90
Hebrew and Greek, study of, 220–21
Henry II, king of France, 12, 32,
    87–88, 221–23
Henry IV, king of France, 38
Hercole d'Este, great-grandfather of
    Alfonso II, 89
    Hercole II d'Este, 87

heresy, destruction of, 193
    and heterodoxy, xiv
    lives of clergy, 60
    problem of, in Venice, 192, 202
Holy Office of the Inquisition
    (Venice). *See* Inquisition (Venice)
Holy Spirit, gifts of, 211
    guide of, 204–5, 207
hope, prophetic, 244
Huguenots, 33–36, 42, 88, 185, 242
    Catherine de'Medici, 223
    Dionisio Gallo, 237
    errors of the Crown, 224
    league of princes, 92
humanism, of Dionisio Gallo and
    Spinola, F., 184, 246
humiliation, for Christ, 162, 174
Hungary, invasion of, 87
Hurault de Baistaille, Jean, French
    ambassador, Venice, friend of F.
    Spinola, 178–79
Hutter, Jakob, 27

ideas, apocalyptic, and Dionisio, 210
Il libro della divina ordinatione, 117, 121
illumination, divine, 247
    Savonarola and opinion of, 162
Il modo del sovvenire a poveri, of Vives, 21
Incurabili, Hospital of, 255
Index of Paul IV, 84
infusion, divine, 196
inquisition, of Dionisio, 158–61,
    165–66, 171
Inquisition, Roman, 83
Inquisition (Venice) (Holy Office of
    the Inquisition), xvii–xix, 6, 63,
    97
    accusations of Dionisio against, 152,
        182, 190
    banishment of Dionisio, 256
    lay members of, 191, 197
    and Postel, G., 102
    seating plan of, 155
    trial of Dionisio, 151–76

Ippolito II d'Este, brother of Francesco d'Este, 91
Isaac, pratriarch, 117
Isaiah, prophet, 78, 95–96, 210
   description of Edom, 232
   third king, 229
Italy, admiration of Dionisio for, 74

Jacob, patriarch, 113, 117, 230, 232
Jacoff, Michael, 256
Jacopone da Todi, 162
Jan-Cain, 254
Jean de Montluc, bishop of Valence, 12
Jeanne d'Albret, 91
Jeremiah, prophet, 94, 154
Jerusalem, new, 25, 244
   and Anabaptists, 26
   John's vision of, 80
   paradigm of *Ecclesia militans*, 198
Jesuits, 101–2
   and G. Postel, 255
   reform, 219–20
   work in Venice, 102
Joachim of Fiore, xviii, 109, 112, 116, 122, 124–25, 131, 210, 216
   Age of the Spirit, 20, 205
   apocalyptic thought, 213
   commentary on Apocalypse, 44, 194–95
   Espositio . . . in Apocalipsim, 228
   generalis capitaneus, 128
   health of the Church, 53
   manna, 227–29
   mosaics of San Marco, 22–23, 44–45, 113–14
   prophecies for Venetians, 109–10
Joannes a Boteren (Joannes ab Hoboken Antwerpiens) rector of *iuristarum* (1566), Studio of Padua, 147
Joel, prophet, 67
Johanna of Austria, wife of Prince Francesco de'Medici, sister of Maximillian, emperor, 71
Johanna, mother (Giovanna), 114–18
   as *Papa Reformatore*, 116
   prophecies to Postel, 115
   vessel of Christ, 116
John, the Evangelist, and Dionisio's identification with, 44, 210, 239
John of Paris, and *Tractatus de anti-Christo*, 111
John, Saint, 127
John, Saint, Lateran, Church of, 61
Joris, David, leader of Dutch Anabaptists, 101
Joseph of Arimathea, and holy shroud, 39
Jubilees, Book of, 230
judges, as "gods," 397 n. 141
judgment, good, and reason, 45
Julius III, pope, 50
jurisdiction, of pope and of Venetian Inquisition, 189
justice, iconography of Venice as, 198–200, 253
   essence of, 203
   and myth of Venice, 258
   nature of, 148–49
   new world order, 221
   and Venice, Doge of, 2, 241
justification, debate on, 40

"king of the Gauls," Dionisio as, 14, 15
king, third, 195–96, 227–29, 231
   king and high priest, 234
kingdom, of God, on earth, 244
Koran, 101

Laçarus de Soardis, Venetian publisher, 112
La Fosse, Jehan de, Abbé, and his *Journal*, 15, 238
Lainez, Diego, and Council of Trent, xviii, 219–20
language, Etruscan-Aramaic, 69
   of Ignatius Loyola, 89
   metaphoric, of Dionisio, 75–76, 240

prophecy, 89, 241, 249, 254
Scripture, 240
Languedoc, arrival of Dionisio in, 16–18, 238
Lapicida, Nicolas, messenger of the Venetian Holy Office, 6, 175
Laurentius da Monte, fra, 103–4, 116
Law of Moses. *See* Decalogue
Lazzarelli, Lodovico, 21, 161
League of Cambrai, 165
  and Cardinal of Lorraine, 90
  of Italian princes, 58, 86, 92, 94, 151
  Montluc's proposal for, 90–91
Le Fèvre de la Boderie, Guy, 242
legates, papal, like medicine, 153
Legatio, of Dionisio Gallo, and resolution of divided Christianity, xvii, 93, 158–61, 186
  response to, of Charles IX, 10
leggenda, and prophetic origin of Venice, 99
Leonora de'Medici, daughter of Cosimo I, 87
Le prime nove del altro mondo, 117, 121
Les très merveilleuses victoires des femmes . . . , and Postel, G., 249
Leu and Gilles, Saints, parish of, 15
Levant, defense of, 47
L'Hôpital, Michel de, 12, 32, 221
Libellus ad Leonem (1513), 107, 169
Liber, quem Nullus aut in codo aut in terra . . . , 70 76
Libro d'oro vecchio, proemio dogale of, 3–4, 200
libro grande, and G. Siculo, 134
Lichtenberger, Reinhard, 216
Lippomano, Girolamo, ambassador of Venice, in Savoy, 39
Lisieux, and "mystical anointment" of Dionisio Gallo, 14, 93, 222
literature, prophetic and devotional, and Joachim, and Savonarola, 23
Livorno, 103
Lodovico XII, 22
Loredan, Antonio, Venetian nobleman and religious reform, 146–47

Leonardo, doge, 104
Lorraine, Cardinal of, Charles de Guise, 90
  desire for Council of Gallican Church, 12
Lotto, Lorenzo, 116
Louis XI, king of France, and San Francesco di Paolo, 28
Louis XII, king of France, husband of Louise of Savoy, and reverence for San Francesco di Paolo, 28
Louise, of Savoy, and prophecy, 28
Lovedo, villa, 145
Loyola, Ignatius, Saint, 27–28, 101, 219–20
  Spiritual Exercises, 89
Lucrezia de'Medici, daughter of Cosimo I, and wife of Alfonso II, 87
Luigi d'Este, cardinal, brother of Alfonso II, 91
Lutherans, 102
Luther, Martin, 24, 112, 122, 130, 169, 235
  and *Address to the Nobility of the German Nation*, 19
Lyon, 88

Machiavelli, Niccolò, xv
Mâcon, 33
madness, feigned, 162
Madonna di Campagna, and Capuchins, 38
Madruzzo, Cristoforo, cardinal, bishop of Trento, 40
Maggior Consiglio, 141
magistracy, most perfect, 200
Magno, Paolo, lawyer, 143
Malamocco, port of, 76
Malipiero
  Alvise and Polo, Venetian noblemen and religious reform, 146–47
  Giacomo, and religious reform, 146–47,
  and Spinola, F., 178

Malta, Knights of, 38
manna, hidden, and relation to white stone, 228
Mantua, and Gonzaga, family of, 46
Marcellus II, pope, 50
Marconlini, Francesco, Venetian printer, 125
Marguerite of France, duchess of Berry, 249
Marguerite of Navarre, 10
Mark, Saint, patron and protector of Venice.
  and Decalogue, 3–4
  and Descent from Levital tribe, 56–57
  as *medicus*, 257
  and Moses, 251–53
  as patron of Venice, 250–52 fig. 19
  and translation of body from Alexandria, 2
  as winged lion, 241, 243 fig. 18
Marot, Clement, translation of the Psalms, and reform, 10, 11, 214
Martin des Champs, Saint, monastery of, and Postel, 249, 254–55
Martin, John, 338 n. 209
Martyr, Peter, and Renée of France, 88
Mazzochis
  Andrea de, father of Rocho, 141
  Anzola de, daughter of Rocho, will of, 143
  Giacomo de, son of Rocho, 143
  Rocho de, Venetian citizen, xvi, xviii, 95, 139–47, 191, 214, 246, 255
  Zuanmaria de, son of Rocho, 143
Medici, family of, 47
  expulsion, 103
  medicine, need of by Church, 18, 51, 53, 233–34
Melanchthon, Philip, 169
Memoires de Condé, and Dionisio Gallo, 15, 16
Menchi-Seidel, Silvana, 100
Meos, 33

Merlin, prophet, 109, 129, 216, 337 n. 191
Messiah, and third king, 196
Messer San Marco, 2. *See also* Mark, Saint
messengers, of God, 209–10
Methodius, 216
Michel, Saint, Feast of, 33
Michelangelo, 27
Michiel, Alvise, archbishop of Spalato, 145
Midi, Dionisio Gallo in, 16–19, 31, 250
Milan, 178
Milanese, Francesco, heretic, 61
Mirabilis Liber (1524), 23, 63, 213, 231
  and creative interpretation, 23
  reform of the Church, and revelation, 22
Miracolo fatto dal glorioso San Francesco de Paulo nella città di Venetia, 28, 29 fig.4
Moab, 78
Mocenigo
  Alvise, ambassador of Venice, to court of Rome, 50
  Alvise and Antonio, sons of Leonardo, pupils of F. Spinola, 178
  Alvise, Venetian nobleman, and religious reform, 146
  Leonardo, and employment of F. Spinola, 178
monarchy, universal, and G. Postel, 218
Mondovì, 37–38
Montargis, and desire of Renée of France to be Protestant city, 88
Montavano, Antonio, de Bozzolo, 137
Montluc, Blaise de, 90
Mont Marsan, 13–15, 223, 237, 255
  and challenge of Dionisio to king, in, 94
Montmorency, house of, and feud with Guise, 90
  Anne, constable of France, 9, 13
  Henri de, duke of Damville, 16, 18
Moravia, 27

Morel, François, sieur of Colonges, friend of Calvin and adviser of Renèe of France, 88
Moro, Alvise, 141
Moro, Baldassare, Venetian patrician, patron of Rocho de Mazzochis, 141–43
Morone, Giovanni, cardinal, 40, 52, 83, 170
Moro, Stefano, Venetian nobleman, 203
Morosini, dalla Sbarra, family of, 145–46, 158
  Benetto, 145
  Giusto, Venetian patrician friend of Dionisio, career of, 140–47, 158, 191, 198, 246
  Marco, one of Tre Savi sopra Eresia, 154, 158, 191, 263 n. 24
  Pietro Antonio, father of Giusto, 145
  Vittorio, cousin of Giusto, 145
mosaics, in Basilica di San Marco, and Apocalypse, 44
  Corazzaro, B., 131
  and prophecy, 126–27, 213
Moses, 112, 136, 204, 228
  ascension to Mt. Sinai, 211
  God's Law, 4, 196
  new type of messiah and prophet, 211
  and Saint Mark, 251, 259
Mula, Lorenzo da, 121
Müntzer, Thomas, 26–27
mysticism, of Dionisio, 203
  Jewish, and Dionisio, 227
mystics, feminine, as sign of divine protection, 151
myth. *See* Venice, myth of

Nadal, Jerónimo, 220
Nani, Bartholomeo, Venetian patrician, 141
  and Palazzo Nani, 144
  Piero, Venetian patrician, 113
Nascimbeni, Nascimbene, 136–37

nature, book of, 76
Nesi, Giovanni, disciple of Marsilio Ficino, 161
nexus, political-religious, of Venice, 253
Niccolia, Otlavia, 20, 27, 69, 101, 154
Nice, 36
Niclaes, Hendrick, and Family of Love, 101
Noah, 69, 232
nobilitas, generosa, 202–3
nobility, concept of, 238
  Venetian, as "mother and father," 198
Nola, Pomponio da, extradition of, to Rome (1555), 189
Normandy, 223
Nostradamus (Nostredame, Michel de) 28,
  Catherine de'Medici, 14, 237
  predictions for future, 246
Novegrado, Marco da, 179, 182

Ochino, Bernardino, 102–103, 242
Old Testament, prophets of, 94, 99
O'Malley, John W., 259 n.
Onus mundi, 26
Oratio de circumcisione dominica, of P. Galatinus, 22
Oratorio of Divine Love, 170
Ospedaletto, 102, 114, 116–117

Padua, 117, 121, 147, 234
  and Dionisio, 149
  followers of F. Spinola, 178
  poor in, 192
  Studio of, 107
Palazzo Ducale (Venice) cortile and significance of, 1, 55, 152, 156, 253
  iconography of, 198
  prisons of, 154
  sacred space, 67, 242
  seat of justice, 2
  significance of justice column, 4
Pandochaeus, Elias, 254
Panevino, Giulio, ally of F. Spinola, 179

Paracelsus, 216
Paris, 155, 222, 25
   Carthusian monastery, in, 175
   great storm in, 14
   influence of Duke of Damville, in, 16
   Parlement of, 16
   and preaching of Dionisio in, 237
Parma, 47
Pasqualigo, Andrea, Venetian patrician, 120, 126
Pasqualitius, Paul, notary of Tragurien, and criticism of wealth of bishops of Church, 63–64
Paul, Saint, 18, 57, 73–74, 156, 162, 207, 234, 239
   apostalate among Gentiles, 193
   Holy Spirit, 206
   language of, 95
Pellegrini, Vincenzo, 120
Pentecost, day of, and white dove, 198
   Feast of, 152
Pescara, marchese, di, 41
Peter, leader of Church Militant, 193
Peter, Saint, 18
   apostalate among Jews, 193
   Basilica of, 61
Petrus Anusius Synesius Venetus, 254
Philip II, king of Spain, and league of princes, 41, 56, 90–91
Piazza San Marco, 1
piazzetta, of San Marco, 2
Piedmont, 41
Piero de'Medici, 103
Pinerolo, 47
Pisa, University of, 103
   and Savonarola's idea in regard to the poor, 247
Pisani, Alvise, cardinal, 148
Pisani, Marc'Antonio, father of Zuan Francesco, 156
   Zuan Francesco, magistrate, 156–57
Plato, and *Timaeus*, 123
Pocock, J. G. A., xv, xvi

Poissy, Colloquy of, and Renée of France, 88
Polanco, Juan Alfonso de, 220
Pole, Reginald, cardinal, 21, 40, 123, 170
politia, and role of Dionisio, 67
politics, blending of, with religion, 150–51
Ponte, Andrea da, 120
poor, cries of, 93
   members of Christ, 235
   misery of, 77
   responsibility of princes for, 224
   sustenance of 192–94, 215
   and wealth of the Church, 86
pope, angelic, 231, 242
   Dionisio Gallo and Guillaume Postel, 254
   imaginary dialogue of Dionisio with, 235
   medieval concepts of, 68, 82
   name of, 216
   new name, 64
   new Moses. *See* Ferrer, Zacharias
   temporal prince, 188
popes
   Paul II, 28
   Paul III, 49, 101
   reform commission, 19
   Paul IV, xix, 50; Index of, 84
   Pius IV, 40, 85, 178
   Pius V, 40, 48, 50, 66, 85–86, 248; accusations against rector of Studio of Padua, 147–48; challenge of Dionisio, 93; desire for reform of Church, 60–61; displays of piety, 61; election of, 193–94; extradition of Guido da Fano, 189–90; extradition of Pietro Carnesecchi, 73; Italian princes, 19; refusal to invest fiefs of Church to illegitimate sons of princes, 96–97; sensitivity to criticism against indulgences, 62
Porta della Carta, 4, 198, 241

Portianus, heretical prince, 206
Portogruaro, 120
Postel, Guillaume, xiii, xvi, xix, 21, 28, 126, 199–200, 240–42, 256–57
  concept of king and angelic pope, 217–18
  and Dionisio Gallo, 17
  emphasis upon Saint Mark, 251
  extradition to Rome, 189
  "immutation" of, 125
  influence on Dionisio, 247
  interpretation of man from Edom, 231–32
  interpretation of Esau, 391 n. 104
  meaning of Edom, 196
  mosaics of Basilica di San Marco, 114
  prophecy, 245–46
  reform: of French court, 27; of pope, 20; of world, 249–50
  royal reader, 220
  universalism, 254
  Venetian Inquisition, 101–2, 116–17
  warning to Capi del Consiglio dei Dieci, 121
poverty, Dionisio's concept of, 304 n. 51, 305 n. 58
  Franciscan, 102
Praise of Folly, 17
preachers, in Venice, 99
  prophetic, 100–101
prelates, and residence in parishes, 215
priests, and erudition and honor, 219
princes, Christian, and reform, 224, 240
  piety of Italian, 20
  role of princes in suppression of heresy, 75–169
prisons, Venetian,
  conversations in, 179
  letters of Dionisio from, 201–2
  in Palazzo Ducale, xix, 6
  suffering of Dionisio in, 207
  violence in, 163–64, 177
Priuli, Alvise, 123

Giralamo, diarist, 104–6
Giralamo, doge, 5, 151
Lorenzo, 300 n. 29
Problemata, of Zorzi, Francesco, 27
program, utopian, of Dionisio, 213–14
propaganda, anti-Venetian, 104
prophecy, xv, xvi, 258
  angelic pope, 67–68
  and artisans of Venice, 127–32
  Cinquecento, importance of, 241–45
  concept of Savonarola, 162
  discovery of America, 27
  "ghetto de Zudei," 127
  God's kingdom on earth, 258
  humanists, 245
  interpretation of Dionisio, xix
  Jewish, and hopes of Christians, 136
  Medieval, 231, 245
  Mestre, 111
  Nani, Piero, 113
  Old Testament, 203, 229
  reform of the Church, 246
  Sansovino, Francesco, 113
  Venice, 99
prophet
  audience of, in Cinquecento, xix
  exaltation of, 21, 161
  innovator, xv
  leadership in reform, 92
  meaning of, in Old Testament, xix, 94
  political context, xv
  role of, and Dionisio, 65–67, 161
Prophetia de maometani et altre cose Turchesche, 54
prophets
  age of gold, 216
  court circles, 245
  life of, 235
  "lunatic fringe," 246
  representation of, in Churches, (Venetian), 99

Protestantism, in France, and Concordat of Bologna, 215
power of, 11
"proxy," of Dionisio, 18
Prudentia, 241
Prudentius, 217
purgatory, Dionisio's opinion of, 226–27
Purification of the Virgin, Feast of, 56
Psalms, 44, 203, 229, 234, 240
  interpretation of, 129
Psalter, Genevan, 214
Pseudepigrapha, 230
Pseudo-Methodius, 210
pseudonyms, use of, by Postel, G., 254

Quadriga Domini, xvi, 256–57
Querini, Vincenzo, 107

rapture, God given, 70
Rauaiolis, Ioannes Baptista de, 130–31, 337–38 nn. 200, 209
reason, and good judgment, 45
Rebekah, wife of Isaac, 117, 230, 232
Reeves, Marjorie, 20, 216
reform, of the Church, 102, 151, 233–35, 244
  as art and method, 75
  and clergy and French Crown, 11
  Dionisio, 10, 90
  Italian princes, 170, 207, 240
  Joachim, 109
  judicial and administrative systems in France, 221
  political and social sphere 21, 79, 239
  pope and Curia, 61, 67, 220, 228
  practices of, 46
  problems of, 86
  sol pastore, 130
  truth, 75
  union of male and female, 198
Reginald, teacher in Dominican Order, and anointment, 112
Reiniero, Daniel, magistrate, 6, 153

religio, and role of Dionisio, 67
religion, Christian, loss of, in Asia, Africa, and parts of Europe, 61
  role of Dionisio, 67
Renée of France, 10
  and friendship with John Calvin, 87–88
renovatio mundi, and Savonarola, 161–62
respublica mundana, 218
restitution, beginning of, in 1566, 250
restoration, and good judgment, 45
Reuchlin, Johannes, 227
Revelationes, of Saint Bridget, 26
Rialto, 143
rights of the poor, 14
Rizzo, Antonio, 1
Rocho de Mazzochis. *See* Mazzochis, Rocho de
Rochus, Venetus, 139, 158, 198. *See also* Mazzochis, Rocho de
rod, iron and rule over wicked with, 195
Romanus, Vincentius Julianius, dom 124
Rome, 155
  arrival of Dionisio in, 49
  influence of Damville in, 16
  key to reformation, 24–25
  league against disturbance of peace in Italy, 75
  stage for prophetic preaching, 49
romito, itinerant prophet, 154
Ronsand, Pierre de, 10
Rouen, Senate of, 47, 223
Rousillon, Château of, 88
Rupescissa, John of, 216
Rusticanus, 201
Sadoleto, Jacopo, cardinal, 40
saints. *See* individual saints
saints, cult of, in Venice, 99
Salmerón, Alfonso and Council of Trent, xviii
Salmon, J. H. M., 222
San Clemente, Chapel of, 253

San Fantin, Campo of, and conventicle, 120, 146
San Faustino, monastery of, (Brescia), 136
San Francesco di Paolo, and Louise of Savoy, 28
San Giacomo, altar of, 113
San Giovanni in Bragora, prisons of, 121, 126, 163
San Giovanni Eleemosinarii di Rialto, Church of, 6
San Lazzaro, Religion of, 38. *See also* San Maurizio
San Magno, bishop of Altin, 131
San Marco, Basilica di, 22, 253–54, 257
  mosaics of, 257
  Piazza, 144
  procurators of, 225
  San Marco, brothers of (Florence), 248
San Mattio di Rialto, and preaching, 146
San Maurizio, religion of, 38
San Moisé, and *mezado* of Rocho de Mazzochis, 144
San Paolo, Compagnia di, 38–39
San Paternian, contrada of, 144
San Pietro in Castello, contrada of, 145
Sansovino, Francesco, and prophecy, 59, 113, 119
Sansovino, Jacopo, and figures of Mars and Neptune, 2
Sant'Andrea della Certosa, Carthusian monstery of, 174–75
Sant'Apostoli, prisons of, 163
Santa Maria Formosa, and family of Morosini, 145
Sanudo, Marino, 104–7, 113
Sanuto, Livio, author of *Astrologia divinativa*, 39
Sara, wife of Abraham, 117
Sarpi, Paolo, 165
Satan, mock dialogue with, by Dionisio, 79–80

Savigliano, 47
Savonarola, Hieronimo, fra, xvi, xviii, 23, 65, 83–84, 103, 105 fig. 8, 163, 185, 234–35
  attitude toward poor, 247
  commentary on Old Testament prophets, 135
  God's fool, 17, 248
  ills of the Church, 62–63
  impiety of the clergy, 181
  influence on Dionisio, 247, 249
  on Italian princes, 22
  Oracolo, 147
  prophetic fervor, 249
  reform, 22, 206
  spirituali, 205–6
Savoy, 31, 249
  activities of Dionisio in, 16
  relations with France, 32
  relations with Venice, 35
  renewal of spiritual life, 38
Savoyards, and affection for France, 35
Scala dei Giganti, 1–2
Scandella, Domenico, xiv
Scarsela, Cesare, and banishment of Dionisio, 176
Schigniragni, a Provençal, heretic, 36
Scholem, Gershom, 230
Scudieri, Francesco, fra, 101
"seals," of Adam, Noah, Shem, Abraham, Moses, David and Solomon, 129, 240
Seidel-Menchi, Silvana. *See* Menchi-Seidel, Silvana
Senate, Venetian, and opinion of Dionisio about right to judge, xvi, 5, 102, 191, 254
senators, Venetian, on tribunal, and Dionisio, 192
senser di biave (grain official), 140, 143. *See also* Mazzochis, Rocho de
Severo, Francesco, physician of Argenta, 133–34, 136–37

Sforza
  Francesco, duke of Milan, 103
  Lolovico, 22
Shroud of Jesus, 39
Sibyls, 216
sickness, of Church, 210
Siculo, Giorgio, Benedictine monk, 33–37, 119, 162, 170
Signori di Notte, prisons of, 163–64, 177, 195
Simoncelli, Paolo, 83, 162
simony, and shepherds of Church, 233, 384 n. 5
Sinai, 252
Sitto e forma delle chiesa di Santo Marcho posta in Venetia, 149
Soardis, Laçarus de, Venetian publisher, 112
Society of Jesus, 249. See also Jesuits
  and Postel, Guillaume, 27
Sodom and Gomorrah, 192
sodomy, problem of, in Venice, 192, 202
  sins of, 207
soldier of Christ, clothing of, 69
Soliman II, emperor of the Turks, 87
Sol pastore, and *sol ovile*, 127
Soranzo, Girolamo, ambassador of Venice, to Rome, 50–51, 147–48, 169, 188
sources, of Dionisio, 243
Southcott, Joanna, English mystic, 117
space, sacred, 4, 150, 241–42, 260 n.5
Spain, 42
Speranza, Zan della, *libraro*, 118
Spinola, Francesco, humanist, 76–86, 120, 138, 146–47, 192
  death of, 185–86
  defense of, by Dionisio, 182–85
  preaching in prison, 178–79
Spiritual Exercises of Ignatius Loyola, 255
spirituali, and prophetic religion, 123–26, 205–6
spirituality, medieval, continuity of, in Cinquecento, 25

state
  universal, 214
  Venetian, and problems in, 192
Staupitz, and Anabaptist community, 27
Stella, Aldo, 27
Stephanus de Franciscis, 6
Stephanus, subdeacon, San Zuane di Rialto, 157
stone, white, 211, 228
Strasbourg, and Anabaptists, 26
strife, religious in France, xix
Strozzi, Giovanni Battista, 72–73
Studio of Padua, 147
Surian, Michiel, Venetian ambassador (1565), 75, 86, 188, 224
Switzerland, Protestants in, 40
symbolism, and clothing of Dionisio, 149–50, 154–55

Talmud, 101
Temperantia, 241
Targum, and annotations of Brocardo, G., 122
Telesforo da Cosenza, 45, 201, 216–18, 231
Terapeuti (Esseni), 257
Thamar, 115
Tharisia, Gioan Domenico, translator of Vives, 21
Theatini, 170
theocracy, utopian political, and Dionisio, 216
Theodore, Saint, Chapel of, 126
Thiphineo, Jacobus, French priest, acquaintance of Dionisio, 174
thinkers, utopian, of Cinquecento, 244
"third party," 12
Tiepolo, Baiamonte, 118
  second Catiline, 108
Tiepolo, Paulo, ambassador of Venice, to Rome, 61, 62, 73
  pressure from pope, 188–90
Todesco, Pietro, 136
Toulouse, 16, 31, 47

league in, 90
Tournon, and "papists," 12
Tractatus de antichristo. See John of Paris
Trattato utilissimo del Beneficio di Gesu Christo crocifisso, 21
Tratto della reuelatione della reformatione della Chiesa, 65
Tre Savi sopra Eresia, 121–22, 207, 246
Trent, 90. *See also* Council of Trent, 90
Trevisan, Giovanni, inquisitor of Venice, 1566, xv
Trevisan, Ioannes, patriarch of Venice, 154, 175
Treviso, 104
Trinity, 95
Trismegistus, Hermes, 161
Tron, Vincanzo, ambassador of Venice, in Savoy, 42
truth, Dionisio's concept of, 204
  desire for 55, 66
  as Reformatrix, Extirpatrix, Consolatrix, Reconciliatrix, Victrix, Imperatrix, 55
Turchi, Floriano, 137–38
Turin, 19, 31, 36, 38–39, 42, 47
Turk, cellmate of Dionisio and abuses of, 177
Turks, 54
  advance of, in Venetian dominion, 96
  conquest of, 130
  conversion of, 69, 213
  resistance against, and reform of clergy, 85
  threat of, 27

Ubertino da Casale, 162
Ugoni, Andrea di, friend of F. Spinola, 178
universalism, of Dionisio and Postel, 254

Valais, 47
Valaresso, Federico, 121
Valenza, 33
Valois, Margaret, duchess of Berry, 32–33, 36, 40
  family of and personal tragedy, 34, 47
  interest in humanists, 32
  religious strife in France, 32–34
Vancimugio, Zuane de, Vicentino, 141
Vasoli, Cesare, 20, 27, 114, 123
Vatable, François, 220
Venetian Virgin, and Postel, xiii
Venetians, bravery of, 106
  and "good sailors," reform of, 129
Venetus, Rochus. *See* Mazzochis, Rocho de
Venice, xvii, 16, 30, 99, 250
  accusations of pope against, 186
  and arrival of Dionisio Gallo, in 1566, 15
  charity of, 225
  dangers to republic, 121–22
  decline of power, 104
  and dedication to justice, 2, 4
  defender of justice, xvi
  divine mission, 4
  expansion on the *terraferma,* 105
  as *Gerusalemme nuova* and *Roma nuova,* 102
  and Holy Office of the Inquisition, xiii
  as justice, 198–99 fig. 15
  and laudatory terms, of Dionisio, 201
  love of God for, 121
  as most perfect magistracy, 200
  myth of, 251, 258
  as new Jerusalem, 112, 198
  and origin, prophetic, 116
  poor in, 192
  praise and blame of, by Dionisio, 201–2
  and prisons, xiv
  as prophetic city, 4, 111, 132
  prophetic challenge of Dionisio, 82, 99
  protection of Saint Mark, 250
  question of papal authority, 188

Venice (cont'd)
  as receptacle of God's Law, 200
  and reformation of the world, 122
  reform of the Church, 103, 197, 256;
    of clergy, 25, 139
  relations with Savoy, 33, 35, 39
  and religious strife in France, 33
  role in history, 102
  Rome, relationship with before
    Interdict of 1606, 188
  Senate of, and divine right to judge,
    197
Venier
  Francesco, and criticism of papal
    legates, 153
  Laura, Venetian noblewoman,
    mother of Giusto Morosini, 145
  Maffeo, procuratore sopra la heresia, 102, 121
Vergerio, Pietro Paolo, 102
Vicenzo, guard of the prisons,
  172–73
Villanova, Asti d', 47
Viret, Peter, and Renée of France, 88
Virgin Mary, 112, 250
  and anointment of Dionisio, xiii,
    xvi, 8, 198, 205
Virgin, Venetian. *See* Johanna
  (Giovanna), Mother
virtue, standards of, in regard to all
  religious, 215
virtues
  Christian, and Graeco-Roman, 108
  of mercy, pardon and charity, 215
  and Porta della Carta, 241
Visconti, Carlo, patron of Spinola, F.
vision, prophetic, of Dionisio, 241
visionaries, Venetian, 136
Viterbo, Egidio, da, cardinal, 22
Vives, Juan Luis, 20–22, 215, 269 n. 65,
  271 n. 87
voice, prophetic, of Dionisio, 242

Waldenses (Waldensians), 40, 170
Wars of Religion, in France, 7, 242
Weinstein, Donald, 20, 103
Wolters, Wolfgang, 260 n. 9, 261 n. 10
writings, of Dionisio, 379–80 n. 1

Xavier, Francis, 101

youths, Venetians, and F. Spinola, 178

Zarri, Gabriella, 151
zecchino d'oro, 253
Zion, holy mountain, 195–96
Zohar, 123, 127
  and influence on Camillo, G.
    123–24
  spirituali, 123–24
Zorzi, (Giorgi) Francesco, fra, 27, 114,
  123, 242–43
  and *De harmonia mundi* and *In Sacram
    Scripturam Problemata*, 123
Zuana. *See* Johanna, Mother
Zuane de Vancimugio, xviii